Lecture Notes in Computer Science　　7513

Commenced Publication in 1973
Founding and Former Series Editors:
Gerhard Goos, Juris Hartmanis, and Jan van Leeuwen

James J. Park   Albert Zomaya
Sang-Soo Yeo   Sartaj Sahni (Eds.)

Network and Parallel Computing

9th IFIP International Conference, NPC 2012
Gwangju, Korea, September 6-8, 2012
Proceedings

 Springer

Volume Editors

James J. Park
SeoulTech, Department of Computer Science and Engineering
172 Gongreung 2-dong, Nowon-gu, Seoul 139-743, Korea
E-mail: parkjonghyuk1@hotmail.com

Albert Zomaya
The University of Sydney, School of Information Technologies
Building J12, Sydney, NSW 2006, Australia
E-mail: albert.zomaya@sydney.edu.au

Sang-Soo Yeo
Mokwon University, Division of Computer Engineering
88 Do-An-Buk-Ro, Seo-gu, Daejeon 302-729, Korea
E-mail: sangsooyeo@gmail.com

Sartaj Sahni
University of Florida
Computer and Information Science and Engineering Department
CSE 301, Gainesville, FL 32611, USA
E-mail: sahni@cise.ufl.edu

ISSN 0302-9743   e-ISSN 1611-3349
ISBN 978-3-642-35605-6   e-ISBN 978-3-642-35606-3
DOI 10.1007/978-3-642-35606-3
Springer Heidelberg Dordrecht London New York

Library of Congress Control Number: 2012953907

CR Subject Classification (1998): D.3.4, C.2.1-2, C.2.4, F.2.2, H.3.4-5, C.2.0,
D.4.1-2, K.6.5, C.1.4

LNCS Sublibrary: SL 1 – Theoretical Computer Science and General Issues

Typesetting: Camera-ready by author, data conversion by Scientific Publishing Services, Chennai, India

Printed on acid-free paper

Springer is part of Springer Science+Business Media (www.springer.com)

Preface

The IFIP International Conference on Network and Parallel Computing is an international conference aimed at providing an exciting platform and forum for researchers and developers from academia and industry to present their latest research in the field of parallel computing systems and applications.

This year NPC fostered state-of-the-art research in the area of converging information technologies, including virtualization techniques, tools, and applications; parallel programming models and languages; parallel language compiler and run-time support; parallel and distributed systems; network architecture and protocol design; network security; network storage; network reliability, security, and dependability; network algorithms; communication technology, scheduling and load balancing; advanced Web and proxy services; middleware frameworks and toolkits; performance modeling, prediction, and tuning; multi-core and cluster computing; ubiquitous communications and networks; USN and RFID; embedded and pervasive computing; peer-to-peer networks, social network and services; multimedia communications; cloud computing and networks; machine-to-machine communications; runtime systems; operating systems; resource management; data mining as well as algorithms and performance evaluation and measurement in parallel computing. The NPC 2012 conference also provided an opportunity for academic and industry professionals to discuss the latest issues and progress in the area of convergence of future computing technologies and applications.

We are proud to have had a prestigious set of keynote speakers, and would like to thank them for their distinguished keynote speech:

- Leonard Barolli (Fukuoka Institute of Technology, Japan)
- Fatos Xhafa (Technical University of Catalonia, Spain)
- Ned Kock (Texas A&M International University, USA)
- Yang Xiao (The University of Alabama, USA)
- Juan Carlos Augusto (The University of Ulster, UK)
- Habib F Rashvand (The University of Warwick, UK)

Owing to many high-quality paper submissions and the lack of space in proceedings, the review process was very tough and we had no choice but to reject several good papers. Each paper was assessed by at least three peer reviewers. The call for papers attracted a total of 136 submissions to the main conference, and only 38 papers were selected for presentation and are included in this volume.

Additionally, we are sure that the distinguished workshop papers from the officially selected five workshops added to the diverse coverage spectrum of our conference. We would like to thank all organizers and all authors of ATIMCN-12, ATSME-12, Cloud&Grid-12, DATICS-12, and UMAS-12.

Finally, we would like to thank all the participants, authors, reviewers, and Organizing Committee members.

September 2012

James J. Park
Albert Zomaya
Sang-Soo Yeo
Sartaj Sahni

Organization

Executive Committee

Honorary Chair

Daesik Ko — President of KI-IT, Korea

General Chairs

James J. (Jong Hyuk) Park — SeoulTech, Korea
Albert Zomaya — University of Sydney, Australia
Zhiwei Xu — Institute of Computing Technology, China

Program Chairs

Sang-Soo Yeo — Mokwon University, Korea
Yu Chen — State University of New York, USA
Sartaj Sahni — University of Florida, USA
Li Zha — Chinese Academy of Sciences, China

Workshop Chairs

Changhoon Lee — SeoulTech, Korea
Weisong Shi — Wayne State University, USA
Chun-Cheng Lin — National Chiao Tung University, Taiwan

Steering Committee Chair

Kemal Ebcioglu — Global Supercomputing, USA

Steering Committee

Hai Jin — Huazhong University of Science and Technology, China
Chen Ding — University of Rochester, USA
Jack Dongarra — University of Tennessee, USA
Guangrong Gao — University of Delaware, USA
Daniel Reed — University of North Carolina, USA
Yang Xiang — Central Queensland University, Australia
Zhiwei Xu — Institute of Computing Technology, China
Yoichi Muraoka — Waseda University, Japan
Jean-Luc Gaudiot — University of California Irvine, USA
Guojie Li — Institute of Computing Technology, China

Publicity Chairs

Hoojin Lee — Hansung University, Korea
Nazim Agoulmine — University of Evry, France

Hsi-Ya Chang	National Center for High Performance Computing, Taiwan
Ibrahim Kamel	University of Sharjah, UAE
Li Shen	NUDT, China

Finance Chair

Yang-Sun Lee	Mokwon University, Korea

Program Committee

Ishfaq Ahmad	University of Texas at Arlington, USA
Gail-Joon Ahn	North Carolina University, USA
Sadaf Alam	Swiss National Supercomputing Centre, Switzerland
Shawkat Ali	CQ University, Australia
Bourgeois Anu	Georgia State University, USA
Sulieman Bani-Ahmad	Al-balqa Applied University, Jordan
Yungang Bao	Institute of Computing Technology, China
Taisuke Boku	Tsukuba University, Japan
Luc Bouge	ENS Cachan, France
Azzedine Boukerche	University of Ottawa, Canada
Mats Brorsson	Royal Institute of Technology, Sweden
Pino Caballero-Gil	La Laguna University, Spain
Massimo Cafaro	University of Salento, Italy
Jian Cao	Shanghai Jiaotong University, China
Jae-Woo Chang	Chonbuk National University, Korea
Arun Chauhan	Indiana University, USA
Hsing-Lung Chen	National Taiwan University of Science and Technology, Taiwan
Wenguang Chen	Tsinghua University, China
Wang Chien-Min	Academia Sinica, Taiwan
Chi-Yin Chow	City University of Hong Kong, Hong Kong
Randy Chow	University of Florida, USA
Yang Chu-Sing	National Cheng-Kung University, Taiwan
Stelvio Cimato	Milan University, Italy
Robert Cohn	Intel, USA
Miguel Pupo Correia	Lisbon University, Portugal
Wang Da-Wei	Academia Sinica, Taiwan
Akshaye Dhawan	Ursinus College, USA
Jack Dongarra	Tennessee University, USA
Christine Eisenbeis	INRIA, France
Karatza Eleni	Aristotle University of Thessaloniki, Greece
Xiang Fan	Central Queensland University, Australia
Yungchin Fang	Dell, USA
Xia Feng	Dalian University of Technology, China

Xiaobing Feng	Institute of Computing Technology, China
Christian Fensch	University of Edinburgh, UK
Yaoqing Gao	IBM Toronto, Canada
Yunjun Gao	Zhejiang University, China
Cecile Germain-Renaud	Paris-Sud University, France
Domingo Gimenez	University of Murcia, Spain
Teofilo F. Gonzalez	UC Santa Babara, USA
Richard Graham	Oak Ridge National Laboratory, USA
Shuai Han	Harbin Institute of Technology, China
Yijie Han	University of Missouri Kansas City, USA
Wim Heirman	Ghent University, Belgium
Nakashima Hiroshi	Kyoto University, Japan
Michael Hobbs	Deakin University, Australia
Bo Hong	Georgia Institute of Technology, USA
Shi-Jinn Horng	National Taiwan University of Science and Technology, Taiwan
Rui Hou	ICT, China
Wei-Chung Hsu	National Chiao Tung University, Taiwan
Yo-Ping Huang	National Taipei University of Technology, Taiwan
Zhiyi Huang	University of Otago, New Zealand
Song Jiang	Wayne State University, USA
Guohua Jin	AMD, USA
Hai Jin	Huazhong University of Science and Technology, China
Yong-Kee Jun	Gyeongsang National University, Korea
David Kaeli	Northeastern University, USA
Mu-Cheol Kim	KISTI, Korea
Graham Kirby	University of St. Andrews, UK
Sy-Yen Kuo	National Taiwan University, Taiwan
Kuan-Chou Lai	National Taichung University, Taiwan
Chul Ung Lee	Korea University, Korea
Chin-Laung Lei	National Taiwan University, Taiwan
Keqin Li	State University of New York, USA
Kuan-Ching Li	Providence University, Taiwan
Xiaoming Li	University of Delaware, USA
Xiuqi Li	North Carolina at Pembroke University, USA
Yamin Li	Hosei University, Japan
Zhuowei Li	Xiamen University, China
Azman Osman Lim	National Institute of Information and Communications Technology, Japan
Jianxun Liu	Hunan University of Science and Technology, China
Shaoshan Liu	Microsoft, USA

Paul Lu	University of Alberta, Canada
Zhonghai Lu	KTH, Sweden
Yingwei Luo	Peking University, China
Miroslaw Malek	Humboldt University, Germany
Vanneschi Marco	University of Pisa, Italy
Kiminori Matsuzaki	University of Tokyo, Japan
Teo Yong Meng	National University of Singapore, Singapore
Phil Mucci	University of Tennessee, USA
Alfredo Navarra	University of Perugia, Italy
Amiya Nayak	University of Ottawa, Canada
Dimitris Nikolopoulos	Foudation for Research and Technology Hellas (FORTH), Greece
Maurizio Palesi	University of Catania, Italy
Liu Pangfeng	National Taiwan University, Taiwan
Seung-Jong Park	Louisiana State University, USA
animesh pathak	INRIA, France
Sushil K. Prasad	Georgia State University, USA
Apan Qasem	Texas State University, USA
Guangzhi Qu	Oakland University, USA
Omer F. Rana	Cardiff University, UK
Rajiv Ranjan	The University of New South Wales, Australia
Chang Ruay-Shiung	National Dong Hwa University, Taiwan
Srinivas Sampalli	Dalhousie University, Canada
Madria Sanjay	Missouri University of Science and Technology, USA
Mitsuhisa Sato	University of Tsukuba, Japan
Sven-Bodo Scholz	Heriot-Watt University, UK
Stanislav G. Sedukhin	University of Aizu, Japan
Zhiyuan Shao	Huazhong University of Science and Technology, China
Jun Shen	University of Wollongong, Australia
Weidong Shi	Nokia, USA
Wen-Chung Shih	Asia University, University
Gaurav Singh	CSIRO, Australia
Oliver Sinnen	University of Auckland, New Zealand
Evgenia Smirni	The College of William and Mary, USA
Haoyu Song	Huawei Technologies, US Research Center, USA
Leonel Sousa	INESC/IST, Portugal
Yuzhong Sun	Chinese Academy of Sciences, China
Yutaka Takahashi	Kyoto University, Japan
Makoto Takizawa	Seikei University, Japan
El-Ghazali Talbi	INRIA Lille Nord Europe, France
Chunqiang Tang	IBM, USA

Xinmin Tian	Intel Corporation, USA
Muntean Traian	Université de la Mediterranée, France
Putchong Uthayopas	Kasetsart University, Tailand
Clark Verbrugge	McGill University, Canada
Luis Javier Garcia Villalba	Universidad Complutense de Madrid (UCM), Spain
Abhinav Vishnu	Pacific Northwest National Laboratory, USA
Sheng-De Wang	National Taiwan University, Taiwan
Jia Weijia	City University of Hong Kong, Hong Kong
Andrew Wendelborn	University of Adelaide, Australia
Michal Wozniak	Wroclaw University of Technology, Poland
Chao-Chin Wu	National Changhua University of Education, Taiwan
Jan-Jan Wu	Academia Sinica, Taiwan
Zheng Da Wu	Bond University, Australia
Dong Xiang	Tsinghua University, China
Bin Xie	InfoBeyond Technology LLC, USA
Qin Xin	UCL, Belgium
Chao-Tung Yang	Tunghai University, Taiwan
De-Nian Yang	Academia Sinica, Taiwan
Laurence T. Yang	St. Francis Xavier University, Canada
Baoliu Ye	Nanjing University, China
Xinfeng Ye	Auckland University, New Zealand
Hsu-Chun Yen	National Taiwan University, Taiwan
Qing Yi	University of Texas in San Antonio, USA
Mehmet Yildiz	IBM Australia, Australia
Andy Yoo	Lawrence Livermore National Laboratory, USA
Shui Yu	Deakin University, Australia
Yijun Yu	Open University, UK
Xin Yuan	Florida State University, USA
Jianfeng Zhan	Chinese Academy of Sciences, China
Weizhe Zhang	Harbin Institute of Technology, China
Yu Zhang	University of Science and Technology of China, China
Weimin Zheng	Tsinghua University, China
Zhiyun Zheng	Zhenzhou University, China
Shuigeng Zhou	Fudan University, China
Wanlei Zhou	Deakin University, Australia
Wen Tao Zhu	Chinese Academy of Sciences, China
Chen Zizhong	Colorado School of Mines, USA
Cliff Zou	Central Florida University, USA
Deqing Zou	Huazhong University of Science and Technology, China

Table of Contents

Algorithms, Scheduling, Analysis, and Data Mining

Network Architecture and Protocol Design

Network Security

Parallel, Distributed, and Virtualization Techniques

Performance Modeling, Prediction, and Tuning

Resource Management

Ubiquitous Communications and Networks

Web, Communication, and Cloud Computing

ATIMCN

ATSME

Cloud & Grid

An Application-Level Scheduling with Task Bundling Approach for Many-Task Computing in Heterogeneous Environments

Jian Xiao, Yu Zhang, Shuwei Chen, and Huashan Yu[*]

School of Electronic Engineering and Computer Science, Peking University
Beijing 100871, P.R. China
{xiaojian,zhangyu,csw}@net.pku.edu.cn, yuhs@pku.edu.cn

Abstract. Many-Task Computing (MTC) is a widely used computing paradigm for large-scale task-parallel processing. One of the key issues in MTC is to schedule a large number of independent tasks onto heterogeneous resources. Traditional task-level scheduling heuristics, like Min-Min, Sufferage and MaxStd, cannot readily be applied in this scenario. As most of MTC tasks are usually fine-grained, the resource management overhead would be prominent and the multi-core nodes might become hard to be fully utilized. In this paper we propose an application-level scheduling with task bundling approach that utilizes the knowledge of both applications and tasks to overcome these difficulties. Furthermore we adapt the traditional task-level heuristics to our model for MTC scheduling. Experimental results show that these application-level scheduling approaches, when equipped with task bundling, can deliver good performance for Many-Task Computing in terms of both Makespan and Flowtime.

Keywords: application-level scheduling, many task computing, task bundling, traditional scheduling heuristics.

1 Introduction

Many-task Computing (MTC) [1] [2] is a loosely coupled computing paradigm that is widely used for scientific applications such as parameter sweep, Monte Carlo simulations, data parallelism, bioinformatics (like BLAST) and image manipulation [2], and the major goal of which is to complete a large number of independently-schedulable tasks within a short period of time. The application in this paradigm is usually developed upon abundant legacy executables accumulated in scientific domain. A scientific computing problem is represented as a MTC job, which could contain as many as thousands to millions fine-grained tasks, and thus the computation complexity could be extraordinarily demanding. The developments of large-scale processing techniques such as Supercomputer, Grid and Cloud in recent years have made it possible for MTC jobs to get results in a reasonable timeframe [1].

To efficiently execute MTC tasks in these large-scale heterogeneous environments, task scheduling is a key issue. However, scheduling MTC tasks is not a trivial

---

[*] Corresponding author.

J.J. Park et al. (Eds.): NPC 2012, LNCS 7513, pp. 1–13, 2012.

problem. The difficulty of MTC scheduling comes from not only the heterogeneity and dynamicity of resources, but also the large number of relatively-small tasks, which the latter might result in huge scheduling cost and starving a lot of computing nodes, and result in severe resource waste for multi-processor computers.

In this paper, we propose an application-level scheduling with task bundling solution to this problem. The proposed approach divides the scheduling process into two stages. In the first stage, the algorithm works at application and job level, matching job and resource by application-resource pairing and job selection, so as to improve the job's computing performance and resource's utilization simultaneously; then in the second stage, the algorithm works at task level to select a package of tasks (task selection) from the previously selected job and then allocates the package to the selected resource in one dispatch, so as to amortize the resource management overhead among tasks in same package and meanwhile exploit the intra-node capacity.

The remaining of the paper is organized as follows. Section 2 describes the problem. Section 3 reviews related works. In Section 4 we present our scheduling approach. Section 5 presents the experimental results. Finally Section 6 concludes the paper.

2   Problem Statement

Terminologies in this paper are used as in [3]. An application refers to a type of jobs, while a job is an instance of some application. Instances/jobs of the same application run the same program and use the same data resources, but read different inputs. And a job is a collection of independent tasks. We will use the terms "application" and "job type", "application instance" and "job" interchangeably.

A typical example of MTC application is Genome Alternative Splicing [4] in bioinformatics that predicts a genome's all possible transcriptomes. An application instance/job in this context refers to an actual genome submitted by some user intending to find the genome's transcriptomes, and a task is a run of the program to search all possible transcriptomes of a single gene. Generally a genome consists of tens of thousands of genes, which means such a job may contain tens of thousands of independent tasks. In our practice, 70% or more of tasks in a typical job was completed within 1 second [5].

We assume multiple applications $A_1, ..., A_p$, each of which may contain several jobs. Applications are heterogeneous, which means every application has its own pattern of computing-resource requirement, preferring such as I/O or CPU speed, and this constitutes the application-resource knowledge to utilize.

In our work we consider a large-scale heterogeneous system $\mathfrak{R} = \{R_1, ..., R_m\}$, consisting of network-connected single- or multi-processor computing nodes, for these applications processing. Processors of each computing node in $\mathfrak{R}$ are homogeneous, providing equal processing speed for the jobs of the same type, whereas processors from different nodes are heterogeneous.

2.1   Job Model and Task Model

A job is a large collection of independent and relatively-small tasks sharing the same computing-resource requirement. The k-th instance of application A_i is denoted as $J_{i,k} = \{\tau_{i,k}^{(h)} : h = 1, \ldots, n_{i,k}\}$, $k=1,2,..$, N_i, where N_i is the job number of application A_i, $n_{i,k}$ is the task number of job $J_{i,k}$ and $\tau_{i,k}^{(h)}$ is a task contained in this job. Conventionally, the estimated execution time of each task $\tau_{i,k}^{(h)}$ is supposed to be available in advance.

2.2   Scheduling Many Tasks as a Challenge

To schedule MTC tasks in a large-scale heterogeneous system would be a real challenge, as two traditionally negligible factors become prominent now:

- **Resource Management Overhead.** For a computing node to execute task, it should be allocated and configured first, and be released after the computation. The time cost of this resource management would be significant, compared with a single MTC task's computing cost itself.
- **Intra-Node Resource Utilization.** MTC tasks are often the small-scale parallel or even sequential programs which require only few resources to complete, so a single MTC task is unable to fully exploit the power of the today's multi-core computing node, and thus cause intra-node resource waste.

2.3   Objectives

This work aims to make a trade-off between Makespan and Flowtime, so as to optimize these two competing objectives [6] simultaneously.

We denote interval $[s_{i,j}^{(k)}, e_{i,j}^{(k)}]$ as the k-th period when job i occupied node j, from time $s_{i,j}^{(k)}$ to $e_{i,j}^{(k)}$. This means that node j is processing the tasks from job i during this period, and there may be several non-intersect time periods for this job on the same node. The Makespan and Flowtime of job i are given by

$$makespan_i = \max_j \{\max_k \{e_{i,j}^{(k)}\}\} \qquad (1)$$

$$flowtime_i = \sum_j \sum_k cn_j \times (e_{i,j}^{(k)} - s_{i,j}^{(k)}) \qquad (2)$$

where cn_j is the core number of R_j.

Based on these, three metrics are derived for performance comparisons:

- Overall Makespan: the maximum of all $makespan_i$, used for measuring overall computing performance.
- Overall Flowtime: the sum of all $flowtime_i$, used for measuring the CPU cost to achieve the overall computing performance.
- Average Job Makespan: the average of all $makespan_i$, used for measuring the QoS of the scheduling.

3   Related Work

As a well-abstracted model, optimal scheduling of tasks for multiple processors is a NP-complete problem [7], and thus many heuristics and meta-heuristics are proposed in literatures. Heuristics are directly designed for tasks scheduling, such as MinMin [8], Sufferage [9] and MaxStd [10], while meta-heuristics are combinatorial optimization techniques used indirectly for task scheduling, and the representative meta-heuristics include Genetic Algorithm (GA) [8], Simulated Annealing (SA) [8], Particle Swarm Optimization (PSO) [11] and Chemical Reaction Optimization (CRO) [6]. These algorithms work at task level, and require the prediction of each task's execution time on each machine, forming an ETC (Expected Time to Compute) matrix [8].Though both heuristics and meta-heuristics are classic solutions to traditional HTC (High Throughput Computing) [1], they are not suitable for MTC. The drawback is, when scheduling hundreds of thousand or even more tasks to large-scale resources, the overhead would be overwhelming. What's more, as these algorithms neglect the cost for resource management, the task-level scheduling for MTC may cause a great waste in repeatedly creating and releasing runtime environment.

Several research works consider multiple applications scheduling in context of Bag-of-Tasks (BoT) [12] or cloud computing [3], but mainly focus either on ETC based task-level scheduling or homogeneous cluster environment. And these works pay litter attention to the applications' differences in resource requirements, which is an important knowledge for scheduling optimization.

Few researches exist on task bundling strategy that dispatches a package of tasks rather than a single task to the resource at every scheduling event. In [13], fixed number of tasks bundling policy is used, but it is too simple for practical use. An improved strategy proposed in [14] bundles the tasks according to the size of input file and tries to balance the task packages in terms of total input file size in the package.

Some recent works concern not only the performance but also the resource cost for this performance. In [6] and [11], meta-heuristics CRO and PSO are adopted to minimize Makespan and Flowtime simultaneously. These works verified the value of meta-heuristics for multi-objective optimization. However, the applicable conditions of these meta-heuristics are confined to small number of large tasks and negligible runtime environment preparation time (compared to task granularity).

4   Scheduling Algorithm

Our scheduling algorithm is performed in a centralized manner. The computing node sends a task request to the scheduler whenever it has no task to make a local allocation; the scheduler processes the request by assigning one or more tasks to the computing node.

Figure 1 shows the algorithm's framework. Firstly, a job-resource pair is determined, indicating the job which the computing node is allocated to; then a subset of tasks from the selected job is allocated to the computing node in one dispatch. The algorithm exploits the following knowledge about applications and tasks.

Scheduling framework
1 $(J_{i,k}, R_j)$ ←Job-resource matching
2 Task-package B←Task-bundling $(J_{i,k}, R_j)$
3 Dispatch task package B to R_j

Fig. 1. Scheduling framework

• **Application's Parallel Degree, $D_{i,j}$.** Application-resource knowledge, reflecting the match between application's intrinsic nature in I/O or CPU preference and the resource's system architecture. Due to the I/O bottleneck, when the processor number of a node exceeds some limit, giving more processors will not help to improve parallel speed. We denote this limit as $D_{i,j}$, the degree of parallelism of application A_i on node R_j. $D_{i,j}$ is an integer between 1 and the processor number cn_j of R_j, represents the *logical processor* number that R_j offers to A_i and can be obtained by historical execution log.

• **Application's Processing Rate, $r_{i,j}$.** The other kind of application-resource knowledge. We denote $r_{i,j}$ as the processing rate of each R_j's logical processor for application A_i. This concept comes from the fact that, for any two computing nodes and different tasks from the same application, the ratio of each task's execution times on the two nodes will be quite stable and close to each other. To get the $r_{i,j}$ matrix, we can choose a *reference node*, say R_1, and let $r_{i,1}=1$; for $j \neq 1$, the $r_{i,j}$ is the ratio of Benchmark task's execution time on node R_1 and R_j.

• **Task's Estimated Execution Time.** This is the typical task-resource knowledge, usually denoted as the ETC matrix in literatures. We define the *task's estimated complexity* as the estimated execution time on the reference node. So given the task's estimated complexity, the task's estimated execution time on any other node can be derived by using the application's processing rate matrix. We use task's estimated complexity to measure the task's granularity and workload.

4.1 Job-Resource Matching

The job-resource matching stage will select a job and a node from the candidates, and allocate the chosen node to the job. We consider both the requesting node's (system utilization) and the application's (computing performance) perspectives, so as to optimize the Makespan and Flowtime simultaneously.

1) Application's perspective
Given the requesting node R_j, all candidate applications are competing for this resource. We use the Node Importance (NI) to quantify how important R_j is for application A_i to achieve high computing performance, which is determined by

$$NI_{i,j} = \sum_{k=1}^{m} \omega_{i,k} \times \frac{r_{i,j} - r_{i,k}}{\overline{r_{i,\cdot}}} \qquad (3)$$

where $\overline{r_{i,.}}$ is mean value of the i-th row of processing rate matrix and $\omega_{i,k}$ is the weight that satisfies $\omega_{i,1} + \cdots + \omega_{i,m} = 1$ for any i. In this definition, $r_{i,j} - r_{i,k}$ is similar to the suffer value in Sufferage heuristic in traditional HTC, and it measures the importance gain in allocating A_i to R_j when comparing the processing rate offered by R_j with that offered by R_k, and $\dfrac{r_{i,j} - r_{i,k}}{\overline{r_{i,.}}}$ is the normalization of this value. If $r_{i,j} > r_{i,k}$, it is more beneficial to get R_j rather than R_k for application A_i, so the importance gain in this comparison is positive; otherwise the gain will be negative. And thus the NI value of R_j for A_i shall be the sum of importance gains in all those possible comparisons. When sum these values up, we follow the intuition of traditional HTC heuristic Sufferage, which gives larger weight to the sufferage incurred from the failure to choose better option(actually it is a 0-1 weight assignment, 1 for the difference between the best option and the second best one, and 0 for others), but adopt a smoothed weight assignment policy:

$$\omega_{i,k} = r_{i,k} / \sum_{l=1}^{m} r_{i,l} \tag{4}$$

For a requesting node R_j, each application A_i will measure it by NI value; If $NI_{i,j} > NI_{k,j}$, R_j is more important to A_i than A_k, and we should allocate A_i to R_j.

2) Requesting node's perspective
Similar to the above case, but the importance now is measured in terms of resource utilization (described by the parallel degree). Specially, when an application is going to choose a computing resource, we use Application Importance (AI) to quantify how important is A_i for R_j to achieve high resource utilization, which is given by

$$AI_{i,j} = \sum_{k=1}^{p} \lambda_{k,j} \times \frac{D_{i,j} - D_{k,j}}{\overline{D}_{.,j}} \tag{5}$$

$$\lambda_{k,j} = D_{k,j} / \sum_{l=1}^{p} D_{l,j} \tag{6}$$

where $\overline{D}_{.,j}$ is the mean value of the j-th column of parallel degree matrix, and $\lambda_{k,j}$ is the weight similar to $\omega_{i,k}$. When $AI_{i,j}$ is larger than $AI_{i,k}$ for two competing resources R_j and R_k, A_i is more important to R_j, so we should allocate R_j to A_i.

3) The global importance value
After determining the AI and NI, a global importance (GI) value is calculated for every possible pair A_i and R_j, so as to support the application-resource matching. This value is given by

$$GI_{i,j} = \mu_{i,j}NI_{i,j} + (1 - \mu_{i,j})AI_{i,j} \qquad (7)$$

where $0 \leq \mu_{ij} \leq 1$, reflecting the trade-off between the optimization of computing performance (Makespan) and utilization (Flowtime). We provide each GI_{ij} a private weight to accommodate more flexibility. To this end, we measure for application A_i that how spread out the processing rates it achieves on different resources is, and for node R_j that how spread out the utilization it achieves in processing different applications is. So the weight value is given by

$$\lambda_{i,j} = r\,cv_i / (r\,cv_i + c\,cv_j) \qquad (8)$$

where rcv_i and ccv_j are the Coefficient-of-Variance (CV) values of the i-th row of processing rate matrix $r_{i,j}$ and j-th column parallel degree matrix $D_{i,j}$ respectively. This weight assignment policy ensures that more opportunities are given to the side whose achievable processing rates or utilization ratios are more dispersed, and it is reasonable to prioritize those decisions.

Job-resource matching
1 For every candidate application-resource pair (A_i, R_j)
2   Compute global importance value $GI_{i,j}$;
3 $(A_i^*, R_j^*) \leftarrow argmax\{GI_{i,j}\}$; //the pair whose GI is maximal
4 $J_{pre} \leftarrow$ previously processed job of R_j^*
5 If $(J_{pre} \neq \emptyset)$
6   return pair (J_{pre}, R_j^*);
7 Else
8     $J_{i,k}^* \leftarrow$ job with least total complexity over all jobs of A_i^*
9   return pair $(J_{i,k}^*, R_j^*)$;

Fig. 2. Job-resource Matching Algorithm

Given an application-resource pair, the rest of the job-resource matching work is just to select an instance of the targeted application (job selection). Figure 2 shows the whole job-resource matching algorithm. The time complexity is $O(mp(m + p) + N_i)$, but in practice we can pre-compute the GI values to reduce the complexity to just $O(N_i + mp)$ (from step 3 to 9). The job selection policy here tends to reuse the runtime environment between task packages and thus reduce resource management overhead.

4.2   Task Bundling

After node R_j is allocated to job $J_{i,k}$, we need further to decide which tasks of $J_{i,k}$ will be dispatched to R_j. Unlike the traditional HTC scheduling, we select a package of tasks rather than a single task in one dispatch. This task bundling approach is exactly the way to amortize the resource management overhead among tasks in the same package and increase the intra-node system utilization.

Our task selection approach considers the parallel degree $D_{i,j}$ of the application A_i on the node R_j, and chooses a subset of tasks of job $J_{i,k}$ by a bin-packing approach. The upper bound workload that each of $D_{i,j}$ bins can hold is determined by

$$\alpha = \max\{c_1 \times M_{i,k}, c_2 \times (T\_trans + T\_env_{i,j})\} \tag{9}$$

where $M_{i,k}$ is granularity of the largest task in job $J_{i,k}$, T_trans is the transmission startup overhead, $T\_env_{i,j}$ is the cost of runtime environment preparation for application A_i on R_j, and c_1 and c_2 are multipliers. Figure 3 shows the detail of the proposed scheme. The complexity is $O(s \log n_{i,k})$ (implemented by balanced Binary Search Tree), where s is the number of tasks in package. This is efficient enough for MTC applications even when there are millions of tasks.

The merits of this scheme are two-fold: 1) the workload of each job can be better balanced among different nodes by picking the largest task first; 2) the intra-node workload can be better balanced among processors as we have already simulated the intra-node scheduling by bin-packing.

Task-bundling ($J_{i,k}$, R_j)

1 Determine the bin upper bound workload α

2 Empty all $D_{i,j}$ bins: $B_h = \emptyset$

3 For each bin B_h

3.1 Find largest task $\tau \in J_{i,k}$, such that $|\tau| \leq \alpha - |B_h|$

3.2 If no such τ, complete the packing of B_h

3.3 Otherwise $J_{i,k} = J_{i,k} - \{\tau\}$, $B_h = B_h \cup \{\tau\}$; go to 3.1

4 Bundle tasks: $B = \cup B_h$

5 Dispatch task package B to R_j

Fig. 3. Task Bundling Algorithm

5   Experiment

To study the proposed algorithm, we compare it with traditional heuristics, including MaxStd, MinMin and Sufferage. For MTC task scheduling, these heuristics can be used in two ways. The bare way is to schedule MTC tasks based on ETC matrix as in HTC. The other way is to revise them to fit into our scheduling framework. The revised heuristics run based on processing rate matrix rather than ETC. They play the role just as the first 3 steps of job-resource matching algorithm showed in Figure 2. The rest part of job-resource matching algorithm and the whole task-bundling algorithm will remain unchanged for revised heuristics.

5.1 Simulation Method and Parameters

The major parameters include node number m, application number p, job number n and task number for each job. And the generating methods for other items are as follows:

• **Node.** The core number of each node is uniformly sampled from {1, 2, 3, 4, 6, 8, 10, 12, 16, 32}.

• **Application.** An *IO-to-CPU ratio* is attached to each application, representing the application's preference for I/O or CPU speed. The ratio value is uniformly sampled from range (0,1). Large values indicate IO-intensive applications and small ones the CPU-intensive applications.

• **Application's parallel degree matrix $D_{i,j}$.** The $D_{i,j}$ value is determined by $D_{i,j} = \lceil (1 - \gamma_i) \times cn_j \rceil$, where γ_i is IO-to-CPU ratio of application A_i, and cn_j is the core number of node R_j.

• **Application's processing rate matrix $r_{i,j}$.** We use the CVB method proposed in [15] to generate the application-resource processing rate matrix. In CVB method, μ_{task}, V_{task} and $V_{machine}$, which represent the mean of task execution time, CV of tasks and the CV of machines, are the three parameters to control the ETC matrix. In the context of application processing rate, V_{task} is actually $V_{application}$, indicating the heterogeneity level of application; $V_{machine}$ remains the same meaning; and μ_{task} becomes a scale parameter without any significance, and is assigned a fixed value 100. $V_{machine}$ and $V_{application}$ will be varied with values {0.1, 0.6}, representing low and high heterogeneity respectively.

• **Job.** Each job belongs to exactly one of the p applications, uniformly. The tasks' *actual task complexity* of each job is drawn from a Power Law distribution, with mean granularity 100 seconds and minimum granularity 1 second measured on the reference node.

• **Task.** Based on the *actual task complexity*, the *estimated task complexity* is sampled from a truncated Gaussian distribution $N(actual\_complexity, \theta \times actual\_complexity)$ as in [9], where θ is a coefficient controlling the inaccuracy of prediction. The inaccuracy level is application-specific, and is uniformly drawn from range [0.5,1.5].

• **Resource management overhead.** For application A_i, this value is $Overhead_i = 10 \times \sigma(\gamma_i)$, where σ is logistic function with 0.5 as location parameter and 0.1 as shape parameter, and 10 is a parameter controlling the maximal overhead.

Under the same parameters set, experiment will be repeated 10 times and the results will be averaged to eliminate casual effects.

5.2 Evaluation of the Proposed Algorithm

This experiment is to evaluate the application-level scheduling with task bundling algorithm (**ALSTB**) against the traditional heuristics comprehensively. Values of the major parameters are listed in Table 1. Value of task number per job here is set to be much smaller than real MTC cases, as the traditional task-level scheduling is too slow for larger values.

Figure 4(a) shows that when number of tasks is small, traditional heuristics behave pretty well; but as the task number increase, the proposed algorithm becomes better.

This proved that the traditional heuristics cost more time in resource management and thus deteriorate the performance. Figure 4(b) shows a gradually bigger advantage of ALSTB in terms of Average Job Makespan when increasing the number of tasks. The reason is, unlike ALSTB, the bare traditional heuristics treat tasks from different jobs indiscriminately, which in its extreme case may schedule tasks from different jobs alternately and result in bad Average Job Makespan. Figure 4(c) shows a clear margin between ALSTB and other three heuristics. We note that the bare heuristics schedule one task every time and cannot fully utilize a modern multi-core node, while the ALSTB considers the intra-node capacity exploitation and workload balancing by the bin-packing task-bundling strategy. This makes the significant difference of Overall Flowtime observed in graph.

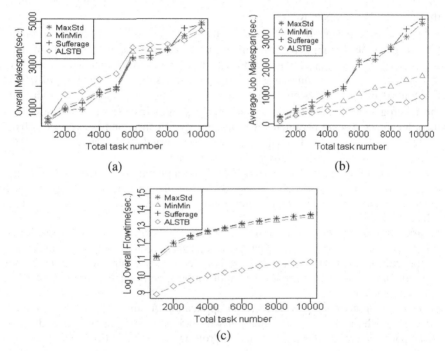

Fig. 4. Performance impact of task number on Overall Makespan, Average Job Makespan and Overall Flowtime

5.3   Evaluation of the Revised Heuristics

This experiment is to evaluate the revised heuristics (denoted as R-MaxStd, R-MinMin and R-Sufferage) that have been adapted to fit into our scheduling model. The experiment is put in real MTC conditions, as listed in Table 2. Every job's task number is uniformly between 10,000 and 50,000, and the total number of processed tasks will range from 1,000,000 to 5,000,000.

Table 1. Major parameters (I)

NodeNum	ApplicationNum	JobNum	TaskNumPerJob
100	10	20	50-500

Table 2. Major parameters (II)

NodeNum	ApplicationNum	JobNum	TaskNumPerJob
1,000	50	100	10,000-50,000

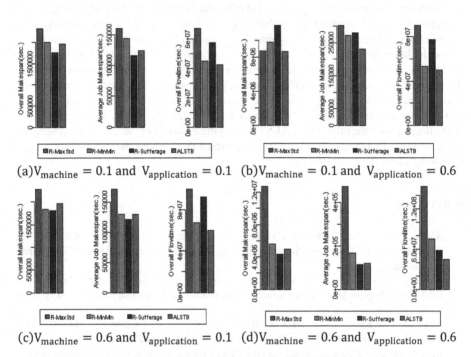

(a)$V_{machine} = 0.1$ and $V_{application} = 0.1$ (b)$V_{machine} = 0.1$ and $V_{application} = 0.6$

(c)$V_{machine} = 0.6$ and $V_{application} = 0.1$ (d)$V_{machine} = 0.6$ and $V_{application} = 0.6$

Fig. 5. Performance of the revised heuristic V.S. ALSTB in 4 settings

Figure 5(a) shows the results when both application and resoruce heterogeneity are low. R-Sufferage is the best in terms of Overall Makespan and Average Job Makespan, whereas ALSTB achieves the best Overall Flowtime.The reason shall be that ALSTB has taken both the application and resource's perspectives into consideration and tend to make a balanced scheduling decision. Figure 5(b) shows the results for high application heterogeneity and low resource heterogeneity, where ALSTB exhibits better than three other heuristics in all metrics. Figure 5(c) shows the results for low application heterogeneity and high resource heterogeneity, which is similar to Figure 5(a). Finally Figure 5(d) shows the results for high application heterogeneity and high resource heterogeneity. The algrithms' performance is more dispersed than other settings, especially that R-MaxStd is far worser than others.

We can read two things in these four results. First, compared to the bare heuristics, the performance of revised heuristics are greatly improved, which could even compete with ALSTB; this verifies the merit of the proposed scheduling strategies. Second, ALSTB still has its advantage in that it gives lower Flowtime in all four settings.

6   Conclusions

In this paper, we propose the ALSTB algorithm, which divides the whole scheduling into a job-resource matching algorithm and a bin-packing based task-bundling algorithm for multiple MTC applications scheduling in heterogeneous environments. The proposed algorithm is compared against both bare and revised traditional heuristics, where the latter are adapted from the former to fit into our scheduling framework. The simulation experiments show that our algorithm gets better results than the bare traditional heuristics, and outperforms the revised ones in Flowtime and meanwhile achieves performance in Makespan comparable to them. So the conclusions are two-fold: on one hand, ALSTB provides a way for multiple applications many-tasks scheduling, and on the other hand, ALSTB gives the balanced optimization of Makespan and Flowtime. In future, our research will concern the fairness issues involved in the multi-user Many-Task Computing.

References

1. Raicu, I., Zhang, Z., Wilde, M., Foster, I.T., Beckman, P.H., Iskra, K., Clifford, B.: Toward Loosely Coupled Programming on Petascale Systems. IEEE/ACM Super Computing (2008)
2. Raicu, I., Foster, I., Zhao, Y.: Many-Task Computing for Grids and Supercomputers. In: IEEE Workshop on Many-Task Computing on Grids and Supercomputers, MTAGS 2008 (2008)
3. Isard, M., Prabhakaran, V., Currey, J., Wieder, U., Talwar, K., Goldberg, A.: Quincy: Fair Scheduling for distributed Computing Clusters. In: OSDI 2010 (2010)
4. Kim, N., et al.: ECgene: Genome-based EST clustering and gene modeling foralternative splicing. Genome. Res. 15, 566–576 (2005)
5. Yu, H., Li, Y., Wu, X., Xiao, J., Li, X.: A Self-Optimizing Computation Partitioning Algorithm for Distributed Many-task Computing. In: China Grid 2010 (2010)
6. Xu, J., Lam, A.Y.S., Li, V.O.K.: Chemical reaction optimization for task scheduling in grid computing. IEEE Trans. Parallel Distrib. Systems (2011)
7. Garey, M.R., Johnson, D.S.: 'Strong' NP-CompletenessResults: Motivation, Examples, and Implications. J. Association for Computing Machinery 25(3), 499–508 (1978)
8. Braun, T.D., Hensgen, D., Freund, R.F., Siegel, H.J., Beck, N., Boloni, L.L., Maheswaran, M., Reuther, A.I., Robertson, J.P., Theys, M.D., Yao, B.: A comparison of eleven static heuristics for mapping a class of independent tasks onto heterogeneous distributed computing systems. J. Parallel and Distributed Comput. 61(6), 810–837 (2001)
9. Maheswaran, M., Ali, S., Siegel, H.J., Hensgen, D., Freund, R.F.: Dynamic matching and scheduling of a class of independent tasks onto heterogeneous computing systems. In: Proceedings of the Eighth Heterogeneous Computing Workshop (1999)

10. Munir, E.U., Li, J.-Z., Shi, S.-F., Zou, Z., Yang, D.: MaxStd: A Task Scheduling Heuristic for Heterogeneous Computing Environment. Information Technology Journal, ISSN-1812-5638
11. Izakian, H., Ladani, B.T., Zamanifar, K., Abraham, A.: A Novel Particle Swarm Optimization Approach for Grid Job Scheduling. In: Proc. Third Int'l Conf. Information Systems, Technology and Management, vol. 31, pp. 100–109 (March 2009)
12. Iosup, A., Sonmez, O.O., Anoep, S., Epema, D.H.J.: The performance of bags-of-tasks in large-scale distributed systems. In: International Symposium on High-Performance Distributed Computing (HPDC), pp. 97–108. ACM (2008)
13. Raicu, I., et al.: Falkon: a Fast and Light-weight task execution framework. IEEE/ACM Super Computing (2007)
14. Li, Y., Wu, X., Xiao, J., Zhang, Y., Yu, H.: A Scheduling Algorithm Based on Task Complexity Estimating for Many-Task Computing. In: SKG 2010 (2010)
15. Ali, S., Siegel, H.J., Maheswaran, M., Ali, S., Hensgen, D.: Task execution time modeling for heterogeneous computing systems. In: Proceedings of the Ninth Heterogeneous Computing Workshop, pp. 185–200 (2000)

DGraph: Algorithms for Shortgun Reads Assembly Using De Bruijn Graph

Jintao Meng[1,2,4], Jianrui Yuan[2,3], Jiefeng Cheng[2], Yanjie Wei[2],
and Shengzhong Feng[2,*]

[1] Institute of Computing Technology, CAS, Beijing, 100190, P.R. China
[2] Shenzhen Institutes of Advanced Technology, CAS, Shenzhen, 518055, P.R. China
[3] Central South University, Changsha, 410083, P.R. China
[4] Graduate University of Chinese Academy of Sciences, Beijing, 100049, China
{jt.meng,jr.yuan,jf.cheng,yj.wei,sz.feng}@siat.ac.cn

Abstract. Massively parallel DNA sequencing platforms have become widely available, reducing the cost of DNA sequencing by over two orders of magnitude, and democratizing the field by putting the sequencing capacity of a major genome center in the hands of individual investigators. New challenges include the development of robust protocols for generating sequencing libraries, building effective new approaches to resequence and data-analysis. In this paper we demonstrate a new sequencing algorithm, named DGraph, which has two modules, one module is responsible to construct De Bruijn graph by cutting reads into k-mers, and the other's duty is to simplify this graph and collect all long contigs. The authors didn't adapt the sequence graph reductions operations proposed by RAMANA M.IDURY or Finding Eulerian Superpaths proved by Pavel A.Pevzner or bubble remove steps suggested by Danial Zerbino, As the first operations was computing expensive, and the second one was impractical, and the last one did not benefit either the quality of contigs or the efficiency of the assembler. Our assembler was focused only on efficient and effective error removal and path reduction operations. Applying DGraph to the simulation data of fruit fly Drosophila melanogaster chromosome X, DGraph (3min) is about six times faster than velvet 0.3 (19 mins), and its coverage (92.5%) is also better than velvet (78.2%) when k = 21. Compare to velvet, the results shows that the algorithm of DGraph is a faster program with high quality results.

Keywords: De Bruijn graph, graph algorithm, short read assembler.

1 Introduction

Each cell of a living organism contains chromosomes composed of a sequence of DNA base pairs. This sequence, the genome, represents a set of instructions that controls the replication and function of each organism. The automated DNA sequencer gave birth to genomics, the analytic and comparative study of genomes, by allowing scientists to decode entire genomes.

---

* Corresponding author.

J.J. Park et al. (Eds.): NPC 2012, LNCS 7513, pp. 14–21, 2012.

Although genomes vary in size from millions of nucleotides in bacteria to billions of nucleotides in humans and most animals and plants, the chemical reactions researchers use to decode the DNA base pairs are accurate for only about 600 to 700 nucleotides at a time.

The process of sequencing begins by physically breaking the DNA into millions of random fragments, which are then "read" by a DNA sequencing machine. Next, a computer program called an assembler pieces together the many overlapping reads and reconstructs the original sequence. This general technique, called shotgun sequencing, was introduced by Fred Sanger in 1982. Recently, new sequencing technologies have emerged [1] (Metzker 2005), for example, pyrosequencing (454 sequencing) [2] (Margulies et al. 2005) and sequencing by synthesis (Solexa) [3] (Bentley 2006), both commercially available. Compared to traditional Sanger methods, these technologies produce shorter reads, currently ~200 bp for pyrosequencing and 35bp for Solexa. Until recently, very short read information was only used in the context of a know reference assembly, either for sequencing individuals of the same species as the reference, or readout assays.

Sequencing remains at the core of genomics. Current sequencing approaches are classed into two strategies. The first one is overlap-layout-consensus, its applications includes TIGR assembler [4], Phrap[5], and CAP3 [6]; the second one is graph-theoretical approach, and its applications includes VCAKE[7], SSAKE[8], Velvet[9].

The assembler following the first approach must first build the graph by computing all possible alignments between the reads. A second stage cleans up the graph by removing transitive edges and resolving ambiguities. The output of this stage comprised a set of nonintersecting simple paths in this refined graph, each such path corresponding to a contig. A final step generates a consensus sequence for each contig by constructing the multiple alignments of the reads that is consistent with the chosen path. Although this approach are relatively easy to implement, but they are inherently local in nature and ignore long-range relationships between reads, which could be useful in detecting and resolving repeats. In addition, all current implementations of the greedy method require huge memory. This limits their applicability on current available hardware to organisms with gnomes of 32 Mbp or less.

The second approach to shotgun sequence assembly uses a sequencing-by-hybridization technology. The idea is create a virtual SBH problem by breaking the reads into overlapping n-mers, where an k-mer is a substring of length k from the original sequence. Next, the assembler builds a directed De Bruijn graph in which each edge corresponds to an k-mer from one of the original sequence reads. Finally, the problem of reconstructing the original DNA molecule corresponds to finding a path that uses all the edges-that is, an Eulerian path. In theory, the Eulerian path approach is computationally far more efficient than the overlap-layout-consensus approach because the assembler can find Eulerian paths in linear time while the problems associated with the overlap-layout-consensus paradigm are NP-complete. Despite this dramatic theoretical difference, the actual performance of existing algorithms indicates that overlap-layout-consensus approach is just as fast as the SBH-based approach.

The algorithm proposed in this paper fell into the graph-theoretical approach. As computation time and quality of contigs still limit the practical use of these implementations adopting de Bruijn graphs approach to genomes on the order of a billion base in size. Compared with the previous works, DGraph will pay attention to these two points. For this result, the authors didn't adapt the sequence graph reductions operations proposed by RAMANA M.IDURY or Finding Eulerian Superpaths proved by Pavel A.Pevzner or bubble remove steps suggested by Danial Zerbino, As the first operations was computing expensive, and the second one was impractical, and the last one did not benefit either the quality of contigs or the computation efficiency of the assembler. Our assembler was focused only on efficient and effective error removal and path reduction operations.

We organize the paper as follows, Section 2 will introduce the operations of two modules in detail. The experiment and performance will be demonstrated in Section 3, and the last section will discuss the weak points of the algorithm and our further work.

2   Algorithmic Approach

The processes of the algorithm DGraph was descript in figure 1. DGraph has two modules, the first one is graph construction, which is responsible to construct De Bruijn graph by cutting reads into k-mers, and the second one is graph simplification whose duty is to simplify this graph.

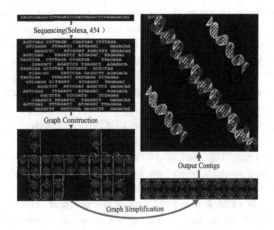

Fig. 1. The processes of algorithm DGraph

2.1   Graph Construction Module

In the De Bruijn graph, each node represents a k-mers, and adjacent k-mers overlap each other with k-1 nucleotides. Each node N is attached to the node ~N, which represents the reverse series of reverse complement k-mers. The adjacent nodes are connected by arc, for each node A to B, a symmetric arc goes from ~B to ~A.

For each read, we cut it into k-mer (k must be an odd number, k<32) and keep it into a hash table. For each k-mers, the hash table will keep this string of k-mers and its node ID in the graph. Each k-mer has a reverse complement.

Then, all adjacent k-mers (or nodes) in the same read are connected. Its reverse complement is also linked with a reverse arc. Each arc has a weight to record how many reads contain this two k-mers. The Construction module of DGraph processes each reads and connects all adjacent k-mers to build a De Bruijn graph.

2.2   Graph Simplification Module

2.2.1   Error Link Removal

Generally speaking, 1%~3% errors will be imported into De Bruijn graph from input reads because of the precision of modern sequencing machines. All low coverage arcs will be thought as error links and must be deleted.

There will be a threshold θ for each arc in the De Bruijn graph, if the weight of arc is less than θ, this arc will be deleted. Then if some node is disconnected with other nodes we will also delete that node.

2.2.2   Path Simplification

This step is to simplify the De Bruijn graph. When a node A has only one outgoing arc that points to node B, then the two nodes can be merged, and their reverse complements should be merged too.

Our module will degrade each chain of nodes into one node. After simplification, the number of nodes will be greatly declined. There possibly are some isolated nodes, we simply delete all of these isolated nodes, as we think it was introduced by error reads.

2.2.3   Tips Removal

Tip is a chain of node which disconnected on one end. All tips will be removed if it is shorter than 2k, this parameter is a cutoff length which was chosen to delete all erroneous constructs.

After that our algorithm produced a much more simply graph without loss of information. We did not do any further operations as the other algorithm does, because we did not agree that bubbles removing step was appropriate operation in velvet[9], it simply combined two path from node A to node B into one, but these two path may actually exist in the finally contigs. We also did not apply graph reduction operation mentioned in [10], in principle, this algorithm was great, it did give a way to simplify the De Bruijn graph; However it is not practical to realize the graph reduction, and the complexity on maintain the data structure defined in [10] is enormous high, not to mention their complex mathematic operation. Even the prototype developed by the authors of [8] will use 10s on assembling 20k data.

3   Experimental Results

The sequence data is produced from Drosophila melanogaster (fruit fly) chromosome X (its sequence size is 21.7M, the NCBI reference sequence ID is NC_004354.3). Our reads producer program will cut NC_004354.3 into short reads with length range from 200bp to 400bp, and the coverage of our read set is 30. Errors rate of 1% was introduced into the read set. The final size of the read set is about 571M.

The DGraph algorithm was compared with velvet 0.3 in our Evaluation in both contig quality and algorithm performance.

The read set will be assembled by DGraph and velvet. We ran the entire test with different parameter k, which was an odd number ranged from 19 to 31. We verified the assemblies by aligning the resulting contigs to the reference sequence by NCBI blast [11] to calculate the quality of the results.

First, the quality analysis of the resulting contigs was illustrated from figure 2 to figure 7. Figure 2 shows that the number of resulting contigs produced by DGraph are about two-third as many as the number of contigs output by velvet. In max length of contigs, DGraph is two times longer than velvet according to figure 3. The same trend also happens in figure 4 on their N50 length. Figure 5 demonstrated that DGraph has less number of contigs larger than N50 compared to velvet, which means that contigs produced by DGraph are mainly consisted with a few long contigs and a large amount of short contigs. All in all, the four figure shows that DGraph has much less but much longer contigs longer than N50 compared with velvet. What's more, the coverage of DGraph's resulting contigs (92.5%) is slightly better than the coverage of velvet's according (78.2%) to figure 6.

Second, In figure 7, DGraph consumed about one-sixth as much cpu time as velvet did, which is 3minutes and 19minutes respectively. But in terms of memory consumption DGraph is two times larger than velvet. Generally speaking, DGraph can produce higher quality of resulting contigs with one-sixth cpu time used by velvet, only at the cost of more memory.

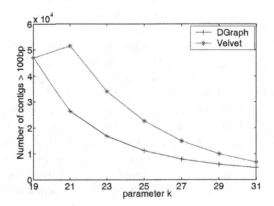

Fig. 2. Number of contigs with length larger than 100bp

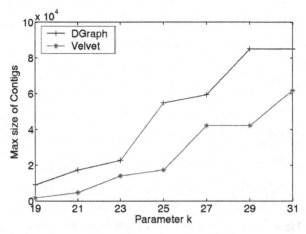

Fig. 3. Max length of contigs

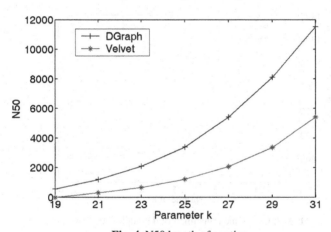

Fig. 4. N50 length of contigs

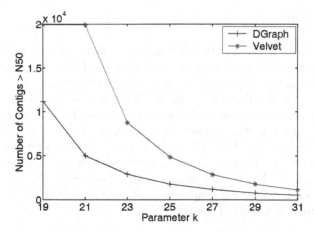

Fig. 5. Number of contigs with length longer N50

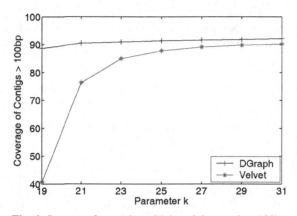

Fig. 6. Coverage for contigs with length longer than 100bp

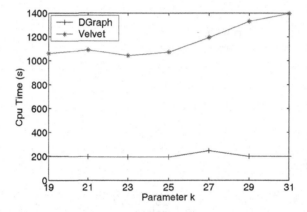

Fig. 7. CPU time consumed by DGraph and Velvet

4   Discussion

The DNA sequencing technology field has become a quickly moving target, Fast and high quality Algorithms that can assemble millions of small DNA fragments into gene sequences are located in our research scope. DGraph, a new de novo sequencing algorithm was proposed in this paper, Core operations, such as graph construction and graph simplification was implemented effectively to support high quality configs. The experiment demonstrated that DGraph outperformance velvet both on assembler speed and contigs' quality. DGraph was just a basical assembler framework on resequencing, father optimization on memory consumption and code parallelization was urgent work in the development of next version. Last, but not least, is there exist a practical method to reduce the simplified graph, Can this method work efficiently and indeed improve the quality of resulted contigs.

Acknowledgements. This work is supported by NSFC (Grant No. 61103049) and Shenzhen Research Fund (Grant No.JC201005270342A). The author also thanks Lin Fang, Bingqiang Wang and their teammates from BGI, and Sitong Sheng from HYK Gene for their supports and suggestions on this work.

References

1. Metzker, M.L., Lu, J., Gibbs, R.A.: Electrophoretically Uniform Fluorescent Dyes for Automated DNA Sequencing. Science 5254(271), 1420–1422 (2009)
2. Margulies, M., et al.: Genome sequencing in microfabricated high-density picolitre reactors. Nature 441(4) (2006)
3. Bentley, D.R.: Whole-genome re-sequencing. Current Opinion in Genetics & Development 6(16), 545–552 (2006)
4. Sutton, G.G., White, O., Adams, M.D., Kerlavage, A.R.: TIGR Assembler: A New Tool for Assembling Large Shotgun Sequencing Projects. Genome Science and Technology 1(1), 9–19 (1995)
5. Green, P.:
   http://bozeman.mbt.washington.edu/phrap.docs/phrap.html
6. Huang, X., Madan, A.: CAP3: A DNA Sequence Assembly Program. Genome Research (9), 868–877 (1990)
7. Kreuze, J.F., Perez, A., Untiveros, M., Quispe, D., Fuentes, S., Barker, I., Simon, R.: Complete viral genome sequence and discovery of novel viruses by deep sequencing of small RNAs: A generic method for diagnosis, discovery and sequencing of viruses. Virology 1(388), 1–7 (2009)
8. Warren, R.L., Sutton, G.G., Jones, S.J.M., et al.: Assembling millions of short DNA sequences using SSAKE. Bioinformatics 4(23), 500–501 (2007)
9. Zerbino, D.R., Birney, E.: Velvet: algorithms for de novo short read assembly using De Bruijn graphs. Genome. Res. 5(18), 821–829 (2008)
10. Idury, R.M., Waterman, M.S.: A New Algorithm for DNA Sequence Assembly. Journal of Computational Biology (1995)
11. blast,
    http://www.ncbi.nlm.nih.gov/blast/producttable.shtml#mega

Knowledge-Based Adaptive Self-Scheduling[*]

Yizhuo Wang, Weixing Ji, Feng Shi, Qi Zuo, and Ning Deng

School of Computer Science and Technology, Beijing Institute of Technology
{frankwyz,jwx,sfbit,zql127,dunning}@bit.edu.cn

Abstract. Loop scheduling scheme plays a critical role in the efficient execution of programs, especially loop dominated applications. This paper presents KASS, a knowledge-based adaptive loop scheduling scheme. KASS consists of two phases: static partitioning and dynamic scheduling. To balance the workload, the knowledge of loop features and the capabilities of processors are both taken into account using a heuristic approach in static partitioning phase. In dynamic scheduling phase, an adaptive self-scheduling algorithm is applied, in which two tuning parameters are set to control chunk sizes, aiming at load balancing and minimizing synchronization overhead. In addition, we extend KASS to apply on loop nests and adjust the chunk sizes at runtime. The experimental results show that KASS performs 4.8% to 16.9% better than the existing self- scheduling schemes, and up to 21% better than the affinity scheduling scheme.

Keywords: loop scheduling, self-scheduling, multiprocessor system.

1 Introduction

Loops are the dominant source of parallelism for many applications [1]. In general, loops fall into two categories: DOALL loops and non-DOALL loops. DOALL loops, also known as parallel loops, do have not any loop-carried dependence. Hence, different iterations of a DOALL loop can be easily executed on concurrent threads. In this paper, we focus on DOALL loops to exploit loop level parallelism (LLP). The main problem encountered with LLP is on partitioning and allocating loop iterations among threads in a multiprocessor environment. Loop scheduling schemes have been extensively studied to deal with this problem.

Existing loop scheduling schemes can be classified as static and dynamic. Static scheduling schemes partition loop iterations at compile time and statically assign iterations to processors. The static scheduling scheme results in a low runtime scheduling overhead but poor load balancing. Dynamic scheduling determines the division of iterations among processors at runtime. It leads to runtime overhead, but achieves dynamic load balancing.

Self-scheduling schemes are the most successful and widely used dynamic scheduling schemes. They partition loop iterations into chunks before execution. A chunk

---

[*] This work was supported by the National Natural Science Foundation of China (60973010).

J.J. Park et al. (Eds.): NPC 2012, LNCS 7513, pp. 22–32, 2012.

is assigned to an idle processor at each scheduling step at runtime. Thus, the time spent in determining how many iterations should be scheduled is saved. Most self-scheduling algorithms have decreasing size chunks, which is a result of the trade-off between load balancing and scheduling overhead.

Some features of the loop and runtime environment affect the execution time of chunks. On one hand, different loops have different types of workload distribution. Non-uniform workload results in different execution times for same size chunks. On the other hand, processor speed and usage are important runtime features that determine the execution time of a chunk. Existing self-scheduling schemes are oblivious to these features. In this paper, we propose an adaptive self-scheduling scheme that utilizes the knowledge of the workload and the runtime environment with the aim of reducing synchronization costs, improving load balancing, and exploiting locality.

The rest of the paper is organized as follows. Section 2 reviews loop scheduling strategies and discusses related work. Section 3 presents the knowledge-based adaptive self-scheduling scheme in detail. Experimental results are presented in section 4, and the conclusion is presented in Section 5.

2   Background and Related Work

The simplest of all scheduling algorithms is static scheduling, which assigns an even number of loop iterations to each processor. It keeps the scheduling overhead to a minimum, but does not balance the load dynamically compared with the other schemes. The first self-scheduling scheme [2] is another extreme. It assigns one iteration to an idle processor each time. Hence, processors finish at nearly the same time and the workload is well balanced. However, the scheduling overhead maybe unacceptable because of the large number of scheduling steps. Self-scheduling with fixed size chunks [3] is a tradeoff between these two rival techniques. It assigns a chunk, which consists of successive iterations, to an idle processor each time. This procedure reduces the number of scheduling steps needed, which therefore, reduces the scheduling overhead.

Some self-scheduling schemes with decreasing chunk sizes were proposed to achieve better load balancing than fixed size chunking self-scheduling. They schedule large chunks at the beginning to ensure locality and reduce overhead, while scheduling small chunks at the end to balance the workload. In these self-scheduling schemes, guided self-scheduling (GSS, [1]), factoring self-scheduling (FSS, [4]), and trapezoid self-scheduling (TSS, [5]) are the most successful and widely used. The difference among them is the computation process for chunk sizes. None of the three schemes takes the characters of the loop and runtime factors into account. Our self-scheduling scheme quantifies these factors and uses them in calculating chunk sizes.

Some dynamic self-scheduling schemes [6, 7] adjust chunk sizes at run time or exploit processor affinity when mapping chunks to processors. Affinity scheduling proposed by Markatos et al. [8], employs per-processor work queues, which is similar with our scheme. However, the size of each work queue is not determined based on the knowledge of loop and runtime environment in affinity scheduling. Some groups [9, 10] have undertaken self-scheduling studies on particular architectures, considering the features of the system architecture. Our technique could be easily extended to these architectures.

3   Knowledge-Based Adaptive Self-Scheduling

In this section, we describe the details of the knowledge-based adaptive self-scheduling scheme (KASS). The problem to be considered is the scheduling, across p processors $P_1, P_2 \ldots$, and P_p, of N iterations on a parallel loop. KASS has two phases:

Static Partitioning Phase: A knowledge-based approach is used to partition iterations of the parallel loop into local queues of processors, which makes the total workload, not the number of iterations, equally distributed onto processors approximately.

Dynamic Scheduling Phase: Based on self-scheduling rule, every local work queue is partitioned into chunks with decreasing sizes. Each processor allocates a chunk from its local queue to execute. A processor steals a chunk from another processor to execute when it finishes the execution of all the chunks in its local queue.

3.1   Static Partitioning

The execution time of each iteration can be obtained via loop profiling. Let t_i denote the execution time of ith iteration. The mean execution time is μ_t and the variance is σ_t. Let l_j and u_j denote the lower and upper bounds of the local queue assigned to processor j. Assuming that all the processors have the same capacity to execute the loop, static partitioning will only relate to the workload distribution of the loop. Thus, the bounds $\{(l_j, u_j) \mid j = 1, 2, ..., p\}$ can be calculated by

$$\sum_{i=l_j}^{u_j} t_i \approx \frac{N\mu_t}{p} \tag{1}$$

Note that

$$l_1 = 1; \quad l_{j+1} = u_j + 1, \quad j = 1, 2, ..., p-1; \quad u_p = N. \tag{2}$$

Parallel loop normally has regular workloads. Thus, t_i could be well estimated by profiling [11]. In addition, prior knowledge about the loop only contributes to the static load balancing. The dynamic scheduling will further balance the workload in our scheme. Thus, prior information need not be accurate. For example, if the workload distribution of the loop is almost uniform, no profiling is needed, and t_i (i=1, 2..., N) could just be set to any fixed number.

In addition to loop features, differences in processor speed, load running, and architecture can significantly impact performance. We use a_i to represent the capacity of processor P_i to execute the loop. In a simple case, let s_i denote the speed of P_i and b_i denote how much of P_i's capacity is used in the execution of this application. Then, $a_i = s_i b_i$. We normalize a_i with a_1. For instance, a_1=1 and a_2=2, which means that the execution time of the same workload on P_1 is twice as that on P_2. Subsequently, the loop bounds of the local queues can be calculated using the following equations under the assumption that the loop is uniform.

$$l_1 = 1; \quad l_{j+1} = u_j + 1; \quad u_j = \left\lceil \left(\sum_{i=1}^{j} a_i \bigg/ \sum_{i=1}^{p} a_i \right) N \right\rceil, j = 1, 2, ..., p-1; \quad u_p = N. \tag{3}$$

Considering the aspects of loop workload distribution and processor capacity, the bounds should be determined using

$$\frac{1}{a_j}\sum_{i=l_j}^{u_j}t_i \approx \sum_{j=1}^{p}\left(\frac{1}{a_j}\sum_{i=l_j}^{u_j}t_i\right)\bigg/p \tag{4}$$

where the discrete function of t_i is approximately equally partitioned among p processors. Unfortunately, the approximation of (4) does not provide a simple computation. We propose a heuristic method to calculate the loop bounds $\{(l_j,u_j)\,|\,j=1,2,...,p\}$. Let l'_j and u'_j denote the bounds calculated using equation (1). Let l''_j and u''_j denote the bounds calculated using equation (3). We initialize the bounds as follows:

$$l_1 = 1;\quad l_{j+1} = u_j + 1;\quad u_j = \left\lfloor\frac{u'_j + u''_j}{2}\right\rfloor, j=1,2,...,p-1.\quad u_p = N; \tag{5}$$

Consequently, the execution time of iterations from l_j to u_j on processor P_j is calculated as follows:

$$T_j = \frac{1}{a_j}\sum_{i=l_j}^{u_j}t_i, j=1,2,...,p. \tag{6}$$

The mean of T_j is μ_T and the variance is σ_T. Our goal is to make all T_j as equal as possible, i.e., all the processors finish the execution at approximately the same time. For a processor P_j, if T_j is greater than μ_T, the processor has much workload, thus, we need to decrease the number of iterations assigned to P_j that results in the adjustment of the bounds, and vice versa. The change is defined as $(\mu_T - T_j)/\bar{t}$, where $\bar{t}$ is the mean execution time of iterations, which is defined as $\bar{t} = \sum_{j=1}^{p}T_j\bigg/N$.

The above procedure is repeated to adjust the bounds until one of the following conditions is met:

1) The maximum number of steps, which is user inputted, is reached.
2) The coefficient of variation (c.o.v.) of T_j (σ_T/μ_T) becomes less than a threshold value, which is set to 0.1 in our experiments.
3) The variance (σ_T) in the current step is greater than that in the last step.

To summarize, we determine the loop bounds of the local queues in the static partitioning phase using the following rules:

1) If the c.o.v of the execution time of iterations (σ_t/μ_t) is less than 0.1, the bounds are calculated using equation (3). Since the loop has nearly uniform workload distribution in this case, we just take the capacities of the processors into account.
2) If the c.o.v of the capacities of the processors (σ_a/μ_a) is less than 0.1, the bounds are calculated using equation (1). The processors have almost same capacity in this case, thus, we just take the workload distribution into account.
3) In other cases, the heuristic method introduced above is used.

3.2   Dynamic Scheduling

In the dynamic scheduling phase, each local iteration queue is partitioned into chunks. A self-scheduling algorithm is then applied to assign a chunk to an idle processor in each scheduling step. A chunk size tuning parameter k_i is set for processor P_i ($i=1,2,...,p$) to balance between data locality and parallelism. Each processor always removes k_i of the remaining iterations in its local queue for execution. P_i turns to help other heavily loaded processors after completing the execution of the iterations in its local queue. In our implementation, P_i allocates k_i of the remaining iterations from the next unfinished work queue for execution. Considering synchronization cost, a chunk should not be too small. Thus, another parameter α, which is the minimal number of iterations in a chunk, is identified. The sketch of KASS is presented in Fig. 1.

Algorithm 1. Knowledge-based Adaptive Self-Scheduling

Master:
```
for (i = 1; i ≤ p; i++)       // initial partition
    assign_iterations(i, li, ui);  // assign iterations li to ui to processor Pi.
for (i = 1; i ≤ p; i++) {    // create workers
    create_thread(Ti);
    Set Ti running on processor Pi;
}
```
Wait for all worker threads to complete.

Worker:
```
get_iterations(l, u, k){   // get a chunk from a work queue.
    if (u−l < 2α){ // ensure chunk size is larger than α.
        chunk.begin = l;   chunk.end = u;
    }else{
        chunk.begin = l;   chunk.end = l + (u−l)k;
    }
    l = chunk.end + 1; // update the lower bound.
}
while (true) {
    // get a chunk in the local work queue of current processor Pi.
    chunk = get_iterations(li, ui, ki)
    if(chunk = NULL){
        Lock( );
        j = find_unfinished_workqueue( );
        // processor Pj has remaining iterations.
        if( j = 0) // all the iterations have been scheduled.
        { Unlock( );    thread_exit( ); }
        chunk = get_iterations(lj, uj, ki)   // steal a chunk from Pj.
        Unlock( );
    }
    execute_loop(chunk);
}
```

Fig. 1. The sketch of KASS

Next, we present the identification of tuning parameters k_i and α. Previous work in [12] shows that the chunk size should range from $R/2p$ to R/p in a self-scheduling scheme with a central work queue to have reasonable load imbalance and synchronization overhead. R is the number of the remaining iterations. The chunk size would range from $0.5 R$ to R when the same principle is applied to per-processor work queues. Therefore, the range of k_i should be $[0.5, 1]$. The selection of k_i relates to two factors: the "*error*" of static partitioning and the dynamic changes of runtime environment. We use c.o.v (σ/μ) to represent the *error* of static partitioning. Three cases in static partition phase were noted, as described in section 3.1. We use σ_d/μ_a when $\sigma_t/\mu_t < 0.1$; use σ_t/μ_t when $\sigma_a/\mu_a < 0.1$; use σ_T/μ_T for other cases. The range of σ/μ is $[0, 0.1]$. Let Δ denote the dynamic changes in the runtime environment, which ranges from 0 to 0.4 to enforce k_i ranging from 0.5 to 1. The chunk size tuning parameter k_i is defined as

$$k_i = 1 - \mu / \sigma - \Delta, \qquad i = 1, 2, ..., p. \tag{7}$$

The value of Δ is user inputted. Our experiment results suggest that it is optimal to set Δ to 0.1 when the system is relatively stable. Thus, the value of k_i is 0.8.

The tuning parameter α limits the minimal size of a chunk. If the time that a processor spends to steal a chunk from another processor is longer than the execution time of this chunk, it is clear that chunk stealing need not be done. Performance penalty of work stealing in the present comes from two aspects. One is the synchronization overhead, which refers to the time cost of the critical sections in shared memory multiprocessor systems. Another is the loss of data locality, which is mainly the cache miss penalty in shared memory systems, and is considered as communication cost in distributed memory systems. The execution time of the critical section used to allocate a chunk via profiling is obtained. Let T_{cs} denote it. The minimal number of iterations of a chunk is defined as $\alpha = 2T_{cs}/\mu_t$, where, μ_t is the mean execution time via profiling. The above equation does not take the effect of locality into account because locality is hard to quantify. Hence, we enlarged the synchronization cost to fill up the loss.

3.3   KASS for Loop Nests

For loop nests with sequential outer loop and parallel inner loop, we improve the KASS algorithm by adaptively changing k_i for each processor. A counter C_i is set for processor P_i. C_i is increased by one each time the processor P_i removes a chunk from another processor P_j. Accordingly, C_j is decreased by one. The counters are initially set to zero at the beginning of every step in the outer loop. At the end of the outer loop step, the processors are classified into three types based on the value of the counters:

- Lightly loaded: the C_i value of the processor is greater than a positive integer θ, which is a threshold set by the user. We set θ to 1 in our experiments.
- Normally loaded: the C_i value of the processor is within the range of $[-\theta, \theta]$.
- Heavily loaded: the C_i value of the processor is less than $-\theta$.

If P_i is a heavily loaded processor, less iterations should be assigned to it at each scheduling step so that more iterations remaining in the heavily loaded processor can be executed by the lightly loaded processors. k_i is decreased to realize the adjustment. On the contrary, k_i is increased for lightly loaded processors so that these processors can

finish the chunks in their local work queue as soon as possible, and then start to help
heavily loaded processors. The value of k_i is adjusted to k_i' as follows:

$$k_i' = \begin{cases} \min(0.9, k_i + 0.1) & \text{if } C_i > \theta \\ k_i & \text{if } \theta \geq C_i \geq -\theta \\ \max(0.5, k_i - 0.1) & \text{if } C_i < -\theta \end{cases} \tag{8}$$

The KASS algorithm for loop nests is similar to the affinity scheduling proposed by
Markatos et al. [8]. Both of these algorithms use per-processor work queues and utilize
work-stealing to balance the workload. Three important differences between KASS and
affinity scheduling exist. First, static partitioning in KASS is knowledge-based, whereas affinity scheduling makes equivalence partitioning. Second, chunk sizes are
adaptively changed by the adjustment of k_i in KASS. In affinity scheduling, chunk sizes
are fixed during multiple execution times of the inner DOALL loop. Third, KASS
limits the minimal chunk size, whereas affinity scheduling does not. Excessive partitioning as in some cases in affinity scheduling causes harmful effects on data locality
and overall performance.

4   Experiments

In this section, we present our experimental setup and results. KASS is compared with
other popular loop scheduling schemes in two cases studies: one for outer most parallel
loops; another for loop nests.

For the case study on outermost loops, we extracted several kernels from SPEC
CPU2000/2006 benchmarks. The detail of the kernel set is presented in Table 1. For the
case study on loop nests, the selected application kernels are Successive
Over-Relaxation (SOR), Jacobi Iteration (JI), and Transitive Closure (TC) [8]. The
detailed experimental setup is provided in Table 2.

4.1   Study on Outermost Parallel Loops

GSS, FSS, and TSS are widely used loop scheduling schemes in practice. For each
kernel in Table 1, we compare execution times obtained with static scheduling, GSS
[1], FSS [4], TSS [5], and KASS. Experiments were run by varying the number of
threads from 2 to 16. All worker threads are bound on different cores.

Several artificial loads are added to processors P_1, P_3, P_5,..., and P_{15} when testing.
Thus, $a_i = 1$ ($i = 1, 3, ..., 15$) and $a_i = 2$ ($i = 2, 4, ..., 16$) in the static partition phase of
KASS. $L1$ to $L9$ use equation (3) to calculate the bounds of local partitions. $L10$ has
obvious non-uniform workloads. Hence, the heuristic method is applied to obtain the
bounds. k_i is set to 0.8 because there are no other unknown loads running in the system.
The parameter α is determined via profiling for each kernel.

We report the speedups over sequential versions of the codes for each scheduling
scheme in Fig. 2. The execution time of the sequential versions is the average value of
the execution times in loaded and unloaded environments on one core. We observed

that for all ten kernels, both KASS and the classic self-scheduling schemes (GSS, FSS, and TSS) show significant improvement over static scheduling. Although static scheduling has better data locality than other schemes of scheduling and has no synchronization cost, poor load balancing made it much worse than self-scheduling.

Table 1. Kernel Set

Kernel	Suite	Benchmark	File, line
L1	SPEC2000	179.art	scanner.c, 317
L2	SPEC2000	188.ammp	rectmm.c, 405
L3	SPEC2000	183.equake	quake.c, 462
L4	SPEC2006	470.lbm	lbm.c, 186
L5	SPEC2006	433.milc	quark_stuff.c, 1523
L6	SPEC2006	462.libquantum	gates.c, 89
L7	SPEC2006	464.h264ref	mv-search.c, 394
L8	SPEC2006	482.sphinx3	vector.c, 512
L9	Matrix Multiplication		mm.c
L10	Matrix Transpose		mt.c

Table 2. Experimental Setup

Processor	4 X Intel®Xeon™ X7350 (4 cores/chip) @ 2.93GHz
L1 Data Cache	32 KB
L2 Cache	2 X 4 MB
Memory	8 GB
Compiler	gcc 4.2.4
Compiler Flags	-O2 -lpthread -lrt -lm
Thread Library	NPTL 2.7
OS	Linux ubuntu 2.6.22.14

Figure 2 shows that KASS is the most effective self-scheduling scheme. Comparing KASS with GSS, FSS and TSS, we observe that KASS is 16.9% faster than GSS on average with 8 threads, which is the best case, and 4.8% faster than FSS on average with 16 threads, which is the worst case. Again, we notice that GSS is worse than other self-scheduling schemes on average due to the large chunk size allocated in the first scheduling step.

The performance gains obtained from KASS can be attributed to load balancing, synchronization overhead and data locality. KASS only needs synchronization during work stealing. In the ideal case, the number of locks can be as low as the number of threads if the workload was balanced perfectly in the static partition phase. For the other three self-scheduling schemes, the number of locks equals the number of chunks, and the value never changes during numerous executions times.

Aside from synchronization overhead, data locality is another significant benefit of using distributed work queues. For the outmost parallel loop, spatial locality is improved because most chunks in the local queue are executed successively by the local processor. For nested loops, distributed work queues enforce processor affinity with the data set. Therefore, temporal locality is improved. To gain better insight into the performance issues, we collected L1 and L2 cache misses with Pfmon2 for each kernel and each self-scheduling scheme. Figure 3 shows the results when 4 threads are used. Cache misses are normalized against cache misses in GSS. KASS has less L1 data cache misses than others. L2 cache misses decrease slightly except for L10. The matrix size in L10 is 3200 x 3200, thus, it cannot be loaded into the L2 cache entirely. Moreover, matrix transposition has decreasing workload distribution. Therefore, L10 presents much variation in cache misses.

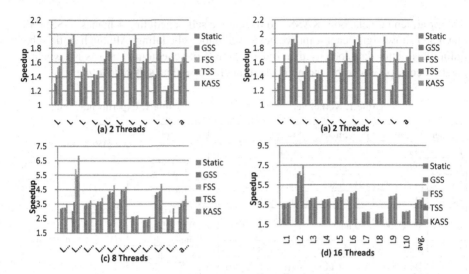

Fig. 2. Speedup over sequential execution

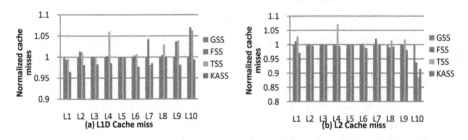

Fig. 3. Cache misses when 4 Threads used

4.2   Study on Loop Nests

To the best of our knowledge, affinity scheduling is most similar with our technique for loop nests. We implemented KASS algorithm as presented in Section 3, and the affinity scheduling algorithm (AFS) in [8]. Three applications (SOR, JI, and TC) were run on 2 cores to 16 cores with N = 10000. The average execution times are reported in Fig. 4. KASS performs better than AFS in all cases. The speedups of KASS over AFS in the figure are also labeled. The maximal speedup is 1.27, which makes KASS 21% faster. As discussed in Section 3, the attained performance is mainly attributed to knowledge-based static partition and adaptive adjustment with tuning parameters.

Both KASS and AFS exploited processor affinity with distributed work queues. Work stealing happens when load imbalance arises between initial partitions. A significant disadvantage with the AFS scheduling scheme exist where work stealing has dramatically increased scheduling overhead when more processors are used.

Therefore, KASS should achieve greater speedup when more processors are used because of relatively balanced initial partition and adaptive adjustments, which result in less work stealing than AFS. This trend has been noticed in Fig. 4(b).

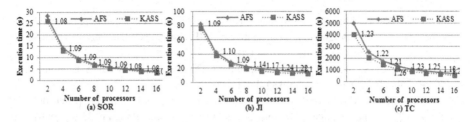

Fig. 4. Execution time of SOR (a), JI (b) and TC (c)

5   Conclusion

A knowledge-based adaptive self-scheduling (KASS) algorithm for parallel loops has been proposed in this paper. An experimental study was performed to compare the KASS algorithm with classic self-scheduling algorithms (GSS, TSS, and FSS), static scheduling, and affinity scheduling algorithm. The major conclusions from the study are: Dynamic scheduling schemes perform well for all kernels. KASS performs better than classic self-scheduling and static scheduling for the outermost loops. For loop nests, KASS not only exploits processor affinity, but also adaptively adjusts chunk partitions. Therefore, KASS achieved better performance compared with affinity scheduling. Future work would be geared towards implementing KASS on heterogeneous computing systems.

References

1. Polychronopoulos, C.D., Kuck, D.J.: Guided self-scheduling: a practical scheduling scheme for parallel supercomputers. IEEE Trans. Computers 36(12), 1425–1439 (1987)
2. Smith, B.J.: Architecture and Application of the HEP Multiprocessor Computer System. In: Real Time Signal Processing IV, vol. 298 (1981)
3. Tang, P., Yew, P.C.: Processor self-scheduling for multiple nested parallel loops. In: ICPP, pp. 528–535 (1986)
4. Flynn-Hummel, S., Schonberg, E., Flynn, L.E.: Factoring: A method for scheduling parallel loops. Communications of the ACM 35(8), 90–101 (1992)
5. Tzen, T.H., Ni, L.M.: Trapezoid self-scheduling: a practical scheduling scheme for parallel computers. IEEE Transactions on Parallel and Distributed Systems 4(1), 87–98 (1993)
6. Tabirca, T., Freeman, L., Tabirca, S., Yang, L.T.: Feedback guided dynamic loop scheduling: convergence of the continuous case. J. Supercomput. 30(2), 151–178 (2004)
7. Cariño, R.L., Banicescu, I.: Dynamic load balancing with adaptive factoring methods in scientific applications. J. Supercomput. 44(1), 41–63 (2008)

8. Markatos, E.P., LeBlanc, T.J.: Using processor affinity in loop scheduling on shared-memory multiprocessors. IEEE Trans. Parallel Distrib. Syst. 5(4), 379–400 (1994)
9. Srivastava, S., Banicescu, I., Ciorba, F.M.: Investigating the robustness of adaptive Dynamic Loop Scheduling on heterogeneous computing systems. In: IPDPS Workshops, pp. 1–8 (2010)
10. Yang, C., Wu, C., Chang, J.: Performance-based parallel loop self-scheduling using hybrid OpenMP and MPI programming on multicore SMP clusters. Concurrency Computation Practice and Experience 23(8), 721–744 (2011)
11. Kejariwal, A., Nicolau, A., Polychronopoulos, C.D.: History-aware Self-Scheduling. In: ICPP, Columbus, Ohio, USA, pp. 185–192 (2006)
12. Liu, J., Saletore, V.A., Lewis, T.G.: Safe Self-Scheduling: A Parallel Loop Scheduling Scheme for Shared-Memory Multiprocessors. Int. J. Parallel Program. 22(6), 589–616 (1994)

Communication Locality Analysis of Triplet-Based Hierarchical Interconnection Network in Chip Multiprocessor

Shahnawaz Talpur[1,2], Feng Shi[1], and Yizhuo Wang[1]

[1] Beijing Institute of Technology, Beijing P.R. China
[2] Department of Computer Systems Engineering,
Mehran University of Engineering & Technology Jamshoro, Sindh, Pakistan
talpur@bit.edu.cn, frankwyz@126.com

Abstract. Interconnection topology inside chip multiprocessor acts as fundamental role in communication locality. Considering compiler optimization data locality has been an inmost hypothesis in the high performance computing. Conversely, data locality sphere has several troubles when its degree of dimension is two or higher. In mesh network of two dimensions, each core is connected with its four neighbors. The data locality can potentially be exploited in two dimensions considering the specified processor's perspective. A Triplet-Based Hierarchical Interconnection Network (TBHIN) has straightforward topology and fractal attribute for chip multiprocessor. In this paper, a static (no contention) performance analysis of TBHIN and 2-D mesh is presented, based on the premise of locality in communication. The dynamic (contention) software simulation of TBHIN shows that the stronger the locality in communication, the lower the delay of the communication.

Keywords: Chip multiprocessor, communication locality, interconnection network, mesh.

1 Introduction

In computing, performance can be achieved by reducing data access latency, which is dependent on interconnect network on-chip. The issue of the highest performance on significant applications is the main effort of the microprocessor architecture, which also meets the limitation in the design time, power consumption and the area [1]. CMP is much more promising because it is partitioned into individual processing cores and has simple design scalability with great performance/power ratios and the potential to provide higher peak throughput [2].

In parallel with interconnection network, Cache organization has also the main impact on data latency which can affect the performance of multicore. Association of memory hierarchy, the operational work load and interconnection on-chip are the factors on which data access latency is built-up. Rapid path or routes are assembled for reducing latency in several Network-on-chip designs, utilizing communication

J.J. Park et al. (Eds.): NPC 2012, LNCS 7513, pp. 33–41, 2012.

locality [3]. Latency on data stored in cache on-chip can be suffered by interconnection network, while the distance in blocks of data stored on cache can be affected by cache association. This affects the overall communication model against NoC.

Multicore has one decisive issue, the locality, which is alienated in temporal and spatial. When two or more cores access shared data in short time, it is known as temporal locality, whereas; in flat time, one core's data is accessed constantly by other core(s), known as spatial locality. Data latency will be even more critical issue as the number of cores increases in the system.

Packet interconnection network is an extensive approach in recent research, for controlling on chip communication. Wires deliver the suitable electrical constraint in structured network, which allows high recital circuits to raise bandwidth and dipping latency [4][5]. Researchers conclude that the power efficiency should be balanced with wire utilization through topologies.

The mature topologies, explored by parallel computing, such as complete connection, torus and cube are all too complex to implement on a single chip. Recently, 2-D mesh is much focused for implementation as interconnection network in CMP [6]. Although it is not expected that it will benefit at all.

The rest of the paper is prepared as follows: Section 2 presents TBHIN topology and node addressing. The static analysis and dynamic analysis are given in Section 3. We compare TBHIN with 2-D mesh on the condition of existence of communication locality. Section 4 consists of related work and Section 5 concludes this paper.

2   Triplet-Based Hierarchical Interconnection Network

Fig 1 illustrates the basic TBHIN topology and it can be seen that its structure is similar to Sierpinski Gasket, which is a fractal object. Iterartor Function System (IFS) produces Sierpinski Gasket according the theory of fractal geometry [7].

Single node in a scalable and hierarchical interconnection network described as a lowest level 0 TBHIN. On next step level 1 three cores shaping one triangle. The level 2 consists of three triangular shape communication links [8], as shown in Fig.1.

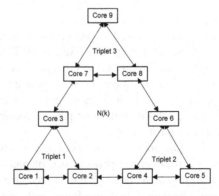

Fig. 1. Triplet-Based Hierarchical Interconnection Network Level 2(TBHIN)

Using Iterated Function System (IFS), higher levels of TBHIN can be generated from level 1. Assume that IFS for this design is IFS {F1, F2, F3}. Level 1 TBHIN N(1) is the outcome after one iteration of IFS and N (k) represents level k, after kth iteration that is the result of IFS. Then the procedure of TBHIN structure can be represented by

$$N_{k+1} = \bigcup_{i=1}^{3} F_i(N_k) \qquad (1)$$

Based on level 1 each core builds an upper level TBHIN. For the convenience three sub-networks of N(k) are described here as Triplet 1, Triplet 2 and Triplet 3 [9]. However; in order to understand the organization and binary representation of basic addressing scheme of TBHIN, we show only the 2 levels of TBHIN in the following Table 1.

Table 1. TBHIN Adressesing

Triplet 1(01)			Triplet 2(10)			Triplet 3(11)		
Core 1	Core 2	Core 3	Core 4	Core 5	Core 6	Core 7	Core 8	Core 9
0101	0110	0111	1001	1010	1011	1101	1110	1111

The ratio of the result of sum of minimal path lengths between two nodes to the total number of paths in the networks is known as mean minimal distance (MMD) of network [10]. The estimated MMD of TBHIN can be calculated as [11]:

$$P_{avg} = \frac{D_k}{3^k \times 3^k} = \frac{3^k \times \left(3 + \frac{16 \times (6^{k-1}-1)}{5} - 3^{k-1}\right)}{3^k \times 3^k}$$

$$= \frac{1}{3^{k-1}} + \frac{16 \times (6^{k-1}-1)}{5 \times 3^k} - \frac{1}{3} \qquad (2)$$

Where D_k is sum of all shortest distance and, k is level of TBHIN.

3   Performance Analysis of Network

This section analyzes the performance of TBHIN. Through this analysis, it is showing the advantages of this interconnection network in comparison to 2-D Mesh, most commonly used network on chip. TBHIN uses less number of links than 2-D mesh, but it provides larger MMD. Section 4.1 presents a performance analysis assuming that there is no contention. Section 4.2 presents contention analysis and the simulation experiments that are on the queuing analysis.

3.1   Analysis with No Contention

Here, we consign all assumptions and performance comparison standards proposed in [12]. In this paper, we consider α as the probability at both the source and destination nodes of a message in the same sub-network, whereas; in [12] α is the probability at both the source and destination nodes of a message in the same cluster. Therefore $(1-\alpha)$ represents the probability of different sub-networks communication. Communication locality is stronger if the value of α is larger. Denoting q_m the probability of both source and destination nodes of a message being in N (m) and q_m' is the probability of a message being in N (M), but not in the same sub-network N (m-1). For N (k), we have:

$$q_1 = \alpha = 1 - (1-\alpha)$$
$$q_2 = q_1 + q_2' = 1 - (1-\alpha)^2$$
$$\cdots \tag{3}$$
$$q_{k-1} = q_{k-2} + q_{k-1}' = 1 - (1-\alpha)^{k-1}$$
$$q_k = q_{k-1} + q_k' = 1$$

$$q_2' = \alpha\,(1 - q_1) = \alpha\,(1-\alpha)$$
$$q_3' = \alpha\,(1 - q_2) = \alpha\,(1-\alpha)^2$$
$$\cdots \tag{4}$$
$$q_{k-1}' = \alpha\,(1 - q_{k-2}) = \alpha\,(1-\alpha)^{k-2}$$
$$q_k' = 1 - q_{k-1} = (1-\alpha)^{k-1}$$

For larger value of α, the probability of inter-sub-networks communication will be smaller. As in [12], the cost and complexity of network N(k) is represented with L_k, and P_k, that is used to present the efficiency of the network N(k). Therefore, a useful measure is the product of L_k, and P_k ($L_k \times P_k$), which gives a cost-benefit part of static performance and should be minimized. For N(k), the total number of links can be presented as:

$$\begin{cases} L_1 = 3 \\ L_k = 3L_{k-1} + 3 \end{cases} \tag{5}$$

From Eq. (11) we can know that:

$$L_k = 3 \times (3^k - 1)/2 \tag{6}$$

Denote P_k' as the source and destination nodes, which reside within the same network of N(k), but not within the same network of Triplet.

$$P_k = P_1 q_1' + P_2' q_2' + P_3' q_3' + \cdots + P_k' q_k'$$
$$= \alpha P_1' + \alpha(1-\alpha) P_2' + \alpha(1-\alpha)^2 P_3' + \cdots + \alpha(1-\alpha)^{k-2} P_{k-1}' + (1-\alpha)^{k-1} P_k' \quad (7)$$

According to [11] suppose v_i and v_j are two nodes and they belongs to two different Triplets.

$$P_k' = \frac{\sum\limits_{i=1}^{3^{k-1}}\sum\limits_{j=1}^{3^{k-1}} d(v_i, v_j)}{3^{k-1} \times 3^{k-1}} = \frac{\sum\limits_{i=1}^{3^{k-1}}\sum\limits_{j=1}^{3^{k-1}} (d(v_i, v_{12})) + 3^{k-1} \times 3^{k-1} \times 1 + \sum\limits_{i=1}^{3^{k-1}}\sum\limits_{j=1}^{3^{k-1}} (d(v_{21}, v_j))}{3^{k-1} \times 3^{k-1}}$$

$$= \frac{3^{k-1} \times \sum\limits_{i=1}^{3^{k-1}} d(v_i, v_{12}) + 3^{k-1} \times 3^{k-1} \times 1 + 3^{k-1} \times \sum\limits_{j=1}^{3^{k-1}} d(v_{21}, v_j)}{3^{k-1} \times 3^{k-1}} \quad (8)$$

$$= \frac{2 \times 3^{k-1} \times Q_{k-1} + 3^{k-1} \times 3^{k-1} \times 1}{3^{k-1} \times 3^{k-1}}$$

From Eq. (8) and already calculated sum of shortest distance from any node with Triplet N(K)[11]

$$P_k' = \frac{2 \times Q_{k-1} \times 3^{k-1} + 3^{k-1} \times 3^{k-1} \times 1}{3^{k-1} \times 3^{k-1}} = \frac{2^{k+1} - 1}{3} \quad (9)$$

And because

$$P_1 = \frac{D_1}{3 \times 3} = \frac{6}{3 \times 3} = \frac{2}{3} \quad (10)$$

Thus from Eq. (7), Eq. (9) and Eq. (10) we can know:

$$P_k = \alpha - \frac{1}{3} + \frac{8 \times \alpha(1-\alpha) - 2^{k+1}(1-\alpha)^k}{3 \times (2\alpha - 1)} \quad (11)$$

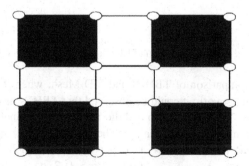

Fig. 2. The group scheme for 2-D mesh

To compare with TBHIN, every four nodes of 2-D mesh are grouped together as a sub-network, as shown in Fig. 2. After that four groups constitute a bigger group. Analogically, the 2-D mesh with $N = 4^k$ nodes can be considered as a k hierarchy network. The number of links and MMD of 2-D mesh are listed below:

$$L_k = 2 \times \left(N - \sqrt{N} \right) = 2 \times \left(4^k - 2^k \right) \tag{12}$$

$$P_{avg,k} = \frac{2(N-1)}{3\sqrt{N}} \approx \frac{2}{3}\sqrt{N} = \frac{2}{3} \times 2^k \tag{13}$$

Like TBHIN, suppose the probability of communication locality is α, yielding:

$$\begin{cases} P_1 = \dfrac{16}{4 \times 4} = 1 \\ P_k = \alpha P_1 + \alpha(1-\alpha)P_2' + \alpha(1-\alpha)^2 P_3' + \cdots + \alpha(1-\alpha)^{k-2} P_{k-1}' + (1-\alpha)^{k-1} P_k' \end{cases} \tag{14}$$

P_k' is given by:

$$P_k' = \frac{P_{\text{arg},k} \times 4^k \times 4^k - 4 \times P_{\text{arg},k-1} \times 4^{k-1} \times 4^{k-1}}{4^k \times 4^k - 4 \times 4^{k-1} \times 4^{k-1}} = \frac{7 \times 2^k}{9} \tag{15}$$

Eq. (14) and Eq. (15) then give:

$$P_k = \alpha + \frac{28\alpha(1-\alpha) - 7 \times 2^k (1-\alpha)^k}{9(2\alpha - 1)} \tag{16}$$

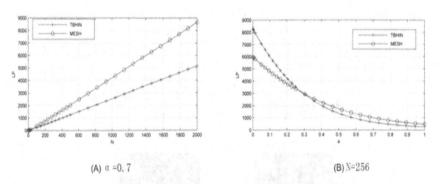

(A) α =0.7   (B) N=256

Fig. 3. The comparison of LP with α=0.7 and N=256

Fig. 3(A) gives LP comparison of TBHIN and 2-D Mesh, when α is 0.7 as function of the all nodes in the network; it could be observed that TBHIN has lower LP than 2-D Mesh. In Fig. 3(B), N is fixed at 256 and the value of α is increased, to increase the probability of communication locality. The graph of Fig. 3(B) indicates that TBHIN has lower LP value when α is larger than 0.3, which proves better cost benefit ration than 2-D mesh on the condition of $\alpha > 0.3$. This condenses; TBHIN is applicable in the fields having higher communication locality.

3.2   Analysis with Contention

The analysis with contention becomes more complex, since we have to consider the competition for communication resources among messages. In order to simulate the transition of messages over network, we assume that every link is full-duplex in the network. Each full-duplex link in our study is conceptually sub divided in two half-duplex links, each of which is modeled as a queuing center [12]. Between the source and destination nodes, all messages are routed over the shortest path. We also suppose that all the messages have the same size and the capacity of link buffers is unlimited.

The simulation process is composed of consecutive steps; following tasks should be finished within each step:

1. Each node generates λ pieces of messages, whose source and destination nodes are randomly obtained according to the distribution of probability. The shortest path from source node to destination nodes is calculated using the algorithm proposed in section IV. Meanwhile, the message is sent to the waiting queue of the first link. Additionally, the shortest path is attached to the corresponding message.
2. Each link picks up μ pieces of messages from the waiting queue, and sends the message to the next link according to the attached routing information. When message reaches the destination node, calculate the total delay and delete the message.
3. Calculate the average delay by dividing the total number of messages into total delay of all messages.

Fig. 4(A) gives the average delay of messages along with the simulation steps. As we can see, the higher the communication locality, the shorter will be average delay. What's more, the network will be stable much more quickly. In reverse, the average delay becomes longer. And what is worse, the network may paralysis due to the heavy workload. In fig. 4(B), the average delay of TBHIN is around 25% lower than 2-D mesh when $\alpha = 0.6, N = 81, \lambda = 1, \mu = 2$. Therefore, Triplet-Based Hierarchical Interconnection Network dynamically performs much better than 2-D mesh.

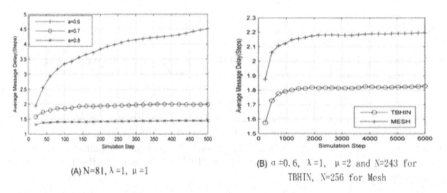

(A) N=81, λ =1, μ =1

(B) α =0.6, λ =1, μ =2 and N=243 for TBHIN, N=256 for Mesh

Fig. 4. The comparison of message delay

4   Related Work

Interconnection network on-chip emphasized more intensely as a prominent factor in Communication locality. In [3], interconnection for cache scheme and design circuit is classified periodically for the improvement in communication latency. Study essential diverse approach focuses on hindrance in locality and partitioning internal memory between cores in CMP shared memory system for reducing locality obstruction [13]. When data is shared among processors, allowing diverse application, optimal data locality scheme has been expressed with inimitable characteristic [14]. Parallel program and locality is achieved by enabling direct manipulation of tiles expressed in [15]. Optimal behavior of cache memory is stated and using sampling techniques elucidate the predictable scheme for CMEs solution in [16]. In literature survey of [17][18], latency improvement is explored in hop count, topology mapping, different mesh dimensions and interconnects graph etc. Data in groups is accessed collectively with reference to the association in memory as expressed in [19]. Despite the fact that, many of the researcher's proposed simple 2D packet-switched mesh interconnects for the cache.   The novelty of our analysis demonstrates that Triplet based hierarchical internetwork can be replaced as improved one. Due to different attributes of each methodology for data accessing, cache/memory hierarchy can't fully benefit from 2D interconnections.

5   Conclusion

In this paper, we investigate communication locality between Triplet-Based Hierarchical Interconnection Network and 2-D mesh. It has been found that TBHIN is easily scalable and has better cost benefit ratio than 2-D mesh in case of higher communication locality. It is also observed that TBHIN dynamically performs much better than 2-D Mesh because of having lower average delay. Due to the facility of hardware implementation, it can be used as the interconnection network of CMP.

References

1. Codrescu, L., Wills, D.S.: Architecture of the Atlas chip-multiprocessor: dynamically parallelizing irregular applications. In: International Conference on Computer Design, ICCD 1999 (2002), 10.1109/ICCD.1999.808577
2. Kumar, R., Zyuban, V., Tullsen, D.M.: Interconnections in Multi-Core Architectures: Understanding Mechanisms, Overheads and Scaling. In: International Symposium on Computer Architecture, ISCA, pp. 408–419 (2005), doi:10.1109/ISCA.2005.34
3. Ahmed, A., Jones, A.K., Rami, M.: Codesign of NoC and Cache Organization for Reducing Access Latency in Chip Multiprocessors. IEEE Transactions on Parallel and Distributed Systems 23 (2012)
4. Dally, W.J., Towles, B.: Route Packets, Not Wires: On-Chip Interconnection Networks. In: Proceedings of the 38th Design Automation Conference, pp. 681–689 (2001)

5. Ching, D., Schaumont, P., Verbauwhede, I.: Integrated Modeling and Generation of a Configurable network-on-chip. In: Proceedings 18th International Parallel and Distributed Processing Symposium, p. 139 (2004)
6. Kumar, S., Jantsch, A., Soininen, J.-P., Forsell, M., Millberg, M., Oberg, J., Tiensyrja, K., Hemani, A.: A network on chip architecture and design methodology. In: Proc. Symposium on VLSI, pp. 117–124 (April 2002)
7. Feng, S., Weixing, J., Baojun, Q., Bin, L., Haroon, R.: A Triplet Based Computer Architecture Supporting Parallel Object Computing. In: Proceedings of the Eighteenth International Conference on ASAP, pp. 192–197 (July 2007)
8. Baojun, Q., Feng, S., Weixing, J.: A New Routing Algorithm in Triple-based Hierarchical Interconnection Network. In: The First International Conference on Innovative Computing, Information and Control, pp. 725–728. IEEE, Beijing (2006)
9. Bin, L., Zhi-Chen, T., Yu-Jin, G.: Triplet-based architecture and its process migration mechanism. In: 2009 International Conference on Machine Learning and Cybernetics, vol. 5 (2009), 10.1109/ICMLC.2009.5212644
10. Dong, Y., Wang, D., Zheng, W.: Exact Computation Of The Mean Minimal Path Length of N-MESH and N-TORUS. Journal of Software 20(4) (1997)
11. Weixing, J., Feng, S., Baojun, Q., Liu, B.: Study on an interconnection network for complex embedded systems. Chinese High Technology Letters 17(9), 886–890 (2007)
12. Dandamudi, S., Eager, D.: Hierarchical Interconnection Networks for Multicomputer Systems. IEEE Transactions on Computers 39(6), 786–797 (1990)
13. Min Kyu, J., Doe Hyun, Y., Dam, S., Mike, S., Ikhwan, L., Mattan, E.: Balancing DRAM Locality and Parallelism in Shared Memory CMP Systems. In: 2012 IEEE 18th International Symposium on High Performance Computer Architecture, HPCA (2012)
14. Kandemir, M.: Data locality enhancement for CMPs. In: Proc. ICCAD (2007)
15. Bikshandi, G., Jia, G., Daniel, H.: Programming for parallelism and locality with hierarchically tiled arrays. In: Proc. PPOPP (2006)
16. Xavier, V., Nerina, B., Josep, L., Antonio, G.: A fast and accurate framework to analyze and optimize cache memory behavior. In: TOPLAS 2004 (2004)
17. Abhinav, B., Laxmikant, V.K.: Benefits of Topology Aware Mapping For Mesh Interconnects. Parallel Processing Letters (April 16, 2010)
18. Abhinav, B., Eric, B., Laxmikant, V.K.: Optimizing communication for Charm++ applications by reducing network contention. Concurrency and Computation: Practice and Experience (2009); 00-17 Prepared using cpeauth.cls (Version: 2002/09/19 v2.02)
19. Zhang, C., Yutao, Z., Youfeng, W.: A hierarchical model of data locality. In: Proc. POPL (2006)

A Scoring System for Short Answers
on the Test in a Large Group

Jae-Young Lee

Department of Computer Engineering, Hallym University, Gangwon, Korea 200-702
jylee@hallym.ac.kr

Abstract. In this paper, we have developed the scoring system that scores short answers based on the score table updated by average scores of non-existing answers. The accuracy and the consistency are very important, because the score influences a life. Automatic mark systems have consistency but need more accuracy. In the paper and pencil, a consistency is difficult to maintain. To achieve accuracy and consistency, the scoring system consists of three passes. The first pass is to score the applicant's answers based on the ready-made score table if it is in the table. If not, the second pass updates the table with the average of credits for which committee members evaluate the non-existing answer. Finally, the third pass is to score non-existing answer based on the updated table.

Keywords: remote education, subjective-type evaluation, automatic scoring system, Internet-based scoring system.

1   Introduction

Learners in an information society can learn immediately the knowledge and technologies they need at any time and at any place and educational activities, such as, learning, testing, and evaluation, are done freely between huge learners and teachers in cyber education via the Internet [1] and [2].

The important thing in this education is fair evaluation for subjective questions to increase the quality of education. How to evaluate the learners' abilities can normally be classified as multiple choices or subjective tests. The multiple-choices can increase fairness and reliability but decrease the quality of education. On the other hand, the subjective tests can improve the quality of education by measuring the cognitive abilities, but lower the fairness and reliability. The biggest drawback of evaluating subjective tests is the lack of fairness.

There were several researches to solve these problems in evaluation of the subjective test.

After applicants solve the subjective questions through Internet, raters are informed the finish of the test by Internet, or telephone. Then, the raters should quickly score the answers through Internet, and the system notifies each result to applicant [3].

In automatic scoring, Park and Kang [4] proposed the model which grades for the subjective-type evaluation, and designs and implements the evaluation system using

J.J. Park et al. (Eds.): NPC 2012, LNCS 7513, pp. 42–47, 2012.
© IFIP International Federation for Information Processing 2012

the synonym thesaurus and the system results the 73% success rate. Kim et. Al. [5] had developed an intelligent grading system, which scores descriptive examination papers automatically, based on Probabilistic Latent Semantic Analysis(PLSA) and it can acquire about 74% accuracy of a manual grading, 7% higher than that from the Simple Vector Space Model. Kang [6] designed and implemented a subjective-type evaluation system using syntactic and case-role information and the system results the 75% success rate. Scores have a great influence on applicants' life, such as, admissions and promotions, the automatic scoring system needs more accuracy. On the other hand, subjective tests and the answers written in pencil for large group exam are scanned to grade the pencil-and-paper test. Internet-based scoring system that two or three raters score the scanned paper instead of the pencil-and-paper test to increase the reliability was studied [7]. It also has the drawback that raters can score unfairly with subjective judgments.

To solve the problems, we have proposed the scoring system that particularly scores non-existing answers based on the new score table updated by average of new scores. The new scores are evaluated non-existing answers by members of committee. This system has three passes to score fairly. The first pass is to score the applicant's answers based on the ready-made score table if it is found in the table. If not, committee members evaluate the non-existing answer and return new credits to the system. The second pass updates the table with the average of the new credits. Finally, the third pass is to score non-existing answers based on the updated score table.

2   Paper and Pencil Scoring

In the paper and pencil scoring, raters evaluate each item of the subjective questions by writing score by hand. It is used for evaluating a small group, specifically, the group of high-quality human resources, but is not suitable for large group because of fairness. In the major field on the secondary teacher certification test at domestic, there are six steps to process between setting the subject test and scoring the answers by hand as follows [7]:

[Step 1] Setting questions:
   -To set questions to majors for the measurement of higher-order thinking skills.
[Step 2] Making answer sheets and the criteria of scoring:
      - At first, every member of committee scores each item of question.
      - And then every member should systematically check the validity and relevance of
        the contents through group discussion.
[Step 3] Simulation to score 3 times:
   - Every rater or committee member scores 3 times each question of every majors and
     a group updates answer sheets and the criteria of scoring after analyzing the results.
[Step 4] Determining the final answer sheets and the final criteria of scoring:
   - Committee members and raters should determine final answer sheets and the criteria of
     scores after checking the validity and relevance of the contents and confirming
     the purpose of the questions through group discussion.

[Step 5] Scoring:
- Each question is independently scored three raters.
- Final score of each can be calculated as the average of 3 scores.
[Step 6] Transfer of Score results:
- Education office in-local or city will take over the score results and test papers from raters.

The reason for these complex procedures to score the subjective questions is to increase the reliability in Paper and pencil scoring. However, it increases processing time and cost because it needs complex procedures to reduce problems occurred by the difference of individuals among members, to maintain the consistency of the scoring, and to inform scoring results to raters.

3   A Scoring System for Short Answers

In this paper, the scoring system for short answers on the test accepts questions and score tables from the committee and then saves them in the database. The table consists of pair of correct answer and its credit, or another pair of similar answer and its credit. The system should not only show questions to the applicants but also store the answer received from the applicants into the database. There are three passes to score the answers. The first pass is to score automatically the applicant's answers based the score table if it is the same as the correct answer, or, similar answer. If not, raters evaluate the non-existing answer and return new credits, and the second pass updates the table with the average of new credits. Finally, the third pass is to score non-existing answers based on the updated score table. Such a clients and server system including database is shown in Fig. 1.

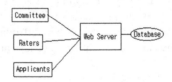

Fig. 1. A scoring system for short answer question

4   A Scoring Algorithm for Short Answers

In the process of scoring short answer questions, it's said that the feature of the short answers tends to classify an answer, so the feature will make answers easier on the test in a huge group. On the other hand, the feature of the essay question is difficult to classify an answer, so it is not useful to score on the test in a huge group.

The scoring system for short answers on the test accepts questions and score tables from the committee. For scoring, the system score an answer based on the ready-made table. But for the non-existing answers that are not in the table, non-existing answers are grouped to make score easier. Rater gives a score every group. The system updates the table with the average of various new credits which raters give and score again the non-existing answers based on the updated score table. Such an algorithm consisting of 3 passes is as follows:

Pass 1: The procedure to score answers in the score table

[Step 1] If there is any applicant's answer, then read the answer and go to [Step 2].
      Otherwise, go to Pass 2.
[Step 2] Look up the answer in the score table.
[Step 3] If the answer and credit exist in the score table, then the answer will be scored based on the score table and go to [Step 1].
[Step 4] Otherwise, the answer will be appended in the table and go to [Step 1].

Pass 2: The procedure to update the table with the average of new credits for non-existing answers

[Step 1] Send the score table including non-existing answers to committee members.
[Step 2] Average the scores evaluated by members of committee.
[Step 3] Update the score table with the average and go to Pass 3.

Pass 3: The procedure to score non-existing answers

[Step 1] If there is non-existing answer, read the non-existing answer and go to [Step 2], else stop.
[Step 2] Look up the non-existing answer in the updated table.
[Step 3] If the non-existing answer and new credit exist in the updated table, then the answer will be scored based on the updated table and go to [Step 1].
[Step 4] Otherwise, go to [Step 1].

The score table consists of number, question, a pair of an answer and a credit, as shown in Table 1. The pair can be one of four types: a pair of correct answer and credit, or a pair of similar answer and credit for Pass 1, or a pair of non-existing answer and credit for Pass 2 and Pass3.

Table 1. Score table consisting of questions, answer, and credit

NO	Question	Answer	Credit
1			
2			
3			

5 Comparative Analysis

Performance of scoring is able to meet a certain number of criteria. The most important things of these are accuracy, fairness, consistency, processing time, and human resource.

Accuracy $A(x)$ is the probability of scoring answers correctly. Fairness $F(x)$ is the probability of scoring answers with objectivity justly. Consistency $C(x)$ is the probability that the same score is given to the same answer from first to the end. Processing time $T(x)$ is the time that scores from first to the end. Human resource $H(x)$ is the number of humane needed to score from first to the end.

The most important thing to evaluate subjective questions is accuracy, fairness, and consistency, because the evaluation results have a significant impact on the lives. The criteria of accuracy, fairness, and consistency are more important than time.

In these respects, there are comparisons of three types of scoring: the automatic scoring system, the paper and pencil scoring, and the scoring system for short answers.

First, the performance of the automatic scoring system is as follows:

$$Pa(x) = Aa(x) + Fa(x) + Ca(x) + 1/Ta(x) + Ha(x) = Aa(x) + 1/Ta(x). \qquad (1)$$

Where $Aa(x)$, $Fa(x)$, $Ca(x)$, $Ta(x)$, and $Ha(x)$ mean accuracy, fairness, consistency, processing time, and human resources for the automatic scoring system, respectively. The accuracy $Aa(x)$ of this system falls, so this system is not suitable. Particularly, a wrong result is a fatal influence on a person's life, although fairness and consistency are perfect and process is very fast. The answers are scored by computer instead of human resources.

In teacher appointment tests, the paper and pencil scoring is still carried out because of the accuracy problem. The performance of this scoring is as follows:

$$Pp(x) = Ap(x) + Fp(x) + Cp(x) + 1/Tp(x) + Hp(x). \qquad (2)$$

Where $Ap(x)$, $Fp(x)$, $Cp(x)$, $Tp(x)$, and $Hp(x)$ mean accuracy, fairness, consistency, processing time, and human resources for the paper and pencil scoring, respectively. The accuracy $Ap(x)$ is better than $Aa(x)$, so this system have been used for evaluating a small group of high-quality human resources, although fairness and consistency are not perfect and it needs a few days, many raters, and high cost.

Before analyzing the scoring system for short answers, let us compare pass 2 in the scoring algorithm and [Step 4] in the paper and pencil scoring.

To search similar answers of all possible cases before scoring in the paper and pencil scoring, raters should make score 3 times for every question and then check both answer sheets and the criteria of scoring, as shown in [Step 3]. In the [Step 4], the committee members and raters should determine final answer sheets and the criteria of scoring after checking the validity and relevance of the contents and purpose of the questions through group discussion. To do these, many human resources, lots of processing time, and high costs are needed.

In the scoring algorithm for short answers, on the other hand, [Step 3] and [Step 4] in the paper and pencil scoring is simply replaced by the pass 2. The key point of the credit in the non-existing answers is to use the average of credits evaluated by every rater, instead of the criteria after their discussion. The discussion is the important factor to increase time, human resource and cost.

Thus, the performance of the algorithm is as follows:

$$Ps(x) = As(x) + Fs(x) + Cs(x) + 1/Ts(x) + Hs(x) = As(x) + 1/Ts(x) + Hs(x). \quad (3)$$

Where $As(x)$, $Fs(x)$, $Cs(x)$, $Ts(x)$, and $Hs(x)$ mean accuracy, fairness, consistency, processing time, and human resources for the scoring system for short answers, respectively. In the scoring system, the accuracy $As(x)$ is better than $Ap(x)$. The fairness and consistency are perfect and process is fast. The raters is to score only non-existing answers, and this scoring requires much less labor than the paper and pencil scoring, so it is suitable for scoring short answers in huge group. Therefore, the algorithm has the advantage to reduce human resources, processing time, and costs.

6   Conclusions

The most important thing to evaluate subjective questions is an accuracy and consistency, because the evaluation results have a significant impact on the lives of applicants. In this respect, automatic mark systems have consistency but need more accuracy. In the paper and pencil, a consistency is difficult to maintain.

To achieve accuracy and consistency, the scoring system scores the applicant's answers based on the ready-made score table, and it then updates the table with the average of various new credits for the non-existing answer. Finally, it scores non-existing answer based on the updated table.

In this paper, the algorithm for short answers has more accuracy than automatic mark system and less costs than the paper and pencil scoring.

Acknowledgments. This research was supported by Hallym University Research Fund, 2012(HRF-2012-06-001).

References

1. Reiser, R.A., Kegelmann, H.W.: Evaluating instructional Software: A review and critique of current method. Education Technology Research and Development 42(3), 63–69 (1994)
2. Jang, S.P., Lee, Y.M.: Alternative Formative Evaluation in Web Based Learning System. Journal of KACE 3, 43 (2000)
3. Bang, H., Kang, T.H., Kim, W.J., Won, D.H., Lee, J.Y.: A Web-based Grading System for Classifying Answers of Subjective Test. Proceeding of KIPS 28, 673–675 (2001)
4. Park, H.J., Kang, W.: Design and Implementation of a Subjective-type Evaluation System Using Natural Language Processing Technique. Journal of KACE 6, 207–216 (2003)
5. Kim, Y.S., Oh, J.S., Lee, J.Y., Chang, J.H.: An intelligent grading system for descriptive examination paper based on probabilistic latent semantic analysis, pp. 1141–1146. Springer, Heidelberg (2004)
6. Kang, W.S.: Design and Implementation of a Subjective-type Evaluation System Using Syntactic and Case-Role Information. Journal of KACE 10, 61–69 (2007)
7. Cho, J.M., Kim, K.H.: A Study on Design of the Internet-based Scoring System for Constructed Responses. Journal of KACE 10, 89–100 (2007)

Reference Variables for Dynamic, Reliable Packet Operations

Ralph Duncan, Peder Jungck, Kenneth Ross, and Dwight Mulcahy

CloudShield Technologies, A Science Applications International Corporation (SAIC) Company
212 Gibraltar Drive, Sunnyvale, CA 94089 USA
rduncan@cloudshield.com

Abstract. A classic 'reference' variable provides an indirect way to access a variable or aggregate. packetC, [1] a language for network packet processing, has specialized requirements for references that apply to aggregates, based on domain-specific, extended data types. The primary functional requirement is to defer selecting particular aggregates until runtime. In addition, requirements for high program reliability and security are paramount. Thus, packetC reference constructs must guarantee that a selected aggregate (i.e., the value of a runtime dereference) always constitutes a legal aggregate for the involved operation. Both reliability concerns and current domain implementation practice discourage references based on addresses (detailed below). A secondary requirement is to support chaining aggregate operations, where the aggregate used in an operation depends on the result of the previous operation. Our design and implementation of packetC references provides a useful case study in how secure, reliable references can meet these requirements by combining strong typing features (e.g., declaration rules), simple mechanics (encoded ordinal values) and appropriate technical attributes for references, such as reseatability and non-nullability.

1   Introduction

In its most general sense, a programming language reference is a construct that provides an indirect means for referring to a variable, aggregate or object's values. Thus, the reference's actual value, such as a memory address, is distinct from the value(s) to which it provides access.

Key reference characteristics include whether a variable with a reference type can

- Be set to a null value or nullability (be in a state where it provides no indirect access to underlying values)
- Be assigned a new value after its declaration or reseatability
- Expose its actual values to the user.

The particular set of characteristics a language's reference types and variables possess depends on the primary roles the constructs play in the language.

J.J. Park et al. (Eds.): NPC 2012, LNCS 7513, pp. 48–60, 2012.

packetC [1], is a heavily extended C dialect for network packet processing. It is being employed to develop commercial and military systems by users that include the U.S. Air Force, IBM and Harris Corporation. packetC uses references to defer until runtime specifying the specific aggregate (extended-type data structure) on which classic packet searching or matching actions will operate. A major use case involves chaining, such that the identity of the aggregate used in one operation depends on the result of a previous one. A packetC user can achieve this by exploiting a simple scheme of reference array indexing. Otherwise, users would have to explicitly code each possible combination of secondary operation and primary operation result value (e.g., in a C-style switch statement), a process prone to errors and omissions.

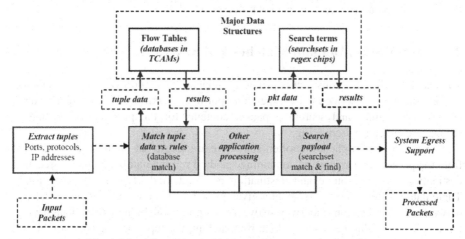

Fig. 1. Matching and searching operations on network packets
©CloudShield Technologies, 2011

Packet processing is an unforgiving application domain. It rewards processing at wire-speed, i.e., processing and outputting packets at the same 1-40 gigabits per second (gbps) speed at which the packets are arriving. Thus, time-consuming exception handling is infeasible and error-free application logic is paramount. This need for reliability requires two technical characteristics of packetC references:

- Strong typing, since trying to apply an operation to a data structure of the wrong type is a major runtime fault.
- Non-nullability, since trying to apply an operation to no data structure at all is prohibitively unreliable.
- In addition, the need to determine at runtime which aggregate will be used for certain operations requires packetC references to have the attribute of
- Reseatability (assignability), especially when references need to be assigned values according to an operation result.

Finally, the demand for a high degree of security, especially for military and telecommunications infrastructure precludes simply using memory addresses as C-style reference values. Even if this were not the case, current implementation practices with specialized chips often mean that the aggregates of interest are not accessible via classic memory addresses.

We hope that these distinctive, domain-oriented requirements will make packetC reference constructs relevant to students of both language design and network packet processing.

The remainder of the paper is organized as follows. We quickly review classic packet matching and searching operations. We then describe packetC matching and searching aggregate types, showing how reference variables are declared, initialized and dereferenced for each. After describing our implementation mechanics, we present experimental results to show how the scheme plays out in a commercial, parallel execution environment for packet processing.

2   Application Domain Matches and Searches

The packetC reference construct is primarily intended to support two classic network packet operations described below: matching portions of extracted packet header data against large tables and searching packet contents for the presence of particular strings or character patterns (Fig. 1).

Network packet applications often start by extracting a set or tuple of basic data from the packet header (portion containing standard routing data), e.g., the source and destination address, source and destination port and kind of protocol being used. Tuple data is often used to associate a given packet with a current flow, essentially a networking conversation underway between two points of the network. Classifying packets in this fashion is usually done by matching the tuple data against a table of current flows, sometimes termed a table of (matching) rules.

Some applications search the packet payload, the non-header portion containing user-specific data, an operation described as deep packet inspection (DPI). Searches are conducted in terms of matching one or more strings or regular expressions.

As a language for network packet processing packetC supports these classic network operations with extended data types and associated operators. The sections that immediately follow describe these constructs and their relation to references.

3   Preview of ref and deref Operators

Before we encounter the code examples below, we offer descriptions of packetC ref and **deref** operators. We use this explicit syntax to emphasize that, unlike * and & in C, these operators do not use memory addresses or support 'pointer arithmetic.'

The **ref** operator takes a single operand, which must be either:

- The name of a *database* with the same structure base type as the reference variable's base type.
- The name of a *searchset* with a string or regular expression type that matches the **string** or **regex** keyword in the reference variable declaration.

The **deref** operator takes a reference variable operand. It is not as if all the aggregate's values were present at that source code location but, rather, it is as if the aggregate identifier had been hard-coded there. A packetC dereference produces an lvalue that indicates an entire aggregate object. Thus, it acts as a substitute for the lvalue at that source code location. This property can lead to unusual code forms (much as pointer dereferencing does in C); however, it provides capabilities for compact, generic programming, as some code examples and experiments below show.

4   Strong Typing, Reseatability and Non-nullability for Database Matching

In packetC[1] flow tables can be implemented via a database extended type [1]. Each element of a database is a C-style structure. Since network application matching against flow tables often selectively uses only a portion of the tuple data, packetC databases are essentially arrays of symmetrical structures, where each structure is, in turn, composed of a data half and corresponding mask half that have a common structure base type. A field of the data portion is only used in matching operations if the bits of the corresponding mask field are set, rather than zeroed. Example declarations follow.

```
struct stype { short dest; short src;};
database stype virusFlows  [300];
```

Matching operations are performed on a database via a **match** operator, expressed with C++ method-style syntax. When a match's required first argument is a structure, it must have the same type as the database's base type. A successful match returns the matching element's index, while a failure to match any element must be handled by packetC's C++-style system of try and catch constructs. Example match code is shown below.

```
try {

    rownum = virusFlows.match( myStruct );// match my-
Struct vs. entire database }
catch ( ERR_DB_NOMATCH ) {…}
```

Because database match operators only make sense if the match operand and database have the same structure base type, packetC reference variables for databases are declared in terms of a base type and can only reference databases with that base type. To further ensure that dereferencing such a variable always produces a legal runtime value, the declaration must set the reference variable to a legal, non-null value (see below). (A packetC structure tag names a type without needing a typedef).

```
struct stype { short dest; short src;};
database stype malwareFlows[500];
database stype virusFlows  [300];
```

```
// declare a database reference var of 'stype' base type
reference db : stype refDB = ref(virusFlows);
...
// 'reseat' reference to DB of 'stype'
refDB = ref(malwareFlows); // legal

// ERROR: try to reseat to DB of another type
database tuple5Type currentFlows[4000];
refDB = ref(currentFlows); // ERROR
```
A dref operation on a database reference variable can be
used anywhere that a database identifier could be used:
```
// Using types from above, deref a database
structVar.dest = deref( refDB )[2].dest;
// At runtime the above construct equals StructVar.dest =
malwareFlows[2].dest
```

5   Strong Typing, Reseatability and Non-nullability for Searchset (Payload) Matching

packetC searchsets [1] supply terms for payload searching in the form of an ordered
set of strings or set of regular expressions. Because these two forms have different
restrictions on what methods can be applied to them, a searchset's elements cannot
mix strings and regular expressions. The code example below shows string and regex
searchset declarations.

```
searchset sSet[3][3]    = {"dog","cat","bat"};
regex searchset regSet[2][7] = {".*?from",".*?mail"};
```

The packetC find method searches for each searchset element, s, starting anywhere
within the argument (which is often the packet payload). When a searchset is declared without the regex keyword qualifier, attempts to find searchset string elements
are made in the same order as their declaration: searching terminates when a match is
found. When a regex qualifier is used, the matching sequence and behavior depends
on the characteristics of the regular expressions involved. Results are returned with
the predefined structure type shown below.

```
struct SearchResult {
   int index;    // searchset elem matched
   int position;// search area where match ends
};
```

The code example below shows the appearance of a find operator expression and the
required use of an associated try/catch construct to handle the appropriate exception if
no search term is found.

```
searchset petSset[3][3] = {"dog","cat","bat"};
SearchResult ansStruct;
  try { // search the entire packet
    ansStruct  =  petSset.find( pkt );
  }
  catch ( ERR_SET_NOTFOUND ) {...}
```

Searchsets also have a match operator, which compares a searchset element of length n to the first n bytes of the match operand. Because regular expressions cannot be used in this way, only searchsets composed of strings can be used with the searchset match operator. Thus, to ensure that a searchset reference variable can be legally dereferenced in any context where the referent could be used, searchset reference variables are declared in terms of being string or regex searchsets.

```
reference set: string refStr = ref(petSset);
//
searchset regSet[2][7] ={".*?from",".*?mail"};
reference set: regex  refReg = ref(regSet);
```

Using the types defined above the code below shows dereferencing applied to both kinds of searchset reference variable.

```
// reference a string searchset for match, using an array
slice operand
result = deref(refStr).match(pkt[64:66]);
// reference a regex searchset for find, using an array
slice operand
// result = regSet.find(pkt[0:end]);
result = deref(refReg).find(pkt[0:end]);
```

The packetC language is agnostic about how references are implemented in that it does not prescribe what kind of values are used to indicate particular databases or searchsets. The language simply specifies that the implementation values cannot be exposed to user examination or manipulation. The next two sections describe our implementation mechanics and how our host platform influences them.

6   Host System Impacts on Reference Implementation

The following aspects of current CloudShield Technologies' platforms [2] affect how we implement references.

- The packetC tool-chain is built atop an interpreted program scheme; thus, the packetC compiler emits bytecodes for an interpreted virtual machine, rather than assembler code.

- CloudShield Technologies' platforms are heterogeneous architectures that use multi-core network processing units (NPUs); thus, dereferencing operations are ultimately executed by NPU microcode.
- Databases and Searchsets are implemented on Ternary Content Addressable Memory (TCAM) chips and regex processors respectively.
- Our bytecodes identify specific databases or searchsets by an integer value assigned on a per-application basis.

Taken together, these characteristics encourage using straightforward mechanics to implement reference values and dereferencing operations. Both are described in the section that follows.

7   Reference Implementation

Our basic approach is to encode the unique integer value associated with databases or searchsets within a 32-bit integer to serve as the basis for reference variables. However, there are two complications:

- Searchsets can be implemented by both a classic searchset table (for the find operation) and a compiler-generated database (for match operations on string searchsets); thus, our reference variables must be able to encode more than just a single compiler-assigned integer identifier.
- The need to keep some additional house-keeping data adds a few additional bits to the 32-bits of encoded data.

Hence, we implement a reference variable as a 32-bit integer with several smaller integer values packed inside it. At worst, dereferencing a packetC reference variable involves a bitwise AND operation to discard the unwanted values and a SHIFT to reposition the remaining value.

The example below shows a searchset find operation chained to the results of a preceding database match, which selects which of three searchsets to use. In this case, the dereferencing only requires an AND operation.

```
searchset bad[2][8]={"bad.com," "evil.com"};
searchset sly[2][6]= {"mal.com", "bat.com"};
searchset incomp[2][5] = {"@!*&!","%^&*"};
reference set:string refArr[3] = {ref(bad), ref(sly),
ref(incomp)};

// match on packet origins in header info
flowRow = flowTab.match( rec );
// search payload, based on packet origins
loca = deref( refArr[flowRow]).find( pkt );
```

A readable snapshot follows of the bytecodes emitted by the compiler for the packetC code above.

```
// match on packet origins in header info; store matching
row in rowNum
DBMATCH 5, msknd, rec.data, rec.mask. rowNum
// use rowNum to put selected reference values into
ssetNum
MCOPY ssetNum, refArr[rownum]
// discard unwanted bits of reference value; remaining
bits are searchset ID num
AND ssetNum, 65535
// perform the chained search, using searchset indicated
by ssetNum
SEARCH_PKT ssetNum, strtIdx, finIdx, resultLoc
```

Thus, with the simple encoding scheme, we can meet our primary requirements for dynamic selection of extended data type aggregates and do so in a secure, reliable manner. In addition, we can provide dynamic, chained operations that are typical of the domain at the cost of two or three elementary operations. The next section presents performance data for these constructs.

8   Reference Performance in a Parallel Environment: Chained Operation Example

A reference implementation that accesses encoded ordinal values by shifting and masking instructions is obviously unlikely to incur significant performance overhead simply on that account. However, the target domain is high-speed packet processing and it is not self-evident how accessing multiple aggregates (stored in specialty chips) by these means plays out in practice. Thus, this section compares a 'brute-force' source code approach to chaining operations with a simple use of references, both hosted on one of our parallel platforms where 96 contexts are processing packets.

The experiment used a CloudShield PN41 [3] 10 Gigabit Ethernet blade hosting the packetC application. The DPPM blade contains an Intel Corporation® IXP 2800 NPU and custom Xilinx, Inc.® Virtex® 5 FPGAs. Netlogic, Inc.® NSE 5512 TCAM chips implement the databases. Searchsets are implemented by an IDT PAX.port 2500 content inspection engine [4]. We used an IXIA® XM12 traffic generator [5] to generate network traffic at a maximum of 10 gigabits per second (Gbps) and approximately 14 million packets per second (pps).

The experimental application defines a packetC database with each of the four database rows geared to matching one of the following kinds of network traffic: HTTP, VoIP, email, DNS. Based on which of the four database cases a packet matches, the program searches the packet payload for matches with strings in one of four possible searchsets. The database declaration and flow matching is conducted in terms of a structure with packet protocol information, as shown below.

```
struct ipv4Tuple {
  int    scrAddr;    int    destAddr;
```

```
    short srcPort;    short destPort;
    byte protocol;
};
database ipv4Tuple flowTable[4] = {…};
try { matchRow = flowTable.match( flow ); }
catch ( ERR_DB_NOMATCH ) {…exit; }
// searchset declarations for each kind of network traf-
fic we are handling follow.
searchset httpVerbs[2][4] = {"GET", "POST"};
searchset sipVerbs[2][6]  = {"INVITE","BYE"};
searchset badGuys[5][20]  = {"aca-
pone","jdillinger","pbfloyd","bonnie", "clyde"};
searchset sites[4][20]
={"yahoo.com","google.com","purepeople.com","cnn.com"};
```

8.1   Version 1: Without References

The version without references must explicitly code each possible searchset operation that could occur, using the relevant identifier for each one. Since only one of the searchsets could be used after a given database match, the code for the possible searchset operations must be structured conditionally, e.g., by using a switch statement as we did to implement this version.

```
try { matchedRow = flowTable.match(flow); }
catch ( ERR_DB_NOMATCH ) {…}

try { // do the desired chained operation
  switch (matchedRow) {
  case 0:
    result=httpVerbs.find(pkt[0:end]);     // throws
ERR_SET_NOTFOUND if no match
    break;
  case 1:
    result = sipVerbs.find(pkt[0:end]);   // throws
ERR_SET_NOTFOUND if no match
    break;
  case 2:
    result = badGuys.find(pkt[0:end]);     // throws
ERR_SET_NOTFOUND if no match
    break;
  case 3:
    result = sites.find(pkt[0:end]);       // throws
ERR_SET_NOTFOUND if no match
    break;
  default:
```

```
    exit;
}
catch ( ERR_SET_NOTFOUND ) {…}
```

8.2   Version 2: Using References

To exploit the reference construct in this situation, we need an array of references in which the:

- Index values correspond to the database rows (records) to be matched during the initial operation.
- Array element values correspond to the searchsets to be used for the next operation.

The relevant array declaration is shown below.

```
reference set:string refSet[4] ={ref(httpVerbs),
ref(sipVerbs), ref(badGuys), ref(sites)};
```

We can now replace coding find operations for each of the possible database match results (i.e., for each possible searchset name) with a single searchset find, abstracting out the individual searchset names and replacing them with a solitary variable holding the reference array's index values. Using the deref operator on an element of that reference array at runtime effectively delivers the referenced aggregate as the searchset upon which the find method will operate (shown below).

```
try { matchedRow = flowTable.match(flow);
    result =
deref(refSet[matchedRow]).find( pkt[0:end] );}
catch (…) {…}
```

8.3   Results: Source Code Reduction and Performance

Our experiments suggest that, for this application domain and hardware, using reference constructs does not cause meaningful performance differences. Fig. 2 shows that, when measuring throughput in gigabits per second (gbps), the application's throughput for packet sizes 300 and 1000 bytes do not vary for hundredths of a gbps. Only at a packet size of 2000 bytes is there a discernable difference, with the using-references version achieving 6.15 gbps and the without-references version running at 6.14 gbps. This small variation could be an artifact of experiment mechanics.

We were concerned that the overhead of moving packet data to the regex chip for the searchset find operation was dwarfing all other effects. To check this, we coded a version of the application in which the second operation was another database match operation, one that involved four alternative databases. The results in Fig. 2(c). show no meaningful performance difference caused by references being used or not.

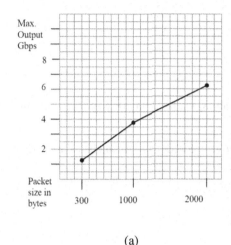

Database op-> searchset op		
Packet size in bytes	Throughput with references (Gbps)	Throughput without references (Gbps)
300	1.16	1.16
1000	3.88	3.88
2000	6.15	6.14

(b)

Database op#1->database op#2		
Packet size in bytes	Throughput with references (Gbps)	Throughput without references (Gbps)
300	0.582	0.582
1000	1.9	1.9
2000	3.9	3.9

(a)   (c)

Fig. 1. Performance with and without references. (a) Throughput sensitivity to packet size (database result drives searchset selection). (b) Database result drives searchset selection. (c) Database result drives 2nd database selection. © CloudShield Technologies, 2011

In these tests the version without references will require comparison and jump by-tecodes to execute the switch statement control flow. The versions that use a refer-ence will employ 2-3 instructions to mask off (and sometimes shift) portions of the encoded data. Any performance differences in these two small instruction sets will be dwarfed by the time spent to move data to the TCAM/regex subsystems or to per-form classic packet matching and searching operations, whether they are implemented with specialized processors or not. Thus, it is not surprising that the experiments show no meaningful performance increase from using references. Our contention is that the increased code simplicity shown above is a significant benefit and that it does not come at a cost of decreased performance. Before presenting final conclusions, the next section quickly compares packetC references with similar constructs in other languages.

9   Reference Constructs in Other Languages or Contexts

Since our approach emphasizes choosing language characteristics as much as imple-mentation mechanics, this penultimate section provides a concise comparison of such characteristics in packetC references and several similar constructs: C pointers, Java pointers, and C++ references (Table 1). Recall that references play a variety of roles, including the following:

- Facilitating the creation and destruction of dynamically-allocated objects (e.g., Java, C).
- Exposing array layout and indexing mechanics (C).
- Passing a parameter that has an aggregate (composite) data type without copying its contents to call-stack slots (C++).

Table 1. Comparing C pointers, C++ references and packetC references. ©CloudShield Technologies, 2011.

Construct/ Attribute	C pointer/ Java reference	C++ reference	packetC reference
New value can be assigned (reseatable).	Yes	No	Yes
Can be assigned NULL value.	Yes	No	No
Can be referenced as itself in source code.	Yes	No	Yes
Must be assigned at declaration.	No	Yes	Yes

A C pointer holds a memory address in the form of a numeric value. Despite some implementation variability, users can depend on a pointer holding the value of an address (or null value) and being amenable to pointer arithmetic operations [6]. Java references share C pointers reseatability, nullability and independence from their referent; however, Java reference values are not generally user-accessible or available for arithmetic operations [7].

In contrast, a packetC reference is not constrained to be an address; it is simply a designation that uniquely indicates one of a finite set of aggregates, which share a common type signature and are visible from the reference variable's scope. Users cannot assume a particular internal organization for reference variables in a given implementation.

A C++ reference [8] is more restricted than a C pointer or a packetC reference: it must be declared with a non-null value that cannot be changed. Source code cannot refer to a reference identifier as an entity in itself, since an occurrence of the identifier indicates the referenced object, instead.

As Table 1 shows, packetC's collection of classic reference characteristics is similar to that of several familiar reference constructs, without being identical to any of those reviewed here. We call attention to packetC references, however, not because their general characteristics are unusual but, instead, because of their specific role for practical operations in a specialized domain. It is this aspect that the conclusions explore below.

10   Summary

Our primary finding is that a programming language can exploit relatively simple reference declaration constructs and implementation mechanisms to deliver significant practical benefits:

- Strong typing and non-nullability to guarantee a legal operand at run-time in a domain where time pressures make most exception handling infeasible.

- Reseatability to enable dynamic selection of operands: in this case, to select entire aggregates of considerable complexity and to construct complex chains of dependent operations.
- Hidden reference values (and avoidance of memory addresses as reference values) to discourage malicious exploits.
- Source code compaction and increased extensibility by replacing a system of switch statement case alternatives with a single dereferencing expression.

Taken separately, the language constructs and implementation mechanics used to provide each of these advantages are fairly ordinary: using base types, requiring and restricting initial values, encoding ordinal values as identifiers. However, the whole is greater than the sum of its parts and provides practical lessons in applying reference constructs to a domain-specific language, especially to one with high reliability and security requirements.

Acknowledgements. Peder Jungck, Dwight Mulcahy and Ralph Duncan are the co-authors of the packetC language. Andy Norton, Greg Triplett, Kai Chang, Mary Pham, Alfredo Chorro-Rivas and Minh Nguyen provided valuable help in many areas for this effort. Thanks are also due the SAIC individuals who secured export approval 12-SAIC-0305-550 for the paper.

References

1. Jungck, P., Duncan, R., Mulcahy, D.: packetC Programming. Apress, New York (2011)
2. CloudShield Technologies. CS-2000 Technical Specifications. Product datasheet available from CloudShield Technologies, 212 Gibraltar Dr., Sunnyvale, CA, USA 94089 (2006)
3. International Business Machines Corporation. IBM Blade Center PN41. Product datasheet available from IBM Systems and Technology Group, Route 100, Somersm, New York, USA 10589 (2008)
4. Chao, H.J., Liu, B.: High Performance Switches and Routers, pp. 562–564. John Wiley and Sons, Hoboken (2007)
5. IXIA. XM12 High Performance Chassis. Retrieved from,
   http://www.ixia.com/products/chassis/
   display?skey=ch_optixia_xm12 (January 24, 2011)
6. ISO/IEC 9899:1999. Standard for the C programming language (May 2005) (version, 'C99')
7. Gosling, J., Joy, B., Steele, G., Bracha, G.: The Java Language Specification, 3rd edn. Addison-Wesley (June 2005)
8. ISO/IEC ISO/IEC 14882:2003 (corrected version of the 1998 C++ standard)

Are Heterogeneous Cellular Networks Superior to Homogeneous Ones?*

Shelly Salim, Christian H.W. Oey, and Sangman Moh**

Dept. of Computer Engineering, Chosun University, Gwangju, South Korea
smmoh@chosun.ac.kr

Abstract. In this paper, the performance of homogeneous cellular networks (HMCNs) and heterogeneous cellular networks (HTCNs) is evaluated and compared. The HTCN discussed in this paper consists of three kinds of cells: macrocells, microcells and femtocells. The macrocells are evenly deployed. The microcells are densely deployed in the offices and public areas and sparsely deployed in the universities areas. The femtocells are deployed in the residential areas. And, a user mobility pattern is defined to model real communication environment. Our simulation results show that the HTCN requires less power (in Watt/km^2/Mbps) and achieves higher throughput compared to the HMCN.

Keywords: Heterogeneous cellular network, user mobility, energy, throughput.

1 Introduction

There are rising concerns about energy conservation in information and communication technology (ICT) field. ICT contributes approximately 2% of global carbon emission and it is predicted to reach 2.8% by 2020 [1]. Among ICTs, the base stations of cellular mobile networks are the most energy consuming component that consumes about an average of 25MWh per year. Millions of base stations are deployed and they will be increased in developing regions. Therefore, the efforts to suppress base stations' power consumption are desperately needed. Besides environment friendly aspect, reducing power consumption of the base stations would also advantage the network operators by lowering the operators' expenditure. The efforts to reduce the power consumption of cellular networks coined the trendy term "green cellular network".

The continuous demand of higher data rate is considered to be the main reason of increasing energy consumption in cellular networks. Users' traffic growth could reach 400% per year, for both data and voice traffic [2]. Therefore, on one hand, the service providers need to reduce the energy consumption of the cellular network, but on the other hand, they also have to meet the demand for higher data rate.

---

* This work was supported in part by the MKE (The Ministry of Knowledge Economy), Korea, under the ITRC (Information Technology Research Center) support program supervised by the NIPA (National IT Industry Promotion Agency) (NIPA-2012-H0301-12-2008).
** Corresponding author.

J.J. Park et al. (Eds.): NPC 2012, LNCS 7513, pp. 61–68, 2012.
© IFIP International Federation for Information Processing 2012

Various strategies have been proposed to reduce power consumption in cellular networks. In [3], two approaches are mentioned; one is by utilizing energy-aware components in the base stations and the other is by employing energy-aware network deployment. Detailed discussions are provided in a survey paper [4], which categorizes the energy saving solutions into architectural, network planning, and system design approaches. The architectural approach focuses on energy saving in the base stations, such as cooperative base stations and renewable energy sources implementation. New technologies, such as cognitive radio and cooperative relays, are considered in the system design approach, in addition to energy-aware communication protocols, resource management, cross-layer design, etc. This paper is especially attracted to the network planning approach, which is about the deployment of heterogeneous cellular networks (HTCN), since it is a promising candidate to achieve both energy conservation and higher data rates.

The straightforward method to increase power efficiency is by decreasing the propagation distance, since it will reduce the transmission power. Therefore, the deployment of smaller cells forming a heterogeneous network is a promising solution. The common base stations of large area coverage, called macrocells, are mainly designed to cover a large transmission area rather than to provide high data rates. While the base stations of small area coverage, called microcells, are low power base stations capable to handle dense traffic. Also, smaller cells could utilize higher frequency bands, allowing them to support high data rates. Moreover, smaller cells encourage spectral efficiency by increasing spatial frequency reuse. In this paper, HTCN consisting of macrocells, microcells and femtocells is introduced with a user mobility pattern and it is compared to the homogeneous cellular network (HMCN) of macrocells only in terms of energy efficiency and system throughput.

The rest of this paper is organized as follows: Some related works are summarized in the following section. A HTCN is presented as a design under test with a user mobility pattern. The performance of the HTCN is evaluated and compared in Section 4. Finally, conclusions are covered in Section 5.

2   Related Works

To the best of our knowledge, the works on HTCNs consider either joint deployment of macrocells and microcells (picocells) or joint deployment of macrocells and femtocells, without the consideration of the three of them deployed simultaneously. In this paper, the HTCN consists of macrocells, microcells and femtocells. Also, a user mobility pattern is included to model real mobile communication environment.

There are many works proposed in the field of cellular networks energy conservation. Some of them concentrate on the deployment of heterogeneous cellular networks or small scale cellular networks. The work in [5] studied the energy efficiency of joint macrocells and picocells network. It concluded that joint deployment strategy could reduce the total energy consumption in urban areas by up to 60%.

The energy efficiency of cellular networks with femtocells is studied in [6]. It presented an energy consumption modeling framework where the base stations have three states, those are: 'turn-off state', 'radio-off state' and 'radio-on state'. Each state represents different energy consumption. The simulation results in [6] showed that as femtocells penetration rate is increased, the normalized energy consumption per cell is decreased; as the number of open access mobile nodes is increased, the system throughput is increased. In [7], simulation-based case studies of macrocells offloading benefits in UMTS (Universal Mobile Telecommunications System) and WiMAX (Worldwide Interoperability for Microwave Access) networks are presented. Both results support femtocells deployment in macrocells. However, those works stated above excluded user mobility or did not consider user mobility into their simulation. There is one work that considered users movement [8], where the macrocell users moved at a walking speed of 1 m/s. The work also introduced an idle mode for femtocells based on user activity detection.

Recently, the authors in [9] proposed a novel design of cellular networks, which is called "small-cell networks (SCNs)". SCNs are defined as cellular networks with very dense deployment of self-organizing, low-cost, low-power base stations. It is believed that SCNs are both cost and energy efficient solution to meet the forecasted traffic growth. However, it is also recognized that the realization of SCNs will encounter considerable challenges, especially because the conventional cellular networks have existed for a long time with enormous number of large-coverage base stations (macrocells) deployed all around the world. Since replacing those base stations with "small-cells" is supposed to be highly unlikely to take place in the near future, the possible target of SCNs would be the regions where cellular networks are not deployed yet.

3   A Heterogeneous Cellular Network: Design under Test

Network providers planning to expand their service in a new area should consider the base station deployment strategy in order to minimize the power consumption. There are some options, namely, (1) to employ a small number of macrocells with high transmission power, (2) to employ a large number of microcells with low transmission power, or (3) a combination of both creating a HTCN.

Since smaller cells consume less power, the deployment of smaller cells is encouraged with respect to energy efficiency. Typical coverage of a microcell is a few hundred meters. Smaller coverage in order of a few meters of indoor area can be achieved in femtocells. Usually, microcells are deployed in addition to the existing macrocells in the areas with high traffic, while femtocells are deployed in indoor areas to provide indoor 3G (3rd generation mobile telecommunications) coverage. According to the case study [1], femtocell deployment could result in 7:1 operational energy advantage ratio compared to macrocell networks for similar service.

In this paper, the HTCN contains macrocells, microcells and femtocells, with the topology as shown in Fig. 1(b). The HTCN is compared to HMCN with the topology as shown in Fig. 1(a). A network area can be divided into three kinds of regions: office and public places (O), universities (U), and residential (R) as shown in Fig. 2. In the HTCN, microcells are deployed densely in the O regions and sparsely in the U

regions, while femtocells are deployed distributively in the R regions. This consideration is taken to model real operation condition, where many mobile users exist at the
same places at the same time.

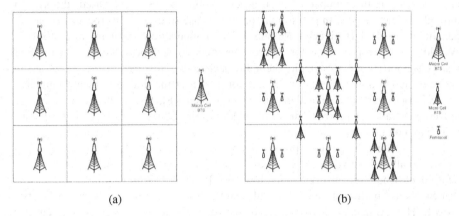

(a)   (b)

Fig. 1. (a) A homogeneous cellular network and (b) A heterogeneous cellular network

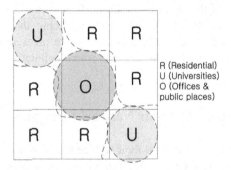

Fig. 2. Three kinds of regions in a network

A user mobility pattern is adapted on the basis of usual human mobility in daily
life. By using this mobility pattern, the performance study is expected to be more
realistic compared to random mobility pattern. Moreover, in HTCN, the users' location is especially significant to determine which base stations should provide service
to certain users, and to clearly compare dense populated areas with scarce ones. In the
proposed user mobility pattern, the overall population of mobile users is divided into
3 classes labeled A, B and C, and their mobility is defined according to certain time
slots as follows (illustrated in Fig. 3):

- 40% of total population: users A. They start from area R, and then move towards
  area O and stay there or move around for some time. After that, some of them
  move around area O before move back to area R or directly return to area R and
  stay until the end of simulation time. Users A reflect office workers.
- 30% of total population: users B. They start from area R, and then move towards
  area U and stay for some time (lower than users A stay time in area O). After that,

they move around area O before move back to area R or directly return to area R and stay until the end of simulation time. Users B reflect academics.

- 30% of total population: users C. Some of them merely stay in area R, and the rest of them move towards area O and then return to area R and stay until the end of simulation time. Users C reflect the rest of the population not belonging to class A or B, such as housewives.

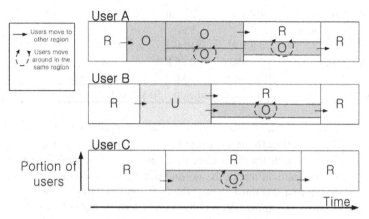

Fig. 3. User mobility pattern

4 Performance Evaluation

4.1 Simulation Environment

To compare the performance of HMCN and HTCN, a simulation is conducted with the settings as shown in Table 1. The HMCN contains macrocells and mobile users, while the HTCN contains all elements of macrocell, microcell, femtocell, and mobile users. The type of macrocell, microcell, and mobile nodes (handset) are the recent technology UMTS base stations, UMTS microcells, and UMTS/3G mobile phone, respectively, whereas the femtocells are assumed to be compatible with that technology. The numerical parameters are adapted from the reference papers.

All network elements, except macrocell, have sleep mode, which is to turn off some electronics equipments when there is no traffic to serve. Despite there are some works proposing idle/sleep mode for macrocells, the real adaptation of such a system is not exist yet. The microcells, femtocells, and mobile nodes are assumed to have idle/sleep mode by default. Therefore, macrocells consume power equal to its total power consumption (1.85 KW) all the time. Based on the power consumption distribution in base stations [4], the proportion of power consumed in idle mode and sleep mode are defined. In the sleep mode, only the power supply is needed, which takes 7.5% of total power consumption. In the idle mode, air conditioning is turned on, which adds 17.5% of total power consumption, resulting in 25% of total power consumption. Both settings are applied for microcells and femtocells, while mobile nodes have only sleep mode which consumes 0.017 W.

Table 1. Simulation settings

Parameter	HMCN HTCN	- HTCN	- HTCN	HMCN HTCN
	Macrocell	Microcell	Femtocell	Mobile users
Number of BS/users	9	16	12	90
Type	UMTS	UMTS	Femtocell	UMTS/3G
Transmission range	1000 m	250 m	10 m	-
Idle mode & sleep mode	No	Yes	Yes	Yes
Transmission power	0.8 KW	10 W	0.1 W	0.25 W
Power consumption	1.85 KW	0.25 KW	7 W	1 W
Data rate	384 Kbps	5 Mbps	14.4 Mbps	-
Backbone	B-ISDN, bandwidth 150 Mb, delay 100 ms			

The traffic is voice traffic [10] which divided into 2 types: normal traffic and femtocell traffic. The normal traffic is executed between random pairs of source and destination, whereas femtocell traffic is executed between source nodes that possess a femtocell to random destinations. In the normal traffic, the simulation time is divided into 3 phases. At the first and third phases, the traffic is low (10 sessions, i.e., 10 pairs of caller and receiver) and at the second phase, the traffic is high (35 sessions). These specifications are to model high traffic during the noon or working hours. The femtocell traffic is moderate (6 sessions out of 12 femtocells) and constant. In the simulation, both normal traffic and femtocell traffic are applied simultaneously. Our simulation is performed on Network Simulator 2 (NS-2) [11].

4.2   Simulation Results and Discussion

In our performance study, normalized power consumption, which is power consumed by each base station divided by its coverage area, is primarily taken into account. Throughput is also observed in terms of user data rate, and normalized power per throughput is evaluated and compared as a combined metric of power consumption and throughput.

Since the macrocells do not have neither idle mode nor sleep mode, one could predict that the HTCN, with more network elements added, would result in higher total power consumption. Fig. 4 shows the normalized power consumption of HMCN and HTCN. The total power consumption of HTCN is 905.16 W/Km^2, which is higher that of HMCN, 783.0 W/Km^2. In case macrocells in both HMCN and HTCN do not have idle/sleep mode, apparently HTCN would consume higher total operational power since it has more network elements (microcells and femtocells). However, macrocells in HTCN has higher activity than the ones in HMCN, showing higher utilization. Therefore, if macrocells have idle/sleep mode, HTCN might perform better energy conservation and utilization compared to HMCN.

Fig. 5 shows the throughput and drop rate of HTCN and HMCN. The throughput of HTCN is 12.5% higher and its drop rate is 7.5% lower than HMCN. If the normalized power consumption is divided by throughput, called normalized power per throughput, then HTCN outperforms HMCN. In HTCN, the normalized power per throughput is 139.81 W/Km^2/Mbps, while it is 143,68 W/Km^2/Mbps in HMCN. For that reason, HTCN is able to achieve higher data rate in energy-efficient manner. Moreover, the microcells and femtocells of HTCN are found to be underloaded. In dense traffic, HTCN is expected to achieve higher throughput than HMCN.

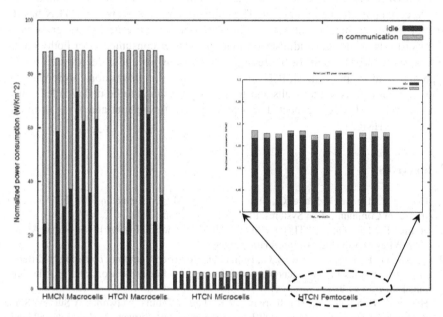

Fig. 4. Normalized power consumption of the whole base stations of HMCN and HTCN

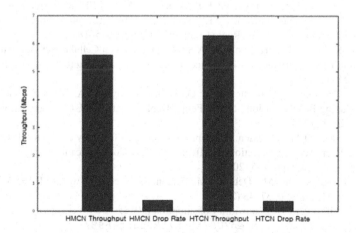

Fig. 5. Throughput and drop rate of HMCN and HTCN

5   Conclusions

In this paper, we have studied the performance of HTCN and HMCN, in terms of power consumption and data rate (throughput). HTCN consists of macrocells, microcell and femtocells, whereas the HMCN consists of macrocells only. The network area is divided into three regions and a user mobility pattern is defined to model real mobile communication environment. The simulation results show that HTCN has the potency to support higher user data rate in energy-efficient manner. However, because the macrocells do not have idle/sleep mode, the power consumption of both cellular networks is relatively high. In the future, if macrocells have idle/sleep mode, HTCN is predicted to outperform HMCN in term of energy conservation. Moreover, the simulation on HTCN's microcells and femtocells are found to be underloaded. Thus, in dense traffic, HTCN is expected to achieve higher throughput and lower drop rate compared to HMCN.

References

1. Forster, C., Dickie, I., Maile, G., Smith, H., Crisp, M.: Understanding the Environmental Impact of Communication Systems. Plextex Final Report (2009)
2. Holma, H., Toskala, A.: LTE for UMTS – OFDMA and SC-FDMA Based Radio Access. John Wiley & Sons Ltd., Chippenham (2009)
3. Arnold, O., Richter, F., Fettweis, G., Blume, O.: Power consumption modeling of different base station types in heterogeneous cellular networks. Future Network and Mobile Summit, 1–8, 16–18 (2010)
4. Hasan, Z., Boostanimehr, H., Bhargava, V.K.: Green Cellular Networks: A Survey, Some Research Issues and Challenges. IEEE Communications Surveys & Tutorials, 524–540 (2011)
5. Claussen, H., Ho, L.T.W., Pivit, F.: Effects of Joint Macrocell and Residential Picocell Deployment on the Network Energy Efficiency. In: 19th IEEE International Symposium on Personal, Indoor and Mobile Radio Communications, pp. 15–18 (2008)
6. Chee, D., Kang, M., Lee, H., Jung, B.: A Study on the Green Cellular Network with Femtocells. In: Third International Conference on Ubiquitous and Future Networks (ICUFN), pp. 235–240 (2011)
7. Calin, D., Claussen, H., Uzunalioglu, H.: On Femto Deployment Architectures and Macrocell Offloading Benefits in Joint Macro-Femto Deployments. IEEE Communications Magazine 48, 26–32 (2010)
8. Ashraf, I., Ho, L.T.W., Claussen, H.: Improving Energy Efficiency of Femtocell Base Stations via User Activity Detection. In: IEEE Wireless Communications and Networking Conference (WCNC), pp. 1–5 (2010)
9. Hoydis, J., Kobayashi, M., Debbah, M.: Green Small-cell Networks. IEEE Vehicular Technology Magazine 6, 37–43 (2011)
10. Voice Over IP – Per Call Bandwidth Consumption (2012),
    http://www.cisco.com/en/US/tech/tk652/tk698/
    technologies_tech_note09186a0080094ae2.shtml
11. The Network Simulator - ns-2 (2012), http://www.isi.edu/nsnam/ns/

Dynamic Spray and Wait Routing Protocol
for Delay Tolerant Networks

Longbo Zhang, Chen Yu, and Hai Jin

Services Computing Technology and System Lab
Cluster and Grid Computing Lab
School of Computer Science and Technology
Huazhong University of Science and Technology, Wuhan, 430074, China
{yuchen,hjin}@hust.edu.cn

Abstract. *Delay Tolerant Networks* (DTN) is one of the mobile wireless networks that cannot set up the end-to-end communication path between the source and destination nodes pair in most of time. In this paper, we propose an improved routing protocol named as *Dynamic Spray & Wait* (DS&W), which is based on Spray and Wait routing strategy attempting to gain the higher delivery ratio benefits of replication-based routing as well as the lower resource utilization benefits of forwarding-based routing. But different from S&W, DS&W routing strategy focus on dynamic control to reduce the scale of the messages' flooding by calculating the delivery success probabilities to destinations. DS&W routing protocol can dramatically reduce the overhead ratio in DTNs. Simulation results also evident that DS&W protocol outperforms other existing DTN routing protocols.

Keywords: Delay Tolerant Network (DTN), mobile networks, epidemic routing, Spray & Wait routing, dynamic control.

1   Introduction

Delay Tolerant Networks (DTN) [1] often refer to sparse mobile ad hoc network, where a routing path does not necessarily exist. In DTNs, both nodes and links may be unreliable. Many emerging communication networks fall into this paradigm including wildlife tracking and habitat monitoring sensor networks (IPN) [2], interplanetary networks [3], nomadic communities networks [4], etc.

Many challenges affect the routing in DTNs such as the changing network topology, low delivery ratio and high delay. The problems can be mitigated by using flooding-based scheme or by predicting the network topology [5] to ensure the delivery ratio and delay. Many works shows that flooding-based scheme has a better performance on delivery ratio and delay than predicting scheme, but it will generate numbers of redundant copies and increase the overhead ratio which would have negative impact on the efficiency, if the flooding scale can not be controlled in a suitable scale, it would lead to network congestion. Thus, the efficiency of a flooding-based scheme DTN routing protocol relies essentially on the appropriate scale of message flooding.

J.J. Park et al. (Eds.): NPC 2012, LNCS 7513, pp. 69–76, 2012.

In this paper, we propose DS&W, a routing protocol for DTNs, which dynamically control the scale of message flooding by predicting the delivery probabilities. The contributions presented in this paper are: we propose a suitable method to control the scale of message flooding; based on the dynamic control, we propose DS&W, a novel routing protocol which relies on the control of the scale of flooding. With DS&W protocol, the scale of message flooding is dynamically changeable, and different from other flooding-based scheme routing protocols, it could reduce the overhead ratio with little effect on delivery ratio and delay.

The paper is organized as follows. Section 2 presents the state of the art for DTN routing and the traditional method of the message flooding. Section 3 presents the dynamic control and DS&W protocol. Section 4 provides the simulation results of DS&W routing and related discussion. Finally, section 5 concludes the paper.

2   Related Works

Several routing protocols have been proposed for DTNs. These protocols can be classified into two categories: single-copy routing protocol [6] and multi-copy routing protocol [7]. With the single-copy routing protocols, only one copy of the message is transported by the topology knowledge of the network. In order to increase the delivery success probabilities, the topology knowledge should be predicted by historical encounters between nodes, location information or others [8]. The Direct Delivery protocol and the First Contact protocol are the use of this strategy. With the multi copy routing, the node carrying the message sends a copy to each encountered node. This is repeated until the destination receives the message. In this case, the contacts are assumed to be totally opportunistic. PRoPHET protocol [9], Epidemic Routing protocol [10], and Spray & Wait routing protocol [11] are the use of this strategy. Due to the low delivery ratio and long delay of the single-copy routing, the multi-copy routing is the mainstream routing protocol.

PRoPHET protocol determines the delivery probability in each node, which is related to the history of the encounters. Transfer is done only for an encountered node, which has a good probability to deliver the message to its final destination. The delivery probability used by each node is recalculated according to three rules:

(a) When the node M encounters another node E, the probability for E is increased:

$$P(M,E)_{new} = P(M,E)_{old} + (1 - P(M,E)_{old}) \times L_{encounter} \tag{1}$$

where $L_{encounter}$ is an initialized constant.

(b) The predictabilities for all destinations D other than E are *aged*:

$$P(M,D)_{new} = P(M,D)_{old} \times \gamma^k \tag{2}$$

where γ is the aging constant and k is the number of time units that has elapsed since the last aging.

(c) Predictabilities are exchanged between M and E and the *transitive* property of predictability is used to update the predictability of destinations D for which E has a value on the assumption that M is likely to meet E again:

$$P(M,D)_{new} = P(M,D)_{old}$$
$$+ (1 - P(M,D)_{old}) \times P(M,E) \times P(E,D) \times \beta \tag{3}$$

where β is a scaling constant.

In PRoPHET protocol, if a node i encounter another node j, node i will decide whether to send the message to node j based on the delivery probability of them.

Epidemic routing can be described as following: the source node, which has N neighbor nodes, sends N copies of the message to its N neighbor nodes. Afterwards, each neighbor node judges whether the received message copy has been received before or not. If it has, the neighbor node discards the copy; otherwise the neighbor node will keep this message copy and send the same copy to all its neighbor nodes until the message reaches the destination node. In the ideal situation, epidemic routing is considered to be the most effective strategy, but in reality, the overhead ratio is high and it is faced with serious network congestion.

In order to solve these problems, fixing the number of copies is the most common method. Spray & Wait routing protocol uses this solution. In Spray & Wait routing, there are two phases: spray phase and wait phase. In spray phase, the source node of a message initially starts with L copies of this message, which is related with the number of nodes and the requirements for delay. Any node A that has $n>1$ message copies (source or relayed), when it encounters another node B with no copies, it hands over to $B^{\lfloor n/2 \rfloor}$ copies and keeps $B^{\lceil n/2 \rceil}$ copies for itself; when A is left with only one copy, it switches to direct transmission. L can be calculated from:

$$\left(H_M^3 - 1.2\right)L^3 + \left(H_M^2 - \frac{\pi^2}{6}\right)L^2 + \left(a + \frac{2M-1}{M(M-1)}\right)L = \frac{M}{M-1} \tag{4}$$

where M is the number of nodes; a is multiples of the time units; $H_n^\tau = \sum_{i=1}^{n}\frac{1}{i^\tau}$ is the nth Harmonic number of order of τ.

The multi-copy routing protocol can achieve higher delivery ratio and lower delay than the single-copy routing protocols, but it will increase the overhead ratio and wastes energy. Although Spray & Wait routing to a certain extent solves the above problems, these problems still exist. Considered Spray & Wait routing, the number of copies L is not appropriate in all cases such as the following situation: in spray phase, a message sends copies to other nodes after a period of time, set the number of nodes L_1, then it will continue to flooding message to the left node until the number of nodes reaches L; then the routing protocol goes in the wait phase. If the message is successfully forwarded by a node in L_1, we can consider the spray phase after L_1 is useless.

3   Dynamic Control and DS&W Routing Protocol

We can find the limitation of Spray & Wait routing is that it has to fix the copies of message to control the overhead ratio; the spray phase will not stop until the message get to the destination or wait phase. The flooding scale L related with the network size can guarantee the maximum delivery delay and stationary message flooding, but it will increase some messages' flooding. For some messages, a smaller L can not only guarantee the delivery ratio and delay, but also decrease the overhead ratio. Since the redundant message flooding in spray phase, the routing efficiency drops. So, if the spray phase can be controlled dynamically, it will have a better performance than Spray & Wait protocol. In order to ensure the delivery ratio and delay, the scale of message flooding should also not be too small. So how to ensure the changeable flooding scale appropriate is very important. Next, we will give our method using the probability of nodes to realize the dynamic control.

Considering PRoPHET routing protocol, it gives a method to evaluate the probability to deliver the message. In the spray phase, we can calculate the total probability of the nodes. When the probability is high enough to ensure the delivery ratio and delay while the spray phase is not end, we can force it end, so that the spray phase can be controlled dynamically. The following section will prove that our assumption is correct, the method of dynamic flooding is effectively. Based on the dynamic flooding, we will give the pseudo code of DS&W routing protocol.

In order to prove our assumption, we do the following works. For the delay, we divided it into two parts: T_s and T_w, means the spray phase and wait phase. It is certain that if we reduce the number of copies T_s will decrease and T_w will increase. Assume that the node can meet another node after t_{unit}, and the node's average delivery probability as $\overline{p}$. In spray phase, expect of T_s is: $T_s = \log_2^L t_{unit}$. In wait phase, all nodes carrying packets is connected with the destination with the probability of $1-\left(1-\overline{p}\right)^L$, so expect of T_w is: $T_w = \dfrac{t_{unit}}{1-\left(1-\overline{p}\right)^L}$. The delivery delay is:

$$T = \log_2^L t_{unit} + \frac{t_{unit}}{1-\left(1-\overline{p}\right)^L} \tag{5}$$

If we decrease the number of nodes to λL ($\lambda \in (0, 1)$), then in spray phase, expect of T_s' is: $T_s' = \log_2^{\lambda L} t_{unit}$. In wait phase, when the number of node is L if the transmission node is in the node of λL, the wait phase is $T_w' = \dfrac{t_{unit}}{1-\left(1-\overline{p}\right)^L}$, if the node is not in the nodes of λL, the message will be transported by the λL nodes, then $T_w' = \dfrac{t_{unit}}{1-\left(1-\overline{p}\right)^{\lambda L}}$, so the expect of T_w is: $T_w' = \dfrac{\lambda t_{unit}}{1-\left(1-\overline{p}\right)^L} + \dfrac{(1-\lambda)t_{unit}}{1-\left(1-\overline{p}\right)^{\lambda L}}$. The delivery delay is:

$$T' = \log_2^{\lambda L} t_{unit} + \frac{\lambda t_{unit}}{1-\left(1-\overline{p}\right)^L} + \frac{(1-\lambda)t_{unit}}{1-\left(1-\overline{p}\right)^{\lambda L}} \quad (6)$$

$$\Delta T = T - T' = \left[\log_2^{\frac{1}{2}} + \frac{1-\lambda}{1-\left(1-\overline{p}\right)^L} - \frac{1-\lambda}{1-\left(1-\overline{p}\right)^{\lambda L}}\right] t_{unit} \quad (7)$$

Derivative of ΔT, we find that $\Delta T'_{\lambda=1} < 0$ and $\Delta T'_{\lambda=0} > 0$, the function graph is similar to a parabola. $\Delta T'_{\lambda=1} = 0$, which means there is a λ that makes $\Delta T_\lambda > 0$, and T is smaller than T, and limit of $\Delta T_{\lambda=0}$ is negative infinity. So when λ is close to 1, the deliver delay is shorter than spray & wait routing, and there should be a minimal value of the delay. After that when λ gets smaller, the delay gets larger. By calculating the total probability, we can make the λ in a suitable scope. By the research, we reach the following conclusions: with the dynamic control, the routing reduces the overhead while has little influence on the delivery ratio and delay.

By the calculation and analysis, the routing forwarding algorithm can be described as: (1) maintain the delivery probability of each node which is related to the history of the encounters; (2) send messages to its neighbor node, calculate the total delivery probability when nodes are connection, and update the record of the messages and the number of copies; (3) if the total delivery probability is higher than p_{max} or L is equal to 1, switches to wait phase. Next is the pseudo code for DS&W forwarding algorithm:

```
Algorithm: Core of DS&W routing
Spray phase
Connect with neighbor
if (neighbor=destination) transport message; jump end;
else transport message;
    total probability=1-(1- total probability)*(1- neighbor. total probability);
    L=L/2;
    if (total probability> p_max or L=1) jump wait phase;
        else jump spray phase;
Wait phase
Connect with neighbor
if (neighbor=destination) transport message; jump end;
else jump wait phase;
End;
```

4   Performance Evaluation

To demonstrate and evaluate the performance of DS&W, we use ONE1.4.1 [12], an *Opportunistic Network Environment* simulator which provides a powerful tool for generating mobility traces, running DTN messaging simulations with different routing protocols, and visualizing both simulations interactively in real-time and results after their completion. 125 nodes are distributed in Helsinki, capital of Finland, about 448km², the nodes are divided into four groups. Group 1 and 4 simulate the pedestrians' nodes, they all have 10MB memory, 1Km/h move speed, 100m transmit range, but move in different area. Group 2 and 3 simulate the car nodes, they have 15MB memories, 150m transmit range, move only on the rode of city, but have different speeds: 2Km/h and 3Km/h. The flowing figures show the performance comparison of three routing protocols.

Table 1. Delivery-ratio of DS&W routing and S&W routing

Routing	DS&W-0.98	DS&W-0.95	DS&W-0.93	DS&W-0.9	DS&W-0.85	DS&W-0.8	S&W
Delivery-ratio	0.4508	0.4486	0.4545	0.4494	0.4228	0.4169	0.4649

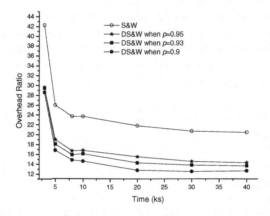

Fig. 1. Overhead ratio comparison between DS&W and S&W

Table 1 shows the delivery ratio of S&W routing and DS&W routing with different p_{max}. We find that when the total probability is from 0.9 to 1, the delivery ratio is similar to S&W routing, this corresponds with our conclusion: if the total probability is high enough, there is negligible affection on delivery ratio. If the total probability gets lower, the delivery ratio would have slightly bad performance.

Figure 1 and 2 show the performance comparison between DS&W routing and S&W routing. We can find that when $p=0.95$, the overhead ratio reduces about 30.07%, and the delay reduces about 5%; when $p=0.93$, the overhead ratio reduces about 33.24%, and the delay is basically unchanged; when $p=0.9$, the overhead ratio reduces about 38.22%, and the delay increases about 13%. It shows a good performance in reducing the burden of network and the delay corresponds with our conclusion: when λ is close to 1, the deliver delay is shorter than Spray & Wait routing, and there should be a minimal value of the delay, after that when λ gets smaller, the delay gets larger. So, when p_{max} is higher than 0.93, the routing can reduce overhead ratio obviously without influencing the delay, when it is from 0.93-0.9, it will increase the delay, but it is still acceptable.

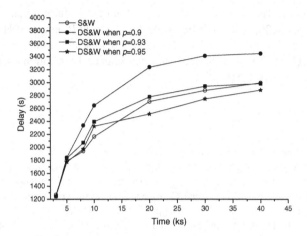

Fig. 2. Delay comparison between DS&W and S&W

Further, we consider the situation when p_{max}=0.85, overhead ratio reduces about 49.5%, and the delay increases about 42.4%. If the network is troubled by the network congestion and is not stringent on delay, this performance still can be acceptable; but when p get lower to 0.8, the overhead ratio reduces about 58.75%, the delay increases about 61.04%, this is unacceptable. So, if p gets smaller, the routing should be regarded as failed.

Table 2. Comparison of low p-DS&W and S&W

Routing	DS&W-0.85	DS&W-0.8	S&W
Overhead-ratio	10.3094	8.4273	20.4340
Delay (ms)	4267.6299	4809.0593	2996.4775

Through our analysis, we can summarize that when $p \in (0.9, 1)$, the DS&W routing shows a good performance in reducing the burden of network while with little influence to delay; when $p \in (0.85, 0.9)$, the DS&W routing protocol can be suitable for the network that is troubled by the burden of network and not particularly stringent requirements on delay.

5   Conclusions

In this paper, we propose a new routing protocol, named DS&W, which is suitable for mobile delay tolerant networks. DS&W routing protocol is based on multi-copy routing protocol and predicts probabilistic using history of encounters and transitivity. DS&W uses the total probability of the nodes carrying message to dynamically control the number of copies. In this way, the overhead-ratio can be reduced, and delivery-ratio and delay will not change much. Simulation results show that DS&W routing protocol outperforms Spray & Wait routing protocol.

Acknowledgement. The work is supported by National Natural Science Foundation of China (No.61003220), Research Fund for the Doctoral Program of Higher Education of China (No.20090142120025), Fundamental Research Funds for the Central Universities (HUST:2010QN051) and Natural Science Foundation of Hubei Province of China (No.2010CDB02302).

References

1. Delay tolerant networking research group, http://www.dtnrg.org
2. Juang, P., Oki, H., Wang, Y., Martonosi, M., Peh, L.S., Rubenstein, D.: Energy-efficient Computing for Wildlife Tracking: Design Tradeoffs and Early Experiences with Zebranet. In: Proceedings of 10th International Conference on Architectural Support for Programming Languages and Operating Systems, pp. 96–107. ACM Press, California (2002)
3. Burleigh, S., Hooke, A., Torgerson, L., Fall, K., Cerf, V., Durst, B., Scott, K.: Delay-tolerant Networking: An Approach to Interplanetary Internet. IEEE Communications Magazine 41, 128–136 (2003)
4. Doria, A., Udn, M., Pandey, D.P.: Providing Connectivity to the Saami Nomadic Community. In: Proceedings of 2nd International Conference on Open Collaborative Design for Sustainable Innovation (2002)
5. Singh, J.P., Dutta, P.: Temporal Behavior Analysis of Mobile ad hoc Network with Different Mobility Patterns. In: Proceedings of International Conference on Advances in Computing, Communication and Control, pp. 696–702. ACM Press, Mumbai (2009)
6. Spyropoulos, T., Psounis, K., Raghavendra, C.S.: Single-copy Routing in Intermittently Connected Mobile Networks. In: Proceedings of 1st IEEE Communications Society Conference on Sensor and Ad Hoc Communications and Networks, pp. 235–244. IEEE Press, Santa Clara (2004)
7. Spyropoulos, T., Psounis, K., Raghavendra, C.S.: Multiple-copy Routing in Intermittently Connected Mobile Networks. Technical Report, USC (2004)
8. Chen, X., Murphy, A.L.: Enabling Disconnected Transitive Communication in Mobile ad hoc Networks. In: Proceedings of Workshop on Principles of Mobile Computing collocated with PODC 2001, ACM Press, Rhode Island (2001)
9. Lindgren, A., Doria, A., Schelen, O.: Probabilistic Routing in Intermittently Connected Networks. SIGMOBILE Mobile Computing and Communications Review 7(3), 19–20 (2003)
10. Vahdat, A., Becker, D.: Epidemic Routing for Partially Connected ad hoc Networks. Technical Report CS-200006, Duke University (2000)
11. Spyropoulos, T., Psounis, K., Raghavendra, C.S.: Spray and Wait: An Efficient Routing Scheme for Intermittently Connected Mobile Networks. In: Proceedings of 2005 ACM SIGCOMM Workshop on Delay-Tolerant Networking, pp. 252–259. ACM Press, New York (2005)
12. Opportunistic Network Environment (ONE),
   http://www.netlab.tkk.fi/tutkimus/dtn/theone/

A Dynamic Popularity-Aware Load Balancing Algorithm for Structured P2P Systems

Narjes Soltani, Ehsan Mousavi Khaneghah,
Mohsen Sharifi, and Seyedeh Leili Mirtaheri

School of Computer Engineering
Iran University of Science and Technology
Tehran, Iran
{emousavi,mirtaheri,msharifi}@iust.ac.ir,
narjes_soltani@comp.iust.ac.ir

Abstract. Load balancing is one of the main challenges of structured P2P systems that use distributed hash tables (DHT) to map data items (objects) onto the nodes of the system. In a typical P2P system with N nodes, the use of random hash functions for distributing keys among peer nodes can lead to O(log N) imbalance. Most existing load balancing algorithms for structured P2Psystems are not proximity-aware, assume uniform distribution of objects in the system and often ignore node heterogeneity. In this paper we propose a load balancing algorithm that considers node heterogeneity, changes in object popularities, and link latencies between nodes. It also considers the load transfer time as an important factor in calculating the cost of load balancing. We present the algorithm using node movement and replication mechanisms. We also show via simulation how well the algorithm performs under different loads in a typical structured P2P system.

Keywords: Structured P2P Systems, Load Balancing, Node Movement, Replication.

1 Introduction

In most structured Peer-to-Peer (P2P) systems distribution of objects among nodes is done through distributed hash tables (DHT) mechanisms that use consistent hashing to map objects onto nodes [1]. Using this mechanism, a unique identifier is associated with each data item (object) and each node in the system. The identifier space is partitioned among the nodes that form the P2P system and each node is responsible for storing all data items that are mapped to an identifier in its portion of the space.

If node identifiers are chosen at random (as in [1]), a random choice of item IDs result in O(log N) imbalance factor in the number of items stored at a node. Here N is the total number of nodes in the system. Furthermore imbalance may result due to non-uniform distribution of objects in the identifier space and a high degree of heterogeneity in object loads and node capacities, memories, and bandwidths.

J.J. Park et al. (Eds.): NPC 2012, LNCS 7513, pp. 77–84, 2012.
© IFIP International Federation for Information Processing 2012

Several solutions are offered to solve the load balancing problem like the one proposed in [2], but these solutions usually have some shortcomings. For instance lots of them do not consider system dynamicity, nodes and objects heterogeneity, link latency between nodes, and the popularity level of moved items. Our algorithm uses two mechanisms namely nodes moving and replication to balance the load between nodes with consideration of items popularities.

The rest of the paper is organized as follows. In Section 2, we formulate the load balancing problem more explicitly and in Section 3, we discuss the related work. In Section 4, we describe our algorithm and we evaluate it in Section 5. We discuss conclusion in Section 6.

2   Definitions and Problem Formulation

We define node load as the temporal average number of bytes which is transferred by that node in each unit of time. In the same way we define the node capacity as the maximum number of bytes that node can transfer per time unit. A node is overloaded if its load is more than an upper threshold which is defined relevant to node capacity.

Our load balancing algorithm aims to minimize the load imbalance factor in the system while also minimizing the moved load. Calculation of load destination cost in our algorithm is based on its load and uptime and also its proximity to the overloaded node. Since there is no global information in P2P systems, we do not claim to select the best node in the system to move load to, but our algorithm does this in a group of nodes. Later we explain how these groups are formed. So when we want to move some load from a node i to a node j the destination cost is formulated as below:

$$DestinationCost=w_1*load_j/cap_j+w_2*(loc_i-loc_j)/distance_{max}+w_3*(uptime_j/t) \qquad (1)$$

In (1) cap and loc denote the capacity and location of a node in order. To normalize the location parameter in the above formula, we divide subtract of locations by $distance_{max}$ which stands for the distance between i and the farthest node j in the mentioned group. In the above formula t is the period of time our experiment lasts and we divide uptime of node j by it to normalize the uptime parameter. Also w_i $(1<=i<=3)$ is the weight given to different cost function parameters and $\sum w_i=1$ is always held. These weights are application-defined.

The load of each node j is defined as the summation of its data items loads. The load of each object k is defined as follows:

$$Load_k=size_k*access\_frequency_k \qquad (2)$$

In the above formula we want to calculate the average amount of bytes that is transferred in each unit of time in relation with object k. We calculate frequency access periodically and in distinct intervals. This means that we consider r intervals each last for t' seconds, then divide the number of access in each interval by the subtract result of $r*t'$ and t_{first}. Starting intervals times from zero in each round of simulation, t_{first} stands for the beginning time of each interval namely it is set to $0, t', 2t', \ldots$ and $(r-1)t'$ in order for each of the r intervals. These intervals can be stored in a cyclic queue with limited size in which the old intervals are replaced with the new ones in a cyclic manner. Next we sum the achieved values to calculate the *access_frequency* parameter.

$$access\_frequency = \sum_{p=0}^{r-1} objAccessNo_{p+1} / (r*t'-p*t') \qquad (3)$$

Defining a node n utility as $load_n/capacity_n$, the goal of our algorithm is to close nodes' utilities to each other as much as possible. However it is not always the case because our algorithm balances the load with considering its cost.

3   Related Work

Generally load balancing protocols are divided to two main groups in structured P2P systems. The first group is based on uniform distribution of items in identifier space and the second group has no such assumption [3]. Suppose that there are N nodes in the system, load balancing is achieved in the first group if the fraction of address space covered by each node is O(1/N). Most of algorithms have used the notion of virtual servers, first introduced in [1] to achieve this goal. A virtual server is similar to a single pear to the underlying DHT and has its own routing table and successors list.

Chord suggests each physical node hosts O(log N) virtual servers which leads to each node has some constant number of items with high probability [1]. CFS [4] accounts for nodes heterogeneity by allocating to each node some number of virtual servers proportional to the node capacity. In [2] Rao et.al. have proposed three different mechanisms to balance the load using virtual servers, yet their mechanisms are static and ignore data items popularities.

Using virtual servers in any algorithm leads to some common disadvantages. The first is that it leads to churn increase. Another disadvantage about virtual servers is that using them causes a great increase in routing table entries. Considering the above problems about virtual servers, our algorithm does not use of virtual servers [5].

Protocols which do not assume uniform item distribution use two different mechanisms to achieve load balance, namely item movement [3] and node movement [6]. Moving items break the DHT assignment of items to nodes, so that items cannot easily be found any more. Moving nodes by letting them to choose their own addresses arbitrarily increase the threat of Byzantine attack which can prevent some items from being found in the network.

Replicating data items is another way to achieve load balance. Although, some simple replication mechanisms have been proposed in structured P2P systems like chord [1], but none of them does this dynamically and with consideration of variant system loads.

4   Load Balancing Scheme

4.1   Nodes Load Information

When a node wants to join the system, a unique key is given to it using a hash function we call *"First Hash"*. For the purpose of load balancing a set of load directories, each called *LoadDir* is designed in the system to which nodes send their loads, capacities, locations, and uptimes information periodically. A node's uptime is defined as the average of continuous time it stays in the system.

To prevent Byzantine attack we use the proposed way in [6]. Each node connects to a central authority once, i.e. the first time it joins the system and obtains a directory identifier, we call *IDdir* that specifies to which *LoadDir* the node should send its information. The number of distinct directory identifiers is limited and determines the number of load directories in the system.

Grouping of nodes in our load balancing algorithm is done based on their directory identifiers. This means the nodes with the same value of *IDdir* send their information to the same *LoadDir* and in case of overloading, our algorithm first tries to move load between the nodes in the same group. A directory with the identifier *d* is stored in the first node whose identifier is equal to or follows *d* and when this node wants to leave system it has to send its stored load directory to its successor.

The central authority periodically sends the directory identifiers to the related nodes, so that each directory is aware of other directories.

4.2   Load Balancing Algorithm

A node starts load balancing algorithm when it notices its load more than its upper threshold. In the simulations it is proved that setting each node upper threshold to 95% of its capacity generates the best result.

Every node checks its load periodically and in case of overloading; it puts its popular items in a list called *popular-item-list*. This list is stored separately in each node and in relation with its own items. In our algorithm an item is popular if more than a quarter of the node load is due to that item load.

Our algorithm uses two mechanisms namely nodes moving and replication to balance the load between nodes with consideration of items popularities. In the following parts we explain these mechanisms in detail.

Node Movement
Node movement is done when one of the following cases arise:

1. A node gets overloaded due to the high popularity of more than one of its items.
2. A node gets overloaded because of high amount of data items put on it while none of them is highly popular.

Considering the above conditions, if a node *n* is overloaded, it sends a request to its relevant directory asking it to find a proper underloaded node for moving load. The selected under-loaded node should leave its previous location in the overlay and join at a new location specified by the *n*'s directory called *"split point"*. The overloaded node's directory selects some of *n*'s data items, starting from the item whose key has the most distance from node key and checks whether *n* load reaches to a normal level by moving this data item or not. If so, the split point is set to that data item key; Otherwise selection of data items continues in the same order until *n* load gets normal or the only remained data item be the one whose key is equal to overloaded node key, in this case the only remained data item is of course a very popular data item and by iterative execution of our algorithm, the next time this node is an eligible candidate for the second load balancing mechanism and its load is balanced by that way.

Finally the split point is set to the last selected item's key. In simulation we show setting normal load of any node to 75% of its capacity is an appropriate choice.

Selection of a proper under-loaded node is done in two steps and as follows. In the first step the overloaded node's directory searches in its stored information, calculates the destination cost function stated in section 2 for each of its entries and selects the one with the minimum cost. The selected node m should move to the specified split point, so all of its assigned keys should be reassigned to its successor. In the second step the directory checks two conditions. The first is that the reassignment process does not lead to the m's successor overloading and the second is moving selected items from n to m do not end up with m's overloading. If both of these conditions are held, m is the proper node we are searching for and it should leave and rejoin to system at the specified split point. If any of the conditions is not held, the selection process is repeated from the first step. If necessary, this directory can connect to other directories and selects a proper node from them.

Replication

If a node is overloaded because of the high popularity of one of its items, it is probable that due to its increasing popularity rate, moving this item to another node causes that node to get overloaded too and it is better to replicate it.

For the purpose of replication, we use a second hash function called *SecHash* and also a set of replication directories each called *RepDir*. Each entry of these directories consists of two parts, namely the name of replicated data item and the destination of replication. Creation of replication directories is done dynamically throughout system operation. If a node wants to replicate one of its items named A, it should search for successor of *SecHash(A)* to find the *RepDir* where it should add an entry.

The replication destination is specified by the overloaded node's *LoadDir*. This directory calculates the destination cost function stated in section 2 for each of its entries and at last the one with the minimum cost is selected if by moving half of the A's load to it, it does not change to an overloaded node. If this condition is not held, the next minimum cost nodes are tested until an appropriate node is selected. Again this directory can connect to other directories if necessary. A is replicated in the found node in association with another field where *FirstHash(A)* is stored. This field is used during search process as we explain later.

The overloaded node can then refuse the replicated item's received requests until it reaches to a normal load state. By this way if a node is searching for a replicated item, it may receive no result after a period of time which means a timeout has occurred. If this is the case, the requester node uses the second hash function to find the relevant *RepDir* and reads the replication destination from it. The above process can be extended to include replicating on more than one node if necessary.

4.3   Search Mechanism

Every time a node receives a request with key k, it checks whether k falls in the interval it is responsible for or not. If it is the case, this node returns the requested item. Otherwise the node should forward the request to another node with respect to its finger table [1], but in our algorithm this step delays with another step in which the node checks whether a replica of the searched item is stored in itself. Since intermediate nodes have no information about the name of requested items during search process and work only with hashed keys, the node checks the requested item key with the fields associated to replicated items on it. If no match is found, it forwards the request to another node with respect to its finger table, otherwise it response to the requester node.

To make the system fault tolerant, we can backup replication directories in the l next successors of the nodes where they are stored. The value of l is defined with consideration of the fault tolerance level needed in system.

5   Simulation Results

To evaluate our algorithm, we have designed and implemented a simulator in java based on Chord structured P2P system. Throughout the simulation we have shown the way our algorithm balances the load and also the importance of proximity factor in bandwidth consumption.

Our simulated nodes are completely heterogeneous and with different capabilities, so Pareto node capacity distribution with parameters shape=2 and scale=100 is used. In our simulated environment, nods can leave or join the system at any time. As stated before our algorithm aims to close nodes' utilities to each other as much as possible. It is not however always the case, because our load balancing algorithm considers the imposed cost.

Fig.1(a) shows nodes utilities in the system before applying any load balancing algorithm. It illustrates the large difference between nodes utilities. In this situation, lots of nodes are overloaded while there are also a lot of nodes with very low or even zero load. Applying our load balancing algorithm, the results change as in Fig.1(b).

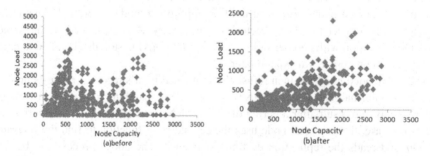

Fig. 1. Load balancing performance (a)Before load balancing (b)After load balancing

To demonstrate the importance of proximity in our algorithm, Fig.2 displays the bandwidth consumption of load transfer through the hops passed during load balancing process. As it is shown, when we have relaxed the proximity factor, the passed physical hops is much more than the case we have regarded this factor.

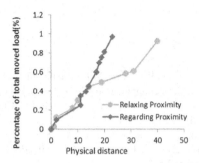

Fig. 2. Changing of links delay while load balancing

In Fig.3 we show the effectiveness of our algorithm by comparing it with three other algorithms, namely Rao et.al. algorithm [2], CFS algorithm [4] and log(N) virtual Server algorithm[1]. As we have mentioned previously Rao et.al. proposed three different schemes to balance the load using virtual servers. In this section we compare our algorithm with the "one-to-one" scheme in which one node contacts a single other node per unit time as two other schemes are said to utilize nodes similarly.

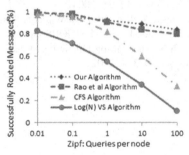

Fig. 3. Percent of successfully routed queries for trace-driven simulation with varying load

The focus was put on the percentage of successfully routed queries for trace-driven simulations with varying loads. To this end we have used Zipf query distribution. This experiment examines how the load balancing algorithms responded to different degrees of applied workload. In almost all cases, we found our algorithm performs the same as or better than the other algorithms.

6   Conclusion

This paper presents a load balancing algorithm which considers items non-uniform distribution, heterogeneous nodes, system dynamicity, and objects different and variable popularities. Also two important factors namely the uptime and proximity are considered during load transfer process. For the purpose of load balancing we have used different mechanisms including moving node and replication. Simulation results show that running our algorithm causes node's utilities to close to each other in most cases.

References

1. Stoica, I., Morris, R., Karger, D., Kaashoek, M.F., Balakrishnan, H.: Chord: a scalable peer-to-peer lookup service for internet applications. In: Proceedings of the 2001 Conference on Applications, Technologies, Architectures, and Protocols For Computer Communications, New York, NY, pp. 149–160 (2001)
2. Rao, A., Lakshminarayanan, K., Surana, S., Karp, R., Stoica, I.: Load Balancing in Structured P2P Systems. In: Kaashoek, M.F., Stoica, I. (eds.) IPTPS 2003. LNCS, vol. 2735, pp. 68–79. Springer, Heidelberg (2003)
3. Ruhl, J.M.: Efficient algorithms for new computational models, USA, Techreport (2003)
4. Dabek, F., Kaashoek, M.F., Karger, D., Morris, R., Stoica, I.: Wide-area cooperative storage with CFS. SIGOPS Oper. Syst. Rev. 35(5), 202–215 (2001)
5. Sharifi, M., Mirtaheri, S.L., Mousavi Khaneghah, E.: A Dynamic Framework for Integrated Management of All Types of Resources in P2P Systems. The Journal of Supercomputing 52(2), 149–170 (2010)
6. Rieche, S., Petrak, L., Wehrle, K.: A thermal-dissipation-based approach for balancing data load in distributed hash tables. In: Proc. of 29th Annual IEEE Conference on Local Computer Networks (LCN), Germany, pp. 15–23 (2004)
7. Castro, M., Druschel, P., Ganesh, A., Rowstron, A., Wallach, D.S.: Secure routing for structured peer-to-peer overlay networks. In: ACM SIGOPS Operating Systems Review, OSDI 2002: Proceedings of the 5th Symposium on Operating Systems Design and Implementation, New York, NY, USA, pp. 299–314 (2002)

NCCPIS: A Co-simulation Tool for Networked Control and Cyber-Physical System Evaluation

Jinzhi Lin, Ying Wu, Gongyi Wu, and Jingdong Xu

College of Information Technical Science, Nankai University
Weijin Road 94, Tianjin, 300071, China
linjinzhi@mail.nankai.edu.cn,
{wuying,wgy,xujd}@nankai.edu.cn

Abstract. As the researches on Networked Control & Cyber-Physical System (NCCPS) are growing, the requirement of reliable evaluation tools for these systems is urgent. There are several simulators, such as TureTime, Ptolemy II and so on, can be used, but they usually focus on modeling of the control dynamics, and are too simple and abstracted on the simulation of network communication. In this work, a co-simulation tool, NCCPIS is presented, which integrates the dynamic control system simulator, Ptolemy II and the network simulator, NS-2. We demonstrate the validation of the tool by presenting a case study of platoon longitudinal control in AHS (Automatic Highway System).

Keywords: Co-simulation, Ptolemy II, NS-2, Evaluation tool, NCS, CPS.

1   Introduction

In recent years, more and more researches focus on Cyber-Physical Systems (CPS), which integrate computation with the physical process. Actually, a CPS is often monitored and controlled by a Networked Control System (NCS). In this paper, we call them together as Networked Control & Cyber-Physical System (NCCPS). Basically, a NCCPS is composed of three components: physical process, computation and network [9]. The researches of NCCPS include investigating problems at the intersection of control systems, networking, and computer science [8], exploring compositional verification and testing methods [15], and so on.

Design and evaluation of NCCPS can not be accurately conducted without considering the effect of networks, it is important to develop a verification tool that not only has the ability of simulating the dynamics of the system's plant and controller, but also can simulate the realistic network environment for communication. To build a brand new tool from scratch satisfying the requirement is very difficult and unnecessary. There are several powerful model-based tools being used to simulate control systems in the academia, such as Ptolemy II [14], Simulink [11], ViSim [19], and so on. On the other hand, there are a few network simulators can exactly emulate detailed network communication, such as NS-2 [12], OpNET [4], OMNet++ [13], and so on. The feasibility of integrating a control system simulator and a network simulator to evaluate NCCPS is foreseeable.

J.J. Park et al. (Eds.): NPC 2012, LNCS 7513, pp. 85–93, 2012.

By considering the flexibility, reliability and technical supporting, we choose to integrate both open source simulators, Ptolemy II and NS-2, to build our co-simulation tool called NCCPIS. The challenges are significant, including designing the framework of NCCPIS and coordinating the synchronization of event time and data exchange in both sides of the simulators.

This paper is organized as follows. In section 2, we introduce the related work. In section 3, we present the implementation of NCCPIS. Time and data synchronization are discussed in section 4. A case study is given in section 5. Finally, this paper is concluded in section 6.

2   Related Work

As a most popular tool for validating NCS, TrueTime [7] extends Matlab/Simulink with platform related modeling concepts (i.e., network, clock and schedulers) and supports simulation of networked and embedded control systems with implementation effects [3]. However, in TureTime, the modeling of network dynamics are highly abstracted, thus it's not appropriate to evaluate the systems that require detailed low layer network communication.

For different considerations, combining different control system simulators with network simulators, some similar ideas of seeking co-simulating methods exist in a few articles. In [16], an evaluation tool called NCSWT was developed, which integrated Matlab/Simulink and NS-2 using the HLA standard for coordinating data communication and time synchronization. In [1], two approaches of extending NS-2 and one of integrating Modelica and NS-2 have been proposed. In [6], for WNCS (Wireless NCS) over MANET (Mobile ad-hoc Network), the SIMULINK-OPNET co-simulation was investigated.

3   NCCPIS Implementation

3.1   Ptolemy II and NS-2

In Ptolemy II, actors are the basic computation units that can execute concurrently and communicate through messages sent via interconnected ports [14]. There may be a special actor in a model called *Director*, which manages the execution of this model. Actors have the key flow of control methods [2, 10]:

- *setup*: Initialize the actor.
- *prefire*: Test preconditions for firing.
- *fire*: Read inputs and produce outputs.
- *postfire*: Update the state.
- *wrapup*: End execution of the actor.

The CT (continuous-time) domain in Ptolemy II aims to help the design and simulation of systems that can be modeled using ordinary differential equations (ODEs).

ContinuousDirector is the main *Director* of CT domain. It contains an *ODESolver* who's responsible to determine the integration step sizes according to ODEs or time points of interest so as to achieve an accurate simulation. Meanwhile, Ptolemy II implements a *ContinuousStepSizeController* interface to support accurate time advancement. Any actors implemented the interface can influence the passage of simulation time. The interface has following methods [10]:

- *isStepSizeAccurate*: to see if the current step is accurate.
- *suggestedStepSize*: suggests the next step size.
- *refinedStepSize*: if *isStepSizeAccurate* returns false, this method will be called, returns the step size this actor wants to refine currently.

Moreover, there is a *ContinuousStatefullComponent* interface which has a *rollBackToCommittedState* method. It's for the actors who have tentative state to roll back if the current step size is not accurate. Figure 1 shows the process of the *fire* method of *ContinuousDirector*.

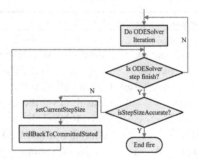

Fig. 1. The process of fire method of *ContinuousDirector*

3.2   Framework and Integration

Figure 2 shows the framework of NCCPIS. Considering supporting separated hosts simulating, we integrate the two simulators through sockets, and design a few commands for synchronization shown in table 1. On the Ptolemy II side, *NS2Node* actors are considered as the shadows of *Nodes* in NS-2, they directly participate in the simulation of Dynamic Control System. Once they have state (e.g., position and velocity) updated or packets to send, they ask *NS2Coordinator* to send the corresponding commands to NS-2 through its socket thread, and waiting for the response commands from NS-2 so as to continue the simulation. The actor *NS2Coordinator* implements *ContinuousStepSizeController* and *ContinuousStatefull-Component* interfaces intrduced previously, every time before *postfire*, *Continuous-Director* invokes *isStepSizeAccurate*, then *NS2Coordinator* turns to consult NS-2 whether the current step size is accurate. On the NS-2 side, similarly, we develop the class *ptIIEngine* as the proxy to coordinate synchronization with Ptolemy II.

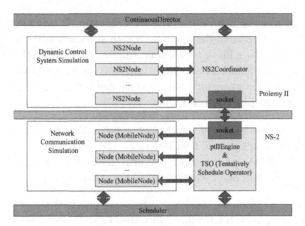

Fig. 2. The framework of NCCPIS

Table 1. Synchronization Commands

Comm	Sender	Response comm	Description
setdest	Ptolemy II	setdest_ok	Coordinate MobileNode to update position
broadcast	Ptolemy II	broadcast_ok	Coordinate MobileNode to broadcast packet
send_pkt	Ptolemy II	send_pkt_ok	Coordinate MobileNode to send packet
iSSA	Ptolemy II	iSSA [true/false]	Consult NS-2 if the step size is accurate
rSS	Ptolemy II	rSS [t]	Consult NS-2 the step size
sSS	Ptolemy II	sSS [t]	Consult NS-2 the next step size
rB [t]	Ptolemy II	rB_ok	Ask NS-2 to roll back to time t
runTo [t]	Ptolemy II	runTo_ok	Ask NS-2 to run to time t
recvdata	NS-2	recvdata_ok	Coordinate NS2Node to generate packet

Note: iSSA = isStepSizeAccurate, rSS = refinedStepSize, sSS = suggestedStepSize, rB = rollBackTo

4   Time and Data Synchronization

Synchronization is critical for co-simulation tools. In NCCPIS, the time when nodes send and receive a packet should be same in both simulations. For wireless network simulation, the position and velocity of nodes are essential for packet transmissions, thus, we need to synchronize the position and velocity of nodes in both simulations.

Position and velocity synchronization is simple. The position and velocity of *NS2Node* can only change in the "*Do Solver Iteration*" process shown in figure 1, as long as *NS2Node* detects the change of its state, it delegates *NS2Coordinator* to send a "*setdest*" command to NS-2. Respectively, when NS-2 receives that command, as shown in figrue 2, *ptIIEngine* inserts an *AtEvent* like "*ns at t 'nn setdest x y v'*" into scheduler, and records it in *TSO* to prepare for following up "*rollBackTo*" command. *TSO* records all events generated by the synchronization commands from Ptolemy II, if *ptIIEngine* receives a "*rollBackTo*" command, it could remove these events from the scheduler, however, if receive a "*runTo*" command, just clear them from *TSO*.

Synchronization of sending packets is similar to that of position and velocity. But, to synchronize the time of receiving packets is a little hard. As shown in figure 3, the simulation time of Ptolemy II is always ahead of NS-2, while the time NS-2 receiving packets is unpredictable, thus we can't generate a future receiving packets event for Ptolemy II in advance. As a result, the time NS-2 receiving packets is always before or equal to (if the receiving time is equal to the time Ptolemy II invokes *postfire*) the current simulation time in Ptolemy II. Obviously, we should ensure that the time NS-2 receiving packets are exactly the time Ptolemy II invokes *postfire*. To accomplish this, as shown in figure 4, we invoke *isStepSizeAccurate* to ask NS-2 to check that if there are packet receiving events in the scheduler before the current simulation time (the time Ptolemy II is going to ask NS-2 to "runTo" if all actors' *isStepSizeAccurate* return true). If existing these events, return false and return the earliest time of all events when the upcoming command "*refinedStepSize*" is invoked, else return true.

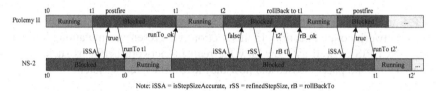

Note: iSSA = isStepSizeAccurate, rSS = refinedStepSize, rB = rollBackTo

Fig. 3. The synchronization between Ptolemy II and NS-2

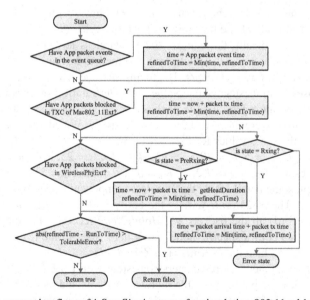

Fig. 4. The processing flow of *isStepSizeAccurate* for simulating 802.11 ad-hoc networks

Actually, to NCCPIS, only application packets matter. While invoking *isStepSize-Accurate*, we can check the event queue of the scheduler in NS-2 to see if there are packet receiving events going to happen in the Application Layer. But there is a dependency problem needs to be considered, that after some related packet events in router, data link layer, physical layer, etc., being scheduled, packet receiving events in Application Layer may appear. By analyzing the simulation mechanism of NS-2, we found that before a packet received in application layer, it is either in the event queue of the scheduler for the upcoming scheduling, or blocked in a queue, a MAC layer, a physical layer and a channel for waiting to be put in the event queue. This means that we should check the event queue and the NS-2 components which may block the application packets for *isStepSizeAccurate* invoking. Specifically, figure 4 depicts the *isStepSizeAccurate* process flow for simulating 802.11 ad-hoc networks. There is a *TolerableError* in NCCPIS due to the *timeResolution* in Ptolemy II meaning the time precision. The default value of *timeResolution* is *1e-10*. As we can see, the time synchronization between Ptolemy II and NS-2 is within this time precision.

5   Case Study

NCCPIS in this work is intended to provide a co-simulation of dynamic control system and network communication. In this section, we present a simulation scenario to validate NCCPIS as well as show how the realistic network performs such as time-varying delays and packet losses and how they affect the overall system.

5.1   Experiment Setup

We consider a platoon of 16 vehicles running on a highway with 15 vehicles followed a lead vehicle. The lead vehicle transmits its position, velocity and acceleration measured by sensors periodically through an 802.11 wireless ad-hoc network to all the vehicles within the platoon. All vehicles are assumed to be initially traveling at the steady-state velocity of $v_0 = 17.9m/s$. Beginning at time $t = 0s$, the lead vehicle's velocity increases from its steady-state value of $17.9m/s$ until it reaches its final value of $25.9m/s$: the maximum jerk and the peak acceleration values corresponding to this velocity time profiles were $2m/s^3$ and $2m/s^2$, respectively. We adopt the control law in [17] and choose the same values for the coefficients: $c_{al} = 15$, $c_{vl} = 74$, $c_{pl} = 120$, $k_{al} = -3.03$, $k_{vl} = -0.05$; $c_a = 5$, $c_v = 49$, $c_p = 120$, $k_a = 10$, $k_v = 25$, and the coefficients of vehicle dynamics are, for $i op= 1,2,…$, $K_{di} = 0.3$, $\tau_i = 0.2$, $d_{mi} = 5$, $m_i = 1464$.

Figure 5 depicts the detail inside the *Wireless* component configured in Ptolemy II for each vehicle. The *NS2MobileNode* is the entity of *NS2Node* as discussed above. The *Recorder* records all the packets *NS2MobileNode* received, but outputs the currently received packet of a specific node which here is set to the lead vehicle until a new packet arrives, in fact, the *Recorder* is a *ZeroHolder*.

In NS-2, we set the network parameters consistent with IEEE 802.11p as shown in table 2, and employ the public available highway patterns and ns traffic trace generation tools presented in [5] to obtain a realistic scenario with a dynamic network topology. We consider a 6km long highway composed of 6 lanes (3 in each direction) with high traffic density, where in total 523 vehicles pass along the road in both directions with an average speed of 120km/h (33.3m/s). For this scenario, we add a 7-th lane for the platoon with the lead vehicle's initial position at 2.5km of the highway. All the normal vehicles in the highway periodically broadcast packets, thus they interfere the communication of the platoon. We conduct three experiments with the normal vehicles broadcasting at different rates and packet sizes: (a) 500 bytes per packet, 5 packets per second; (b) 500 bytes per packet, 10 packets per second; (c) 1500 bytes per packet, 10 packets per second. The lead vehicle of the platoon broadcasts its state every 100ms by setting the interval of the *PeriodicSampler* shown in figure 5 to 0.1.

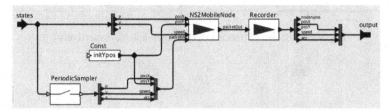

Fig. 5. The detail of the *Wireless* component configured in Ptolemy II for each vehicle

Table 2. Simulation configuration in NS-2

Category	Parameter	Value
PHY	Frequency	5.9 GHz
	Power Monitor Threshold	-102 dBm
	Transmission Power	1 mW
	SINR Preamble Capture	4 dB
	SINR Data Capture	10 dB
MAC	Slot Time	13 us
	SIFS Time	32 us
	Header Duration	40us
	Symbol Duration	8us (3 Mbps)
	Modulation Scheme	BPSK

5.2   Evaluation

Figure 6, 7 respectively shows the delays and loss of packets that the platoon vehicles received from the lead vehicle. We can see that broadcasting of non-platoon vehicles have obvious effect on communication of platoon.Figure 8 shows the co-simulation results. Compared to [17], we can infer that our co-simulation results are valid. Compared to [18], our platoon performances are better, because in our law, we used the information of the lead vehicle by adding the wireless network communication to the simulation. In addition, due to the delay and loss of packets, the performances of experiment a, b and c shown in figure 8 are worse and worse. That also proves the validation of our co-simulation. In this case study, Ptolemy II and NS-2 are both running on a RedHat virtual machine with 1GB memory on an XP host with 2GB memory and a 2.80GHz dual-core CPU. The overall 18 seconds co-simulation has taken five minutes. The communications of the 523 *MobileNodes* for the normal vehicles in NS-2 and the frequent "*rollback*" in Ptolemy II cost most all of the time.

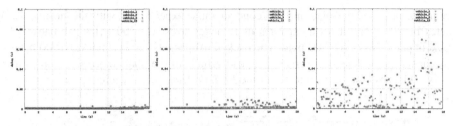

Fig. 6. The delays of packets (Experiment a, b, c, respectively)

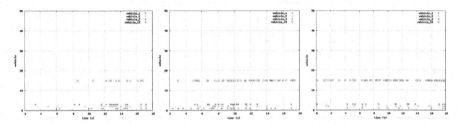

Fig. 7. The losses of packets (Experiment a, b, c, respectively)

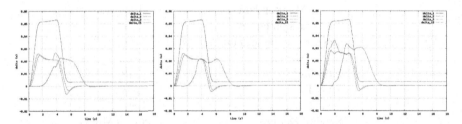

Fig. 8. The platoon performances of $\triangle_1$, $\triangle_2$, $\triangle_3$ and $\triangle_{15}$ (Experiment a, b, c, respectively)

6   Conclusion

In this work we present NCCPIS, a co-simulation tool integrating a control system simulator, Ptolemy II and a network simulator, NS-2. By studying the architectures of them, we have designed the framework of NCCPIS, developed data exchange and time synchronization mechanism. At the same time, we demonstrate the validation of the tool by presenting case studies of platoon longitudinal control in AHS. As Ptolemy II is a tool orienting multi-domains and aiming to simulate hybrid systems, we will import the co-simulation of multi-domains to NCCPIS and validate it.

Acknowledgments. This work was supported by the Research Fund for the Doctoral Program of Higher Education of China (No. 20110031110026), and the National Natural Science Foundation of China (No. 61103214).

References

1. Al-Hammouri, A.T., Branicky, M.S., Liberatore, V.: Co-simulation Tools for Networked Control Systems. In: Egerstedt, M., Mishra, B. (eds.) HSCC 2008. LNCS, vol. 4981, pp. 16–29. Springer, Heidelberg (2008)
2. Brooks, C., Lee, E.A., Liu, X., Neuendorffer, S., Zhao, Y., Zheng, H.: Heterogeneous Concurrent Modeling and Design in Java (vol. 2: Ptolemy II Software Architecture). EECS Department, University of California, Berkeley, USA (2008)
3. Cervin, A., Ohlin, M., Henriksson, D.: Simulation of Networked Control Systems using Truetime. In: 3rd International Workshop on Networked Control Systems: Tolerant to Faults, Nancy, France (2007)
4. Chang, X.: Network Simulations with Opnet. In: Proc. of Simulation Conference. Phoenix, USA (1999)
5. Chevillat, P., Jelitto, J., Truong, H.L.: Dynamic Data Rate and Transmit Power Adjustment in IEEE 802.11 Wireless LANs. International Journal of Wireless Information Networks 12(3), 123–145 (2005)
6. Hasan, M., Yu, H., Carrington, A., Yang, T.: Co-simulation of Wireless Networked Control Systems over Mobile Ad Hoc Network using Simulink and Opnet. IET Communications 3(8), 1297–1310 (2009)
7. Henriksson, D., Cervin, A., Arzen, K.E.: Truetime: Real-time Control System Simulation with Matlab/Simulink. In: Proc. of Nordic MATLAB Conference. Copenhagen, Denmark (2003)
8. Baillieul, J., Antsaklis, P.J.: Control and Communication Challenges in Networked Real-time Systems. Proc. of the IEEE 95(1), 9–28 (2007)
9. Lee, E.A.: CPS Foundations. In: 47th Design Automation Conference, Anaheim, USA, pp. 737–742 (2010)
10. Lee, E.A., Zheng, H.: Leveraging Synchronous Language Principles for Heterogeneous Modeling and Design of Embedded Systems. In: 7th ACM & IEEE International Conference on Embedded Software, New York, USA, pp. 114–123 (2007)
11. Simulink, http://www.mathworks.com/products/simulink/
12. The Network Simulator: ns-2, http://www.isi.edu/nsnam/ns/
13. Omnet++: Discrete event simulation system, http://www.omnetpp.org
14. Ptolemy II, http://ptolemy.eecs.berkeley.edu/ptolemyII/index.htm
15. Rajkumar, R., Lee, I., Sha, L., Stankovic, J.: Cyber-physical Systems: the Next Computing Revolution. In: 47th Design Automation Conference, Anaheim, USA, pp. 731–736 (2010)
16. Riley, D., Eyisi, E., Bai, J., Koutsoukos, X., Xue, Y., Sztipanovits, J.: Networked Control System Wind Tunnel (NCSWT)- An Evaluation Tool for Networked Multi-agent Systems. In: SIMUTools 2011, Barcelona, Spain, pp. 9–18 (2011)
17. Sheikholeslam, S., Desoer, C.A.: Longitudinal Control of a Platoon of Vehicles. In: American Control Conference, San Diego, USA, pp. 291–296 (1990)
18. Sheikholeslam, S., Desoer, C.A.: Longitudinal Control of a Platoon of Vehicles with no Communication of Lead Vehicle Information: A System Level Study. IEEE Transactions on Vehicular Technology 42(4), 546–554 (1993)
19. Vissim, http://www.vissim.com/products/vissim.html

Dempster-Shafer Theory to Identify Insider Attacker in Wireless Sensor Network

Muhammad Ahmed, Xu Huang, and Dharmendra Sharma

Faculty of Information Sciences and Engineering,
University of Canberra, Australia
{muhammad.ahmed,xu.huang,dharmendra.sharma}@canberra.edu.au

Abstract. Due to the construction and network infrastructure of wireless sensor network (WSN) are known to be vulnerable to variety of attacks. In order to ensure its functionality especially in malicious environments, security mechanisms are essential. Several works have been done to secure WSN, but identification of insider attacker has not been given much attention. In the WSN system the malicious node behavior is different from the neighbor nodes. Instead of relying the untrustworthy neighbor node we use Dempster-Shafer theory (DST) of combined evidence to identify the insider attacker in WSN. This theory reflects with the uncertain event or uncertainty as well as uncertainty of the observation. The mathematical calculation shows the DST capability of identifying the insider attacker.

Keywords: Wireless Sensor Networks, Insider Attacker, Security, Dempster-shafer theory.

1 Introduction

Wireless sensor networks are a new technology for collecting data with autonomous sensors. Recently, this technology became more popular because of its application and cost. It consists of large number of low cost, low power and multifunctional sensors embedded with short range wireless communication capability. Sink in which all data is transmitted in an autonomous way has high capacity of storage and analysis power. The application of WSN includes battlefield surveillance, border monitoring, habitat monitoring, intelligent agriculture, home automation, etc.

In this information age the world is interconnected via various communications. Security provisioning is a critical requirement for any communication network. Security in the wireless sensor network is challenging and important task because of its characteristics that include, open nature of wireless medium, unattended operation, limited energy, memory, computing power, communication bandwidth, and communication range. Considering those characteristics many algorithms have developed for the secure functionality of WSN. Most of the work has focused on the pair wise key establishment, authentication access control and defense against attack. Most importantly those works mainly focused on the traditional cryptographic information, data authentication in order to build the relationship between the sensors.

J.J. Park et al. (Eds.): NPC 2012, LNCS 7513, pp. 94–100, 2012.

However, the unreliable communications through wireless channel made the communication technique vulnerable by allowing the sensor nodes to compromise and release the security information to the adversary [1]. The compromised entity of the network acts as a legitimate node. So it is easy for the adversary to perform the insider attacks. When insider attack occurs for a node, this node will behave abnormally such as tampering the massage from other member, dropping the data or broadcast excessive data.

So far, not much attention has been given to save the network from the insider attacker that caused by the abnormally behaved node. In this paper, we have proposed Dempster–Shafer theory (DST) based insider attacker identification mechanism with neighbor nodes parameters observation as DST has the feature of dealing with uncertainty. In our proposed method the system does not need to have any prior knowledge of the pre-classified training data of the nodes.

The paper is organised as follows: section 2 is comprised of the overview of the related work followed by the system architecture and network model in section 3. The detail of the dempester-shafer theory for insider attacker identification process is described in section 4. The evaluation in WSN and mathematical calculation is given in section 5 followed by conclusion in section 6.

2   Related Work

To identify insider attacker in wireless sensors networks several work has been done in the past but DST based method was not given significant attention.

For detection of abnormal behavior of the nodes or insider attacker Staddon et al [2] proposed to trace the failed nodes in sensor networks at the base station assuming that all the sensor measurement will be directed along the sinker based on the routing tree. In this work the sinker has the global view of the network topology and can identify the failed nodes through route update message and it is directional.

Watchdog like technique was proposed by Marti [3], this technique can detect the packet dropping attack by letting nodes listen to the next hope nodes broadcasting transmission. In this multiple watchdog work collaboratively in decision making and reputation system is necessary to provide the quality rating of the participants.

Zhang et al [4] proposed a scheme which is the first work on intrusion detection in wireless ad hoc networks. A new architecture is investigated for collaborative statistical anomaly detection which provides protection from attack on ad hoc routing.

These developments somehow solve the mathematical problems with certain constrain but does not take the insider attacker identification in consideration with the uncertainty of observation by neighbor nodes.

3   System Architecture and Network Model

In our system we have considered the neighbor nodes or observer nodes evidence to identify the insider attacker. The neighbor nodes will share their independent observation about the suspected insider attacker behavior. The data from the neighbor nodes we will consider as evidence, which can be in the form of malcounts (number of occurrences of misbehavior). We will combine the independent pieces evidence and take the decision based on the DST.

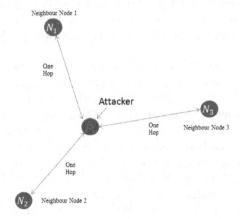

Fig. 1. Three neighbor observing the attacker with one hop

In WSN the neighbor with one hop will observe the data as node behavior. Temperature measurement wireless sensor network scenario neighbor will check the temperature reading and that will be become the evidence. The neighbors can obtain degrees of belief about the proposition from related proposition subjective probabilities. In the figure (1), neighbor nodes N_1, N_2 and N_3 will share their independent observation about the insider attacker before taking the decision. The neighbor nodes will be the nodes with nearest euclidian distance.

4   Methodology

The Bayesian theory is the canonical method for statistical inference problems. The Dempster-Shafer decision theory is considered a generalized Bayesian theory. It allows distributing support for proposition, not only to a proposition itself but also to the union of propositions that include it. [5] In Dempster-Shafer Theory (DST) a node can hold either supportive or uncertain opinion toward an event. It addresses the solution by representing the uncertainty in the form of belief functions. The idea is neighbor or observer nodes can obtain degree of belief about the proposition from the related proposition's subjective probabilities.

4.1   Bayesian Interface

In order to understand the Dempster-Shafer Theory beyesian approach is often studied. Bayesian inference derives a posterior probability distribution as a consequence of two antecedents, a prior probability and likelihood, probability model for the data to be observed. [6]Bayesian inference computes the posterior probability by conditioning, according to the rule of Bayes for proposition of H and Evidence E.

$$P(H) = \frac{P(E \mid H)P(H)}{P(E)} \qquad (1)$$

According to Bayesians interpret, $P(H)$ the priori reflects the initial degree of belief in H in the absence of evidence E. $P(H|E)$, the posteriori probability as a measure of belief about a hypothesis or proposition H that updates in response to evidence.

In figure one we consider node N_1, N_2 and N_3 has the representative pieces of evidence e_{N_1}, e_{N_2} and e_{N_3}, in order to support the hypothesis H. So, the posteriori probability becomes

$$P(H \mid e_{N_1}, e_{N_2}, e_{N_3}) = \frac{P(e_{N_1}, e_{N_2}, e_{N_3} \mid H)P(H)}{\begin{array}{c} P(e_{N_1}, e_{N_2}, e_{N_3} \mid H)P(H) + \\ P(e_{N_1}, e_{N_2}, e_{N_3} \mid \sim H)(1 - P(H)) \end{array}} \qquad (2)$$

In which ~H is not H hypothesis means node A is an attacker. The neighbor nodes observes the attacker independently, hence the computation of the equation 2 can be simplified as in equation 3 by factorization process.

$$P(H \mid e_{N_1}, e_{N_2}, e_{N_3}) = P(e_{N_1} H)P(e_{N_2} H)P(e_{N_3} H) \qquad (3)$$

Complete knowledge of the prior and conditional probabilities is a significunt requirement for this approach which is difficult to determine in practice. In this approach estimation of the prior probabilities is done from the empirical data. Hence, this method does not have capability to deal with the states of ignorance.

4.2   Dempster-Shafer Framework

In DST, probability is replaced by an uncertainty interval bounded by belief and plausibility. Belief is the lower bound of the interval and represents supporting evidence. Plausibility is the upper bound of the interval and represents the non-refuting evidence. In this reasoning system, all possible mutually exclusive hypothesis (or events) of the same kind are enumerated in the frame of discernment Ω. A basic belief assignment (BBA) or mass function is a function m: $2^\Omega \rightarrow [0, 1]$, and it satisfies two following conditions

$$m(\partial) = 0 \qquad (4)$$

$$\sum_{A \subseteq \Omega} m(A_j) = 1 \qquad (5)$$

In which ∂ is the empty set and a BBA that satisfy the condition $m(\partial) = 0$. The basic probability number can be translated as $m(A)$ because the portion of total belief assigned to hypothesis A, which reflects the evidences strength of support. The assignment of belief function maps each hypothesis B to a value $bel(B)$ between 0 and 1. This defined as

$$bel(B) = \sum_{j:A_j \subseteq A} m(A_j) \tag{6}$$

The upper bound of the confidence interval is the plausibility function, which accounts for all the observations that do not rule out the given proposition. It maps each hypothesis B to a value $pls(B)$ between 0 and 1, can be defined as follows.

$$pls(B) = \sum_{j:A_j \cap B \neq \partial} m(A_j) \tag{7}$$

The plausibility function is a weight of evidence which is non-refuting to B. equation (8) shows the relation between belief and plausibility.

$$pls(B) = 1 - bel(\sim B) \tag{8}$$

The hypothesis not B is representing by $\sim B$. The functions basic probability numbers, belief and plausibility are in one-to-one correspondence and by knowing one of them, the other two functions could be derived.

Assuming $m_1(A)$ and $m_2(A)$ are two basic probability number by two independent items of evidence means two independent neighbor node which act as observers in the same frame of discernment. The observations (the pieces of evidence) can be combined using Dempster's rule of combination (known as orthogonal sum) as in equation (9).

$$m(B) = (m_1 \oplus m_2)(B) = \frac{\sum_{i,j:A_i \cap A_j = B} m_1(A_i) m_2(A_j)}{1 - \sum_{i,j:A_i \cap A_j = \partial} m_1(A_i) m_2(A_j)} \tag{9}$$

More than two belief function can be combined with pairwise in any order.

5   Evaluation in WSN

In temperature collection WSN we consider the normal temperature range is T= 8 to 10 degree centigrade based on the Gaussian distributing with 1 sigma based on the approach taken by holder el at [7] , and $\sim T$ means the temperature is out of range and consider the node A is attacked. So, the frame of discernment consists of two probabilities concerning the attacker node A: $\Omega = \{T, \sim T\}$. Hence, for Ω the power set has three focal elements: hypothesis $H = \{\sim T\}$, $H = \{T\}$ and universe hypothesis

$U= \Omega$ meaning node A is either attacked or a good node. We consider that neighbor node N_1 is a trusted node with the probability β. Based on the node N_1 information if node A is an attacker, the basic probability assignment will be as follows.

$$m_1(H) = 0;$$
$$m_1(\sim H) = \beta;$$
$$m_1(U) = 1 - \beta; \qquad (10)$$

If A is a good node the basic probability assignment will be

$$m_1(H) = \beta;$$
$$m_1(\sim H) = 0;$$
$$m_1(U) = 1 - \beta; \qquad (11)$$

Using the same approach we can construct the basic probability assignment m_1 and m_2 for neighbor node N_2 and N_3.

The combined belief of N_1, N_2 and N_3 in H is bel(H) = m(H) = $m_1(H) \oplus m_2(H) \oplus m_3(H)$ following the Dempster rule of combination based on equation (9). It is possible to combine any pair of arguments and then combine the remaining argument. m_1 and m_2 combination can be written as follows.

$$(m_1 \oplus m_2)(H) = \frac{1}{k}[m_1(H)m_2(H) + m_1(H)m_2(U) + m_1(U)m_2(H)]$$

$$(m_1 \oplus m_2)(\sim H) = \frac{1}{k}[m_1(\sim H)m_2(\sim H) + m_1(\sim H)m_2(U) + m_1(U)m_2(\sim H)]$$

$$(m_1 \oplus m_2)(U) = \frac{1}{k}[m_1(U)m_2(U)] \qquad (12)$$

Where,

$$K = \frac{m_1(H)m_2(H) + m_1(H)m_2(U) + m_1(U)m_2(H) + m_1(\sim H)m_2(\sim H)}{+ m_1(\sim H)m_2(U) + m_1(U)m_2(\sim H) + m_1(U)m_2(U)}$$

After combining the reports from the neighbor's nodes we can identify the insider attacker.

5.1   Example

In the paper we have given some mathematical calculation and results for the combined degree of belief that the node A is insider attacker.

Table 1. Combine degree of belief calculation

Trust probability of the neighbor node			
N_1	N_2	N_3	Combined degree of Belief
0.9	0.8	0.2	0.975
0.2	0.2	0.9	0.878
0.8	0.8	0.8	0.828

In the table 1 we can see that the calculation is done by assigning the different trust probability to the neighbor and combine degree of belief is 0.975, 0.878, 0.828 respectively. From the high belief is it concluded that the node is an attacker.

6   Conclusion

In this paper an insider identification framework in wireless sensor network is proposed with Dempster-Shafer theory of evidence combination method. the mathematical calculation shows that the result depends on the neighbor nodes reliability. Moreover, the conflict increases with the number of sources.

In future, we would like to create a database for the nodes normal behavior form that we can decide about the reliability of the nodes and employ extended dempster-shefer theory.

References

1. Zhou, Y., Fang, Y., Zhang, Y.: Securing wireless sensor networks: a survey. IEEE Communications Surveys & Tutorials (3rd Quarter, 2008)
2. Staddon, J., Balfanz, D., Durfee, G.: Efficient tracing of failed nodes in sensor networks. In: WSNA 2002, Atlanta, USA, pp. 122–130 (2002)
3. Marti, S., Giuli, T.J., Lai, K., Baker, M.: Mitigating Routing Misbehavior in Mobile Ad Hoc Networks. In: ACM MOBICOM 2000, Boston, USA, pp. 255–265 (August 2000)
4. Zhang, Y., Lee, W.: Intrusion Detection in Wireless Ad-hoc Networks. In: ACM MOBICOM 2000, Boston, USA, pp. 275–283 (August 2000)
5. Sentz, K.: Combination of Evidence in Dempster-Shafer Theory. System Science and Engineering Department, Binghamton University, SAND 2002-0835 (April 2002)
6. Koks, D., Challa, S.: An Introduction to Bayesian and Dempster-Shafer Data Fusion. DSTO Systems Sciences Laboratory, Australia (2005)
7. Holder, C., Boyles, R., Robinson, P., Raman, S., Fishel, G.: Calculating a daily Normal temperature range that reflects daily temperature variability. American Meteorological Society (June 2006)

MIB-ITrace-CP: An Improvement of ICMP-Based Traceback Efficiency in Network Forensic Analysis

Bo-Chao Cheng[1], Guo-Tan Liao[1], Ching-Kai Lin[1], Shih-Chun Hsu[1],
Ping-Hai Hsu[2], and Jong Hyuk Park[3]

[1] Dept. of Communications Engineering, National Chung Cheng University, Taiwan
[2] Information and Communications Research, ITRI, Taiwan
[3] Dept. of Computer Science and Engineering, SeoulTech, Korea
bcheng@ccu.edu.tw, becker@itri.org.tw,
{loboyoh,hisa918203}@gmail.com,
{ganes0503,parkjonghyuk1}@hotmail.com

Abstract. A denial-of-service (DoS) / distributed-denial-of-service (DDoS) attack may result in rapid resource depletion along the attack path. For stepping-stone and masquerading techniques typically used in DoS/DDoS attacks such as internet protocol (IP) or Media Access Control (MAC) address spoofing, tracing the intrusion back to the true attacker becomes a challenging task for network security engineers. Although the Internet Engineer Task Force (IETF) has proposed an Internet Control Message Protocol (ICMP) based Traceback solution, it faces severe difficulties in practice in regard to justifying the interoperability of deployed routers as well as the correctness of Traceback with multiple attack paths. This research proposes a novel approach to embed the essence of a management information base (MIB) into iTrace messages, named MIB-ITrace-CP, in order to improve the accuracy and efficiency of the original ICMP-based Traceback. Through our implementations on a Testbed@TWISC platform, we validated our approach and demonstrated the feasibility of practical network forensics.

Keywords: DoS, Spoofing, Forensics, Traceback, ITrace-CP.

1   Introduction and Background

For Internet service providers (ISP), a denial-of-service (DoS) / distributed-denial-of-service (DDoS) attack is one of the more difficult problems faced. This is because attackers can attack either using a real or a fake internet protocol (IP) address, rendering it difficult to find the real attacker and prevent the attack. Identification of the attackers' IP address is even not possible for computer forensics [1] nowadays. In conventional IP networks, there are three famous Traceback models that provide fundamental foundations on a range of different researches: Logging [2], Probabilistic Packet Marking (PPM) [3] and ICMP-based Traceback [4] discussed by IETF [5].

With respect to various ICMP-based Traceback [6-8], we found that there are some weaknesses. For example, mobile attacker, multiple attack sources, multiple attack

J.J. Park et al. (Eds.): NPC 2012, LNCS 7513, pp. 101–109, 2012.
© IFIP International Federation for Information Processing 2012

paths and spoofing attack make Traceback more difficult to correctly locate the attacker's address over multiple paths. Here, we show the progressive improvement of ICMP-based Traceback mechanisms as below. Initially, this ICMP Traceback (ITrace) idea was presented as an industry standard of IETF (Internet Engineering Task Force) on 2000, available at draft-ietf-itrace-00.txt. In 2001, S. Felix Wu et al. proposed intention-driven ITrace [9], whose concept is to use an extra intention bit in the routing (e.g., the community attribute in BGP routing table) for controlling the forward ITrace option to achieve a much better tracing performance about the statistic problem of ITrace. The latest version of ITrace draft "draft-ietf-itrace-04.txt" [4] was updated in 2003. Then in 2007 A. Izaddoost et al. [10] proposed an accurate ICMP Traceback model based on intention-driven ITrace to reconstruct attack paths accurately by generating more effective ICMP Traceback packets. The ITrace message is emitted randomly by routers along the path and sent randomly to the destination (to provide useful information to the attacked party) or to the origin (to provide information to decipher reflector attacks).

On the other hand, Henry C.J. Lee et al. in 2003 proposed a so-called ICMP Traceback with Cumulative Path (ITrace-CP) [6], which is an enhancement of the ITrace approach. ITrace-CP messages are made to carry a part of entire attack path information, the same as ITrace messages, so as to accelerate the attack path construction in the event of a DDoS attack. In ITrace-CP, it proposed three kinds of schemes, where the scheme 3 is "Hash-based Packet Identification with indicator bit" involving three mechanisms: 1) Basic Packet Identification (BPI), 2) Hash function, 3) Indicator bit. About scheme 3 of ITrace-CP [6], it solves the problem of how to identify corresponding IP packets and ITrace-CP messages, and reduces the storage requirement.

With reference to ITrace draft [4], the probability of Traceback generation should not be greater than 1/1000, adjustable by the operator of the router. In 2005, V. Thing [7] proposed the distribution of generation probability in an exponential manner. For example, the probability at each router is computed by: $p=d^x/c$ where d is the distance from current router to the victim, x is the exponent and c is a constant. The enhanced ITrace-CP [7] shows an idea that the furthest router from the victim has the highest probability, and has better Traceback performance than ITrace when the distance between an attacker and a victim is near the diameter of a network. Inspired from that Traceroute works by increasing the Time To Live (TTL) value of each successive set of packets sent until the destination host receives the packets and returns an ICMP Echo Reply message, H. Tsunoda et al. [8] propose a countermeasure against TTL spoofing by TTL-based calculation of generation probability of ITrace-CP messages.

As mentioned above, conventional ICMP-based Traceback approaches have weaknesses in the issues of multiple attack sources and multiple attack paths to correctly identify the attacker's location. We proposed MIB-ITrace-CP approach, which embeds Management Information Base (MIB) [11] information into ITrace-CP message combined with benefits of various ICMP-based Traceback schemes including the Hash-based Packet Identification scheme [6], intention-driven model [9], TTL-based calculation of probability [8]). The goal of MIB-ITrace-CP is to improve the ICMP-based Traceback's correctness and efficiency, and we have used Testbed@TWISC [12] as the platform for our experiments.

2   System Model and Assumption

In the original ITrace-CP method, due to a flaw in the algorithm, it does not work well in a diversified topology. In particular, serious mistakes can result with multiple paths. Thus, to improve the original solution, we propose our MIB-ITrace-CP that not only applies the Hash-bashed Packet Identification (HPI) with indicator bit, the same as intention-driven model, but also embeds extra MIB data into original ITrace-CP message. We consider a scheme for the generation probability of MIB-ITrace-CP message. Firstly, the main assumptions are as follows:

(**A1**) All MIB-ITrace-CP messages (m) should store the source (S), the destination (D), the initial originator ($\bar{S}$) of m and which interface (ifName), a path (from $\bar{S}$'s previous node (N_P) to the last expected node), and two hash values for a packet (P). In addition, if $\bar{S}$ is just the source S, the N_P field will be filled in with itself ($\bar{S}$). The intention-driven hash $H_R^1(P)$ is varied with the current generator of MIB-ITrace-CP message (N_G), but the flow-classification hash $H_R^2(P)$ is unique and determined by $\bar{S}$ during the transmission to D.

(**A2**) Furthermore, using the Management Information Base (MIB) [RFC 1156, 1213, 2863], it enables routers to handle more efficient information. Besides of the interface identifier mentioned in A1 (such as "ifName", N_P and N_N (the next node of the current node from the routing table)), we use another two external pieces of data which are "ifEntry::ifSpeed" and "ifEntry::ifOutUcastPkts" provided by MIB module. By providing more information for the victim to perform better judgments, it also increases the accuracy in determining the attacker's real address and would not cause a problem for computer forensics. The two data is detailed as follows:

- ifEntry::ifSpeed (interfaceSpeed): Provide every connected device's bandwidth and take "bits per second" as the unit of measurement. ifSpeed (S_i) will represent the current operational speed of the interface in bits per second. In other words, the ifSpeed object defined in MIB-II's interfaces table provides "an estimate of the interface's current bandwidth in bits per second".
- ifEntry::ifOutUcastPkts: Provide the number of packets in the high-level protocol. What we want is to get the packet number (P_i) sent between two subsequent MIB-ITrace-CP messages originated from the same interface that can be calculated by a register).

(**A3**) The additional packet marking information, embedded into a packet (P), is the indicator bit, which indicates that a MIB-ITrace-CP message has been generated for a specific IP packet P, as well as the intention-driven hash $H_R^1(P)$ when the indicator bit (*ITRACE_CP_DONE*) is set.

Typically, the so-called Basic Packet Identification (BPI), set by the source ($\bar{s}$), is a value ($UN_{TimeWindow}$) that must be unique for that source-destination pair and protocol for the time the packet will be active in the Internet. HPI is the hash of BPI, used to reduce the storage requirement instead of storing the BPI of a packet. In this paper, we use two HPI of different context information for intention-driven model and flow classification. We define the 1st hash value, calculated in the router R and whose four inputs are N_G, D, *Protocol* from m and the new N_N from the routing table of R for P, is the so-called intention-driven hash $H_R^1(P)$. The 2nd hash value, calculated in the router R and whose four inputs are S, D, *Protocol* of the packet P and $UN_{TimeWindow}$ for the flow of P, is the so-called flow-classification hash $H_R^2(P)$. And, for intention-driven check in each router, there is a table T kept for a short time period and composed of two attributes, the intention-driven hash value ($H_R^1(P)$) and the next hop (N_N) corresponding to a packet (P).

We propose MIB-ITrace-CP to improve the ICMP-based Traceback. If the victim experiences DoS attacks in traffic, MIB-ITrace-CP method can still determine the attacker's real address with high accuracy and the path it passed through. The packets received by a victim can be separated into three kinds according to their types: 1) packets without the indicator bit set, 2) packets with the indicator bit set, 3) MIB-ITrace-CP messages with MIB information for attack graph reconstruction. And, the system architecture of MIB-ITrace-CP involves three parts, namely "Originating", "Forwarding" and "Path reconstruction", described as follows.

- Implementation of Generation Probability

Originally, all routers use the same probability for generating Traceback messages in ITrace. In order not to cause heavy overhead, it is suggested that the probability should not be greater than 1/1000. As the average maximum diameter (H_{max}) of the Internet is 20 hops, a default value of probability about 1/20000 is suggested. Inherited from the improvement of previous generation probability [7, 8], we adopt the idea of TTL value to determine a probability p. And we propose a practical method by the assessment of H_{max} to calculate the probability for generating MIB-ITrace-CP messages. In theory, the equations are formulated as Eq. (1), and we specially focus on the exponent $x=1$ and modify as shown in Eq. (2).

$$p = d^x / c, \quad \sum_{d=1}^{H_{max}} (d^x / c) = 1/1000 \tag{1}$$

$$p = d / c, \quad c = 500 \cdot H_{max} \cdot (H_{max} + 1), \quad d = H_{max} - d_{src} \tag{2}$$

As for easy calculation for adjusting H_{max}, using the case $x=1$ of Eq. (1) has its advantages. The near from the flow source, the higher probability for generating MIB-ITrace-CP messages. And, the source node also adopts the highest probability as H_{max}^x / c. In overall, using the view of d_{src} to set p is better than that from d_{dst} (to destination) because it can promote the efficiency in terms of Traceback time. Furthermore, it can integrate with judgment of the regular TTL value (255, 128, 64 or 32) to defeat against TTL spoofing.

- Forwarding of Traceback Message

Moreover, a key point is to achieve the intention-driven model by simply comparing intention-driven hash values of the packet and the corresponding MIB-ITrace-CP message (m). After identification of the expected m, a router R decides to send a new

m' embedded R's address to N_N if matched or send a new message m' to D without making any changes to the payload of m if mismatched. Especially when the new expected MIB-ITrace-CP message (m') is generated, it should be transmitted to N_N of T as far as possible. In detail, the m' of transmitted to the expected next hop keeps the original information of m, including S, D, $\overline{S}$, $Protocol$, $H_{\overline{S}}^{2}(P)$, P_i, S_i and the route path from $\overline{S}$'s previous hop to R's previous hop (N_P), and then also embeds R's address and $H_R^1(P)$.

- Path Reconstruction

Firstly, speaking about two categories of MIB-ITrace-CP messages received at a victim, one category (C_1) with the corresponding intention-driven hash $H_R^1(P)$ value is sent triggered from the previous node (NP), and the other (C2) with mismatched $H_R^1(P)$ is forwarded by N_P. Fig. 1 shows how path reconstruction is done through the MIB-ITrace-CP system, how bandwidth is set to judge whether DoS attacks have occurred or not, and how collected information from the victim is used, threshold calculation, data comparison in MIB-ITrace-CP messages, and filtering of the MIB-ITrace-CP messages produced by DoS attacks. Using this pseudo code, we thus improved on the ITrace-CP, enabling it to work with multiple paths and increasing its efficiency. With the information of MIB-ITrace-CP messages (C_1), it can help reconstruct more exact attack graph. On the other hand, as a mobile attacker sends a huge number of packets to the victim, the victim can infer that attacker's movement by those MIB-ITrace-CP messages (C_2).

After the victim has finished collecting MIB-ITrace-CP messages, it performs path reconstruction and tries to find the attacker's real address using the information given by MIB-ITrace-CP messages. MIB-ITrace-CP is an algorithm based on ICMP-based Traceback's basic structure and addresses the limitations of ICMP-based Traceback. Inside this part, apart from path reconstruction, it also contains a filter. The filter's main function is to filter the MIB-ITrace-CP messages (m) produced by DoS attacks. It is useful, by filtering the message m_i with Ψ_i lower than a threshold value Ψ_θ, for finding the correct attack path from multiple paths and filters using Ψ_θ as shown in Eq. (3) where α represents the weighted factor that is defined and executed by the administrator or the intrusion detection system, P_{avg} represents the average of P_i and S_{avg} represents the average of S_i. For example, for SYN attacks, Teardrop attacks or DoS-like attacks, if SYN flood attacks are found, $\alpha=0.8$. This is because SYN flood attacks will produce a large amount of packets. If the α value is higher, it means that P_{avg} weight will be higher and the selection will be more accurate. Conversely, if Teardrop attacks occur, then $\alpha=0.2$. This is because Teardrop attacks may create a series of IP fragments with overlapping offset fields in a high network traffic flow. As the α value is lower, the S_{avg} weight ($1-\alpha$) is also higher and the threshold value will be more accurate. For MIB-based calculation, each MIB-ITrace-CP message (m_i) includes the two MIB information, P_i and S_i.

$$\begin{cases} \Psi_\theta & = \alpha \cdot P_{avg} + (1-\alpha) \cdot S_{avg} \\ \Psi_i & = \alpha \cdot P_i + (1-\alpha) \cdot S_i \end{cases} \qquad (3)$$

Path reconstruction procedure at victim V:

Two categories of MIB-ITrace-CP messages: C_1 and C_2

C_1 is triggered from the previous node N_P;

C_2 is forwarded by N_P with failure of intention-driven check

List a table sorted according to the master column "S-D pair" (S, D), $H_R^2(P)$ and C_i

Get the suspect ITrace-CP messages with key $H_R^2(P)$ and (S, D)

Select the path of C_1 whose entry has $H_R^2(P)$ to form an attack graph G_1 (reliable)

Select the path of C_2 whose entry has (S, D) to form an attack graph G_2 (inferable)

Execute MIB-based calculation of Ψ_i for C_1 in according to the parameter α of Ψ_θ by Eq.(3)

Select the paths, filtered by comparing Ψ_i with Ψ_θ, to form an attack graph G_3 (reasonable)

Identify attack paths and attackers' location by G_1, G_2 and G_3

Fig. 1. Pseudocode of attack path reconstruction by MIB-based ITrace-CP at a victim

- Example

For example, as shown in Fig. 2, there are two source nodes that generate DoS attacks (Node A) and normal traffic (Node H) respectively. The victim collects all the packets and five MIB-ITrace-CP messages (m_i) with path information in the example, as shown in Table 1. The convention ICMP-based approaches are not able to identify the real attach path (A→B→C→D→E→F) based on these five ITrace-CP messages because the victim collects a normal traffic flow path (H→I→J→C→D→E→F) at the same time. Now, we show how MIB-ITrace-CP to solve this multiple-path problem via extra MIB information (P_i and S_i) embedded in MIB-ITrace-CP messages. First, we can obtain Ψ_θ and Ψ_i based on Eq.(3) as $\alpha=0.8$. Since Ψ_3 and Ψ_5 are less than Ψ_θ, m_3 and m_5 would be skipped. As such, m_1, m_2 and m_4 would be noticed as the attack graph G_3 (reasonable) for path reconstruction.

In summary, it yields an attack graph (G_1) which can trace back to node A and node H. It is possible to find out the real attacker as well as finding a regular source which makes huge traffic. Moreover, MIB-ITrace-CP with the availability of more information would make the analysis more effective, as only the attaching path (A→B→C→D→E→F) in the attack graph G_3.

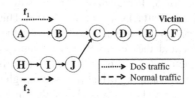

Fig. 2. Example of path reconstruction

Table 1. Example of MIB model calculation

m_i	S-D	$H_R^2(P)$	C_i	$\overline{S}$	Interface	TTL	P_i	S_i(bps)	Ψ_i	Cumulative Path
1	A-F	x	C_1	B	B_1	61	135000	20000	112000	A→B→C→D→E
2	A-F	x	C_1	C	C_1	62	130000	21000	108200	B→C→D→E
3	I-F	x	C_1	C	C_2	62	60000	5000	49000	J→C→D→E
4	I-F	x	C_1	E	E_1	64	170000	26000	141200	D→E
5	I-F	x	C_1	I	I_1	60	50000	6000	41200	H→I→J→C→D→E
							109000	15600	90320	← Ψ_θ (as α=0.8)
							(P_{Avg})	(S_{Avg})	(Ψ_θ)	

3   Experiment and Analysis

In this section, we first discuss the research application and the flow of the experiments. Our research used Testbed@TWISC [12] as the experimental environment. Testbed@TWISC (Taiwan Information Security Center) provides an integrated lab environment that fulfills the requirements of being quarantined, closed, recordable, controllable and storable for researchers. In accordance with the MIB-ITrace-CP system, the experiment was built to verify that path reconstruction under DoS attacks will be reconstructed effectively. The simulated environment uses a multiple path topology as shown in Fig. 3, similar with [10]. Next, we make experiments and show the analysis of effectiveness on multiple traffic flows. And, MIB-ITrace-CP is conducted under the parameters x=1, H_{max}=20 and c=210000 in Eqs. (1)–(2).

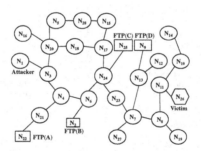

Fig. 3. Topology of the experimental network

In our experiments, we only discuss DoS attack by MIB-ITrace-CP with α=0.8. For the experiment of multiple paths, an attack path from the attacker (N_1) to the victim (N_{26}) is N_1→N_3→N_4→N_6→N_{24}→N_{23}→N_7→N_8→N_{11}→N_{26}, and there are four FTP servers (N_2, N_9, N_{22} and N_{25}) in Fig. 3. The FTP traffic is simulated by the download of data with 10Mbps from each FTP server to the victim. And, the attack traffic is launched by SYN flood attack of 2500 SYNs/sec. Firstly, as shown in Fig. 4(a), the x-axis represents the number of FTP servers and the y-axis represents the number of packets received at the victim until it gets an MIB-ITrace-CP message with full path for tracing the DoS attacker. The performance metric is expressed as the convergence time as the minimum threshold number of packets required. In this scenario, because the minimum hop from the source (N_1) to the victim (N_{26}) is only 9, so the results of ITrace-CP are better than that of the Enhanced ITrace-CP as the parameters $x=1$, $H_{max}=20$ and $c=210000$. On an average, the MIB-ITrace-CP method has the best performance and can get the key Traceback message of full path in the shortest time.

Secondly, as shown in Fig. 4(b), the x-axis represents the number of FTP servers (b/w=10Mbps) and the y-axis represents the percentage of effective Traceback messages, which are triggered from the attack flow, among total Traceback messages received at the victim as the attacker sends out 150,000 SYN packets. Here, please note the performance evaluation for MIB-ITrace-CP is based on the results which are filtered by MIB-ITrace-CP's path reconstruction algorithm presented in Fig. 1. In sum, the MIB-ITrace-CP method has the best performance due to efficient filter although it can quickly gather more Traceback messages for path reconstruction. The results show that MIB-ITrace-CP can perform good Traceback performance and support effective path identification.

The main advantage of MIB-ITrace-CP is that could trace back to multiple attackers quickly and effectively as well as under the condition that normal traffic occurred simultaneously by a weighted α value for different types of attack to facilitate Traceback identification.

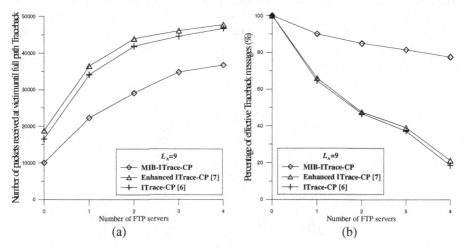

Fig. 4. Efficiency analysis of multiple flows among SYN attacks (a) Traceback convergence time (b) percentage of effective Traceback message

4   Conclusion

Upon being attacked on the Internet, all victims desire to locate the real attacker. For network forensics, in this paper, we use information provided by MIB embedded in ITrace-CP message. As DoS attacks usually generate a large amount of traffic flow or packets to debilitate a server's connection, the additional information enables filtering of Traceback packets and is useful for promoting the efficiency of ITrace-CP. The addition of the MIB system is not only lightweight, but also helps the victim gather more information to forensic teams. Further, this paper proposes a flow-classification concept, working with intention-driven, to promote the accuracy of attack path reconstruction. And, the experiments on Testbed@TWISC platform ensures that the results obtained would be closer to real-world conditions.

Acknowledgement. This research was supported by the Industrial Technology Research Institute, Taiwan.

References

1. US-CERT, Computer Forensics (2008),
   http://www.us-cert.gov/reading_room/forensics.pdf
2. Snoeren, A.C., Partridge, C., Sanchez, L.A., Jones, C.E., Tchakountio, F., Kent, S.T., Strayer, W.T.: Hash-Based IP Traceback. In: SIGCOMM 2001 (August 2001)
3. Savage, S., Wetherall, D., Karlin, A., Anderson, T.: Network Support for IP Traceback. IEEE/ACM Transactions on Networking (TON) 9(3), 226–237 (2001)
4. Bellovin, S., Leech, M., Taylor, T.: ICMP Traceback Messages. Internet Draft (February 2003), http://www.ietf.org/proceedings/03mar/I-D/draft-ietf-itrace-04.txt
5. Internet Engineer Task Force (IETF), http://www.ietf.org/
6. Lee, H.C.J., Thing, V.L.L., Xu, Y., Ma, M.: ICMP Traceback with Cumulative Path, An Efficient Solution for IP Traceback. In: 5th International Conference on Information and Communications Security, pp. 124–135 (October 2003)
7. Thing, V.L.L., Lee, H.C.J., Sloman, M., Zhou, J.: Enhanced ICMP Traceback with Cumulative Path. In: IEEE 61st Vehicular Technology Conference (VTC 2005-Spring), vol. 4, pp. 2415–2419 (2005)
8. Tsunoda, H., Tochiori, T., Waizumi, Y., Kato, N., Nemoto, Y.: Improving the Efficiency of DoS Traceback Based on the Enhanced ITrace-CP Method for Mobile Environment (Invited Paper). In: Third International Conference on Communications and Networking in China (ChinaCom 2008), pp. 680–685 (2008)
9. Mankin, A., Massey, D., Wu, C.L., Wu, S.F., Zhang, L.: On Design and Evaluation of Intention-Driven ICMP Traceback. In: IEEE Int' 10th Conf. Computer Communications and Networks, pp. 159–165. IEEE CS Press (2001)
10. Izaddoost, A., Othman, M., Rasid, M.F.A.: Accurate ICMP Traceback Model under DoS/DDoS ATTACK. In: 15th International Conference on Advanced Computing and Communications (ADCOM 2007), pp. 441–446 (December 2007)
11. IEEE Draft Standard for Management Information Base (MIB) Definitions for Ethernet. P802.3.1/D3.0 (November 2010)
12. Testbed@TWISC, Network Emulation Testbed, http://testbed.ncku.edu.tw/

Breaking a Robust Remote User Authentication Scheme Using Smart Cards

Ding Wang[1,2], Chun-guang Ma[1], Sen-dong Zhao[1], and Chang-li Zhou[1]

[1] College of Computer Science and Technology, Harbin Engineering University
145 Nantong Street, Harbin City 150001, China
wangdingg@mail.nankai.edu.cn
[2] Automobile Management Institute of PLA, Bengbu City 233011, China

Abstract. Understanding security failures of cryptographic protocols is the key to both patching existing protocols and designing future schemes. Recently, Yeh et al. showed that Hsiang and Shih's password-based remote user authentication scheme is vulnerable to various attacks if the smart card is non-tamper resistant, and proposed an improved version which was claimed to be efficient and secure. In this study, however, we find that, although Yeh et al.'s scheme possesses many attractive features, it still cannot achieve the claimed security goals, and we report its following flaws: (1) It cannot withstand offline password guessing attack and key-compromise impersonation attack under their non-tamper resistance assumption of the smart card; (2) It fails to provide user anonymity and forward secrecy; (3) It has some other minor defects. The proposed cryptanalysis discourages any use of the scheme under investigation in practice. Remarkably, rationales for the security analysis of password-based authentication schemes using smart cards are discussed in detail.

Keywords: Cryptanalysis, Authentication protocol, Offline password guessing attack, Smart card, Forward secrecy.

1 Introduction

With the development of distributed computer networks, it is easy for user terminals to share information and computing power with hosts [1,2]. The distributed locations of service providers make it efficient and convenient for subscribers to access the resources, and it is of great concern to protect the systems and the users' privacy and security from malicious adversaries. Accordingly, user authentication becomes an essential security mechanism for remote systems to assure one communicating party of the legitimacy of the corresponding party by acquisition of corroborative evidence. Among numerous methods for user authentication, password based authentication with smart cards is one of the most promising techniques and has been widely adopted over insecure networks to validate the legitimacy of users.

In 1981, Lamport [3] introduced the first password authentication scheme to authenticate a remote user over an insecure channel. This seminal scheme was later refined and used in a number of applications, notably Haller's famous S/KEY one-time password system [4]. Later on, Chang and Wu [5] introduced the smart cards

J.J. Park et al. (Eds.): NPC 2012, LNCS 7513, pp. 110–118, 2012.

into remote user authentication schemes, since then there have been many smart card based password authentication schemes proposed [6-10]. In such schemes, the user is equipped with a smart card and a password as identification verifiers. When the user wants to login to the server, she provides the card with her password, which is used to construct a login request that is sent to the server. Upon receiving the request, the server authenticates these messages and provides the desired service if the verifiers are found valid. If mutual authentication occurs, the client is also convinced that the corresponding server is authentic. More admired schemes also achieve session key agreement for securing the subsequent data communications.

The common adversary model to evaluate the security of authentication protocols using smart cards assumes an attacker with full control over the communication channel between the user and the remote server [7,10,11]. Accordingly, all the messages exchanged can be blocked, intercepted, deleted, or modified by the attacker, and the attacker can also insert his/her own fabricated messages. Secondly, protocols must assume that the attacker can temporarily get access to the legitimate user's smart card, which is reasonable in practice. What's more, since recent research results have shown that the secret data stored in the common smart card could be extracted by some means, such as monitoring the power consumption [12,13] or analyzing the leaked information [14], the smart card should be assumed to be non-tamper resistant, i.e., the secret information stored in the smart card can be revealed.

As mentioned in [10,15], a sound password authentication scheme should be able to withstand a number of sophisticated distinct types of attacks, such as replay attack, password guessing attack, parallel session attack, denial of service attack, stolen verifier attack, and user/server impersonation attack. As resistance to these passive and active attacks is a basic security requirement for authentication protocols, the following desirable attributes are also of great importance in the case of an authentication scheme with session key establishment [16,17]:

i.   Resistance to known key attack. A protocol still achieves its security goal in the face of an adversary who has learned some previous session keys.

ii.   Provision of forward secrecy. Even if long-term private key of one or more entities are compromised, the secrecy of previous session keys is not affected.

iii. Resistance to unknown key-share attack. The entity i cannot be coerced into sharing a key with entity j without i's knowledge, i.e., when i believes the key is shared with some other entity k, where $k \neq j$.

iv.   Resistance to key-compromise impersonation attack. It is desirable that the leakage of entity i's long term private key does not enable an adversary to impersonate other entities to i.

In 2009, Hsiang and Shih [8] showed that Yoon et al.'s scheme [6] is susceptible to user impersonation attack, offline password guessing attack and parallel session attack. To overcome these defects, Hsiang and Shih presented an enhanced version. Later on, Sood et al. [9] showed that Hsiang and Shih's scheme still suffers from offline password guessing attack and user impersonation attack, and user anonymity is not preserved. More recently, Yeh et al. [18] identified that, besides the security flaws found by Sood et al., Hsiang and Shih's scheme is also prone to undetectable online password guessing attack. Consequently, Yeh et al. proposed a further improved version to eliminate the aforementioned security flaws. In this paper, however, we will demonstrate that Yeh et al.'s scheme is still vulnerable to the offline password guessing attack and key-compromise impersonation attack. Moreover, their scheme fails to provide the property of forward secrecy and user anonymity.

The remainder of this paper is organized as follows: in Section 2, we briefly review Yeh et al.'s authentication scheme. Section 3 describes the weaknesses of Yeh et al.'s scheme. Finally, we conclude this paper in the last section.

2   Review of Yeh et al.'s Scheme

In this section, we briefly review the first scheme, i.e. the improvement on Hsiang and Shih's scheme, proposed by Yeh et al. in [18]. Their scheme, summarized in Fig.1, consists of four phases, namely, the registration phase, the login phase, the verification phase and password update phase. For ease of presentation, we employ some intuitive abbreviations and notations listed in Table 1.

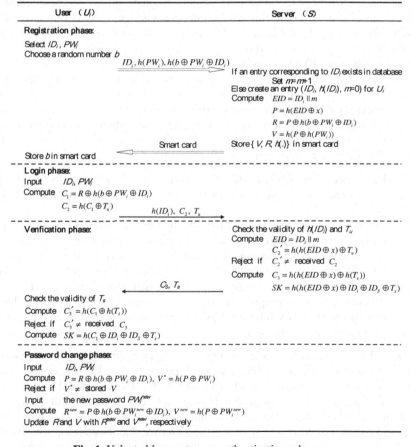

Fig. 1. Yeh et al.'s remote user authentication scheme

Table 1. Notations

Symbol	Description
U_i	i^{th} user
S	remote server
ID_i	identity of user U_i
PW_i	password of user U_i
x	the secret key of remote server S
$h(\cdot)$	collision free one-way hash function
$\oplus$	the bitwise XOR operation
$\parallel$	the string concatenation operation
$A \Rightarrow B : M$	message M is transferred through a secure channel from A to B
$A \rightarrow B : M$	message M is transferred through a common channel from A to B

2.1   Registration Phase

The registration phase involves the following operations:

Step R1. U_i chooses his/her identity ID_i, password PW_i, and a random number b.

Step R2. $U_i \Rightarrow S$: $\{ID_i, h(PW_i), h(b \oplus PW_i \oplus ID_i)\}$.

Step R3. On receiving the registration message from U_i, the server S creates a new entry $(h(ID_i), ID_i, m)$ with the value $m = 0$ for U_i in the backend database, or sets $m = m+1$ in the existing entry. Then, S computes $EID = ID \parallel m$, $P = h(EID \oplus x)$, $R = P \oplus h(b \oplus PW_i \oplus ID_i)$ and $V = h(P \oplus h(PW_i))$.

Step R4. $S \Rightarrow U_i$: A smart card containing security parameters $\{V, R, h(\cdot)\}$.

Step R5. U_i enters b into his/her smart card.

2.2   Login Phase

When U_i wants to login to S, the following operations will be performed:

Step L1. U_i inserts his/her smart card into the card reader, and inputs ID_i and PW_i.

Step L2. The smart card computes $C_1 = R \oplus h(b \oplus PW_i \oplus ID_i)$ and $C_2 = h(C_1 \oplus T_u)$, where T_u is the current timestamp on user side.

Step L3. $U_i \rightarrow S$: $\{C_2, h(ID_i), T_u\}$.

2.3   Verification Phase

After receiving the login request from user U_i, S performs the following operations:

Step V1. S first checks the validity of $h(ID_i)$ and T_u, computes $EID = ID_i \parallel m$ and $C_2' = h(h(EID \oplus x) \oplus T_u)$, and then compares the computed C_2' with the received C_2. If they are equal, S computes $C_3 = h(h(EID \oplus x) \oplus h(T_s))$ and session key $SK = h(h(EID \oplus x) \oplus ID_i \oplus ID_S \oplus T_s)$, where ID_S denotes the identity of S. Otherwise, S rejects the request.

Step V2. $S \rightarrow U_i$: $\{C_3, T_s\}$.

Step V3. Upon receiving the reply message, U_i checks the validity of T_u. If the verification fails, U_i terminates the session. Then, U_i computes $C_3' = h(C_1 \oplus$

$h(T_s)$), and then compares the computed C_3' with the received C_3. If the verification holds, U_i computes $SK=h(h(EID \oplus x) \oplus ID_i \oplus ID_S \oplus T_s)$. Otherwise, U_i terminates the session.

Step V4. After authenticating each other, U_i and S use the same session key SK to secure ensuing data communications.

2.4   Password Change Phase

When U_i wants to change the old password PW_i to the new password PW_i^{new}, the following operations will be involved:

Step P1. U_i insert his/her own smart card into card reader, keys ID_i and PW_i.

Step P2. The smart card computes $P=R \oplus h(b \oplus PW_i \oplus ID_i)$ and $V^*=h(P \oplus h(PW_i))$, and checks whether V^* equals V. If the verification fails, smart card rejects.

Step P3. U_i keys his/her new password PW_i^{new}.

Step P4. The smart card computes $R^{new}=P \oplus h(b \oplus PW_i^{new} \oplus ID_i)$ and $V^{new}=h(P \oplus h(PW_i^{new}))$, and updates R and V with the new R^{new} and V^{new} respectively.

3   Cryptanalysis of Yeh et al.'s Scheme

There are two assumptions explicitly made in Yeh et al.'s scheme [18]:

(i) The adversary $\mathcal{A}$ has total control over the communication channel between the user U and the remote server S. In other words, the adversary can insert, delete, alter, or intercept any messages transmitted in the channel.

(ii) The secret parameters stored in the smart card could be extracted out once a legitimate user's card is somehow (e.g. stolen or picked up) obtained by $\mathcal{A}$.

Note that the above two assumptions, which are also made in the latest works [7,9,10], are indeed reasonable: (1) Assumption *i* is accordant with the common adversary model introduced in Section 1; and (2) Assumption *ii* is also practical in consideration of the state-of-art side-channel attack techniques [12-14]. In the following discussions of the security flaws of Yeh et al.'s scheme, based on the above two assumptions, we assume that $\mathcal{A}$ can extract the secret values $\{V, R, b\}$ stored in the legitimate user's smart card, and the attacker can also intercept or block the login request message $\{C_2, h(ID_i), T_u\}$ from U_i and the reply message $\{C_3, T_s\}$ from S.

As described in Yeh et al.'s scheme, mainly two countermeasures are employed to remedy the identified flaws in Hsiang and Shih's scheme: (1) user's *ID* is concealed by use of a non-invertible hash function to double the difficulty of mounting an offline password guessing attack; (2) a session key is agreed to resist against server impersonation attack. However, as will be shown in the following, the first countermeasure is not effective enough, and the later one lacks key security considerations yet.

3.1   Offline Password Guessing Attack

A remote user authentication scheme vulnerable to the offline password guessing attack must satisfy the two conditions: the user's password is weak, and there exists a piece of password-related information used as a comparison target for password guessing. In Yeh et al.'s scheme, a user is allowed to choose his/her own password *PW* at will during the registration and password change phases; the user usually tends to select a password, e.g., his phone number or birthday, which is easily remembered for his convenience. Hence, these easy-to-remember passwords, called weak passwords [19], have low entropy and thus are potentially vulnerable to offline password guessing attack. Inevitably, user's *ID*, chose by the user in the same way with *PW* as described in the scheme, is exposed to the same threat.

Let us consider the following scenarios. In case a legitimate user U_i's smart card is stolen by an adversary $\mathcal{A}$, and the stored secret values such as R, V and b can be extracted. With a previously eavesdropped message $\{C_2, h(ID_i), T_u\}$, $\mathcal{A}$ can acquire U_i's password PW_i by performing the following malicious attack procedure:

Step 1. Guesses all possible values ID_i^* of U_i's identity, and compares the value of $h(ID_i^*)$ with $h(ID_i)$. If the computed $h(ID_i^*)$ equals the intercepted $h(ID_i)$, it implies $ID_i^* = ID_i$ and U_i's identity is found, and proceeds to Step 2.

Step 2. Guesses the value of PW_i to be PW_i^* from the password space $\mathcal{D}$.

Step 3. Computes $C_1^* = R \oplus h(b \oplus PW_i^* \oplus ID_i)$, where the value of b and R are revealed from the smart card and the value of ID_i is obtained through Step 1.

Step 4. Computes $C_2^* = h(C_1^* \oplus T_u)$, as T_u is previously intercepted.

Step 5. Verifies the correctness of PW_i^* by checking if C_2^* equals the intercepted C_2.

Step 6. Repeats Steps 2, 3, 4 and 5 of this phase until the correct value of PW_i is found.

Since the size of password dictionary, i.e. $|\mathcal{D}|$, often is very limited, the above attack procedure can be completed in polynomial time. Halevi and Krawczyk [20] have proved that, under the Dolev-Yao adversary model [11], no password protocol can be free from offline password guessing attack if the public-key techniques are not employed. Therefore, the feasible solution is to reduce the success probability of this attack. Following this principle, Yeh et al.'s scheme thwarts this threat to nearly half success probability as compared to that of Hsiang and Shih's original scheme, which can be easily confirmed from the above attack procedure.

However, we have found that, some minor technical modifications to Yeh et al.'s scheme can quadratically but not linearly reduce the success possibility of this attack. Due to space constraints, we do not give the complete remedy here, and recommend readers to refer the literature [10] for details. The idea of the remedy is not particularly complicated: whenever PW_i appears, it is concatenated with the identity ID_i, while ID_i is concealed in dynamic-ID(s). Therefore, the mechanism employed by Yeh et al. to resist against offline password guessing attack is not effective enough as minor revision may thwart this threat to a more desirable extent.

3.2   Key-Compromise Impersonation Attack

In the case of key-compromise impersonation, the question is whether the knowledge of a communicating party A's private key allows a malicious attacker $\mathcal{A}$ not only to impersonate A to others but also to impersonate other uncorrupted parties to A. Schemes that prevent this kind of reverse impersonation are said to withstand key-compromise impersonation attack.

Suppose the long-term secret key x of the server S is leaked out by accident or intentionally stolen by the adversary $\mathcal{A}$. Once the value of x is obtained, with previously intercepted $h(ID_i)$ transmitted in U_i's authentication process, $\mathcal{A}$ can impersonate the legitimate user U_i through the following method:

Step 1. Guesses U_i's identity to be ID_i^* from a dictionary of all possible 'weak' identities, and verify the guess by checking whether $h(ID_i^*)$ equals $h(ID_i)$.

Step 2. Assumes $m = 0$, where m denotes the re-registration times of U_i.

Step 3. Computes $EID=ID_i \parallel m$ and $P=h(EID \oplus x)$, where ID_i is derived through Step 1 and x has also been learned.

Step 4. Let $C_1 = P$ and $C_2 = h(C_1 \oplus T_m)$, where T_m is the current timestamp.

Step 5. Sends the fabricated login request $\{C_2, h(ID_i), T_m\}$ to server S.

Step 6. Waits for the reply for a reasonable interval. If no response comes, set $m = m+1$ and goes back to Step 3, else proceeds to the next step.

Step 7. Receives the reply $\{C_3, T_s\}$ from server S and computes the session key $SK= h(h(EID \oplus x) \oplus ID_i \oplus ID_S \oplus T_s)$.

Since the value of m, i.e. the re-registration times of U_i, should be very limited in common practice, at most a few dozen, the iteration of the above procedure will come to an end very quickly. The rest of the question is whether Step 1 can be completed in polynomial time. In Yeh et al.'s scheme, a user is allowed to choose his/her own identity ID at will during the registration and password change phases; the user usually tends to select an identity that is human-memorable short strings but not high-entropy keys. In other words, they are chosen from the dictionaries of small size. Therefore, the above attack is feasible.

3.3   Failure to Achieve Forward Secrecy

As with resistance to key-compromise impersonation attack, the property of forward secrecy is also concerned with limiting the effects of eventual failures, in case the disclosure of server's long-term private keys. Let us consider the following scenarios. Suppose the server S's long-term private key x is leaked out by accident or intentionally stolen by an adversary $\mathcal{A}$. Once x is obtained, with previously intercepted messages $\{h(ID_i), T_s^j, C_3^j\}$ transmitted during any one of U_i's authenti-cation process (without loss of generality, assume it is U_i's jth authentication process), $\mathcal{A}$ can derive the session key SK^j of S and U_i's jth encrypted communication through the following method:

Step 1. Guesses U_i's identity to be ID_i^* from a dictionary of all possible 'weak' identities, and verify the guess by checking whether $h(ID_i^*)$ equals $h(ID_i)$.

Step 2. Assumes $m = 0$, where m denotes the re-registration times of U_i.

Step 3. Computes $EID=ID_i \parallel m$ and $C_3^{j*} = h(h(EID \oplus x) \oplus h(T_s^j))$, where ID_i is derived through Step 1 and x has also been learned.

Step 4. Compares C_3^{j*} with the intercepted C_3^j, this equivalence implies the correct value of m is found. Otherwise, sets $m = m+1$ and goes back to Step 3.

Step 5. Computes $SK^j = h(h(EID \oplus x) \oplus ID_i \oplus ID_s \oplus T_s)$.

The computation complexity of Step 1, Step 3 and Step 4 has been analyzed in Section 3.2, and it's evident that the whole procedure described above can be completed in polynomial time. Once the session key SK^j is obtained, the entire jth session will become completely insecure. Consequently, the property of forward secrecy is not provided in Yeh et al.'s scheme, while the provision of forward secrecy is a basic requirement for a secure key agreement scheme.

3.4   No Provision of User Anonymity

In Yeh et al.'s scheme, the user U_i's identity ID_i is wrapped up in hashing, i.e. $h(ID_i)$, which is static and specific to user U_i in all the transaction sessions, an adversary can easily obtain the hashed identity of this communicating client once the login messages were eavesdropped, and hence, different login request messages belonging to the same user can be traced out and may be interlinked to derive some secret information related to the user. Furthermore, U_i's identity ID_i may be derived from $h(ID_i)$ through the method introduced in Section 3.1. Hence, user anonymity is not preserved.

3.5   Some Practical Pitfalls

In the registration phase, U_i's password PW_i is just submitted in a hashed form to S, and thus it can be easily derived by S. If U_i uses this PW_i to access several servers for his/her convenience, the insider of S can impersonate U_i to access other servers. Hence, it's an insecure factor to commit just a hashed password to the server.

Another pitfall in Yeh's scheme is the slow wrong password detection [15]. If U_i inputs a wrong password by mistake, this wrong password will be only detected by the remote system in the verification phase. Therefore, their scheme is slow to detect the user's wrongly input password.

4   Conclusion

Smart card-based password authentication technology has been widely deployed in various kinds of security-critical applications, and careful security considerations should be taken into account when designing such schemes. In this paper, we have shown that Yeh et al.'s scheme still suffers from the offline password guessing attack and key-compromise impersonation attack. In addition, their scheme fails to provide the property of forward secrecy and user anonymity. Some other minor defects have also been found. In conclusion, although Yeh et al.'s scheme has many attractive features, it, in fact, does not provide all of the security properties that they claimed and only radical revisions of the protocol can possibly eliminate the identified defects. Therefore, the scheme under study is not recommended for practical application.

Acknowledgements. This research was supported by the National Natural Science Foundation of China (NSFC) under Grants No. 61170241 and No. 61073042.

References

1. Vicente, A.G., Munoz, I.B., Galilea, J.L.L., del Toro, P.A.R.: Remote automation laboratory using a cluster of virtual machines. IEEE Transactions on Industrial Electronics 57(10), 3276–3283 (2010)
2. Barolli, L., Xhafa, F.: JXTA-OVERLAY: A P2P platform for distributed, collaborative and ubiquitous computing. IEEE Transactions on Industrial Electronics 58(6), 2163–2172 (2010)
3. Lamport, L.: Password authentication with insecure communication. Communications of the ACM 24(11), 770–772 (1981)
4. Hailer, N.M.: The S/Key One-time Password System. In: Proceedings of the Symposium on Network and Distributed System Security, pp. 151–158. IEEE Press, New York (1994)
5. Chang, C.C., Wu, T.C.: Remote password authentication with smart cards. IEE Proceedings-E 138(3), 165–168 (1993)
6. Yoon, E.J., Ryu, E.K., Yoo, K.Y.: Further improvement of an efficient password based remote user authentication scheme using smart cards. IEEE Transactions on Consumer Electronics 50(2), 612–614 (2004)
7. Yang, G., Wong, D.S., Wang, H., Deng, X.: Two-factor mutual authentication based on smart cards and password. Journal of Computer and System Sciences 74(7), 1160–1172 (2008)
8. Hsiang, H.C., Shih, W.K.: Weaknesses and improvements of the Yoon-Ryu-Yoo remote user authentication scheme using smart cards. Computer Communications 32(4), 649–652 (2009)
9. Sood, S.K., Sarje, A.K., Singh, K.: An improvement of Hsiang-Shih's authentication scheme using smart cards. In: Proceedings of ICWET 2010, pp. 19–25. ACM Press, New York (2010)
10. Ma, C.-G., Wang, D., Zhang, Q.-M.: Cryptanalysis and Improvement of Sood et al.'s Dynamic ID-Based Authentication Scheme. In: Ramanujam, R., Ramaswamy, S. (eds.) ICDCIT 2012. LNCS, vol. 7154, pp. 141–152. Springer, Heidelberg (2012)
11. Dolev, D., Yao, A.C.: On the security of public key protocols. IEEE Transactions on Information Theory 29(2), 198–208 (1983)
12. Kocher, P., Jaffe, J., Jun, B.: Differential Power Analysis. In: Wiener, M. (ed.) CRYPTO 1999. LNCS, vol. 1666, pp. 388–397. Springer, Heidelberg (1999)
13. Messerges, T.S., Dabbish, E.A., Sloan, R.H.: Examining Smart-Card Security under the Threat of Power Analysis Attacks. IEEE Transactions on Computers 51(5), 541–552 (2002)
14. Mangard, S., Oswald, E., Standaert, F.X.: One for all-all for one: unifying standard differential power analysis attacks. IET Information Security 5(2), 100–110 (2011)
15. Tsai, C., Lee, C., Hwang, M.: Password authentication schemes: current status and key issues. International Journal of Network Security 3(2), 101–115 (2006)
16. Blake-Wilson, S., Johnson, D., Menezes, A.: Key Agreement Protocols and Their Security Analysis. In: Darnell, M.J. (ed.) Cryptography and Coding 1997. LNCS, vol. 1355, pp. 30–45. Springer, Heidelberg (1997)
17. Krawczyk, H.: HMQV: A High-Performance Secure Diffie-Hellman Protocol. In: Shoup, V. (ed.) CRYPTO 2005. LNCS, vol. 3621, pp. 546–566. Springer, Heidelberg (2005)
18. Yeh, K.H., Su, C.H., Lo, N.W.: Two robust remote user authentication protocols using smart cards. Journal of Systems and Software 83(12), 2556–2565 (2010)
19. Klein, D.V.: Foiling the Cracker: A Survey of, and Improvements to, Password Security. In: 2nd USENIX Security Workshop, pp. 5–14. USENIX Association, Portland (1990)
20. Halevi, S., Krawczyk, H.: Public-key cryptography and password protocols. ACM Transactions on Information and System Security 2(3), 230–268 (1999)

An Analysis of Privacy Preserving Data Aggregation Protocols for WSNs

Irfana Memon

ERISCS Research Group, Aix-Marseille Université, France
Irfana.MEMON@univ-amu.fr

Abstract. Wireless sensor network (WSN) technology has the potential to change the way we live, work, protect and do business, with applications in entertainment, travel, industry, telemedicine, disaster and emergency management. Data aggregation is key technique for power-efficient information acquisition in WSNs. However, data privacy during data aggregation is an important issue when the WSN is deployed in sensitive data applications, such as telemedicine. If the issues associated with data privacy are not seriously considered, the technology would not be trustingly used for many valuable applications. The existing privacy preserving data aggregation protocols provide a method to sustain privacy of collected sensor's data from external and internal adversaries during data aggregation in WSNs. The basic aim of the paper is to investigate the critical aspects of the existing privacy preserving data aggregation protocols for WSNs and highlight their major limitations. We claim that in future such limitations can be corrected. Our ongoing work is to propose an alternative solution to overcome such limitations, but this will be presented in a future paper.

1 Introduction

A WSN can be generally described as a network of nodes that cooperatively monitor environmental or physical conditions such as temperature, vibration, pressure, location or motion from unattended locations. Recently, WSNs have found their way into a wide variety of applications like disaster relief, emergency rescue operation, military surveillance, habitat monitoring, remote health care applications, environmental monitoring [1]. WSNs are usually deployed in hostile environments, where the deployment of sensors, their maintenance, recharging or replacing their batteries are not always feasible. Sensor nodes are resource constrained (i.e., have limited resources in terms of power, memory and transmission range). Previous studies such as [2] have shown that data communication between sensor nodes requires a large portion of the total energy consumption of the WSNs, thus finding an optimal approach to minimize the messages transmitted in the network is particularly important.

Data aggregation is a key feature for power-efficient information acquisition in resource-constrained WSNs. It is the process of combining data from different sensor nodes by using some functions such as suppression or filtering (eliminating duplicates), min, max and average; to minimize data transmission and removing

J.J. Park et al. (Eds.): NPC 2012, LNCS 7513, pp. 119–128, 2012.

redundancy. Several studies address data aggregation schemes in WSNs to minimize data transmission [[3]-[6]].

If privacy of the collected sensor's information is not preserved, it is not safe to deploy the WSNs for sensitive data applications, such as telemedicine and military applications. Data privacy in WSNs has to be guaranteed end-to-end (that is, each node should know its own data, but has no knowledge about neighbors data in the network and only base station could read final aggregation result). Very little work has been proposed to address Privacy preserving Data Aggregation (PDA) in WSNs. The purpose of this paper is to review the ewisting PDA protocols and to highlight their limitations. Up to now, to the best of our knowledge, there have been two surveys of this literature so far, one by Na Li et al., [7] and another by Rabindra Bista et al., [8]. However, they do not provide analysis of the protocols in the terms of communication and computation cost, security, and fault tolerance. The rest of the paper is organized as follows. In section 2, we give a critical analysis of existing PDA protocols. Section 3 presents basic requirements for designing PDA protocol. Section 4 presents the conclusion and future work.

2   An Analysis of Existing Privacy Preserving Data Aggregation (PDA) Protocols

In this section, we review the existing PDA protocols for WSNs and classify them in three classes according to schemes adopted to satisfy data privacy: privacy homomorphism, perturbation, and shuffling.

2.1   Privacy Homomorphism

Privacy homomorphism scheme allows arithmetic operations to be performed on encrypted data without need of decryption. The protocols proposed in [9], [11], and [12] are based on this scheme.

2.1.1   Concealed Data Aggregation (CDA) [9]
In this scheme, sensor nodes share a common symmetric key with the base station that is kept hidden from intermediate aggregators. Aggregators carry out aggregation functions that are applied to encrypted data without decrypting. This provides the advantage of aggregators not to carry out costly decryption and re-encryption operations. CDA employs the privacy homomorphic encryption function proposed by Domingo-Ferrer [10]. In CDA, each sensor node splits its sensed data into 'd' parts (d≥2), encrypts each part and sends encrypted data to the aggregator node. The aggregator node aggregates received encrypted data without decryption and sends it to the base station. Base station decrypts the encrypted aggregated data to derive the original data.

Complexity Analysis
Communication and Computation Cost: In CDA, each node divides its data into d parts, encrypt each part and sends it to aggregator node. As a result, CDA suffers from excessive computational complexity and communication overhead.

Security: CDA ensures data privacy against aggregators but does not guarantee the privacy of individually sensed data against other nodes because all sensor nodes share the same encryption key with the base station.

2.1.2   Efficient Aggregation of Encrypted Data [11]

This scheme is essentially a stream cipher and its homomorphic property relies on the synchronization among the key-stream generators, i.e., all sensors in the field must share the same key-stream generator. In this scheme, aggregator node can aggregate received data from its children without decryption. The main idea of this approach is to use modular addition (+) instead of xor (Exclusive-OR) operation that is found in the stream ciphers. To minimize trust assumptions, this scheme assumes that each sensor n_i share a distinct long-term key k_i with the BS. This key is originally derived, using a pseudo-random function (PRF), from the master secret K, which is only known to the BS. Sensor nodes encrypt their data using key k and then forwards it to aggregator, who aggregates all received encrypted data of its children without decrypting. The base station can decrypt and derive original data.

Complexity Analysis

Communication Cost: In this scheme, BS needs to know the IDs of all nodes. Therefore, each aggregator needs to append the IDs of its children that did not reply to the query to the aggregate, which generates high communication overhead.

Security: Although the proposed scheme provides end-to-end privacy, but it is vulnerable to false data injection attacks. An external attacker can add an arbitrary value to an aggregate cipher text. Moreover, it is difficult to ensure the confidentiality of the commonly shared key-stream generator in this scheme.

2.1.3   Efficient and Provably Secure Aggregation of Encrypted Data [12]

This is an improved scheme of [11] for privacy-preserving additive aggregation based on homomorphic encryption. Compared to earlier work [11], this paper provides the details of a concrete construction using a pseudo-random function (PRF).

In this scheme, the key is generated by a certain deterministic algorithm (with an un-known seed) such as a pseudo-random function [13]. Two components are used in construction: a pseudo-random function 'f' and a length-matching hash function 'h'. The output of the pseudo-random function can be hashed down by some length-matching hash function. The purpose of 'h' is to shorten a long bit-string, rather than to produce a fingerprint of a message. For instance, 'h' can be implemented by truncating the output of a PRF and taking l least significant bits as output. Note that the parameter l should still be chosen large enough to ensure reasonably low probability of success for a random guess.

Complexity Analysis

Communication Cost: In this scheme, hash function 'h' is used to shorten a long bit-string. Therefore, communication cost is less than the scheme presented in [11]. But, still in this scheme, base station needs to know the IDs of all nodes. Therefore, each aggregator needs to append the IDs of its children that did not reply to the query in the aggregate, that generates high communication cost.

Computation Cost: To encrypt its data, a node performs one PRF invocation, one length matching hash, and one mod M addition. It also performs one extra addition for aggregation. The authors considered the cost of evaluating 'h' to be negligible in the calculation of overall computation cost for encryption. As a result, the cost of encryption is dominated by a single PRF invocation.

Security: This scheme allows aggregators to aggregate encrypted data of their children without having to decrypt. As a result, even if an aggregator is compromised, it cannot learn the data of its children, resulting in much stronger privacy. This scheme is vulnerable to message loss, the base station will obtain bogus aggregate with a single message loss.

2.2   Perturbation Scheme

In Perturbation scheme, sensor nodes use encryption keys and private/public seeds generated by randomization techniques. Cluster based Private Data Aggregation (CPDA) [14] and Contie et al. scheme [16] are perturbation based protocols.

2.2.1   Cluster Based Private Data Aggregation (CPDA) [14]

In CPDA, sensors are randomly grouped into clusters using a distributed protocol proposed in [14]. In each cluster, cluster leader is responsible for aggregating data received from the cluster members. To maintain data privacy, all sensors within a cluster share a common (non-private) knowledge of non-zero numbers, referred to as seeds, which are distinct with each other. Sensors in each cluster customize their private data into k-1 polynomial using shared seeds and random numbers (private), where k is the total number of nodes in a cluster. Then, each sensor encrypts its customized value by using a unique shared key between sensors. Sensor S_i keeps one share, and exchange remaining shares with (k-1) nodes in same cluster. Each sensor S_i assembles all the data including its own by using the additive property of polynomials and sends them to their respective cluster leader. Finally, cluster leader computes the aggregate value and forwards the derived sum of the cluster to the base station along the TAG routing tree [15]. Fig.1. illustrates the CPDA scheme step by step among the three nodes, where A is the cluster leader of this cluster and B and C are cluster members.

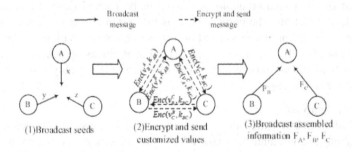

Fig. 1. CPDA scheme

Complexity Analysis
Communication Cost: Cluster formation step in CPDA has a complexity of $O(p_c N)$, where p_c is the probability of a node indepently becoming a cluster leader and N is the number of nodes in the network. In addition, exchanging of seeds within a cluster takes $O(k)$ messages and exchanging their encrypted customized data within a cluster takes $O(k)$ message. Where k is the number of nodes in cluster. This is done in each cluster. Hence, the CPDA approach suffers from the high communication overhead.

Node Failure: When cluster leader failure occurs, data aggregation within the cluster fails. When a cluster member sends data partially to a few nodes and then fails, it results a loss in accuracy.

2.2.2   Privacy-Preserving Robust Data Aggregation [16]

This scheme has following key elements: First, establishment of twin-keys for different pairs of sensors in the network, which is an anonymous process that prevents each node in a pair from deriving the identity of the other node (twin-node). Second, for each aggregation phase, sensor node uses an anonymous liveness announcement protocol to declare the liveness of each twin-key, so that each node becomes aware of whether a twin-key it possesses will be used by the anonymous twin-node. Finally, during the aggregation phase, each node encrypts its own value by adding shadow values computed from the alive twin-keys it holds. As a result, the contribution of the shadow values for each twin-key will cancel out each other and the correct aggregated result is finally obtained. This scheme consists of three steps: local cluster formation, twin-key establishment and data aggregation. In the local cluster formation step, nodes are grouped into several clusters using a cluster algorithm proposed in [17]. Each cluster forms a different logical Hamiltonian circuit, and each pair of neighboring nodes in the circuit shares a pair-wise key. In the twin-key establishment step, it is assumed that each node contains a pre-deployed key-ring of K symmetric key, using the set-up procedure of Eschenauer and Gligors protocol [18]: the K keys are randomly chosen from a larger key-pool of size P. Each node n_i anonymously checks which ones of its K keys are also shared with other nodes in the same cluster and establishes a number of twin keys with the other nodes. In particular, a node n_i establishes a twin key with another node (twin-node) in the cluster when n_i is aware there is a node sharing a key with it. Data aggregation step is further divided into two parts: First, each cluster computes the the aggregated value of its nodes, together with a twin-key liveness announcement procedure. During this phase an aggregate is routed twice along the Hamiltonian circuit. Each node adds its own sensed value to the aggregate. At the same time, for each alive twin-key it adds (or removes, in accordance with the liveness announcement) a corresponding shadow value. The cluster head obtains the correct aggregate for the cluster. The liveness announcement guarantees that any shadow value, computed from a twin-key that is added in the aggregation by one node will be removed by another node that shares the same twin-key. Second, by using a tree structure [15], the cluster heads contribute to the aggregate with the cluster. Finally, the base station receives the aggregated results of the cluster heads. Fig.2. show the data aggregation with shadow values and aggregation of the cluster aggregates, respectively.

Complexity Analysis

Communication and Computation Cost : In this scheme, an aggregate is routed twice along the Hamiltonian circuit and each node is required to test each of its pre-distributed keys to find out the required twin-keys shared with other nodes. Each node has to send out the hash values corresponding to its twin-keys that have not yet been declared alive by other nodes. Furthermore, each node has to compute the hash for each of its pre-distributed keys and to encrypt each message it sends out. For each agreed twin-key, k, each node has to compute two hash values. One hash is computed for the verification of the liveness announcement of k. The other hash is computed for the k's corresponding shadow value added in the aggregated value. Therefore, the computation of each node in the worst case is 2A hash computations, considering A agreed twin-keys. This scheme suffers from high computation and communication cost.

Security: This scheme preserves data privacy from external and internal adversaries. It is resilient to eavesdropping attack due to the pair-wise encryption between nodes. In this scheme, each node value is protected by one or more shadow values, hence it is resilient to node compromise attacks. The secrecy of the shadow value, in turn, is protected by the secrecy of the twin- keys. To compromise the privacy of non-captured node, n_i, the attacker has to obtain the keys used to generate the shadow values that n_i uses to protect its own privacy.

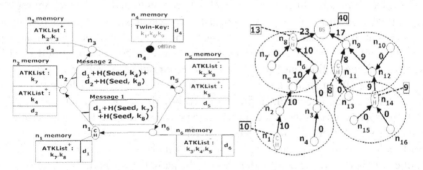

(a) Data aggregation with shadow values   (b) Aggregation of the cluster aggregates

Fig. 2. Conti et al. Scheme

2.3   Shuffling Scheme

In shuffling scheme, each sensor node slices its sensed data randomly into a certain number (say, n) of pieces, and one piece is kept on itself, the remaining n-1 pieces are securely distributed to n-1 neighbor nodes. After the data pieces are received from the neighboring nodes, all the sensors decrypt the data by using their shared keys, sums up all the received data slices, and sends the sum to their parent node. SMART[14] and iPDA[19] are shuffling based protocols.

2.3.1 Slice-Mix-AggRegaTe (SMART) [14]

This scheme guarantees data privacy through data "slicing and assembling". In SMART, base station runs key distribution scheme [18] to generate and distribute key ring in all nodes. The key ring for sensor S_i is represented by k_i and K is the union set of all key rings. SMART scheme consists three steps: In the first step, each sensor S_i (i = 1,2,...,N), randomly select J neighbor nodes in h hops (J is a design parameter). Sensor S_i then slices its private data into J pieces. One piece is kept at sensor S_i itself, the remaining J-1 pieces are encrypted and sent to nodes in the randomly selected set of S_i. In the second step, on receiving data pieces from the neighbors, all sensors decrypt the data by using their shared keys and sum all the received data slices. In the third step, when a node receives all data slices, it forwards a message of the sum to its parent, which in turn forwards the message to the base station using tree-based routing protocol [15]. Eventually the aggregation reaches the base station.

Complexity Analysis

Communication Cost: Each sensor node randomly selects a set of J nodes within h hops. Furthermore, Data pieces are sent out appropriately by each sensor node. Hence, this scheme suffers from the high communication overhead. Furthermore, randomly selected set of J nodes are not necessary in immediate communication range. Hence lot of power consumption is expended for communication.

Node Failure: Sensor node's failure results to loss in accuracy of the final result.

2.3.2 Integrity-Protecting Private Data Aggregation (iPDA) [19]

In this scheme, data privacy is achieved through data "slicing and assembling" scheme discussed in [14]; and data integrity is achieved through redundancy by constructing disjoint aggregation trees. Fig.3. shows two disjoint aggregation trees which are separately rooted at base station. Each sensor node sends its reading to both aggregation trees. The disjoint aggregation trees perform data aggregation individually. Hence, base station can detect data pollution attacks by comparing aggregation results along the disjoint aggregation trees. If the aggregation results received along both trees are same, the base station will accept the result. Otherwise, the base station knows that there exist either data pollution attacks or node failures, or both; hence base station reject it. In iPDA, each sensor node hides its individual data by slicing the data and sending encrypted data slices to different neighboring nodes, then the aggregators aggregate the received data and sends aggregated results to the base station.

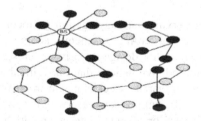

Fig. 3. iPDA scheme (Two disjoint aggregation trees)

This scheme suffers same complexity issues as described earlier in the complexity analysis of SMART protocol. In addition this scheme has a high communication overhead due to the slicing technique and each sensor node has to send its reading to both aggregation trees. In this scheme, base station can detect data pollution attack, but does not propose any solution to protect from the attack.

3   Criteria, Challenges and Requirements to Design Privacy Preserving Data Aggregation Protocols

The following criteria summarize the required characteristics of privacy preserving data aggregation protocols for WSNs.

Data Privacy: Data privacy ensures that the original data of any sensor node S_i should not be revealed to an adversary, or any other trusted participating nodes in the network.

Energy Efficiency: Sensor's lifetime is strictly dependent on its power resource, thus the protocol should intelligently use power for preserving their energy. Privacy protection in WSNs consumes additional power, that can not be avoided. A good and efficient protocol should keep that additional communication overhead, computation cost, memory and payload size as small as possible.

Data Accuracy: Data may be lost due to node failure or wireless link during transmission, hence the accuracy of the final aggregated result can be affected. In the applications of WSNs where aggregated results are used to make some critical decision, the accuracy of final aggregated result at the base station is very important with the restriction that private data of sensor node is not disclosed. Therefore, an appropriate method is required to determine an accurate aggregated result in WSNs.

Fault Tolerance: Sensor nodes are prone to failure due to lack of energy, hardware failure, and malicious attack. Wireless sensor network must be robust against failure of sensor node and the network functionality must be maintained. New nodes can be added into the network to compensate for failure nodes. A good protocol should allow node addition during data aggregation for maintain network functionality.

4   Conclusion and Future Work

In this paper, privacy preserving data aggregation protocols for WSNs have been analyzed and classified them according to schemes adopted to satisfy data privacy. Requirements and challenges for designing privacy preserving data aggregation protocols have been identified. We believe that our critical analysis of the existing protocols will provide new researchers guidelines to improve the existing protocols and to design new energy efficient privacy preserving data aggregation protocols for WSNs. The existing privacy-preserving data aggregation protocols have used different schemes to achieve data privacy, such as privacy homomorphism, perturbation, and shuffling. Each type of the above schemes has some advantages and limitations which are summarized as:

(1) The protocols based on privacy homomorphism allow aggregation directly on encrypted data. Therefore, it minimizes possibility of attack at aggregator node. However, these schemes can only apply to some query based aggregation functions (e.g, sum, average, etc); hence they limits our ability to perform aggregation in network. Therefore, an efficient privacy homomorphic scheme is required that could support all aggregation functions.

(2) The protocols based on perturbation scheme maintain privacy by exchanging seeds (non-private numbers) and exchanging of their encrypted customized data within a cluster, which results in high communication and computation overhead. Therefore, an optimal method is required to minimize communication overhead while maintaining privacy.

(3) The protocols based on shuffling guarantees data privacy through data `slicing and assembling' with randomly selected J nodes within h hops. Selection of nodes is done only once (i.e., initially). Since sensors are prone to failure due to lack of energy during data aggregation, that results in loss of data and loss in coverage. So, to maintain accuracy and privacy of the remaining data, each node in the J-list of the failed node, after recognizing the failure should broadcast the failure message to their corresponding J-list nodes to discard the failed node data and continue the operation with remaining nodes. Such a broadcast takes $O(JN)$ messages.

Protocol should support node addition for maintaining sensing coverage during data aggregation. This is not addressed in any existing privacy preserving data aggregation protocol.

Our ongoing work is to propose an energy efficient Privacy Preserving data Aggregation (EPPA) for WSNs where a secure key management along with shuffling technique will be adopted that will provide strong security and energy efficient system. In our scheme, nodes maintain privacy through `slicing and assembling' with their siblings within the immediate transmission range. In our work, we propose a new tree construction protocol, which we refer to as Secure Coverage Tree (SCT) protocol and a tree-reconstruction scheme which make it resilient to node failure. We implement our proposed EPPA protocol on top of the Secure Coverage Tree (SCT) protocol. We strongly believe that our proposed scheme will performs better than the existing protocols in terms of communication overhead, security, and fault tolerance.

References

1. Singh, S.K., Singh, M.P., Singh, D.K.: Applications, Classifications, and Selections of Energy-Efficient Routing Protocols for Wireless Sensor Networks. International Journal of Advanced Engineering Sciences and Technologies (2010)
2. Hill, J., Szewczyk, R., Woo, A., Hollar, S., Pister, D.C.K.: System architecture directions for networked sensors. In: Proceedings of the 9th International Conference on Architectural Support for Programming Languages and Operating Systems (2000)

3. Maraiya, K., Kant, K., Gupta, N.: Wireless Sensor Network: A Review on Data Aggregation. International Journal of Scientific and Engineering Research (2011)
4. Madden, S., Szewczyk, R., Franklin, M., Culler, D.: Supporting aggregate queries over ad-hoc sensor networks. In: Workshop on Mobile Computing and Systems Applications (2002)
5. Wagner, D.: Resilient aggregation in sensor networks. In: Proceedings of the 2nd ACM Workshop on Security of Adhoc and Sensor Networks (2004)
6. Intanagonwiwat, C., Estrin, D., Govindan, R., Heidemann, J.: Impact of Network Density on Data aggregation in Wireless Sensor Networks. In: Proceedings of the 22nd International Conference on Distributed Computing Systems (2002)
7. Li, N., Zhang, N., Das, S.K., Thuraisingham, B.: Privacy-preserving in wireless sensor networks: A state-of-the-art survey. Ad Hoc Networks (2009)
8. Bista, R., Chang, J.-W.: Privacy-Preserving Data Aggregation Protocols for Wireless Sensor Networks: A Survey. Sensors (2010)
9. Westhoff, D., Girao, J., Acharya, M.: Concealed data aggregation for reverse multicast traffic in sensor networks: encryption key distribution and routing adaptation. IEEE Transactions on Mobile Computing (2006)
10. Domingo-Ferrer, J.: A Provably Secure Additive and Multiplicative Privacy Homomorphism. In: Proc. Information Security Conf., pp. 471–483 (October 2002)
11. Castelluccia, C., Mykletun, E., Tsudik, G.: Efficient Aggregation of Encrypted Data in WSN. In: MobiQuitous. IEEE Computer Society (2005)
12. Castellucia, C., Chan, A.C.-F., Mykletun, E., Tsudnik, G.: Efficient and Provably Secure Aggregation of encrypted data in WSNs. ACM Transactions on Sensor Networks 5(3) (May 2009)
13. Goldreich, O., Goldwasser, S., Micali, S.: How to construct random functions. Journal of the Association for Computing Machinay (1986)
14. He, W., Liu, X., Nguyen, H., Nahrstedt, K., Abdelzaher, T.: PDA: privacy-preserving data aggregation in wireless sensor networks. IEEE INFOCOM (2007)
15. Madden, S., Franklin, M.J., Hellerstein, J.M.: TAG: A Tiny AGgregation Service for Ad-Hoc Sensor Networks. OSDI (2002)
16. Conti, M., Zhang, L., Roy, S., Pietro, R.D., Jajodia, S., Mancini, L.V.: Privacy-preserving robust data aggregation in WSNs. Secur. Commun. Netw. (2009)
17. Choi, H., Zhu, S., La Porta, T.F.: SET: Detecting Node Clones in Sensor Networks. In: Proceedings of IEEE 3rd International Conference on Security and Privacy in Communication Networks (2007)
18. Eschenauer, L., Gligor, V.D.: A key-management scheme for distributed sensor networks. In: Proceedings of the 9th ACM Conference on Computer and Communications Security (November 2002)
19. He, W., Nguyen, H., Liu, X., Nahrstedt, K., Abdelzaher, T.: iPDA: An integrity-protecting private data aggregation scheme for wireless sensor networks. In: Proceedings of IEEE Military Communication Conference, MILCOM, San Diego, CA, USA (November 2008)

Hybrid Obfuscated Javascript Strength Analysis System for Detection of Malicious Websites

R. Krishnaveni, C. Chellappan, and R. Dhanalakshmi

Department of Computer Science & Engineering,
Anna University, Chennai, India
{rskichu10,dhanalakshmisai}@gmail.com, drcc@annauniv.edu

Abstract. JavaScripts are mostly used by the malicious websites to attack the client systems. To detect and prevent this, static and dynamic analysis systems are used which has problems like longer analysis time, setting up of virtual environment and prone to real attacks. Hence a new hybrid analysis system is proposed which reduces the shortcomings of the static and dynamic analysis systems. Additional features such as keywords to words ratio, average line length, presence of suspicious URLs and tags, whitespace percentage, number of redirections, and enigmatic variable names are used to measure the strength of the obfuscation. In this system performance is improved and the number of false positives and negatives are reduced. Based on the strength of obfuscation in the JavaScript code, a website is determined to be benign or malicious.

Keywords: Malicious Web Sites, JavaScript Obfuscation, JavaScript Extraction, Hybrid Strength Analysis System.

1   Introduction

Normally, the attacker uses the Internet to insert an attack code into the web site, or downloads the attacking program in the client's system without the user's knowledge. JavaScripts are the most convenient tools for the attackers to create a malicious web site. JavaScript obfuscation techniques are also used to hide the JavaScript containing the attack code.

Attack Sites are Web sites that try to infect our computer with malware when we visit. These attacks can be very difficult to detect; even a site that looks safe may be secretly trying to attack us. Sometimes the Web site's owner won't even know that the site has been turned into an Attack Site. Some malicious codes get distributed only under certain conditions; some installs silently, without alerting the user. There are three common ways for a website to become an attack site:

- The site is created for malicious purposes.
- The site serves malicious content from an ad network or other third-party content provider.
- The site is infected through a security weakness in the site or the Webmaster's computer.

J.J. Park et al. (Eds.): NPC 2012, LNCS 7513, pp. 129–137, 2012.

A malicious website facilitates the distribution of malware, either intentionally or because it has been compromised. Most malicious websites distribute malware without the knowledge of the sites' owners.

1.1   JavaScript Obfuscation

Obfuscated JavaScript is a source or machine code that has been made difficult to understand for humans. Obfuscators transform readable code into obfuscated code using various techniques. There are mainly four methods in which JavaScript can be obfuscated.

- Using ASCII values and Unicode values
- Using an XOR operation
- Splitting a string
- Compressing a string and replacing with a meaningless string

2   Literature Survey

2.1   Static Analysis Systems

Static analysis system downloads and analyzes the source of the web site. This system has less vulnerability against the attack, as the attack is not directly made. The shortcomings are that the person should analyze the source code manually and takes a longer amount of time to detect a variant and generate a signature.

Malzilla,[1] proposed in "Rhino:Javascript for java" by Mozilla is the method of downloading the source codes by entering the URL of the web site and then analyze them. Until the normal JavaScript is obtained, decoding of the obfuscated codes takes place. There is a shortcoming in analyzing whether the detected JavaScript code is an attack JavaScript that induces malicious behavior or not.

The method proposed in "Automatic detection for JavaScript Obfuscation Attacks in web pages through string pattern analysis"[2] by YoungHanChoi analyzes the pattern of web page strings. It separates obfuscated JavaScript codes from normal ones using N-gram entropy and string size. If JavaScript is found to exceed the certain threshold value, the web site will be considered as a malicious web site. As the characteristic of the malicious code is not considered, it could be difficult to detect a malicious web site that contains normal JavaScript.

The method in "Access Log Generator for Analyzing Malicious Website Browsing Behaviors"[3] by Chu Hsing Lin proposed an access log generator to generate access logs with characteristics of browsing behaviors for the particular website under investigation. We also include malicious behaviors into the generated access log, which is combined with actual access log of the website for further tests and analyses. The disadvantage of this concept is that the website is not checked for malicious scripts at run time. The method is slow and prone to attack before the access logs are analyzed.

The approach in "Beyond Blacklists: Learning to Detect Malicious Web Sites from Suspicious URLs"[4] by Justin Ma for detection of malicious websites analyzes the lexical properties of the URL. The disadvantage of this method is that only the suspicious URL is analyzed to find whether a website is benign or malicious.

The anomaly semantics approach in "Malicious Web Page Detection Based on Anomaly Semantics"[5] by D.J.Guan for detecting malicious web pages is based on URL features, non content-based features, content-based features, potential dangerous tags and tag attributes. The disadvantage of this method is that it mainly concentrates on the HTML tags and attributes and does not concentrate more on JavaScript.

2.2 Dynamic Analysis Systems

The dynamic analysis system visits the web site to check if any of the web pages causes any change in the user's system in order to analyze malicious behavior of the web site. The web site obfuscated with JavaScript is not directly decoded. Instead, JavaScript codes are executed, and then the result is analyzed to check malicious behavior.

In Wepawet proposed by Marco Cova in "Detection and Analysis of Drive-By-Download Attacks and Malicious Javascript Code"[6] visits the web site using the entered web site address from the virtual environment system, developed for analysis and the visit result is analyzed. The virtual environment system analyzes whether the visited web site is obfuscated, whether any malicious behavior is committed or not and shows the analysis result.

MonkeyWrench proposed by Armin Buscher in "Throwing a MonkeyWrench into Web Attack Plans"[7], analyzes the web page using an analysis method similar to Wepawet.

Therefore, malicious behavior can be analyzed only when that particular application has been developed in a virtual environment in advance. Hence, much time and efforts are required to build these analysis environments.

The dynamic analysis method is fast and shows more accurate examination results than the static analysis method. It has the advantage of analyzing JavaScript codes that are generated dynamically. The dynamic analysis method can check the malicious nature of the web site within shorter time than static analysis. However, an environment should be created that allows execution of malicious behavior contained in the malicious obfuscated web site.

2.3 Hybrid Analysis System

The method proposed in "Suspicious Malicious Web Site Detection with Strength Analysis of a JavaScript Obfuscation" by "Byung-Ik Kim"[8], detect malicious websites based on JavaScript obfuscation strength check system. They analyze using limited characteristic features such as density, frequency and entropy. Due to this, accuracy and detection rate might be less.

3   System Architecture

An URL of the website is given as an input to the system. The codes of the website are analyzed and the JavaScript codes are extracted separately. The extracted

JavaScript code is analyzed using the metrics such as presence of suspicious URLs, density, frequency, enigmatic variable names, quasi- tautology, number of redirections, empty code branches and presence of suspicious URLs and scored based on the metrics. Based on the scores got by each website, a website is determined to be benign or malicious.

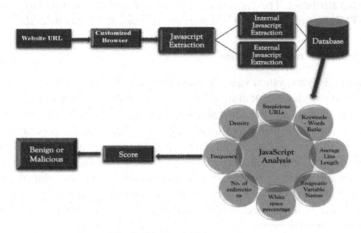

Fig. 1. System Architecture

4   Modules

The modules in the system are Custom Browser Creation, JavaScript Extraction, Obfuscated Javascript strength analysis and Scoring Mechanism.

4.1   Custom Browser Creation

A Web browser is a software application used to locate, retrieve and also display content on the World Wide Web, including Web pages, images, video and other files. As a client/server model, the browser is the client run on a computer that contacts the Web server and requests information. The Web server sends the information back to the Web browser, which displays the results on the computer or other Internet-enabled device that supports a browser. A custom Web Browser is created to illustrate how this system can be integrated into the real time Web Browser.

4.2   JavaScript Extraction

The JavaScript present in the webpage is extracted from the other codes for analysis. This module extracts both internal javascript and external javascript. The internal javascript are extracted using the regular expressions by matching the patterns within the script tag. All the contents present inside the script tag are extracted and stored for analysis.

The external javascripts are scripts that are stored in a separate file and are referenced by the websites which uses it. The external javascript has the extension

'.js'. All reference to the '.js' file from the website are searched and the contents of the '.js' files are extracted and stored.

4.3   Obfuscated JavaScript Strength Analysis

The JavaScript that are thus extracted are analyzed using the following features to determine whether a website is malicious or benign.

1) Presence of suspicious URLs: All the URLs that are present in the website code are extracted separately and stored into the database. These URLs are compared with the already blacklisted URLs that are collected from various sources. The database contains around 60,000 blacklisted suspicious URLs, which are compared with.

$$\% \text{ of Suspicious URLs} = \frac{\text{No.of links matching with blacklist}}{\text{Total No. of links in the website}}$$

2) Density: Generally, the obfuscated string is longer than the normal string. The length of a string tends to increase while encoding a string or replacing it with a meaningless string. Therefore, this feature checks if the length of a single string is longer than 200 characters, if so, the website is considered to be malicious website.

$$\text{Density} = \frac{\text{Strings having more than 200 characters}}{\text{Total Number of Strings}}$$

3) Frequency: The JavaScript obfuscation strength check system uses the frequency of the particular function, encoding mark, and % symbol occurrence, as the detailed check items to check frequency. The proposed system checks the possibility of obfuscation, by checking the use frequency of these functions. Those that are considered dynamic functions are also checked.

$$\text{Frequency} = \frac{\text{Number of suspicious functions and symbols}}{\text{Total Number of Strings}}$$

4) Number of Redirections: The web page redirects the user to the different web pages automatically or through user's action such as clicking some ads, etc. The redirected web page may contain malicious code, which will be downloaded to the user's computer.

$$\text{Redirection Percentage} = \frac{\text{No. of redirections}}{\text{Total No. of Links}}$$

5) Presence of white spaces: Number of extra white spaces, line feeds and tabs are used in the code to confuse the strength analysis system.

$$\text{Whitespace Percentage} = \frac{\text{Number of whitespaces}}{\text{Total Number of Strings}}$$

6) Enigmatic Variable Names: The strings used in the javascript code may be meaningless when compared with the normal javascript code.

$$\text{Enigmatic Variable names} = \frac{\text{Number of meaningless variables}}{\text{Total Number of variables}}$$

7) Average Line Length: A normal javascript code might have a line length of less than 120. Traditional line length of javascript is 80. The obfuscated malicious javascript code might contain the lines which are greater than 120.

$$\text{Average Line Length} = \frac{\text{Number of lines having with length more than 120}}{\text{Total number of lines}}$$

8) Keywords to words ratio: In the malicious javascript code, the use of these keywords is limited due to large use of other operations such as multiple instantiations, declarations, function calls, etc. So in a normal javascript code the keywords are used more than in a malicious javascript code.

$$\text{Keywords} - \text{words ratio} = \frac{\text{Total keywords in javascript}}{\text{Total Number of words}}$$

4.4   Scoring Mechanism

A scoring mechanism is developed using the features that are used to check the websites. Each feature is tested whether the website satisfies its criteria. Each feature is deemed to be positive based on the analysis and by using the following scores.

- Presence of suspicious URLs – If more than 10% of URLs that are present in the website matches with the blacklisted URLs in the database, then this criterion is positive.
- Length – All the length of the strings present in the javascript code are calculated and if more than 30% of strings in the code is having more than the length of 200, then this feature is positive.
- Frequency – The number of suspicious functions present in the javascript code is found and if more than 30% of the string in the code is suspicious function strings, then this feature is positive.

- Number of redirections – If the percentage of number of redirected links to the number of actual links present in the website is more than 30%, then this feature is positive.
- Presence of whitespaces – if the ratio of whitespace to strings in the code is more than 30%, then this feature is positive.
- Enigmatic Variable Name – if more than 30% of variable names are meaningless in the javascript, then feature is positive.
- Average line length – if more than 30% of lines in the website has length of more than120, then this feature is positive.
- Keywords to words ratio – if only less than 10% of strings in the website are keywords, then this feature is positive.

Based on these scores, as shown in Fig 2, if a website is tested to have more than 2 features positive, then it is deemed to be malicious. If even only one of these feature i.e. presence of suspicious URLs or frequency is positive, then this website is found to be malicious. Here, we consider a sample of 100 malicious websites, and based on the proposed scoring mechanism, we observe that if we consider 1 positive feature alone as threshold the false positive rate is high and if 3 or more positive features are considered as threshold the detection rate decreases, hence the performance is poor. Hence the threshold is chosen as shown in Fig 2 which gives a better performance when tested.

```
If(no.of      positive      criteria>=2||presence      of      suspicious
urls=true||frequency=true)
   then
      open the alert page and block the malicious website from the user.
   else
      Open the website directly to the user.
Endif
```

Fig. 2. Scoring Pseudo Code

5   Performance Analysis

5.1   Analysis

Accuracy is the ratio of the number of correctly classified websites to the number of total websites. Correctly classified websites are the benign websites detected as benign websites and malicious websites detected as malicious websites.

$$\text{Accuracy Rate} = \frac{N_{cor}}{N_{total}} = \frac{N_{Ben-Ben} + N_{Mal\text{-}Mal}}{N_{total}}$$

Detection Rate is the ratio of number of malicious websites detected as malicious websites to the number of total malicious websites and ratio of number benign websites detected as benign websites to the number of total benign websites.

$$\text{Detection Rate} = \frac{N_{Ben-Ben}}{N_{Ben}} + \frac{N_{Mal-Mal}}{N_{Mal}}$$

$N_{Mal-Mal}$ = Number of malicious websites detected as malicious websites

$N_{Ben-Ben}$ = Number of benign websites detected as benign Websites

N_{cor} = Number of correctly classified websites

N_{total} = Number of total websites taken for analysis

5.2   Result

The table 1 shows the results of analysis of the websites. A total of 30 websites were taken for analysis and the above results were obtained. The accuracy is improved by 14% and detection rate is improved by around 2%.

Table 1. Comparison of the proposed system with existing system

Performance parameter	Existing System	Proposed System
Accuracy	83%	97%
Detection Rate	96%	98%
False Negative Rate	3.84%	0%
False Positive Rate	12.13%	4.35%

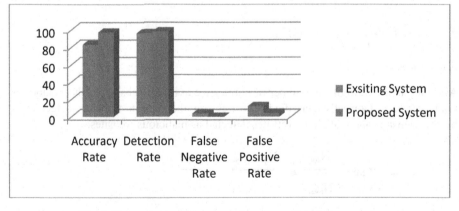

Fig. 3. Comparison of the proposed system with existing system

Fig. 3 shows the graph comparing the accuracy, detection, false negative, false positive rates of the existing system and the proposed system.

6   Conclusion and Future Work

A new hybrid obfuscated java script strength analysis system was developed. The java script from the websites were extracted and analyzed for features such as presence of suspicious URLs, density, frequency, number of redirections, presence of whitespaces, average line length, enigmatic variable names and keywords to words ratio. A score was made based on these features which determined the website to be malicious or benign.

Analysis can be performed deeply to improve the scoring mechanism and processing speed which are considered as a future work. The system can also be extended to other scripts also.

References

1. Malzilla.org Rhino: JavaScript for Java, http://www.mozilla.org/rhino
2. Choi, Y.H., Kim, T.G., Choi, S.J.: Automatic Detection for Javascript Obfuscation Attacks in Web Pages through String Pattern Analysis. International Journal of Security and Its Applications 4(2), 13–26 (2010)
3. Lin, C.-H., Liu, J.-C., Chen, C.-R.: Access Log Generator for Analyzing Malicious Website Browsing Behaviors. In: Fifth International Conference on Information Assurance and Security (2009)
4. Ma, J., Saul, L.K., Savage, S., Voelker, G.M.: Beyond Blacklists: Learning to Detect Malicious Web Sites from Suspicious URLs. In: KDD 2009, Paris, France (2009)
5. Guan, D.J., Chen, C.-M., Luo, J.-S., Hou, Y.-T.: Malicious Web Page Detection Based on Anomaly Semantics. In: Fourth Joint Workshop on Information Security (JWIS 2009), Kaohsiung, Taiwan (2009)
6. Cova, M., Kruegel, C., Vigna, G.: Detection and Analsis of Drive-by-Download Attacks and Malicious JavaScript Code. Management of Computing and Information Systems (2010)
7. Böscher, A., Meier, M., Benzmöller, R.: Throwing a MonkeyWrench into Web Attacks Plans. In: International Fedration for Information Processing, pp.28–39 (2010)
8. Kim, B.-I., Im, C.-T., Jung, H.-C.: Suspicious Malicious Web Site Detection with Strength Analysis of a JavaScript Obfuscation. International Journal of Advanced Science and Technology 26 (2011)

Detection and Mitigation of Web Application Vulnerabilities Based on Security Testing[*]

Taeseung Lee[1], Giyoun Won[2], Seongje Cho[2], Namje Park[3], and Dongho Won[1,**]

[1] College of Information and Communication Engineering, Sungkyunkwan University,
300 Cheoncheon-dong, Jangan-gu, Suwon-si, Gyeonggi-do, 440-746, Korea
tslee@kisa.or.kr, {tslee,dhwon}@security.re.kr
[2] Department of Computer Science & Engineering, Dankook University, Korea
kgyoun4@gmail.com, sjcho@dankook.ac.kr
[3] Department of Computer Education, Teachers College,
Jeju National University, Jeju, Korea
namjepark@jejunu.ac.kr

Abstract. The paper proposes a security testing technique to detect known vulnerabilities of web applications using both static and dynamic analysis. We also present a process to improve the security of web applications by mitigating many of the vulnerabilities revealed in the testing phase, and address a new method for detecting unknown vulnerabilities by applying dynamic black-box testing based on a fuzzing technique. The fuzzing technique includes a structured fuzzing strategy that considers the input data format as well as misuse case generation to enhance the detection rate compared to general fuzzing techniques.

Keywords: web application, security testing, vulnerability, security.

1 Introduction

Software security testing analyzes the security of applications from the viewpoint of attackers and is not really concerned with the functionality of the software. Such testing consists of static testing and dynamic testing. The advantage of code-based static testing is its ability to efficiently analyze software in its entirety, but this testing often has a high false detection ratio, and can hardly be applied to commercial software whose source code is not given. Execution-based dynamic testing can be applied to commercial software and has a low false detection ratio, but analysis time is long and code coverage is limited [1].

---

[*] This research was supported by the KCC(Korea Communications Commission), Korea, under the R&D program supervised by the KCA(Korea Communications Agency) (KCA-2012-12-912-06-003).
[**] Corresponding author.

J.J. Park et al. (Eds.): NPC 2012, LNCS 7513, pp. 138–144, 2012.
© IFIP International Federation for Information Processing 2012

This paper proposes a vulnerability detection and mitigation technique to increase the security of web applications. The vulnerability detection technique used in this paper is a software security test that combines both static and dynamic analysis from the viewpoint of the attacker, not the developer; and the vulnerability mitigation technique used here is the secure coding method. To this end, automated static analysis tools and dynamic analysis tools are applied to the web application to detect known vulnerabilities. Then a "fuzzing" technique for detecting new vulnerabilities is proposed. "Fuzzing" is a technique that generates/mutates input data either randomly or structurally and injects it into the application then monitors the results of application execution to detect vulnerabilities [2]. This paper proposes an abuse case generation and testing strategy for efficient fuzzing as well. Third, to mitigate or remove detected web application vulnerabilities, a process for applying the secure coding technique is shown.

2   Security Testing Integration and Vulnerability Mitigation

2.1   Integration of Static and Dynamic Testing

Static analysis and dynamic analysis are complementary. The advantages of integrating them are as follows:

- Expansion of analysis scope and analysis targets: The code coverage of the code review of static analysis is high, while the code coverage of dynamic analysis is low. On the contrary, source codes are given in case of code review, but dynamic analysis can be applied to commercial software as well.
- Increased accuracy: Static analysis has a high false detection ratio, while dynamic analysis is accurate. So if they are integrated, the accuracy of vulnerability detection can be increased.
- Increased detection ratio: It is very difficult for fuzzing to detect vulnerabilities. It can be supplemented by vulnerability scanning or code analysis that has a high detection ratio.
- Expansion of detection areas: Code review and vulnerability scanning can detect known vulnerabilities. If fuzzing is applied, new unknown vulnerabilities can be detected as well.

2.2   Fuzzing

Vulnerabilities of web applications are caused mostly by wrongly implemented source codes, but sometimes by web application servers. This paper proposes the fuzzing process for finding vulnerabilities of web applications and servers.

2.2.1   Input Format Considerations

To create misuse cases used for fuzzing, the input format of web applications must be analyzed. The request message, which is the input of web applications, can be divided into the "URI of the Request Line," and the "message header and message body."

The first part, the URI, is a standard command system indicating the location of documents and resources on the Internet. Its format is "protocol name://domain name/path name (parameter)." It is used as the input for the browser address window or for the Request Line of the request message. If components like the protocol, domain name and path name are invalid, the input cannot reach the web applications. As attacks are made by changing the input for the URI parameter in general, fuzzing can be done for the values of the parameters.

The second part of the request message is the message header and body. The header includes additional information of the HTTP message, and the body describes the data necessary for the request. Fuzzing can also be attempted by altering the parameter values of the header and body of the request message.

2.2.2   Fuzzing Strategy

There are four fuzzing techniques for discovering vulnerabilities: simple random, simple mutation, structured random and structured mutation. For more information on these techniques, please see a previous study of the authors [3].

- Simple random: This method randomly generates input data without taking the input format into consideration. As fuzzing is done with completely random data without a basic input format, and most web applications process errors unawares, no exception will occur.
- Simple mutation: This method brings a valid URL or request message and changes it as much as desired in units of single bytes. If the field perceiving the path of the URL or request message in web applications is mutated, it will not be perceived as a correct input, thereby lowering efficiency.
- Structured random: This method adds the path of the URL or the header of the request message to the randomly generated data. If a header with a certain level of format is applied to the simple random data, web applications will perceive it as a normal format.
- Structured mutation: This method gets actual input data, grasps the data format structure, and mutates desired parts. For example, the data of the request message is mutated, or the header size may be mutated, etc.

2.2.3   Technique for Generating Abuse Cases for Fuzzing

It is important to generate abuse cases when using the fuzzing technique. This study collected and analyzed information on existing known vulnerabilities to generate abuse cases, and generates abuse cases in consideration of the fuzzing technique (See Figure 1) [4].

The information on disclosed vulnerabilities of JEUS Web Application Server (WAS) for generation of abuse cases was searched. If JEUS vulnerabilities are searched through CVE (Common Vulnerabilities and Exposure), vulnerabilities related to the Alternate Data Stream can be found as shown in Figure 2.

The Alternate Data Stream is a function of the Windows NT File System that prevents users from seeing a file through Windows Explorer by loading this file onto another file. This method is also used by attackers to prevent the attack file from being detected by hiding it in another file. If this is used to make a request like "test.jsp::$DATA," JEUS will perceive it as a general file, not a jsp file, thereby exposing the source [5].

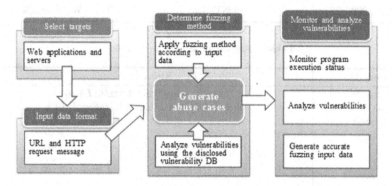

Fig. 1. Abuse case generation

Name	Description
CVE-2008-6528	NTFS TmaxSoft JEUS 5 before Fix 26 allows remote attackers to read the source code for scripts by appending ::$DATA to the URL, which accesses the alternate data stream.

Fig. 2. JEUS vulnerabilities

To collect and analyze information on more vulnerabilities, vulnerabilities regarding the Alternate Data Stream of other products similar to the disclosed vulnerabilities of JEUS were investigated. <Table 1> shows that web servers are the main targets of attacks, and as for types of abuses, most of the input data is divided into filename and data stream.

Table 1. Results of an Alternate Data Stream vulnerability search

CVE-ID	Types of abuses	Targets of attack
CVE-2209-2445	test.jsp::$DATA	Sun ONE Web Server
CVE-2008-6528	test.jsp::$DATA	JEUS
CVE-2006-5715	HTTP GET request::$DATA	EFS Easy Address Book Web Server
CVE-2006-5714	HTTP GET request::$DATA	EFS Easy File Sharing Web Server
CVE-2006-1475	filename:stream syntax	Windows XP Firewall

Other vulnerabilities similar to data stream vulnerabilities that were also analyzed are shown in Table 2. The analysis result showed that they were the buffer overflow of the HTTP request message due to the input value of Post: or Host:. Accordingly, the association between the input value of each field in the HTTP request message and the occurrence of vulnerabilities may be considered, and abuse cases can be generated in consideration of this.

Table 2. Results of searching vulnerabilities related to the HTTP request message

CVE-ID	Types of abuses	Targets of attack
CVE-2008-4678	Long HTTP Host Header	WebSphere
CVE-2008-3257	POST /.jsp	Oracle WebLogic Server

Table 3. Abuse case generation method

Applied to	Abuse case
URL filename URL data stream HTTP request message field	*http://....../bugTrack/**FuzzDATA**.jsp* *http://...../bugTrack/Default.jsp**FuzzDATA***
| | ```
Accept: image/gif, image/jpeg, image/pjpeg, image/pjpeg, app:
Accept-Language: ko
User-Agent: Mozilla/4.0 (compatibl          ws NT 5.:
Accept-Encoding: gzip, deflate     FuzzDATA
Host: localhost:8088
Connection: Keep-Alive
Cookie: JSESSIONID=3aUAmyRb3WJIEjKFjKO1eR          fycgyOUNAB1rLWW!

&catid=AAA&catid=AAA&catid=AAA&catid=AAA&c  id=AAA&catid=AAA
=AAA&catid=AAA&catid=AAA&catid=AAA&catid=AAA&catid=AAA&catid
atid=AAA&catid=AAA&catid=AAA&catid=AAA&catid=AAA&catid=AAA&c
AA&catid=AAA&catid=AAA&catid=AAA&catid=AAA&catid=AAA&catid=A
``` |

As for the method of generating abuse cases, the types of abuses in <Table 1> were analyzed, and the structured mutation method was applied to the filename of the URL and the data stream, which are normal input data, as shown in <Table 3>. At this time, the types of abuses in <Table 2> were analyzed, and test cases were generated for each field of the header and body of a normal HTTP request message.

2.2.4   Monitoring and Vulnerability Analysis

Fuzzing can discover abnormal terminations or unique bugs only, and it is impossible to accurately analyze vulnerabilities with this information alone. Accordingly, the next step is to monitor the input process of the fuzz data, and analyze exceptions to classify vulnerabilities.

As for web applications, the response message of the client can be used to check if there was any exception. As for web servers, process monitoring tools like Process Explorer can be used to look at the status of processes. It is possible to use register information, stack information and exception information at the time when vulnerabilities occurred through debugging using OllyDbg.

2.3   Vulnerability Mitigation

For starters, if there are source codes, a code review tool can be used to detect source code implementation errors, and then vulnerability scanning and fuzzing conducted for the complete application. Vulnerability scanning detects known vulnerabilities based on the inspection rules made through analyzing information on existing vulnerabilities. To detect unknown vulnerabilities, fuzzing can be applied.
```

Mitigation measures should be implemented for detected vulnerabilities. For example, as there is a limit in blocking Cross Site Scripting (XSS) and injection vulnerability of the OWASP TOP 10 (2010) with a web firewall, removing or mitigating it can be a more fundamental solution. To mitigate vulnerabilities detected through security testing, vulnerabilities will be searched in the list of vulnerabilities that can be mitigated through secure coding. Vulnerabilities detected by applying the mitigation technique to the vulnerabilities found in the list can be mitigated.

3   Conclusion

In this paper, static testing and dynamic testing were applied to web applications to detect security vulnerabilities which were then removed. In other words, code review, vulnerability scanning and fuzzing were conducted to detect vulnerabilities, and a process of using secure coding to mitigate vulnerabilities was proposed. Also, this paper proposed a fuzzing technique for discovering new vulnerabilities as well as an abuse case generation technique, which is the key to efficient fuzzing.

References

1. Ernst, M.D.: Static and dynamic analysis: synergy and duality. In: Proc. of WODA 2003 (ICSE Workshop on Dynamic Analysis) (2003)
2. Godefroid, P., Levin, M.Y., Molnar, D.: Automated Whitebox Fuzz Testing. NDSS (2008)
3. Kim, D.J., Cho, S.J.: Fuzzing-based Vulnerability Analysis for Multimedia Players. Journal of KIISE: Computing Practices and Letters 17(2) (2011)
4. Kim, G., Cho, S.: Fuzzing of Web Application Server Using Known Vulnerability Information and Its Verification. Proc. of the KIISE Korea Computer Congress 2011 38(1-B), 181–184 (2011)
5. Security Focus Vulnerability Database: Vulnerability Summary for BID: 32804, Security Focus (2008)
6. Park, N., Kwak, J., Kim, S., Won, D., Kim, H.: WIPI Mobile Platform with Secure Service for Mobile RFID Network Environment. In: Shen, H.T., Li, J., Li, M., Ni, J., Wang, W. (eds.) APWeb Workshops 2006. LNCS, vol. 3842, pp. 741–748. Springer, Heidelberg (2006)
7. Park, N.: Security Scheme for Managing a Large Quantity of Individual Information in RFID Environment. In: Zhu, R., Zhang, Y., Liu, B., Liu, C. (eds.) ICICA 2010. CCIS, vol. 106, pp. 72–79. Springer, Heidelberg (2010)
8. Park, N.: Secure UHF/HF Dual-Band RFID: Strategic Framework Approaches and Application Solutions. In: Jędrzejowicz, P., Nguyen, N.T., Hoang, K. (eds.) ICCCI 2011, Part I. LNCS, vol. 6922, pp. 488–496. Springer, Heidelberg (2011)
9. Park, N.: Implementation of Terminal Middleware Platform for Mobile RFID computing. International Journal of Ad Hoc and Ubiquitous Computing 8(4), 205–219 (2011)
10. Park, N., Kim, Y.: Harmful Adult Multimedia Contents Filtering Method in Mobile RFID Service Environment. In: Pan, J.-S., Chen, S.-M., Nguyen, N.T. (eds.) ICCCI 2010, Part II. LNCS (LNAI), vol. 6422, pp. 193–202. Springer, Heidelberg (2010)

11. Park, N., Song, Y.: AONT Encryption Based Application Data Management in Mobile RFID Environment. In: Pan, J.-S., Chen, S.-M., Nguyen, N.T. (eds.) ICCCI 2010, Part II. LNCS (LNAI), vol. 6422, pp. 142–152. Springer, Heidelberg (2010)
12. Park, N., Song, Y.: Secure RFID Application Data Management Using All-Or-Nothing Transform Encryption. In: Pandurangan, G., Anil Kumar, V.S., Ming, G., Liu, Y., Li, Y. (eds.) WASA 2010. LNCS, vol. 6221, pp. 245–252. Springer, Heidelberg (2010)
13. Park, N.: The Implementation of Open Embedded S/W Platform for Secure Mobile RFID Reader. The Journal of Korea Information and Communications Society 35(5), 785–793 (2010)

Small World Asynchronous Parallel Model
for Genome Assembly

Jintao Meng[1,2,4], Jianrui Yuan[2,3], Jiefeng Cheng[2], Yanjie Wei[2], and Shengzhong Feng[2]

[1] Institute of Computing Technology, CAS, Beijing, 100190, P.R. China
[2] Shenzhen Institutes of Advanced Technology, CAS, Shenzhen, 518055, P.R. China
[3] Central South University, Changsha, 410083, P.R. China
[4] Graduate University of Chinese Academy of Sciences, Beijing, 100049, China
{jt.meng,jr.yuan,jf.cheng,yj.wei,sz.feng}@siat.ac.cn

Abstract. Large de bruijn graph based algorithm is widely used in genome assembly and metagenetic assembly. The scale of this kind of graphs - in some cases billions of vertices and edges - poses challenges to genome assembly problem. In this paper, a one-step bi-directed graph is used to abstract the problem of genome assembly. After that small world asynchronous parallel model (SWAP) is proposed to handle the edge merging operation predefined in the graph. SWAP aims at making use of the locality of computing and communication to explore parallelism for graph algorithm. Based on the above graph abstraction and SWAP model, an assembler is developed, and experiment results shows that a factor of 20 times speedup is achieved when the number of processors scales from 10 to 640 when testing on processing C.elegans data.

Keywords: parallel computing, De Bruijn graph, genome assembly.

1 Introduction

Current sequencing technology (Illumina Solexa [1], Applied Biosystems SoLiD[2], and Helicos Biosciences Heliscope[3]) allows one to read millions of short 35 to 100 nucleotide sequences per hour. Due to experimental errors, gaps, and genomic repeats, a much higher coverage depth of 50-fold to 300-fold is needed for accurate assembly. These factors contribute to a 300-fold to 1000-fold increase in the number of reads, which means there are billions of reads need to be processed, and this significantly complicate the genome assembly problem.

De Bruijn Assembler based on de-bruijn graph strategy [4,5] is well suitable for the current generation high throughput short reads assembly. In De Bruijn graph each vertex represents a length-k substring (k-mer) in a length-L read or its reverse complement. A directed edge connects two vertex u and v, if the k-1 length suffix of u is the same as the k-1 length prefix of v. Each input read is a path in the graph. By connecting such vertex pairs through edges, this approach will output the longest path without any branches as contigs. We denote the assemblers using De Bruijn graph strategy as De Bruijn assembler.

J.J. Park et al. (Eds.): NPC 2012, LNCS 7513, pp. 145–155, 2012.
© IFIP International Federation for Information Processing 2012

The first De Bruijn assembler, EULER assembler [5] was proposed by Pevzner, who had transformed the fragment assembly problem into a variation of the classical Eulerian path problem by dividing reads into k-mers and then constructing k-mers into a path graph. This opens new possibilities for repeat resolution and generating error-free solutions of the large-scale fragment assembly problem. Programs such as Velvet[6], SOAPdenovo[7], and IDBA[8] implicitly use this framework but are slightly different in local details. Velvet manipulates these De Bruijn graphs efficiently to both eliminate errors and resolve repeats by error correction algorithm. SOAPdenovo implement pre-assembler error correction on human genome assembly, after this operation the proportion of error free reads was improved from 64% to 70%, and nearly 60% percent of k-mers was filtered from the graph. IDBA also adopt pre-assembler error filtering technique, which can save nearly 40-80% of memory compared with velvet. The second feature of IDBA is that it iterates from small k-mer to large k-mer to get longer contigs. So the quality of contigs is better than other tools.

The above assemble tools can only run on single machine, the human genome assembly with current sequencing technology needs about 1TB memory and takes weeks or even months on single server. The situation will be even worse for larger genome assembly or meta-genome assembly.

Parallel algorithm for sequencing assembly is an alternative to solve the problem. Parallel assemblers included ABySS[9] and YAGA[10-12], are both based on De Bruijn graph strategy. ABySS distributes k-mers to multi-servers to build a distributed De Bruijn graph, and error removal and vertex merging were implemented over MPI communication messages. YAGA constructs the distributed bi-directed De Bruijn graph by maintaining edge tuples in a community of servers. Unanimous chain compaction problem in YAGA was transformed to undirected list ranking, and then the authors designed a modified sparse ruling set algorithm for undirected lists. The computational complexity of YAGA is given by $O(n/p)$ compute time, $O(n/p)$ communication volume, and $O(log^2 n)$ communication rounds, where n is the number of nucleotides in all reads, p denotes the number of processors .

Efficient and scalable frameworks or libraries for distributed graphs are essential to parallel assembly based on De Bruijn graph. Existing works, such as BSPlib [13-15], CGMgraph [16], PBGL [17,18], Prejel [19], are based on BSP [20] model. The BSP model has advantage on simple computation-communication programming model, whereas the barrel principle exists in the computation-communication phase and the synchronous phase over large clusters limits the scalability of the model. To our knowledge, the scalability these implementations under BSP model has not been evaluated beyond several hundreds of computers [19]. No genome assembly tools have adapted the BSP library, although YAGA has used the BSP idea in its design on parallel list ranking algorithm implicitly. Another parallel programming model, MapReduce [21], has strength in loosely coupled work such as frequency statistics, sorting, indexing, and machine learning etc, and these works can be easily distributed to clusters. However graph algorithm is a tight coupled work and dividing one graph into several meaningful sub-graphs is still a challenging problem.

This paper first demonstrates a one-step bi-directed graph for the problem of genome assembly. Genome can be recovered by merging semi-extended edges to full-extended edges. Then small world asynchronous parallel (SWAP) model is proposed to realize edge merging over a distributed one-step bi-directed graph. Specially, we implement an assembler using the SWAP model. Given the number of processes p, the complexity of this problem is reduced to $O(n/p)$ parallel compute time, $O(n/p)$ communication round, and $O(nlog(n)/p)$ communication volume, here n is total length of input sequences. Simulation shows that Assembler has a factor of 20 times speedup when the number of processors scales from 10 to 640.

The rest of the paper is organized as follows: Section 2 abstracts the De Bruijn graph based genome assembly problem; Section 3 describes the SWAP model for large scale graphs with small world property, then an assembler, as SWAP's first application, is illustrated. Experimental results will be present in section 4. Finally section 5 concludes this paper.

2   Abstraction of De Bruijn Assembly

Let $s \in M^l$ be a string of length L, where $M = \{a,t,c,g\}$. Any substring $\alpha = s[j]s[j+1]...s[j+k-1]$, $0 \le j < L-k+1$ is a k-mer of s. The set of all k-mers of a given string s is written as $\mathbb{Z}(s,k)$, here k must be odd. The reverse complement of a k-mer α, denotes by α', is obtained by reversing α and complementing each base ($\alpha'[i] = \alpha[k-i+1]'$) by the following bijection of $\Sigma, \Sigma : \{a \to t, t \to a, c \to g, g \to c\}$. Note that $\alpha[i] = \alpha[i]''$ and $\alpha = \alpha''$.

A k-molecule $\hat{\alpha}$ is a pair of complementary k-mers $\{\alpha, \alpha'\}$. Let $\ge$ be the partial ordering relation among the string of equal length such that $\alpha \ge \beta$ indicates that the string α is lexicographically larger than β. We designate the lexicographically larger of the two complementary k-mers as the positive k-mer, denoted as α^+, and the lexicographically smaller one as the negative k-mer, denoted as α^-, here $\alpha^+ \ge \alpha^-$. We choose the positive k-mer α^+ as the representative k-mer $\hat{\alpha}$ of the k-molecule. The set of all k-molecules of a given string s is called the k-spectrum of s and is written as $\mathbb{S}(s,k)$. Noted that $\mathbb{S}(s,k) = \mathbb{S}(s',k)$.

The notation $suf(a, l)$ ($pre(a, l)$, respectively) is used to denote the length l suffix (prefix, respectively) of string a. Let the symbol $\circ$ denotes the concatenation operation between two strings, and the number of edges attached to k-molecule $\hat{\alpha}$ is denoted as $degree(\hat{\alpha})$. The number of edges pointing out from k-molecule $\hat{\alpha}$ is denoted as $\deg ree(\hat{\alpha})$.

Definition 1. The vertex set V_s is defined as k-spectrum of s,

$$V_s = \mathbb{S}(s,k) \tag{1}$$

Definition 2. The 1-step bi-directed edge set E_s^1 is defined as follows:

$$E_s^1 = \{e_{\alpha\beta}^1 = (\alpha, \beta, d_\alpha, d_\beta, c_{\alpha\beta}^1) \mid \forall \hat{\alpha}, \hat{\beta} \in \mathbb{S}(s,k), suf(\alpha, k-1) \tag{2}$$
$$= pre(\beta, k-1) \wedge (\alpha \circ \beta[k-1] \in (\mathbb{Z}(s,k+1) \vee \mathbb{Z}(s',k+1)))\}$$

Equations (2) declares that any two overlapped k-molecules can be connected with a 1-step bi-directed edge, if they are continuous in sequence s or its complementary. Here d_α is the direction of k-mer α, if $\alpha = \alpha^+, d_\alpha = '+'$, otherwise $d_\alpha = '-'$. Set $c_{\alpha\beta}^1$ is initialized with one element $\beta[k-1]$, and $suf(\alpha \circ c_{\alpha\beta}^1, k) = \beta$.

Property 1. Given two k-molecules $\hat{\alpha}, \hat{\beta} = \mathbb{S}(s,k)$, there will be four possible connections, and for each type of connection exactly two equivalent 1-step bi-directed edge exist,

1. $e_{\alpha^+\beta^+}^1 = (\alpha^+, \beta^+, +, +, c_{\alpha^+\beta^+}^1), e_{\alpha^-\beta^-}^1 = (\alpha^-, \beta^-, -, -, c_{\alpha^-\beta^-}^1)$,

2. $e_{\alpha^+\beta^-}^1 = (\alpha^+, \beta^-, +, -, c_{\alpha^+\beta^-}^1), e_{\alpha^-\beta^+}^1 = (\alpha^-, \beta^+, -, +, c_{\alpha^-\beta^+}^1)$,

3. $e_{\alpha^-\beta^+}^1 = (\alpha^-, \beta^+, -, +, c_{\alpha^-\beta^+}^1), e_{\alpha^+\beta^-}^1 = (\alpha^+, \beta^-, +, -, c_{\alpha^+\beta^-}^1)$,

4. $e_{\alpha^-\beta^-}^1 = (\alpha^-, \beta^-, -, -, c_{\alpha^-\beta^-}^1), e_{\alpha^+\beta^+}^1 = (\alpha^+, \beta^+, +, +, c_{\alpha^+\beta^+}^1)$.

In each type of connection, the first bi-directed edge and the second one correspond to the same bi-directed edge, but in different form. Within a distributed edge representation situation, the first bi-directed edge in each type will be attached with k-molecule $\hat{\alpha}$, and the second one will be with $\hat{\beta}$. Figure (1) illustrates four possible connections and examples of a 1-step bi-directed edge graph.

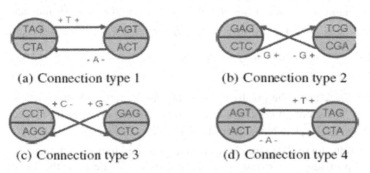

(a) Connection type 1   (b) Connection type 2

(c) Connection type 3   (d) Connection type 4

Fig. 1. The illustration of four possible connections

Definition 3. 1-step bi-directed de bruijn graph of order k for a string s can be:

$$G_k^1(s) = \{V_s, E_s^1\} \tag{3}$$

Definition 4. Given two 1-step bi-directed edge $e_{\alpha\beta}^1 = (\alpha, \beta, d_\alpha, d_\beta, c_{\alpha\beta}^1)$ and $e_{\beta\gamma}^1 = (\beta, \gamma, d_\beta, d_\gamma, c_{\beta\gamma}^1)$, if $e_{\alpha\beta}^1.d_\beta = e_{\beta\gamma}^1.d_\beta$ and $degree(\hat{\beta}) = 2$, we can get

2-step bi-directed edge $e_{\alpha\gamma}{}^2 = (\alpha, \gamma, d_\alpha, d_\gamma, c_{\alpha\gamma}{}^2)$ by merging $e_{\alpha\beta}{}^1$ and $e_{\beta\gamma}{}^1$. Here $c_{\alpha\gamma}{}^2 = c_{\alpha\beta}{}^1 \circ c_{\beta\gamma}{}^1$. Let the symbol $\oplus$ denote **edge merging operation** between two bi-directed edges attached to one k-molecule, then **edge merging operation** can be written as,

$$e_{\alpha\gamma}{}^2 = e_{\alpha\beta}{}^1 \oplus e_{\beta\gamma}{}^1 \tag{4}$$

$$\text{or } e_{\gamma\alpha}{}^2 = e_{\gamma\beta}{}^1 \oplus e_{\beta\alpha}{}^1 \tag{5}$$

According to property 1, equation (4) and equation (5) correspond to one edge merging operation. Then z-step bi-directed edge can be defined as:

$$e_{\alpha\gamma}{}^z = e_{\alpha\beta}{}^x \oplus e_{\beta\gamma}{}^y, iff \exists \beta, e_{\alpha\beta}{}^x.d_\beta = e_{\beta\gamma}{}^y.d_\beta, \deg ree(\widehat{\beta}) = 2, z = x + y \tag{6}$$

Definition 5. Given an n-step bi-directed edge $e_{\alpha\beta}{}^m = (\alpha, \beta, d_\alpha, d_\beta, C_{\alpha\beta}{}^m)$, if k-molecule α or β has only one another bi-directed edge $e_{\gamma\alpha}{}^t = (\gamma, \alpha, d_\gamma, d_\alpha, C_{\gamma\alpha}{}^t)$ or $e_{\beta\gamma}{}^t = (\beta, \gamma, d_\beta, d_\gamma, C_{\beta\gamma}{}^t)$ respectively, then $e_{\alpha\beta}{}^m$ can be extended by $e_{\gamma\alpha}{}^t$ or $e_{\beta\gamma}{}^t$, we regard this edge as semi-extended edge, and the corresponding k-molecule as semi-extended vertex. If $e_{\alpha\beta}{}^m$ cannot be extended by any edge, we call this edge a full-extended edge.

Given a set of string or reads $S = \{s_1, s_2, \ldots, s_h\}$, a one-step bi-directed De Bruijn graph of S with order of k is $G_k^1(S) = \{V_S, E_S^1\} = \{\bigcup_{1 \leq i \leq h} V_{s_i}, \bigcup_{1 \leq i \leq h} E_{s_i}{}^1\}$. The key property of this bi-directed De Bruijn graph $G_k^1(S)$ is that each read can be recovered by traversing the corresponding path in either direction, concatenating (k-1)-molecule prefix of the first node and the edge labels on the path. As all input reads of assembler are derived from chromosomes, each chromosome can now be seen as a long path in this graph. However because of read errors, and repeats in the sequence, we cannot expect to see continuity in sampling, our goal is to recover the genome as a large set of contigs by merging semi-extended edges into full-extended edges.

3   Assembler over SWAP

Vertices in large scale real world graph (such as social network, web link graph, et) always have limited number of neighbors, little computing work, and constant number of edges randomly connected to other vertices, this phenomenon is denoted as small world property. For a given vertex, its small world includes all its edges, neighbors and itself. Then any computing and communication work of a vertex can be done in its small world. As long as the work of a vertex on a graph does not interrupt others, we can run computational work of those vertices in parallel. Here we will present our work on pursuing parallelism in the computation of bi-directed graph for genome assembly.

Inspirited from CSMA/CA in wireless networks [22], Small World Asynchronous Parallel model (SWAP) aims to improve parallelism on processing large scale graph problem with small world property. After having distributed graph over a network of processors, the main schedule of SWAP can be defined as a combination of following three steps:

1. **Lock** operation is applied to each vertex's small world, which includes itself and its neighbors.
2. **Computation** and modification will be performed in each vertex's small world..
3. **Unlock** operation will be triggered after each computation step.

The basic schedule of SWAP is Lock-Computation-Unlock. Because of the locality of computing and communication in the small world, SWAP model utilizes local synchronization and global asynchronization mechanism to maximize underline parallelism for the graph algorithm.

An assembler over SWAP is the first application using SWAP model. In the following paragraphs we will describe its data structure on distributed de brujin graph, strategy on error removal, and the edge merging algorithm, respectively.

3.1   Parallel Constuction of Distributed One-Step Bi-directed De Bruijn Graph

$S = \{s_1, s_2, \ldots, s_m\}$ is m sequences sampled from a genome of length g, the total length of all these sequence is n. we aim to construct a one-step bi-directed De Bruijn graph $G_k^1(S)$ with $O(n)$ vertexes and edges distributed among p processors such that each processor store $O(n/p)$ vertices.

Input sequences can be broken into overlapping k-molecules by sliding a window of length k along the input sequence. Each processor maintains a hash table to store k-molecules, and each k-molecule is represented as a base-4 number of its positive k-mer.   Numerical values $\{0,1,2,3\}$ are assigned to bases $\{A,C,G,T\}$. The location of a given k-molecule can be computed by take the mod of a large prime number and then take the mod of the number of processors. The large prime number is used to evenly distribute k-molecules to all processors.

A single k-molecule can have up to eight edges, and each of them corresponds to a one-base extension, $\{A, C, G, T\}$ in either direction. The adjacent k-molecule can be easily generated by adding the base extension in the edge set to the source k-molecule.

The construction of one-step bidirected De Bruijn graph can be achieved in $O(n/p)$ parallel compute time, $O(1)$ round of all-to-all communication, and $O(n/p)$ parallel communication volume.

3.2   Error Removal

Sequencing errors make the assembly problem more complex. To identify errors, we assume that the errors are random, and they are unlikely to occur twice in the same base. As each base in the genome is sampled on average as many times as the overage number, the erroneous k-molecule will have lower frequency compared to the correct ones. According to this principle, we identify all k-molecules with low frequency as erroneous k-molecules, and delete all of them from our vertex set of the graph. The complexity of this step is $O(n/p)$ parallel compute time.

3.3   Edge Merging

One step bidirected graph generated in the previous section will likely have many long chains, and each corresponds to a sequence that can be unambiguously assembled into a single contig. We will merge these chains into full-extend edges using **Algorithm 1**.

Algorithm 1 Edge Merging Operation Algorithm

Iteration:
1: **Element selection operation**
   For each semi-extended k-molecule $\hat{\alpha}$ in V_i, if $\hat{\alpha}$'s two neighbors $\hat{\beta}$ and $\hat{\gamma}$ are connected by edge $e^u_{\beta\alpha}$ and $e^v_{\alpha\gamma}$, then $e^u_{\beta\alpha}$ and $e^v_{\alpha\gamma}$ can be merged as $e^{u+v}_{\beta\gamma} = e^u_{\beta\alpha} \bigoplus e^v_{\alpha\gamma}$, $e^{u+v}_{\gamma'\beta'} = e^v_{\gamma'\alpha'} \bigoplus e^u_{\alpha'\beta'}$
2: **Lock**
   In order to merging $e^u_{\beta\alpha}$, $e^v_{\alpha\gamma}$, we need to send Lock messages to lock k-molecules $\hat{\alpha}$, and its neighbours $\hat{\beta}$, $\hat{\gamma}$.
3: **Computing**
   $e^u_{\beta\alpha}$, $e^v_{\alpha\gamma}$ and $e^v_{\gamma'\alpha'}$, $e^u_{\alpha'\beta'}$ will be merged into one edge $e^{u+v}_{\beta\gamma}$. That means the original two edges $e^u_{\beta\alpha}$, $e^v_{\alpha\gamma}$ will be deleted, and new edge $e^{u+v}_{\beta\gamma}$, $e^{u+v}_{\gamma\beta'}$ between $\hat{\beta}$ and $\hat{\gamma}$ will be added.
4: **Unlock**
   k-molecule $\hat{\alpha}$ sends unlock messages to unlock k-molecule $\hat{\alpha}$, $\hat{\beta}$ and $\hat{\gamma}$.
Output:
   Return Full-extended edges.

A subset of vertices and their associated edges are stored in processor i, and the set of semi-extended vertices stored in this processor is denoted as V_i. We aim to delete all semi-extended vertices and merge their associated semi-extended edges to form full-extended edges.

As the bi-directed graph $G^1_k(S)$ is distributed over p processors, each processor will store a subset of semi-extended k-molecules V_i and the average number of k-molecules in V_i is $O(n/p)$. Then the expected computational complexity of each processor on edge merging is given by $O(n/p)$ parallel compute time, $O(n/p)$ communication round, and $O(nlog(n)/p)$ communication volume.

4   Experimental Results

The assembler is written in C++ and MPI. The hardware and software architecture supporting this assembler is demonstrated in Fig 2. We use Dawning 5000 as high performance cluster, which has 40 16-core servers with 32GB memory. The distributed file system is lustre. All the components are interconnected with infiniband 20Gbit Router.

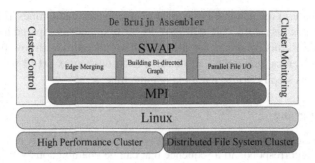

Fig. 2. Hardware and software architecture of the assembler on SWAP

Perl scripts [23] are used to generate the following two theoretical datasets: 50x coverage of Yeast chromosomes containing 17 million reads, and 50x coverage of C.elegans chromosomes containing 141 million reads. The error rate is set to be 1%, and the length of reads ranges from 36bp to 50bp. The primary goal of this experiment is to demonstrate the scalability of SWAP model on handling large-scale graphs using parallel system with distributed memory.

We first test the performance of this assembler on Yeast dataset. The runtime of assembler is displayed in figure 3, and the time is divided into three phases, Parallel File I/O, graph building, and edge merging. The first phase is the time spent on reading dataset from a distributed file system, the second phase is the time used to construct the one-step bi-directed graph over the cluster, and the last phase is the time cost on edge merging operations. The run time is dominated by the third phase, where hundreds of processors are sending messages to lock their neighbors, merging edges, deleting semi-extended nodes and edges, and unlocking their neighbors. Figure 3 shows that this phase has good scalability. The speedup is about 50 when the number of processor scales from 10 to 640 and the overall runtime of assembler on Yeast dataset is reduced by a factor of 30.

The C.elegans dataset is nearly ten times larger than Yeast, and its corresponding data on time usage is demonstrated in figure 4. In this figure, the time used in parallel

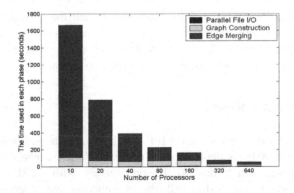

Fig. 3. Time usage analysis in three phase on Yeast dataset

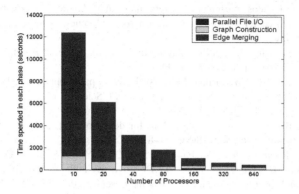

Fig. 4. Time usage analysis in three phase on C.elegans dataset

file I/O is very short compared to the other two phases. The graph construction phase has a decreasing trend on its running time. This phase have a speedup of 35x. This speedup is slightly smaller than that of the yeast dataset. The total speedup of all three phases on C.elegans dataset is about 20.

5   Conclusion

In this paper, we abstracted the problem of genome assembly using De Bruijn strategy. By constructing the one-step bi-directed graph over k-spectrum of input sequences, the unanimous path compaction problem in generic genome assembly was transformed to merge semi-extended edges in our bi-directed graph, and the final contigs are full-extended edges in our method. The proposed SWAP introduced local synchronization and global asynchronization mechanism to maximize the parallelism in the graph algorithm. SWAP model applies the Lock-Computation-Unlock scheme to each vertex's small world. Based on SWAP model, we developed a De Bruijn assembler, and simulation results show that when the number of processors scales from 10 to 640, a factor of 30 and 20 speedup, can be achieved for   assembling Yeast and C.elegans genomes, respectively.

Acknowledgements. This work is supported by NSFC (Grant No. 61103049) and Shenzhen Research Fund (Grant No.JC201005270342A). The author also thanks Bingqiang Wang from BGI, and Prof. Francis Y.L. Chin from HKU for their suggestions on this work.

References

1. Bennet, S.: Solexa ltd. Pharmacogenomics 5(4), 433–438 (2004)
2. Pandey, V., Nutter, R.C., Prediger, E.: Applied Biosystems SOLiDTM System: Ligation-Based Sequencing. In: Next Generation Genome Sequencing: Towards Personalized Medicine. Wiley (2008)

3. Business Wire, Helicos biosciences enters molecular diagnostics collaboration with renowned research center to sequence cancer-associated genes. Genetic Engineering and Biotechnology News (2008)

4. Idury, R.M., Waterman, M.S.: A New Algorithm for DNA Sequence Assembly. Journal of Computational Biology 2(2), 291–306 (1995)

5. Pevzner, P.A., Tang, H., Waterman, M.S.: An Eulerian path approach to DNA fragment assembly. Proceedings of the National Academy of Sciences of the United States of America (PNAS) 98(17), 9748–9753 (2001)

6. Zerbino, D.R., Birney, E.: Velvet: algorithms for de novo short read assembly using De Bruijn graphs. Genome Research 18(5), 821–829 (2008)

7. Li, R., Zhu, H., Ruan, J., Qian, W., Fang, X., Shi, Z., Li, Y., Li, S., Shan, G., Kristiansen, K., Li, S., Yang, H., Wang, J., Wang, J.: De novo assembly of human genomes with massively parallel short read sequencing. Genome Research 20(2), 265–272 (2010)

8. Peng, Y., Leung, H.C.M., Yiu, S.M., Chin, F.Y.L.: IDBA – A Practical Iterative de Bruijn Graph De Novo Assembler. In: Berger, B. (ed.) RECOMB 2010. LNCS, vol. 6044, pp. 426–440. Springer, Heidelberg (2010)

9. Simpson, J.T., Wong, K., Jackman, S.D., Schein, J.E., et al.: ABySS: a parallel assembler for short read sequence data. Genome Research 19(6), 1117–1123 (2009)

10. Jackson, B.G., Aluru, S.: Parallel Construction of Bidirected String Graphs for Genome Assembly. In: Proc. of the 37th International Conference on Parallel Processing (ICPP 2008), pp. 346–353 (September 2008)

11. Jackson, B.G., Schnable, P.S., Aluru, S.: Parallel short sequence assembly of transcriptomes. BMC Bioinformatics 10(S-1) (2009)

12. Jackson, B.G., Regennitter, M., Yang, X., Schnable, P.S., Aluru, S.: Parallel de novo assembly of large genomes from high-throughput short reads. In: Proc. of the 24th International Symposium on Parallel & Distributed Processing (IPDPS 2010), Atlanta (2010)

13. Miller, R.: A Library for Bulk-Synchronous Parallel Programming. In: Proc. British Computer Society Parallel Processing Specialist Group Workshop on General Purpose Parallel Computing (1993)

14. Goudreau, M.W., Lang, K., Rao, S.B., Suel, T., Tsantilas, T.: Portable and Effcient Parallel Computing Using the BSP Model. IEEE Transactions on Computers 48(7), 670–689 (1999)

15. Bonorden, O., Juurlink, B.H.H., von Otte, I., Rieping, I.: The Paderborn University BSP (PUB) Library. Parallel Computing 29(2), 187–207 (2003)

16. Chan, A., Dehne, F.: CGMGRAPH/CGMLIB: Implementing and Testing CGM Graph Algorithms on PC Clusters and Shared Memory Machines. International Journal of High Performance Computing Applications 19(1), 81–97 (2005)

17. Gregor, D., Lumsdaine, A.: The Parallel BGL: A Generic Library for Distributed Graph Computations. In: Proc. of Parallel Object-Oriented Scientific Computing, POOSC (2005)

18. Gregor, D., Lumsdaine, A.: Lifting Sequential Graph Algorithms for Distributed-Memory Parallel Computation. In: Proc. of the 20th Annual ACM SIGPLAN Conference on Object-Oriented Programming, Systems, Languages, and Applications(OOPSLA 2005), pp. 423–437 (2005)

19. Malewicz, G., Austern, M.H., Bik, A.J.C., Dehnert, J.C., Horn, I., Leiser, N., Czajkowski, G.: Pregel: a system for large-scale graph processing. In: SIGMOD 2010 Proceedings of the 2010 International Conference on Management of Data, New York, pp. 135–146 (2010)

20. Valiant, L.G.: A bridging model for parallel computation. Communications of the ACM 33(8) (August 1990)
21. Dean, J., Ghemawat, S.: MapReduce: simplified data processing on large clusters. Communications of the ACM - 50th Anniversary Issue: 1958 - 2008 51(1) (2008)
22. Tanenbaum, A.S.: Computer Networks. Prentice Hall, New Jersey (2003)
23. Zhang, W., Chen, J., Yang, Y., Tang, Y., Shang, J., Shen, B.: A practical comparison of de novo genome assembly software tools for next-generation sequencing technologies. PLoS ONE 6(3) (March 2011)

UKCF: A New Graphics Driver Cross-Platform Translation Framework for Virtual Machines

Haitao Jiang[1], Yun Xu[1], Yin Liao[1], Guojie Jin[2], and Guoliang Chen[1]

[1] School of Computer Science and Technology,
University of Science and Technology of China, Hefei, China
[2] Institute of Computing Technology Chinese Academy of Sciences, Beijing, China
jhtjht1@mail.ustc.edu.cn

Abstract. Virtual machine with dynamic binary translation system is the key technology to solve software compatibility problem. But traditional user space binary translation systems can't translate hardware drivers such as graphics drivers in operating system kernel directly, instead, they need translate the entire operating system. To solve this problem, we designed a new binary translation framework. This framework has a user space translator and a kernel space translator working coordinated and can translate graphics drivers directly. Compared with traditional binary translation systems, this framework can significantly improve the performance of the virtual machine. Based on our experiment, the multimedia performance of virtual machines can been improved about 30%.

Keywords: virtualization, binary translation, operating system, driver, cross-platform.

1   Introduction

At present, with the innovation of computer architecture, Software compatibility issue has become increasingly prominent. Virtual machine (VM) can run binary format software on different architectures without modifying of source code, and thus become an important technology to solve this problem[1][7]. Graphic driver translation is a key problem in software compatibility issue because most multimedia softwares need graphic drivers working with them.

The key technology to run software on different architectures is binary translation which can translate an instruction stream based on one ISA (Instruction System Architecture) into the corresponding instruction stream based on another ISA[2]. There are two kinds of binary translation systems: static binary translation system and dynamic binary translation system. Interactive virtual machines always use dynamic translation system, which translates instructions dynamically during execution of programs.

Traditional virtual machines with dynamic binary translation run upon host operation system (such as VMware[3], QEMU[5][6], virtualbox[4]), these virtual

J.J. Park et al. (Eds.): NPC 2012, LNCS 7513, pp. 156–163, 2012.

machines have some advantages: clean hierarchy, easy to use, easy to migrate from one compute to another. But, they can't translate hardware drivers such as graphic drivers in operating system kernel directly; instead, they need translate the entire operating system[3][4][5]. This kind of translation mode brings about significant additional time consuming. At present, large-scale multimedia software usually need huge amount of computing resources and very high performance requirement, so this kind of low efficiency translation mode usually can't meet the demand.

To solve this problem, we designed a new binary translation framework (User space translator and Kernel space translator Cooperate Framework, UKCF). This framework has two translators, one works in user space, and the other works in operating system kernel space to translate the graphic driver directly. Compared with traditional binary translation systems, UKCF needn't translate the instructions of the entire operating system; instead, it only need translate the instructions of the application software's operating system kernel module (such as a graphic driver). UKCF can significantly improve the performance of the virtual machine because it reduces the number of instructions which need to be translated.

The remainder of this paper is as follows. In section 2, we introduce existing widely used virtual machines, discuss why they can't translate graphic driver directly. In section 3, we introduce the design and structure of UKCF. The experiment results and analysis are drawn in section 4.

2   Existing Technology

VMware is a widely used business virtual machine. It provides an abstraction of x86 PC hardware to run multiple operating systems at the same time. As a mature business system used by millions of users, VMware has high stability and efficiency. But, it has no dynamic binary systems and can't run application softwares on different ISA, such as MIPS. So it can't be used to solve the graphic driver translation problem.

Virtualbox is a powerful x86 virtualization software for enterprise and home use which is freely available as Open Source Software under the terms of the GNU General Public License (GPL). It has comparative performance with VMware. It also has no dynamic binary systems, and is not a solution to graphic driver translation problem.

QEMU is a multihost, multitarget virtual machine. It can run on multiple host ISA, such as X86,   X86-64, MIPS, PowerPC and so on, and it can emulate multiple guest ISA too[6]. So it can be used to resolve software compatibility problem. QEMU runs upon host operating systems and it can only translate the instructions in user space. Graphic drivers are embedded in operating system kernel space, so it can't translate the instructions of graphic drivers directly. Fig. 1 gives a clear view of this problem.

Kernel-based Virtual Machine (KVM)[9], is a subsystem of Linux operating system which leverages virtualization extensions of commodity x86 processors to add a virtual machine monitor capability to Linux. Using KVM, multiple virtual machines can run on Linux operating system. This is an operating system level virtualization system which can run in kernel space. But it has no dynamic binary translation module so can't be used to solve the graphic driver translation problem.

From fig. 1 shows that, to translate graphic drivers directly, we need to translate and execute the instructions of graphic drivers in operating system kernel space (as fig. 2 shows). In view of this point, we designed UKCF, a new binary translation framework with an operating system kernel space translator to solve this problem.

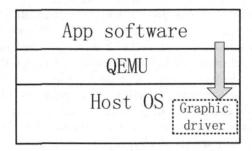

Fig. 1. The locations of QEMU and graphic drivers

Fig. 2. The locations of graphic drivers and kernel translator

3 Design of UKCF

3.1 Workflow of Traditional Graphic Drivers

Graphic drivers are embedded into operating system kernels. When an application software needs to use the graphic driver, it first calls an operating system kernel API and traps into the kernel, and then call the functions of the graphic driver. During the execution of the graphic driver, it may call other operating system kernel functions. Fig. 3 shows the workflow of graphic drivers.

Two calling processes of fig. 3 must be handled by UKCF, one is the calling process from the kernel API to the graphic driver, and the other is the calling process from the graphic driver to the operating system kernel. When a kernel API calls a function of the graphic driver, UKCF needs intercept the calling action and start the translation mechanism to execute the instructions of the graphic driver. When the

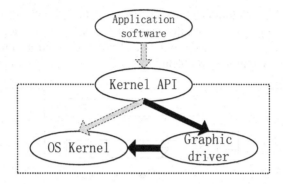

Fig. 3. The workflow of graphic drivers

graphic driver calls a function of the operating system kernel, UKCF needs end the translation mechanism and give the execution control to the operating system kernel. The detail method of this switching will be introduced in next section.

3.2 Workflow of the Graphic Driver in UKCF

In UKCF, instructions of the graphic driver and instructions of the operating system kernel have incompatible ISA, so, traditional kernel module loading method[8] can't embed the graphic driver into the kernel. To embed the graphic driver into the kernel, we treat the graphic driver as a stream of data and use an array in the operating system kernel to store it. When a function of the graphic driver is called, UKCF will get the address of the function, translate and execute the instructions of the function.

During the application software's execution, only a part of the instructions needs to be translated, and the other instructions must be executed directly. To solve this problem, UKCF needs to do two additional works, one is monitoring entrance points and exit points, and the other is saving and loading the translation context.

When the operating system kernel calls a function of the graphic driver, the function's address is an entrance point. We use function shell technology to catch the entrance point. To work with the operating system kernel, the graphic driver must register its functions to the kernel[8]. To catch the functions' calling time, UKCF doesn't allow the graphic driver register its functions to the kernel directly, instead, UKCF register the shelled functions of the graphic driver to the operating system kernel. Fig. 4 shows this technology.

The shell of a function is another function, it is registered to the calling point of the shelled function. So when the kernel calls the shelled function, the shell function is called. When the shell function is called, it sends the address of the shelled function to UKCF, UKCF loads the translation context and starts the translation. The shell function also saves the return address of the shelled function, and when the shelled function ends, UKCF save the translation context and return to this address. This solves the entrance point monitoring problem.

UKCF monitors all the jump instructions' target address, if the target address is not in the content of the graphic driver, this means the target address is a kernel function. UKCF changes the pc to the target address and gives the control to the kernel. This solves the exit point monitoring problem.

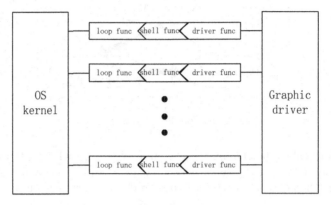

Fig. 4. The shelling technology of UKCF

3.3   Structure of UKCF

Fig. 5 shows the structure of UKCF. It contains six modules: a user space translator, a kernel space translator, a graphic driver shell, a jump monitor, and two CPU simulators. The user space translator is the first starting module of UKCF, it loads the application software and translates it. CPU simulator simulates a guest ISA CPU to execute the instructions. In UKCF, the CPU simulator is the same as traditional virtual machines[5]. The graphic driver shell monitors the entrance point of the graphic driver and gives the entrance address to the kernel space translator. The

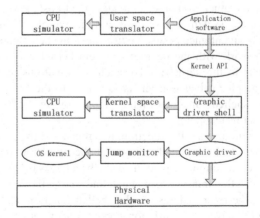

Fig. 5. The structure of UKCF

kernel space translator works together with the jump monitor, when the jump monitor catches a call from the graphic driver to the operating system kernel, the kernel space translator stops translation, saves the translation context, modifies the pc and gives control to the operating system kernel.

4   Experiment and Analysis

Traditional user space binary translation systems can't translate graphic drivers in operating system kernel directly, instead, they need translate the entire operating system. UKCF can translate graphic drivers directly in kernel space, so the number of instructions needing to be translated is reduced. To analyse the performance of UKCF quantitatively, we defined the concept of performance loss ratio (PLR), for a given instruction stream i with execution time t_1 on its original ISA platform, if its execution time on a different ISA platform with a binary translation system is t_2, then the instruction stream PLR_i of the binary translation system is:

$$PLR_i = t2/t1 \tag{1}$$

The PLR of the binary translation system is the average of the PLR_i:

$$PLR = \sum_{i=1}^{n} PLR_i / n \tag{2}$$

In order to facilitate the presentation, we call the traditional translation mode (translating the entire operating system) scheme 1, call the UKCF's translation mode (translating the graphic driver directly) scheme 2. We use NUM_1 to identify the number of instructions needing to be translated by scheme 1, NUM_2 to identify the number of instructions needing to be translated by scheme 2, t to identify the average execution time of one instruction, $TIME_1$ to identify the execution time of scheme 1, $TIME_2$ to identify the execution time of scheme 2, then:

$$TIME_1 = t \times NUM_1 \times PLR \tag{3}$$
$$TIME_2 = t \times NUM_2 \times PLR + t \times (NUM_1 - NUM_2) \tag{4}$$

So the performance improved percentage of UKCF is:

$$P = (TIME_1 - TIME_2) / TIME_1 = \frac{(NUM_1 - NUM_2)(PLR-1)}{NUM_1 \times PLR} \tag{5}$$

Formula 5 shows a fact that, the execution time saved depends on the reduction percentage of the instructions needing to be translated.

We tested the reduction percentage of the instructions needing to be translated, the host ISA platform is the Loongson 3A platform[10][11], which has a MIPS compatible ISA. The host operating system is Linux, the guest ISA is x86 IA-32. The compared binary translation system is QEMU, which has been proven to be a very fast dynamic binary translation virtual machine[6]. We used mplayer[13] and a group of videos as the testing set, the results are shown by fig. 6:

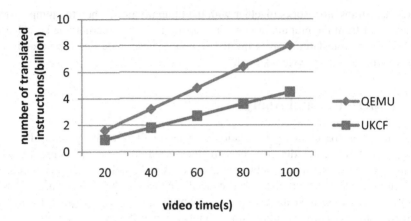

Fig. 6. Experimental results: the numbers of translated instructions of QEMU and UKCF

Fig. 6 shows that, UKCF only needs to translate about 60% instructions. In our experiment environment, the PLR of QEMU is about 6. We can compute the performance improved percentage of UKCF using formula 5, the result is about 33%. We tested the result based on real videos played by mplayer, the experiment results are shown by fig. 7:

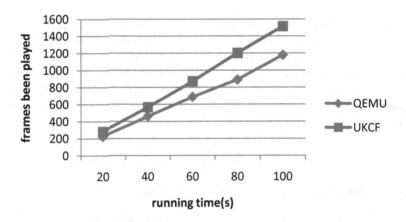

Fig. 7. Experimental results: the performance compare of QEMU and UKCF

From fig. 7 we can see that, during the same time, UKCF can play about 30% more frames than QEMU, this result confirms the analysis based on formula 5.

5   Conclusion

This paper designed a new graphics driver cross-platform translation framework named UKCF for virtual machines. Compared with existing dynamic binary translation system needing translate the entire operating system to run the graphic driver, UKCF can translate and execute the graphic driver in operating system kernel directly. Experiment results improved that UKCF runs faster than existing binary translation systems about 30%.

How to improve the performance is the key problem of binary translation systems. How to make good use of the advantages of kernel space, such as memory allocation privilege and direct hardware access privilege, to further improve the performance of UKCF, is the future research goal.

References

1. Smith, J.E.: A unified view of virtualization. In: Proceedings of the 1st ACM/USENIX international Conference on Virtual Execution Environments (June 2005)
2. Sites, R.L., Chernoff, A., Kirk, M.B., et al.: Binary translation. Communications of the ACM CACM Homepage Archive 36 (1993)
3. http://www.vmware.com
4. http://www.virtualbox.org
5. http://wiki.qemu.org
6. Bellard, F.: Qemu, a fast and portable dynamic translator. In: Proceedings of the USENIX 2005 Annual Technical Conference, pp. 41–46 (2005)
7. Altman, E.R., Kaeli, D., Sheffer, Y.: Welcome to the Opportunities of Binary Translation. IEEE Computer 33 (2000)
8. http://www.linux.org
9. Kivity, A., Kamay, Y., Laor, D., Lublin, U., Liguori, A.: kvm: the Linux virtual machine monitor. In: OLS 2007: The 2007 Ottawa Linux Symposium, pp. 225–230 (July 2007)
10. Hu, W.-W., Wang, J., Gao, X., et al.: Godson-3: A Scalable Multicore RISC Processor with x86 Emulation. IEEE Micro. 29, 17–29 (2009)
11. Hu, W.-W., Wang, J., Gao, X., et al.: Micro-architecture of Godson-3 Multi-Core Processor. In: Proceedings of the 20th Hot Chips (2008)
12. http://www.spec.org
13. http://www.mplayerhq.hu

Fast Parallel Garner Algorithm for Chinese Remainder Theorem

Yongnan Li, Limin Xiao, Aihua Liang, Yao Zheng, and Li Ruan

School of Computer Science and Engineering, Beihang University,
Beijing, 100191, China
{liyongnan1984,liangah,zyshren}@cse.buaa.edu.cn,
{xiaolm,ruanli}@buaa.edu.cn

Abstract. This paper presents a fast parallel garner algorithm for Chinese remainder theorem. The variables in garner algorithm are divided into public parameters that are constants for fixed module and private parameters that represent random input integers. We design the parallel garner algorithm by analyzing the data dependencies of these arithmetic operations for computing public variables and private variables. Time complexities and speedup ratios of the parallel algorithm and the sequential algorithm are calculated to make the quantitative comparison based on our previous work about some fundamental parallel algorithms. The performance evaluation shows high efficiency of the proposed parallel algorithm compared to the sequential one.

Keywords: garner algorithm, Chinese remainder theorem, parallel processing, balanced binary tree.

1 Introduction

The Chinese remainder theorem [1], which is creatively put forward by Sun Tzu, an ancient Chinese military strategist who composed the brilliant military writing "The Art of War", is a constructive algorithm to find the solution of a positive integer divided by some given divisors. In recent years, this theorem has received considerable attention in many modern computer applications, especially in the field of information security. There are many scientists dedicated to simplifying and accelerating the operation of Chinese remainder theorem to reduce the computation complexities in these applications. These works about parallelization of Chinese remainder theorem are mainly focused on fault-tolerant technology [2,3], binary reverse converter [4-6], distributed key distribution scheme [7,8] and fast encryption/decryption of cryptographic algorithm [9-11]. However, there is less deep study on more general parallel algorithms concerning multiple-precision integers for Chinese remainder theorem.

In this paper, we propose a fast parallel garner algorithm concerning basic algebra and modular arithmetic operations of multiple-precision integer to increase the efficiency of Chinese remainder theorem. The general parallel methods including balanced binary tree and prefix computation circuit are chosen to design the proposed parallel algorithm based on analyzing the data dependencies of the mathematical

J.J. Park et al. (Eds.): NPC 2012, LNCS 7513, pp. 164–171, 2012.

operations. This parallel algorithm achieves high speedup and could be applied to many types of applications by improving their efficiencies.

The rest of this paper is organized as follows. Next section introduces the garner algorithm and section 3 presents time complexities of several basic arithmetic algorithms. Section 4 proposes the fast parallel garner algorithm. The performance evaluation is presented in section 5. The last section concludes the whole paper and points out some future works briefly.

2   Garner Algorithm

The following algorithm is the garner algorithm, by means of which can be found the solution of variables divided by the given divisors in Chinese remainder theorem. For more details about Chinese remainder theorem, please refer to [1]. Product M of the dividers m_i represents the module in Chinese remainder theorem while sequences $(v_1, v_2, \ldots, v_t)$ map given remainders in different finite field m_i.

Garner Algorithm

Input: positive integer $M = \prod_{i=1}^{t} m_i > 1$, for $\forall i \neq j, gcd(m_i, m_j) = 1$,
$\qquad v(x) = (v_1, v_2, \ldots, v_t)$.
Output: integer x.
1. for i from 2 to t, repeat:
$\qquad$ 1.1 $C_i \leftarrow 1$.
$\qquad$ 1.2 for j from 1 to $(i-1)$, repeat:
$\qquad\qquad u_j \leftarrow m_j^{-1} mod\ m_i, \quad u_j \leftarrow u_j \bullet C_j mod\ m_i$.
2. $u \leftarrow v_1, \ x \leftarrow v_1$.
3. for i from 2 to t, repeat:
$\qquad u \leftarrow (v_i - x)C_i mod\ m_i, \quad x \leftarrow x + u \bullet \prod_{j=1}^{i-1} m_j$.
4. return (x).

---

3   Time Complexities of Basic Algorithms

As depicted in [12], time complexities of basic multiple-precision algorithms are listed in Table 1. We set the runtime of single-precision multiplication as the basic measurement unit. Time complexities of multiple-precision addition and deduction are $O(1)$.

Table 1. Time complexities of basic algorithms

Operation	Parallel		Sequential
	computation	*communication*	
Multiplication	$O(n^2/s + 2)$	$+O(n^2/s + 2n)$	$O(n^2 + 2n)$
	computation	*communication*	
Barrett reduction	$O(2n^2/s + 8)$	$+O(2n^2/s + 4n)$	$O(n^2 + 4n + 5)$
Inversion-multiplication	*computation* $O(3\lceil \lg X \rceil + 3\lceil \lg P \rceil)$	*communication* $+O(2\lceil \lg X \rceil + 2\lceil \lg P \rceil)$	$O(4\lceil \lg X \rceil + 4\lceil \lg P \rceil)$

The meanings of the variables in Table 1 list as follows:

- n : multiple-precision of operand.
- s : process number for computing multiplication.
- X: numerator of inversion-multiplication.
- P: denominator of inversion-multiplication.

4   Parallel Garner Algorithm

This section discusses the proposed parallel garner algorithm for Chinese remainder theorem. This algorithm contains three public parameters (C_i, $m_j^{-1} \bmod m_i$ and $\prod_{j=1}^{i-1} m_j$) and two private parameters (v_i and x). The public parameters are fixed integers and only need to be computed one time for the same module M, while the private ones are used to compute the random number x divided by the given divisors.

4.1   Parallelization of Inversion

Inversion $m_j^{-1} \bmod m_i$ is one particular case of inversion-multiplication, in which the dividend is integer 1, and the parallel complexity and sequential complexity could be looked up in Table 1. For every m_i in substep 1.2, $(i - 1)i/2$ times inversion operations should be calculated. These inversion operations have no data dependency, which means that all of them could be computed simultaneously. Therefore, the parallel runtime and sequential runtime are

$$T_p = \overbrace{O(3\lceil lg\ X\rceil + 3\lceil lg\ P\rceil)}^{computation} + \overbrace{O(2\lceil lg\ X\rceil + 2\lceil lg\ P\rceil)}^{communication}. \tag{1}$$

$$T_s = (t(t - 1)(t + 1)/6)O(4\lceil lg\ P\rceil). \tag{2}$$

Assume that the word length of the computer we used is k bit, and then total runtime lists as follows

$$T_{p1} = \overbrace{O(6kn_{max})}^{computation} + \overbrace{O(4kn_{max})}^{communication}\ where\ n_{max} = \{n_1, n_2, \ldots, n_{t-1}\}. \tag{3}$$

$$T_{s1} = \sum_{i=2}^{t}(i - 1)O(8kn_i). \tag{4}$$

4.2   Parallelization of Computing C$_i$

In substep 1.2, we could obtain the solution of C$_i$ by computing $\prod_{j=1}^{i-1} u_j \bmod m_i$. Then computing C$_i$ is a classical balanced binary tree problem, which is one of the general parallel questions. Fig.1 shows one example of computing C$_i$ by using balanced binary tree. In every layer of the balanced tree, one multiplication and one reduction must be executed. The depth of the balanced tree is $\lceil lg(i - 1)\rceil$, so the parallel runtime for computing C$_i$ is

$$T_p = \lceil lg(i-1) \rceil \Big(\underbrace{O(3n_i^2/s + 10)}_{computation} + \underbrace{O(3n_i^2/s + 6n_i)}_{communication} \Big). \qquad (5)$$

All of public parameters C_i have no data dependency, so they can be parallel calculated. Then the parallel runtime for computing all C_i is

$$T_{p2} = Max \Big\{ \lceil lg(i-1) \rceil \Big(\underbrace{O(3n_i^2/s + 10)}_{computation} + \underbrace{O(3n_i^2/s + 6n_i)}_{communication} \Big) \Big\}. \qquad (6)$$

In sequential algorithm, $(i-1)$ times multiplications and $(i-1)$ times reductions are needed. The sequential runtime is

$$T_s = O(\textstyle\sum_{j=1}^{i-1}(2n_j^2 + 6n_j + 5)). \qquad (7)$$

Therefore, the sequential runtime for computing all C_i is

$$T_{s2} = O(\textstyle\sum_{i=2}^{t} \sum_{j=1}^{i-1}(2n_j^2 + 6n_j + 5)). \qquad (8)$$

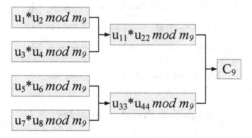

Fig. 1. An example of computing C_i

4.3   Parallelization of Product of Subset Module

M_i is defined as $\prod_{j=1}^{i} m_j$ for clarifying expression of the parallel procedure of this series of multiplication operation. We adopt the high-low prefix computation circuit, a general parallel method to handle suffix computation problem, to calculate this operation and Fig.2 shows one example of computing $\{M_1, M_2, \ldots, M_{t-1}\}$.

As depicted in Fig.2, $\lceil lg(t-1) \rceil$ communication time units and $\lceil lg(t-1) \rceil$ round multiplications are required when computing $\{M_1, M_2, \ldots, M_{t-1}\}$. Along with the execution of the high-low prefix computation circuit, the multiple-precision of the parameters are doubled. Therefore, the parallel runtime for computing $\{M_1, M_2, \ldots, M_{t-1}\}$ is

$$T_{p3} = \textstyle\sum_{i=1}^{\lceil lg(t-1) \rceil} \Big\{ \underbrace{O((in_{max})^2/s + 2)}_{computation} + \underbrace{O((in_{max})^2/s + 2in_{max} + 1)}_{communication} \Big\}. \qquad (9)$$
$$where \ n_{max} = max\{n_1, n_2, \ldots, n_{t-1}\}$$

If the multiple-precisions of two parameters in multiplication are l_1 and l_2 respectively, the sequential time complexity would be $O(l_1 l_2 + l_1 + l_2)$. In sequential algorithm of computing $M_i = M_{i-1} \bullet m_i$, the multiple-precision of M_{i-1} is $\sum_{j=1}^{i-1} n_j$ and the one of m_i is n_i. Therefore, the sequential runtime of computing $M_{i-1} \bullet m_i$ is

$$T_s = O\left((\textstyle\sum_{j=1}^{i-1} n_j)n_i + \textstyle\sum_{j=1}^{i} n_j\right). \tag{10}$$

Then the total sequential runtime for computing $\{M_1, M_2, \ldots, M_{t-1}\}$ is

$$T_{s3} = O\left(\textstyle\sum_{i=2}^{t}\left((\textstyle\sum_{j=1}^{i-1} n_j)n_i + \textstyle\sum_{j=1}^{i} n_j\right)\right). \tag{11}$$

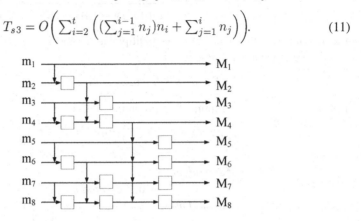

Fig. 2. An example of computing M_{t-1}

4.4   Parallelization of Computing Private Variables

The private variables in garner algorithm concerns only two operations in step 3. Degrading the multiple-precision of x is helpful to simplify the computation of $(v_i - x)C_i \bmod m_i$, so one reduction needs to be executed firstly. If v_i is smaller than $x \bmod m_i$, one multiple-precision addition would be needed and the probability is 0.5. To sum up, this operation consists of 0.5 multiple-precision addition, one multiple-precision deduction, one multiplication and two reductions. Then the parallel runtime and sequential runtime of computing $(v_i - x)C_i \bmod m_i$ are

$$T_p = \overbrace{O(5n_i^2/s + 19.5)}^{computation} + \overbrace{O(5n_i^2/s + 10n_i)}^{communication}. \tag{12}$$

$$T_s = O(3n_i^2 + 10n_i + 11.5). \tag{13}$$

Therefore, the total runtime of this operation for all rounds in this loop are

$$T_{p4} = \textstyle\sum_{i=2}^{t}\left(\overbrace{O(5n_i^2/s + 19.5)}^{computation} + \overbrace{O(5n_i^2/s + 10n_i)}^{communication}\right). \tag{14}$$

$$T_{s4} = \textstyle\sum_{i=2}^{t} O(3n_i^2 + 10n_i + 11.5). \tag{15}$$

In every round of the loop in step 3, the multiple-precision of u and M_{i-1} are n_i and $\sum_{j=1}^{i-1} n_j$ respectively. The operation $(x + u \bullet M_{i-1})$ contains one multiplication and one multiple-precision addition. Therefore, the parallel runtime and sequential runtime of every round are

$$T_p = \overbrace{O\left(n_i\left(\sum_{j=1}^{i-1} n_j\right)/s + 3\right)}^{computation} + \overbrace{O\left(n_i\left(\sum_{j=1}^{i-1} n_j\right)/s + \sum_{j=1}^{i} n_j\right)}^{communication}. \quad (16)$$

$$T_s = O\left(n_i(\sum_{j=1}^{i-1} n_j) + \sum_{j=1}^{i} n_j + 1\right). \quad (17)$$

The total runtime of this operation are

$$T_{p5} = \sum_{i=2}^{t} \overbrace{O\left(n_i\left(\sum_{j=1}^{i-1} n_j\right)/s + 3\right)}^{computation} + \overbrace{O\left(n_i\left(\sum_{j=1}^{i-1} n_j\right)/s + \sum_{j=1}^{i} n_j\right)}^{communication}. \quad (18)$$

$$T_{s5} = \sum_{i=2}^{t} O\left(n_i(\sum_{j=1}^{i-1} n_j) + \sum_{j=1}^{i} n_j + 1\right). \quad (19)$$

5   Performance Discussion

This section evaluates the performance of the parallel garner algorithm and sequential garner algorithm. In order to analyze the performance of this algorithm, we choose the special remainder module in which all given dividers have the same multiple-precision in garner algorithm. In other words, all n_i are equal in this algorithm and we assign value n_a to it. For simplification of performance evaluation, we also assume that the value of s is n_a and that the word length of the computer is 32. Then parallel runtime of all operations could be simplified as the following expressions with only two variables:

$$T_{p1} = \overbrace{O(192n_a)}^{computation} + \overbrace{O(128n_a)}^{communication}. \quad (20)$$

$$T_{p2} = \lceil lg(t-1) \rceil \left(\overbrace{O(3n_a + 10)}^{computation} + \overbrace{O(9n_a)}^{communication} \right). \quad (21)$$

$$T_{p3} = \sum_{i=1}^{\lceil lg(t-1) \rceil} \left(\overbrace{O(i^2 n_a + 2)}^{computation} + \overbrace{O(i^2 n_a + 2in_a + 1)}^{communication} \right). \quad (22)$$

$$T_{p4} = (t-1) \left(\overbrace{O(5n_a + 19.5)}^{computation} + \overbrace{O(15n_a)}^{communication} \right). \quad (23)$$

$$T_{p5} = \overbrace{O((t-1)tn_a/2 + 3(t-1))}^{computation} + \overbrace{O((t^2 - 1)n_a)}^{communication}. \quad (24)$$

And so are the simplifications of the sequential runtime of all operations:

$$T_{s1} = O(128t(t-1)n_a). \quad (25)$$

$$T_{s2} = O(t(t-1)(2n_a^2 + 6n_a + 5)/2). \quad (26)$$

$$T_{s3} = O((t-1)tn_a^2/2 + (t-1)(t+2)n_a/2). \quad (27)$$

$$T_{s4} = O\big((t-1)(3n_a^2 + 10n_a + 11.5)\big). \tag{28}$$

$$T_{s5} = O\big((t-1)tn_a^2 + (t-1)(t+2)n_a/2 + t - 1\big). \tag{29}$$

The speedup is

$$S = (T_{s1} + T_{s2} + T_{s3} + T_{s4} + T_{s5})/(T_{p1} + T_{p2} + T_{p3} + T_{p4} + T_{p5}). \tag{30}$$

We assign the independent parameters (n_a and t) into different values to make the quantitative comparison between the parallel algorithm and the sequential algorithm on condition that the communication time unit is 20 percent of computation time unit. As showed in Fig.3, the proposed method could significantly accelerate the speed of incorporating the parameters in the subset of Chinese remainder theorem. The quantitative performance evaluation demonstrates acceleration up to 9~55 times speedup while the parameter t varies from 5 to 11 and parameter n_a increases from 5 to 40. We also make other assumption of relationship between communication time unit and computation time unit. The same conclusion could be derived by analyzing the performance comparison on different conditions.

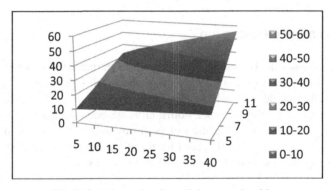

Fig. 3. Speedup ratio of parallel garner algorithm

6   Conclusions

This paper proposes a fast parallel garner algorithm designed for Chinese remainder theorem, which concerns basic algebra and modular arithmetic operations of multiple-precision integer, for rapid calculation of a random number divided by some given divisors. The parallel algorithm is designed through a separate consideration of the constants for given module that is called public variables and random given parameters named as private variables. The public variables only need to be computed one time for the same module. Our previous work about time complexities of some basic operations serves as a simple and convenient criterion for the proposed algorithm. The performance evaluation and the comparison demonstrate that the fast parallel garner algorithm achieves remarkable speedup.

The analysis of this parallel algorithm is only a theoretical one and it just make performance comparison by considering different multiple precision integers of the variables in garner algorithm. We are likely to implement the parallel garner algorithm on GPU to verify the validity and high efficiency of this algorithm. Future research efforts may also focus on the application of this fast parallel garner algorithm in the field of fault-tolerant technology, binary reverse converter, distributed key distribution scheme, fast encryption/decryption, etc.

Acknowledgments. This study is sponsored by the National "Core electronic devices high-end general purpose chips and fundamental software" project under Grant No. 2010ZX01036-001-001, Beijing Natural Science Foundation under Grant No. 4122042, the Hi-tech Research and Development Program of China (863 Program) under Grant No. 2011AA01A205 and the National Natural Science Foundation of China under Grant No. 60973008.

References

1. Wikipedia,
   http://en.wikipedia.org/wiki/Chinese_remainder_theorem
2. Chen, H.: CRT-based high-speed parallel architecture for long BCH encoding. IEEE Transactions on Circuits and Systems II: Express Briefs 56(8), 684–686 (2009)
3. Sundaram, S., Hadjicostis, C.N.: Fault-tolerant convolution via Chinese remainder codes constructed from non-coprime moduli. IEEE Transactions on Signal Processing 56(9), 4244–4254 (2008)
4. Abdelfattah, O., Swidan, A., Zilic, Z.: Direct residue-to-analog conversion scheme based on Chinese remainder theorem. In: 2010 IEEE International Conference on Electronics, Circuits, and Systems, pp. 687–690. IEEE Press, Athens (2010)
5. Hariri, A., Navi, K., Rastegar, R.: A new high dynamic range moduli set with efficient reverse converter. Computers and Mathematics with Applications 55(4), 660–668 (2008)
6. Bi, S., Gross, W.J.: The mixed-radix Chinese remainder theorem and its applications to residue comparison. IEEE Transactions on Computers 57(12), 1624–1632 (2008)
7. Zhou, J., Ou, Y.-h.: Key Tree and Chinese Remainder Theorem Based Group Key Distribution Scheme. In: Hua, A., Chang, S.-L. (eds.) ICA3PP 2009. LNCS, vol. 5574, pp. 254–265. Springer, Heidelberg (2009)
8. Wen, T.Z.: Analyzing euler-fermat theorem based multicast key distribution schemes with Chinese remainder theorem. In: 2008 IFIP International Conference on Network and Parallel Computing, pp. 11–17. IEEE Press, Shanghai (2008)
9. Song, B., Ito, Y., Nakano, K.: CRT-based DSP decryption using montgomery modular multiplication on the FPGA. In: 2011 IEEE International Symposium on Parallel and Distributed Processing Workshops and Phd Forum, pp. 532–541. IEEE Press, Anchorage (2011)
10. Li, Y., Xiao, L., Chen, S., Tian, H., Ruan, L., Yu, B.: Parallel Extended Basic Operations for Conic Curves Cryptography over Ring Zn. In: 9th IEEE International Symposium on Parallel and Distributed Processing with Applications Workshops, pp. 203–209. IEEE Press, Busan (2011)
11. Li, Y., Xiao, L., Qin, G., Li, X., Lei, S.: Comparison of Three Parallel Point-Multiplication Algorithms on Conic Curves. In: Xiang, Y., Cuzzocrea, A., Hobbs, M., Zhou, W. (eds.) ICA3PP 2011, Part II. LNCS, vol. 7017, pp. 43–53. Springer, Heidelberg (2011)
12. Li, Y., Xiao, L., Hu, Y., Liang, A., Tian, L.: Parallel algorithms for cryptosystem on conic curves over finite field Fp. In: 9th International Conference on Grid and Cloud Computing, pp. 163–167. IEEE Press, Nanjing (2010)

dMPI: Facilitating Debugging of MPI Programs via Deterministic Message Passing

Xu Zhou, Kai Lu, Xicheng Lu, Xiaoping Wang, and Baohua Fan

School of Computer, National University of Defense Technology
Changsha, Hunan, China, 410073

Abstract. This paper presents a novel deterministic MPI implementation (dMPI) to facilitate the debugging of MPI programs. Distinct from existing approaches, dMPI ensures inherent determinism without using any external support (e.g., logs), which achieves convenience and performance simultaneously. The basic idea of dMPI is to use deterministic logical time to solve message races and control asynchronous transmissions, thus could eliminate the nondeterministic behaviors of the existing message passing mechanism. To avoid deadlocks introduced by dMPI, we also integrate dMPI with a lightweight deadlock checker to dynamically detect and solve these deadlocks. We have implemented dMPI and evaluated it using NPB benchmarks. The results show that dMPI could guarantee determinism with incurring modest overhead (8% on average).

1 Introduction

Parallel programs written in the Message Passing Interface (MPI) are inherently nondeterminism due to message races and asynchronous transmission of messages. Nondeterminism hampers the debugging of MPI programs and makes cyclic debugging a particularly challenging task [1-5].

Currently, researchers adopt the approaches of *record & replay* to eliminate the nondeterminism of MPI. These approaches record the nondeterministic events of messages, and deterministically replay the MPI programs according to the recorded logs. Since determinism is not an inherent character, these systems have limitations. First, these systems do not guarantee *first-run determinism* (default determinism), i.e., a program can be deterministic only after it is recorded. Moreover, one set of logs only make a certain execution of a program deterministic. When the inputs change, the program will undergo a different execution path, which is still nondeterministic. Second, deploying a record & replay system in the production environment is difficult, as they are constrained by maintaining logs. In some systems, the logging rate could be nearly 1 GB per minute for large-scale programs [3], which presents a great challenge for the deployment of these systems. Third, these approaches are prone to cause large recording overhead, which may be unacceptable for some performance-critical programs. For example, the state-of-the-art hybrid record & replay system reported an average of 27% runtime overhead [3].

J.J. Park et al. (Eds.): NPC 2012, LNCS 7513, pp. 172–179, 2012.

The major problem of record & replay systems is they rely on external support to implement determinism instead of making determinism as a default property. To improve this weakness, we propose a novel *deterministic Message Passing Interface* (dMPI) that guarantees inherent determinism of MPI program without using any external support (e.g., logs). By using dMPI, programs are deterministic even at their first execution, thus any heisenbugs related to the message passing mechanism could be captured and debugged.

The basic design of dMPI is to conduct message transmissions and mappings according to a deterministic logical time. For any asynchronous transmission operation, dMPI forces the transmission of the message to be finished at a specific logical time, so that the process will always perceive the finishing of transmission at deterministic program point. For any promiscuous receiving operation, dMPI orders the incoming messages according to logical time to solve the nondeterminism of message races. The difficulty of this design is each process should see the distributed logical time consistently and timely to make a correct and efficient decision. To overcome this difficulty, we design the *world clock* and use the small-sized control messages to propagate clock values. As we put constraints on the actions of sending and receiving messages, it may cause deadlocks. To make a practical implementation, we design a lightweight deadlock checker to detect and solve these deadlocks. We have implemented dMPI as a compatible MPI library—programs only need to be linked to the dMPI library to gain the deterministic feature.

2   Design and Implementation

2.1   Nondeterminism of MPI

There are two major sources of nondeterminism in MPI: (1) the asynchronous operations and (2) the wildcard receiving operations [1, 2]. The calling of asynchronous operations (e.g., *MPI_Isend*, *MPI_Irecv* and *MPI_Iprobe*, etc.) may have nondeterministic effects on program states depending on the timing of message transmissions. The wildcard receiving operations (e.g., the calling of *MPI_Recv* with the wildcard parameter) may accept an arbitrary message if several messages are racing to arrive.

The design of dMPI is to eliminate these nondeterministic effects while preserving performance maximally. Note that there may be other kinds of non-determinism in MPI programs (e.g., the nondeterminism of thread concurrency inside one process). As these problems could be addressed by existing approaches (e.g., deterministic scheduling [6]), they are not discussed in this paper.

2.2   Design Overview

The basic design principle of dMPI is to use logical time to guide the sending and receiving of messages. Following this principle, we design dMPI as shown in Figure 1. We set a local logical clock in each process to time stamp every concerning event (e.g., the calling of *MPI_Send*). We add two mechanisms to ensure determinism: the *deterministic waiting* mechanism and the d*eterministic mapping* mechanism. The deterministic waiting mechanism sets a Deterministic Transmission Point (DTP) for each asynchronous transmission operation. DTP is a fixed program point in the instruction stream of a process. The positions of DTPs are defined by logical time to ensure determinism. The deterministic waiting mechanism forces the transmission of asynchronous message to be finished exactly at its corresponding DTP (as shown in Figure 1), which hides the nondeterminism of asynchronous message transmission. The deterministic mapping mechanism dominates the message mapping of wildcard receiving operations according to logical timestamp of messages. For each wildcard receiving operation, it should only accept the *earliest message* (message with the smallest logical timestamp among all the unaccepted messages at now and in the future). Therefore, no matter when the message arrives, the wildcard receiving operation will always accept a determinate message (as shown in Figure 1, the wildcard receive always accepts M(2-4)). In this way, the deterministic mapping mechanism resolves the nondeterminism of message races.

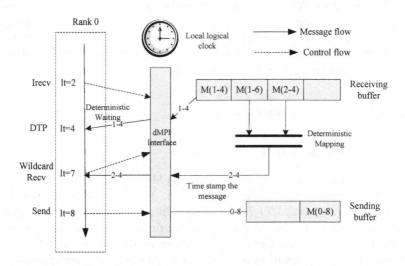

Fig. 1. The design overview of dMPI. "M(1-4)" indicates a message whose source is rank 1 and whose logical time is 4. "lt=2" indicates current logical time is 2.

2.3   Clock and Logical Time

Logical time is used to order messages and label DTPs in dMPI. To maintain a deterministic logical time, we propose the *world clock* which is a hybrid of Lamport clock [12] and vector clock [11]. World clock is a clock vector set in each process to monitor the time of all processes (including the local process). Each slot in the clock vector is corresponding to a process in the process network, describing the time of the process already seen by the local process. Different from vector clock [11], world clock only time stamp messages with a scalar value of the local time (we add an

8-bytes field to all kinds MPI packets). This design simplifies the mechanism of normal vector clock and reduces the communication overhead. In the clock vector, only the local time (the logical time of the local process) is precise, as it is driven by local events (e.g., calling of MPI operations, etc.). The times of other processes may be old values, as they are driven by external messages—when an incoming message is accepted, the timestamp piggybacked in this message will be used to refresh the corresponding clock vector slot if the timestamp is bigger.

To provide a correct and efficient support for message ordering and DTP creation, the driven of local logical time must meet two requirements: (1) local logical time must be precise enough to distinguish DTPs and messages, and (2) the speed of local logical time should reflect the physical time of the process execution well. The first requirement is achieved by interposing MPI APIs (e.g., *MPI_Send*, *MPI_Recv*, etc.). By doing so, no two MPI function calls will happen at the same logical time, thus messages and DTPs are easily distinguished by logical time.

The second requirement is achieved by compile-time instrumentation and the using of empirical statistics. At compile-time, we insert a *time_tick* event for each function call to increase the local logical time. The increased value of this function is derived from the function length (the predicted execution time of the function is based on instruction count). The compile-time instrumentation works well for memory-only codes, but is not suitable for system calls, as their execution time is hard to predict (e.g., the calling of Sleep(1) and Sleep(3) will differ much in execution time). To reflect the execution time well, we set an empirical studying table to describe the logical time values of special operations. For example, the calling of Sleep(1) is corresponding to 1000 logical time unit in our empirical studying.

2.4   Deterministic Waiting

The logical time is used to setup DTPs to confine the finishing points of transmission operations. For any asynchronous transmission operation (e.g., *MPI_Isend*), the corresponding DTP is inserted at the program point that is K logical time units after the function call. Note that the value K should be constant so as to ensure determinism (In the example of Figure 1, $K = 2$).

dMPI enforces that the transmission of message be finished right at its corresponding DTP. When an asynchronous request is posted, dMPI adds a DTP for that request. If the message arrives earlier, dMPI postpones the declaration of its arrival until the process reaches the DTP. Therefore, the issued testing function (e.g., *MPI_Test* or *MPI_Probe*) before the DTP could not perceive the arriving of the message. In the contrary, if a message is late, dMPI forces the process to wait at the DTP until the message arrives. Therefore, the testing function after the DTP will always detect the message. Note that the design of DTP only constrains the declaration of the finishing of message transmissions, while the underlying transmission is not affected. In this way, DTP creates a deterministic environment for the upper applications. To mitigate the performance degradation caused by DTP waiting, we also adopt a buffer-strategy to pre-receive messages that cannot be accepted at once.

2.5   Deterministic Mapping

The deterministic mapping mechanism solves the non-determinism of message race. When a message arrives, dMPI tries to map it with a posted receiving request. If the receiving request is not a wildcard receiving, normal mapping mechanism is used. Otherwise, we check if this message is the earliest by its timestamp. The earliest message is an unaccepted incoming message that has a smaller timestamp than any other unaccepted incoming messages (including the incoming messages that is on the way or have not been sent). We leverage the world clock to determine the earliest messages. The world clock records the logical time of all processes, thus dMPI simply compares the timestamp of the message with the values in the clock vector. If the timestamp is smaller than or equal to all the values in the clock vector, the message is considered to be the earliest and it is accepted directly. Otherwise, the message is not the earliest and the process must wait until the earliest message appears.

Since the world clock only refreshes time values of other processes upon messages arrivals, the time values seen by the local process may be out-of-date, which may cause process being blocked for a long time. To mitigate this problem, we introduce the small-sized *control messages* to exchange information between MPI processes. The typical use of control message is to update clock vectors. We design an *on-demand strategy* to minimize communication overhead. The on-demand strategy works as follows. If the checking of the earliest message fails because of a smaller value in the clock vector, the process will send a *Request* (a control message used to ask for the logical time of another process) to the corresponding process to refresh its time. The process that receives the *Request* will schedule an *Answer* based on the local logical time. As the *Request* contains the expected logical time, the replying process only need to send the *Answer* when its logical time is greater than the expected value.

2.6   Dead Locks

The deterministic mechanisms in dMPI may introduce *deterministic deadlocks* which are caused by the extra wait-for dependencies. We propose a *lightweight deadlock checker* (LW-DC) to detect and solve these deadlocks. Different from existing general deadlock detectors [10], LW-DC is supposed to be a special deadlock detector for deterministic deadlocks only. LW-DC is a hybrid approach of timeout deadlock detector and dependency analysis detector. Since the wildcard receiving will accept a determinate message in dMPI, it greatly simplifies the design. The working procedure of LW-DC is as follows. Each process will start to check for deadlock when it stops for a while (100ms in our implementation). Then LW-DC will collect the wait-for dependency using control messages. Once LW-DC detects a cyclic dependency, it simply relaxes the deterministic mechanism to break the deadlock. Due to space limitation, we do not discuss LW-DC in detail in this paper.

3   Evaluation

3.1   Methodology

We implemented dMPI based on MPICH2 (version 1.4) [7]. Our evaluation hardware is consisted of 2 AMD servers connected with a 1GB/s switch. Each server has a 2.2GHz CPU with 4 cores, 1GB memory and a 1GB/s Ethernet card, running Fedora 12 with Linux kernel version 2.6.31.5. We used the NPB benchmarks [8] to test dMPI. Each benchmark is configured with 8 processes which are equally distributed among the two servers.

We verified the determinism of dMPI by (1) examining the outputs of programs, (2) checking the return value for each testing function, and (3) checking the accepted message for each wildcard receiving. We ran each benchmark 100 times, and recorded the above information. We compared the results of different runs for each benchmark. Note that dMPI does not address the nondeterministic events caused by system calls (e.g., *gettimeofday*). Therefore, when comparing the normal program outputs, we ignored the time-related data.

To evaluate the performance, we setup a baseline execution (the performance of the standard MPICH2). We compared the performance of dMPI with the baseline execution. For each benchmark, we ran it 10 times to collect the mean value.

3.2   Execution Time

The performance of dMPI is shown in Figure 2. We divide the execution time of each benchmark into three parts: (1) the *application time* which is the execution time of normal program codes; (2) the *instrument overhead*, which is the execution time of the instrumented codes; (3) the *determinism overhead*, which is caused by the deterministic mechanisms. Overall, the average overhead of dMPI is small (below 8%).

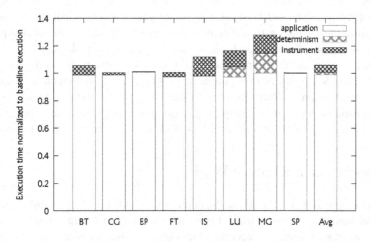

Fig. 2. The execution time of dMPI compared with that of the standard MPI library

Table 1. The Detailed Information of Programs Running with dMPI

benchmark	dMPI profiling			Normal messages		Control messages		
	DTP	wildcard	deadlock	count	size (Byte)	count	size (byte)	count rate (%)
bt	2418	0	0	2436	283918712	0	0	0
cg	1680	0	0	1683	46658367	0	0	0
ep	0	0	0	9	780	0	0	0
ft	0	0	0	40	201330833	0	0	0
is	0.75	0	0	128	92358592	0	0	0
lu	510	510	13.25	31661	122780595	789	3194	2.5
mg	714	714	9	867	32057558	622	2490	71.7
sp	4818	0	0	4836	493724232	0	0	0
avg	1267.5	153	2.78	2436	283918712	176.4	710.5	29

In Table 1, we provide the detailed profiling data of programs running under dMPI. As seen from this table, the impact of our deterministic message passing mechanism is trivial: For each program on average, dMPI additionally handles about 1200 DTPs (Column 2), 150 wildcard receiving operations (Colum 3), 2 or 3 deadlocks (Column 5). The introduced control messages are also trivial compared with the normal messages in size and number (Column 5-9).

4   Related Work

Record & replay is a typical method to eliminate the nondeterminism of MPI [1-5]. Some of them record the nondeterministic message order in the recording phase, and force the messages to follow the order of the recorded logs in the replay phase [1]. Some others record the contents of messages instead of their orders [4]. A hybrid method—MPIWiz [3] record both message order and contents. Distinct from these works, we provide a solution for inherent determinism without any external supports (e.g., logs), which is efficient in performance and is convenient to deploy.

Inherent determinism has been introduced in the shared-memory multi-processing field to facilitate debugging of multi-threaded programs [6, 9]. Although we share the same concept of inherent determinism with these works, our work is to address the nondeterministic problem of the message passing mechanism in the distributed environment, which is different from the problem of the shared-memory environment.

5   Conclusion and Future Work

This paper designs dMPI to facilitate the debugging of MPI programs. dMPI ensures inherent determinism by using logical time to control the finishing points of asynchronous transmissions and the accepted messages of wildcard receiving operations. We implemented and evaluated dMPI to demonstrate its practicality. The evaluation results show that the overhead of dMPI is practical and low (8%). In the future work, we will use buffering and speculation mechanism to further mitigate the performance impact of dMPI.

Acknowledgment. This work is partially supported by National High-tech R&D Program of China (863 Program) under Grants 2012AA01A301, and by National Science Foundation (NSF) China 61103082, 61003075, 61170261 and 61103193.

References

1. de Kergommeaux, J.C., Ronsse, M., De Bosschere, K.: *MPL**: Efficient Record/Replay of Nondeterministic Features of Message Passing Libraries. In: Margalef, T., Dongarra, J., Luque, E. (eds.) PVM/MPI 1999. LNCS, vol. 1697, pp. 141–148. Springer, Heidelberg (1999)
2. Clémençon, C., Fritscher, J., Meehan, M., Rhl, R.: An Implementation of Race Detection and Deterministic Replay with MPI. In: Haridi, S., Ali, K., Magnusson, P. (eds.) Euro-Par 1995. LNCS, vol. 966, pp. 155–166. Springer, Heidelberg (1995)
3. Xue, R., Liu, X., Wu, M., Guo, Z., Chen, W., Zheng, W., Zhang, Z., Voelker, G.: MPIWiz: Subgroup reproducible replay of MPI applications. In: PPoPP, pp. 251–260 (2009)
4. Maruyama, M., Tsumura, T., Nakashima, H.: Parallel program debugging based on data-replay. In: PDCS, pp. 151–156 (2005)
5. Kranzlmüller, D., Schaubschläger, C., Volkert, J.: An Integrated Record&Replay Mechanism for Nondeterministic Message Passing Programs. In: Cotronis, Y., Dongarra, J. (eds.) PVM/MPI 2001. LNCS, vol. 2131, pp. 192–200. Springer, Heidelberg (2001)
6. Joseph, D., Brandon, L., Luis, C., Mark, O.: DMP: deterministic shared memory multiprocessing. In: Proceeding of the 14th International Conference on Architectural Support for Programming Languages and Operating Systems. ACM, Washington, DC (2009)
7. MPICH2, http://www.mcs.anl.gov/research/projects/mpich2/
8. Bailey, D., Harris, T., Saphir, W., van der Wijngaart, R., Woo, A., Yarrow, M.: The NAS Parallel Benchmarks 2.0. Technical Report NAS-95-020, NASA Ames Research Center, Mail Stop T 27 A-1, Moffett Field, CA 94035- 1000, USA (December 05, 1995)
9. Bocchino Jr, R.L., Adve, V.S., Adve, S.V., Snir, M.: Parallel programming must be deterministic by default. In: Proceedings of the First USENIX Conference on Hot Topics in Parallelism, p. 4 (2009)
10. Luecke, G.R., Zou, Y., Coyle, J., Hoekstra, J., Kraeva, M.: Deadlocks detection in MPI programs. Concurrency and Computation: Practice and Experience 14, 911–932 (2002)
11. Fidge, C.J.: Partial orders for parallel debugging. In: ACM SIGPLAN/SIGOPS Workshop on Parallel and Distributed Debugging, vol. 24(1), pp. 183–194 (January 1989)
12. Lamport, L.: Time, clocks, and the ordering of events in a distributed system. Communications of the ACM 21, 558–565 (1978)

On Dynamic Communication Performance of a Hierarchical 3D-Mesh Network

M.M. Hafizur Rahman[1], Asadullah Shah[1], and Yasushi Inoguchi[2]

[1] Dept. of Computer Science, KICT, IIUM, Gombak-53100, Malaysia
[2] Center for Information Science, JAIST, Ishikawa 923-1292, Japan
{hafizur,asadullah}@iium.edu.my, inoguchi@jaist.ac.jp

Abstract. A Hierarchical 3D-Mesh (H3DM) Network is a 2D-mesh network of multiple basic modules (BMs), in which the basic modules are 3D-torus networks that are hierarchically interconnected for higher-level networks. In this paper, we evaluate the dynamic communication performance of a Hierarchical 3D-Mesh (H3DM) network using a deadlock-free routing algorithm with minimum number of virtual channels under the uniform and non-uniform traffic patterns; and compare it with other networks to show the superiority of the H3DM network over other networks. We have also evaluated the dynamic communication performance of the mesh and torus networks. It is shown that H3DM network yields low average transfer time than that of mesh and torus networks. The trade-off between throughput and latency of these networks shown that H3DM network provide better dynamic communication performance than that of mesh and torus networks before saturation.

Keywords: Interconnection network, H3DM network, Deadlock-free routing algorithm, Traffic patterns, Dynamic communication performance.

1 Introduction

High-performance computing is necessary in solving the grand challenge problems in many areas such as development of new materials and sources of energy, development of new medicines and improved health care, strategies for disaster prevention and mitigation, weather forecasting, and for scientific research including the origins of matter and the universe. This makes the current supercomputer changes into massively parallel computer (MPC) systems with thousands of node (Kei, Cray XT5-HE), that satisfy the insatiable demand of computing power. In near future, we will need computer systems capable of computing at the petaflops or exaflops level. To achieve this level of performance, we need MPC with tens of thousands or millions of nodes. Interconnection networks play a crucial role in the performance of MPC systems [1]. Many recent experimental and commercial parallel computers use direct networks for low latency and high bandwidth of interprocessor communication. For future MPC with millions of nodes, the large diameter of conventional topologies is intolerable. Hence, the hierarchical interconnection network (HIN) provides an alternative efficient way in which several network topologies can be integrated [2] together to construct the future MPC [2]. A variety of hypercube based HINs found in the literature, however, its huge

J.J. Park et al. (Eds.): NPC 2012, LNCS 7513, pp. 180–187, 2012.

number of physical links make it difficult to implement. To alleviate this problem, k-ary n-cube based HIN [3, 4] is a plausible alternative way.

A Hierarchical 3D-Mesh (H3DM) Network [5] is a 2D-mesh network $(n \times n)$ of multiple basic modules (BMs), in which the BMs are 3D-torus networks $(m \times m \times m)$ that are hierarchically interconnected for higher-level networks. Wormhole routing [6] has become the dominant switching technique used in contemporary multicomputers. This is because it has low buffering requirements and it makes latency independent of the message distance. Deterministic, dimension-order routing is popular in MPC because it has minimal hardware requirements and allows the design of simple and fast routers. Wormhole routing relies on a blocking mechanism for flow control, deadlock can occur because of cyclic dependencies over network resources during message routing. Virtual channels (VCs) [7] are used to solve the problem of deadlock in wormhole-routed networks. Since the hardware cost increases as the number of VCs increases, the unconstrained use of VCs is not cost-effective in MPC systems. The static network performance of the H3DM network is evaluated and presented in [5]. And in our another study, we have presented a deadlock-free routing algorithm for the H3DM network using 2 VCs [8]. The main objective of this paper is to study the dynamic communication performance of the H3DM network.

The remainder of this paper is organized as follows. In Section 2, we briefly describe the basic structure of the H3DM network. In Section 3, we recall the deadlock-free dimension order routing for the H3DM network. Section 4 discusses the evaluation of dynamic communication performance. Finally, in Section 5, we conclude the results presented in this paper.

2   Interconnection of the H3DM Network

The *H3DM* network [5] is a HIN consisting of multiple BM that are hierarchically interconnected for higher level networks. The BM of the H3DM network is a 3D-torus network of size $(m \times m \times m)$, where m is a positive integer. m can be any value, however the preferable one is $m = 2^p$, where p is a positive integer. The BM of a $(4 \times 4 \times 4)$ torus, as depicted in Figure 1(a), has some free ports at the contours of the *xy*-plane. A $(m \times m \times m)$ BM has $(4 \times m^2)$ free ports for higher level interconnection. All free ports, typically one or two, of the exterior Processing Elements (PEs) are used for inter-BM connections to form higher level networks. Successively higher level networks are built by recursively interconnecting lower level subnetworks in a 2D-mesh of size $(n \times n)$, where n is also a positive integer. As portrayed in Figure 1(b), a Level-2 H3DM network can be formed by interconnecting 16 BMs as a (4×4) 2D-mesh network. Similarly, a Level-*3* network can be formed by interconnecting n^2 Level-*2* subnetworks, and so on. Each BM is connected to its logically adjacent BMs.

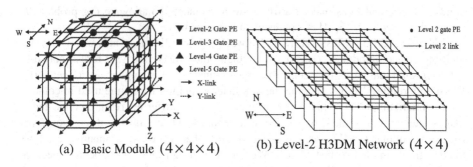

(a) Basic Module $(4\times4\times4)$ (b) Level-2 H3DM Network (4×4)

Fig. 1. Interconnection of a H3DM Network

For each higher level interconnection of H3DM network, a BM must use $4m\left(2^q\right)$ of its free links: $2m\left(2^q\right)$ free links for y-direction and $2m\left(2^q\right)$ free links for x-direction interconnections. Here, $q \in \{0,1,...,p\}$, is the inter-level connectivity, where $p = \left\lfloor \log_2^m \right\rfloor$. $q = 0$ leads to minimal inter-level connectivity, while $q = p$ leads to maximum inter-level connectivity. It is depicted in Figure 1(a) that the $(4\times4\times4)$ BM has $(4\times4^2 = 64)$ free ports. With $q = 0$, $(4\times4\times2^0 = 16)$ free links are used for each level interconnection, 8 for y-direction and 8 for x-direction interconnections as portrayed in Figure 1(b). The highest level network which can be built from a $(m\times m\times m)$ BM is $L_{max} = 2^{p-q} +1$. With q = 0, Level-5 is the highest possible level to which a $(4\times4\times4)$ BM can be interconnected. The total number of nodes in a network having $(m\times m\times m)$ BMs and $(n\times n)$ higher level is $N = [m^3 \times n^{2(L_{max}-1)}]$. Thus, the maximum number of nodes which can be interconnected by the H3DM network is $N = [m^3 \times n^{2(2^{p-q})}]$. If m = 4, n = 4, and q = 0, then $N = 4^3 \times 4^8 = 4194304$, i.e., about 4.2 million.

The address of a PE at Level-L H3DM network is represented by Eq. 1.

$$A^L = \begin{cases} \left(a_z\right)\left(a_y\right)\left(a_x\right) & \text{if } L=1 \\ \left(a_y{}^L\right)\left(a_x{}^L\right) & \text{if } L \geq 2 \end{cases} \tag{1}$$

More generally, in a Level-L H3DM, the node address is represented by:

$$A = A^L A^{L-1} A^{L-2} .... A^3 A^2 A^1 = a_\alpha a_{\alpha-1} a_{\alpha-2} a_{\alpha-3} .... a_2 a_1 a_0$$
$$= \left(a_{2L} a_{2L-1}\right)\left(a_{2L-2} a_{2L-3}\right)........\left(a_4 a_3\right)\left(a_2 a_1 a_0\right) \tag{2}$$

Here, the total number of digits is $\alpha = 2L+1$, where L is the level number. In particular, i^{th} group $\left(a_{2i}\ a_{2i-1}\right)$ indicates the location of a Level-$(i-1)$ subnetwork within the ith group to which the node belongs; $2 \leq i \leq L$.

3   Routing Algorithm for H3DM Network

3.1   Routing Algorithm

Routing of messages in the H3DM network is first done at the highest level network; then, after the packet reaches its highest level sub-destination, routing continues within the subnetwork to the next lower level sub-destination. This process is repeated until the packet arrives at its final destination [10]. For messages routing using dimension-order routing in H3DM network, first find the nonzero offset in the most significant position by subtracting the current address from the destination. Then make a step towards nullifying the offset by sending the packet in descending order. When the offset along a dimension is zero, then the routing message is switched over to the next dimension. Routing dimension is strictly followed in the dimension order routing. Routing at the higher level H3DM is performed first in the y-direction and then in the x-direction. In a BM, the routing order is z-direction, y-direction, and x-direction, respectively.

Routing H3DM (s,d);

source node address: $s_\alpha, s_{\alpha-1}, \dots s_2, s_1, s_0$

destination node address: $d_\alpha, d_{\alpha-1}, \dots d_1, d_0$

tag: $t_\alpha, t_{\alpha-1}, t_{\alpha-2}, \dots t_2, t_1, t_0$

for i = n : 3
   if (i /2 = 0 and t_i > 0), routedir = North, endif;
   if (i/2 = 0 and t_i < 0), routedir = South, endif;
   if (i%2 = 1 and t_i > 0), routedir = East, endif;
   if (i%2 = 1 and t_i < 0), routedir = West, endif;
   while (t_i ≠ 0) do
     $Nz = outlet_z(s, d, L, routedir)$
     $Ny = outlet_y(s, d, L, routedir)$
     $Nx = outlet_x(s, d, L, routedir)$
     BM_Routing (Nz, Ny, Nx)
     if routedir = North or East
         move packet to next BM;
     if routedir = South or West
         move packet to previous BM;
     $t_i = t_i - 1$;
   endwhile
endfor
   BM_Routing (t_z, t_y, t_x)
end

BM_Routing ();
BM_tag $t_2, t_1, t_0 = (r_2, r_1, r_0) - (d_2, d_1, d_0)$
for i = 2 : 0
   if(t_i > 0 and t_i ≤ m/2) or (t_i < 0 and t_i = 1 - m)
     movedir = positive; endif;
   if(t_i > 0 and t_i = m - 1) or (t_i < 0 and t_i ≥ - m/2)
     movedir = negative; endif;
   if(movedir = positive and t_i > 0), dist = t_i; endif;
   if(movedir = positive and t_i < 0), dist = m+t_i; endif;
   if(movedir = negative and t_i < 0), dist = t_i; endif;
   if(movedir = negative and t_i > 0), dist = t_i-m; endif;
endfor
while (t_2 ≠ 0 or $dist_2$ ≠ 0) do
   if movedir = positive, move packet to +z node
     $dist_2 = dist_2 - 1$; endif;
   if movedir = negative, move packet to -z node
     $dist_2 = dist_2 + 1$; endif; endwhile
while (t_1 ≠ 0 or $dist_1$ ≠ 0) do
   if movedir = positive, move packet to +y node
     $dist_1 = dist_1 - 1$; endif;
   if movedir = negative, move packet to -y node
     $dist_1 = dist_1 + 1$; endif; endwhile
while (t_0 ≠ 0 or $dist_0$ ≠ 0) do
   if movedir = positive, move packet to +x node
     $dist_0 = dist_0 - 1$; endif;
   if movedir = negative, move packet to -x node
     $dist_0 = dist_0 + 1$; endif; endwhile
end

Fig. 2. Dimension-Order Routing Algorithm of the H3DM Network

Routing in the H3DM network is strictly defined by the source node address and the destination node address. Let a source node address be $s_\alpha, s_{\alpha-1}, s_{\alpha-2}, \dots,$ $\dots s_2, s_1, s_0$, a destination node address be $d_\alpha, d_{\alpha-1}, d_{\alpha-2} \dots d_2, d_1, d_0$, and a routing tag be $t_\alpha, t_{\alpha-1}, t_{\alpha-2} \ldots \ldots t_2, t_1, t_0$, where $t_i = d_i - s_i$. The source node address of H3DM is expressed as $s = (s_{2L}, s_{2L-1}), (s_{2L-2}, s_{2L-3}) \ldots \ldots (s_2, s_1, s_0)$. Similarly, the destination address is expressed as $d = (d_{2L}, d_{2L-1}), (d_{2L-2}, d_{2L-3})$ $\ldots \ldots (d_2, d_1, d_0)$. Figure 2 shows the routing algorithm for the H3DM network.

3.2   Deadlock-Free Routing

A deadlock-free routing algorithm can be constructed for a wormhole routed interconnection network by introducing VCs [7]. Since the hardware cost increases as the number of VCs increases, the unconstrained use of VCs is prohibited for cost-effective parallel computers. A deadlock-free routing algorithm with a minimum number of VCs is preferred. In our previous study [8], we proved that the dimension-order routing algorithm on H3DM network is deadlock-free using 2 VCs and 2 is the minimum number of VCs for the H3DM network.

Theorem 1. *A H3DM network is deadlock-free with 2 virtual channels [8].*

4   Dynamic Communication Performance

The overall performance of a MPC system is affected by the performance of the interconnection network as well as by the performance of the node. Low performance of the underlying interconnection network will severely limit the speed of the entire MPC system. Therefore, the success of a MPC is highly dependent on the efficiency of their interconnection networks.

4.1   Performance Metrics

The dynamic communication performance of a MPC system is characterized by message latency and network throughput. Message latency refers to the time elapsed from the instant when the first flit (header) is injected into the network from the source to the instant when the last data flit of the message is received at the destination. Network throughput refers to the maximum amount of information delivered per unit of time through the network. For the network to have good performance, low latency and high throughput must be achieved.

4.2   Simulation Environment

We have developed a wormhole routing simulator using C language to evaluate the dynamic communication performance. We use a dimension-order routing and uniform and bit-flip traffic patterns. In the evaluation of performance, flocks of messages are sent through the network to compete for the output channels. Packets are transmitted by the request-probability r during T clock cycles and the number of flits which reached at destination node and its transfer time is recorded. Then the average transfer time and throughput are calculated and plotted as average transfer time in the horizontal axis and throughput in the vertical axis. The process of performance evaluation is carried out with changing the request-probability r. We have considered that the message generation rate is constant and the same for all nodes. Flits are transmitted at 20,000 cycles i.e., $T = 20000$. In each clock cycle, one flit is transferred from the input buffer to the output buffer, or vice versa if the corresponding buffer in the next node is empty. Thus, transferring data between two nodes takes 2 clock cycles. The message length is considered as short (16 flits), medium (64 flits), and long (256 flits); and the buffer length of each channel is 2 flits. For fair comparison of dynamic communication performance, two VCs per physical link are simulated, and the VCs are arbitrated by a round robin algorithm.

4.3   Dynamic Communication Performance Evaluation

We have evaluated the dynamic communication performance of several networks using deadlock-free dimension order routing with minimum number of virtual channels under the uniform and bit-flip traffic patterns. For fair comparison we should have equal number of nodes for all the considered network. If $m = 4$, $n = 4$, and $L = 2$, then the total number of nodes in the H3DM network is 1024. 32 × 32 mesh and 32 × 32 torus networks also have 1024 nodes.

Uniform Traffic Pattern
The most frequently used, simplest, and most elegant traffic pattern is the uniform traffic pattern where the source and the destination are randomly selected, i.e., every node sends messages to every other node with equal probability [9]. Figure 3 (a), (b), and (c) show the average transfer time as a function of network throughput under uniform traffic pattern for different networks. The average transfer time at no load is called zero load latency. As shown in Figure 3, for all message length, the zero load latency of the H3DM network is lower than that of the mesh and torus networks.

The throughput and latency of a network is increased with the increase of load. Because the links and VCs become congested and the message competes to each other for the network resources, links and channels. With the injection of more and more messages and in course of time, the network becomes saturated. After saturation, the message latency is increasing dramatically while the network throughput will not increase anymore. Up to saturation the trade-off between throughput and latency of the H3DM network is better than that of mesh and torus networks as illustrated in Fig. 3. The limited connectivity of higher level links of 2D-mesh network becomes congested with the increase of packet in the network. On top of this 2D-mesh network saturates earlier due to lack of symmetry. However, the maximum throughput of the mesh and torus network is higher than that of H3DM network as shown in Fig. 3. The number of channels required deadlock-free routing for mesh network is one; however, we used two VCs for fair comparison. With this additional channel the congestion of the mesh network is relief and the throughput is increased. It is portrayed in Figure 3(b) and (c) that the relative difference of maximum throughput between H3DM and mesh network is diminishing with the increase of message length. In torus network all the end-to-end nodes are connected by long length wrap-around links. These links provides a by-pass path for messages which in turns increase the throughput.

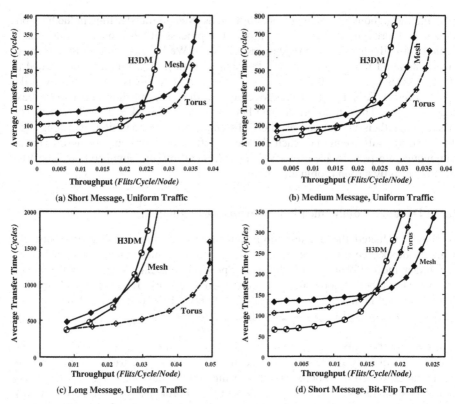

Fig. 3. Dynamic communication performance of various networks using dimension-order routing: 1024 nodes, 2 VCs, and 2 flits buffers

Bit-Flip Traffic Pattern

In a bit flip traffic, a node with binary address $\text{Node}(b_{\beta-1}, b_{\beta-2} \ldots \ldots b_1, b_0)$ sends messages to Node $(\overline{b_0}, \overline{b_1}, \ldots \ldots \overline{b_{\beta-2}}, \overline{b_{\beta-1}})$. Figure 3(d) portrays the result of simulations under bit-flip traffic pattern for the various networks for short message. It is seen that the average transfer time at zero load of the H3DM network far lower than that of the mesh and torus networks. Up to saturation the trade-off between throughput and latency under bit-flip traffic of the H3DM network is better than that of mesh and torus networks. However, the maximum throughput of the mesh and torus network is higher than that of H3DM network as depicted in Figure 3(d).

5   Conclusion

A deadlock-free routing algorithm using dimension order routing with a minimum number of VCs was proposed for the H3DM network. It is proven that 2 VCs per physical link are sufficient for the deadlock-free routing algorithm of the H3DM network; 2 is also the minimum number of VCs for dimension order routing. By using the deadlock-free dimension-order routing and the uniform and bit-flip traffic patterns, we have evaluated the dynamic communication performance of the H3DM, mesh, and torus networks. The average transfer time of H3DM network is lower than that of the mesh and torus networks. Maximum throughput of the H3DM network is also higher than that of those networks. A comparison of dynamic communication performance reveals that the H3DM outperforms mesh and torus networks because it yields low latency and high throughput, which are indispensable for next generation high performance massively parallel computer systems. The important issue of assessing the dynamic communication performance improvement of the H3DM network by the adaptive routing algorithm remains a subject for further exploration.

Acknowledgment. This work is supported in part by IIUM Endowment-B research fund EDW B11-169-0647, RMC, IIUM, Malaysia and Postdoctoral Fellowship by Japan Society for the Promotion of Science, No. P09058. The authors are grateful to the anonymous reviewers for their constructive comments which helped to greatly improve the clarity of this paper.

References

1. Dally, W.J.: Performance Analysis of k-ary n-cube Interconnection Networks. IEEE Trans. on Computers 39(6), 775–785 (1990)
2. Abd-El-Barr, M., Al-Somani, T.F.: Topological Properties of Hierarchical Interconnection Networks: A Review and Comparison. Journal of Electrical and Computer Engineering, 12 pages (2011)
3. Lai, P.L., Hsu, H.C., Tsai, C.H., Stewart, I.A.: A class of hierarchical graphs as topologies for interconnection networks. Theor. Comp. Science 411, 2912–2924 (2010)
4. Liu, Y., Li, C., Han, J.: RTTM: A New Hierarchical Interconnection Network for Massively Parallel Computing. In: Zhang, W., Chen, Z., Douglas, C.C., Tong, W. (eds.) HPCA 2009. LNCS, vol. 5938, pp. 264–271. Springer, Heidelberg (2010)
5. Horiguchi, S.: New Interconnection for massively Parallel and Distributed System. Research Report, 09044150, JAIST, pp. 47–57 (1999)
6. Ni, L.M., McKinley, P.K.: A Survey of Wormhole Routing Techniques in Direct Networks. IEEE Computer 26(2), 62–76 (1993)
7. Dally, W.J.: Virtual-Channel Flow Control. IEEE Trans. on Parallel and Distributed Systems 3(2), 194–205 (1992)
8. Hafizur Rahman, M.M., Shah, A., Inoguchi, Y.: A Deadlock-Free Dimension Order Routing for Hierarchical 3D-Mesh Network. In: Proc. of the ICCIS 2012 (2012)
9. Najaf-abadi, H.H., Sarbazi-Azad, H.: The Effect of Adaptivity on the Performance of the OTIS-Hypercube Under Different Traffic Patterns. In: Jin, H., Gao, G.R., Xu, Z., Chen, H. (eds.) NPC 2004. LNCS, vol. 3222, pp. 390–398. Springer, Heidelberg (2004)
10. Holsmark, R., Kumar, S., Palesi, M., Mekia, A.: HiRA: A Methodology for Deadlock Free Routing in Hierarchical Networks on Chip. In: Proc. of the 3rd ACM/IEEE NOCS, pp. 2–11 (2009)

An Elastic Architecture Adaptable to Millions of Application Scenarios

Yunji Chen[1,2], Tianshi Chen[1,2], Qi Guo[1,2], Zhiwei Xu[1], and Lei Zhang[1]

[1] Institute of Computing Technology, Chinese Academy of Sciences, Beijing 100190, China
[2] Loongson Technologies Corporation Limited, Beijing 100190, China
{cyj,chentianshi,guoqi,zxu,zlei}@ict.ac.cn

Abstract. With the rapid development of computer industry, the number of applications has been growing rapidly. Furthermore, even one application may correspond to different application scenarios which impose different requirements on performance or power. This trend raises the following question: how to design processors that best suit millions of application scenarios? It is impractical to design a dedicated processor for each single application scenario. A better alternative is to design a general-purpose processor architecture that can generate different architecture instances on demand. This paper proposes a novel CPU architecture called Elastic Architecture (EA), which can be dynamically configured into different architecture instances to suit different application scenarios. By employing reconfigurable architecture components (instruction set, branch predictor, data path, memory hierarchy, concurrency, status & control, and so on), the EA can achieve considerable elasticities on each application, which enables the EA to meet the performance or power requirements associated with each application scenario. We validate the effectiveness of the EA on a prototype implementation called Sim-EA. We demonstrate that Sim-EA exhibits large elasticities over 26 benchmarks of SPEC CPU2000, enabling Sim-EA to reduce the average energy-delay product (EDP) by 31.14% of a fixed baseline architecture.

1   Introduction

Since the appearance of the first electronic computer, millions of computer applications have emerged. Each single application (e.g., an internet game application running on hand-held terminals or desktop computers) may correspond to several *application scenarios,* which specify not only the concrete application but also the requirements imposed on the responses (response refers to some execution expenditure such as performance, power, performance-power tradeoff). To cope with the requirements of millions of application scenarios, more and more processor types are devised and used. For instance, the processor products of Intel increased from 5 types to near 30 types between 1999 and 2009 [10, 11]. However, the problem of having a processor matching different application scenarios at the runtime and maintaining low costs in processor design and manufacture is not solved.

J.J. Park et al. (Eds.): NPC 2012, LNCS 7513, pp. 188–195, 2012.
© IFIP International Federation for Information Processing 2012

To address this problem, we propose a novel CPU architecture called the *Elastic Architecture* (EA) whose architecture components can be dynamically reconfigured to suit (adapt to) different application scenarios. The reconfigurable components in an EA may include instruction set, branch predictor, data path, memory hierarchy, concurrency, status & control, and so on. Through dynamically reconfiguring these components, the processor can be adjusted on demand. The EA can potentially be configured to a considerable number of *architecture instances[1]*, which is significantly larger than the number of architecture instances that can be activated by conventional architectures. For example, a modern processor with the Dynamic Voltage/Frequency Scaling (DVFS) technique, whose frequency can be dynamically configured to 1 GHz, 1.5 GHz, or 2 GHz, only has three different architecture instances. In contrast, this paper shows that the EA can be reconfigured into more 70 million architecture instances. Consequently, the EA can offer higher *elasticity* (defined as *the ratio of the worst-case response to the best-case response*) for each application scenario, compared with conventional designs. Taking again the processor with DVFS as an example, its *performance elasticity* is at most 2 (the ratio of execution times when running at 1 GHz and 2 GHz) for all applications. Such a small elasticity of the conventional architecture makes it hard to meet sophisticated requirements on responses (e.g., the power consumptions should be less than 100 Watt while the execution should be as fast as possible), while the EA is capable of tackling such requirements for various application scenarios.

We implement a prototype design of EA, named Sim-EA. Sim-EA can be reconfigured into more than 70,000,000 architecture instances. We evaluate the elasticity of performance-power tradeoff with EDP (Energy-Delay Product) of the EA, using 26 benchmarks of SPEC CPU2000. The arithmetic average EDP elasticity of Sim-EA is 5.41, and such a large elasticity indicates that selected reconfigurable components have crucial impacts on the performance-power tradeoff. To demonstrate the effectiveness of EA, we also compare the achieved EDPs of Sim-EA with those of a traditional fixed baseline architecture. Experimental results show that the EA can provide near-optimal EDPs for all benchmark applications, which results in 31.14% average EDP reduction.

2   Elastic Architecture

2.1   Concept

The EA is a flexible CPU architecture whose architecture components can be dynamically reconfigured so as to adapt to different application scenarios. The reconfigurable components may include instruction set, branch predictor, data path, memory hierarchy, concurrency, status & control, and so on. For an application scenario with

---

[1] An architecture instance is a runtime configuration of an architecture, in which all architecture components are fixed, and an application can be executed with fixed performance and power (if random disturbance is ignored).

high-performance requirement, the EA can be configured into a high-performance CPU architecture instance. For an application scenario with low-power requirement, the EA can work as a low-power CPU. For an application scenario without a specific requirement, the EA can select an architecture instance with efficient performance-power tradeoff. The concrete configurable features of an EA may include:

1. The configurable instruction set mainly requires a configurable instruction decoder, which is sufficient to support instruction set variations. It enables an EA to support applications developed for different but closely-related computer families.
2. The configurable branch predictor enables the EA to adopt suitable branch prediction strategies (e.g., global history predictor, local history predictor, and so on) for applications with different types of branch behaviors.
3. The configurable data path provides flexible computational ability for the EA. Through configuring data path, the number and functionality of computational units can be adjusted to meet specific performance and power requirements.
4. The configurable memory hierarchy is crucial to the EA, since the memory hierarchy may consume half of the area in a state-of-art CPU. There are many important memory hierarchy parameters, such as cache size, cache line size, cache way, cache replacement strategies, and so on. Each of these parameters has a non-negligible impact on the performance and power.
5. The configurable concurrency includes not only TLP, but also ILP. Concretely, the concurrency configurations can include core number, issue width, instruction window size, and so on.
6. The configurable status & control include voltage adjustment, frequency adjustment, kernel-mode resource adjustment, and other miscellaneous CPU configurations.

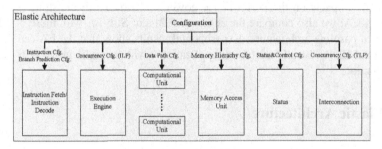

Fig. 1. In an elastic architecture, the instruction fetch&decode model, execution engine, computational units, memory access unit, status, and interconnection can be dynamically configured

Figure 1 illustrates the concept of EA, in which a central configuration module controls the other modules (instruction fetch & decode module, execution engine, computational units, memory access unit, status and core interconnection) through several configuration buses (instruction config bus, branch prediction config bus, concurrency config bus, data path config bus, memory hierarchy config bus, and status & control config bus).

It is worth noting that an EA does not require that all the above features of the CPU are reconfigurable. In other words, for a certain EA, it always consists of a part of fixed features and a part of reconfigurable features. Hence, determining which part to reconfigure and how to reconfigure should cautiously trade off between the design complexity and obtained benefits. An empirical guideline to determine the reconfigurable features is that such reconfigurable parts can provide large elasticities for applications, which can offer great adaptivity to a wide range of application scenarios.

2.2 Implementation of EA

To demonstrate the feasibility and merit of EA, we implement Sim-EA, a prototyping of EA on a simplescalar-like C simulator [2]. As shown in Table 1, there are ten configurable parameters in the EA, which include the issue width (WIDTH), the number of floating-point functional unit (FUNIT), the number of integer functional unit (IUNIT), the size of L1 data cache (L1DC), the size of L1 instruction cache (L1IC), the size of L2 cache (L2UC), the size of gshare branch history table (GSHARE), the size of branch target buffer (BTB), the size of reorder buffer (ROB), and the size of load store queue (LSQ). We choose the above parameters to be configurable, not only because these parameters can be conveniently configured, but also because they are critical to control the overall performance/power of the processor, i.e., most of such parameters are closely related to the ILP, e.g., WIDTH, FUNIT, IUNIT, GSHARE, BTB and ROB etc. Among these parameters, WIDTH, FUNIT, IUNIT, ROQ and LSQ can be reconfigured in about ten cycles. Once the pipeline is flushed, they can take effect immediately. L1DC, L1IC, L2UC, GSHARE and BTB need relatively long time to be reconfigured, since the corresponding RAMs need to be flushed before reconfiguring these parameters. The detailed costs of reconfiguring such parameters are also shown in Table 1.

Table 1. Reconfigurable parameters in processor with EA

Abbr.	Parameter	Value	Reconfiguration Costs
WIDTH	Fetch Width	2,4,6,8	~10 cycle (flush pipeline)
FUNIT	FPALU/FPMULT Units	2,4,6,8	~10 cycle (flush pipeline)
IUINT	IALU/IMULT Units	2,4,6,8	~10 cycle (flush pipeline)
L1IC	L1-ICache	8-256KB: step 2*	~2000 cycle (flush L1D cache)
L1DC	L1-DCache	8-256KB: step 2*	~2000 cycle (flush L1D cache)
L2UC	L2-UCache	256-4096KB: step 2*	~10000 cycle (flush L2 cache)
ROB	ROB size	16-256: step 16+	~10 cycle (flush pipeline
LSQ	LSQ size	8-128: step 8+	~10 cycle (flush pipeline)
GSHARE	GShare size	1-32K: step 2*	~200 cycle (flush GShare table)
BTB	BTB size	512-4096: step 2*	~100 cycle (flush BTB)
Total	**10 parameters**	**70,778,880 options**	

3   Experiments

3.1   Experimental Methodology

To evaluate the EDP elasticity and the EDP reduction of Sim-EA, we employ the 26 benchmarks of SPEC CPU2000 as the representative applications for real life applications in different fields. As shown in Table 1, 10 crucial features of Sim-EA are variable, resulting in a design space consisting of more than 70 million architecture instances. As defined in Section 1, the EDP elasticity is the ratio of the worst-case EDP to the best-case EDP, which means that we should determine such two extreme architecture instances (i.e., achieving the best and worst EDPs) from the design space for each application. Furthermore, we also want to obtain the EDP reduction compared with a baseline architecture, which also requires us to obtain the optimal architectures from such a design space for each application via machine learning techniques (e.g., model tree algorithm [17]).

For fair comparison, we employ average Cycle-per-Instruction (CPI) to measure the performance of each architecture instance in the design space. In addition to the performance metric, we also estimate the *average power consumption* of each architecture instance with a widely-used metrics on performance-power tradeoff, i.e., Energy Delay Product (EDP) [7], which equals to $CP I^2 \times power$.

3.2   Elasticity

As the first step of experiments, for each of the 26 benchmark applications we employ predictive modeling techniques to explore the design space. For each application, we first randomly sample 500 architecture instances as the training set, that is, we simulate each application with 500 different architecture instances to obtain the corresponding performance/power responses. Then, such information is collected as the training data to build two predictive models i.e., model trees, for performance and power, respectively. After that, the performance/power with respect to a given architecture instance can be rapidly deduced by such models. Since we can easily know the performance/power responses with the help of predictive models, it is straightforward to find the two architecture instances with the best and the worst EDP for each application.

Once we can obtain the best and worst case EDP of Sim-EA, we can show the elasticity over 26 applications in SPEC CPU2000 in Fig. 2. We observe that the elasticity ranges from 3.31 (*sixtrack*) to 14.34 (*art*), and the arithmetic average elasticity is 5.41. Briefly, an application corresponding to larger elasticity implies that the applications are more sensitive to Sim-EA, which provides larger freedom for the EA to dynamically reconfiguring the architecture features on demand. For example, the elasticity of *art* is 14.34, which indicates that *art* is most sensitive (among all investigated 26 applications) to 10 reconfigurable parameters in Sim-EA. Moreover, the average elasticity as 5.41 indicates that the selected 10 reconfigurable parameters

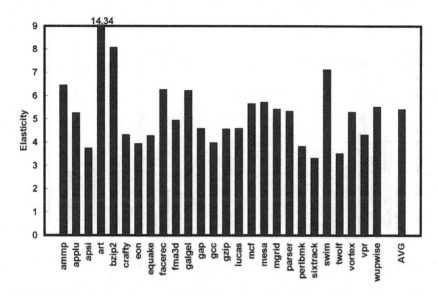

Fig. 2. EDP elasticities of the Sim-EA over different applications

offer considerable freedom for Sim-EA to obtain an appropriate EDP for real-life scenarios. Similar situations can be observed when using performance or power as the alternative response for estimating the elasticity (i.e., performance elasticity or power elasticity).

3.3   EDP Reduction

By integrating the optimal architecture instances (obtained for 26 benchmarks respectively) as the candidate running modes, Sim-EA can reconfigure its architecture to achieve promising EDP over different applications. The default architecture as a classical superscalar architecture in SimpleScalar Tool Suite, as shown in Table 2, is employed as the baseline. Fig. 3 shows the EDP reduction of Sim-EA to the baseline architecture, i.e., $(1 - EDP_{Sim-EA}/EDP_{baseline}) \times 100\%$. It can be observed that, for all applications, Sim-EA can reduce the EDP of baseline architecture significantly, and the arithmetic average EDP reduction is 31.14%. The benefit of Sim-EA is highlighted by application *art*, which can reduce 82.84% EDP compared with the baseline architecture. However, for *eon*, it can only achieve 6.26% EDP reduction, an insignificant improvement on EDP. To be specific, the CPI and *Power* of Sim-EA on *eon* are 0.79 and 14.43 respectively, while the CPI and *Power* of the baseline are 0.69 and 19.14, respectively. In fact, the baseline architecture has already been at the Pareto Frontier of the performance-power tradeoff function [16], and it is a near-optimal architecture instance with respect to EDP. In this case, the EDA reduction of the Sim-EA is not significant.

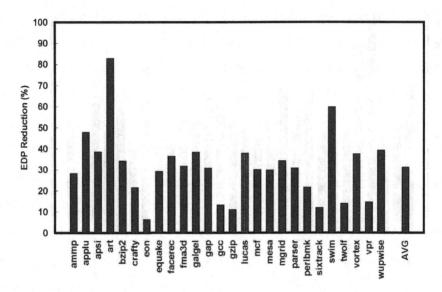

Fig. 3. EDP reduction over the baseline architecture. The arithmetic average EDP reduction is 31.14%, ranging from 6.26% (eon) to 82.84% (art) for 26 applications in SPEC CPU2000.

Table 2. Baseline architecture

Parameter	WIDTH	FUNIT	IUNIT	L1IC	L1DC	L2UC	ROB	LSQ	GSHARE	BTB
Value	4	4	4	16KB	16KB	128KB	16	8	2048	2048

4   Conclusion

With the advance of computer industry, the programmers and end users have put more and more requirements on processors. For different application scenarios, they hope that the processors can adapt to specific requirements on performance/power. Such requirements cannot be satisfied with a processor diversity approach, and may lead to excessive processor market segmentation, which increases the overall cost of processor design and manufacture. A promising solution is to make the processor elastic, which has many configurable features (e.g., instruction set, data path, memory hierarchy, concurrency, and so on). In this paper, we propose a Elastic Architecture and a prototype design of EA, which is named Sim-EA. Experimental results show that with respect to the SPEC CPU2000 benchmark suite, the elasticity of Sim-EA ranges from 3.31 to 14.34, with 5.41 in arithmetic average, provides great flexibility to fulfill the different performance/power requirements in different scenarios. Moreover, Sim-EA can significantly reduce the energy-delay product by 31.14% in average compared with a baseline fixed architecture.

In the future development of EAs, it is possible that more architecture features are designed to be reconfigurable, resulting in advanced EAs. An advanced EA is said to be *downward compatible* with a former EA if the advanced one can reconfigure all architecture features that can be reconfigured by the former. Driven by the rapid development of the microprocessor industry, a new concept called *computer tribe* may emerge, which is the set of consecutively-developed processors adopting downward compatible EAs.

Acknowledgement. This work is partially supported by the National Natural Science Foundation of China (under Grants 61003064, 61100163, 61173006, and 60921002), the National S&T Major Project of China (under Grant 2010ZX01036-001-002), the National 863 Program of China (under Grant 2012AA012202), and the Strategic Priority Research Program of the Chinese Academy of Sciences (under Grant XDA06010401-02).

References

1. Abella, J., Gonzalez, A.: On reducing register pressure and energy in multiple-banked register files. In: ICCD (2003)
2. Austin, T., et al.: Simplescalar: An infrastructure for computer system modeling. Computer 35, 59–67 (2002)
3. Balasubramonian, R., et al.: Memory hierarchy reconfiguration for energy and performance in general-purpose processor architectures. In: MICRO-33 (2000)
4. Blaauw, G., Brooks Jr., F.: The structure of SYSTEM/360: Part I: Outline of the logical structure. IBM Systems Journal 3(2) (1964)
5. Dubach, C., et al.: A predictive model for dynamic microarchitectural adaptivity control. In: MICRO-43 (2010)
6. Folegnani, D., González, A.: Energy-effective issue logic. In: ISCA (2001)
7. Gonzalez, R., Horowitz, M.: Energy dissipation in general purpose microprocessors. IEEE Journal of Solid-State Circuits 31(9), 1277–1284 (1996)
8. Hoste, K., Eeckhout, L.: Microarchitecture-independent workload characterization. IEEE Micro 27(3), 63–72 (2007)
9. Hughes, C.J., et al.: Saving energy with architectural and frequency adaptations for multimedia applications. In: MICRO-34 (2001)
10. Intel, annual report (1999),
    http://download.intel.com/museum/archives/pdf/1999AR.pdf
11. Intel, annual report (2009), http://www.intc.com/intelAR2009/
12. Ipek, E., et al.: Core fusion: accommodating software diversity in chip multiprocessors. In: ISCA (2007)
13. Ipek, E., et al.: Efficiently exploring architectural design spaces via predictive modeling. In: ASPLOS-XII (2006)
14. Kontorinis, V., Shayan, A., Tullsen, D.M., et al.: Reducing peak power with a table-driven adaptive processor core. In: MICRO-42 (2009)
15. Liu, F., et al.: Understanding how off-chip memory bandwidth partitioning in chip multiprocessors affects system performance. In: HPCA (2010)
16. Mariani, G., et al.: An industrial design space exploration framework for supporting runtime resource management on multi-core systems. In: DATE (2010)
17. Quinlan, J.R.: Learning with continuous classes. In: AI (1992)

Demystifying Performance Predictions of Distributed FFT3D Implementations

Daniel Orozco[1], Elkin Garcia[1], Robert Pavel[1], Orlando Ayala[2],
Lian-Ping Wang[2], and Guang Gao[1]

[1] Electrical and Computer Engineering,
[2] Mechanical Engineering,
University of Delaware
{orozco,egarcia,rspavel,omayalah,lwang}udel.edu,
ggao@capsl.udel.edu

Abstract. This paper presents a comprehensive story of the development of simpler performance models for distributed implementations of the Fast Fourier Transform in 3 Dimensions (FFT3D). We start by providing an overview of several implementations and their performance models. Then, we present arguments to support the use of a simple power function instead of the full performance models proposed by other publications. We argue that our model can be obtained for a particular problem size with minimal experimentation while other models require significant tuning to determine their constants.

Our advocacy for simpler performance models is inspired by the difficulties found when estimating the performance of FFT3D programs. Correctly estimating how well large-scale programs (such as FFT3D) will work is one of the most challenging problems faced by scientists. The significant effort devoted to this problem has resulted in the appearance of numerous works on performance modeling.

The results produced by an exhaustive performance modeling study may predict the performance of a program with a reasonably good accuracy. However, those studies may become unusable because their aim for accuracy can make them so difficult and cumbersome to use that direct experimentation with the program may be preferable, defeating their original purpose. We propose an alternative approach in this paper that does not require a full, accurate, performance model. Our approach mitigates the problem of existing performance models, each one of the parameters and constants in the model has to be carefully measured and tuned, a process that is intrinsically harder than direct experimentation with the program at hand.

Instead, we were able to simplify our approach by (1) building performance models that target particular applications in their normal operating conditions and (2) using simpler models that still produce good approximations for the particular case of a program's normal operating environment.

We have conducted experiments using the Blue Fire Supercomputer at the National Center for Atmospheric Research (NCAR), showing that our simplified model can predict the performance of a particular implementation with a high degree of accuracy and very little effort when the program is used in its intended operating range.

J.J. Park et al. (Eds.): NPC 2012, LNCS 7513, pp. 196–207, 2012.

Finally, although our performance model does not cover extreme cases, we show that its simple approximation under the normal operating conditions of FFT3D is able to provide solid, useful approximations.

1   Introduction

The Fast Fourier Transform (FFT)[1] is an important tool in physics and engineering, and it is relevant to numerous High Performance Computing (HPC) applications.

This paper addresses the issue of how to efficiently select an FFT algorithm for the particular case of large-scale distributed scientific simulations. Examples of large-scale scientific applications that use FFT include Cloud Physics[2], Molecular Dynamics[3], calculation of Coulomb Energies [4], Seismic Imaging [5] and Computational Geosciences [6].

Understanding the performance of FFT in large scale systems is important because FFT plays a significant role in many scientific programs. For example, the turbulent droplet collision simulation developed by Wang et al [7] uses a pseudo-spectral method for the flow simulation that requires multiple 3-Dimensional FFTs during each timestep of the computation. In fact, profiling of the flow simulation alone reveals that the 3D FFT alone can take up to 90\% of the total execution time in the program.

Because the FFT is not the objective of the computation in many cases, but rather a tool used to help it, it is of paramount importance to understand the effect of design choices on the overall program. For example, there may be a certain overhead in the passing of arguments to the FFT. The partitioning of the data may force the use of certain FFT strategies, or even the physical location of the compute nodes may greatly affect the performance of particular FFT strategies.

The necessity to understand the performance of FFT implementations and its relationship to the program using it has prompted researchers to build performance models that aim to predict the performance of particular implementations. These previous approaches [8-11] have resulted in very detailed performance models that include many factors such as computation time, communication time, the presence of overlapping or pipelining, the location of the memory and so on.

The biggest drawback to building a performance model is that correctly developing each performance model requires significant effort: the algorithm must be considered, constants in the model have to be measured, and the model may only work for certain architectures or interconnects. The difficulties of building performance models are so great that when one is correctly found it is published in a recognized venue (*e.g.* Dimitruk published his model in the *Parallel Computing* Journal [8] and Ayala's model[11]is currently under review in the same journal).

Instead, we have looked at alternatives that would allow scientists to make decisions about 3-Dimensional FFT implementations without the burden of developing full performance models. We have approached the problem by studying the nature of the 3D-FFT computation itself and existing performance models for different 3D-FFT strategies to see if there is a simpler way to efficiently select a particular 3D-FFT implementation over a set of alternatives.

We have sought to understand the performance of different 3D-FFT implementations on distributed memory machines through preliminary experiments (Figure 1) conducted on the Bluefire Supercomputer from the National Center for Atmospheric Research (NCAR).

Figure 1 shows the results of using two very different implementations of FFT3D on data of the same size. The differences in performance between the two techniques shown are due to differences in the implementation such as communication strategy and algorithm used.

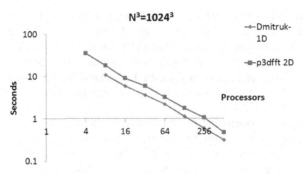

Fig. 1. Performance of two different FFT3D techniques. The relationship between time to execute and the number of processors appears to follow a straight line in this logarithmic plot.

Our experiments, which focus on large-scale systems, suggest an alternative approach to analyze FFT3D implementations: The running time of a particular FFT3D implementation can be approximated by a line in a logarithmic graph. This approximation corresponds to a power function. The power-function approach has the advantage of being significantly easier to use and build while still allowing the estimation (albeit with reduced accuracy when communication latency is high) of the performance of particular 3D-FFT implementations.

To test our hypothesis regarding the validity of our power-law approximation, we have assembled several 3D-FFT implementations. A brief overview for each one of them is given in Section 2, along with their performance models, when they are available.

We develop our prediction model in Section 3 and we conduct experiments to test the validity of our model in Section 4. Finally, we provide some conclusions in Section 5.

2   Background on FFT3D Algorithms

Many techniques have been investigated and developed to perform a distributed 3-dimensional FFT. For the purpose of this study, we focused on approaches that did not change the underlying FFT algorithm but instead changed the decomposition of the data and the communication patterns. The algorithms presented here leverage the principle that a 3-dimensional FFT can be performed by executing a 1-dimensional FFT along each one of the three dimensions of the data.

We will use the notation in Table 1 to aid us in our explanation of the FFT3D algorithms and models.

Table 1. Parameter and constant definitions

N^3: Problem size	P: Number of processors
B_w: Inter-process bandwidth	k_c: Average computation rate (FLOPS)
k_m: A constant associated with main memory bandwidth	T: Predicted execution time
k_s: A constant associated with the startup time for a message	

2.1   1D Domain Decomposition: "Slabs"

The first decomposition we studied is the 1D domain decomposition, as seen in Figure 2. This decomposition is often referred to as a ``slab" decomposition where each processor is responsible for a single slab. In the case of Figure 2, each processor initially holds a slab of size $N*N*(N/P)$.

Because a slab must have a width of at least one element, the parallelism of 1D decomposition implementations is limited to using at most N processors.

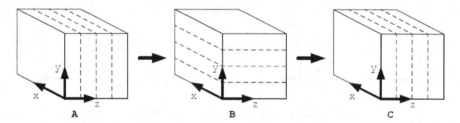

Fig. 2. 1D domain (slab) decomposition for FFT 3D

Dmitruk's 1D Domain Decomposition

Dmitruk's solution to the problem of the 3-Dimensional FFT [8] is to partition data in one of the space dimensions.

Each of the P processors is responsible for a single slab. First, each processor performs N/P 2D FFTs along the xy plane. Then, a transpose is performed such that the data in the z direction is now saved in the y direction and vice versa. With this transposed data, the required 1D FFTs are performed. Finally, a second transpose may be performed to restore the data to its original orientation, depending upon the needs of the application.

However, the essence of Dmitruk's work is in his implementation of the transpose. There are three methods that work on the principle of breaking the slab into ``blocks", moving the blocks to the appropriate processors, and then locally rearranging the data. What differs is the communication scheme used. The first method involves a cyclic strategy: Each processor sends data to the next processor in the list while receiving data from the previous processor. This is repeated until every processor has traversed the entire list of processors. The second strategy is similar in that each processor sends to the processor that is currently receiving from via a temporary pairing strategy. This is repeated in parallel until every processor has paired with every other processor. Finally, MPI collectives in the form of the ``all-to-all" operator were used for the third method. Of these three methods, the second method's pairwise strategy gave the best performance under Dmitruk's tests.

Equation 1 shows the full performance model presented by Dmitruk's paper[8].

$$T = \frac{2N^3}{B_w P} + \frac{15}{2\log(2)} \frac{N^3 \log(N)}{k_c P} + \frac{3N^3}{k_m P} + 2k_s P \tag{1}$$

2.2   2D Domain Decomposition: "Pencils"

A 2D domain decomposition strategy is a natural extension to the 1D idea. The 2D domain decomposition can be done along X axis, referred to as X-pencil, Y axis (Y-pencil) or Z axis (Z-pencil).

Assuming that the P processors are arranged in a grid so that $P = P_y * P_z$, Figure 2 shows a case where each pencil is of size $N * (N/P_y) * (N/P_z)$ and each processor is responsible for a single pencil.

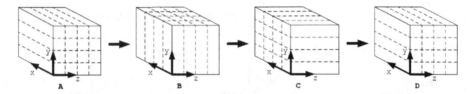

Fig. 3. 2D domain (pencil) decomposition for FFT 3D

The three libraries studied below follow the same general pattern. Three sets of 1D FFTs are performed along each axis with a transpose used to reorder data. In the case of Figure 3, this means 1D FFT in the x-direction, transpose, y-direction, transpose, and then z-direction. Depending on the application, a final transpose will be performed to restore the data. These libraries differ in how the transpose is handled.

2DECOMPFFT

2DECOMPFFT [9] is designed for applications using 3-dimensional structured mesh and spatially implicit numerical algorithms. It implements a general-purpose 2D pencil decomposition for data distribution on distributed memory platforms. The transpositions are done using the MPI ``all-to-all" operator, but with a complex communication pattern according to the orientation of pencils and their associated memory pattern.

p3dfft

The p3dfft algorithm [10] is an algorithm developed by Pekurovsky that uses a 2D pencil decomposition with the objective of maximizing parallelism. p3dfft was written in Fortran and MPI and uses FFTW[12] as the underlying library for FFT. Communication operations are done using MPI ``all-to-all" operations.

Pekurovsky's FFT3D requires a total of 3 transpositions to compute a transformation. Data is redistributed during each step using call to MPI All-to-All that requires internal redistribution of data. In each of the 3 communication steps, each processor transfers a block of size N^3/P with a bandwidth of B_W. Equation 2 summarizes these steps into a performance model.

$$T = \frac{3N^3}{B_w P} + 3\frac{N^3 \log(N)}{k_c P} + \frac{3N^3}{k_m P} + 2k_s(P_y + P_z - 2) \tag{2}$$

Ayala's 2D Domain Decomposition
Ayala and Wang[11]built upon the work of Dmitruk et al. As with the other libraries, a 2D Pencil Decomposition is used. Due to the target application of Direct Numerical Simulation, the last transpose is not necessary in Ayala's method.

As with Dmitruk's work, the optimization of the transpose plays a large part in improving performance. In this case, Ayala chose to follow Dmitruk's cyclic strategy. This provides better performance because during a transpose for a 2D Decomposition, only processors in the same plane as the transpose need to communicate. For example, a transpose along the x and y axes will only require communication between processors in the same xy plane to communicate.

Equation 3 presents a performance model taken from Ayala and Wang's paper[11].

$$T = \frac{4N^3}{B_w P} + \frac{15}{2\log(2)}\frac{N^3\log(N)}{k_c P} + \frac{6N^3}{k_m P} + 2k_s(P_y + P_z - 2) \tag{3}$$

2.3   3D Domain Decomposition: "Blocks"

Finally, we studied the 3D Domain Decomposition in which the data is broken up into blocks. The P processors that participate in the computation are arranged in a 3-Dimensional grid so that $P = P_x * P_y * P_z$. The amount of data held by each processor (Figure 4) is $(N/P_x) * (N/P_y) * (N/P_z)$.

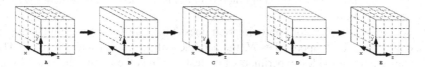

Fig. 4. 3D domain (block) decomposition for FFT 3D

3Decomp
3Decomp computes FFT3D by executing four data transpositions as shown in Figure 4. In each case the communication is done using nonblocking point-to-point MPI calls. Due to the differences in topology between each step, each processor needs to communicate with several other processors. The local 1-Dimensional FFT transforms required are computed using the FFTW[12] library.

The performance model of 3Decomp (Equation 4) is obtained by analyzing its data movement and the amount of computation per-formed: Four communication steps are used where all data held by each processor (N^3 /P in size) is reorganized locally and then sent to another processor. Each processor, in parallel, computes $3N^2$ /P one-dimensional FFTs, each of complexity $N \setminus \log(N)$.

$$T = \frac{4N^3}{B_w P} + 3\frac{N^3 \log(N)}{k_c P} + \frac{4N^3}{k_m P} + 2k_s(2P_x + P_y(P_x + P_z) - 4) \qquad (4)$$

3   A Simplified Model Approach for FFT3D

Section 2 presented a selection of algorithms for FFT3D and their performance models.

Correctly developing and using performance models such as those presented in Equations 1, 2, 3 and 4 require a significant effort: It requires a reasonable understanding of the implementation, and it requires extensive testing on the machine to identify the constants of the model.

Our previous experiments (Figure 1) showed a case where plotting execution time as a function of the number of processors resulted in a straight line when plotted on a logarithmic scale, indicating a power-function behavior. These results have motivated us to approximate the performance models of FFT3D as a power function as presented in Equation 5.

$$T_N(P) = A_N \times P^{-B_N} \qquad (5)$$

Equation 5 is significantly simpler than other performance models, such as those presented in Section 2, and it is appropriate to represent the behavior observed in Figure 1.

The power-function approximation is intended to provide estimates of parallelism for large scale systems in a range of situations where there is enough parallelism available. *i.e.* Equation 5 will provide a reasonable approximation for a particular number of processors if the FFT3D implementation is able to scale reasonably well up to that number of processors.

It is worth noting that our approximation doesn't account for the startup latency of a message. Thus, as P approaches N, the accuracy of our model may decrease. The following section provides experiments that test our hypothesis and the usability of our simplified performance model, even under these circumstances.

4   Experiments

We conducted experiments to confirm the validity of our claims. Specifically, we wanted to test whether or not the use of the power-law model of Equation 5 was sufficient to predict the performance of particular implementations of FFT3D.

Our experiments were conducted on the Bluefire Supercomputer at the National Center for Atmospheric Research (NCAR). The Bluefire supercomputer possesses

4096 Power6 processors running at 4.7GHz and having 2GB of memory. Bluefire's processors are connected by eight 4X infiniband DDR links with a total bandwidth of 2.5GB/s. Further information about Bluefire's hardware can be obtained from NCAR's website[13].

The experiments seek to establish whether or not it is possible to predict the performance of FFT3D implementations using the model of Equation 5. As explained in Section 3, the power-law model attempts to predict the performance of a particular implementation in common situations.

To test our hypothesis, we have ran the implementations described in Section 2. In our experiments, we chose several input sizes ($N^3=256^3$, $N^3=512^3$ and $N^3=1024^3$) for FFT3D that are typical of large-scale programs such as in cloud microphysics studies by direct numerical simulations. For each implementation, we run each problem size while the number of processors was changed. Due to memory, execution time, or processor count constraints, not all combinations of problem sizes and processor counts were possible.

The results of our experiments are reported in Figures 5, 6 and 7. To confirm the validity of our model, we have built simplified performance models for each implementation in the style of Equation 5. For each case, the constants A_N and B_N found in Equation 5 have been found using a least squares regression model.

The resulting models are presented in Table 2. The table shows the models as well as an indication (R^2 parameter) of how well the models are able to represent the experimental data obtained ($R^2=1$ means perfect match).

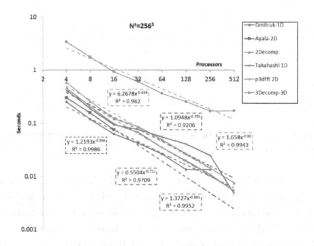

Fig. 5. FFT3D performance for $N^3=256^3$. Solid lines show actual experimental data. Dashed lines show a prediction using a power function.

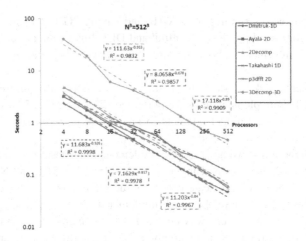

Fig. 6. FFT3D performance for $N^3=512^3$. Solid lines show actual experimental data. Dashed lines show a prediction using a power function.

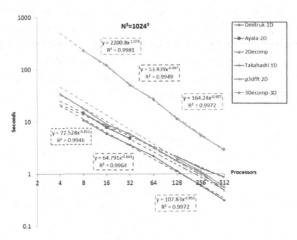

Fig. 7. FFT3D performance for $N^3=1024^3$. Solid lines show actual experimental data. Dashed lines show a prediction using a power function.

As can be seen from Figures 5, 6 and 7 and Table 2, the power function approxi-mation works remark-ably well. In most situations, the R^2 parameter is greater than 0.99, indicating that the model was able to fit the data with a high degree of accuracy.

Figures 5, 6 and 7 also give an intuitive indication of the quality of our models: The predicted models, represented with dashed lines, agree with the data gathered (plotted with solid lines).

The high level of similarity between the solid lines (measured) and dashed lines (model) and the high value of the R^2 indicator lead us to conclude that our model is an effective way to predict the performance of FFT3D implementations in their normal operating range. This is an important conclusion because the simple, power-function model can be quickly obtained with as few as only two measurements, one at low processor counts, and one at high processor counts. This is significantly simpler than the other models presented in Section 2 while still presenting good accuracy.

Of particular interest was the issue of startup latency and congestion when the maximum parallelism of a problem is approached. This is most evident for Dmitruk's 1D Domain Decomposition when $N=P$. Figure 5 does show this limitation. However, as the problem size is increased, the impact of the startup latency is greatly decreased, and our approximation's accuracy remains high.

The experimental information obtained here supports our hypothesis: A simplified performance model for FFT3D is enough to make sufficiently accurate predictions when those predictions pertain normal operating conditions. Our model has the advantage of being significantly simpler while still being useful.

Table 2. Power-function models for several FFT3D implementations

Models for $N^3 = 256^3$		
Implementation	**Function**	R^2
Dmitruk-1D	$T_{256} = 0.550P^{-0.722}$	0.970
Ayala-2D	$T_{256} = 1.22P^{-0.996}$	0.999
2Decomp	$T_{256} = 1.658P^{-0.86}$	0.994
Takahashi 1D	$T_{256} = 1.095P^{-0.765}$	0.921
p3dfft 2D	$T_{256} = 1.373P^{-0.883}$	0.995
3Decomp-3D	$T_{256} = 6.268P^{-0.634}$	0.962
Models for $N^3 = 512^3$		
Implementation	**Function**	R^2
Dmitruk-1D	$T_{512} = 7.163P^{-0.817}$	0.998
Ayala-2D	$T_{512} = 11.683P^{-0.926}$	0.9998
2Decomp	$T_{512} = 17.118P^{-0.89}$	0.991
Takahashi 1D	$T_{512} = 8.066P^{-0.678}$	0.986
p3dfft 2D	$T_{512} = 11.203P^{-0.84}$	0.997
3Decomp-3D	$T_{512} = 111.63P^{-0.913}$	0.9832
Models for $N^3 = 1024^3$		
Implementation	**Function**	R^2
Dmitruk-1D	$T_{1024} = 64.791P^{-0.843}$	0.996
Ayala-2D	$T_{1024} = 77.528P^{-0.812}$	0.995
2Decomp	$T_{1024} = 164.24P^{-0.907}$	0.997
Takahashi 1D	$T_{1024} = 53.839P^{-0.667}$	0.995
p3dfft 2D	$T_{1024} = 107.83P^{-0.853}$	0.997
3Decomp-3D	$T_{1024} = 2200.8P^{-1.074}$	0.998

5   Summary and Conclusions

We demonstrated that a simplified performance model is enough to capture the behavior of distributed-memory implementations of FFT3D in the particular case of large-scale systems. We have targeted our efforts at predicting the performance of implementations under their typical operating conditions. That is, when enough parallelism is available and the number of processors used is reasonably large.

Preliminary results showed that the performance of FFT3D implementations followed a power-function trend. Our full set of experiments, conducted on NCAR's Bluefire supercomputer has shown that the use of a power function model is adequate to represent the performance of FFT3D implementations on traditional distributed-memory machines.

The R^2 indicator, which provides a quantitative way to measure the fidelity of an approximation, shows, in all cases, a high degree of accuracy for our method. In most cases, the R^2 indicator was greater than 0.99, further validating the effectiveness of our approach.

An important feature of the power function model is that obtaining it re-quires very little experimentation. The constants of the model can be obtained with as little as two measurements, while still producing useful predictions.

Our current model has been designed to produce predictions related to the execution of programs over data of a particular size. To study data of a different size, experiments must be run to determine the adjusted constants. Our future work will focus on extending our model to be a function of problem size in addition to the number of available processors.

Acknowledgments. This research was made possible by the generous support of the NSF through grants CCF-0833122, CCF-0925863, CCF-0937907, CNS-0720531, and OCI-0904534.

References

1. Cooley, J.W., Tukey, J.W.: An algorithm for the machine calculation of complex fourier series. Mathematics of Computation 19(90), 297–301 (1965), http://www.jstor.org/stable/2003354
2. Ayala, O., Grabowski, W.W., Wang, L.P.: A hybrid approach for simulating turbulent collisions of hydrodynamically-interacting particles. J. Comput. Phys. 225(1), 51–73 (2007), http://dx.doi.org/10.1016/j.jcp.2006.11.016
3. Laasonen, K., Pasquarello, A., Car, R., Lee, C., Vanderbilt, D.: Car-parrinello molecular dynamics with van-derbilt ultrasoft pseudopotentials. Physical Review B 47(16), 10142 (1993)
4. Bylaska, E.J., Valiev, M., Kawai, R., Weare, J.H.: Parallel implementation of the projector augmented plane wave method for charged systems. Computer Physics Communications 143(1), 11–28 (2002), http://www.sciencedirect.com/science/article/pii/S0010465501004131
5. Calandra, H., Bothorel, F., Vezolle, P.: A massively parallel implementation of the common azimuth pre-stack depth migration. IBM J. Res. Dev. 52(1/2), 83–91 (2008), http://dl.acm.org/citation.cfm?id=1375990.1375998
6. Stellmach, S., Hansen, U.: An efficient spectral method for the simulation of dynamos in Cartesian geometry and its implementation on massively parallel computers. Geochemistry, Geophysics, Geosystems 9, 5003 (2008)

7. Wang, L., Ayala, O., Parishani, H., Grabowski, W., Wyszogrodzki, A., Piotrowski, Z., Gao, G., Kambhamettu, C., Li, X., Rossi, L., et al.: Towards an integrated multiscale simulation of turbulent clouds on petascale computers. Journal of Physics: Conference Series 318, 072021 (2011)
8. Dmitruk, P., Wang, L.P., Matthaeus, W., Zhang, R., Seckel, D.: Scalable parallel fft for spectral simulations on a beowulf cluster. Parallel Computing 27(14), 1921–1936 (2001), http://www.sciencedirect.com/science/article/pii/S016781910100120X
9. Li, N., Laizet, S.: 2decomp fft a highly scalable 2d decomposition library and fft interface. Cray User Group 2010 (2010)
10. Pekurovsky, D.: Ultrascalable fourier transfroms in three dimensions. In: Proceedings of the 2011 TeraGrid Conference: Extreme Digital Discovery, TG 2011, pp. 9:1–9:2. ACM, New York (2011), http://doi.acm.org/10.1145/2016741.2016751
11. Ayala, O., Wang, L.P.: Parallel implementation and scalability analysis of 3d fast fourier transform using 2d domain decomposition. Parallel Computing (submitted, 2012) (under review)
12. Frigo, M., Johnson, S.: Fftw: An adaptive software architecture for the fft. In: Proceedings of the 1998 IEEE International Conference on Acoustics, Speech and Signal Processing, vol. 3, pp. 1381–1384. IEEE (1998)
13. Bluefire User Guide, http://www2.cisl.ucar.edu/docs/bluefire-user-guide

MAP-*numa*: Access Patterns Used to Characterize the NUMA Memory Access Optimization Techniques and Algorithms

Qiuming Luo[1,2], Chenjian Liu[2], Chang Kong[2], and Ye Cai[1,2,3,*]

[1] National High Performance Computing Center (NHPCC), Shenzhen, China
[2] College of Computer Science and Software Engineering, Shenzhen University, China
[3] State Key Laboratory of Computer Architecture, Institute of Computing Technology, Chinese Academy of Sciences, Beijing, China
wiselcj@126.com, clarkong89@gmail.com,
{lqm@szu,caiye}@szu.edu.cn

Abstract. Some typical memory access patterns are provided and programmed in C, which can be used as benchmark to characterize the various techniques and algorithms aim to improve the performance of NUMA memory access. These access patterns, called MAP-*numa* (Memory Access Patterns for NUMA), currently include three classes, whose working data sets are corresponding to 1-dimension array, 2-dimension matrix and 3-dimension cube. It is dedicated for NUMA memory access optimization other than measuring the memory bandwidth and latency. MAP-*numa* is an alternative to those exist benchmarks such as STREAM, pChase, etc. It is used to verify the optimizations' (made automatically/manually to source code/executive binary) capacities by investigating what locality leakage can be remedied. Some experiment results are shown, which give an example of using MAP-*numa* to evaluate some optimizations based on Oprofile sampling.

Keywords: Memory Access Patterns, NUMA, Benchmark, Oprofile.

1 Introduction

NUMA has been the source of performance problems for high performance computing on large scale distributed shared memory platforms for years. In these systems a processer core can access nearby memory faster than remote memory. To maximize the aggregate memory bandwidth all processes must simultaneously access data from their own local memory location. It means that multithreaded codes in NUMA platform should sustain sufficient locality of memory access and minimize access to remote data to obtain a high performance.

The importance of the data locality is well documented [1][2][3][4] and there are some OS-provided NUMA APIs to control it [5][6][7][8]. Linux traditionally had ways to bind threads to specific CPUs/Cores and NUMA API extends that to

---

*Corresponding author.

J.J. Park et al. (Eds.): NPC 2012, LNCS 7513, pp. 208–216, 2012.
© IFIP International Federation for Information Processing 2012

allow programs to specify on which node memory should be allocated. Some more complicated APIs are based on these basic policies, such as MAi [7] and MaMI [9].It is not an easy task to apply these API because it is much difficult to find the communication pattern in shared memory platform than message passing platform, because it is implicit and occurs through the memory accesses. Recently, some tools are available to guide a program developer on where to judiciously apply these API within a large parallel code [10][11][12]. But it is still a hard problem to find the best mapping of the access patterns, which is considered NP-Hard [13]. [12] used a heuristic algorithm to map threads and data on the machine based on the Edmonds matching algorithm [14]. [18] presents a strategy which used the Dual Recursive Bipartition algorithm for process placement to reduce communication time of parallel applications that have a steady communication pattern on clusters of multi-core machines. [19] introduced the Locality-Aware Mapping Algorithm (LAMA) for distributing individual processes of a parallel application across the processing resources in an HPC system paying particular attention to on-node hardware topologies and memory locality.

But all those works are using the traditional test tools or benchmarks to evaluate their efforts. To our best knowledge, there are no benchmark dedicate to validate the various optimizations for memory access on NUMA platform. How to qualify and characterize an optimization technology or algorithm is still need further study. One benchmark that can tell how the memory locality leakage can be remedied by an optimization would be the answer. And this benchmark should be an abstraction of typical applications which is architecture independent. This is the motivation of MAP-numa (Memory Access Patterns for NUMA, short for MAP).

The rest of the paper is organized as follows. In section 2, we discuss related work. Section 3 focuses on MAP and the memory access patterns. In section 4 we present an application example of MAP in a NUMA optimization based on memory traces (obtained via Oprofile). Finally in section 5 the conclusion is drawn and some future work is discussed.

2   Related Work

There exist plenty of researches that focus on NUMA memory access optimization. They can be classified into three categories if the verification method is considered. Some of them use well-known benchmarks for high performance computing, some use a particular application, and some other use memory benchmarks.

Memphis [11] evaluated its effectiveness by applying the NPB (NAS Parallel Benchmarks), HYCOM (a production ocean modeling application), XGC1 (a production Fortran90 particle-in-cell code that models several aspects of plasmas in a tokamak thermonuclear fusion reactor) and CAM (the Community Atmosphere Model). MAi [7] used two kernels (FFT and CG) from NPB and ICTM [15]. SPLASH2, PARSEC and Advention (a part of the Brazilian Regional Atmosphere Modeling System) were used in [13]. NPB is also used in [12][16][17]. They measured the runtime before and after the optimization with the well known scientific benchmarks to demonstrate their effectiveness.

The second category use particular applications other than using benchmarks. Gaussian computational chemistry code is used in [10]. H.264 video encoding code is used in [17]. Essentially, they are similar to the first category.

The last category try to setup some memory testing code customized to NUMA characteristic. ForestGOMP [9] made some modification to STREAM benchmark. STREAM measures sustainable memory bandwidth and the corresponding computation rate for simple vectors. The first modification is called nested-STREAM, which creates the threads by two steps. The threads in outer parallelism create a team of threads in inner parallelism. Each team works on its own set of STREAM vectors. The other modification is called twisted-STREAM. It contains two distinct phases. The first one behaves exactly as nested-STREAM. During the second phase, each team works on a different data set instead the one it was given in the first phase. ForestGOMP also considered the irregular applications with imbalanced parallelism and derived a modified version call imbalanced-STREAM.

Using the well known high performance computing benchmarks can demonstrate the effectiveness of various optimizations to sustaining the memory locality on NUMA. And so do those particular applications. But it cannot give us more details about how and what the optimization really contributes, except the reduction of running time. Nested-STREAM, twisted-STREAM and imblanced-STREAM reveal some more details about how and what ForestGOMP help to improve the memory performance in these three different circumstances. Keeping that idea in mind, we are trying to figure out one set of code that can help to understand characteristics of various optimization techniques and algorithms.

3   MAP-*numa*

MAP is designed under some guide lines or objectives. First of all, it should represent the typical memory access patterns used in today's high performance computing, or it will be useless. Secondly, it should cover a wide range of applications. The third objective is to be capable of revealing different kinds of potential memory locality leakages, and to be able to characterize an optimization in various aspects. The forth objective is to achieve platform independence. And the last one is to limit the use of cache, or the NUMA effect will be conceal under the enormous cache hits.

3.1   Data Set and Thread Affinity

Most computing programs used 1D array, 2D matrix (2D array) or 3D cubic (3D array) as their work data set. MAP uses those types of data sets too. But what is more important is the relationship between the computing threads and the data subset they access.

The first type of data set used by MAP is 1D array and the access patterns include shared, divided, interleaved and partial shared. Fig.1-(a) stands for the shared case, where all the threads share the entire array equally. The access sequence can be serialized of randomized. Fig.1-(b) stands for the divided case, where each thread accesses the dedicated memory zone separately. Fig.1-(c) stands for the interleaved case, where each thread accesses the entire memory area in an interleaved pattern. Fig.1-(d) stands for the case between shared and divided, each thread accesses its dedicated memory and shares a portion of it with its neighbor. These access patterns should have cover most applications that using 1D array as their working data set.

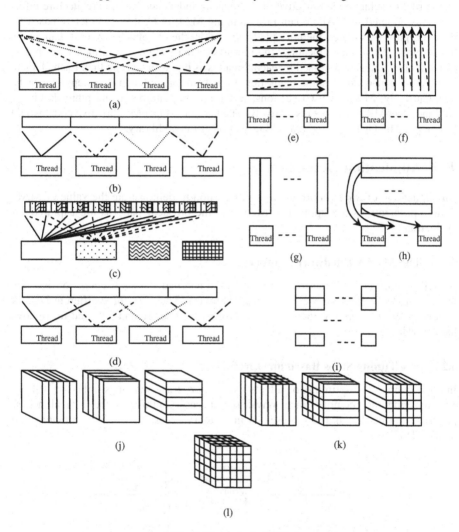

Fig. 1. Data sets in MAP

For 2D matrix cases, the data set can be accessed in more patterns. If it is shared, the access sequence may be scanning in horizontally or vertically, or randomly. As for divided cases, it can be divided in horizontal, in vertical or in 2D mesh. All the patterns are drawn in Fig. 1-(e)~(i). The 3D array in MAP is accessed in three fashions shown as Fig. 1-(j)~(l).

The STREAM benchmark uses four types of operations (COPY: a(i) = b(i), SCALE : a(i) = q*b(i) SCALE : a(i) = q*b(i), SUM : a(i) = b(i) + c(i) and TRIAD :

a(i) = b(i) + q*c(i)).While in MAP, the emphasis is NUMA memory access and the arithmetic operation should be eliminated. The basic operations (read, write and read/write) are chosen to perform without any arithmetic operations.

In order to achieve the objective of architecture independence, no architecture information is adopted in MAP. When programming MAP in C, it is completely based on the concept of one shared memory platform, and let the OS and compiler to handle the thread binding and data allocating. In order to eliminate the cache influence, each data element of the data set accessed by each thread is as big as one cache line. Each element in the array is padded by some blank field to make it long enough to occupy one cache line. Currently, MAP has two versions, which are programmed using pthreads library API and OpenMP directives respectively. The later one, OpenMP directive code, would be compiled by GCC with pthreads library or other thread library.

4   Application Example

An application example is provided in this section to demonstrate the value of MAP. Some optimizations are applied to MAP and the physical patterns are captured for evaluation.

4.1   The NUMA Hardware Platform

An HP 32-core NUMA platform is used as the test bed. Each 4 cores consists one memory node. 8 NUMA nodes are connected by HT. There are three different NUMA factors (relative latency values), 10 stands for native one, 16 and 22 stand for remove latency values.

4.2   The Tuning Steps Based on Oprofile

In this example, the optimization adopts the memory trace scheme similar to [10][13]. By analyzing the memory trace, physical patterns (contrast to the logical access patterns) can be drawn and represented in memory access matrix or communication matrix [16].

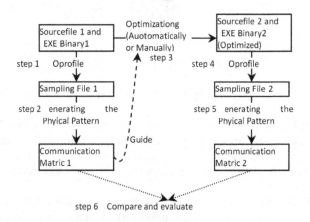

Fig. 2. The optimization steps

On AMD Opteron, with the Instruction-Based-Sampling (IBS)[20], it can provide the following information for sampled instructions that *load* data or *store* data.

☐ The precise program counter of the instruction.
☐ The virtual address of the data referenced by the instruction.
☐ The physical address of the data referenced by the instruction.

Only the samples with correct TID are kept and analyzed. Then they are classified into load and write categories. They are further labeled by node number according their physical address. The communication matrix is generated by accumulating the item with same source node and target node. The whole process is shown by Fig.2.

4.3   The Experiment Results

Three optimization methods, Linux NUMA API functions, *numactl* command-line tools and rewriting the source code manually, are applied to MAP's 1D data set to

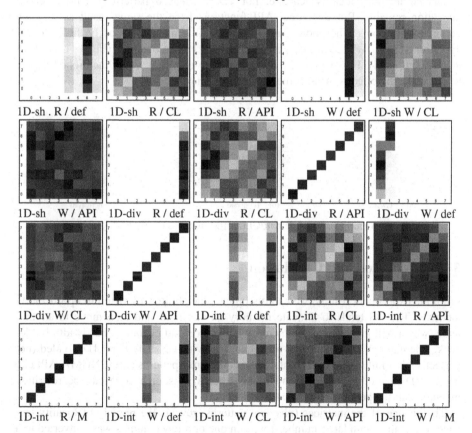

Fig. 3. Communication matrices of MAP-*numa* before and after the optimizations (1D stands for 1D data set, sh/div/int stand for shared/divided/interleave, R/W stands for read or write, def/CL/API/M stand for default/command line tools/NUMA API functions/Manually rewrite)

make comparison. The following communication matrices (vertical axis represents the nodes ID that issue the accesses and the horizontal axis represents the accessed nodes ID, the darker means more accesses) are obtained by Oprofile sampling.

For 1D shared pattern (Fig.1-a), OS allocates the data without particular policy and with influence from other processes' memory allocation (Fig. 3, 1D-sh R/def and 1D-sh W/def). Because the allocation tends to take place in one node, the communication matrix is focus on one (or a few) node. While applying numactl command-line tools (with --interleave option) to binary executable file or NUMA API functions into source file, the matrix become more flattened(Fig3, 1D-sh R/CL, 1D-sh W/CL, 1D-sh R/API and 1D-sh W/API). For 1D divided pattern (Fig.1-b), the default matrix (Fig. 3, 1D-div R/def and 1D-div W/def) still focus on one (or a few) node. Using numactl command-line tools (with --interleave option) can make the matrix more flattened (Fig.3 1D-div R/CL and 1D-div R/CL). By adding NUMA API functions into source code, the matrix can be diagonalized (Fig.3 1D-div R/API and 1D-div R/API), which means no memory locality leakage. For 1D interleaved pattern (Fig.1-c), default allocation remains. But this time, API functions have the same result as *numactl* command-line tools. They both flatten the matrix. If manually modify the code and applying NUMA API functions, a diagonal matrix can be obtained (Fig.3 1D-int R/M and 1D-int W/M). Fig. 4 give the execution time of all the cases mentioned above, which make the effectiveness of these optimization obvious.

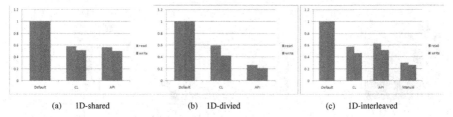

(a)   1D-shared   (b)   1D-divied   (c)   1D-interleaved

Fig. 4. Execution time of default/CL/API/M methods on MAP's 1D data set

5   Discussion and Conclusion

From the experiment results, we can distinguish the abilities of different optimization methods. The OS tends to allocate memory on one node and then move to another node, which will give rise to the memory contention and become a bandwidth bottleneck. The *numactl* command-line tools can deal with 1D-shared and 1D-divided (not perfectly), but fail to handle 1D-interleaved and multi-patterns cases. NUMA API can handle 1D-shared, 1D-divided and multi-patterns. If source code can be rewritten manually, all the patterns can be handled nicely.

The change of the matrices (physical patterns) reveals the remedy of locality leakage. If a matrix with large number focus on one or a few columns was converted to a more flat matrix, which means the potential memory bandwidth bottleneck is removed. If a matrix with large number focus on one or a few rows was converted to a more flat matrix, which means the threads are distribute to more nodes and improving the parallelism. If an evenly distributed matrix is converted to a diagonalized matrix, it means the best placement is achieved where there is no remote memory access.

So, we used table 1 to summarize their ability. It is hard to compare two optimizations, if they are only applied to one particular application. Instead, MAP consists of various typical access patterns and is able to verify whether (and what) locality leakages can be remedied by an optimization method. Actually, Table 1 can have more details if all the patterns are applied.

Table 1. Abilities of *nuamctl*, NUMA API and rewrite manually methods

	default	*numactl*	NUMA API	rewrite manually
1D-shared	×	√	√	√
1D-divided	×	√	√	√
1D-interleaved	×	×	×	√
multi-patterns	×	×	√	√

MAP is applicable to the source code methods as well as the methods modify binary executable file. The optimizations made by manually coding, or with the help of compiler, don't make any difference when being evaluated. So MAP is good start point of a general purpose benchmark to evaluate all kinds of optimizations.

As future work, we intend to profile some real world parallel applications to get the memory access patterns ,which are contained by our MAP access patterns. Further more, we can use the proper way described in Table 1 to optimize the applications.

Acknowledgements. This work was supported by the project (NO. 2011A090100037) funded by Guangdong Province and Chinese Academy of Sciences, and the project funded by State Key Laboratory of Computer Architecture, ICT,CAS.

References

1. Zhang, X., Qin, X.: Performance Prediction and Evaluation of Parallel Processing on a NUMA Multiprocessor. IEEE Trans. Software Eng. 17(10), 1059–1068 (1991)
2. LaRowe Jr., R.P., Ellis, C.S., Holliday, M.A.: Evaluation of NUMA Memory Management Through Modeling and Measurements. IEEE Transactions on Parallel and Distributed Systems, 686–701 (1992)
3. Brecht, T.B.: On the importance of parallel application placement in NUMA multiprocessors. In: Proc. of SEDMS IV, Symposium on Experiences with Distributed and Multiprocessor Systems, pp. 1–18. USENIX Association (1993)
4. Holliday, M.A., Stumm, M.: Performance Evaluation of Hierarchical Ring-Based Shared Memory Multiprocessors. IEEE Trans. Computers 43(1), 52–67 (1994)
5. Drepper, U.: What every programmer should know about memory (2007), http://people.redhat.com/drepper/cpumemory.pdf
6. Kleen, A.: A NUMA API for linux. Technical report, Novell Inc., Suse Linux Products GmbH (2005)

7. Ribeiro, C.P., Méhaut, J.-F., Carissimi, A., Fernandes, L.G.: Memory Affinity for Hierarchical Shared Memory Multiprocessors. In: 21st International Symposium on Computer Architecture and High Performance Computing, pp. 59–66 (2009)

8. Lameter, C.: Local and remote memory: Memory in a Linux/NUMA system (2006), ftp://ftp.tlk-l.net/pub/linux/kernel/people/christoph/pmig/numamemory.pdf

9. Broquedis, F., Furmento, N., Goglin, B., Wacrenier, P., Namyst, R.: ForestGOMP: An Efficient OpenMP Environment for NUMA Architectures. International Journal of Parallel Programming (Spring 2010)

10. Yang, R., Antony, J., Rendell, A., Robson, D., Strazdins, P.: Profiling Directed NUMA Optimization on Linux System: A Case Study of the Gaussian Computational Chemistry Code. In: 2011 IEEE International Parallel&Distributed Processing Symposium, pp. 1046–1057 (2011)

11. McCurdy, C., Vetter, J.: Memphis: Finding and Fixing numa-related performance problems on Multi-core platforms. In: Proceedings of ISPASS, pp. 87–96 (2010)

12. Cruz, E., Pousa, C., Alves, M., Carissimi, A., Navaux, P., Mehaut, J.-F.: Using Memory Access Traces to Map Threads and Data on Hierarchical Multi-core Platforms. In: 2011 IEEE International Parallel & Distributed Processing Symposium, pp. 551–558 (2011)

13. Diener, M., Madruga, F., Rodrigues, E., Alves, M., Schneider, J., Navaux, P., Heiss, H.U.: Evaluating thread placement based on memory access patterns for multi-core processors. In: 2010 12th IEEE International Conference on High Performance Computing and Communications, pp. 491–496 (2010)

14. Osiakwan, C., Akl, S.: The maximum weight perfect matching problem for complete weighted graphs is in pc. In: Proceedings of the Second IEEE Symposium on Parallel and Distributed Processing, pp. 880–887 (1990)

15. Castro, M., Fernandes, L.G., Ribeiro, C.P., Méhaut, J.-F., de Aguiar, M.S.: NUMA-ICTM: A Parallel Version of ICTM Exploiting Memory Placement Strategies for NUMA Machines. In: PDSEC 2009: Parallel and Distributed Processing Symposium, International, pp. 1–8 (2009)

16. Cruz, E., Alves, M., Carissimi, A., Navaux, P., Pousa, C., Méhaut, J.-F.: Memory-aware Thread and Data Mapping for Hierarchical Multi-core Platforms. International Journal of Networking and Computing, 97–116 (2012)

17. Tudor, M., Teo, Y., See, S.: Understanding Off-Chip Memory Contention of Parallel Programs in Multicore Systems. In: 2011 International Conference on Parallel Processing, pp. 602–611 (2011)

18. Rodrigues, E.R., Madruga, F.L., Navaux, P.O.A., Panetta, J.: Multi-core aware process mapping and its impact on communication overhead of parallel applications. In: ISCC, pp. 811–817 (2009)

19. Hursey, J., Squyres, J.M., Dontje, T.: Locality-Aware Parallel Process Mapping for Multi-Core HPC Systems. In: 2011 IEEE International Conference on Cluster Computing, pp. 527–531 (2011)

20. Drongowski, P.J.: Instruction-Based Sampling: A New Performance Analysis Technique for AMD Family 10h Processors. Advanced Micro Devices, Inc. (2007)

mHLogGP: A Parallel Computation Model for CPU/GPU Heterogeneous Computing Cluster

Gangfeng Liu, Yunlan Wang, Tianhai Zhao, Jianhua Gu, and Dongyang Li

Center for High Performance Computing, Northwestern Polytechnical University, Xi'an, China
wangyl@nwpu.edu.cn

Abstract. CPU/GPU heterogeneous computing has become a tendency in scientific and engineering computing. The conventional computation models cannot be used to estimate the application running time under the CPU/GPU heterogeneous computing environment. In this paper, a new model named mHLogGP is presented on the basis of mPlogP, LogGP and LogP. In mHLogGP, he communication and memory access is abstracted based on the characteristic of CPU/GPU hybrid computing cluster. This model can be used to study the behavior of application, estimate the execution time and guide the optimization of parallel programs. The results show that the predicted running time approaches to the actual execution of program.

Keywords: CPU/GPU Heterogeneous computing, Parallel Computation Model, Parallel Computing.

1   Introduction

The compute-capable graphics processing units (GPUs) are attractive as accelerators for high-performance parallel computing. According to the top500 supercomputer sites, three out of the top five fastest supercomputers in November 2011, employ GPUs. CPU and GPU have their own advantages respectively. CPU is suitable for complex arithmetical, logical, and input/output operations. GPU consists of hundreds of smaller cores which gives high compute performance. Therefore, heterogeneous CPU/GPU computing provides new and powerful computing architecture.

The conventional parallel computation models are not suitable for the new emerging heterogeneous computing environment. The PRAM [1] is unrealistic because it assumes that all processors work synchronously. The bulk-synchronous parallel model (BSP) [2] models asynchronously processors, communication latency and limited bandwidth. The LogP model [3] is capable of predicting the communication time for short messages but cannot accurately predict the communication time for long messages. The LogGP [4] extends it and adds an additional parameter for long messages, which captures the bandwidth constraints for long messages. The PlogP [5] considers the varying communication overheads for different message sizes. The memory LogP [6], $\log_3 P$ and $\log_n P$ [7] models draw characteristics of data movement in the traditional parallel computer. However, all the models mentioned above ignore the new characteristics of communication and memory access in the heterogeneous computing system. MMGP [8] is a multi-dimensional parallel computation model for steering the

J.J. Park et al. (Eds.): NPC 2012, LNCS 7513, pp. 217–224, 2012.

parallelization process on heterogeneous multi-core processors. However, it ignores the influence of data movement across computational cores. mPlogP [9] is also a model for heterogeneous multi-core computer. It extends PLogP and adds another level on top of the conventional level to model behaviors of computational cores. However, the characteristics of CPU/GPU hybrid computing environment is not considered in this model.

In this paper, a new model named mHLogGP is proposed, which is on the basis of mPlogP, LogGP and LogP. In order to analyze the characteristics of CPU/GPU heterogeneous computing cluster, some related parameters are defined to estimate the time performance of the parallel program.

2   mHLogGP Model

2.1   Abstract Hardware Architecture of GPU and CPU

Fig.1(a) shows GPU abstract architecture [10]. Each thread processors has private memory and parallel data cache. The thread processors visit each other through the parallel data cache and global memory. Fig.1 (b) shows CPU abstract architecture, the CPU cores exchange message via the bus and the host memory.

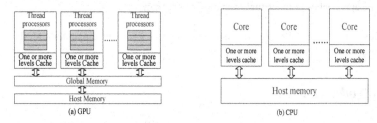

Fig. 1. Hardware Abstraction of Processor Architecture

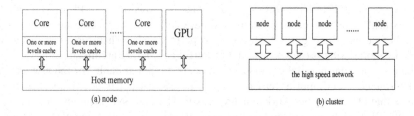

Fig. 2. Hardware Abstraction of a node(a) and cluster(b)

The hardware abstraction of computer node which includes GPU and CPU is showed in Fig.2(a). The host memory is shared by GPU and CPU. GPU exchanges information with CPU by accessing host memory.

The hardware abstraction of the widely used CPU/GPU computer cluster is shown in Fig.2(b). A computer cluster consists of dozens to thousands computers that are connected by high performance network such as Infiniband, 10-Gigabit Ethernet, etc.

2.2   The Parameters of the Model

o(Overhead): the time needed by processor to send or receive a message, $o \cdot \{o_s, o_r\}$. o_s $\cdot \{o_{sg}, o_{sc}\}$, o_{sg} is the time that GPU sends messages to host memory. o_{sc} is the time that CPU sending messages. $o_{sc} \cdot \{o_{scd}, o_{scn}\}$, o_{scd} defined as the time that CPU sends messages to global memory. o_{scn} is the time that CPU sending messages to another computer node. $o_r \cdot \{ o_{rgb}, o_{rm}, o_{rd} \}$, o_r is the time that a processor receive a message. o_{rgb} is the time of initializing the GPU. o_{rm} (o_{rd}) is defined as the time that CPU (GPU) engaged reception of each message.

l : latency, or delay, incurred in communicating a message from its sender to receiver. $l \in \{ l_g, l_c, l_{dm}, l_{nn}\}$, l_g denotes the latency between the parallel data cache and the global memory. l_c denotes the latency from the core of CPU to the host memory of another node. l_{dm} denotes the latency between the global memory and the host memory. l_{nn} is defined as the delay from one node to another.

G: the Gap per byte for long messages, which is defined as the time per byte for a long message. The reciprocal of G characterizes the available communication bandwidth per processor for long messages.

g: the gap, defined as the time interval between consecutive message transmission or reception. The reciprocal of g corresponds to the available communication bandwidth per-processor and the speed of accessing the memory. $g \in \{ g_g, g_c, \}$, g_g means the time interval between consecutive message transmission or reception in the global memory of GPU. g_c denotes the time interval for sending a message from the host memory to network cache.

P: the number of computer nodes. P is mostly used to model the collective communication.

3   Usage of the Model

3.1   Point-to-Point Communication

In this section, the performance of point-to-point communications is predicted. In the CPU/GPU hybrid computing environment, the cost of sending short message between two nodes can be predicted as $o_{s1} + l + o_{r1}$(LogP), where l is the latency of communicating a message from its sender to receiver, o_{s1}, o_{r1} is the time of sending or receiving the first message, where G is the Gap per byte. For long message, the Point-to-Point Communication time can be predicted as follows:

$$T = o_{s1} + (k_1 - 1)G + l + o_{r1} \quad \text{(LogGP)} \tag{1}$$

As shown in Fig.3, if the non-blocking communication is used to send 'm' consecutive messages, the transmission time is as follows:

$$T = o_{s1} + (k_1 - 1)G + \sum_{i=1}^{m-1} \max(((k_{i+1} - 1)G + g_{c(i+1)} + o_{s(i+1)}), l_{nni}) + l_{nnm} + o_{rm} \tag{2}$$

Where k_{i+1} is the size of the (i+1)-th message. o_{si}, o_{ri} is the time of sending or receiving the i-th message, It is obvious that network bandwidth and the speed of accessing the memory have a great influence on inter-node communication time.

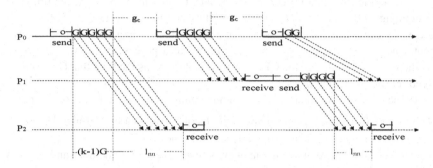

Fig. 3. Sending and receiving messages

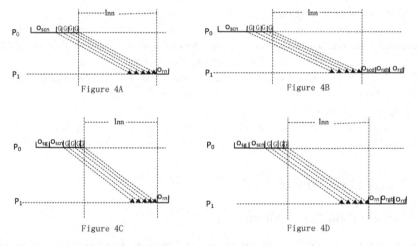

Fig. 4. Half-round trip sender/receiver communication cost

The communication cost varies with different sender and receiver. If messages are send from CPU of one node to CPU of another node (Fig.4A), the communication cost can be expressed by (2) where $o_s = o_{scn}$ and $o_r = o_m$. If messages are send from CPU of one node to GPU of another node (Fig.4B), $o_s = o_{scn}$, for the first message, $o_r = o_{rgb} + o_m + o_{rd}$, for other messages, $o_r = o_m + o_{rd}$. If messages are sent from GPU of one node to CPU of another node (Fig.4C), $o_s = o_{sg} + o_{scn}$, $o_r = o_m$. If messages are send from GPU of one node to GPU of another node (Fig.4D), $o_s = o_{sg} + o_{scn}$, for the first message $o_r = o_{rgb} + o_m + o_{rd}$, for other messages $o_r = o_m + o_{rd}$.

3.2   Broadcast Communication

We take the MPICH2 as example. For the short message or the number of nodes less than 8, the broadcast communication ids taken by the short message algorithm, namely, binomial tree. If the number of nodes is P and the size of the message is k. it needs lgP steps in broadcast communication. Each byte travels through the network for l_{nn}. Under the CPU/GPU heterogeneous computing environment, the broadcast communication cost can be predicted as follows:

$$T_{broP} = lgP * o + lgP * k * (G + l_{nn}). \qquad (3)$$

For medium-size messages and power-of-two number of nodes, the broadcast communication uses a recursive doubling algorithm. This costs approximately $T_{broP} = 2*lgP*o + 2*k*(P-1)/P*(G+l_{nn})$. For long messages or medium-size messages and non-power-of-two node situations the broadcast communication use a ring algorithm, which takes P-1 steps, so the total cost is $T_{broP} = (lgP + P-1)*o + 2*k*(P-1)/P*(G+l_{nn})$.

4   Validating the Model

Our experimental platform is the Dawning TC3600 Blade system with Intel X5650 processors and NVIDIA Tesla C2050 GPUs at the National Super Computer Center in Shenzhen, China. The computing network is 40Gb InfiniBand.

Table 1. Sender and receiver overheads between Global memory and host memory

Message Size	1B	4KB	16KB	64KB	256KB	1MB	4MB	16MB	256MB
o_{scd}, o_{rd}(μs)	3	45	52	64	173	381	1243	4754	71799
O_{rg}(μs)	20	22	26	50	174	824	1329	4803	70209
O_{scn}(μs)	4	4	8	17	32	65	128	904	20426
O_{rgb}(μs)	102055	103537	109984	109455	114427	111911	101656	101410	103542
o_{rn}(μs)	3	5	8	15	32	67	129	1002	21527
l_{nn}(μs)	141	149	225	268	339	755	2589	10461	161469

It can be shown in Table 1 that o_{scd} remains unchanged when the message size is less than 256 KB. It increases linearly when the message size is larger than 256 KB. So does o_{rg}, o_{scn} and o_{rn} when the size is larger than 64KB. Since the GPU must be initialized, no matter the size of message short or large, the value of o_{rgb} has no large variation. Because the speed of intra-node communication is very high, the value of l_g, l_c and l_{dm} can be ignored. l_{nn} denotes the intra-node delay. The experiments show that l_{nn} is random from 100 μs to 700 μs when the size of a message is less than 1MB. It increases linearly when the message size is larger than the 1MB.

As shown in Table 2, G is not stable when the size of a message is less than 1MB. When the message size larger than 1MB, it approaches a constant. g_g and g_c has changed little   when   the size of the data varies.

As shown in Table 3, for the messages size larger than 64KB, the total cost of broadcast communication is accord with ring algorithm. There may be errors of the test function, and other factors deviating from the principle of broadcast communication when the messages size less than 64KB.

Table 2. Overheads per byte for a long message

Message Size	1B	256B	1KB	16 kB	64kB	256kB	1MB	16MB	64MB
G(us/B)	141	0.578125	0.145508	0.014710	0.004577	0.001537	0.000845	0.000737	0.000749
g_e(μs)	4	4	4	4	4	7	68	104	249
g_c(μs)	0	0	0	42	39	40	41	55	35

Table 3. Overheads of broadcast communication

size time(us) nodes	1B	256B	16KB	64KB	256kB	1MB	4MB	16MB	64MB	256MB
2	83667	85284	97732	106578	106578	95334	101449	140239	211425	417945
4	132472	142002	140794	188769	213175	197967	234129	284768	392290	805469
8	207340	203330	291777	294295	299879	300807	472381	599026	822744	1804826

5   Experiments Validation

The matrix multiply [11] is adopted to validate mHLogGP. The implementation of algorithm mainly adopts the point-to-point communication and broadcast communication. Let A and B be two matrices, n represents the number of lines in matrices A. Matrices A is divided into p parts. The master process sends every part and broadcast matrices B to p slave processes. The slave processes receive the data and do the calculation by GPU and send the results to the master process. The master process receives the results and save the information. The overhead of program can be estimated based on the formulas in Section 3.

Table 4. The comparison between computing cost and total cost

Matrix size	64*64	128*128	256*256	512*512	1024*1024	2048*2048	4192*4192	8192*8192
Total cost(μs)	110268	109819	115474	115553	119466	219825	964722	6999979
Computing cost(μs)	164	166	241	300	423	1042	2854	11284

The cost of sending messages (for the master process) is:

$$T_{ptop1}= o_{scn1} +(k_1 -1)G+\sum_{i=1}^{p-1}\max(((k_{i+1}-1)G+g_{c(i+1)}+o_{scn(i+1)}),l_{nni})+l_{nnp}+o_{mp}+o_{rgbp}+o_{rdp}$$

The cost of receiving messages (for the master process) is:

$$T_{ptop2}=\sum_{i=1}^{p}(o_{sgi}+o_{scni}+(k_i -1)G+l_{nni}+o_{mi})$$

The cost of the broadcast Communication (for the master process) is:

$$T_{broP} = (\lg P + P - 1) * o + 2 * k * (P-1) / P * (G + l_{nn})$$

The value of parameters is based on the experiments data in section 4. For single GPU, the computing cost and total cost is shown in Table 4. The computing time in matrix multiply is very short compared to communication time, so it is ignored.

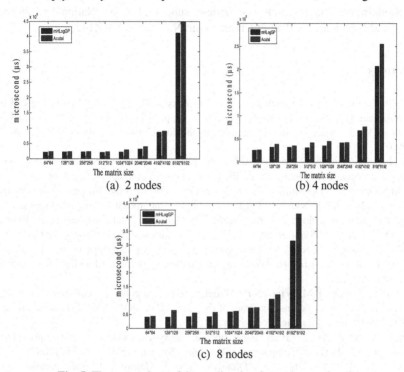

(a) 2 nodes   (b) 4 nodes

(c) 8 nodes

Fig. 5. The comparison of the predicted and actual execution time

The experiments are done on a cluster with 8 nodes including GPU. The comparison of the predicted and actual running time is showed in Fig.5. It is shown that our model could get competitive accuracy. With the increase of computation scale, the errors of the predicted running time increases. But, at worst, when matrix size becomes 8192*8192 on 8 nodes, the error of our model is 15-25%.

6   Conclusion and Future Work

Nowadays, CPU/GPU heterogeneous computing is a tendency. The conventional computation models do not fit in with the emerging CPU/GPU heterogeneous computing environment. In this paper, a new model named mHLogGP is presented. In mHLogGP, communication and memory access is abstracted by considering the characteristic of the CPU/GPU heterogeneous computing environment. This parallel computation model can be used to estimate the communication time and running time of parallel program, to find the bottleneck and guide the optimization of parallel programs in heterogeneous computing environment. The evaluation experiments show that this computation model is valid. In the future, the computing time of parallel program will be concerned. We will also study the execution time of concurrent parallel programs under the heterogeneous computing environment with dynamic load.

Acknowledgment. This research was partially supported by the National High-Tech Research and Development Plan of China (Grant No. 2009AA01Z142).

References

1. Steven, F., James, W.: Parallelism in Random Access Machines. In: Proceedings of the 10th Annual Symposium on Theory of Computing, pp. 114–118 (1978)
2. Leslie, G.V.: A bridging model for parallel computation. Commun. of the ACM 33, 103–111 (1990)
3. David, C., Richard, K., David, P., Abhijit, S., Klaus, E.S., Eunice, S., Ramesh, S.: Thorsten v. E.: Logp: Towards a realistic model of parallel computation. In: Proc. of the 4th ACM SIGPLAN Symposium on Principles and Practice of Parallel Programming (1993)
4. Albert, A., Mihai, F.I., Klaus, E.S., Chris, S.: LogGP: incorporating long messages into the logp modeláone step closer towards a realistic model for parallel computation. In: Proc. of the 7th Annual ACM Symposium on Parallel Algorithms and Architectures (1995)
5. Thilo, K., Henri, E.B., Kees, V.: Fast measurement of logp parameters for message passing platforms. In: Proc. of the 4th Workshop on Runtime Systems for Parallel Programming, RTSPP (2000)
6. Qasim, A., Samuel, P.M., Vijay, S.P.: Modeling advanced collective communication algorithms on cell-based systems. In: Proc. of the 15th ACM SIGPLAN Symposium on Principles and Practice of Parallel Computing (2010)
7. Kirk, W.C., Rong, G.: $log_n P$ and $log_3 P$: accurate analytical models of point-to-point communication. IEEE Trans. Computers on Distributed Systems 56(3), 314–332 (2007)
8. Filip, B., Xizhou, F., Kirk, W.C., Dimitrios, S.N.: Modeling multi-grain parallelism on heterogeneous multicore processors: A case study of the cell be. In: Proc. of the 2008 International Conference on High-Performance Embedded Architectures and Compilers, Goteborg, Sweden (2008)
9. Liang, L., Xingjun, Z., Jinghua, F., Xiaoshe, D.: mPlogP: a Parallel Computation Model for Heterogeneous Multi-core Computer. In: Proc. of 10th IEEE/ACM International Conference on Cluster, Cloud and Grid Computing (2010)
10. Sunpyo, H., Hyesoon, K.: An Analytical Model for a GPU Architecture with Memory-level and Thread-level Parallelism Awareness. In: Proceedings of the 36th Annual International Symposium on Computer Architecture, ISCA 2009, pp. 152–163 (2009)
11. Karunadasa, N.P., Ranasinghe, D.N.: Accelerating High Performance Applications with CUDA and MPI. In: Proc. of Fourth International Conference on Industrial and Information Systems, ICIIS 2009, Sri Lanka, December 28-31 (2009)

Estimating Available Bandwidth in Cooperative Multi-hop Wireless Networks

Wei Feng, Jian Liu, Jiannong Cao, Liang Yang, and Qin Xin

China Transportation Telecommunication and Information Center, China
Hong Kong Polytechnic University, Hong Kong
University of the Faroe Islands, Denmark
{fengwei,liujian}@cttic.cn, {csjcao,csliangy}@comp.polyu.edu.hk,
qinx@setur.fo

Abstract. Estimating available bandwidth (EAB) is an important and challenging task for providing QoS support in wireless networks. Existing works on EAB did not consider cooperative communication which can improve available bandwidth of wireless networks. To fill this void, this paper studies the problem of estimating available bandwidth in cooperative multi-hop wireless networks, which is formulated as an optimization problem, called Cooperative Available Bandwidth Estimation problem (Coop-ABE). Given a new connection request, the Coop-ABE problem targets at finding the maximum available bandwidth that can be provided to the new connection subject to that existing flows are kept free from interference. We propose a centralized algorithm to solve the Coop-ABE problem.

Keywords: Cooperative, QoS, routing, scheduling.

1   Introduction

Estimating available bandwidth (EAB) is an important and challenging task for providing QoS support in multi-hop wireless networks. For example, before admitting a new connection request to a multi-hop wireless network, it is important for us to know the maximum available bandwidth that the network can provide to this new connection. If the maximum available bandwidth is larger than the bandwidth demand of the new connection, the new connection will be accepted. Otherwise, it will be blocked. Moreover, cooperative communication is a new technology, which can improve poor links' transmission capacity with other nodes' help. Hereafter, we denote the node which helps other links retransmit packets by helper node.   The cooperative communication provides us a new method to improve the available bandwidth of a multi-hop wireless network, but no existing works [1],[2],[3] on EAB consider it. This paper tries to fill this void, and studies how to estimate available bandwidth in cooperative multi-hop wireless networks.

We formulate the problem of estimating available bandwidth in cooperative multi-hop wireless networks as an optimization problem, called Cooperative Available Bandwidth Estimation problem (Coop-ABE). Compared with existing works about

J.J. Park et al. (Eds.): NPC 2012, LNCS 7513, pp. 225–232, 2012.

EAB problem, the Coop-ABE problem needs to address following new issues. For example existing works only consider routing and scheduling issues, and they do not consider how to select helper nodes for forwarding links in the routing path. However, in the Coop-ABE problem, we need to consider how to jointly select routing path and helper nodes to achieve the maximum available bandwidth. Moreover, the Coop-ABE problem needs to consider more complicated interference relationship and capacity model.

We make following contributions while solving the Coop-ABE problem. First, we construct a new virtual graph to represent the new interference relationship and new capacity model. In the new virtual graph, we add some virtual links to represent the links working in the cooperative transmission mode. We redefine the interference relationship and capacity for these virtual links. By doing this, we significantly simplify the interference relationship among links and the capacity model. Second, we transform the Coop-ABE problem to a simpler problem which targets at finding a single-path rouging and the corresponding scheduling scheme in the virtual graph. Third, we propose a centralized polynomial approximation algorithm to solve the Coop-ABE problem, referred to as the centralized Coop-ABE algorithm.

2   System Model and Problem Formulation

2.1   System Model

In this paper, we consider a cooperative multi-hop wireless network. We adopt the $\Omega(1)$ model introduced in [4] to bound the distance between node pairs: the distance between any two nodes may not fall below a constant d_0. This assumption is reasonable because in the real wireless network there are physical limitations on how close to each other two nodes can be placed. We model the network as an undirected graph $G(V,E)$, where V denotes a set of n nodes, and E denotes a set of m links.

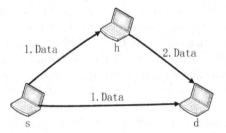

Fig. 1. DF cooperation scheme

We assume that a Decode-and-Forward cooperation scheme (DF) is adopted to improve poor links' transmission capacity. The capacity for links working on DF mode under the two-time-slot structure is given [5].

$$C_{DF}(s,h,d) = W * I_{DF}(s,h,d) \tag{1}$$

$$I_{DF}(s,h,d) = \frac{1}{2} * \min\{\log_2(1+SINR_{sh}), \log_2(1+SINR_{sd}+SINR_{hd})\} \quad (2)$$

The capacity for direct transmission is described as follows.

$$C_{direct}(s,d) = W * \log_2(1+SINR_{sd}) \quad (3)$$

To simplify our analysis, we use the Additive White Gaussian Noise (AWGN) model in [6] to approximate one link's SINR.

$$SINR_{ij} = \frac{P}{d(l_{ij})^\alpha N_0 W} \quad (4)$$

Here, W is the bandwidth, N_0 is white noise level, α is path loss factor, $d(l_{ij})$ is the distance between node i and j. Because W, N_0, and α are all constants, each link's SINR and capacity are fixed.

2.2 Problem Formulation

We formally define Coop-ABE problem as follows.

Definition1. (Cooperative Available Bandwidth Estimation problem, Coop-ABE) Given a network $G(V,E)$, each link's *SINR* and *ATF*, a set of existing flows, and a new connection request $\rho(s,t)$ with bandwidth requirement *RBW*, the problem is to determine whether request $\rho(s,t)$ can be accommodated by finding the maximum available bandwidth that the network can provide to connection $\rho(s,t)$ subject to that existing flows are kept free from interfere. We need to find a cooperative routing path P from s to t, and a scheduling scheme for links in P to achieve the maximum available bandwidth. We mathematically describe the problem as follows.

Objective: Maximize($BW(P)$)
subject to:

- Path bandwidth constraint:

$$BW(P) = C(l_{i,i+1}, h_i) * TF(l_{i,i+1}, h_i, \rho) \quad (5)$$

- Flow conservation constraint:

$$\forall l_{i,i+1}, l_{j,j+1} \in P, C(l_{i,i+1}, h_i) * TF(l_{i,i+1}, h_i, \rho) = C(l_{j,j+1}, h_j) * TF(l_{j,j+1}, h_j, \rho) \quad (6)$$

- Feasible scheduling constraint:

$$\forall l \in IS(P), \sum_{e \in IS(l)} TF(e, \rho) \le ATF(l) \tag{7}$$

- Relay constraint:

$$\forall i, j, m \in V, \$ \sum_{m \in V} x(m, P) + \sum_{l_{ij} \in P} y(m, l_{ij}, P) \le 1 \tag{8}$$

Here, $BW(P)$ denotes the available bandwidth of path P, $IS(P)$ denotes the set of links interfering with links in P, $IS(P) = \bigcup_{l \in P} IS(l)$. $C(l_{i,i+1}, h_i)$ denotes the capacity of link $l_{i,i+1}$ working in the cooperative transmission mode with node h_i as its helper. $TF(l_{i,i+1}, h_i, \rho)$ denotes the time fraction consumed by link $l_{i,i+1}$ and its helper node h_i when it works in the cooperative transmission mode with node h_i as its helper. The first constraint defines the path available bandwidth. The second constraint denotes the flow conservation constraint. The third constraint denotes each node within interference range of links in P should not be interfered. The fourth constraint denotes that any node can act only once either as a forwarder or a helper in P.

3   Algorithm Design and Analysis

3.1   Construct Virtual Graph

In this subsection, we transform the Coop-ABE problem to a simpler problem by constructing a virtual graph. We show the transformation by an example in figure2, in which node 2 is a helper for link l_{13} and l_{56}. We construct a virtual graph $G'(V', E')$ shown in the right graph of figure 2by following steps.

1) Add virtual nodes and virtual links: We add virtual nodes and virtual links to denote the potential helpers and links working in the cooperative transmission mode. For example, in figure2, node 2 is a potential helper for link l_{56}, we add a virtual node 8 to represent the helper node 2, and two virtual links l_{58} and l_{86} to denote links between node 5 and node 6 working in the cooperative transmission mode. We also add virtual node 7 and virtual links l_{17} and l_{73} since node 2 also works as helper node for links l_{13}. To simplify our presentation, we define the set of virtual links in G' as Virtual link Set of G', denoted by $VS(G')$. We define the set of original links in G' as Original link Set, denoted by $OS(G')$. Given a virtual link v, we also define a link set, L(v), to denote the original links that virtual link v represents. For example, in figure2, $L(l_{17}) = \{l_{12}, l_{13}\}$.

2) Label virtual links: We label virtual links with three metrics, including capacity, ATF and hop-count. Because we divide the transmission of one original link l into two virtual links, the transmission capacity of a virtual link is defined as twice as that of link l working in the cooperative transmission mode. For example, in figure2, we define the transmission capacity of virtual link l_{17} as $C(l_{17}) = C(l_{73}) = 2*C_{DF}(1,2,3)$. When link l works in the cooperative transmission mode, it needs to work cooperatively with other two links. So we set ATF of a virtual link v as the minimum ATF of the original links that link v represents. For example, in figure2, we set ATF of virtual link l_{17} as $ATF(l_{17}) = \min\{ATF(l_{12}), ATF(l_{13})\}$. Because the length of a cooperative routing path is equal to that of a routing path P, we set hop-count for original link as l and that for virtual link as 0.5.

3) Redefine interference relationship: We redefine the interference relationship in the virtual graph by redefining original and virtual links' interference link set (IS). We define IS of an original link l as that of original link l and virtual links which include original links interfering with link l. For example, in figure2, in original graph, we suppose that $IS(l_{13}) = \{l_{12}, l_{23}, l_{34}\}$. In virtual graph, we set $IS(l_{13}) = \{l_{12}, l_{23}, l_{34}, l_{17}, l_{73}\}$. The IS of a virtual link v is defined as set of links interfering with original links included in v, $IS(v) = \bigcup_{l \in L(v)} IS(l)$, L(v) denotes original links included in v. For example, in figure2, $IS(l_{17}) = \{l_{12}, l_{23}, l_{34}, l_{13}, l_{73}\}$.

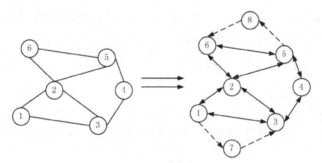

Fig. 2. Example of constructing virtual graph

Based on concept of virtual graph, we transform Coop-ABE problem to a simpler routing problem, which seeks a single-path routing P and a scheduling scheme S to achieve the maximum available bandwidth in the virtual graph.

3.2   Centralized Coop-ABE Algorithm

We propose a centralized algorithm, called centralized Coop-ABE algorithm to solve the Coop-ABE problem. To guarantee that transmission on link l does not interfere with other links, link l cannot occupy time fraction more than ATF of links within its interference range. We define one metric, called Bottle-neck Available Time Fraction

(BTF) to denote the available time fraction of link l while considering interference constraint, $BTF(l) = \min_{e \in IS(l)} ATF(e)$. We define another metric, called Bottleneck Bandwidth (BBW) to denote the available bandwidth of link l when considering the interference constraint, $BBW(l) = \min_{e \in IS(l)} \{C(e) * BTF(e)\}$. Intuitively, we should select links with high BBW to achieve high available bandwidth. We construct a sub-graph, called reserved graph to select links with high BBW. We divide the centralized Coop-ABE algorithm into three phases as follows.

1) Construct reserved graph: We first construct a virtual graph $G'(V', E')$ for the network G(V,E) according to rules in above subsection. To solve the duplicated relay node selection problem, we combine original node and its corresponding helper nodes as a supper node to represent that these links share a helper node. For example, nodes 2,7,8 in the virtual graph of figure2 are combined as a super node 2 in the left graph in figure5. Because we need to select links with high BBW, we construct a sub-graph, called reserved graph, $G^*(V^*, E^*, mid)$ in the right graph of figure3, which only includes the links with BBW higher than the threshold mid. We use binary search method to update the threshold value mid until the shortest cooperative routing P from node s to t in the reserved graph G^* is found. We formally define reserved graph as follows.

Definition 2. (Reserved Graph) Given a weighted graph G(V,E), and a threshold mid, Reserved Graph $G^*(V^*, E^*, mid)$ is defined as a sub-graph of G, which contains links with weights no less than mid, $w(e) \geq mid$.

Algorithm 1. Centralized Coop-ABE

```
Input: Network G(V,E), each link's SINR, ATF, connection
request ρ(s,t) and its required bandwidth RBW.
Output: Cooperative Routing path P, a scheduling scheme
S, BW(P).
Construct virtual graph G'(V',E');
Combine virtual node and its original node;
```
$mid = high = \max_{e \in E'} (BBW(e))$;

$low = \min_{e \in E'} (BBW(e))$;

```
While ( high ≥ low )
{
Construct reserved graph u.distance + uv.hops < v.distance;
For {each node v in V*}
```

```
{ For {each original link l_uv adjacent to node v}
   {    If { u.distance + uv.hops < v.distance }
      { v.distance=u.distance + uv.hops; v.predecessor= u;}
   }
   For {each virtual link pair l_mu , l_uv adjacent to node v}
   {
      If{u.distance+uv.hops+mv.hops<v.distance}
      {     v.distance=u.distance + uv.hops+mu.hops;
         v.predecessor= m, v.helper=u;
      }
   }
}
```

If $\{ \rho \ P \neq \phi \}$

$\{ BW(P) = \min_{e \in P} (BBW(l)/ | PILS(l,P) |)$;

$\forall e \in P, TF(e,\rho) = BW(P)/C(e)$;

```
Break while;
}
Else
{ high= high/2,mid=(high+low)/2;
}
}
```

If $\{ P = \phi \ or BW(P) < RBW \ \}$

```
{    Block the connection request }
Else
{Accept connection request ρ ;}
```

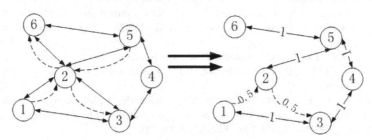

Fig. 3. Example of reserved graph

2) Find the shortest path: We also prefer path with short length because the shortest path leads to less opportunity of interference. We modify Bellman Ford algorithm to find the shortest path in reserved graph $G^*(V^*, E^*, B)$.

3) Estimate available bandwidth}} In this phase, we estimate available bandwidth of the selected cooperative routing path P. We define a link set, called Path Interference Link Set (PILS) to denote the links interfering with link l in path P.

Definition 3. (Path Interference Link Set, PILS) Given a link l and a routing path P, PILS is defined as a set of links in P interfering with link l, $

$$PILS(l,P) = \{e \in E \mid e \in P, e \in IS(l)\}.$$

When considering interference from neighboring links in P, link l in path P can at most achieve following bandwidth, $BW(l) = BBW(l) / \left| PILS(l, P) \right|$. The available bandwidth of path P is determined by the bottle-neck link, $\min_{e \in P} (BBW(e) / PILS(e, P))$. We check whether the connection's bandwidth requirement is satisfied or not. If it is satisfied, we accept the new connection. Otherwise, the new connection is blocked.

4   Conclusion

In this paper, we study the problem of estimating available bandwidth in coop- erative multi-hop wireless networks. We propose centralized algorithms to solve the Coop-ABE problem. We prove that the centralized algorithm can achieve a constant approximation ratio.

References

1. Zhai, H., Fang, Y.: Impact of routing metrics on path capacity in multi-rate and multi-hop wireless ad hoc networks. In: Proceedings of the 14th IEEE International Conference on Network Protocols (ICNP 2006), Santa Barbara, USA (2006)
2. Zhu, C., Corson, M.: Qos routing for mobile ad hoc networks. In: Proceedings of IEEE INFOCOM 2002, New York, USA (2002)
3. Chen, F., Zhai, H., Fang, Y.: Available bandwidth in multirate and multihop wireless ad hoc networks. IEEE Journal on Selected Areas in Communications 28, 299–307 (2010)
4. Kuhn, F., Wattenhofer, R., Zollinger, A.: Worstcase optimal and average case efficient geometric adhoc routing. In: Proceedings of ACM MobiHoc 2003, Annapolis, Maryland, USA (2003)
5. Laneman, J.N., Tse, D.N.C., Wornell, G.W.: Cooperative diversity in wireless networks: Efficient protocols and outage behavior. IEEE Transactions on Information Theory 50, 3062–3080 (2004)
6. Chafekar, D., Kumar, V.S.A., Marathe, M.V., Parthasarathy, S., Srinivasan, A.: Approximation algorithms for computing capacity of wireless networks with sinr constraints. In: Proceedings of IEEE INFOCOM 2008, Phoenix, USA (2008)

Relative Priority Analysis of Korean IS Audit Standard Check Items Using the Constant-Sum Method

Boo-Hyoung Lee, Chi-Su Kim, and Heon-Tag Kong

Kongju National University, S. Korea
bhl1998@kongju.ac.kr

Abstract. Currently, our country have introduced IS audit system to manage and supervise stable development and efficient operation of the IS. IT audit is accomplished by IS auditor using standard check items made by our government. As IT paradigm drastically changes and user's IT service demands level is high, Flexible change or modification of standard check items is inevitable. It is reasonable to change or modify them according to the priority after establishing relative weight inter-standard check items. To do this, domestic standard check items are represented as hierarchical structure using Hierarchical Decision Model (HDM) and relative weights and priority among them are obtained by Constant-sum Method in this paper. This result will give a logical validity enough to modify or change domestic standard check items.

1 Introduction

As Information system (IS) is an integral part in all areas and the dependency on the system is getting larger, it is very important to predict and prevent risks that may take place in developing and operating an information system [1]. The Korean government have introduced the IS Audit System to manage and supervise the stable development and effective operation of IS since July 2006. Also, it is stipulated that every IS development companies which develop programs over 0.5billion ordered by government branches must be IS audited [2].

The IS Audit is defined as activities conducted by an authorized person for the purpose of providing an independent assessment of software products and processes in order to assess compliance with requirements. In general, the auditing is executed based on "The standard check items" by auditing-companies registered in the Minister of Public Administration and Security. After IS audit, the auditing companies should submit the audit results which follows specific rules. The auditing-company must be independent with the audit ordering agency and auditee. The audit ordering agency indicates government branches that order the IS development and the auditee means IS development company [3].

Since the initiation of the Information System Audit at 1987 by National Information society Agency, the foundation of private audit corporations was permitted in 1998 and IS audit was activated, The basis for the Information System Audit is added in Electronic Government Act(Art. 57), and Electronic Government Act Enforcement Decree(Art. 71). According to it, the Ministry of Public Administration and Security released

J.J. Park et al. (Eds.): NPC 2012, LNCS 7513, pp. 233–240, 2012.

『Information System Audit standards 『which stipulates the audit procedures and methods for effective implementation of audit tasks including audit agreement, audit planning, onsite audit, audit report preparation, and inspection of audit result applications. According to Art. 23 in it, National Information society Agency published 『Practical Guide for IS Audit 『which defines the detailed audit procedures and methods, standard check items, format of IS audit plan and report etc[4].

Although IS Audit is executed by such mendatory audit policy and need of it is increased, there are still many negative opinions regarding the effect and quality of the audit. Typical complains are subjective audit results that cannot be agreed or audit results not helping management decision making.There are many studies to solve such problems and enhance audit quality [5-7].

Tae-Won Kyung et al released "a Study on the Priority Analysis of Information System Audit Service Evaluation Items by Means of FuzzyAHP Technique," where he defines the Information System Audit as a service activity, highlights the factors to differentiate and improve the quality of audit services, and endeavors to quantify the priority of such factors[8].

Don-ik Shin suggests the two step auditing method - the process audit and then product audit - in his "a Scientific Method for Information System Audit," and claims the necessity to improve the validity and reliability of audit by means of this method[9].

Gi-chan Nam et al, in his "a Comparative Analysis of Information System Audit and International IT Guidance," analyzes the correlation between the current Audit Standards and international IT guidances, and presents the enhanced audit standard in compliance with the international IT guidance[10].

The above studies are focused on only methods such as introduction of evaluation methods for audit results, improvement of auditor ability and change of the auditing method to improve audit quality. As long as the current audit standards check items continue to be applied in auditing in spite of IT paradigm drastically changes, the system development environment is consistently changing and user demands are becoming more stringent, it is difficult to improve audit quality.

In order to modify or change audit standards check items, it is necessary to prioritize the current audit check items by experts, and then modify or change them based on the priority.

To do this, standard check items are presented in a hierarchical structure by means of HDM method, one of the decision-making methods and then the relative weights among standard check items are measured by means of the Constant-Sum Method, Finally, the priority of each item are drew out. These results make valid basis for modification and change of audit standards that can improve audit quality.

2   Korean IS Audit Check Standard

As stated in the introduction, the fundamental directions for the Information System Audit is based on 『Practical Guide for IS Audit 『published by the National Information society Agency. Especially, the development systems are assessed according to 'Standard check items' in 『Practical Guide for IS Audit 『. The standard check items have the structure of project type based check system. Accordingly, the standard check items have check items which should be assessed by project type. The project type is classified into 6 areas- IT Architecture, IT Strategy, IS System Development, DB Construction, System Operation and Maintenance. In view point of auditing, the project type is considered as the audit field. Each audit field is divided audit time (phase), audit sub-area and detailed check items [11].Table 1 shows the project type based standard check items.

Table 1. The project type based standard check items

Audit Field	Audit Time	Sub-area	Detailed Audit items
IT Architecture	Foundation Set-up& Current Architecture Construction	Foundation Set-up	4 items
		Current Architecture Construction	9 items
		Quality Control	4 items
	Goal Architecture Construction & Implementation Plan	Goal Architecture Construction	6 items
		Implementation Plan	4 items
		Management	4 items
		Quality Control	4 items
IT Strategy	Current step analysis & Strategy development	Task Analysis	7 items
		Technology Analysis	5 items
		Quality Control	3 items
	Improvement Model & Implementation plan	IT plan	9 items
		Quality Control	3 items
IS system Development	Demand Analysis	System Architecture	4 items
		Applied System	5 items
		Database	3 items
	Analysis/Design	System Architecture	5 items
		Applied System	9 items
		Database	6 items
	Implementation	System Architecture	3 items
		Applied System	6 items
		Database	4 items
	Testing	Test Activities	7 items
	Deployment	Preparation for Operation	4 items
DB Construction	Preparation	Data Collection Model Construction	7 items
	Implementation	Data Construction	4 items
		Quality Control	3 items
System Operation	Operation	User-Service	8 items
		User-Service support	6 items
Maintenance	Maintenance	Maintenance	6 items

3   Establishment of the Relative Weights Inter-standard Check Items

This study aims to decide the relative weights among the domestic audit standard check items, and determine the priority. To this end, the Hierarchical Decision Model which is decision-making technique is adapted. The hierarchical decision making   is the technique that divides into hierarchical steps [12]. The decision-making using the Hierarchical Decision Model is as follows:

> First, All elements involved in the decision-making enlists and stratifies by the Hierarchical Decision Model
> Second, 1:1 pair-wise comparison is conducted among elements on the same level in each hierarchical step and score(100 point measure) is given to each element.
> Third, scores are analyzed to decide the relative weights of each element and prioritize them.

The representative Hierarchical Decision methods are The Analytic Hierarchy Process (AHP) and Hierarchical Decision Model (HDM) suggested by Thomas L. Saaty and Dundar F. Kocaoglu, [13][14]. These are the same in that they presents all elements hierarchically, but in the way to obtain the relative weights or priority of items in each hierarchical step, Saaty adopts the 'Eigenvalue method' while Dundar adopts the 'Constant Sum method.' Kocaoglu's HDM and the Constant Sum Method are used in this paper.

3.1   Hierarchical Decision Model(HDM)

HDM Hierarchical Decision Model represents elements to be decided as in Fig. 1 in the three levels - Impact, Targe, and Operational. More specifically, it includes

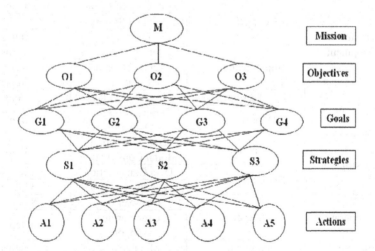

Fig. 1. A Typical Hierarchical Decision Model

MOGSA(Mission/ Objectives/ Goal/ Strategy/ Action) stages. The Impact Level, as the highest stage, is the ultimate goal of decision-making and consists of Mission/ Objectives. The Target Level is the goal level and consists of methodological elements to carry out missions of the highest level. The Operational Level is the level including Strategy/ Action and has more specific activities or alternatives that may affect the mission or the ultimate goal. Elements in the lower level are comparatively specific, and each element on the same level should be comparable with each other.

3.2   Constant-Sum Method

Data Collection To give weight value to elements in each level, 1 to 1 pairwise comparison is conducted inter-elements in each level, and the extent of contribution to the upper-level elements is expressed as the 100 point measure by the Constant-Sum Method. For example, if the relative weight of one element is 4 times higher than that of the other element, then they are given 80 points and 20 points respectively. If the relative weight of one element is a bit higher than that of the other, they are given 52 points and 48 points respectively. If two elements have the same relative weight, then they are given 50 points respectively. Once every element is given the score after comparison, the final matrixes A, B, and C are calculated based on the assigned scores, and the priority is decided [14].

4   Data Collection and Analysis Results

To measure the relative weights and priority of standard audit items, the standard check items are presented as a hierarchical structure by the Hierarchical Decision Model and the pair wise comparison is conducted among elements in the same level to grade each element. The score by the pair wise comparison was obtained through the survey of IS experts. In this study, the standard check items are represented in the 3-stage Hierarchical Decision Structure of HDM for each project type, the survey is conducted to grade items based on the pair wise comparison. 21 IS experts participated in the survey. The scores given by the experts are analyzed to measure the relative weights inter- audit items.

4.1   HDM Structure of Standard Check Items

Korean standard audit items can be represented in the three-stage hierarchical decision model. Fig. 2 shows an example of the hierarchical decision model for standard check items on the IT Architecture in Table 1. In Fig. 2, the IT Architecture consists of the two audit time, 7 audit sub-areas, and 35 detailed check items.

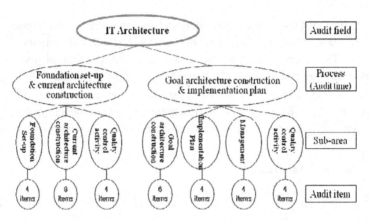

Fig. 2. An example of the hierarchical decision model for IT Architecture

4.2   Results

The relative weights inter-standard check items were measured by means of a pairwise comparison survey conducted by IS experts. Pair-wise comparison was done for elements on audit time and sub-area in each audit field. Among the 21 participants in the survey, 11 are working at IS auditor, and the other 10 were IT experts. Table 2 presents the relative weights of inter-elements on audit time and sub-area in each audit field

Table 2.

Audit Field	Audit Time	Weight	Sub-area	Weight	Final weight	Priority
IT Architecture	Foundation Set-up& Current Architecture Construction	0.55	Foundation Set-up	0.38	0.22	1
			Current Architecture Construction	0.34	0.18	2
			Quality Control	0.27	0.15	3
	Goal Architecture Construction & Implementation Plan	0.45	Goal Architecture Construction	0.29	0.13	1
			Implementation Plan	0.26	0.12	2
			Management	0.23	0.10	3
			Quality Control	0.21	0.09	4
IT Strategy	Current step analysis & Strategy development	0.59	Task Analysis	0.44	0.26	1
			Technology Analysis	0.31	0.18	2
			Quality Control	0.26	0.15	3
	Improvement Model & Implementation plan	0.41	IT plan	0.63	0.26	2
			Quality Control	0.37	0.37	1

Table2. (*Continued*)

IS system Development	Demand Analysis	0.33	System Architecture	0.38	0.13	1
			Applied System	0.29	0.10	3
			Database	0.33	0.11	2
	Analysis/Design	0.24	System Architecture	0.37	0.09	1
			Applied System	0.29	0.07	3
			Database	0.33	0.08	2
	Implementation	0.15	System Architecture	0.20	0.03	3
			Applied System	0.32	0.05	2
			Database	0.48	0.07	1
	Testing	0.15	Test Activities	*	0.15	1
	Deployment	0.13	Preparation for Operation	*	0.13	2
DB Construction	Preparation	0.65	Data Collection Model Construction	*	0.65	1
	Implementation	0.35	Data Construction	0.56	0.20	2
			Quality Control	0.44	0.15	3
System Operation	Operation	*	User-Service	0.54	0.54	1
			User-Service support	0.46	0.46	2
Maintenance	Maintenance	*	Maintenance	*	*	

In table 2, relative weights of inter –element in audit time and sub-area is shown. The final weights are calculated by the relative weight of the certain item multiplied by the upper level item's relative weight. For the project type such as System operation and Maintenance have only one element, it was unable to calculate the relative weight since a pair-wise comparison could not conducted for one element. So it is recorded as *. After final weights are obtained, the priority is calculated based on it. This result gives a logical validity enough to modify or change standard check items.

5   Conclusion

The IS Audit is defined as activities conducted by an authorized person for the purpose of providing an independent assessment of software products and processes in order to assess compliance with requirements. In general, the auditing is executed based on "The standard check items" by auditing-companies registered in the Minister of Public Administration and Security. Although such activity contributes to protecting computer system assets, maintaining the integrity of data and securing the efficiency and effectiveness of the system to a large extent, there have been many negative views on the audit effect and quality. Although there have been a lot of studies on audit effect and quality, most of them focus on improvement of auditor ability human resources, problem-solving for poor audit companies, and quality evaluation for audit results. However, it is essential to flexibly change the audit check items in order to improve the audit quality as information technologies become converged and complex, various technologies emerge, and software becomes more intelligent, larger, and more complicated. To this end, this study calculated relative weight and priority of inter- standard check items using HDM which is a Hierarchical Decision-making Model and the Constant-Sum Method which is a method to give relative weight score. These results will give a logical validity enough to modify or change standard check items.

References

1. National Computerization Agency, A Study on the Audit Programs for Information System the Report of 2004 R&D Results (2004)
2. Electronic Government Act Art. 57 (Information System Audit for Administrative Agencies, etc), Enforcement Decree Art 71 of Electronic Government Law (Information System Audit)
3. Announcement from the Ministry of Public Administration and Security (No. 2010-85), Revision of the Information System Audit Standard
4. National Information Society, Informationalization Project Management Manual (ver. 1.0-2011.07)
5. The Direction of the Information System Audit System. In: Information System Audit Symposium (2009)
6. The Direction of ICT Audit in IT Convergence. In: Information System Audit Symposium (2010)
7. Measures for the Information System Audit in the Future Computing Environment. In: Information System Audit Symposium (2011)
8. Gyeong, T.-W., Kim, S.-G.: A Study on the Priority Analysis of Information Systems Audit Evaluation Factors using Fuzzy-AHP Method. Information Systems Review 10(3), 155–183 (2008)
9. Shin, D.-I.: A Scientific Method of Information System Audit. In: Informationalization Policy, 2nd edn., vol. 15, pp. 3–24 (2008) (Summer Edition)
10. Nam, G., et al.: A Study on Comparative Analysis for Information Systems Audit and International IT Guidance. The final report of issues entrusted to the National Information Society, 12 (2008)
11. Information System Audit Comments Ver. 3.0, National Information Society Agency (2008)
12. Jo, G.-T., Jo, Y.-G., Kang, H.-S.: Analytic Hierarchy Process. Donghyun Publishing Co. (2003)
13. Saaty, T.L.: The Analytic Hierarchy Process. McGraw-Hill, New York (1980)
14. Kocaoglu, D.F.: A participative Approach to Program Evaluation. IEEE Transaction on Engineering Management Em-30(3) (August 1983)

Improving the Performances of Internet-Based Marketplace for Technology: A Korean Case Study

Jong Bok Park

Dept. of Venture & Business, Gyeongnam National University of Science and Technology
150 Chilam-Dong, Jinju, Gyeongnam, South Korea, 660-758
jxpark@gntech.ac.kr

Abstract. Korean governments are experimenting with online approach for promoting technology transfer. Internet-based market for technology has limitations in completing transactions owing to characteristics intrinsic to technologies as subjects of transactions and allows the room for improving its role and function. This paper investigates the performance of the most representative marketplace for technology operating in Korea and explores its obstacles to satisfying the great expectations of stakeholders. The paper reports both quantitative and qualitative evidences through in-depth interview and focus group interview. The concluding remarks focus on management implications to enhance the performances of the Internet-based marketplace for technology.

Keywords: market for technology, technology transfer, Internet-based approach, technology commercialization.

1 Introduction

In Korea, the markets for technology have received great attention from the government and policy makers since the government enacted 'Korean Technology Transfer Promotion Act (KTTP Act)' in 2000. A series of pro-technology transfer programs have been launched in Korea on the basis of the KTTP Act, which resembles the U.S. Bayh-Dole Act of 1980 and the U.S. Stevenson-Wydler Technology Innovation Act of 1980. Because the market for technology was unfledged, the Korean government determined to develop the market for technology rapidly. Most of all, the government opened an Internet-based marketplace called 'National Technology Bank (NTB)' in 2000 based on the KTTP Act.[1]

Basically, markets for technology promote the diffusion and efficient use of existing technology and they can enhance the rate of technological advance by providing additional incentives to invest in R&D (Arora *et al.*, 2001). However, the markets for technology have remained imperfect in contrast to the markets for most products and services. As technological knowledge is usually commercialized by selling products

---

[1] In 2010, NTB was re-abbreviated as 'network for tech-biz.' The website of the NTB is www.ntb.kr.

J.J. Park et al. (Eds.): NPC 2012, LNCS 7513, pp. 241–247, 2012.
© IFIP International Federation for Information Processing 2012

and services, the markets for technology are not common. At the same time, there are many imperfections in these markets, which result in high transaction costs.

Along with the 'information technology-based revolution', many practitioners and policy makers have assumed that Internet could help firms to overcome these market imperfections. In particular, Internet-based marketplaces for technology were expected to encourage inter-organizational technology transactions. A variety of intermediary companies, which are often backed by venture capital, have emerged to facilitate technology trading through Internet platforms. Prominent examples include Yet2.com, NineSigma, InnoCentive, and the Patent & Licenses Exchange (Lichtenthaler & Ernst, 2008).

By the way the NTB, that is, the most representative Internet-based marketplace for technology in Korea, doesn't seem to work effectively not only because of the characteristics intrinsic to technologies but also because of the failures of operation strategies. Very little is known about its success regarding the number of technology transactions that have originated from NTB, and hardly any information is unveiled by the Korean government that runs the marketplace.[2] Therefore, it is needed to diagnose the current status of NTB and to enhance the performances of the Internet-based marketplace in order to meet the great expectations of stakeholders.

2 Methodology

2.1 In-Depth Interview and Focus Group Interview

In-depth interview was used to collect quantitative and qualitative data on NTB. The author asked several KIAT staffs in charge of NTB about their experiences and expectations, and the thoughts they have concerning NTB operations, processes, and outcomes as a result of their involvement in the Internet-based marketplace. Through the one-to-one interviews, comprehensive data on NTB were obtained.

Focus group interview was employed to identify obstacles to facilitating the NTB and to brainstorm the strategies for improving the performances of NTB. Focus group included eight professionals across the sectors of technology seller, buyer, intermediary, and investor. Questions were asked in an interactive group setting where participants were free to talk with other group members.

2.2 Framework for Investigating Performances

It is not easy to find previous research on the performances of Internet-based marketplace for technology to my knowledge. Park (2002) and Seo *et al.* (2003) propose the roles of cyber technology market focusing on online technomart services. Koh *et al.* (2009) suggests a conceptual model including the relationship between the online supporting services of technology intermediary and the performance of technology trading.

---

[2] NTB has been operated by the Korea Institute for Advancement of Technology (KIAT) on behalf of the Korean government.

An Internet-based marketplace for technology is not only a cyber space where technology buyers and sellers meet each other, but also a one-stop total technology transaction support system that enables the systematic technology transaction to be accomplished on it (Park, 2002). In this paper, the performances of NTB were measured by primary performance and secondary performance (refer to Table 1). The primary performance implies the extent of vitalization of online market for technology, which can be classified into technology registration, technology evaluation, and technology marketing. The secondary performance tells how many technologies are licensed or sold online and/or offline after registration on Internet-based marketplace.

Table 1. Indicators measuring the performances of NTB

Classification		Indicator	Operational definition
Primary performance	Technology registration	Technology supply	• Number of technologies registered for sale or licensing
		Technology demand	• Number of technologies registered that potential buyers demand
	Technology evaluation	-	• Incidences that customers utilize the technology evaluation services offered
	Technology marketing	Technology promoting	• Incidences that technologies are promoted effectively
		Networking	• Number of technologies which information is shared by the other Internet platforms
Secondary performance	Technology transaction	-	• Number of licensed or sold technologies among the ones registered

3   Overview of NTB

Several government ministries in Korea have been constructing their own online markets for technology competitively. NTB is the most representative market for technology, considering its biggest size in Korea, which is greater than five times that of the second largest 'IP-Mart' in terms of the number of technologies registered.[3]

NTB is an extended online platform for technology transaction, that is, a network for technology transfer and technology commercialization, which has been operated by KIAT in request of the Ministry of Knowledge Economy. NTB users can be supported by offline services as well as online ones.

Basically, NTB provides five types of services online, which consist of 'technology trading support service,' 'technology evaluation service,' 'technology news service,' 'technology consulting service,' and 'global business support service.' Technology

---

[3] IP-Mart is an abbreviation of Internet Patent Mart and it has been sponsored by the Korean Intellectual Property Office. As of 2010, NTB contains 78,011 cases of technologies supplied and 1,730 cases of technologies demanded.

trading support service allows NTB users to search technologies of their interest by specific areas and technology sellers. Through technology evaluation service, NTB users can have technologies of their interest evaluated as well as compare other related evaluation reports provided by professional technology rating agencies.

In addition, technology news service enables NTB users to obtain various kinds of technology-related news focusing on recent trends of technological development and government funds available. NTB users can also take professional advice when they ask questions on technology transfer and commercialization through technology consulting service. Lastly, global business support service is specialized to provide NTB users with reliable information necessary to put themselves into global marketplaces, including the EU, the United States, China, Japan, and Southeast Asia.

In contrast, offline services of NTB have been offered through technology brokerage events. These are classified into domestic and international technology brokerage events. The former is held every week, and the latter is held about twice a year.

4   Diagnosis of NTB

4.1   Investigation of NTB Performances

With respect to primary performance of NTB, the performance of technology registration signifies how much database of supplied and demanded technologies is constructed in terms of its quantity. Technology supply of NTB has been conducted mainly by public sectors. In 2010, there were few technologies that were supplied by private enterprises (62 cases by large companies; 5 cases by small and medium sized enterprises) and individuals (0 cases) while public research organizations (PROs) including universities and government laboratories registered 3,375 cases of technologies. Technologies on demand have also been of great scarcity except for a few of certified technology intermediaries.[4] Only 37 cases of technologies were explicitly demanded on NTB through certified technology intermediaries in 2010. Thus, technology registration performance of NTB is unbalanced and dominated by public sectors despite of NTB's diverse supporting activities for vitalizing the marketplace for technology.

The performance of technology evaluation could be estimated by investigating how many times technology evaluation services are used. In detail, 'commercialization possibility evaluation service' (397 cases) and 'technology valuation service' (395 cases) were relatively more used than 'corporate technological capability evaluation service' (84 cases) and 'business plan preparing service' (105 cases) in 2010. However, most of certified technology intermediaries that are considered to be major beneficiaries have been employing their own evaluation solutions rather than technology evaluation services of NTB. This tells us that technology evaluation performance of NTB is a little bit measured excessively.

---

[4] The KTTP Act stipulates that the government can certify technology intermediaries that meet some qualification criteria (Park, 2010).

The performance of technology marketing implies how aggressively technologies on NTB are marketed. In 2010, NTB sent 1,638,419 newsletters to its users and about 44% of sent newsletters were received online. 226 cases of technologies on NTB were promoted through domestic and international technology brokerage events. However, its networking with other related Internet platforms or institutions, especially overseas institutions such as 'Asian and Pacific Center for Transfer of Technology', is not facilitated that much. Although NTB shares technology and market information with other Internet platforms, the amount of information shared is considerably limited owing to simple linkages.

Secondary performance of NTB could be represented by the performance of technology transaction, which is measured by licensed or sold technologies among the ones registered on NTB. The performance of technology transaction was on an increasing trend in the past three years (257 cases in 2007; 390 cases in 2008; 484 cases in 2009). Out of technologies transacted, the average cases of technologies traded through offline technology brokerage events were 62 during the past five years of 2005-2009. However, it is hard to measure how much NTB contributed to such technology transactions because technologies registered on NTB could be transferred through alternative channels without its direct assistance.

4.2   Identification of Obstacles to Facilitating NTB

In order to explore obstacles to facilitating NTB and analyze their causes, two steps of activities were performed. First, the obstacles were identified through the in-depth interview with KIAT staffs. According to the 'Survey on service utilization and user satisfaction on NTB' that KIAT administered in 2010, 'lack of public promotion' (27.5%), 'low quality of information and service' (25.5%), and 'inconvenient user interface' (21.1%) were found to be three primary problems of NTB in terms of response rate. Second, the details and causes of these three problems were examined through the focus group interview.

'Lack of public promotion' includes confusion of the meaning on NTB, lack of promotion for success stories on technology transaction via NTB, and technology brokerage events undifferentiated from those of other agencies. This problem may be caused from the fact that NTB is somewhat ill-equipped and under-funded to accomplish its role and mission. Therefore, the majority of potential customers tend to have little interest in NTB while technology transfer managers in PROs are aware of its existence due to the legal duty of registering technologies developed in their organizations.

Next, 'low quality of information and service' implies technical knowledge-biased and/or outdated technology information, missing links of communication channels between technology sellers and potential buyers, low reliability of information linked to other Internet platforms, and low quality of technology consulting service. Several causes for this problem were posed in the focus group interview. Technology transfer managers in PROs were not strongly motivated to provide buyer-friendly technology information since they did not expect to be additionally rewarded for their efforts to register technologies (Choi, 2001). In addition, the ill-equipped and under-funded features of NTB were suggested as one of the major causes of this problem like that of 'lack of public promotion.'

Lastly, 'inconvenient user interface' means heavy searching costs induced by technology seller-friendly arrangements of search results, limitation of the numbers and sizes of technology information files uploaded simultaneously, and uniform e-mailing service with less consideration of recipients. Being in consumers' shoes as well as listening to a variety of users' opinions is critical for improving user interface of NTB.

5   Concluding Remarks: Management Implications

In order to enhance the performances of the Internet-based marketplace for technology in Korea, the future managerial strategies for NTB need to focus on participant's incentives to use NTB and capability to accelerate commercialization.

With regard to participant's incentives, it is desirable that NTB users continue to re-visit and utilize technology information and services. Thus, NTB needs to provide more application-oriented information, because technical knowledge-biased information is not easy for potential buyers to understand. Furthermore, the quality of information regis-tered by sellers should be enhanced by controlling technology registration process and by monitoring the reliability of the information more tightly.

Second, the marketplace and users on NTB need to be segmented in order to differen-tiate technology markets and to customize various kinds of users. Without differentiating markets, technology sellers are not motivated to register their attractive technologies onto NTB. In particular, PROs are likely to supply valueless technologies, subject to the gov-ernment regulation on the obligatory registration of technologies available for technology transfer. By customizing users, their satisfactions may be maximized and therefore they become loyal customers to NTB.

Third, the sector-wise networking communities should be organized and operated online and offline. A lot of opportunities for technology transaction and investment can be created and they can develop further into commercialization projects. It is recommended that the networking communities include investor such as venture capi-tal as well as technology seller, buyer, and intermediary.

Concerning the capability to accelerate commercialization, NTB needs to be improved so that it enables the information and services to be utilized for commercialization. Therefore, NTB needs to provide reference information for technology transaction. In particular, reference information for pricing subject technologies is most demanded. Although NTB has been offering technology evaluation service and technology news service, the information from those services may not be enough to price potential tech-nologies for trading. Thus, NTB may as well provide the primary statistics on technology transactions such as price, running royalty rate, and upfront fee by constructing database using the bi-annual technology transfer reports received from PROs.

Second, NTB needs to strengthen consultation services for technology transfer and commercialization. The current technology consulting services are offered only on the basis of online advising or commenting. It is not easy to find success stories or good experiences that customer benefited from the consultation service. Therefore, NTB may as well add consultation services on the basis of phone call or offline meeting in order to maximize the effect of consultation service.

Third, NTB needs to link related government programs and policies to NTB in order to facilitate technology transfer and commercialization in there. KIAT, the operating agency of NTB, is planning and implementing a lot of government grant programs in the area of technology commercialization on behalf of the Korean government. Unfortunately, it seems that KIAT and the government regard NTB as just one of various programs they manage. Therefore, NTB needs to leverage its attractiveness by combining the other related grant programs in order to induce potential customers into NTB regime.

References

1. Arora, A., Fosfuri, A., Gambardella, A.: Markets for technology: The Economics of Innovation and Corporate Strategy. MIT Press, Cambridge (2001)
2. Choi, J.P.: Technology transfer with moral hazard. International Journal of Industrial Organization 19(1-2), 249–266 (2001)
3. Koh, J., Choi, S.-J., Lim, J.-D., Lee, G.-H.: An Exploratory Study on Online Service Factors Promoting Technology Trade. Korean Journal of Internet e-Commerce 9(3), 285–312 (2009) (in Korean)
4. Lichtenthaler, U., Ernst, H.: Innovation Intermediaries: Why Internet Marketplaces for Technology Have Not Yet Met the Expectations. Creativity and Innovation Management 17(1), 14–25 (2008)
5. Park, H.-W.: A study on improved roles of cyber Technology Market in Korea. Korean Journal of Internet e-Commerce 2(2), 143–165 (2002) (in Korean)
6. Park, J.-B.: Cultivating the technology transfer intermediary in Korea. KIET Industrial Economic Review 15(4), 40–54 (2010)
7. Seo, J., Lim, D., Jeong, H.: A review on the online technomart service and service strategy. Korean Journal of Internet e-Commerce 3(1), 95–117 (2003) (in Korean)

The Day-of-the Week Effects for Cloud-Based Shipment Timing Support System for Stored Apples

Youngsik Kwak[1] and YoonJung Nam[2,*]

[1] Gyeongnam National University of Science and Technology
yskwak@gntech.ac.kr
[2] Hanyang University
jean@hanyang.ac.kr

Abstract. The purpose of this study is to empirically analyze whether the wholesale price of apples sold in the Korean action-based wholesale market is statistically significantly different at the aggregate and disaggregate levels, or not. It means that the researchers in this study empirically analyzed to identify day-of-the-week effects in Korean wholesale price of apples.

The results of this study showed that, when shipped by the order of Monday, Thursday, Wednesday, Friday, Tuesday, and Saturday, the apples can be sold with higher prices, with statistical significance. Monday recorded the highest price while Saturday recorded the lowest price. Based on the results of this study, the growers and sellers of apples may control shipping time so that the apples are sold by auction on days of the week when their profits are maximized. Also, when the day-of-the-week effects is applied to the modeling of supporting system for the apple shipping period presented by the previous studies, more accurate system for shipping period can be constructed. Such system can be used by the growers or sellers of apples at the cloud base.

Keywords: Day-of-the Effect, Stored Apples, Cloud-based Shipment Timing Support System Modeling.

1   Introduction

The day-of-the-week effect indicates a condition that sales volume, price, and profit of a product are different from days of the week [1]. Studies of the effects mainly focus on stock market, and it is rare to research the effects on agricultural and marine products [2].

The characteristics of the previous studies of the day-of-the-week effects on agricultural and marine products are as follows. First, studies on agricultural products are more than those on marine products. Second, the US has measured the day-of-the-week effects on various grains dealt in futures markets, but Korean researchers have studied only seasonings such as garlic, onion, and red pepper[2], indicating that studies on grains

---

* Corresponding author.

J.J. Park et al. (Eds.): NPC 2012, LNCS 7513, pp. 248–255, 2012.

or fruits are insufficient. Third, the analysis unit of the previous studies is the whole sell-ing period during a year, and thus, they are studies at aggregate level. However, as Seo and Kim(2009) pointed out, analysis of selling price is desirable to be conducted by di-viding the whole selling period into several segmented markets [3], indicating that it is needed to be analyzed at segment level or disaggregate level. Fourth, day-of-the-week effects among purchasing time effects has relatively more literature than intra-month or inter-month effects. Fifth, American studies usually focus on future wholesale prices from futures markets, but Korean counterparts are based on prices of present wholesale prices [4]. Future price is a price of certain point of the future and auction wholesale price is sales price of a day, and Korean researchers rather than their American counterparts reflect price interest of sellers or growers more.

Table 1. Dichotomy of Purchasing Time Effect

	Aggregate level	Disaggregate level
the day- of-the-week effect	grains(US), Onion, Halibut, Meat, Rockfish (Korea), Position of this study	Position of this study
intra-month effect	Garlic, Onion(Korea)	
inter-month effect	Garlic, Onion, Spice, Halibut(Korea)	

This study is purported to fill in the research field that has not been dealt in the previous studies. The purpose of this study is to empirically analyze whether the wholesale price of apples sold in a few auction-based wholesale market such as Garak and Gangseo agricultural market is statistically significantly different at the disaggre-gate levels, or not. It means the authors in this study empirically analyzed to identify the day-of-the-week effect in Korean wholesale price of apples.

Based on the results of this study, the sellers of apples may control shipping time so that the apples are sold by auction on days of the week when their profits are max-imized at business perspectives. Also, when the day-of-the-week effects is applied to the modeling of supporting system for the apple shipping period presented by the previous studies, more accurate system for shipping period may be constructed [11]. In terms of academic aspect, this study reports the day-of-the-week effects on fruits, which have hardly been dealt with by the previous studies in agricultural industry.

2   Literature Review for Purchasing Time Effects

Purchasing time effect indicates that sales volume, price, and profits are different from selling time points (day of the week, intra-month, inter-month) [5]. The purchas-ing time effect in the previous studies is roughly classified into 1) cases in which analysis unit is different and 2) cases in which analysis time-point is different.

Studies with different analysis unit may be divided into three types as follows. First, there are studies of differences from time points when volume serves as analysis unit, indicating studies of tracking changes in volumes such as frequency of occurrence, selling volume, and shipping volume on certain day of the week. These may be studies of changes in crime rate or selling volume of clothes by days of the week [6]. Second, there are studies of differences from time points in changes in price level. Such domestic studies include the Korean ones investigating time effects of agricultural and marine products (seasoning vegetables and seafood) on auction prices in Garak market and Noryangjin fish market, and the American ones identifying grain prices in American futures market[2][4][7]. The previous studies have focused on rather wholesale price than retail price. Third, there are studies in which profit is used as analysis unit, indicating studies in which differences in price earnings ratio and bond yield are analyzed in financial management whose time effects have been researched most actively, on bases of days of the week, intra-month, and inter-month.

As for Korean agricultural and marine products, there may be two analysis units in studies of purchasing time effect: volume and price level. The Seoul Agricultural & Marine Products Corporation is making on-line announcement of volume and bid in wholesale markets on a daily basis [8]. Growers or sellers of apple have interest in bid rather than volume, for, in this study, the analysis unit of purchasing time point was the wholesale prices announced by the Garak Agricultural & Marine Products Corporation on-line on a daily basis.

Second, when studies are divided by analysis time-point, purchasing time effects can be classified into day-of-the-week effects, intra-month effects, and inter-month effects. As for the three time effects by industries, certain academic fields tend to focus on certain time effects. Financial management usually have researched day-of-the-week effects, intra-month effects, and inter-month effects, criminology have measured day-of-the-week effects, and agricultural and marine products have studied day-of-the-week effects and intra-month effects. Clothes and sports shoes have researched day-of-the-week effects and intra-month effects, while fashion has rarely studied inter-month effects.

In terms of agricultural and marine products, the sellers are possible to have interest in day-of-the-week effects rather than intra- or inter-month effects. In this context, this study selected day-of-the-week effects as the analysis unit.

Studies of agricultural and marine products have been conducted in the USA and Korea. Most American studies have focused on the day-of-the-week effects of grains in futures markets, while Korean studies have dealt with the daily wholesale bids of seasoning vegetables and some marine products in wholesale markets. Yoon and Yangg (2004) and Ko (2010) identified the day-of-the-week, monthly, and intra-month effects of seasoning vegetable prices, flatfish and Jacopever. Their results showed that time effects were different even in the same seasoning vegetable and fishes [2][0]. Thus, it is indicating that the results of day-of-the-week effects may be different from research subjects. Chiang & Tapley (1983) identified day-of-the-week effects in futures markets. When daily changes in future prices of 21 items were investigated, day-of-the-week effects as in stock market were shown in grains [7].

Chang & Kim (1988) investigated day-of-the-week effects and changes in product prices in future market. Day-of-the-week effects had existed until 1981, but since 1982 such effects had disappeared in future market [4].

The day-of-the-week effects of these American studies showed or did not show based on research period, indicating that determination of research period is a key to studies of day-of-the-week effects. In this context, analysis in this study should be conducted on the basis of data collected in the sufficiently long term. All the above-mentioned articles investigated day-of-the-week effects of the subject products during only certain period. They can be called aggregate level analysis because day-of-the-week effects were analyzed for the entire sample data.

However, Seo and Kim (2009) divided apple shipping period into six sub-periods in researching the shipping period for Korean apple wholesale prices based on risk bearing tendency of apple growers [3]. This may be called disaggregate level analysis.

Seo and Kim (2009) was not a study of day-of-the-week effects; the average prices of each sub-period were all different and the shipping activities of apple growers were different. Thus, such difference in prices and shipping amount might be shown as day-of-the-week effects different from periods. However, there have been no evidences to prove that the division of six sub-periods for shipping periods of Korean stored apples presented by Seo and Kim (2009) is normatively proper. Based on such inference, therefore, the authors of this study measured day-of-the-week effects 1) when the entire data collection period was analysis unit and 2) when the six sub-periods by Seo and Kim (2009) were analysis unit.

3   Research

The wholesale prices of apples used in this study were on-line daily announcement data presented by the Seoul Agricultural & Marine Products Corporation. Because prices of apples are different from varieties, grades, and package units, Fuji 15kg special grade apples were selected to be the subjects. The data was collected between October 14, 2009 and February 25, 2012. The Fuji apples of special grade were first sold by auction on October 14, 2009, and a total 662 apples were observed.

Table 2. Wholesale prices average of Fuji apples by days of the week in the samples

Day	Average price(KRW)	N	SD
Monday	59,189	111	13,004
Tuesday	57,050	106	11,955
Wednesday	57,184	113	13,315
Thursday	58,646	110	12,893
Friday	57,093	112	13,549
Saturday	53,155	110	11,657
Average	57,057	662	12,855

4   Results

4.1   The Day-of-the Week Effects at Aggregate Level

4.1.1 Verification of Differences in Averages by Days of the Week

The average prices by days of the week during the period of data collection are as shown in Table 2; the average prices (57,057 as median) were lowest on Saturday and highest on Monday. ANOVA was conducted to verify whether the auction wholesale prices of a 15kg box of Fuji apples with special grade are statistically significantly different by days of the week. The results of the analysis were as shown in Table 3. The samples of this study were reveal differences in the wholesale prices at 99-percent confidence level by days of the week (F=3.022, p=0.01).

Table 3. ANOVA results for difference in average price for the day-of-the effect

	SS	Df	MS	F	P
Bt groups	2.45E+0.9	5	491872887	3.02	0.01
Within groups	1.06E+11	656	162770720		
Total	1.09E+11	661			

Scheffe test was conducted to empirically verify differences in the wholesale prices among days of the week, and the results are as shown in Table 4. The differences in the wholesale average prices were statistically significant only between Saturday and Monday and between Saturday and Thursday. No statistically significant differences were found in the wholesale average prices at 90-percent confidence level between other days of the weeks.

Based on the results of analysis of the entire samples, apple growers can have profits when they avoid Saturday's auction and ship their apples on any day of the week except for Saturday.

Table 4. Scheffe Test among days of the week in the entire samples based on Saturday

Anchor Day	Day	MD	SE	P
Saturday	Monday	-6034	1,716	0.031
	Tuesday	-3895	1,736	0.413
	Wednesday	-4029	1,708	0.353
	Thursday	-5491	1,720	0.072
	Friday	-3938	1,712	0.383

4.1.2 Regression Analysis of Effects of Day-of-the-Week

However, there may be several variables affecting the wholesale bid of each day of the week. Regression analysis in which such multi variables are independent variables may be helpful in measuring effects of each day of the week on daily wholesale price.

In this study, independent variables included shipment quantity at the previous time t (Q_{t-1}), apple's wholesale price at the previous time t(p_{t-1}), whether the time t is the last week of Chuseok or Lunar New Year's Day (BEFORE), whether the time t is the next week of Chuseok or Lunar New Year's Day (AFTER), number of days passed after shipping of newly harvested apples (DAY), differences in prices between apple and pear during the last period (AP_PEAR $_{t-1}$), and nominal scale expressing days of the weeks. The R-square value of the formula was 0.63.

$$\text{Price}_t = a_t + b_1 Q_{t-1} + b_2 p_{t-1} + b_3 \text{BEFORE}_t + b_4 \text{AFTER}_t + b_5 \text{DAY}_t + b_6 \text{DAY*DAY}_t$$
$$+ b_7 \text{AP\_PEAR}_{t-1} + b_8 \text{Mon}_t + b_9 \text{Tues}_t + b_{10} \text{Wends}_t + b_{11} \text{Thurs}_t + b_{12} \text{Fri}_t + b_{13} \text{Sat}_t \qquad (1)$$

Where a, b1 to b13 are parameters to be estimated.

Table 5. Results of regression analysis to verify variables affecting apple's wholesale prices

Predictors	coefficients	Wald	p-value
Intercept	20063.47	82.0	1.40E-19
Q_{t-1}	-15.15	10.0	1.50E-03
p_{t-1}	0.63	385.8	6.70E-86
BEFORE	3194.42	16.7	4.50E-05
AFTER	-2920.90	19.9	8.40E-06
DAY	100.85	27.8	1.40E-07
DDAY	-0.40	34.6	4.00E-09
AP_Pear $_{t-1}$	-0.04	5.6	0.018
Monday	3898.83		
Tuesday	-1207.58		
Wednesday	716.95	54.4	1.70E-10
Thursday	912.67		
Friday	-458.12		
Saturday	-3862.75		

The results are as shown in Table 5. All the independent variables significantly affected the wholesale prices of apples during this period (p<0.01). The results showed that, when shipped by the order of Monday, Thursday, Wednesday, Friday, Tuesday, and Saturday, the apples can be sold with higher prices, with statistical significance (Wald test=54.4, p=1.70E+10). Monday recorded the highest price while Saturday recorded the lowest price.

Formula (1) can be used as a predictive model for how much are the wholesale prices of apples per the time t, indicating that it can be used as an apples' shipment decision-making support system. When the model is supplied to those who grow and store apples as a cloud-based application, they may record sufficient profits by using the day-of-the-week effects.

4.2 The Day-of-the Week Effects at Disaggregate Level

According to the Seo and Kim (2009)'s classification, te shipping period was divided into six sessions to analyze sub-periods: Period 1 (harvest period, between the middle of October and the first of December), Period 2 (year-end and New Year's time, between the middle of December and the first of January), Period 3 (Lunar New Year's Day, between the middle of January and the middle of February), Period 4 (between the last of February and the last of April), Period 5 (between the first of May and the last of June), and Period 6 (between the first of July and the last of August). The observed values by days of the week were different because auction was not performed during Lunar New Year's Day and Chuseok.

According to the results of the ANOVA for the Period 1, 2, 3, 4, and 6, there were no statistically significant differences in the wholesale prices of the 15kg box of Fuji apples with special grade by days of the weeks, respectively. In case of Period 1, $F=0.527$, $p=0.756$. In case of Period 2, $F=1.382$, $p=0.242$. In case of Period 3, $F=0.598$, $p=0.701$. In case of Period 4, $F=0.396$, $p=0.851$. In case of Period 6, $F=0.396$, $p=0.851$.

The results of ANOVA for the Period 5 showed that statistically significant differences were found in the wholesale prices of the 15kg box of Fuji apples with special grade by days of the weeks in spring days between May and June ($F=2.142$, $p=0.067$). Tukey test was conducted to empirically verify where the differences in the wholesale prices are located between days of the weeks, and the results are as shown in Table 6.

Table 6. Wholesale prices of Fuji apples by days of the weeks during the Period 5

Day	Average price(KRW)	N	SD
Monday	58,861	18	6,651
Tuesday	57,713	18	6,759
Wednesday	59,811	18	7,069
Thursday	58,979	17	7,308
Friday	60,216	16	8,613
Saturday	53,395	17	5,435
Average	58,161	104	7,203

Differences in the wholesale average prices with statistical significance were shown only between Saturday and Wednesday and between Saturday and Friday. Periods between other days of the weeks did now show differences in the wholesale average prices at 90-percent confidence level. During the Period 5, apple growers may have profits when avoided Saturday's auction and shipped their apples on any day of the week except for Saturday.

5   Conclusion

The purpose of this study was to empirically analyze at the aggregate and disaggregate levels whether the differences in the wholesale prices of apples sold in the Korean auction-based wholesale market had statistical significance based on days of the weeks. That is, the researchers empirically analyzed to identify day-of-the-week effects in Korean wholesale price of apples.

The results at the aggregate level showed that apple growers can have profits when they avoid Saturday's auction and ship their apples on any day of the week except for Saturday. In case of analysis at disaggregate level the results produced when shipped by the order of Monday, Thursday, Wednesday, Friday, Tuesday, and Saturday, the apples can be sold with higher prices, with statistical significance. Monday recorded the highest price while Saturday recorded the lowest price. At least, if the apple growers ship the apples on Monday than Saturday, they can improve the profit 7761.59(=3898.83+3862.75) KRW.

On the basis of the results of this study, the growers and sellers of apples may control shipping time so that the apples are sold by auction on days of the week when their profits are maximized at business level. Also, when the day-of-the-week effects is applied to the modeling of supporting system for the apple shipping period presented by the previous studies, more accurate system for shipping period can be constructed as follows;

$$\text{Price}_t = 20063.47 - 15.15 * Q_{t-1} + 0.63 * p_{t-1} + 3194.41 * \text{BEFORE}_t + -2920.9 * \text{AFTER}_t + 100.85 * \text{DAY}_t - 0.4 * \text{DAY} * \text{DAY}_t - 0.04 * \text{AP\_PEAR}_{t-1} + 3898.83 * \text{Mon}_t + - 1207.58 * \text{Tues}_t + 716.95 * \text{Wends}_t + 912.67 * \text{Thurs}_t - 458.12 * \text{Fri}_t - 3862.75 * \text{Sat}_t$$

Such system can be used by the growers or sellers of apples at the cloud base.

Acknowledgements. This work was supported by Gyeongnam National University of Science and Technology Grant in 2012.

References

1. Kahn, B.E., Schmittlein, D.C.: Shopping Trip Behavior: An Empirical Investigation. Marketing Letters 1(1), 55–69 (1989)
2. Yoon, B.-S., Yang, S.-R.: A Study on the Day-of-the-Week, Monthly and Intra-Month Effects in Spicy Vegetable Prices. Agriculture and Economy Research 45(2), 187–210 (2004)
3. Seo, S., Kim, T.: Stochastic Dominance of Expected Income by Sales Timing for Stored Apples in Korea. Journal of Korean Agricultural Economic Association 50(1), 85–101 (2009)
4. Chang, E.C., Kim, C.: Day of the Week Effects and Commodity Price Changes. Journal of Futures Market 8(2), 229–241 (1988)
5. Lee, M., Hwang, S., Kwak, Y.: A Study of Timing Effects in Sports Shoes Market: The Day-of-the Week Effects. The Korean Society of Clothing and Textiles (forthcoming, 2012)
6. Nam, S.: A Study on the Anomaly in Retailing Market: Focused on the day of the week effect of Sales Volume in Fashion Apparel Products Retail Store. Marketing Science Research 16(1), 117–141 (2006)
7. Chinag, R.C., Tapley, T.C.: Day-of-the-Week Effects and the Futures Market. Review of Research in Futures Market 2, 356–410 (1983)
8. Ko, B.-H.: Analysis of Business Operation Trends and Economic Feasibility on Halibut Culture in Jeju Region. Jeju Development Institute (2010)
9. Seo, S., Kim, T.: Operating Statuses of Cold Storage Facilities and Factors of Storage and Sales Decision-Making in Stored Apples. Korean Journal of Agricultural Management and Policy 36(1), 179–197 (2009)
10. Kwak, Y., Song, S.: Shipmen timing support system modeling for stored apples in Korea. Communications in Computer and Information Science 264, 144–152 (2011)

An Empirical View on Opportunistic Forwarding Relay Selection Using Contact Records

Jia Jianbin, Chen Yingwen, and Xu Ming

School of Computer, National University of Defense Technology,
Changsha, 410073, China
{jiajianbin.nudt,csywchen}@gmail.com, xuming@nudt.edu.cn

Abstract. Opportunistic routing schemes usually infer future contact time to select next hop relays. But the effect of relay selected in this way is uncertain. In order to get further understanding of the intrinsic uncertainty characteristic of relay efficiency, this paper makes an empirical investigation on opportunistic forwarding relay selection schemes using contact records. Based on the underlying opportunistic vehicular network extracted from large-scale realistic vehicle traces, we evaluated the efficiency of relay selection and got some intrinsic sight of opportunistic forwarding. The questions we investigated are: What is the probability that a selected relay can make the end-to-end delay reduced? How much the latency can be saved by a properly selected relay? Such an empirical study is meaningful for the protocol design and applications deployment in future opportunistic networks.

Keywords: opportunistic networks, relay selection, residual expected delay, delay reduced ratio.

1   Introduction

In Delay Tolerant Networks (DTN) or Opportunistic Networks (ON), carry-and-forward technique is the major method used for delivering messages. Direct Forwarding (DF) is the most basic scheme, in which messages are carried until the source node contacts with the destination directly. Relays may be involved to assist data exchange in order to obtain better delivery performance. In this case, a primary issue is how to select effective relays. A lot of schemes proposed in previous literatures make relay decision based on the predication of future contact opportunities from history information of connectivity between mobile nodes [1][2].

However, the inaccuracy of predication in practical leads to the selected relay(s) has only an incidental rather than intentional effect on delivery metrics such as end-to-end delay [3]. For example in Fig. 1, if we assume node R_2 is selected as relay, whether the delivery delay of relay assisted forwarding ($S \rightarrow R_2 \rightarrow D$) is really lower than that of direct forwarding ($S \rightarrow D$) is questionable. In addition, whether the selected relay node R_2 has more time saved than other candidate nodes in R_1, R_3, $\cdots$, and R_n is still unclear.

J.J. Park et al. (Eds.): NPC 2012, LNCS 7513, pp. 256–263, 2012.

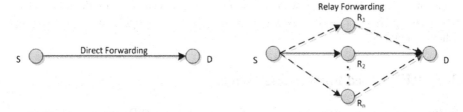

Fig. 1. Example of Relay Assisted Data Delivery

For such "incidental" relay efficiency, this paper provides an empirical study in the background of vehicular DTN. In particular, we mainly focus on the following questions: How to select a proper node as relay? What is the probability that a relay can make the end-to-end delivery delay reduced? How much latency time can be saved by a properly selected relay?

The main contributions of this paper are: (1) We introduce an more effective opportunistic relay selection scheme based on Residual Expected Delay (RED), which utilizes local pairwise contact records and the elapsed time since last encounter to estimate residual encounter time. (2) Based on the underlying vehicular DTN, we investigate relay efficiency in terms of the ratio of delay time can be reduced and the number of possible relays can be selected. Empirical results reflect that the relay efficiency is related to the distribution of direct forwarding delay.

The structure of the paper is organized as follows: The next section presents related work, the third section introduces the RED based relay selection scheme and the estimation framework of RED value. Section 4 gives the detailed evaluation results and analysis of relay efficiency in underlying vehicular DTN. The conclusion of this paper is made in Section 5.

2   Related Works

The core issue of opportunistic messages forwarding is relay selection. Using the knowledge of history contact records between mobile nodes to assist forwarding decision is an important method. S. Jain et al. [4] proposed the Minimum Expected Delay (MED) algorithm in which the value of expected delay is defined as the average waiting time calculated from connectivity schedules of mobile nodes. Evan P. C. Jones et al. [5] improved MED and propose Minimum Estimated Expected Delay (MEED), where the expected delay is calculated using the observed contact history of a sliding history window. While H. Chen et al. in [6] proposed a forwarding scheme that each node decides whether to forward the message to its current encounter by comparing their minimum expected meeting delays (MEMDs) to the destination. The MEMD is calculated based on the past inter-contact times between each pair of nodes and the elapsed time since their last contact.

Our work also uses history contact records to predict residual encounter time with considering the elapsed time from last meeting time. The difference lies in that we focus on the direct forwarding residual delay time and employ a per-contact relay decision scheme. Particularly, we make an empirical investigation on the relay selection methods. Such a work provides some insight into the opportunistic forwarding scheme in practical.

3   RED Based Forwarding Scheme

In this section, we describe the Residual Expected Delay (RED) based relay selection scheme. RED is the estimation value of residual meeting time for a pair of nodes.

3.1   Residual Expected Delay Estimation

Assume each node records the last $n + 1$ meeting times with others. For a pair of nodes, the records are represented by time series $t_1, t_2, \cdots, t_{n+1}$, where t_1 is the most recent record and t_{n+1} is the oldest record. If current time is t, then ET is calculated as $T_E = t - t_1$. Thus, the last n inter contact time (ICT) series can be calculated as $t_1 - t_2$, $t_2 - t_3$, $\cdots$, $t_n - t_{n+1}$. To be described conveniently, we denote the ICT series with $I_1, I_2, \cdots, I_n$, in which the ICTs are sorted by length. Thereby, the residual encounter time for a node pair can be estimated as follow.

Given a set of ICT records of node pair S-D are $I_1, I_2, \cdots, I_n$, where $I_1 \leq I_2 \leq \cdots \leq I_n$. If the elapsed time from last meeting between S and D to the relay decision moment is T_E, and $I_k \leq T_E < I_{k+1}$, then the expectation of residual encounter time T_R for S-D can be calculated by

$$E[T_R] = \frac{1}{n-k}\sum_{k+1}^{n} I_i - T_E \tag{1}$$

Note, when the elapsed time T_E is lower than the minimum value in $\{I_1, I_2, \cdots, I_n\}$, i.e. $T_E < I_1$, the residual delay estimated according to Eq. 1 degrades to the mean inter contact time (MICT). While if T_E is equal to or greater than the maximum value in $\{I_1, I_2, \cdots, I_n\}$, i.e. $T_E \geq I_n$, Eq. 1 is invalid to estimate the residual delay. In this situation, we also use the mean inter contact time as the estimation value as well. Therefore, Eq. 1 is improved to be as the following

$$E[T_R] = \begin{cases} \frac{1}{n-k}\sum_{k+1}^{n} I_i - T_E, & I_k \leq T_E < I_{k+1} \\ \frac{1}{n}\sum_1^n I_i, & T_E < I_1 \text{ or } T_E \geq I_n \end{cases} \tag{2}$$

3.2   Residual Delay Based Relay Selection Decision

Suppose from the time node S injects a message (Msg), which is target to the destination node D, to the time S contact with D directly, S will meet a set of nodes, represented by $\Omega = \{R_1, R_2, \cdots, R_m\}$ in chronological order. In order to reduce the delay time of direct forwarding, S may choose a node from Ω to assist the transmission of Msg. Therefore, Ω can be regarded as potential candidate set of relay. Naturally, the central issue is how to find out an appropriate node from Ω to be utilized as relay.

Residual delay is an effective metric for relay selection decision, which refers to the time from a relay decision moment to the time that the message arriving at destination successfully. Formally, the RED based relay selection strategy is described as following. Assume $T_{R_{XY}}$ represents the residual delay of a message delivered from node X to Y directly. $R_1, R_2, \cdots, R_n$ are the intermediate nodes that source node S met before the target D. The relay selection judgment is determined by comparing the residual expected delay values (calculated according to Eq. 2) of node pairs S-D and R_i-D.

RED Based Strategy: For $R_i \in \{R_1, R_2, \cdots, R_m\}$, if

$$E[T_{R_{SD}}] \geq E\left[T_{R_{R_iD}}\right] \tag{3}$$

then R_i is regarded to be fitting for carrying and forwarding Msg to D.

4   Empirical Evaluation

In this section, we present the empirical investigation results of RED based relay selection strategy. The evaluation is carried out with Cabspotting [7] taxi traces. These taxis operate in San Francisco city Bay area with a core driving coverage of about $11 \times 13 \ km^2$. A Cabspotting trace dataset containing the trace records of 536 vehicles within 25 days can be found in CRAWDAD [8]. We randomly generate a test set composed by 8000 pairs of source-destination (S-D) combination. To avoid the delivery time of S-D sessions being beyond the record time span in the trace dataset, the messages sending requests are randomly injected by node S within the first three days of the records.

To investigate the RED based relay selection method, we design a two-hop opportunistic forwarding algorithm with single copy scheme, in which, only one relay node is needed, and there exists only one replication of message in the network, i.e., if the previous carrier forward the message to the next node, it will discard its own replica. The algorithm uses the per-contact relay decision paradigm, in which the message sender (or carrier) makes a judgment at each time when it meet with a potential relay node, until the message is hand over. Although the two-hop single relay forwarding algorithm is somewhat naive, it is able to generally reflect the relay efficiency of opportunistic forwarding scheme in practical. In addition, we compare RED based forwarding scheme with MICT based scheme [4][5] in which the mean inter contact time value is used as a rough estimation of residual delay time.

4.1   Performance Metrics

We call the constraint conditions used for relay selection as *Qualified Condition*, such as Eq. 1. Nodes satisfying qualified condition are called *Qualified Node*. Generally, a qualified node is expected to have the ability of reducing delivery delay of messages, but whether it can achieve such a benefit is not sure. For distinguishing, we refer to the qualified node satisfying delay reduce expectation as *Good Relay*. Percentage of delay reduced and the ratio of good nodes in qualified nodes reflect the efficiency of the relay qualifying strategy.

Assume the direct forwarding delay is denoted by T_{DF}, and the relay assisted delivery delay is denoted by T_{SRD}. Then, the two metrics to investigate the performance of opportunistic relaying scheme are defined as follows.

- Delay Reduced Ratio (DRR): DRR is measured with the delivery time saved by relay forwarding compared to the delay of direct forwarding. Formally,

$$DRR = \frac{T_{DF} - T_{SRD}}{T_{DF}}$$

- Good Relay Ratio (GRR): GRR is defined as the ratio of good relay number to the qualified node number. Formally,

$$GRR = \frac{N_{good\,relay}}{N_{qualified\,node}}$$

4.2   Delay Reduced Ratio

First, let us look at the average delay reduced ratio of potential relays in different candidate sets. Three relay candidate sets are considered: (1) all potential relays without qualified condition filtering (all the nodes met by S before it meets D); (2) MICT based qualified nodes according to Eq. 3; and (3) RED based qualified nodes according to Eq. 3. As displayed in Table 1, The average DRRs for the three relay candidate sets are about 3.93%, 10.25% and 23.85% respectively. Meanwhile, when only considering good relays in those candidates, the average DRRs are about 27.79%, 32.00% and 44.88% respectively. Such result suggests that taking into account the elapsed time is effective when choosing relays in opportunistic forwarding. And it implies when properly selected a relay with RED based strategy, more than 40% of delay time could be reduced in a general view.

Table 1. Overall Average Delay Reduced Ratio

	Potential Relays	MICT Qualified	RED Qualified
All Relays	3.93%	10.25%	23.85%
Good Relays	27.79%	32.00%	44.88

Table 2. Average Delay Reduced Ratio for First Meet Relay

	Basic FMR	MICT based FMR	RED based FMR
First Relay	6.77%	11.50%	15.20%
First Good Relay	35.60%	37.22%	53.75%

Then, we investigate the distribution of average delay reduced ratio correlated with direct forwarding delay. Fig. 2 shows the average delay reduced ratio in different direct forwarding delay levels. DRR is represented by the vertical axis, while DF delay is represented by the horizontal axis. To reflect DRR under different DF delay levels, we divide the horizontal axis into the unit of a day's time, and then count the average DRR in each DF delay level. For example, the average DRR corresponding to 10 days in horizontal axis means the average DRR of those *S-D* pairs whose direct forwarding delay is larger than 10 days and lower than 11 days.

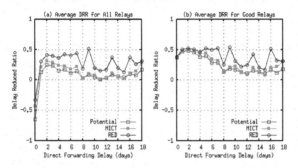

Fig. 2. Delay Reduced Ratio in Average

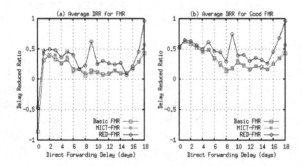

Fig. 3. Delay Reduced Ratio for First Meet Relay

Fig. 2(a) exhibits the average DRR distribution for three kinds of candidate relay sets, and Fig. 2(b) exhibits the corresponding average DRR distribution only considering good candidate relays. Both of the figures show that the average DRR of MICT qualified nodes is a little better than the average of un-qualifying relays. In the same time, the average DRR of RED scheme is much better than others. Particularly, when DF delay is higher than 5 days, RED scheme is more advantageous.

For a determined single relay, if we consider the basic first meet relay (FMR), the average DRRs are exhibited in Table 2 and Fig.3. The basic FMR uses the first met node as the single relay without judgment. MICT-FMT or RED-FMT respectively uses the first met node satisfying MICT or RED based qualified conditions as the single relay. It is apparently that the FMR result is mainly in accordance with the trend of general average situation introduced above. This proves a relay selected with RED is more effective in reducing opportunistic forwarding delay.

Discussion: From Fig. 2(a) and Fig. 3(a), we can also learn that, when the DF delay is lower than one day's time (corresponding to zero in horizontal axis), the average

DRRs of all three schemes are lower than zero. This suggests that under this condition, direct forwarding is likely to be more effective than taking a relay. On the other hand, the corresponding DRRs of good relay showed in Fig. 2(b) and Fig. 3(b) perform quite well. This difference is resulted from that good relays are relatively less in the potential relay candidates, which is the paradigm examined in the next part.

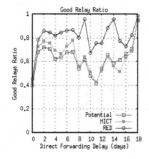

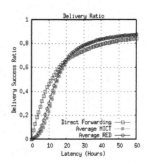

Fig. 4. Average Good Relay Ratio   **Fig. 5.** The CDF of Delivery Delay

4.3   Good Relay Ratio

Fig. 4 shows the average good relay ratio corresponding to different DF delay levels. We can find that when DF delay is higher than one day, the good relay ratio of RED scheme is much better than that of MICT scheme and all potential one's. This indicates that a RED qualified relay has higher probability to make the delivery delay reduced. In other words, it proves the RED based relay selection decision is more accurate than MICT. Another noteworthy feature is that when DF delay time is less than one day, the good relay ratio is also very low. This confirms the observation that direct forwarding is likely more effective than using relay in low DF delay level, where the good relay ratio is only about 40%.

Discussion: Considering DRR and GRR jointly, we can see that when DF delay is high, relaying schemes have better DRR and GRR at the same time. Therefore, relay forwarding is more effective than direct forwarding. Particularly, in the scenario of underlying vehicular DTN, when DF delay is larger than one day's time, it is prefer to use relay scheme. On the other hand, when DF delay is lower than one day, direct forwarding has better delivery performance. This can be confirmed in Fig.5, in which the cumulative distribution of direct forwarding delay, average delivery delay of MICT qualified relay forwarding and average delivery delay of RED qualified relay forwarding are plotted. In fact, the CDF shows when DF delay is lower than 20 hours, direct forwarding is more promising in delivery ratio.

This insight of efficiency transition between direct forwarding and relay forwarding would like to maintain in other opportunistic network scenarios with specific critical DF delay value. From another point of view, this insight suggests it is more proper to use a hybrid multi-copy scheme which uses relay forwarding and also retains direct forwarding. It also reflects that the relay selection scheme only using contact records is inefficient when DF delay is low. More effective method or improvement should be proposed to remedy this drawback.

5   Conclusions and Future Work

In this paper, we introduced a residual expected delay based relay selection scheme, and made an empirical investigation on the opportunistic relay efficiency. We demonstrated the relay efficiency in terms of delay reduced ratio and good relay ratio. Evaluation result shows that the RED based relay selection scheme taking into consider the elapsed time exhibits better performance than the mean inter-contact time based scheme. However, the correlation between relay efficiency and direct forwarding delay implies that when the direct forwarding delay is lower than some value, opportunistic single relay assisted delivery is likely to not obtain benefit in reducing end-to-end delay. Therefore, the helpfulness and harmfulness of opportunistic relay forwarding should be reconsidered.

In the next step, we will look at the performance of multi-relay opportunistic forwarding schemes in different realistic scenarios. Another problem drawing our attention is to deal with the ineffective relay selection in low direct forwarding latency.

Acknowledgments. This research is partially supported by the National Science Foundation of China under Grant No. 61070211 and No. 61003304; and Hunan Provincial Natural Science Foundation of China under grants No. 09JJ4034.

References

1. Lindgren, A., Doria, A., Schelén, O.: Probabilistic Routing in Intermittently Connected Networks. In: Dini, P., Lorenz, P., de Souza, J.N. (eds.) SAPIR 2004. LNCS, vol. 3126, pp. 239–254. Springer, Heidelberg (2004)
2. Nelson, S.C., Bakht, M., Kravets, R.: Encounter-Based Routing in DTNs. In: Proceedings of INFOCOM 2009, pp. 846–854. IEEE Press, New York (2009)
3. Balasubramanian, A., Levine, B.N., Venkataramani, A.: DTN routing as a resource allocation problem. In: Proceedings of SIGCOMM 2007, pp. 373–384. ACM Press, New York (2007)
4. Jain, S., Fall, K., Patra, R.: Routing in a delay-tolerant network. In: Proceedings of SIGCOMM 2004, pp. 145–158. ACM Press, New York (2004)
5. Jones, E.P.C., Li, L., Ward, P.A.S.: Practical routing in delay-tolerant networks. In: Proceedings of the 2005 ACM SIGCOMM workshop on Delay-tolerant networking, pp. 1–7. ACM Press, New York (2005)
6. Chen, H., Lou, W.: On Using Contact Expectation for Routing in Delay Tolerant Networks. In: Proceedings of 2011 International Conference on Parallel Processing (ICPP), pp. 683–692. IEEE Press, New York (2011)
7. Piorkowski, M., Djukic, N.S., Grossglauser, M.: A Parsimonious Model of Mobile Partitioned Networks with Clustering. In: Proceedings of 1st International Conference on COMmunication Systems and NETworkS (COMSNETS), pp. 258–267. IEEE Press, New York (2009)
8. CRAWDAW, http://www.crawdad.cs.dartmouth.edu/

Design and Deployment of Testbed
for Experimental Sensor Network Research

Zeeshan Hameed Mir, Hyeon Park, Young Bag Moon,
Nae Soo Kim, and Cheol Sig Pyo

USN/IoT Convergence Research Division,
Electronics & Telecommunications Research Institute (ETRI), Republic of Korea
{zhmir,hpark,moonyb,nskim,cspyo}@etri.re.kr

Abstract. This paper presents the Ubiquitous Sensor Network (USN) testbed, which is deployed at Electronics and Telecommunications Research Institute (ETRI), in Republic of Korea. USN testbed is a state-of-the-art sensor network experimental facility composed of various components. It includes heterogeneous sensor nodes with variety of sensing module ranging from ultra-low power to high performance hardware platforms, a scalable and reliable Ethernet based wired backplane network to program, interact with and receive/send data from/to the sensor nodes, an easily extendable application software suite which glues and drive everything in a user friendly manner, and an indoor and outdoor deployment space offering various environmental characteristics. We also included two case studies where researchers have put USN testbed into practice for experimental evaluation of algorithms and networking protocols. The case studies cover routing and clustering protocol in wireless sensor networks.

Keywords: Wireless Sensor Network, Experimental Testbed, Heterogeneous.

1   Introduction

For the last few years the importance of sensor network testbed [1] [2] [3] [4] [5] [6] [7] [8] has been continuously on the rise. Researchers are placing a considerable emphasis on the testbed infrastructure to validate theoretical system models as well as to evaluate performances of various sensor network applications. Testbed are also necessary to design, develop, and evaluate algorithms, protocols, and hardware platforms for the sensor network. There have been number of testbeds built to answer the limitations of simulation environment. However, most of these attempts tend to integrate several individual sensor nodes into a common infrastructure to achieve either certain application specific goals or a subset of the overall design objectives.

Sensor nodes must support various sensing modalities to cater diverse requirements impose by wide range of application scenarios. Moreover, the hierarchical organization of most of the sensor network applications demands sensor nodes to be built according to different capabilities at each successive level of the hierarchy.

J.J. Park et al. (Eds.): NPC 2012, LNCS 7513, pp. 264–272, 2012.

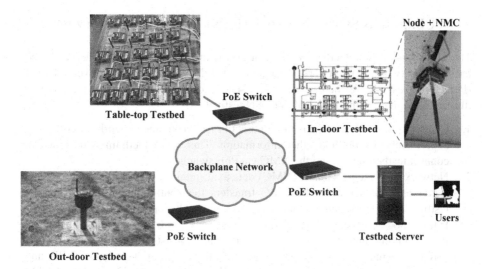

Fig. 1. Main components of the USN testbed

The backplane must be a reliable and scalable infrastructure for node deployment, configuration and monitoring which is vital to any testbed. It is also necessary for the backplane network to operate without causing interference with the experiment itself. The testbed management software which glues and drive everything must be user friendly and easily extendable. Finally, the deployment space of the testbed must provide a wide range of environmental characteristics and propagation attributes in the form of both indoor and outdoor testbed.

There are two main contributions of this paper. Firstly, we describe Ubiquitous Sensor Network (USN) testbed architecture and its main components. USN testbed is a state-of-the-art sensor network experimental facility which is located within the premises of Electronics and Telecommunication Research Institute, Republic of Korea. USN testbed is composed of heterogeneous sensor nodes, an Ethernet based backplane [1] for experiment data collection and system monitoring, a versatile application software suite that allows users to interact with the testbed in an intuitive manner. The USN testbed deployment space not only covers indoor and outdoor environments but it can easily be extended for table-top/bench-top experiments as well. The second contribution is to discuss two case studies, where researchers have put USN testbed into practice for the implementation and testing of sensor network protocols. To demonstrate the different functionalities of the testbed we shared our experiences on routing, and clustering protocols in wireless sensor networks.

The remainder of the paper is organized as follows. In Section 2, we describe the overall architecture and main components of the USN testbed. In Section 3, we discuss in details each of the constituent component namely the deployment space, backplane network, sensor nodes, and the application software suite. In Section 4, we present two case studies where researchers have implemented and tested various protocols and applications for wireless sensor network using the USN testbed. Finally, in Section 5 we conclude this paper.

2   Ubiquitous Sensor Network (USN) Testbed: An Overview

The USN testbad architecture consists of six main components, (1) Ethernet based backplane network, (2) Network Management Card (NMC), (3) Power over Ethernet (PoE) switches, (4) Testbed server, (5) Users, and lastly (6) Sensor nodes. Fig. 1 illustrates the main components of the USN testbed

1. Central to the USN testbed is the Ethernet based backplane network for collecting experimental results and other information. This wired medium is designed to connect testbed server and the NMC via PoE switches.
2. Network Management Card (NMC) acts as a middle-agent between the testbed server and the sensor node. NMC transfers the control signals/data from the testbed server to the sensor node. Likewise, it can also operate to get the feedback from a node to the testbed server. It consists of two layers, main board and interface communication board. The main board consists of micro-controller unit (MCU), memory, power supply and ISP (for program download), USB and JTAG. The interface communication board consists of CC2420 chipset, RS232 and LAN board.
3. Power over Ethernet (PoE) switch is used to supply power to operate the sensor node via NMC and collect data on the Ethernet cabling.
4. The testbed server is used to manage information regarding NMC, sensor nodes, users etc. The testbed server transfers the control commands to the NMC and sends resultant feedback via Ethernet network. The testbed server is designed to support all the required functions and information transfer to the users.
5. USN testbed supports multiple users running sensor network applications. Each user configures nodes to use wireless channel orthogonal to those used by the other users of the testbed.
6. Sensor nodes support various requirements imposed by a wide array of sensor networking application scenarios.

3   Ubiquitous Sensor Network (USN) Testbed: Main Components

3.1   The Deployment Space

Currently, the indoor testbed infrastructure is installed at the 1st and the 5th floors of Building No. 12, at the Electronics and Telecommunications Research Institute (ETRI). However, in the past the indoor testbed was deployed at the Ground and 2nd floors of Building No.7. The nodes at the outdoor testbed are located along the boundaries of soccer and baseball fields within the ETRI premises. Moreover, the architecture of USN testbed can easily be extended by deploying table-top testbed. Some of the main information is given as under.

–   Number of nodes: The indoor and outdoor testbed has a provision of up to 40 and 100 nodes, respectively.

– Intra-node spacing: Indoor testbed (One Side: 3 m and another side: 3.5 m) and Outdoor testbed (10 m).
– Height above the floor (8 cm)/ceiling (2.5 m): 180 degree rotation is possible for various node orientations (useful for studying antenna orientation and its effect on testbed physical environment).

3.2   The Backplane Network

USN testbed employs an Ethernet based backplane network.   The use of wired connections allows following testbed functions in a non-intrusive manner without introducing additional interferences.

– Gather debugging information,
– Real-time performance evaluation statistics collection,
– Transmit command/response to/from sensor nodes,
– Node status check, ON/OFF, and parameter adjustment (like transmit power),
– Remotely downloading code via Network Management Card (NMC),
– Supply power to the sensor nodes.

Out of total 10 PoE switches, five of those switches are allocated for nodes in the outdoor environment, while four are at 5th floor and the last one is at 1st floor of Building No. 12. Each of the PoE switch can have up to 24 ports thus enabling connection to 24 nodes via NMC.

3.3   The Hardware Platform

The sensor nodes follow layered architecture to support diverse requirements imposed by various types of applications. The basic sensor node is composed of different modules such as sensing, micro-controller, RF and power supply module interconnected via inter-module interfaces.

The basic sensor node sensing module captures variety of physical properties from the environment such as Passive Infrared (PIR), light, acoustic, temperature/humidity, magnetic, vibration sensors. The node uses low-power MSP430 micro-controller module for sensor data processing and to provide inter-module and other interfaces such as SPI, ADC, UART, GPIO etc. MSP430 micro-controller is equipped with MSP430F2618 [9], 16-bits processor with Flash (116kB+256kB)/RAM (8kB) memory and 8MB Serial Flash. The MSP430 module drives DC +3.7 V to +3.3 V from the power module to supply power to MSP430F2618, Serial Flash and other circuitry. The RF module is a 2.4GHz CC2420 [10] chipset enabling 10-250kbps for wireless communication. The sensor node is also equipped with SMA-connector in order to connect with a range of external antennas (both Omni-directional and Sectored-antenna). The nodes can be powered either by Power over Ethernet (PoE) connected via Network Management Card (NMC) or through batteries.

The hierarchical organization of most of the sensor networks demand sensor nodes to be built according to certain roles for example, basic, cluster-head and gateway nodes. The ultra-low power design of the basic sensor node supports lightweight medium access protocols, dynamic routing and self-organized networking.

Table 1. The Basic, Cluster-head and Gateway node hardware platform description

Feature	Basic node	Cluster-head	Gateway
MCUs (1)	16Bit RISC/16Mhz	16Bit RISC/16Mhz	16Bit RISC/16Mhz
MCUs (2)	-	32Bit	Xscale/13-520MHz
Communication range	30m	100m	100m-7km
Power supply	Battery/PoE	Battery/PoE	Battery/PoE
Frequency/Data rate	2.45GHz/	433/915Mhz,2.4GHz/	2.45GHz/
(RF 1)	10-250Kbps	40-250Kbps	250Kbps
Frequency/Data rate	-	2.4GHz/	CDMA/
(RF 2)	-	250Kbps	370Kbps-2Mbps
Sensing module		PIR/30m	GPS
/ Sensing range		Acoustic/50m	CDMA
OR		Magnetometer/5m	USB
Interfaces		Seismic/5m	Ethernet

However, to execute more computation and resource intense tasks (like network-wide schedule computation) USN testbed features the cluster-head nodes. Cluster-head nodes include dual micro-controllers (MSP430 and PXA270) for low-power consumption and high performance. At the RF module end, it incorporates options like 433/915 MHz and 2.4 GHz frequency capable of supporting 40 to 250kps of data rates. The sensor module can be enhanced further to capture audio and visual information as well. Hybrid sensor signal processing is provided with both low-power processor (e.g., MSP430F2618) and high performance digital signal processor (e.g., TMS320F28335 DSP [11]). The applications for cluster-head node are multiple target detection, classification and tracking, surveillance and cluster management.

Finally, the role of a gateway node is to converge information from multiple heterogeneous sources either as the final destination or as an intermediate link towards the storage unit. For these purposes, the design of gateway incorporate features of basic and cluster-head nodes with some more that are specific to its own role. For example, it can have an XScale micro-controller, CDMA supporting 370kbps to 2Mbps data rates, USB, Ethernet, GPS and power connections. The potential target applications of the gateway node are remote communication (e.g., inter-networking with Multimedia Terminal Mobile (MTM), hybrid MAC protocols (e.g., fusing TDMA and CSMA), GPS-based localization etc. Table 1, summarizes the hardware platform description of basic, cluster-head and gateways nodes.

3.4   The Software Management Tool

The software management tool is actually an application software suite. It includes Graphical User Interfaces (GUIs) to, (1) Issue commands and views the final data and performance evaluation statistics. (2) Apply topology and communication protocol level parameter settings. (3) Download and program the sensor nodes independent of the underlying physical sensor network testbed and embedded operating system. Following are the main software management programs of the USN testbed.

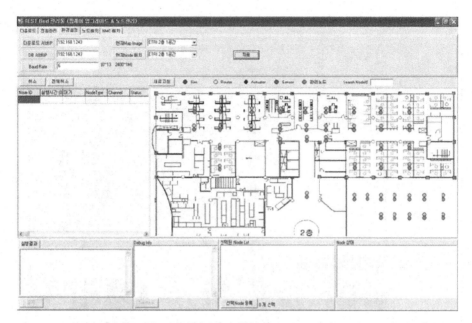

Fig. 2. Snapshot of USN Testbed Manager GUI

Server Program. A user must run the server program to remotely establish a connection with the USN testbed server. Once a successful connection is established the testbed server then configures the connection setting with the sensor node. These connection settings are directed by application software like USN Testbed Manager and the Testbed Tester. After completing the connection setting with the sensor node the testbed server sends the ID Query messages to the sensor nodes. The sensor nodes reply with the (IP, ID) pairs. The testbed server then stores and manages the UDP socket number and ID pair of the sensor nodes. The applications programs uses sensor node's ID to send commands and data to the testbed server. The testbed server lookup the ID-UDP socket number table and report the command to the corresponding sensor nodes via NMC.

Testbed Manager. This application software is a one stop solution for various tasks related with the experiment setup on USN testbed. The GUI is mainly composed of several tabs each offering a range of functions to its users. For example, a user can select nodes by choosing appropriate drop-down location options. The GUI node selection window allows selection/de-selection of a single node or a group of nodes with a simple drag and drop operation. Users then associate the NMC (with an IP address) to a particular node before downloading the source code binary. The source code binary is the compiled version generated separately using the IAR Compiler Software [12]. On successful or failed transmission of source code binary to the sensor node the appropriate result is displayed at the GUI of the user. Moreover, USN Testbed Manager also handles certain node management related function (like RESET). Fig. 2 illustrates the USN Testbed Manager software GUI.

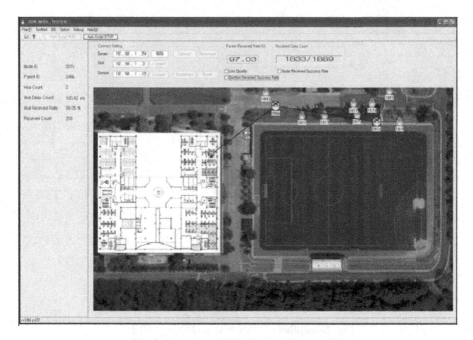

Fig. 3. Snapshot of USN Testbed Tester GUI

Terminal Program. The main purpose of this program is to send command to the sensor nodes and receive data from them at runtime. The interface allows the user to select a node (by the IP address of its attached NMC) and enter any string either in ASCII or hexadecimal format.

Testbed Tester. The actual experiments are executed using the USN Testbed Tester application software. This tool allows its users to configure the network topology, functioning of the nodes and communication protocol parameters based on the experiment requirements. The users can control the number of iterations a particular experiment can run with modified experiment parameters (like packet interval). The Testbed Tester collects and displays real-time performance evaluation statistics (like Packet Success Rate, End-to-End Delay etc.), nodes channel condition (like RSSI, LQI etc.) and sensing information (like light, temperature etc.). A user can also configure experiment to collection traces on per node basis. At the end of the experiments, the generated traces are stored in the spreadsheet software for later data analysis. The Testbed Tester program is easily extendable for various types of communication protocols and customized output generation. Fig. 3 illustrates the USN Testbed Tester software GUI.

4   Ubiquitous Sensor Network (USN) Testbed: Case Studies

The USN testbed has been used to study the performance and analysis of several control protocols including clustering, routing, cross-layer communication and medium access control (MAC) protocols. The testbed infrastructure has also been successfully utilized to deploy sensor network applications such as target detection and classification, surveillance and reconnaissance, pedestrian tracking to name a few.

4.1   Case Study 1: MINT-Based Routing Protocol

The USN testbed has been used to implement and test an enhanced version of the MINT (MINimum Transmission) [13] routing protocol. The enhanced version deals with real-time and reliable transfer of large amount of data (e.g. image) over the sensor network testbed. The application scenario that this protocol caters for include surveillance and reconnaissance.

The enhancement incorporates heterogeneity-aware TCP-like fragmentation mechanism to decide on the network-wide MTU (Minimum Transport Unit) size. Secondly, an improved packet retransmission scheme is proposed that adapt itself to the permissible loss rate sufficient enough to maintain prescribed image quality. Finally, the protocol uses expected number of transmissions along with neighbor status information to find more reliable paths. Extra features were added in the software management tools to visualize various types of node information such as node's neighbor table, details about averaged delivery ratio and delay time etc. It is also extended to take into account several of the new messages format. The sole purpose of these messages is to enable communication between the protocol and the USN Testbed Tester and the terminal program.

4.2   Case Study 2: Static and Dynamic Clustering Protocol

The USN testbed has been used to study the performance of static and dynamic clustering protocols. The static clustering algorithm designates few of the sensor nodes as the cluster-head during the network initialization process. While the dynamic clustering algorithm runs reactively as a result of certain event detection. In both cases the cluster-members will simply forward the data towards the cluster-head. The collected data is then aggregated at the cluster-head before it is sent to the sink node.

NanoQ-Plus [14], an ETRI proprietary operating system for embedded devices has been used to design, develop and load the program code on to the sensor nodes. The Testbed Tester and the terminal program were modified to allow specialized visualization of the results of the clustering algorithms. The sensor nodes take on different shapes and color based on their role in the network as a result of applying the clustering algorithms. Further details on the clustering protocols and test results can be found in [15].

5   Conclusion

This paper describes USN testbed, a state-of-the-art sensor network experimental facility. It is composed of several types sensor nodes deployed at multiple indoor and outdoor locations. The testbed provides an extendable Ethernet based backplane network so that real-time information can be transmitted without interfering and compromising the operation of the sensor network applications and protocol being tested. The USN testbed software component allows multiple users to manage and run separate experiments simultaneously. These software tools are used to program, send/receive messages to/from nodes and to gather real-time debugging information and statistical results of the experiments. We also presented two case studies where the scientists and researchers at ETRI have used the USN testbed for validating their protocols and applications. The presented case studies show the usability and the applicability of the USN testbed infrastructure to understand, apply and improve research and development in sensor networks.

Acknowledgments. This work was supported by the Dual Use Technology program of the DUTC, South Korea [Surveillance and Reconnaissance Sensor Network Development].

References

1. Crepaldi, R., et al.: The Design, Deployment, and Analysis of SignetLab: A Sensor Network Testbed and Interactive Management Tool. In: Proc. of TRIDENTCOM (2007)
2. Bapat, S., et al.: Chowkidar: A Health Monitor for Wireless Sensor Network Testbeds. In: Proc. of TRIDENTCOM (2007)
3. Werner-Allen, G., Swieskowski, P., Welsh, M.: Motelab: A Wireless Sensor Network Testbed. In: Proc. of IPSN (2005)
4. Arora, A., et al.: Kansei: A High-Fidelity Sensing Testbed. Proc. of IEEE Internet Computing 10, 35–47 (2006)
5. Gluhak, A., et al.: A survey on facilities for experimental internet of things research. Proc. of IEEE Communications Magazine 49(11), 58–67 (2011)
6. Rensfelt, O., et al.: SENSEI-A Flexible Testbed for Heterogeneous Wireless Sensor Networks. In: Proc. of TRIDENTCOM (2009)
7. Doddavenkatappa, M., Chan, M.C., Ananda, A.L.: Indriya: A Low-Cost, 3D Wireless Sensor Network Testbed. In: Korakis, T., Li, H., Tran-Gia, P., Park, H.-S. (eds.) TridentCom 2011. LNICST, vol. 90, pp. 302–316. Springer, Heidelberg (2012)
8. des Rosiers, C.B., Chelius, G., Fleury, E., Fraboulet, A., Gallais, A., Mitton, N., Noël, T.: SensLAB: Very Large Scale Open Wireless Sensor Network Testbed. In: Korakis, T., Li, H., Tran-Gia, P., Park, H.-S. (eds.) TridentCom 2011. LNICST, vol. 90, pp. 239–254. Springer, Heidelberg (2012)
9. DataSheet for (TI) MSP430F2618, http://focus.ti.com/
10. Datasheet for Chipcon (TI) CC2420 2.4 GHz IEEE 802.15.4/ZigBee RF Transceiver, http://www.chipcon.com
11. DataSheet for (TI) TMS320F28335, http://focus.ti.com/
12. IAR Systems, http://www.iar.com/
13. Park, H., Ham, Y., Park, S., Woo, J., Lee, J.: Large Data Transport for Real-Time Services in Sensor Networks. In: Proc. of ComputationWorld (2009)
14. Park, S., Won Kim, J., Shin, K., Kim, D.: A Nano Operating System for Wireless Sensor Networks. In: Proc. of IEEE ICACT (2006)
15. Moon, Y., Kim, N., Lim, K., Jung, J., Ko, Y.: Efficient Cluster Head Election in Surveillance Reconnaissance Sensor Network. In: Proc. of ICWN 2010 - World Comp (2010)

Implementation of the Integrated Monitoring System Based on an Automatic Disaster Prevention Device

Yoonsik Kwak

Dept. of Computer Engineering, Korea National University of Transportation
50 Daehak-ro, Chungju-si, Chungbuk 380-702

Abstract. In this paper, we have presented the Integrated Monitoring System based on an automatic disaster prevention device. The Integrated monitoring system aims to collect information related to vehicles' input and output and more. To design and implement the automatic disaster prevention system, production devices for antiseptic water and mining systems- vehicles and their license plate recognition systems- were designed and implemented. As experiment results, we can prove a disinfective function that is related to antiseptic water production device. We also proved that it is possible to monitor disinfected vehicles, moving vehicles and even the drivers at all times. Due to its characteristic of integration management, it can be adapted to remote farming and efficient monitoring in disinfection management.

Keywords: automatic, disaster prevention system, monitoring system, mining.

1 Introduction

Advanced information communication and computer science have changed society in many fields. Especially, the advance in convergence IT technology consistently affected many fields such as the military, geology, agriculture, health service, and more. Developing and advancing these technologies is the trend now. Many researchers have been pointing out interest in these subjects and solving these problems.[1][2]

Specifically, in the case of agriculture in many areas, according to the adopted convergence of IT technology, technology's advancement, and practical use have been persisting to achieve enhancement and competitiveness of the agriculture field. After joining the FTA, the government is supporting domestic agriculture to become competitive against agro and livestock products which is imported from developed countries. As an example of practical use of convergence IT, sensor networks is used for various goals in many fields such as agriculture, livestock, and the fishing industry.[1]

Also, in case of domestic and international, huge nations try to prevent biological disaster. Because S.A.S which occurred in agro and livestock industry frequently heavily damaged people who work in these fields and even gave irrecoverable damage which cannot be sustained individually or nationally.

J.J. Park et al. (Eds.): NPC 2012, LNCS 7513, pp. 273–278, 2012.
© IFIP International Federation for Information Processing 2012

In this paper, in order to overcome these difficulties, we designed and implemented an automatic disaster prevention system and integrated a monitoring system to overcome disasters in the agro and livestock industries. Related to automatic disaster prevent system such as references [3][4], many researchers are engaged in these fields. It is the same for antiseptic water. Also researching with a mining system is conducted actively, especially in traffic. The automatic disinfection system is made up of antiseptic water production devices. And the integrated monitoring system consists of mining and vehicle recognition systems.

2   Integrated Mining System

As shown in figure 1, this displays the proposed architecture system for the Integrated Mining System in this paper.

As shown in figure 1, this system consists of an antiseptic water production device as a disaster prevention device and a mining system that consists of a camera, a communication unit, a vehicle recognition system, and a license plate recognition system. Information which is received from these devices is accumulated to a central integrated monitoring system based on a cloud system.

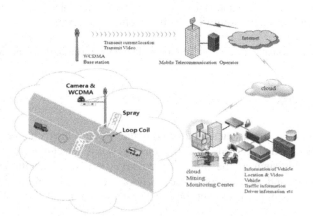

Fig. 1. System Architecture

2.1   Automatic Disaster Prevention System

An automatic disaster prevention system is shown in figure 3. Basically the architecture system consists of an antiseptic water production device, camera, communication, spray, and control unit.

As shown in the following figure, information of a vechiles' license plate which is taken from a camera using signals from a sensing device, and the original vehicles' image is transmitted to the integrated system by Internet or communication unit. Also the spray's function depends on an event signal which is detected from sensors (deployed loop coil).

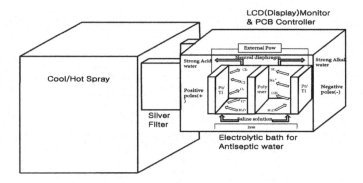

Fig. 2. Production system for antiseptic water

In figure 4, the vehicles' disinfection devices are divided into the storage, spray, connection, and antiseptic water production unit.

Storage part can store water and is able to have a pumping device. The pump will pump water stored in the storage part.

The spray part has water sprayed to vehicles. It is formed at a certain length which stands at each side with a certain distance. It could be assigned to stand on the edge of the road. It includes a pipe and some nozzle.

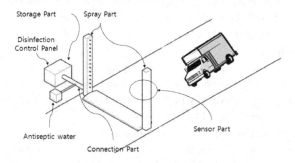

Fig. 3. Automatic Vehicles Disinfection System

The pipe can stand on the ground perpendicularly. The nozzle can be formed in a certain order depending on the direction and length of the pipe.

In the connection part, the storage and spray parts are connected. In this part, there would be an installed pump which pumps storage water.

2.2   Vehicles Recognition System and Integrated Monitoring System

The Integrated monitoring system is designed to get a moving vehicles' video image and its license plate information. Figure 4 is a brief algorithm for vehicle recognition.

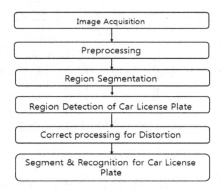

Fig. 4. Algorithm for Vehicles Recognition

In the process of image acquisition, the specification of the camera is an effective pixel(1628Hx1236V), pixel size(1624x1232), and real frame rate(16, 1624x1232, Mono 8) in our system.

Preprocessing, is a process to enhance video image by using the surrounded pixel's relation such as filtering, binary coding, color segmentation. However, in our system, we used the Top – Hat method.[7][8]

Regional detection, is a process to get the region of a car license plate. This process is progressed by Sobel, Gray scale vector, information about hue, brightness, and saturation of vehicles, histogram, and the Run–length method. And many researches are processing study.[7]

Distorting and correcting process, after preprocessing and region detecting, overlapping and blurring can occur at the edges in correcting character region which can cause distortion. To solve this problem, we process distortion correction by the morphology processing method.[9]

In region segmentation and recognition process for character, we divide the plate region into upward and downward regions by horizontal profiling. Each region detaches a character region by perpendicular filing. Next, we split those regions. Finally, we implement an algorithm of character recognition and adapt it to the split character region.

There are many algorithms such as neural networks, structure information, statistical information, circular pattern, and recognition specific base. But in our system, we choose the method based on neural networks.(Figure 5)

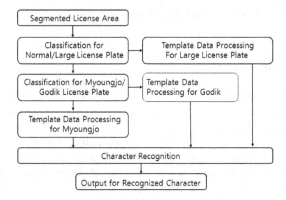

Fig. 5. Flowchart of Character Recognition Algorithm

The Integrated monitoring system collects and manages various vehicles' related information. For example, there are vehicle images, plate information, visiting time, visitor information, and so on. These data are acquired by the vehicle recognition system. And the mining system is designed as component of the integrated monitoring system.

This Monitoring system consists of a real time monitoring part, object management, configuration management, user management, and a login/out part. Our system is designed to monitor at all times, the acquired objects which are monitored real time vehicles. Their information – the object's list, images, and map images are also acquired.

Object management is designed for the object's registration and deletion. Also it manages various information which are related to the objects.

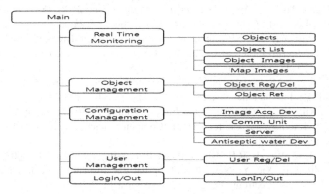

Fig. 6. Integrated Monitoring System Architecture

The components of the configuration management part, are camera, communication unit, server system, and an antiseptic water production device. It is designed to manage information which is related to the system's components.

The user management part, is designed to register and delete users.

Log management, is designed to manage and record the integrated monitoring system's log-in/out.

3   Conclusion

In this paper, we presented an automatic disinfection system and their data monitoring system. This system could contribute to achieve high quality agriculture and overcome biological disasters.

This integrated monitoring system is based on a cloud system to get efficiency and convenience in implementation of the system. By its characters, the system could be installed remotely. And data which collects through remote devices can be accumulated to the central devices effectively.

Using this system in the agro and livestock industry, we can determine the competitiveness of our product's quality and efficiency of management in disasters is assured.

Acknowledgements. This work (Grants No.00047926) was supported by the Business for Cooperative R&D between Industry, Academy, and Research Institute funded Korea Small and Medium Business Administration in 2011.

References

1. Yick, J., Mukherjee, B., Ghosal, D.: Wireless sensor network survey. Computer Networks 52, 2292–2330 (2008)
2. Yoneki, E., Bacon, J.: A survey of Wireless sensor Network technologies:research trends and middleware's role. Technical report Number 646, University of Cambridge
3. Kang, K., et al.: Investigation on the Technology Trend in Electrolyzed Sterilizing Water by the Patent Analysis. Applied Chemistry for Engineering 21(2), 188–194 (2010)
4. Jang, K.I., Lee, J.H., Choi, S.G., Lee, H.B.: Chemistry & Food; Quality of Stored Grape (Vitis Labruscana) Treated with Electrolyzed Acid Water Humidification, Electrolyzed Acid Water Sterilization and Ozone Water Sterilization. Journal of Agriculture & Life Science 42(2), 47–57 (2008)
5. Kassem, A., Jabr, R., Salamouni, G., Maalouf, Z.K.: Vehicle Black Box System. In: IEEE SysCon-IEEE International Systems Conference, pp. 1–6 (April 2008)
6. Zhu, H., Xu, Z.: An Effective Algorithm for Mining Positive and Negative Association Rules. In: International Conference on Computer Science and Software Engineering, pp. 455–458 (2008)
7. Gonzalez, R.C., Woods, R.E.: Digital Image Processing. Prentice Hall (2002)
8. Bai, X., Zhou, F., Xie, Y.: New class of top-hat transformation to enhance infrared small targets. Journal of Electronic Imaging 17(3) (August 11, 2008)
9. Seo, J.H., Lee, J.K., Choi, J.G.: A Decision Method of Front/Back Side Container Images Using Morphological Filters and Projective Transform. Journal of Korean Society for Image Science & Technology 16(3), 33–42 (2010)
10. Oh, H.-C., Choi, J.-H.: A Recognition Algorithm of Car License Plate using Edge Projection and Directivity Vector. The Journal of Korean Institute of Information Technology 6(1), 1–10 (2009)
11. Lee, S.-H., Choi, S.-Y., Lee, S.-Y., Kim, Y.-S.: Licence Plate Recognition Using Improved IAFC Fuzzy Neural Network. Korean Institute of Intelligent Systems 19(1), 6–12 (2009)

Smart Ring: A Model of Node Failure Detection in High Available Cloud Data Center

Lei Xu, Wenzhi Chen, Zonghui Wang, Huafei Ni, and Jiajie Wu

College of Computer Science and Technology, Zhejiang University,
Zheda Rd. 38, Hangzhou 310027, China
{leixu,chenwz,zjuzhwang,20921248,21121176}@zju.edu.cn

Abstract. Nowadays most of cloud data centers deploy high available system in order to provide continuous services, so it's very important for a high available cluster to detect the node failure (physical machine failure) accurately and timely in a low bandwidth occupation way. However, compared to the traditional cluster environment, the scale of cloud data center increases rapidly with the use of virtualization, so traditional node failure detection models have already faced several new problems. In this paper, we present a three roles and two layers node failure detection model, named as Smart Ring, which fits cloud data center well and strikes a balance between accuracy, instantaneity and bandwidth occupation. It can simultaneously detect the status of physical machines and virtual machines and deal well with multiple nodes failure and network partition. Our experiment results show that Smart Ring has a better performance than most existing models.

Keywords: Cloud Data Center, High Availability, Node Failure Detection.

1 Introduction

In the past few years, many kinds of cloud services spew out. These services must serve continuously for 24 hours a day and 365 days a year with minimal maintenance. In addition, in many important fields, such as Finance, Traffic, Telecom and Military, once the system crashes, even if a short stop running, it may bring unimaginable consequences. So cloud data center should deploy high available (HA) system to provide the most stable network service and check out the node failure in time.

In our research we have found several kinds of failure detection models that have been applied in HA system. However, these models designed for traditional clusters can't fit well with data center. Because the number of machines has exploded rapidly in data center, especially the numbers of virtual machines (VM), most existed models have obvious bottlenecks when they are applied in cloud data center. They either consume more time to detect node failure, or occupy more bandwidth or easy to make misjudgments. What's worse, some of these traditional models don't support virtualization architecture that means they can't monitor the status of VM efficiently.

Considering the problems mentioned above, a novel model is proposed in this paper. We firstly introduce several classical node failure detection models in section 2.

J.J. Park et al. (Eds.): NPC 2012, LNCS 7513, pp. 279–288, 2012.
© IFIP International Federation for Information Processing 2012

In section 3, we detail the design of Smart-Ring. Section 4 shows the extended functions of Smart-Ring. In section 5, we implement a prototype system to evaluate the performance of Smart Ring. A summary and plan of our future work are described in section 6.

2   Related Work

HA architecture has been extensively explored by cluster researchers in past years. This has led to the development of various node failure detection models. We have found many existing models used in HA system. These models can be summarized as five categories.

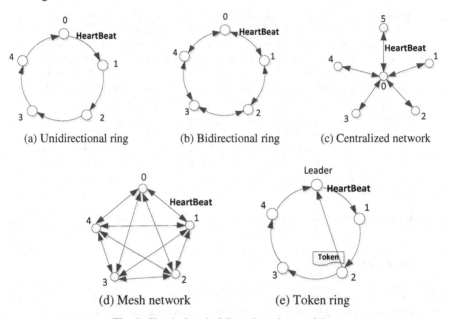

(a) Unidirectional ring   (b) Bidirectional ring   (c) Centralized network

(d) Mesh network   (e) Token ring

Fig. 1. Classical node failure detection models

Unidirectional ring is the simplest model. G Rudolph [1] published a paper talked about parallel clustering on a unidirectional ring in 1993 and a patent of Symantec [2] is also based on unidirectional ring. This model is very easy to make a misjudgment, because its judge logic is too simple.

Bidirectional ring is an upgrade of the unidirectional ring. Wang [3] and Savari [4] et al. have discussed the bidirectional ring network model in their papers. This model can reduce misjudgment rate, because a node is judged invalid only when the precursor and successor both don't get heartbeat. However, it occupies double bandwidth as the unidirectional ring.

Centralized network is a kind of stellate reticulum model. The principle of Linux-HA project [5] is similar with centralized model, Khan et al. [6] and Hamlyn [7] have researched this centralized framework in distribution system. Nevertheless, if the central one is down, the system can't keep running which means it is the bottleneck of system.

Mesh network is a kind of full connection model. Only when all other nodes can't get heartbeat from a node the system judges this node is definitely down. This model has the highest accuracy while occupies the highest bandwidth. A famous HA project named Linux Failsafe [8] developed by SGI & SUSE is based on this model.

Token ring is a classic network model. Nilausen [9], Hutchison [10] and Goapl [11] have done a lot of work around token ring model. This model can enhance reliability, so the grid fault-tolerant middleware GRM [12] and group communication project Corosync [13] both use token ring network model. How-ever, in this model, the cycle of fault detection is too long. It isn't suitable for applied in large scale virtual cluster yet.

Briefly, we can see that all these aforementioned models have their own features. But when focus on HA data center environment, they seem not to be suitable. Because they couldn't support virtualization architecture well and can't strike a balance among accuracy, instantaneity and bandwidth occupation. So based on long time of survey and study, we design a novel model which is fit for large scale HA data center.

3   A Novel Node Failure Detection Model - Smart Ring

Smart Ring has two monitoring layers as depicted in Fig. 2. At the physical machine (PM) layer, each node is monitored by precursor while VMs are monitored by their host PM at the virtual machine layer.

Smart Ring also has three node roles: leader, backup and common. When leader node is invalid, backup node will be elected to be new leader. When backup node is invalid, its first successor common node will change into backup. This process is irreversible. A short introduction about the features of these three roles should be made:

— Common node corresponds to an actual PM running with many VMs. Each common node has an IP list with three records corresponded to leader IP, backup IP and the first successor IP. With the first successor IP a common node can keep heartbeat with it, with leader IP a common node can inform a suspect failure to leader and backup IP will be the new leader IP after leader failure. This IP list is important for Smart Ring to maintain system operation.

— Leader node is also a common node when there are no failures, which means in most of time it works as a common server. This design can make Smart Ring have more equivalence. But the IP list stored in leader node is different with commons'. This IP list records backup IP and all common IP. Only when machines join, exit or malfunction, leader will do some special operations like detecting node failure, updating the IP list of related nodes or modifying the global view which is a relational map of all PMs & VMs.

— Backup node is also a common node just like the leader. The IP list stored in it records leader IP and all common IP. After leader modifies the global view, it should synchronize the view with leader through Sync Info Channel. And if leader is invalid, backup will become a new leader node. With the global view stored on it, it can take over leader's work.

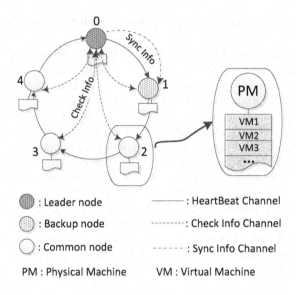

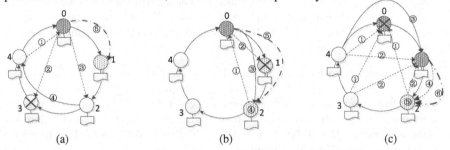

Fig. 2. Smart Ring model

3.1   Physical Machine Failure Detection

As mentioned above, nodes in Smart Ring have three different roles and the detection process of each role is different, we will describe respectively.

Fig. 3. Node Failure Detection Process. (a) Common node failure detection process. (b) Backup node failure detection process. (c) Leader node failure detection process.

Common Node Failure Detection Process: Now we assume node 3 is invalid, as shown in Fig. 3(a), node 4 wouldn't get heartbeat from 3 in appointed timeout. Then 4 will report this suspected fault to the leader node 0, 0 knows 4's precursor is 3 by checking the global view. 0 sends check info to 3 by Check Info Channel. If in the appointed timeout 0 can't get response from 3, in that way we think 3 is invalid, otherwise 3 is active. If 3 is indeed invalid, 0 will inform 4 to set its precursor as 3's precursor that is node 2, and 0 modifies global view and synchronizes with backup node 1. If node 3 is active, it indicates that there is only a link failure between 3 and 4, this link failure doesn't influence the normal work of node 3 and 4, so 0 will record this link failure in system log file, 4 will monitor 3 again after system administrator fixes this link failure.

Backup Node Failure Detection Process: This process shown in Fig. 3(b) is similar with common node failure detection process. The only different is that if 1 is invalid, the leader node 0 will set node 2 which is the first successor of 1 as a new backup node and 0 sets its successor as 2. After that, 0 will update its successor info in its IP list, in the same way, 2 will update its precursor info too. Then 0 modifies global view and synchronizes it with the new backup node 2.

Leader Node Failure Detection Process: If leader is down, 1 wouldn't get the heartbeat from 0. Then 1 will inform all common nodes to check leader's status and then report the result to node 1. 1 will judge whether leader is active or not by all results. If most nodes (more than $Num_{All}/2$, Num_{All} is the number of all nodes) judge leader is invalid, 1 will change itself into new leader and set its successor as new backup and then inform all nodes to modify their leader IP and backup IP info recorded in their own IP lists. Otherwise the leader is normal, and it is just a kind of link failure. Just like common node failure detection process we describe above, system writes down this failure in log file and 1 will monitor 0 again after administrator fixes this failure. This process is described in Fig. 3(c).

3.2 Virtual Machine Failure Detection

The process of virtual machine failure detection is relatively simple. As VMM (Virtual Machine Monitor) can get current status of virtual machines by commands, for example, use "xm list" command in Xen VMM. We should just set a suitable interval, and a daemon process executes this command periodically to get the status of virtual machines repeatedly. If host machine finds a VM fault, it will remove this VM info from the VM list stored in it and then report to leader. After leader gets this VM fault report, it immediately modifies global view and synchronizes with backup without checking again. The command we used is shown as follows:

```
xm list|sed -n '3,$'p|awk '{print $1;print $5}'> xmstatus.info
```

4   Extended Functions of Smart Ring

Node failure detection is just a major and primary function of Smart Ring. Be-yond that, it also has some extended functions which can deal with the problems in traditional HA system, such as multiple nodes fault and network partition.

4.1   Multiple Nodes Failure

In order to ensure that when multiple nodes fail simultaneously HA system still can work normally, we should just set more backup nodes. In a general way, if system meets the condition $Num_{Backup} \geq Num_{Fault}$ Where Num_{Backup} is the number of backup nodes in supporting multiple nodes failure Smart Ring and Num_{Fault} is the maximum number of faulted machines that we want our system to support. This can ensure the normal work of system, because there are enough backup nodes could become leader when leader and several backup nodes fail simultaneously.

There is a new problem after Smart Ring sets multiple backup nodes that is how to keep global view consistency between leader and all backup nodes. For solving this problem, we can import a GCS (Group Communication System) in Smart ring. GCS is a private channel between leader node and all backup nodes, and it can ensure that all group members can receive messages orderly and reliably. Our research group has respectively deployed Apache ZooKeeper and Spread in our Smart Ring to keep global view consistency which are both excellent GCS toolkit.

4.2   Network Partition

Network partition [14] is the condition that exists after all network connections between any two groups of systems fail simultaneously. When this happens, systems on both sides of the partition can restart applications from the other side resulting in duplicate services, or split-brain. A split brain occurs when two independent systems configured in a cluster assume they have exclusive access to a given resource (usually a file system or volume). The most serious problem caused by a network partition is that it affects the data on shared disks. For solving this problem, Smart Ring takes such a strategy:

a) For a subgroup with leader node, it is a valid subgroup and keeps running only when it meets the condition $Num_{Now} \geq Num_{Most}/2$. Meanwhile, the other subgroups are invalid. Num_{Now} is the number of this subgroup and Num_{Most} is the number of nodes in the ring before network partition. Num_{Most} is not a constant, its initial value is equal with the number of PMs and it will update after a network partition.

b) For a subgroup with backup node, first of all, backup changes into new leader. Then it counts up the number of nodes in this subgroup. If it meets the condition $Num_{Now} > Num_{Most}/2$, it is a valid subgroup and forms a new ring. So the other subgroups are invalid and they must quit Smart Ring.

c) For a subgroup with both leader and backup, it is treated as a valid subgroup no matter how many nodes in this subgroup. It will keep running while the other subgroups must quit HA system.

d) For a subgroup without both leader and backup, it is treated as an invalid subgroup no matter how many nodes in this subgroup.

Through this strategy, we can ensure that there is only an optimum sub-group valid and this subgroup can form a new Smart Ring to keep HA system continuously running.

5   Performance Evaluation

For evaluating the performance of Smart Ring, we have implemented a prototype system to observe the time consuming of node failure detection and the bandwidth occupation. Our experiments ran on this environment shown as Table 1:

Table 1. Experiment environment

PM Numbers	VM Numbers	CPU Frequency (GHz)	CPU Cores	Memory (GB)	Network (Mb/s)	Leader Numbers	Backup Numbers	Common Numbers
64	6400	3.3	4	4	100	1	3	60

5.1   Node Failure Detection Evaluation

For the first experiment, we perform three groups of tests for 10 times each group. Firstly, we respectively calculate the average time consuming of one node failure detection among those five models we talked in section 2 and Smart Ring as a comparison. Then we calculate the average time consuming of two nodes failure detection in Smart Ring. At last, we calculate the average time consuming of three nodes failure detection which is the maximum number our experiment environment supports.

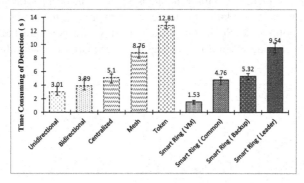

(a) One node failure detection (SmartRing VS other models)

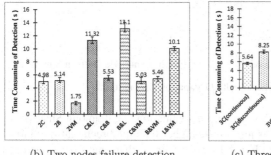

(b) Two nodes failure detection

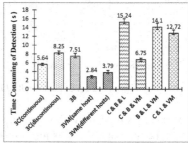

(c) Three nodes failure detection

Fig. 4. Node Failure Detection Testing

As shown in Fig. 4(a), compared to other models, Smart Ring takes less time than the average level. Especially it spends the least time in VM failure detection which is the most possible failure in cloud data center. And we can see in the Smart Ring, VM failure takes the least time, leader failure takes the most and common failure takes the same time as backup approximately. In Fig. 4(b), we examine the capacity of Smart Ring in two nodes failure detection where 2C means two Common nodes failure, 2B means two Backup nodes failure, C & L means a Common node and a Leader node failure and so on. From the results, we can see it takes the same time approximately as the situation of one node failure. We examine the capacity of three nodes failure detection in Fig. 4(c) as well. What to notice is that the time consuming of three continuous common nodes failure detection is different with those discontinuous and three VMs on the same host is different with those on the different hosts as well.

5.2   Bandwidth Occupation Evaluation

Smart Ring takes a tiny bandwidth occupation when HA system runs normally, because only heartbeat messages transferred between adjacent nodes occupy the bandwidth and VM failure detection executed inter physical machine doesn't occupy bandwidth neither. If there is a failure happens, bandwidth occupation will increase until a new ring forms. As we know the leader node which has the largest data flow is the performance bottleneck. So in our second testing, we compare the bandwidth occupation of leader node when a failure happens in Smart Ring with the other five models.

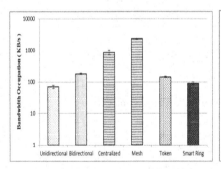
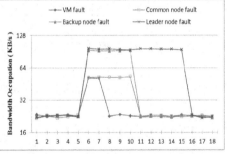

(a) SmartRing VS other models   (b) Different node faults in SmartRing

Fig. 5. Bandwidth Occupation Evaluation

Fig. 5(a) shows the bandwidth occupation evaluation result among Smart Ring and other five models. Smart Ring is just a little higher than unidirectional ring model but a great fewer than others. From Fig. 5(b) we can know that Smart Ring just occupies about 22KB/s when HA system runs normally. But when a fault happens at the 5th second it will increase until a new ring forms. For a VM fault or a common node fault the bandwidth occupation is about 55KB/s, while for a backup node fault or a leader node fault it is about 97KB/s. Because synchronizing the whole of global view occupies a little bandwidth. In addition, we can see the time from bandwidth occupation increases to it restores coincides with our first test results.

6   Conclusion and Future Work

In this paper, we have presented a three roles and two layers node failure detection model. To the best of our knowledge, this work is a kind of novel design and implementation of node failure detection that could be applied in a big scale cluster with plenty of VMs like a cloud data center. We have detailed how to detect a node failure quickly and exactly with a lower cost, support multiple nodes fail simultaneously, solve network partition problem. Moreover, we have evaluated Smart Ring within a 64*100 machines scale cluster. The result shows that Smart Ring has a higher accuracy compared to unidirectional and Bidirectional ring, a lower bandwidth occupation compared to centralized ring and mesh network, and a lower time consuming of node failure detection compared to token ring.

Nevertheless, our design has some limitations that we plan to address in the future. We now can't support discontinuous backup nodes and detect the status of VMs in a simple way through the VMM commands. Finally, it's just a beginning of Smart Ring of design, implementation and performance evaluation. Various other measurements and optimization strategies will need to be explored in the future.

References

1. Rudolph, G.: Parallel clustering on a unidirectional ring. In: Proceedings of the 1993 World Transputer Congress on Transputer Applications and Systems, Aachen, Germany, September 20-22, vol. 36, p. 487. Ios Pr. Inc. (1993)
2. Pasqua, J.: Cluster communication in heartbeat messages. US Patent 7,330,444 (February 12, 2008)
3. Wang, L., Han, X.: Stability and hopf bifurcation analysis in bidirectional ring network model. Communications in Nonlinear Science and Numerical Simulation (2010)
4. Savari, S., Kramer, G.: The multimessage unicast capacity region for bidirectional ring networks. In: 2006 IEEE International Symposium on Information Theory, pp. 763–767. IEEE (2006)
5. Robertson, A.: Linux-ha heartbeat system design. In: Proceedings of the 4th Annual Linux Showcase and Conference, ALS 2000 (2000)
6. Khan, N., Mahajan, A.: Centralized framework with ring broadcasting for real time traffic in vehicular ad hoc networks. In: 2010 3rd International Conference on Emerging Trends in Engineering and Technology, CETET, pp. 842–847. IEEE (2010)
7. Hamlyn, A., Cheung, H., Yang, C.: Computer network distributed monitoring and centralized forecasting of utility distribution system operations. In: IEEE Canadian Conference on Electrical and Computer Engineering, CCECE 2008, pp. 001719–001722 (2008)
8. SGI: Linux failsafe (2009), http://oss.sgi.com/projects/failsafe/
9. Nilausen, J.: Token ring network management: Performance management. International Journal of Network Management 5(1), 47–53 (1995)
10. Hutchison, D., Coffield, D.: Simple token ring local area network. Microprocessors and Microsystems 8(4), 171–176 (1984)

11. Gopal, T., Raja, G., Vijaykumar, D., Sankaranarayanan, V.: Novel fault tolerant token ring network. Microelectronics Reliability 36(5), 707–710 (1996); Fault tolerance; Token ring networks
12. Siddesh, G., Srinivasa, K., Venugopal, K.: Grm: a reliable and fault tolerant data replication middleware for grid environment. In: Proceedings of the International Conference & Workshop on Emerging Trends in Technology, pp. 810–815. ACM (2011)
13. Dake, S., Caulfield, C., Beekhof, A.: The corosync cluster engine. In: Linux Symposium 85
14. Symantec: Network partition (1995),
    http://www.symantec.com/security_response/glossary/
    defin-e.jsp?letter=n&word=network-partition

EaSync: A Transparent File Synchronization Service across Multiple Machines

Huajian Mao[1,2], Hang Zhang[1,2], Xianqiang Bao[1,2],
Nong Xiao[1,2], Weisong Shi[3], and Yutong Lu[1,2]

[1] State Key Laboratory of High Performance Computing, Changsha, Hunan, China
[2] National University of Defense Technology, Changsha, Hunan 410073, China
[3] Wayne State University, 5057 Woodward Ave, Detroit, MI 48202, USA
{huajianmao,nongxiao,ytlu}@nudt.edu.cn, weisong@wayne.edu

Abstract. In our daily life, people increasingly use multiple machines to do their daily work. As platform switching and file modification are so frequently that a way for file synchronization across multiple machines is required to make the files in synchronized. In this paper, we propose EaSync, a transparent file synchronization service across multiple machines. EaSync proposes several key technologies for file synchronization oriented service, including a timestamp based synchronization protocol, an enhanced deduplication algorithm DS-Dedup. We implement and evaluate the EaSync prototype system. As the result shown, EaSync outperforms other synchronization system in operation latency and other metrics.

Keywords: file synchronization, multiple machines, deduplication, EaSync.

1 Introduction

In our daily life, people increasingly use multiple machines to do their daily work. They intermittently work on different platforms in different places, and nomadically do their routine work like document processing, presenting and so on. During the processing of the files on these machines, files may be created, read, modified and deleted which will make different machines have different views and versions of files and folders. As platform switching and file modification are so frequent that a way for file synchronization across multiple machines will be required to make the files on different work platforms in synchronization.

With diving into how users typically process documents on multiple machines, we find that, the essential requirement for a convenience file synchronization service needs to be satisfied is that it should be pervasively accessible and transparent to the applications, and make nomadic access with intermittent connection always latest guaranteed at any location. However, several challenging issues arise in file synchronization across multiple machines. First, data should be accessed at anywhere; however, the network may be partitioned or client may go offline. Second, service should keep working correctly with multiple clients; however conflicts always show

J.J. Park et al. (Eds.): NPC 2012, LNCS 7513, pp. 289–296, 2012.

up. Third, data consistency should be assured; however, network is always partitioned, and it is not easy to keep data consistency in the synchronization service across multiple machines. Forth, synchronization service should be transparent to the applications in the client; however, most of the applications can only do local file operations.

Several new methods like Dropbox[1], UbuntuOne and DBank have been provided as a service for the Internet users. However, Dropbox sometime does not synchronize the files very well, especially when you have multiple person share the files. Also they are all close source project, especially at the server, where much more research issues and large scale data center challenges may be discovered. Also, they only work with the support of connection with their servers, which means, when you only have a local area network connection, the file synchronization will fail, even if the connected machines are actually connected directly.

In this paper, we propose EaSync, a transparent file synchronization service across multiple machines. EaSync enables users to store and sync files online and across multiple computers. EaSync gives users the probability to work anywhere with the freshest data. This paper describes our experience from conception to implementation and evaluation. The main contributions presented in this paper are as follows: First, EaSync states the problem about the file synchronization across multiple machines and make an open source project for both client and server side. Second, several key designs for file synchronization oriented service are proposed in this paper. The designs include a dual-timestamp based synchronization protocol, an enhanced deduplication algorithm DS-Dedup for deduplication. Third, we implement and evaluate the EaSync prototype system. The experiment results show that EaSync outperforms the other platforms in many aspects.

The rest of this paper is organized as follows. We then outline the system model and design of EaSync in detail in Section 2, followed by the implementation in Section 3. We show our experimental results in Section 4. Section 5 presents the prior related work. We conclude our paper and present the future work in Section 6.

2 Design of EaSync

EaSync includes four main components which are EaSync Client, EaSync Gateway, MetaStore, and DataStore. Figure 1 is an overview of EaSync architecture. EaSync client consists of three components which are Local Update Observer (LObsvr), Remote Update Observer (RObsvr), and the synchronization daemon (Syncer). EaSync client runs synchronization protocol with the EaSync Gateway. The synchronization protocol will be discussed in Section 2.2. EaSync client monitors the file update on the client, and starts the synchronization to EaSync Server.

Gateway is the entry of EaSync service. It deals with the requests from both the EaSync clients and the web browser. In order to scale up, load balancing is considered. The main work of the gateway is to route the requests (with Logic Controller) to help the clients to fetch metadata from MetaStore (with a metastore manager instance) and data from DataStore (with a datastore manager instance). MetaStore manages all of the metadata information for the users. Also the synchronization log records are also managed in MetaStore. Another important component in server side is the DataStore where all of the data are store.

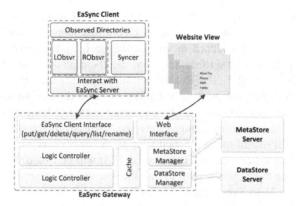

Fig. 1. An overview of EaSync architecture

2.1   Synchronization Protocol

We propose a hybrid timestamp based synchronization protocol to keep the managed files in sync. In this protocol, two timestamps are used, one is the client-side time-stamp as local time, and the other one is server-side one as a global timestamp. The local time is used to record when the update is made, while the global one is used to record when the update is submitted to the EaSync server (by reading the gateway at server side system time).

Figure 2 gives the steps of file synchronization between EaSync client and server. We describe this protocol in detail as following. L.1) The Lobsvr observes the mod-ification of the candidate objects with the notification mechanism. And once an object is modified, client runs step L.2), which inserts a change log into a local to-be-synced pool, and marks the change type to be "changed by local". In this step, the local time-stamp is recorded. After this, L.3) is executed by the Syncer. It reads the updates with type of "changed by local", and starts step L.4) to fetch the freshest data in local, and synchronizes it to the server with step L.5).

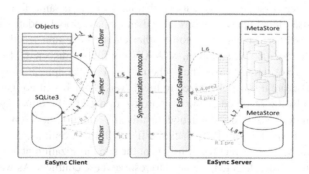

Fig. 2. Timestamp based synchronization protocol

When the gateway receives an update request, L.6) it first starts conflict detection, and if no conflict happens, it then create an global timestamp by reading the server side clock, and updates the record in server side. In L.7), the server responses the EaSync client with the global timestamp, and the client record it in a local snapshot table. On the other side, R.1) The Robsvr periodically polls the server with a global timestamp, which is returned by the last polling, to fetch the change log on server to find which files are changed, and then R.2) inserts the change log batches into the to-be-synced pool, with setting the change type to be "changed by remote". At the meantime, the client will record the responded time as the next query time. Just like L.3) when the periodical Syncer daemon is executed, R.3) will be called. In this step, Syncer firstly query the to-be-synced pool to find the record sets where a remote synchronization is needed. Then Syncer literately runs R.4) and R.5). The former fetches the updated data from EaSync server and the later store them in local.

2.2   Consistency Model

It is common that the network is always partitioned. Also, in some situation, the client even can only access the data in its own device. So it is not possible to maintain all the replications on different machines in a strong data consistency. In EaSync we provide an eventual consistency[8] for the file synchronization. However, in the eventual consistency model, conflicts are unavoidable. To solve conflict problems, there are two key questions to be answered, and they are 1) when to discover the conflict, and 2) whose duty to resolve the conflict.

For the first question, EaSync detects the conflict at the synchronization phase by the client. Basically, in a partitioned network there are two conflict forms: RAW (Read-After-Write) in which a client reads the value of a data item that is being concurrently updated by a second client, and WAW (Write-After-Write) in which two clients update the same data item in incompatible ways.

For both of these two conflict types, we provide an optimistic strategy for conflicts detection: we accept all the user operations in the client and leave the conflict detection at the synchronization phase. When EaSync client starts to synchronize their data, it detects conflicts first. It firstly check whether there is a same file exists on the server side whose global update time is later than the last global update time stored in the client. If it is true, it means that some other clients have updated the data before this synchronization. In this situation, a WAW conflict is detected. RAW conflicts may happen in the eventual consistency schema too. For example, if client A updated some data, and before it is synchronized to the server, client B will not get the freshest data. This can also be resolved at the synchronization phase by either synchronizing the data in which client B does not update this file, or turning RAW conflict into WAW conflict in which client B updates the file. With this optimistic conflict detection strategy, EaSync can detect the conflicts at the synchronization phase.

After the conflicts are detected, we need to resolve these conflicts. As we analyzed in previous, the main conflict is the WAW conflict at synchronization phase. In detail, the problem is how to resolve the situation when there is a file whose update time is later than the last update time on the client. EaSync resolves these conflicts by creating a new version on the server side with a suffix .timestamp.clientname. After the EaSync client finishes its synchronization phase, the user will find the conflict versions. EaSync leaves it to the users, relying on humans effort for resolving conflicts.

3   Optimization and Implementation

In the file synchronization service like EaSync, user data is always revised frequently. There will be a bundle of data which is very similar. If we split the files into chunks, there will be a number of same chunks from different files. In EaSync, we use a deduplication method at the client side. EaSync uses deduplication together with S-RSync[9] and we name this method as DS-Dedup.

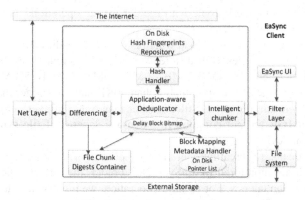

Fig. 3. Overview of DS-dedup

Figure 3 shows the overview of DS-Dedup. When a file is modified, EaSync will send a request to the DS-Dedup module to synchronize the data to serve. DS-Dedup serves EaSync request by the Intelligent chunker. It splits the data into chunks intelligently according to the frequent of file modification.   DS-Dedup uses content defined chunking (CDC) to split for the frequently updated files, and static chunking (SC) for the files not frequently updated. After the file data is split into chunks, the chunks enter into the AAplication-aware Deduplicator (AADedup)[2]. AADedup controls the deduplication of DS-Dedup. When a chunk arrives, it first calculates the fingerprint, and searches in the Hash Fingerprints Repository. It the fingerprint of a chunk exists, AADedup will generate a point to the chunk data and stores it in the On Disk pointer List.   This is done by Block Mapping Metadata Handler. Otherwise, if there is no fingerprint for the new coming data chunk, AADedup will generate a new fingerprint by Hash Handler and add it to the Hash Fingerprints Repository. In order to synchronize data to the EaSync server side with S-Rsync differencing algorithm, an File Chunk Digests Container component is used in DS-Dedup to store the chunks information including the chunk finger print of the file.   When S-Rsync start to check the differences, it reads the chunk fingerprint information and generate the differences with S-RSync algorithm.   After that the difference is then transferred to the EaSync server side with S-RSync algorithm.

4   Evaluation

We set up an experimental platform with 2 PCs and 1 laptop as EaSync clients and Panasas ActiveStor cluster for Gateway, MetaData and DataStore server. The clients and server are connected by a local area network. With this experiment platform, we evaluate EaSync as follows: First, we evaluate EaSync by comparing with an open source project named with iFolder. Second, we have evaluated the EaSync in the aspect of synchronization protocol, in which we compare S-Rsync with Rsync. Finally, we evaluate the benefit and cost of deduplication.

4.1   Performance Comparison

In this section, we compare EaSync with iFolder for the operations latency of creating, updating, renaming and deleting.

We have collected a set of workload which is used and modified in our daily work. We select operations on files with different sizes and different types. The sizes are about 50KB, 100KB, 500KB, 1MB, 5MB, 10MB, 50MB, 100MB, 500MB, 1GB. We do not present the latencies for files smaller than 50KB and files larger than 1GB. The latencies of EaSync and iFolder for files smaller than 50KB are very close. Also, the files larger than 1GB are not common in our usage schema of file synchronization between different devices.

In the experiments, for creating operation, we put the files with different sizes into the folder which are monitored by EaSync and iFolder, then we get the latencies as the creating operation latency. For updating operation, we modify the files by appending 1KB data to the files, and then record the latencies of data synchronization, and make these latencies as the updating latency. Figure 4 shows the latencies of different operations.

As the result shows, EaSync outperforms iFolder for most of the operations including create, update, rename and delete. The main reason for the larger latencies for create and update is that iFolder uses RSync synchronization algorithm to synchronize the differences of the files. While RSync will read data from the server first, then compare the data with that in client side. However, EaSync uses our proposed SRSync algorithm to do the operations, it reduces the cost a lot, as shown in the figure. Another information included in the figure is that when the size of the file increases, the latencies of iFolder increases faster than that of our EaSync. In summary, compared to iFolder, EaSync outperforms in the operation latencies.

4.2   Effect of Ds-Dedup

EaSync uses deduplication to reduce the capacity and transmission cost. In this section we evaluate the effect of deduplication for EaSync. First, we evaluate the storage capacity used by a frequently revised file. We compare DS-Dedup with other strategies with different chunk size settings. As the deduplication method is dependent on the chunk size of file split. In our experiments, we uses static chunk split method with the chunk sizes of 0.5KB, 1.0KB, 1.5KB, and 2.0KB.

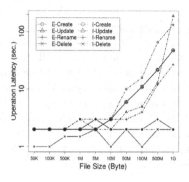

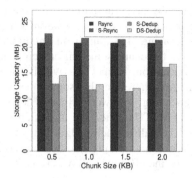

Fig. 4. Operation latencies   **Fig. 5.** Storage capacity used

Figure 5 shows the result of storage capacity used under different strategies. As the result shown, Rsync uses about 20.8MB for the storage capacity. However, S-Rsync uses a little bit more. This is mainly because of that S-Rsync needs to store the chunk digest information for the files. While as S-dedupe uses deduplication method for both the data chunks and the metadata, it costs the least space. For the same reason as S-Rsync to Rsync, DS-Dedup uses a little more space than S-dedupe because of the space cost of chunks digest information.

From the result we can find that, comparing with the strategies with no deduplication methods, DS-Dedup and S-dedup is always better. DS-Dedup can reduce the storage cost to about half of that of Rsync and S-Rsync. Also, it can be found that the storage cost is dependent on chunk size. When deduplication is used, the chunk size should be selected carefully. In this experiment setting, 1.5KB is the best size for deduplication. Another benefit of client side deduplication comes from the transmission cost to synchronize the updated data to the server. As the redundancy of the data is deleted, EaSync only needs to transfer part of the whole data which is enough to reproduce the original data.

5   Related Work

EaSync shares several considerations with the other prior works. Services like Dropbox, UbuntuOne DBank, and Wukong[4] are probably the closest existing work to our EaSync. We share the overall architecture, which is client-server based. However, EaSync is designed not only for the file synchronization service, but also for research purpose, which is designed to be an open source project. While the existing services like Dropbox, UbuntuOne are always close source projects, especially the server side design where much more research issues and large scale data center challenges may be discovered. So EaSync shares these services with similar ideas, but contains more values for research community. EaSync also shares a lot of technologies and ideas with some synchronization methods, like Rsync[6,7], and the version control services. However, most of the traditional synchronizers are invoked explicitly by an action from the user (issuing a synchronization command, clicking the synchronization button, etc.), while EaSync runs a background daemon and synchronize the updates automatically and transparently for the users. It definitely improves the user experience and eases the user's operations which may introduce unconscious errors.

Differencing algorithm is an important technology in file synchronization service. Recently, there are some differencing algorithms aiming at special application or special occasion. Rsync[7] is widely used for synchronization, backup and recovery system. And there are also some other algorithms adopting other consideration like, Delta-encoding. The work[5] uses "delta" vcdiff[3] encoding way to improve performance of HTTP traffic. The algorithm vcdiff is one of the best delta encoding algorithms. Every differencing algorithm has its own advantages on the reasonable size of difference or computing overhead, according to its special scene. Because of the simplicity and efficiency, Rsync is used widely in synchronization system.

6   Conclusion

We present EaSync, a transparent file synchronization service across multiple machines in this paper. EaSync characterizes itself with several unique features: First, it supports file synchronization in local area network environment. Second, it proposes several key technologies for file synchronization oriented service, including a dual-timestamp based synchronization protocol, DS-Dedup. Third, it explorers an open source implementation for research community.

Acknowledgments. The authors would like to thank the anonymous reviewers for their comments and kindly suggestions. This work is supported by the National Natural Science Foundation of China under Grant No. 60736013, Grant No. 61120106005, Grant No. 61025009 and Grant No. 60903040.

References

1. Dropbox, http://www.dropbox.com
2. Fu, Y., et al.: Aa-dedupe: An application-aware source deduplication approach for cloud backup services in the personal computing environment. In: Proceedings of the CLUSTER (2011)
3. Korn, D., et al.: The VCDIFF generic differencing and compression data format (2002)
4. Mao, H., et al.: Wukong: A cloud-oriented file service for mobile Internet devices. Journal of Parallel and Distributed Computing (2011)
5. Mogul, J., et al.: Potential benefits of delta encoding and data compression for http. In: Proceedings of ACM SIGCOMM (1997)
6. Rasch, D., et al.: In-place rsync: File synchronization for mobile and wireless devices. In: Proceedings of the USENIX ATC (2003)
7. Tridgell, A., et al.: The rsync algorithm. Australian Natl. Univ. Canberra (1996)
8. Vogels, W.: Eventually consistent. Communications of the ACM 52(1), 40–44 (2009)
9. Zhang, H., et al.: S-rsync: An efficient differencing algorithm with locally chunk digests generating for file synchronization services. In: Proceedings of the Humancom (2011)

Relationship between Correcting Code and Module Technique in Hiding Secret Data[*]

Phan Trung Huy[1], Nguyen Hai Thanh[2], and Cheonsick Kim[3]

[1] Hanoi University of Science and Technology, Hanoi, Vietnam
huypt-fami@mail.hut.edu.vn, huyfr2002@yahoo.com
[2] Ministry of Education and Training, Hanoi, Vietnam
nhthanh@moet.gov.vn
[3] Dept. of Computer Engineering Sejong University,
98 Gunja-Dong, Gwangjin-Gu, Seoul 143-747, Korea
mipsan@paran.com

Abstract. In this paper, we show the role of modules over rings of finite characteristics in data hiding area. Applications of correcting codes and covering functions in data hiding are shown as special cases of our module approach. Applications of modules over rings of characteristic 2 to design new embedding schemes for hiding secret data in binary images are introduced.

Keywords: module, ring, characteristic 2, data hiding, binary image, steganography, correcting codes, covering function, MSDR.

1 Introduction

Data hiding can be applied in copyright, annotation, and communication, and can be achieved by altering some nonessential pixels in the cover image. For example, in a given color image (including grayscale image), the least-significant bit (LSB) of each pixel can be changed to embed the secret data. However, two color images embedded by secret data are very sensitive and can be easily detected by the human eyes. One of the most challenging problems is hiding the secret data into binary images with a high ratio of secret data, and low image distortion. In case of palette images, ones need to prevent steganalysis, especially to histogram-based attacks (see for examples some analysis in [18], if the alpha ratio of the number of changed pixels to the number of total pixels of a given palette image is lower than 0.1, it is very difficult to guess if the image contains hidden data. In block-based approaches, each binary image is partitioned into binary blocks of the same size N, each block can be seen as an N-bit string of size N. In such a block F of size N, by taking WL scheme [16] one can embed one bit by changing at most one bit of F. From CPT scheme proposed by Chen-Pan-Tseng (2000) [3], in F one can embed $r=\lfloor \log_2(N+1) \rfloor$ bits, by changing at most two bits of F.

---

[*] This work is partially supported by Vietnamese National Foundation for Science & Technology Development (NAFOSTED).

J.J. Park et al. (Eds.): NPC 2012, LNCS 7513, pp. 297–307, 2012.
© IFIP International Federation for Information Processing 2012

By correcting codes approach, with notion of covering codes, Crandall [5] refers to an unpublished article by Bierbrauer [1] that brings deep techniques to data hiding area, based on the point of view of a coding theorist [10,12,13]. The connection between linear covering codes and steganography had also appeared in one paper by Galand and Kabatiansky [6], and covering codes in [13] dating back 1994 by R. Struik. In a nice paper [7] written by J. Bierbrauer and J. Fridrich, the authors described and extended the original Bierbrauer's work[1] which show rich contributions of covering functions to data hiding area. As shown in their paper, in binary images or in binary data formed from LSB planes of three component colors Red, Green, Blue of pixels, in true color images, some schemes have reached the maximum secret data ratio ($MSDR_k$) based on the number of secret bits which can be embedded in a block F of N pixels with the restrictions: in F, at most k bits can be changed ($k=1,2,3$). Several works [2, 4, 5, 6, 7, 9, 14, 15] introduced the powerful applications of approaches based on correcting codes in data hiding.

In this paper, we introduced an application of modules over rings of characteristic 2 to data hiding area, for binary images the main case of our interest. It can be seen that this idea will be easily extended to others characteristics for different formats on multimedia environment. The relationship between two methods in data hiding, by module and by correcting codes methods is considered. It is shown that hiding secret data based on correcting codes is the special case of hiding data by module over rings of characteristic 2. Some new schemes for data hiding by module method are introduced, showing the advantage and flexible of module approach to data hiding area.

The paper is divided into 5 sections. Following the introduction section, section 2 recalls applications of linear correcting codes and covering codes in binary data hiding. Due to [11] we recall the notion "k-maximal secret data ratio" ($MSDR_k$) of secret bits embedded in each block F of N pixels in binary images with the restriction that at most k –pixels can be changed in F. As shown, the results of covering codes which reached these limits. In section 3 we focus on modules over the ring Z_2 of integers modulo 2, the main subject of this paper. Notions of k- base on module and k-embedding scheme are introduced. Some aspects of $MSDR$ are considered. To get new 2-bases of Z_2-modules for new 2-embedding schemes applied to binary images, a designing method is given. In section 4 we show the relationship between correcting codes, covering function with module method, and present in details the arguments via an example of using Hamming code (7,4) in data hiding. As experimental results, some 2-bases obtained by our program are presented and their applications in data hiding schemes are discussed. Conclusion is the content of section 5. The general applications of modules over the rings of characteristics q, $q>1$, specially for the special case of ring Z_q of integers modulo q, are discussed for future study.

2   Error Correcting Codes and Covering Codes

2.1   Correcting Codes in Steganography

As shown in the survey work [7] of J. Bierbrauer and J. Fridrich, the covering function technique is originated from error correcting codes area and this brings to steganography powerful ways to design high quality schemes for embedding secret data. For examples, the matrix encoding technique used in F5 algorithm by Westfeld [15] permit us to modify at most 1 pixel among 2^k-1 pixels to hide k secret bits. The distortion of image then is reduced with the high ratio of the embedding scheme, which reached MSDR$_1$. Matrix encoding technique using correcting codes show that after the embedding phase, the syndromes generated by a parity check matrix in the extracting phase will present exactly secret data embedded in stego-images. In covering code technique, the covering radius of the code reflects the maximal number of pixels changed to embed secret data and the dimension of code reflects the capacity of bits can be embedded, by a scheme used this approach.

Given the linear space $W_n = \mathbf{F}^n_q$ of dimension n over the finite field $\mathbf{F}_q$ and a natural number $d > 1$. Due to Hamming's work origined from 1947, an error correcting code over $\mathbf{F}_q$ is defined as a subset $C \subseteq W_n$ for which d is the minimum distance between two distinct code words $x \neq y \in C$. In error correcting codes area, each codeword $v \in C$ can be seen as an (exact) encoded bit string we need to transmit on a noise channel. If there are at most $r = \lfloor d/2 \rfloor$ errors appear on transmission, that is v is changed to $v'=v+e$ for some error vector e whose Hamming weight $w(e) \leq r$, then we can correct v' to recover v after erasing e, by some methods detecting e. The size of C is defined as $|C|$- the number of code words in C.

If the code is linear, we can find some effective ways to detect the error vector e.

A linear code C of type $[n, k, d]$ is a linear subspace of W_n having its dimension $k < n$, with d the minimum (Hamming) distance between distinct code words $x \neq y \in C$. The covering radius ρ of code C is defined as $\rho = max_{v \in \mathbf{W}}d(v;C)$, where $d(v;C)$ denotes the minimum Hamming distance from the vector v to the code C. A parity check matrix of C is a matrix H *of size* $t \times n$, $t=n-k$, which permit us to obtain for any $v \in W_n$ its syndrome vector $s(v) = H.v^T$, where v^T is the column vector form of v, so that $s(v)= 0$ if and only if $v \in C$. The syndrome $s(v)$ is used to detect and correct the error e if $w(e)=k$ (the number of errors), $k \leq r = \lfloor d/2 \rfloor$, appeared on transmission, to recover the correct message v *from the received message* $v'=v+e$ as follows: since $s(v')=H.v'=H.(v+e)^T=H.v^T+H.e^T=s(v)+s(e)=s(e)$, we find e so that s$(e) = s(v')$ and $w(e) \leq r = \lfloor d/2 \rfloor$, and correct v' to $v = v'-e$. To obtain an efficient way recognizing the error e, *the coset technique* is developed.

A coset $C + v$ is the set of all vectors in W_n with the same syndrome $s(v)$. A vector $l_{r(v)}$ of the minimum weight in $C + v$ can be called a *leader of the coset*. We define the syndrome map $s : W_n \rightarrow W_t$ by $s(v) = H . v^T$.

In steganography (see [7, 9]), one can make use of the syndrome map $s : W_n \rightarrow W_t$ as the extracting map of the embedding scheme $[n, t, \rho]$ which can be defined by:

1. Let n and t be positive integers, $t \leq n$, and let X be a finite set of symbols. An embedding scheme of type $[n, t,\rho]$ over X is given by a pair of maps $c : X^t \times X^n \rightarrow X^n$ and $s : X^n \rightarrow X^t$ such that $s(c(p, v)) = p$ for all (plaintext) $p \in X^t$ and v *(stego-block)* $\in X^n$. Maps c and s are the embedding and the extracting maps, respectively. The

covering radius of the scheme is defined as $\rho = \max\{d(v, c(p, v)) \mid p \in X^t, v \in X^n\}$, where d is the Hamming distance.

2. The embedding scheme $[n\ t,\rho]$ allows us to hide p (as a string of t secret symbols) into v (as an n-string v of n cover symbols), by changing at most ρ of n cover symbols. The following algorithm shows this idea.

Coset Algorithm. *Given p,v*

a) Compute $u = s(v) - p$,

b) Set $v'= c(p;\ v) = v - l_u$, where l_u is a leader of the coset $C + u$ of all the vectors in W_n with the same syndrome of u. The Hamming weigh $w(l_u) = j \leq \rho$ together with vector l_u show the exact j positions on which we need to change with the cover vector v by equation $v' = v - l_u$. So, $s(l_u) = u$. This provides us in the extract phase: by using (a) above, the syndrome $s(v') = s(v)- s(l_u)=s(v)- u = p$ is obtained, the exact plaintext as claimed.

Concretely (see, such as [7]), in case $X = \mathbf{F}_2$ (also $\mathbf{Z}_2$) for designing an embedding scheme $[n,\ t,\rho]$, we can use a covering function $COV(\rho,n,t)$ which permit us to embed any t-bit string p in any n-bit string v (as a block of n bits) by changing at most ρ positions on v.

Good Covering Codes

In [7] the authors show some interest classes of cover functions:

1. COV $(2, 5 \cdot 2^{a-1} - 1, 2a + 1)$ for $a \geq 1$ by equation (1).
2. COV $(2, 6 \cdot 4^{a-1} - 1, 4a)$, $a \geq 2$ by equation (4). The first members of this family are COV $(2, 23, 8)$, COV $(2, 95, 12)$.

By our interest, for high quality of stego-images, in this paper we focus only on small values, especially for $\rho=1, 2$.

2.2   k-Maximal Secret Data Ratio of Embedded Bits

In this part, given an image G, for simplicity we only concentrate on one fixed block $F = (F_1, F_2,.., F_N)$ of N pixels of G, and F is considered as a vector of dimension N). In F each entry F_i can be understood as a pixel whenever the index i is referring, also as the color of this pixel whenever its color value is mentioned. Suppose each color F_i can be changed to q-1 new colors F_i' closed to F_i, by one of q-1 different ways. In the case of binary images, $q=2$. In the general case $q \geq 2$ for color images.

We consider here *k-embedding schemes* in which secret bits can be embedded in each block F by changing at most k entries, with k small, $k = 1, 2$. Together with F, each new block F' after changing pixels of F is called a *configuration*. Denote by $MSDR_k$ the *k-Maximal Secret Data Ratio* which presents the *largest number of embedded bits in each block F of N pixels by changing colors of at most k pixels in F*.

In the case $k=1$, since we change colors in at most one element in F, with N elements, $1+(q-1)N$ ways can be taken. This means that for any 1-embedding scheme, we can hide at most

$$MSDR_1 = \lfloor \log_2(1+(q-1).C(N,1)) \rfloor \text{ secret bits in each block } F.$$

In the cases $k=2$ or 3, similarly, we have

$$MSDR_2 = \lfloor \log_2(1+(q-1).C(N,1)+(q-1)^2.C(N,2)) \rfloor \text{ and}$$
$$MSDR_3 = \lfloor \log_2(1+(q-1).C(N,1)+(q-1)^2.C(N,2))+(q-1)^3.C(N,3)) \rfloor.$$

For example, in binary images, if $N = 5$ then $MSDR_2 = 4$. In the case of grey images, with $N=1$, $q=16$, $MSDR_1 = \lfloor \log_2(1+15.1) \rfloor = 4$. That means in each pixel F (a block of 1 pixel) if its color has 15 other ways to change, then any 4 secret bits can be hidden in F by some appropriate change. This is the case achieved in [8].

3   Modules over Rings of Characteristic 2 in Hiding Secret Data

3.1   Application of Modules in Hiding Secret Data

Each (right) module M over the ring $\mathbf{Z}_q$ is an additive abelian group M with zero 0 together with a scalar multiplication "." to assign each couple (m,t) in $M \times \mathbf{Z}_q$ with an element $m.t$ in M. Let $\mathbf{Z}_q = \{0,1,...,q-1\}$. We need some following basic properties, which will be used in the sequent:

P1) $m.\mathbf{0} = 0; m.\mathbf{1}=m;$
P2) $m+n = n+m$ for all m,n in M.
P3) $m.(t+l) = m.t + m.l$ for all m in M, t,l in $\mathbf{Z}_q$.

Definition 1. Given a natural number $v > 0$, a subset $U \subseteq M-\{0\}$, we call U a v-base of M if for any $x \in M - \{0\}$, x can be presented by a linear combination of at most v elements in U. That means there exist n elements $u_1,u_2,..,u_n$ in U, $n \leq v$, together with $t_1,t_2,...,t_n$ in $\mathbf{Z}_q$ such that $x = u_1.t_1+u_2.t_2+..+u_n.t_n$.

We call a k-embedding scheme any embedding scheme that permits in each block F of N elements ones can change at most k elements to hide data. In the case $v=1$, it is obvious that $U=M-\{0\}$ is the unique 1-base.

In this paper, the main of our interest are the cases $v = 1,2$ for binary images (according to the characteristic $q =2$ and $M =\mathbf{Z}_2 \times \mathbf{Z}_2 \times..\times \mathbf{Z}_2$ is the n-fold cartesian product of $\mathbf{Z}_2$, which can be seen as a (right) $\mathbf{Z}_2$-module. For binary image we have $q=2$. The addition in $\mathbf{Z}_2$ can be seen as the operation XOR (exclusive –OR) on bits, Each element $x=(x_1,x_2,..,x_n)$ in M can be presented as an n-bit string $x=x_1x_2..x_n$, with operations defined as follows:

D1) $x+y = z_1z_2..z_n$ where $z_i=x_i \oplus y_i$, $i=1,..,n$, For $x=x_1x_2..x_n$, $y=y_1..y_n$ in M, k in $\mathbf{Z}_2$,
D2) $x.k= z_1z_2..z_n$ where $z_i=x_i.k = x_i$ AND k.

Given a binary image G, we set $C_G= \mathbf{Z}_2 =\{0,1\}$ as the set of two colors of G. The *color changing function* Next: $\mathbf{Z}_2 \rightarrow \mathbf{Z}_2$ is given by:

(3.1) $c' = c+1 = $ Next(c), for all c in $\mathbf{Z}_2$ and *changing a color c* means that c is replaced by $c' = $ Next(c).

As one can see, an 1-embedding scheme can be reduced from a 2-embedding scheme. Hence, at first we consider 2-embedding schemes.

3.2   Application of 2-Bases for 2-Embedding Schemes

Let $U \subseteq M$-$\{0\}$, U be a 2-base of a $\mathbb{Z}_2$ –module M. Suppose $|U| =n$. Consider any binary block $F =(F_1, F_2,.., F_s)$ of a given binary image G, and binary secret key $K= (K_1, K_2,.., K_s)$, F_i, $K_i \in \mathbb{Z}_2$, i=1, .., N.

Suppose $s \geq n$. For F, we can assign a surjective function $h_F : \{1,2,..,N\} \rightarrow U$ as a weight function of indexes i of F_i. Since F is fixed in the scope, for simplicity we write h instead. We can embed any secret element $d \in M$ in F by *changing colors of at most 2 elements* in F as the following 2-embedding scheme.

3.2.1   Embedding a Secret Element d

Set $S[F,K] = \sum_{1 \leq i \leq N} h(i).T_i$, by taking operations on the $\mathbb{Z}_2$ – right module M.

Step 0) Given a secret key as a binary vector $K=(k_0, k_1,.., k_N)$, $k_i \in \mathbb{Z}_2$.

Change the color F_i of each $F_i \in F$ into a *marked color* $T_i=F_i+k_i$ (in $\mathbb{Z}_2$).

We present this computation by $T=F \oplus K$;

Step 1) Compute $m = S[F,K]$;

Step 2) Compare m and d:

- Case $m = d$: keep F intact;

- Case $d \neq m$: then find $d -m=a$, for some $a \in M$-$\{0\}$. There are two following cases happen:

i) $a \in U$: since h is surjective, there exists F_q in F , such that $h(q) = a =d$-m. Then change the color F_q to new color $F_q'=\text{Next}(F_q)=F_q+\mathbf{1}$.

ii) $a \notin U$: Since U is a 2-base of M - a $\mathbb{Z}_2$-module - we can find (successfully) two elements x,y in U *such that* $a=x+y$, and therefore find two entries F_p, F_q in F such that $h(p)=x$, $h(q)=$y.

Then we change F_p to new color $F_p'=F_p+\mathbf{1}$, and change F_q to new color $F_q'=F_q+\mathbf{1}$;

3.2.2   Extracting the Secret Element Embedded in F

Step 1) Computing $u=S[F,K]$;

Step 2) Return u as the secret element d embedded in S (that is $u=d$) .

Correctness of the Method

Theorem 1. *The element u extracted in step 1 of the extracting stage 3.2.2 above is exactly the secret element d hidden into S in the embedding stage 3.2.1.*

Proof. We need consider only the case $d \neq m$ and prove that $u=d$.

Indeed, if the step (2i) in **3.2.1** is taken place, after changing the color F_q to F_q' $=F_q+\mathbf{1}$ by step 2(ii) in **3.2.1** with $h(q)=a=d$-m, we get $T_q'=T_q+\mathbf{1}$. Then,

$$u = \sum_{1 \leq q \neq i \leq N} h(i).T_i + h(q).(T_q+\mathbf{1}) = \sum_{1 \leq q \neq i \leq N} h(i).T_i + h(q).(T_q) +h(q).\mathbf{1}$$
$$= \sum_{1 \leq i \leq N} h(i).T_i + h(q)=m+d-m =d.$$

For the case that the step (2ii) in **3.2.1** is taken place, using $d - m = a = x + y$, $h(p)=x$, $h(q)=y$, by the same arguments we deduce $T_p'=T_p+1$ and $T_q'=T_q+1$. Therefore by properties of modules

$$u = \sum_{1 \leq p, q \neq i \leq N} h(i).T_i + h(p).T_p' + h(q).T_q = \sum_{1 \leq p, q \neq i \leq N} h(i).T_i + h(p).T_p + h(p) + h(q).T_q + h(q)$$
$$= \sum_{1 \leq i \leq N} h(i).T_i + h(p).T_p + h(q).T_q + h(p) + h(q)$$

$$= \sum_{1 \leq i \leq N} h(i).T_i + h(p) + h(q) = m + a = m + d - m = d. \text{ This completes the proof. } \|$$

Example 1. The subset $U=\{0001,0010,0100,1000,1111\}$ is a 2-base of the module
$M = \mathbf{Z}_2 \times \mathbf{Z}_2 \times \mathbf{Z}_2 \times \mathbf{Z}_2$. Therefore, we can use it to hide data. In any block F of 5 pixels, we can change at most two pixels to hide 4 bits. That is the $MSDR_2$ is obtained: $MSDR_2 = \lfloor \log_2(1+5(5+1)/2) \rfloor = 4 = \lfloor \log_2(|M|) \rfloor$.

Remark 1. Applications of k-bases for k-embedding schemes are similarly established, for any $k>0$, hence we do not mention in details.

3.3   Designing 2 – Bases of $\mathbf{Z}_2^n$

In this part we introduce a method to design 2-bases of $\mathbf{Z}_2^n$ inductively.

Denote by $V_n = \mathbf{Z}_2^n = \mathbf{Z}_2 \times \mathbf{Z}_2 \times .. \times \mathbf{Z}_2$ the $\mathbf{Z}_2$- module whose elements can be presented simply as the form $b = b_n b_{n-1}..b_1$, an n- bit strings.

Denote by $PR_k(V_n)$ the projection getting k right components in V_n and $PL_k(V_n)$ the projection getting k left components in V_n.

Concretely, $PR_k(b_n b_{n-1}..b_r..b_1) = b_k b_{k-1}..b_1$ and $PL_k(b_n b_{n-1}..b_2 b_1) = b_n b_{n-1}.. b_{n-k+2} b_{n-k+1}$.

Denote by $CL_{k,t}$ a class of 2-bases X of V_n satisfying $|X|=2^k + 2^t -3, n=k+t$, and $PL_k(X) = V_k$.

Denote by $CR_{k,t}$ a class of 2-bases X of V_n satisfying $|X|=2^k + 2^t -3, n=k+t$, and $PR_t(X) = V_t$.

Lemma 2. If X is a 2-base of V_n such that $PL_m(X) =V_m$ for some integer $0 < m < n$, then there exist a 2-base Y of V_{n+1} such that $PL_m(Y) =V_m$ and $|Y|=|X|+2^r$, $m+r=n$.

Proof. Define Y is the set of all $n+1$-bit string x in one of two following forms:

(i) $b_n b_{n-1}..b_1 0$, with any $b_n b_{n-1}..b_1$ in X and whose right most bit is 0.
(ii) $00..0x_r x_{r-1}..x_1 1$ with any $x_r x_{r-1}..x_1 \in V_r$.

By assumption on X, any element of the form $y_1..y_m 0$ in V_{n+1} can be presented as a linear combination of at most two elements in Y. For any element of the form $y_1..y_m x_1..x_r 1$ in V_{n+1}, by $PL_m(X) =V_m$ there exists n-bit string of X of the form $y_1..y_m v_1..v_r$, for some r-bit string $v_1..v_r$. So $y_1..y_m v_1..v_r 0$ belongs to Y by definition.

Define $u_1..u_r = x_1..x_r \oplus v_1..v_r$. Then $y_1..y_m x_1..x_r 1 = 00..0u_1..u_r 1 \oplus y_1..y_1 v_1..v_r$. Hence Y is a 2-base of V_{n+1}. Obviously, $|Y|=|X|+2^r$, $m+r=n$ and $PL_m(Y) =V_m$. $\|$

Remark 2. By duality, from a 2-base X satisfying $PR_r(X)=V_r$, we can define a 2-base Z of V_{n+1} having all elements in one of two forms: $1y_1..y_m 00..0$, with any m-bit string $y_1..y_m$ in V_m, and $0x_1..x_m u_1..u_r$, with any n-bit string $x_1..x_m u_1..u_r$ in X.

Theorem 3. *For any $n \geq 4$, there exist 2-bases X in $CL_{m,r}$, Y in $CR_{m,,r}$ such that if m,r >1, $m+r=n$ then $|X|, |Y| \leq 2^m + 2^r - 3$.*

Proof. Firstly, one can see that:

a) $CL_{2,2}$ contains the set $Z=\{0001, 0010, 0100, 1110, 1001\}$, this set satisfies the claim $|Z| = 5 = 2^2 + 2^2 - 3$, and $CR_{2,2}$ contains the set $T=\{1000,0100,0010,0111,1001\}$ with $|T|=5$ which satisfies the claim.

b) For all $CL_{m,r}$, $CR_{m,r}$, $m+r=n$, $n \geq 4$, m, $r >1$, one can prove easily the theorem by induction on n, starting from two 2-bases Z, T above and applying Lemma 2 together with Remark 2 by duality.   □

Example 1

a) the class $CL_{2,1}$ contains the set $X=\{110,100,010,001\}$, and $CR_{1,2}$ contains the set Y $= \{011,001,010,100\}$.

Generally, for any $n>0$, we can define the set X contains all $n+1$- bit strings in one of two forms: $b_n b_{n-1}..b_1 0 \neq 00..0$ and $00..01$. Then X belongs to $CL_{n,1}$. We define the set Y contains all $n+1$- bit strings of two forms: $0b_n b_{n-1}..b_1 \neq 00..0$ and $100..0$, then Y belongs to $CL_{n,1}$.

b) $CL_{2,3}$ contains the set of 9 elements $X = \{00010, 00100, 01000, 11100, 10010,$ $00001, 00011, 00101, 00111\}$

c) $CL_{3,3}$ contains the set of 13 elements $\{000010, 000100, 001000, 011100,$ $010010, 000001, 000011, 000101, 000111, 100000, 110000, 101000, 111000\}$.

4   Correcting Codes and Module Method in Data Hiding

4.1   Correcting Code and Covering Function as Special Cases of Module Method

In data hiding area, by the essential relation between correcting code and covering function, for simplicity we need only to show the relation between correcting codes and module methods. Indeed, by the coset algorithm in the part 2.1, section 2, in the extract phase, a plaintext p hidden in the cover-string v' can be extracted from v' by computing the syndrome of v' as $p = s(v')=H.v'^T$, where $v'= v - l_u$ and H is the parity checking matrix of size $t \times n$ which can be presented as $H = (C_1,..,C_i,..,C_n)$, where each column vector C_i with size $t \times 1$ is considered an element in W_t, a Z_2 - module. Suppose $v'= (x_1,..,x_n)$, $x_i \in Z_2$, $i=1,..,n$. It is obvious that the syndrome $s(v') = H.v' = \Sigma_{1 \leq i \leq n} C_i . x_i$ is exactly the sum we compute by module method, where the weight function h: $\{1,..,n\} \rightarrow M-\{0\}$ is defined by $h(i) = C_i$ for all $i=1,...,n$ with the Z_2- module $M = W_t$. Computing $v'= v - l_u$ means that we need to find some positions on v to flip if in the coset leader l_u of $u = s(v)-p$, the corresponding positions are different from 0. In the following example, we present the arguments in details.

Example 2. The Hamming code can supply us an instance for module approach in hiding data. In details, we have the embedding scheme [7,3,1] by using the Hamming code (7, 4), taking $W_3-\{0\} = \{1,2,..,7\}$ and considering each column $C_1,C_2,..,C_7$ of the parity checking matrix H of size 3×7 as a 3-bit presentation of these numbers

$$H = \begin{pmatrix} 1 & 0 & 1 & 0 & 1 & 0 & 1 \\ 0 & 1 & 1 & 0 & 0 & 1 & 1 \\ 0 & 0 & 0 & 1 & 1 & 0 & 1 \end{pmatrix}$$

$$C_1 \quad C_2 \quad C_3 \quad C_4 \quad C_5 \quad C_6 \quad C_7$$

Fig. 1. Parity checking matrix H in Hamming code (7,4)

Each block F of the binary image can be seen as a column vector u of 7 entries: $u = (x_1, x_2, ..x_7)^T$. Then taking operations on Z_2-module we can write $H.u = C_1.x_1 + C_2.x_2 + ... + C_7.x_7$ where each column C_i can be seen as a vector in $V_3 = Z_2^3$ and the set $C = \{C_1, C_2, C_3, C_4, C_5, C_6, C_7\}$ is nothing but an 1-base in Z_2 - module V_3. For security reason, one can choose an extra binary key k - as a column vector of 7 entries, $k = (k_1, k_2, ..., k_7)^T$ and taking operation XOR, with u we get $v = u \oplus k = (y_1, y_2, ..., y_7)$ and $H.v = C_1.y_1 + C_2.y_2 + .. + C_7.y_7$.

Replacing a position x_j in u by $x_j \oplus 1$ implies that the same position y_j in v is replaced by $y_j \oplus 1$. This gives us the marked vector v' satisfying the equation $H.v' = H.v \oplus C_j$. Now, suppose $H.v = e$ and we need to hide a vector d (of 3 bits) which is considered as an element in W_3. We can flip at most one position x_j in u to hide d as follows:

Case $d = e$, the block u is kept intact, so that in the extracting phase, ones recover $H.v = d$. Case $d \ne e$, or equivalent, $e - d \ne 0$, we can find in C (an 1-base of W_3) a vector C_j so that $C_j = e - d$ (that means $C = e \oplus d$ in W_3). After flip x_j to $x_j \oplus 1$ in u, we have $H.v' = H.v \oplus C_j = e \oplus e \oplus d = d$, the result one needs to recover in the extract phase. Let us remark that the sum $C_1.y_1 + C_2.y_2 + .. + C_7.y_7$ is exactly the result we get by the steps in **3.2.1** where $C_i.y_i$ is nothing but h(i).T_i in that steps, with $h(i) = C_i$ for $i = 1, 2, .., 7$.

4.2   Experimental Results for Finding 2-Bases

As some results generated from our program, we obtained:

(i)   The 2-base $X = \{0001, 0010, 0100, 1110, 1001\}$ and $Y = \{1000, 0100, 0010, 0111, 1001\}$ provide us 2- embedding schemes which permit in each block of 5 pixels, by changing at most two pixels one can hide 4 bits. Hence regarding 2-embedding schemes, our schemes can be seen as some expanded for the list COV $(2, 6 \cdot 4^{a-1} - 1, 4a)$ with $a = 1$, by equation (4)[7] mentioned in section 2.

(ii)   The 2-base $X = \{1, 2, 3, 4, 5, 6, 8, 16, 24, 37, 45, 53, 58\}$ and $Y = \{1, 2, 3, 4, 5, 6, 8, 16, 24, 32, 47, 55, 63\}$ in $W_6 = Z_2^6$ (the numbers can be seen as 6-bit strings). We provide new 2-bases with 13 elements, which permit us to hide 6 bits in each block of 13 pixels. Then we can extend them by the techniques mentioned in Lemma 2 to obtain new 2-bases for hiding 7-bit strings.

5   Conclusion

By flexibility of module approach for which correcting codes and covering function techniques are considered as the special cases, we can offer more new and powerful schemes to hide data without of using radius or distances as in correcting and covering codes.

In color images (24bpp with three channels Red, Green, Blue), or in palette images, especially for grayscale images, ones can obtain a higher ratio of secret bits hiding in each block of images by using some other module, such as $\mathbf{Z}_q$, $q>2$.

Several works consider some ways to hide as much as secret data in each block of pixels with low image distortion if it is possible. In preventing from steganalysis attacks, ones need a very high quality of stego-images, generally in palette images, hiding bits in each pixel is not good enough for security reason. In these situations, changing only a small $k = 1, 2, 3$ pixels in each block of pixels, using a huge number of key matrices to prevent effectively from exhausted attacks, by some k- embedding scheme modified for color images we can obtain stego-images with the high quality. These will be studied in future works.

References

1. Bierbrauer, J.: Crandall's problem (1998) (unpublished),
   http://www.ws.binghamton.edu/fridrich/covcodes.pdf
2. Chang, C.C., Kieu, T.D., Chou, Y.C.: A High Payload Steganographic Scheme based on (7,4) Hamming Code for Digital Images. In: Electronic Commerce and Security 2008 Symposium, pp. 16–21 (2008)
3. Chen, Y., Pan, H., Tseng, Y.: A secure of data hiding scheme for two-color images. In: IEEE Symposium on Computers and Communications (2000)
4. Kim, C., Shin, D., Shin, D.: Data Hiding in a Halftone Image Using Hamming Code (15, 11). In: Nguyen, N.T., Kim, C.-G., Janiak, A. (eds.) ACIIDS 2011, Part II. LNCS, vol. 6592, pp. 372–381. Springer, Heidelberg (2011)
5. Crandall, R.: Some notes on steganography. Posted on steganography mailing list (1998),
   http://os.inf.tu-dresden.de/_westfeld/crandall.pdf
6. Galand, Kabatiansky, G.: Information hiding by coverings. In: Proceedings of the IEEE Information Theory Workshop, pp. 151–154 (2004)
7. Bierbrauer, J., Fridrich, J.: Constructing Good Covering Codes for Applications in Steganography. In: Shi, Y.Q. (ed.) Transactions on DHMS III. LNCS, vol. 4920, pp. 1–22. Springer, Heidelberg (2008)
8. Lee, C.F., Chen, H.L.: A novel data hiding scheme based on modulus function. The Journal of Systems and Software 83, 832–843 (2010)
9. Ould Medeni, M.B., Souidi, E.M.: A Novel Steganographic Protocol from Error-correcting Codes. Journal of Information Hiding and Multimedia Signal Processing 1(4) (October 2010) ISSN 2073-4212
10. Nordstrom, A.W., Robinson, J.P.: An optimum nonlinear code. Information and Control 11, 613–616 (1967)
11. Phan, T.H., Nguyen, H.T.: On the Maximality of Secret Data Ratio in CPTE Schemes. In: Nguyen, N.T., Kim, C.-G., Janiak, A. (eds.) ACIIDS 2011, Part I. LNCS (LNAI), vol. 6591, pp. 88–99. Springer, Heidelberg (2011)
12. Preparata, F.P.: A class of optimum nonlinear double-error-correcting codes. Information and Control 13, 378–400 (1968)
13. Struik, R.: Covering Codes. Ph.D. dissertation, Eindhoven (1994)

14. Zhang, W., Zhang, X., Wang, S.: Maximizing Steganographic Embedding Efficiency by Combining Hamming Codes and Wet Paper Codes. In: Solanki, K., Sullivan, K., Madhow, U. (eds.) IH 2008. LNCS, vol. 5284, pp. 60–71. Springer, Heidelberg (2008)

15. Westfeld, A.: F5-A Steganographic Algorithm High Capacity Despite Better Steganalysis. In: Moskowitz, I.S. (ed.) IH 2001. LNCS, vol. 2137, pp. 289–302. Springer, Heidelberg (2001)

16. Wu, M.Y., Lee, J.H.: Anovel data embedding method for two-color fascimile images. In: Proceedings of International Symposium on Multimedia Information Processing. Chung-Li, Taiwan, R.O.C (1998)

17. Zhang, X., Wang, S.: Analysis of Parity Assignment Steganography in Palette Images. In: Khosla, R., Howlett, R.J., Jain, L.C. (eds.) KES 2005. LNCS (LNAI), vol. 3683, pp. 1025–1031. Springer, Heidelberg (2005)

18. Zhang, X., Wang, S.: Vulnerability of pixel-value differencing steganography to histogram analysis and modification for enhanced security. Pattern Recognition Letters 25, 331–339 (2004)

Different Characteristics of Radio Modules in Wireless Body Sensor Network Systems

Woosik Lee[1], Min Choi[2], and Namgi Kim[1,*]

[1] Computer Science Department, University of Kyonggi
Suwon, Kyonggi, Korea
[2] University of Chungbuk
Heungdeok-gu, Chungbuk, Korea
{wslee,ngkim}@kgu.ac.kr, mchoi@cbnu.ac.kr

Abstract. Wireless body sensor network systems (WB-SNSs) can use diverse radio modules. However, previous studies did not consider different characteristics of radio modules, which deeply impact the performance of WB-SNSs. In this paper, we analyze the performance of WB-SNSs using the representative radio modules CC2420 and CC1000. In this environment, we collected log data from real sensor devices deployed on the human body. After log data collection, we first show that CC2420 and CC1000 have different radio characteristics from diverse views, such as the received signal strength indication (RSSI) average and deviation, transmission power levels, and body movement. Through the analysis, we also find that an efficient transmission power control (TPC) algorithm should consider these diverse factors due to different radio modules.

Keywords: Wireless Body Area Network, Body Sensor System, Radio Module, CC2420, CC1000.

1 Introduction

As IT technologies are developed in pervasive computing, our society is moving toward ubiquitous computing environments. Sensor nodes in ubiquitous computing environments can collect diverse environmental information, such as temperature, humanity, light levels, and so forth. These sensors go beyond the bounds of wireless sensor networks (WSNs), toward wireless body sensor network systems (WB-SNSs). WB-SNSs can consist of various radio modules, such as CC2420, CC1000, and CC1010 [1]. These radio modules have unique characteristics, such as frequency, output power range, and radio propagation. The different characteristics of radio modules deeply impact the performance of WB-SNSs. These characteristics cause various problems, such as TPC failure, packet drops, and excessive energy consumption. Therefore, we must carefully consider the characteristics of diverse radio modules. In this paper, we analyze CC1000 and CC2420 radio modules, which

---

* Corresponding author.

J.J. Park et al. (Eds.): NPC 2012, LNCS 7513, pp. 308–314, 2012.

are representative radio modules in WB-SNSs. For analysis, we first investigated radio properties. We then show diverse results with RSSI values depending on transmission power (TP) levels. Finally, we analyze packet delivery rates (PDRs) and RSSI deviations depending on TP levels in various environments, such as standing, walking, and running.

2   Related Work

Many previous studies focused on particular radio modules [2]-[4]. Natarajan [2] and Shah [3] explored link layer characteristics of CC2420 by collecting log data from many volunteers in different environments. Quwaider [4] proposed a dynamic TPC algorithm using CC1000 radio modules at 433 MHz. However, these studies concentrated on particular radio modules, so their experimental results cannot be applied to other radio modules. On the other hand, Hamalainen [5] investigated a number of experimental data using SkyCross SMT-3TO10M-A antennas on a PHY layer for hospital environment channel modeling. However, this study did not consider either the MAC layer or other popular modules. The IEEE 802.15.6 working group [6] also investigated diverse channel models for WB-SNSs. However, they only concentrated on channel modeling and did not analyze diverse radio modules. Our previous work also only considered link channel characteristics using a CC2420 device [7]. Moreover, its work experiments took place in a static environment and did not consider dynamic environments such as walking and running. Thus, our previous study lacks additional experiments based on diverse radio modules in both static and dynamic environments. Therefore, in this paper, we investigate radio module properties and conduct experiments in real WB-SNSs so as to understand the different characteristics of diverse radio modules.

3   Radio Properties Comparison

In this section, we analyze radio properties of representative radio modules for WB-SNSs, CC2420 and CC1000. Table 1 shows properties of both CC2420 and CC1000. CC2420 and CC1000 have the same RF modules, Zigbee. However, In terms of

Table 1. Properties of CC2420 and CC1000

	CC2420	CC1000
Frequency	2.4 GHz	300 – 1000 MHz
Transmit Bit Rate	250 kbps	76.8 kbps
Power Control	Programmable	Programmable
Output Power Range	-24 to 0 dBm	-20 to 10 dBm
RF Module	Zigbee	Zigbee
Supply Voltage	2.1 to 3.6 V	2.1 to 3.6 V

frequency and transmit bit rate, CC2420 is higher frequency and transmit bit rate than CC1000. It means that CC2420 has more line-of-sight propagation property which can not travel over the horizon or behind obstacles. They also have different output power range. In other words, CC2420 and CC1000 have a different range of TP levels. So, same TP level maybe incur different TPC results.

4   Experimental Environment

Fig. 1 shows the experimental environment, such as sensor placements, the experiment area, and body movements. On the human body, the transmitting node is deployed on the chest and sends packets to the receiving node per 100ms . The receiving node is deployed on the stomach and stores a set of log data. The log data consist of 100 samples that include RSSI values, a power level index, and sequence numbers. After logging data, the host computer collects the log data in the EEPROM of the sensor node. Such setups apply equally to both CC1000 and CC2420. The right side of Fig. 1 shows our experimental area, the total size of which is 360 900cm. Arrows in the figure indicate a moving path and a triangle shape is the starting point. In this environment, we repeatedly experimented with CC1000 and CC2420 radio devices for collecting raw data with respect to standing, walking, and running. A walking stride was approximately 45 cm, and that of running was approximately 90 cm.

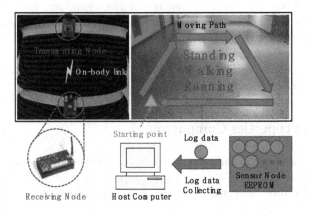

Fig. 1. Experimental environment

5   Radio Transmission Comparison

In Fig. 2, the x-axis represents TP levels and the y-axis RSSI values. As seen in the graph, the CC2420 TP levels are denser than those of CC1000. The range of CC2420 TP levels is from 3 to 31, but CC1000 is from 0 to 22. Through the graph, we see that CC2420 has an exponential shape and CC1000 a linear shape, depending on TP levels. Therefore, TPC algorithms using a linear equation for TP control cannot be applied to CC2420 radio modules. Second, CC1000 does not overlap each TP level, but CC2420 overlaps them from 4 to 8, 8 to 12, and 12 to 14, as seen in Fig. 2. If CC2420 changes TP levels like CC1000, some TP levels will not work well. Thus, CC2420 should coarsely change TP levels for efficient energy management.

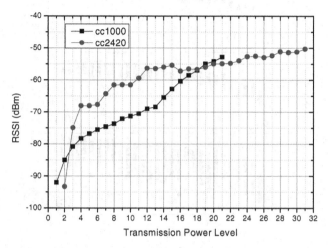

Fig. 2. Average RSSI of CC1000 and CC2420

6   Packet Delivery Rate and RSSI Comparison

Fig. 3 and 4 show total packet delivery rates as red bars and the CC2420 and CC1000 radio module RSSI values as black dots. In the graphs, the x-axis is the TP levels, the left y-axis is the PDRs, and the right y-axis is the RSSI values. These graphs consist of three situations: (a) standing, (b) walking, and (c) running. Through Fig. 3, we know that CC2420 has a lower PDR and higher RSSI deviations when a body is running. In this case, the RSSI deviation depending on TP levels is very large, making it difficult to estimate channel conditions. The fundamental reason for this is that standing is a static environment but running is a dynamic environment. In a static environment, the location of sensors does not change over time. On the other hand, in a dynamic environment, the sensor locations usually change as a result of the person's movements. Fig. 4 shows CC1000 experiment results, like Fig. 3 shows those of CC2420. However, CC1000 has a better PDR and fewer RSSI deviations than those of CC2420 in each situation. Moreover, CC1000 has a linear shape on the RSSI graph, while CC2420 has an exponential shape. Thus, CC1000 can apply to linear TPC algorithms, but CC2420 cannot apply. Furthermore, in dynamic environments, CC1000 has a higher PDR than CC2420 at low TP levels because CC2420 has more line-of-sight propagation than CC1000. Therefore, CC1000 can commute well, with low drop rates in dynamic environments. However, because CC1000 has a low transmit bit rate, we consider diverse radio modules for applications needing a high transmit bit rate.

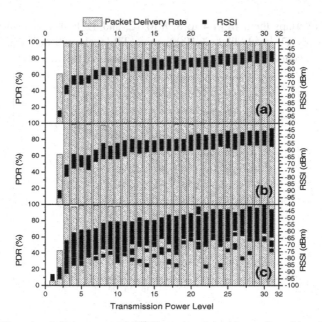

Fig. 3. CC2420 packet delivery rate and RSSI graphs when (a) standing, (b) walking, and (c) running

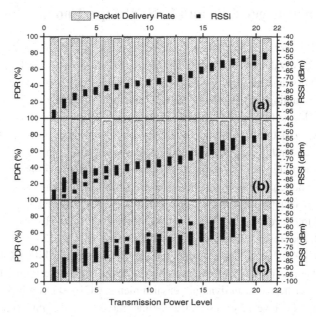

Fig. 4. CC1000 packet delivery rate and RSSI graphs when (a) standing, (b) walking, and (c) running

Fig. 5 shows the RSSI deviations of CC1000 and CC2420. The x-axis shows the TP levels and the y-axis indicates RSSI values during three movements: standing, walking, and running. The top graph is the result of CC1000, and the bottom graph is the result of CC2420. In this graph, we compare the similarities and the differences between body movements in CC1000 and CC2420 modules. Both results show that almost all TP levels have similar results, in that walking has a higher deviation than standing, and running has a higher deviation than walking. This phenomenon is retained even if the TP levels are changed in both modules. Exceptionally, in the case of low TPs such as 1 and 2 in CC2420, the deviation is lower than other TP levels' deviations because of a lower PDR, as illustrated in Figure 3. For the other similarity, a different point depending on radio modules is that CC2420RSSI deviations are higher than those of CC1000 at all TP levels. Therefore, we must consider the differences between CC1000 and CC2420 modules when designing an efficient TPC algorithm.

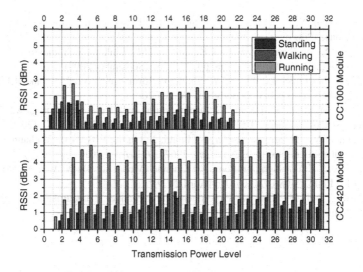

Fig. 5. RSSI deviation of CC1000 and CC2420

7   Conclusion

In this paper, we compare the characteristics of CC2420 and CC1000 radio modules through real experiments. To compare these modules, we first investigated radio properties such as the frequencies, transmit bit rates, power controls, output power ranges, RF modules, and supply voltages of CC2420 and CC1000. Second, we conducted experiments with real sensor nodes. Third, we analyzed the PDR and RSSI experimental results values for both the CC2420 and CC1000 modules. The results showed that CC1000 has a better PDR and less RSSI deviation than CC2420. Moreover, we knew that CC1000 has a linear RSSI shape, and that CC2420 has an exponential shape depending on TP levels. Lastly, the CC1000 and CC2420 RSSI deviations take similar forms according to the movements in this graph. However, the size of the deviations is different in that the CC2420 deviations are larger than those of CC1000. Through these experiments and the analysis, we knew that CC2420 and CC1000 modules have different properties, packet delivery rates, average RSSI values, and RSSI deviations. Consequently, we need a sophisticated TPC algorithm to cover the diverse characteristics of these radio modules. In the future, we will design a new TPC algorithm that can be simultaneously adopted for diverse radio modules.

Acknowledgment. This research was supported by Basic Science Research Program through the National Research Foundation of Korea (NRF) funded by the Ministry of Education, Science and Technology (grant number 2012R1A1A1002133)

References

1. Hall, P.S., Hao, Y.: Antennas and Propagation for Body-Centric Wireless Communications. Artech House (2006)
2. Natarajan, A., de Silva, B., Yap, K.K., Motani, M.: Link Layer Behavior of Body Area Networks at 2.4 GHz. In: MobiCom, pp. 241–252 (September 2009)
3. Shah, R.C., Nachman, L., Wan, C.Y.: On the Performance of Bluetooth and IEEE 802.15.4 radios in a body area network. BodyNets (March 2008)
4. Quwaider, M., Rao, J., Biswas, S.: Body-posture-based dynamic link power control in wearable sensor networks. IEEE Communications Magazine 48, 134–142 (2010)
5. Hamalainen, M., Taparugssanagorn, A., Iinatti, J.: On the WBAN radio channel modelling for medical applications. In: EUCAP, pp. 2967–2971 (April 2011)
6. Yazdandoost, K.Y., Sayrafian-Pour, K.: Channel Model for Body Area Network (BAN). doc: IEEE P802.15-08-0780-09-006 (April 2009)
7. Lee, W.S., Choi, M., Kim, N.: Experimental link channel characteristics in wireless body sensor systems. In: ICOIN, pp. 374–378 (February 2012)

The Development of Sustainable Growth Strategy Model Based on the User Tendency in the Online Game Services

Hyeog-In Kwon, Hi-Yeob Joo, Dae-Jin Kim, and Jong-Seok Park

Chung-Ang University, Art Center 8F-10806, Heukseok-dong, Dongjak-gu,
Seoul, 156-756, Korea
hikwon@cau.ac.kr, hyjoo74@gmail.com,
yauchee@empal.com, mercifulrcy@nate.com

Abstract. Currently the online game market continues growing, but there is an absence of appropriate strategies of corporation. In addition the strategic game management has been required to respond the reaction of customers as time goes by. So in this study, we analyze the typical forms of user types in MMORPG (Massive Multiplayer Online Role Playing Game) based on PLC. We suggested that there is a difference in the ratio of user types as fighter, leader, socialiser and trader of PLC's phase. Also we presented the service lineup for retaining the users in each phase.

Keywords: On-line game, MMORPG, User-type, PLC, PLM, Sustainable Growth Strategy.

1   Introduction

The game industry and user popularity continue growing throughout the world. For the sustained growth, the game developing companies are focusing on finding new and diverse ideas in terms of the way to play and the game contents. According to the Korea Creative Content Agency Report 2011, the worldwide game market is estimated over $84.8 billion which is of 0.2% growth in comparison to the year before. Currently, video games have the biggest market share; arcade games are second, followed by online games, mobile games and PC games. For the recent trend of arcade game shrinks and the fast growth of online game, however, they assumed that the online game would occupy the biggest game market share soon. An online game is an internet-based game which is capable of supporting worldwide multiple players playing together, and MMORPG (Massively Multiplayer Online Role-Playing Games) is a representative form.

In case of MMORPG, thousands of game products just have showed up and got disappeared in a very fast cycle, as opposed to the overall market has been growing. This would be from several reasons, and the first is because MMORPG games have developed in exclusive way; until they open for the public test, the developing process goes strongly under secure. To make one final game product, the whole developing

J.J. Park et al. (Eds.): NPC 2012, LNCS 7513, pp. 315–319, 2012.

process takes high costs and high risks. Thus the game developing companies collect the developing costs early and compose the portfolio for sales diversification. In addition, many of them have imitated few succeeded examples rather than considering user attributes or trends, and it results deterioration of quality in the overall game industry (Hana Financial Management Institute, 2007). Hence, the purpose of this study is to suggest a strategy for promoting sustainable growth of MMORPG game industry by user analysis.

2   Theoretical Background and Previous Research

2.1   MMORPG

MMORPG is a representative genre of internet-based video games. Players perform their given roles by controlling their own avatars, which represent users self in 2D or 3D game environment. MMORPGs provide a naturalistic setting where millions of users voluntarily immerse themselves in a graphical virtual environment and interact with each other through avatars (Yee, 2006). MMORPGs strongly reflect gamers' attributes.

2.2   Product Lifecycle Management(PLM)

In case of most products, user types or attributes keep changing depends on PLC (Product Life Cycle); user types getting more varied and profits increasing until a certain point. PCL shows changes of profit condition from introduction until the dissolution, and it can be divided into four stages: Introduction stage, growth stage, maturity stage and saturation-decline stage.

PLM (Product Lifecycle Management) is the process of constructing information and data share environment for all the interested parties (Jun, 2010). PLM is aimed to find proper strategies for dealing with changing business world. According to Game Planning Theory (2003) published in the Korea Computer Game Society, online games have different characteristics under each lifecycle stage Table 1.

Table 1. The life-cycle of online games

Introduction Stage	Growth Stage	Maturity Stage	Saturation and Decline Stage
- sales game packages - Fee-charging - new customers join in	- new customers increasing - simultaneous log-ins are on the rapid increase - sever extension, updating contents	- server extension slowed down - new customers join stands still - simultaneous log-ins stand still	- existing customers withdraw - new customers decrease - simultaneous log-ins decreasing

2.3   User Classification

At MMORPG's world, the game players interact to each other while playing individually. MMORPG game players' characteristics can be classified by game types, lifecycle stages, and even what server they connect to. We attempt to restructure several former scholars' player type classification.

Bartle's study(1996) classify as 'killer' who feel fun from outstanding themselves among others. And they have a pleasure from attacking and harassing other players. We redefined the 'killer' as 'fighter'. Lim(2007) suggested in MMORPG, players are trying to organize the 'guild' that cause of many kinds of issues as battle or alliances. In this case they keep causing some process that adjusting crisis and conflict or cooperate with each other. In such a confused situation there is a leader who carries out role such as adjusting dispute between clan member, establishing strategy, implementing strategy and assigning the task. There is one type of user that Barttle(1996), Jung(2006), and Do(2009)'s study being classified in common. It is the most common players who consider interaction and relationship with other players importantly. It can be defined as 'socialiser'. According to Jung(2009), games are become more popular, the trade market of the game items and accounts in the real world is more activated. In addition, there are some players who are trying to make money by game playing professionally. It means that there some players who are trying to buy a rare items or high class of avatar because of deficiency of playing time. They can be defined as 'trader'. As mentioned above, we classified user type as 'Fighter', 'Leader', 'Socialiser' and 'Trader'.

3   Developing Process

This research is focused on the analysis of component ratio of players' types and core services that they want. So we plan to conduct a survey of MMORPG players for finding the ratio by user types. We also plan to examine the ratio by user types are depends on the product life cycle stages.

First of all, designate representative game of MMORPG and then proceed our study through user survey. Analysis PLC of game based on time, categorize server that phased opened. And then, analysis user type through survey with a selected sample of user of each server as shown in the Figure 1.

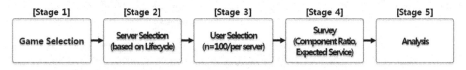

Fig. 1. Research design

4   Expected Outcomes

This study expected outcomes as below of service, major customer, and main properties in MMORPG as shown in the Figures 2 ~ Figure 4.

Game	Server	Lifecycle	Component Ratio				# of Players
			Fighter	Leader	Socializer	Trader	
Lineage I	Server #1	Decline	15%	10%	70%	5%	239
Lineage I	Server #2	Maturity	20%	15%	50%	15%	1,300
Lineage I	Server #3	Growth	7%	14%	68%	11%	1,800
Lineage I	Server #4	Introduction	5%	10%	80%	5%	500
Diablo III	Server #1	Decline	13%	7%	75%	5%	453
Diablo III	Server #2	Maturity	17%	25%	45%	13%	1,730
Diablo III	Server #3	Growth	7%	11%	70%	12%	2,570
Diablo III	Server #4	Introduction	5%	14%	75%	6%	1,300
Lineage II	Server #1	Decline	10%	30%	56%	4%	170
...	...						

Fig. 2. Component ratio of players' types

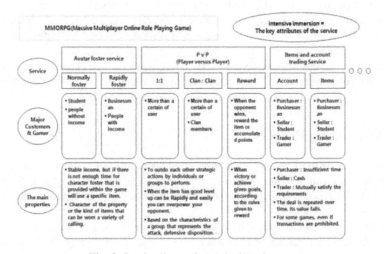

Fig. 3. Service lineup for each player's types

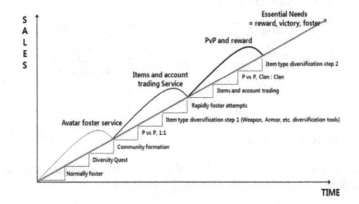

Fig. 4. Core services for sustainable growth

The success of game is decided by the number of paid user. The purpose of MMORPG service is that increasing and sustaining of users steadily. As you can see in the Figure 3, user is formed around user who enjoys game at the beginning. However, the forming of new game service market and item dealing service appear from extending service. So, such as Figure 4 new service has to renew and push ahead service development that is customized user's expectation standards which increase steadily. Through this service development, it's easy to create new opportunities.

5   Conclusions

For the sustain growth of MMORPGs, we suggest to establish strategies on the basis of players' characteristics. Previous studies have shown that game players have different characteristics depending on the PLC process. The findings from this study would suggest the following:

First, promote games to consider user-incentive strategies in conjunction with campaigns; a campaign can be used as a good marketing tool to gather numbers of people with similar characteristics. Second, promotion events should be planned based upon PLC and player characteristics under each stage. It also should never forget that game player characteristics could be constrained on a per-server basis. Teasing out what players need in every product lifecycle stage is very important. Third, note the service delivery strategy from Microsoft, which was based upon their product life cycle. It would give lessons timing to the companies planning for huge projects like most MMORPGs about proper launching timing.

References

1. Childress, M.D., Braswell, R.: Using Massively Multiplayer Online Role-Playing Games for Online Learning. Distance Education 27(2), 187–196 (2006)
2. Nam, B.-C., Bae, K.-T.: Quantitative Analysis of Flow in MMORPG Games. Journal of Korea Game Society 11(3), 73–84 (2011)
3. Product Lifecycle Management: Empowering the Future of Business. ACIM data Report (2002)
4. Yee, N.: The Demographics, Motivations, and Derived Experiences of Users of Massively Multi-User Online Graphical Environments. Presence 15(3), 309–329 (2006)
5. Jun, H.-B.: A Study on the Concept of Product Lifecycle Managementand its Applications for each Lifecycle phase. Enture Journal of Information Technology 9(1), 159–167 (2010)
6. Online Game Industry Research for credit. Hana Institute of Finance (2007)
7. Jung, G.-C.: A study on the MMORPG User Typology. The Graduate School of Korea University (2006)
8. Do, Y.-Y.: Self-recognitions and Self-changes in Online Game World. The Graduate School Yonsei University(2009)
9. Lim, S., Park, N.: MMORPG users' Motivation and the Spill-over Effect on their off-line Leadership Development. Korean Journal of Journalism & Communication Studies 51(5), 322–485 (2007)
10. Jung, H.-W.: A Study on the Legalization of cash Transactions in MMORPG Items. Graduate School of Sangmyung University (2009)
11. Kwon, H.-I., Choi, Y.-S., Lee, S.-W.: A Study on the Way of Online Game service. Korean Journal of Society For Computer Game 24(4), 61–71 (2011)

Computer Education's Teaching-Learning Methods Using Educational Programming Language Based on STEAM Education[*]

Namje Park[**] and Yeonghae Ko

Department of Computer Education, Teachers College,
Jeju National University, Jeju, Korea
{namjepark,smakor}@jejunu.ac.kr

Abstract. STEAM is an acronym of Science, Technology, Engineering, Arts, and Mathematics. To realize the STEAM education, the factors on how to interrelate and integrate science, technology, engineering, art, and mathematics as well as the factors that are needed in realizing the STEAM education in creativity in addition to the considered factors in contents need to be decided, which in reality, makes the creation of STEAM materials into a system science or system engineering. This paper analyzed the statuses of STEAM education. And, suggested factors to realize successful STEAM education materials.

Keywords: STEAM, Computer education, EPL, Science, Technology.

1   Introduction

In June of 2005, the U.S. President's Information Technology Advisory Committee (PITAC) projected that the Computational Science is the most needed and important field in the 21st century academics. In addition, the Association of Computing Machinery (ACM) in May of 2011 pointed out that despite the great contribution of computational sciences not only on the economy but also on the technology that has renovated the general society, the number of students who major in computational sciences has decreased and the interests in K-12 education are also low. As its solution, they advise that the computational sciences and IT need to be mixed in actual learning and the political basis to cultivate licensed teachers need to be established. In other words, the computational sciences education is argued to be the crucial and key education to bring up the global leaders in the elementary school education.

Such computational sciences and IT education can also be found in the concept of STEAM education. Yakman defined the boundaries of Science (S), Technology (T), Engineering (E), Arts (A), and Mathematics (M) in STEAM education. He suggested that the contents of computational sciences belong to the Computer in Engineering

---

[*] This work was supported by the Korea Foundation for the Advancement of Science & Creativity(KOFAC) grant funded by the Korean Government(MEST).
[**] Corresponding author.

J.J. Park et al. (Eds.): NPC 2012, LNCS 7513, pp. 320–327, 2012.

(E) field and the contents of IT belong to informational technology under Technology (T). The STEAM education using IT is an attractive educational method for the digital generation students to easily and pleasantly learn the contents of mathematics, sciences, and technology. The educational methods that integrate IT and other fields of academia have been attempted before STEAM education. In addition, the reason for a brighter footlight for IT as the transition from STEM education to STEAM education occurs is that occupy a large section in the field of Art in the digital era. Korea also needs to reflect such international standardization trends of NFC standardization and also create an appropriate connection platform for Korea through a comparative analysis with the domestic standardization of mobile RFID technology. In addition, the new standardizations need to be reflected internationally in an active manner. For these reasons, this report provides the foundation for domestic distribution of related technologies and standardizations by connecting the two technologies through the analysis of NFC system international standardization activities and trends with mobile RFID technology.

2   STEAM Education

2.1   STEAM Concept

STEAM is an acronym of Science, Technology, Engineering, Arts, and Mathematics. This is an educational curriculum that combined Art to the existing American STEM (Science, Technology, Engineering, Mathematics) curriculum and Yakman (2008) defined the STEAM education in the following two directions.

First, it is an education where Science, Technology, engineering, and mathetmatics include other areas in addition to the standards of their own and second, it is an integrative education that purposefully includes the actual subjects and teaching matters. For a more detailed definition, Yakman (2008) suggested the framework. As shown in the framework, the STEAM education determines the level from the lifelong learning to detailed academic content classification. The first level is the Lifelong learning. This stage signifies our adaptation to our surroundings and sustained learning that are unintended and unavoidable.

Second level is Integrative learning. In this stage, the student learns the basic overview of all of the academic fields and how they are related. The best way is to learn by topics. This stage of learning is appropriate for elementary and middle school education.

The third level is Multidisciplinary learning. This stage allows the student to learn a specific field and how they are related to real life. The best method is to learn the practical uses. This is appropriate for middle school education.

The fourth level is Discipline learning. This stage focuses on each educational stage and is appropriate for middle school education.

The last fifth level is Content Specific learning. This stage deals with detailed research of each field and is appropriate for high school and professional education.

Therefore, STEAM education does not entail a part of education but refers to an overall paradigm from the professional learning to lifelong learning, which is organized with the addition of art to the existing education, especially in the integrated education of Science, Technology, Engineering, Mathematics and Art in elementary school education.

2.2   Need for STEAM Education

As the low interests and accomplishments of American teenagers in math and science, the STEM education started as an educational solution. However, the STEM education was missing a very important piece. This is that Art, a comparatively competitive and innovative field as STEM in creativity, was also needed. In addition, the science education could not keep up with the current changes in science, technology, and engineering and the teenagers who are used to the various advanced technology products were bound to lose interests as well as creating a gap in creativity cultivation in science education during elementary and middle school years.

Therefore, the experts argued for "amicability between science and art" because a dichotomous thought that art is illogical and science is not creative ruined the future and the art and science should be taught together before the concept of STEAM education emerged. In this perspective, the art education is crucial in developing creativity that is highly valued in modern education; therefore, the art education should be added to the education of science, technology, engineering, and mathematics.

3   Factors to Realize Successful STEAM Education Materials

To realize the STEAM education, the factors on how to interrelate and integrate science, technology, engineering, art, and mathematics as well as the factors that are needed in realizing the STEAM education in creativity in addition to the considered factors in contents need to be decided, which in reality, makes the creation of STEAM materials into a system science or system engineering. In other words, the many factors need to harmonize in a creative and appropriate way along with the theoretical foundation and applications in a systematic way.

Many questions on STEAM education include whether only S and T or T and E could be realized, how it is different from the field trips to research centers or science centers, and how different it is from the existing STS education.

First, the materials of STEAM education could hold an important meaning. Therefore, whether to start from current textbook science theories and systematically increase into the engineering and technology or whether to create a new structure of reverse engineering on a topic to allow students find the theories as they dissemble a product could be an issue but to smoothly transition to STEAM project with minimal friction, the former would be more preferable than the latter. This is because if the reverse engineering is utilized for the concept understanding in science education, the students may not fully understand the science theories and may require additional curricular activities.

In reality, the reflecting factors of S, T, E, A, and M in STEAM education are naturally included in the systematic connection based on a key factor of storytelling and the process to describe the variety of science technology engineering. Therefore, the most important yet the most difficult part in STEAM content organization is how to realize the following 7 basic concepts in each section.

1) Connection, combination and fusion
To apply on site without creating conflicts with current curriculum, a systematic connection into the basic science technology engineering is required. In addition, integrative thought or fused thought activities could be organized separately or together with each area of STEAM.

2) Introduction of variability for a creative STEAM education through diverse thoughts on science technology engineering. For creative diverse thoughts, the factors that educate students on how the basic scientific theory can be applied in various technologies and how these are used in diverse ways in real life through engineering are necessary. Therefore, the systematic connection between the STEAM areas in STEAM education and the education and activities on the diverse applications of the areas are crucial in a creative education.

3) For an efficient and creative teaching, the teachers require various creative tools. In creative STEAM education, the development of various creative methods, creative learning tools, and creative experiments is important. However, the term, creative experiment, is being overused currently. The experiments in creative sciences should be based on the STEAM concept.

4) One of the key STEAM educations is cultivating the ability to see the big picture, or the ability to be able to see the forest along with the trees.

5) In the rapidly changing world of integrative technology, science, technology and engineering of 10 years past can be meaningless. Therefore, one of the key factors of STEAM education is just in time education that rapidly responds to the changing integrative technology.

6) First, STEAM education will be a practical and realistic education that can predict the future in a systematic way based on the science technology and engineering as well as the connections to politics, environment, society, economy, and pursuit of values with integrative thoughts and creativity.

7) The integrative design concept in engineering could be an important spirit in STEAM education. The integrative design concept on the group works for the STEAM can be introduced to cultivate the abilities to become ethical, social, cooperative, leading, and considerate and communicative among the students as well as the systematic experiment abilities in science, technology and engineering, which will not only cultivate the scientists, technologists, or engineers with the right character and practical abilities and also the future politicians and social leaders in various areas.

The other factors to consider in STEAM contents development other than the key basic factors are the introductions of STEAM education concept to cultivate creative talents who will contribute to the global society. In other words, it is to cultivate global talents with international senses based on integrative STEAM knowledge in science, technology, and engineering that will consider the anthropological culture, history, politics, economy, and environment and also solve the issues with highly ethical thoughts and science, technology, and engineering. The global integrative talents desired by the current world are people with ethics, strategies, creativity, challenging minds, and sacrificial decision-making abilities. Ultimately, the STEAM education attempts to create integrative science technology talents as a global leader with high ethical standards and minds to harmoniously manage the nature and humans. The basic skills to manage the modern science technology engineering are emphasized in STEAM education. This STEAM education is the driving power for the future and a crucial education system to gain higher grounds in the global competition.

4   Example : EPL-Based STEAM Education

This is example of STEAM education using IT-based EPL. Contents are as follows.

1) Review

- Teacher (T): Let's talk about what we learned last time.
- Student (S): (Talks about what they learned last time.)

2) Motivation

- T: Let's watch how to draw the bracken with a computer program. (Shows the picture of bracken and the fractal shape realization process.)
- S: (Watches the videos.)
- T: Let's watch how to draw the snowflakes with the computer program. (Shows the picture of snowflakes and the Koch snowflake fractal realization process.)
- S: (Watches the videos.)

3) Learning Objectives and Learning Activities

- T: Let's talk about the learning objectives.
- T: Let's talk about the learning activities.

<Learning Activities>
- Activity 1:   Hey, logo! Listen to me!
- Activity 2: Drawing shapes

4) Activity 1: Hey, logo! Listen to me!

- T:Let's talk about the basic screen of the logo program. (Screen organization, command enter window, realization screen, etc.)
- S:(Learns the screen organization.)

- T: Let's talk about the commands of the logo program. (Allow the students to easily understand the commands, such as fd, bk, rt, lt, home, cs, ct, pu, pd, and setpc through the realization screen and allow the students to practice.)
- S:(Learns the basic commands.)
- T: Let's draw simple shapes with the commands with me. (Teach the students to draw simple shapes (many triangles, simple rectangles, etc) with basic commands.)
- S: (Draws simple shapes using the basic commands.)

5) Activity 2: Drawing shapes

- T:Let's draw the shapes on your own using the logo program. First, use the contruction paper to create the shape you want. Do not use curves and make sure to have more than 6 angles. (Teacher shows an example with a large piece of paper.) When you are coming back to the original point, use the command "home" instead of fd, bk, rt, or lt.
- S: (Makes the individual shapes with construction paper and a pair of scissors and then uses the logo program to realize it on the screen.)
- T: If you are done making your own shapes with the logo program, make the shapes that I am giving you. (Reward the top3 based on their accomplishment.)
- S: (Realizes the difficult shapes onto the screen.)

6) Ending and Preview

- T:Let's talk about what we learned today.
- S: We learned about the logo program./ We learned the basic commands of the logo program./ We drew shapes onto the screen, etc.
- T: We will learn (next content) next time we meet.

Accomplishment standards: Can the student understand the use the basic commands of logo program?
  · high: understands the basic commands of logo programs and uses them well.
  · middle: understands and uses the basic commands of logo programs.
  · low: cannot understand nor use the basic commands of logo program.

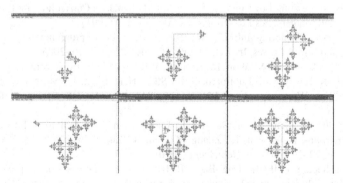

Fig. 1. Fractal geometry screen developed by LOGO Programming

Fig. 2. Students's class working

5   Conclusion

To realize the STEAM education, the factors on how to interrelate and integrate science, technology, engineering, art, and mathematics as well as the factors that are needed in realizing the STEAM education in creativity in addition to the considered factors in contents need to be decided, which in reality, makes the creation of STEAM materials into a system science or system engineering. In other words, the many factors need to harmonize in a creative and appropriate way along with the theoretical foundation and applications in a systematic way.

This paper analyzed the statuses of STEAM education. And, suggested factors to realize successful STEAM education materials.

Acknowledgments. This work was supported by the Korea Foundation for the Advancement of Science & Creativity(KOFAC) grant funded by the Korean Government(MEST).

References

1. Horton, B.: Integrating Logo into the Secondary Mathematics Curriculum. In: Proceedings of LOGO and Mathematics Education Conference, vol. 5 (1991)
2. Sacristan, A.I.: Exploring infinite processes through Logo programming activities of recursive and fractal figures. In: EUROLOGO Conference, vol. 10 (2005)
3. Park, N., Kwak, J., Kim, S., Won, D., Kim, H.: WIPI Mobile Platform with Secure Service for Mobile RFID Network Environment. In: Shen, H.T., Li, J., Li, M., Ni, J., Wang, W. (eds.) APWeb Workshops 2006. LNCS, vol. 3842, pp. 741–748. Springer, Heidelberg (2006)
4. Park, N.: Security Scheme for Managing a Large Quantity of Individual Information in RFID Environment. In: Zhu, R., Zhang, Y., Liu, B., Liu, C. (eds.) ICICA 2010. CCIS, vol. 106, pp. 72–79. Springer, Heidelberg (2010)
5. Park, N.: Secure UHF/HF Dual-Band RFID: Strategic Framework Approaches and Application Solutions. In: Jędrzejowicz, P., Nguyen, N.T., Hoang, K. (eds.) ICCCI 2011, Part I. LNCS, vol. 6922, pp. 488–496. Springer, Heidelberg (2011)

6. Park, N.: Implementation of Terminal Middleware Platform for Mobile RFID computing. International Journal of Ad Hoc and Ubiquitous Computing 8(4), 205–219 (2011)
7. Toenisson, E.: Programming language LOGO in school mathematics and teacher training. In: Proceedings of PME Conference, vol. 21(1) (1997)
8. Freiermuth, K., Hromkovič, J., Steffen, B.: Creating and Testing Textbooks for Secondary Schools An Example: Programming in LOGO. In: Mittermeir, R.T., Sysło, M.M. (eds.) ISSEP 2008. LNCS, vol. 5090, pp. 216–228. Springer, Heidelberg (2008)
9. Park, N., Kim, Y.: Harmful Adult Multimedia Contents Filtering Method in Mobile RFID Service Environment. In: Pan, J.-S., Chen, S.-M., Nguyen, N.T. (eds.) ICCCI 2010, Part II. LNCS (LNAI), vol. 6422, pp. 193–202. Springer, Heidelberg (2010)
10. Park, N.: Customized Healthcare Infrastructure Using Privacy Weight Level Based on Smart Device. In: Lee, G., Howard, D., Ślęzak, D. (eds.) ICHIT 2011. CCIS, vol. 206, pp. 467–474. Springer, Heidelberg (2011)
11. Park, N.: Secure Data Access Control Scheme Using Type-Based Re-encryption in Cloud Environment. In: Katarzyniak, R., Chiu, T.-F., Hong, C.-F., Nguyen, N.T. (eds.) Semantic Methods. SCI, vol. 381, pp. 319–327. Springer, Heidelberg (2011)
12. Park, N., Song, Y.: Secure RFID Application Data Management Using All-Or-Nothing Transform Encryption. In: Pandurangan, G., Anil Kumar, V.S., Ming, G., Liu, Y., Li, Y. (eds.) WASA 2010. LNCS, vol. 6221, pp. 245–252. Springer, Heidelberg (2010)
13. Park, N.: The Implementation of Open Embedded S/W Platform for Secure Mobile RFID Reader. The Journal of Korea Information and Communications Society 35(5), 785–793 (2010)

The Performances Study of EDCF
with Block_Ack in WLANs

Chien-Erh Weng[1,*], Chien-Hung Chen[1], Chiung-Hsing Chen[1], and Jyh-Horng Wen[2]

[1] Department of Electronic Communication Engineering,
National Kaohsiung Marine University
Kaohsiung, Taiwan, ROC
ceweng@mail.nkmu.edu.tw
[2] Department of Electrical Engineering,
Tunghai University
Taichung, Taiwan, ROC
jhwen@thu.edu.tw

Abstract. IEEE 802.11e Enhanced Distributed Coordination Function (EDCF) is a new wireless technology in wireless local area networks (WLANs). It defines a new supplement to the existing IEEE 802.11 MAC protocol. In IEEE 802.11e EDCF, the aim is providing a QoS support in WLANs. While the system services different Access categories (ACs), IEEE 802.11e EDCF does not perform well under high load conditions. In order to improve the efficiency, we pay attention to the EDCF of IEEE 802.11e with Block_Ack mechanism. We first proposed a markov chain model and studied the behavior. We extend the model to support IEEE 802.11e EDCF, and presented a more accurate analysis under non-ideal channel environment. We also compared it with that without Block_Ack mechanism under channel error environment.

Keywords: EDCF, Acs,QoS, Block_Ack.

1   Introduction

In recent years, the WLANs market is experiencing an explosive growth. The medium access control (MAC) protocol is the key element that provides the efficiency in accessing the channel, while satisfying the quality of service (QoS) requirements. IEEE 802.11e EDCF is a new wireless technology which is an enhanced version of IEEE 802.11 distributed coordination function (DCF). The IEEE 802.11e EDCF aims at improving the capabilities and efficiency of the IEEE 802.11 MAC protocol by defining a new mechanism to support the QoS services. While the system services different ACs, EDCF does not perform well under high load conditions. In order to improve the efficiency, EDCF provides two mechanisms named as transmission opportunity (TXOP) and Block_ACK. These two mechanisms are allowed to offer new data transmission services that include the multiple frame delivery [1-3]. There have been many performance analyses of the IEEE 802.11e EDCF. Deng and Chang [4]

---

* Corresponding author.

J.J. Park et al. (Eds.): NPC 2012, LNCS 7513, pp. 328–335, 2012.
© IFIP International Federation for Information Processing 2012

proposed a priority scheme by differentiating the backoff window. Aad and Castelluccia [5] proposed a priority scheme by differentiating inter-frame spaces (IFS's), in which a higher priority class uses IFS, whereas a lower priority class uses a space that equals the sum of IFS and the maximum window size. In [6] Veres and Campbell et al. proposed priority schemes by differentiating the minimum backoff window size and the maximum window size. These performance studies neglected that high load situation. They can't truly reflect the real operation of EDCF with priority schemes. In order to improve the efficiency, IEEE 802.11e EDCF provides two mechanisms named as TXOP and Block_Ack mechanisms. In this paper, we pay attention to the EDCF of IEEE 802.11e with Block_Ack mechanism. We proposed a markov chain model and studied the behavior. We extend the model to support IEEE 802.11e EDCF, and present a more accurate analysis of the IEEE 802.11e EDCF under a non-ideal channel environment. We also compared it with that without Block_Ack mechanism under channel error environment.

The rest of this paper is organized as follows. In section 2, a general description of our proposed model with Block_Ack mechanism is presented. Analytical performance deviations of proposed model including throughput analysis under non-ideal channel scenario are presented in section 3. The numerical results are given with discussion in section 4. Finally, conclusions are drawn in section 5.

2   Enhanced DCF of IEEE 802.11e

IEEE 802.11e EDCF is a new wireless technology which is an enhanced version of IEEE 802.11 DCF. It defines a new supplement to the existing IEEE 802.11 MAC protocol. The IEEE 802.11e EDCF aims at improving the capabilities and efficiency of the IEEE 802.11 MAC protocol by defining a new mechanism to support the QoS services.

2.1   IEEE 802.11e EDCF Scheme

EDCF specifies four default access categories (ACs). Each STA contends for the channel access and independently starts its backoff depending on its associated AC. Each AC uses AIFS[AC], CW_{min}[AC] and CW_{max}[AC] instead of DIFS, CW_{min} and CW_{max} of the DCF [11].

The contention method of EDCF is the same as that in DCF. Each STA having a frame to transmit has to wait for the channel to be idle without interruption for a period AIFS[AC], and then it should start a random backoff process with its own CW[AC]. For each time slot interval, during which the channel stays idle, the random backoff value is decremented. When the backoff counter reaches zero, the frame is transmitted. AIFS[AC] is calculated as follows:

$$AIFS[AC] = AIFSN[AC] \times aSlotTime + aSIFSTime, \qquad (1)$$

where the backoff time is calculated as follows:

$$backoff\ time = random\_integer \times aSlotTime, \qquad (2)$$

where random_integer is uniformly and randomly chosen in the range $[0,CW(AC)]$, instead of $[0,W-1]$ in the DCF. The value of CW_{min} is 15 and CW_{max} is 1023 [12]. Initially, CW of each AC is equal to $CW_{min}[AC]$. After each collision, CW is doubled up to:

$$CW_{max}[AC] = 2^m \times (CW_{min}[AC]),$$ (3)

where m is called the maximum backoff stage. Once it reaches $CW_{max}[AC]$, it remains at this value until it is reset.

2.2   The System Model

We assume in the following that for a given station in the priority i class, $b(i,t)$ is defined as a random process representing the value of backoff counter at time t, and $s(i,t)$ is defined as the random process representing the backoff stage j , where $0 \le j \le m$ and m is the maximum backoff stage. The value of the backoff counter is uniformly chosen in the range $(0,1,...,W_{i,j} -1)$, where $W_{i,j} = 2^j W_{i,0}$ and $W_{i,0} = CW_{min}[i]$.

Let P_i denote the probability that a transmitted frame collides in the priority i class. A Markov chain $\{s(i,t),b(i,t)\}$ can be established to analyze the contention process. Therefore, the state of each station in the priority i class is described by $\{i, j, k\}$, where i is just an index standing for the priority i class, j stands for the backoff stage and takes values $(0,1,...,m)$, and k stands for the backoff delay and takes values $(0,1,...,W_{i,j} -1)$ in time slots. The state transition diagram for the priority i class is shown in Fig. 1, where the state $\{i, -1, 0\}$ stands for the state that the station senses when the channel is idle and when a previous frame transmits successfully, the STA can transmit a frame immediately without activating the backoff stage. The transmission probabilities are listed as follows:

1. The backoff counter freezes when the STA senses that the channel is busy in the priority i class:

$$P\{i, j,k | i, j,k\} = p_i, \ 0 \le k \le W_{i,j} -1, \ 0 \le j \le m.$$ (4)

2. The backoff counter decrements when the STA senses the channel is idle in the priority i class:

$$P\{i, j,k | i, j,k +1\} = 1 - p_i, \ 0 \le k \le W_{i,j} -2, \ 0 \le j \le m.$$ (5)

3. The STA enters the $\{i, -1, 0\}$ state if it has a successful transmission with the previous frame in the priority i class:

$$P\{i,-1,0 | i, j,0\} = 1 - p_i, \ 0 \le j \le m.$$ (6)

4. The STA transmits it frame without entering the backoff process at $\{i, -1, 0\}$ state if it detects that its previous transmitted frame was successfully received and the channel is idle in the priority i class:

$$P\{i,-1,0 | i,-1,0\} = 1 - p_i.$$ (7)

5. The STA defers the transmission of a new frame and enters stage 0 of the backoff process if the STA finds a collision has occurred at $\{i, -1, 0\}$ state in the priority i class:

$$P\{i,0,k|i,-1,0\} = p_i/W_{i,0}, \ 0 \le k \le W_{i,0} - 1. \tag{8}$$

6. The STA chooses a backoff delay of the next stage j after an unsuccessful transmission at stage j-1 in the priority i class:

$$P\{i,j,k|i,j-1,0\} = p_i/W_{i,j}, \ 1 \le j \le m, \ 0 \le k \le W_{i,j} - 1. \tag{9}$$

Let $b_{i,j,k} = \lim P_r\{s(i,t) = j, b(i,t) = k\}$ be the stationary distribution of the Markov chain. We can derive the following relations by chain regularities:

$$b_{i,-1,0} = \frac{2p_i(1-p_i)^2(1-2p_i)}{2p_i(1-p_i)^2(1-2p_i) + W_{i,0}(1-(2p_i)^m)(1-p_i) + (1+W_{i,0}(2p_i)^m)(1-2p_i)}. \tag{10}$$

Let τ_i be the probability that a STA in the priority i class transmits during a time slot e. We then have

$$\tau_i = b_{i,-1,0} + \sum_{j=0}^{m-1} b_{i,j,0} + b_{i,m,0} = \frac{1}{1-p_i} b_{i,-1,0}. \tag{11}$$

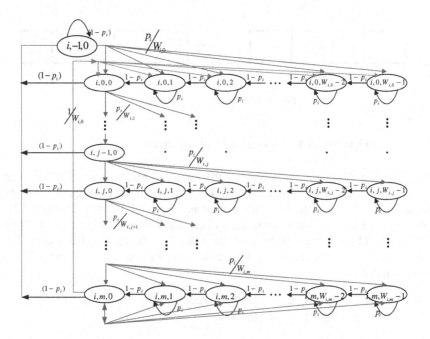

Fig. 1. Markov chain model for the priority i with the backoff window size

2.3   Block_Ack Mechanism

In IEEE 802.11e, a STA must receive an ACK frame to confirm a successful transmission. The Block_Ack is defined in order to reduce the channel wastes due to the
ACK transmission. The Block_Ack mechanism improves channel efficiency by aggregating several ACKs into one frame. This mechanism allows a block of frames to
be transmitted, each separated by a SIFS period, and to be acknowledged by a final
aggregated ACK frame, which is called Block_Ack (B_ACK) frame as shown in Fig.
2. The Block ACK contains information about the reception of the whole block
through a corresponding bitmap, and it is transmitted after an explicit transmitter
makes a request, which is named Block ACK Request (BAR). In the B_ACK mechanism, the sender STA only contends for the channel access before the first frame
of a block. If the STA wins the channel access, the STA sends out a whole block and
a Block ACK Request frame and then waits for the Block ACK frame. Upon receiving the B_ACK frame correctly, the STA must defer a DIFS interval and a backoff
process before sensing the channel again. At the same time, the other STAs should
wait until the STA ends the B_ACK mechanism and then defer another DIFS interval
before counting down their backoff counters for the next round of contention.

In general, the STA sends out a whole block of frames and a BAR frame. If the receiver STA detects a collision, the receiver STA will not send back the B_ACK frame. If
the sender STA cannot receive the B_ACK frame, it must retry the transmission again.

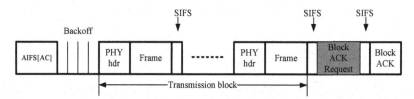

Fig. 2. The B_ACK frame structure

3   Description of the System Performance

The saturation throughput is defined as the frame information in a slot time that is
successfully transmitted in slot duration. There are four types of states in the B_ACK
mechanism: 1) None of the STAs transmit at any time slot, i.e., the channel is idle. 2)
Only one STA transmits at the time slot and the transmission is successful. 3) There is
at least two STAs transmit at the same time slot, i.e., the channel has a collision. 4)
There is at least one frame corrupted in a block, i.e., the channel has an error. We then
can obtain that

$$S_i = \frac{p_{s,i}\left(1-P_{e,i}\right)N_iT_{L_i}}{(1-p_i)\sigma + \sum_{i=0}^{N-1} p_{s,i}\left(1-P_{e,i}\right)T_{S,i} + [p_i - p_{s,i}]T_{C,i} + \sum_{i=0}^{N-1} p_{s,i}\left(P_{e,i}^{RTS}T_{e,i}^{RTS} + P_{e,i}^{CTS}T_{e,i}^{CTS} + P_{e,i}^{L_i}T_{e,i}^{L_i}\right)}. \tag{12}$$

$$T_{S,i} = T_{RTS} + T_{CTS} + 2T_{SIFS} + N_i(T_{L_i} + T_{SIFS}) + AIFS(i) + (T_{BAR} + T_{SIFS} + T_{BA}) + (N_i + 2)T_H. \tag{13}$$

$$T_{C,i} = T_{RTS} + T_{CTS} + 2T_{SIFS} + N_i(T_{L_i} + T_{SIFS}) + T_{BAR} + (N_i + 1)T_H + T_{EIFS,i},$$
$$T_{EIFS,i} = T_H + T_{BA} + AIFS(i) + T_{SIFS}. \tag{14}$$

Where N_i denotes the number of frames in a block. $T_{S,i}$ is the time of the whole block transmission due to a successful transmission for priority i class. σ is the duration of an empty time slot.

4   Simulation Results

The following simulation results have been obtained assuming the parameters are as follows: Frame payload = 1023 bytes, MAC header = 34 bytes, PHY header = 16 bytes, ACK = 14 bytes, RTS = 20 bytes, CTS = 14 bytes, SIFS = 20 us, DIFS = 50 us, propagation delay = 1 us, slot time = 20 us, and $[W_{0,0}\ W_{1,0}\ W_{2,0}\ W_{3,0}] = [16\ 32\ 64\ 128]$.

Fig. 3 and Fig. 4 show the saturation throughput performances of different priority STAs using the RTS/CTS CSMA/CA scheme with/without the B_ACK mechanism under a non-ideal channel scenario. From the results, we can conclude that the STA with B_ACK mechanism got better performance than that without B_ACK mechanism because the B_ACK mechanism improves channel efficiency by aggregating several ACKs into one frame.

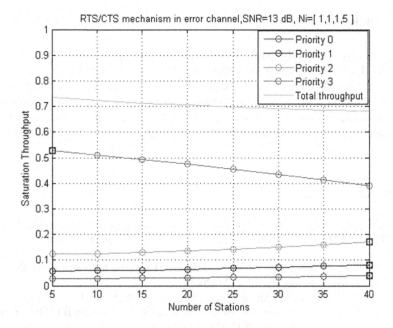

Fig. 3. Saturation throughput of the different priority STAs with the B_ACK mechanism

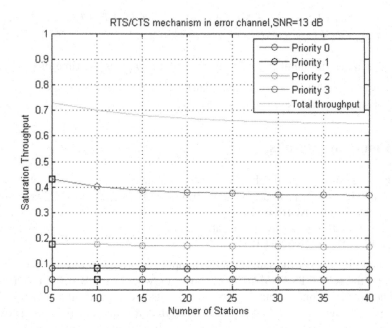

Fig. 4. Saturation throughput of the different priority STAs without the B_ACK mechanism

5   Conclusions

In this paper, we studied the backoff process characteristics of Markov chain model with RTS/CTS CSMA/CA scheme under non-ideal channel scenario. In order to increase the system throughput we integrated the B_ACK mechanism into the model. The model with the B_ACK mechanism under a channel error scenario can achieve a higher performance than that without the B_ACK mechanism due to fact that the model with the B_ACK mechanism is allowed to aggregate several ACKs into one frame.

References

1. Xiao, Y.: QoS guarantee and provisioning at the contention-based wireless MAC layer in the IEEE 802.11e wireless LANs. IEEE Wireless Communications Magazine 13, 14–21 (2006)
2. Gu, D., Zhang, J.: QoS enhancement in IEEE 802.11 wireless local area networks. IEEE Communications Magazine 41, 120–124 (2003)
3. Choi, S., del Prado, J., Sai Shankar, N., Mangold, S.: IEEE 802.11e contention-based channel access (EDCF) performance evaluation. In: Proceedings of the IEEE International Conference on Communications, ICC 2003 (May 2003)
4. Deng, D.J., Chang, R.S.: A priority Scheme for IEEE 802.11 DCF Access Method. IEICE Trans. Communications E82-B(1), 96–102 (1999)

5. Aad, I., Castelluccia, C.: Differentiation Mechanisms for IEEE 802.11. In: IEEE INFOCOM 2001 (2001)
6. Veres, A., Campbell, A.T., Barry, M., Sun, L.H.: Supporting Differentiation in Wireless Packet Networks Using Distributed Control. IEEE J-SAC 19(10), 2081–2093 (2001)
7. Xia, X.: Enhanced DCF MAC scheme for providing differentiated QoS in ITS. In: Proceedings of IEEE Intelligent Transportation Systems Conference, pp. 280–286 (October 2004)
8. Gu, D., Zhang, J.: QoS enhancement in IEEE 802.11 wireless local area networks. IEEE Communications Magazine 41, 120–124 (2003)
9. Ma, J., Liu, Y., Tang, B.: QoS research and design for WLAN. In: Proceedings of IEEE International Symposium on Communications and Information Technology, vol. 2, pp. 865–868 (October 2005)
10. Nakajima, T., Adachi, T., Nishibayashi, Y., Utsunomiya, Y., Tandai, T., Takagi, M.: Compressed block ACK, an efficient selective repeat mechanism for IEEE 802.11n. IEICE Tech. Rep., CS2004-194, pp. 65–70 (January 2005)

A Study of SLA-Based Defense Resource Management Strategy in Network Security Defense System

Wen-Hsu Hsiao[1], Hui-Kai Su[2], Yu-Siang Wei[3], Wei-Sheng Ho[3], and Kim-Joan Chen[3]

[1] Department of Computer Science and Information Technology WuFeng University, Taiwan
shianws@wfu.edu.tw
[2] Department of Electrical Engineering National Formosa University Yunlin, Taiwan
hksu@nfu.edu.tw
[3] Department of Electrical Engineering National Chung Cheng University Chia-Yi, Taiwan
ieekjc@ccu.edu.tw

Abstract. This paper mainly propose a service of network security defense provide by the network service provider, and the service system is built on the original ISP network structure, the security decisions center build on the ISP's core network which is making the policy decisions of security event, and built a defense system on border routers to form a secure domain called security domain, the service provider will join the user who is using the service to the security domain, through the defense system to   network traffic monitoring and filtering malice package to provide users of network security threat defense services. Using Service Level Agreements (SLA) to represent users' needs, so that users can choose services according to their needs, network security defense system provide different type of defense services based on user needs. Finally, we analyze the usage of the defense resource, furthermore we formulate the mechanisms of policy for the client's needs, and how to allocate resources in the case of resource saturation for the defense to satisfy service providers obtain the best benefits of the service strategy, and design the mechanism of resource management.

Keywords: Security Policy Management,SLA.

1   Introduction

In recent years, the network attacks is changed rapidly and it's impossible to defend effectively. For the user who not familiar with the security issue to operate the security software is difficult. In such situation, these users usually use the setting by default, we are not sure whether the default setting can be able to against these attacks or not; On the other hand, for the network administrator is familiar with network security management, will still be subject to the hazards of cyber-attacks. Such as the recent years, Sony and Google was be hacked, and the hackers steal a large number of customers' personal data. Only enterprise collected information alone is not sufficient to prevent attack. These prevention methods are in the user side to install their own network security software or hardware, as well as via the user or the network managers to manage the data information.

J.J. Park et al. (Eds.): NPC 2012, LNCS 7513, pp. 336–348, 2012.

This paper proposes the architecture to provide network security services by the Internet Service Provider (ISP). The service provider is responsible for managing the customer's network security, taking a protection of customers using the Internet from the malicious so that customers do not need to install their own network security software or hardware. The service is known as network security and defense services. However, the degree of network security needs of each customer are different, it must be customer-oriented, according to the security needs of each customer to provide the appropriate network security.

For these motivation, this paper will be based on the security system architecture [4] to explore the application environment and services designed to modify the system according to the needs of the application environment and services, and incorporate the concept of user demand to provide network security system; Finally, we have to analysis of the defense system usage behavior, and further development the mechanisms of customer demand and planning the security management.

2   Background

A.   The Distributed Defense System

In the paper [4] [5] proposed a distributed security system architecture like Fig.1 (Security Policy Decision Server, system architecture, SPDS) as the policy decision, and communication with the other domains to achieve a defense. The routers in the domain of the system are to deploy security router as packet forwarding, monitoring and filtering. And the SPDS policy decision part, just mainly about the mechanisms of the Policy Management security policy.

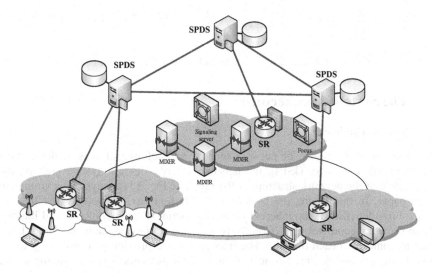

Fig. 1. The system architecture of distributed protection device

B. The Policy Management

Aib, [1] proposed an architecture be called Policy Simulator. The operation of the Policy Manager starts when all new events are loaded. In this architecture, we placed in a framework of SLA management mechanism and set its security policy according to the Business of behavior, as shown in Fig. 2.

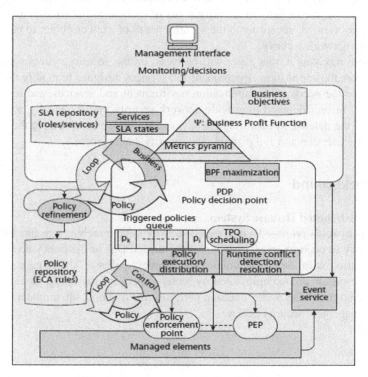

Fig. 2. The architecture of Policy Simulator

3   The System Architecture

3.1   System Environment

This paper proposed to provide network security and defense services by the Internet Service Provider industry (ISPs), the network security defense system built on the original core of the network structure of the ISP. The Fig. 3 is the system environment in this paper. In this figure, the bottom of the system environment for the Internet Service Provider (ISP) is the inherent network structure. The gray cloud, said Internet service provider's core network (Core Network), and in the core network border has a router to connect to each domain. The internet service providers in order to provide network security and defense services to the inherent network structure, setting up the defense system on the entrances and exits of each domain of the core network border router which mainly responsible for network monitoring and defense of each domain. This system called security Router (SR), and the defense domain was monitored as the security domain (security domain).

For the purpose of collecting the network attacks information in a distributed environment, there are more than one security monitoring system to monitor each domain. Furthermore, in the core network can build a security decision center for the policy-making and decision-making, not only collect the network monitoring information but also manage and control the defense system for the SR. The network security decision-making center is through setting a few security policy decision-making systems (security Policy Decision Server, SPDS) which consist of decision-making center. The aim is managing the SR which in their security domain distributed in order to achieve load balancing.

In the Fig. 3, the systems environment context diagram has the solid line and the dotted line, where the solid lines represent the Internet Network, which is the network used by the general user (or customer), while the dotted line represent the private network of defense systems which known as the security Management network also as a communication network between the SPDS and SR devices. There are many different customers in each security domain, and their network security needs are different, as shown in Fig. 3, presents the customers in the security domain may be general user, enterprise or factory and so on.

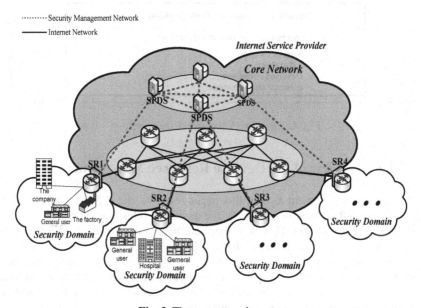

Fig. 3. The system environment

3.2   System Architecture

Network security defense system architecture diagram is divided into two physical components, namely, the defense system (Security Router) and security policy decision-making system, the system works according to our research previously. As shown in Fig. 4.

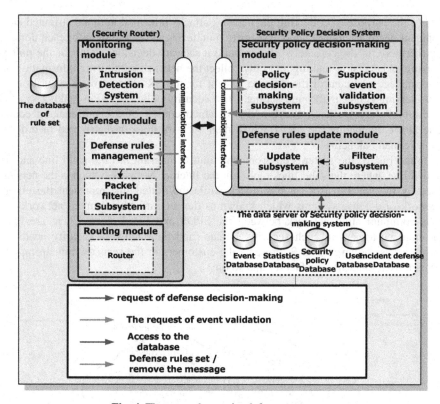

Fig. 4. The network security defense system

4   The Overview of the Defense Resource Management

The defense resources mentioned in this paper refers to the defense module of the defense system (SR), which is used to set the defensive rules, but the resources of the defense system has the limit. However, there are many different demands of customers in each security domain. It means that when the customers increase, the SR has to protect these customers by using more defense resources because each customer's demands are not the same. Owing to the proportion of defense resources for each customer is not the same, when the defense resources become saturation, how to allocate defense resources will be the important issue.

The following will explore the design of the mechanism about the defense resource management, and the network security defense system mechanism show as the Fig. 5.

One of the properties of "Provider Resource" refers to the resources of the defense system, another property of the "user requirements" means the defense requirements of customers, and the "Service Policy" as a service provider business strategy. In this paper, the service strategy of network security and defense services is to get the best interests and benefits for the service providers. So, we will explore how to allocate the use of the fixed defensive resources in order to achieve the best results. The service management mechanism is a mechanism of the entire system operation, and the

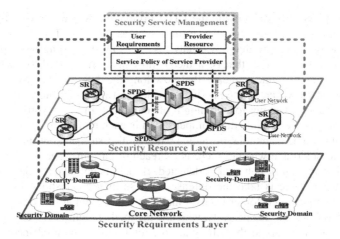

Fig. 5. The service management mechanism

defense resources management also belongs to. So the defense resource management mechanisms must be user demand-oriented, as well as according to the service strategy to manage defense resources.

5   The Network Security and Defense Services

A.   Service environment modeling
First, we assume that the system module of the network security defense system is hardware-based filtering system or firewall system, and the maximum available defense resources for the defense module is   . Furthermore, we assume that the defense module processing performance is not affected by the number of flow size and defensive rules, within the maximum available defense resources.

Assuming that the network service provider industry provide network security and defense services, in accordance with the common network attack types, which can provide several event types of projects for defense to customers to choose such as Table 3. And the maximum available defense resources for the network security defense system which service provider industry provided is   .

As the charges of the service, the service provider is analyzing the characteristics of various types of attacks, then further analysis of the degree of damages for customers, and develop the hazard rating, charges ( ) and the compensation ratio ( ); For the service provider, there were two sets of fee for the different needs of customers, one is the general-type customer and another is enterprise-type customer, However, the hazard rating of the characteristics of both types and the level of charges are different, such as Table 1, and Table 2.

When a customer selected a type, then it will have an SLA contracts to be corresponding to the customer, For example, when a customer was selected general-type, then the SLA contracts will be such as shown in Table 3. The customers will be able to choose the services in the SLA project according to their demand, and to sign a contract with the service providers to complete the purchase of services process. The service providers also can provide the PTP information, which is including the costs of the defense services and the service time, such as shown in Table 4. The information of costs is to indicate that how many resources must be using when the services projects set up the defense, that is, it means how many rules need to set up. The information of defense time is means that how long the defense rules exist for the defense services. However, in the service provider part of the balance sheet of income and compensation planning for the month of settlement, In other words, it will calculate the total revenue and the total compensation in each month.

The total revenue is the total of the fee paid by all customers, but the total compensation has to determine whether there is a breach of customer needs, The criterion is decided when the attack behavior is detected. If there is not take the defense during a certain time, or there is take the defense but less than a threshold, then it will be judged as not to meet customer needs. Finally, it will to sum all the compensation for all unmet customer service projects, which is the total amount of the compensation of the service provider. As to the total gain, the total gain is the total income after deducting the total compensation.

B.   The model of the defense resources usage

This part will analyze the overall operation of the system behavior for the use of defense resources to develop the formula of statistical analysis. This paper presents a scheme for the system management and resource allocation according to the service strategy, which means that the behavior of the overall system operation and the use of resources for defense must be consistent with the goal of the service strategy.

In this paper, the target for the service provider is to get the best benefits, which is to get the best profit. According to the modeling of a service environment mentioned before. We assume that the best benefit the service providers get, the less the amount of compensation is. So, the goal of the statistical analysis is to strive for the maximum benefit basically, and to pay the minimal compensation to customers for the service provider.

However, the need of compensation is decided on whether to meet the customer needs. To meet the customer needs, the service provider need to consume defense resources to defense attacks but do not require compensation to customers; if not, then it do not consume resources to defense attacks but need to compensate customers. The decision-making parameters of statistical analysis is whether the defense to meet customer demand.

The formula of statistical analysis is based on the mode of operation and limitations of the overall system, such as the usage of the defense resources must be lesser than the maximum available, in the meanwhile, when the defense services that the customer does not need and the attack event which has not occurred, then the service provider has not to take the defense. Before introducing the model of defense resource usage, we first described the parameters in Table 5.

The defense resource model developed under the above conditions is as follows :

1)   Decision values :

$X_{st} = \begin{cases} 1 \\ 0 \end{cases}$, Represent that whether there are demand for the s customer in t defense services.

2) Objective :

$$\max\left(\sum_s \sum_t \delta_{st} C_{st} - \sum_s \sum_t \sigma_{st} \delta_{st}(1 - x_{st}) P_{st}\right), \quad s \in S, t \in T$$

3) Subject to :

$$\sum_e \sum_s \sum_t \varepsilon_{est} \delta_{st} x_{st} r_t \leq F \ , \ s \in S, t \in T, e \in E. \tag{1}$$

$$\sum_s \sum_t (1 - \delta_{st}) x_{st} = 0 \ , \ s \in S, t \in T. \tag{2}$$

$$\sum_s \sum_t \sigma_{st}(1 - \delta_{st}) x_{st} = 0 \ , \ s \in S, t \in T. \tag{3}$$

$$\sum_s \sum_t (1 - \sigma_{st})(1 - \delta_{st}) x_{st} = 0 \ , \ s \in S, t \in T. \tag{4}$$

$$\sum_s \sum_t \varepsilon_{est} = 1 \ , \ \forall e = 1, \ldots, m \ , \ s \in S, t \in T. \tag{5}$$

$$\prod_e (1 - \varepsilon_{est}) = (1 - \sigma_{st}), \ \forall s = 1, \ldots, n \quad \forall t = 1, \ldots, 5 \quad e \in E. \tag{6}$$

The objective of the analysis of the defense resources model is getting the maximum benefit; the model has following six limitations :

(1) The usage of resources must be less than F.
(2) During the first s customer in t defense type has no attacks ($\sigma_{st} = 0$), the x_{st} equal 0.
(3) When the first s customer in t defense type has no demand ($\delta_{st} = 0$), the x_{st} equal 0.
(4) When the condition conform the limitation (2) and (3), then the x_{st} also equal 0.
(5) Each event will only attack one customer, and only belongs to one type of event;
(6) As limiting the first s customer in t defensive types of projects (σ_{st}), which is 1 when the events occurred, and 0 represent not events occurred.

Table 1. The hazard rating of the general customers

Hazard level (l)	Harmful behavior	Charge	Compensation ratio
1	Be unauthorized manipulation of the computer (or server)	NT\$ Rev_1	P_ratio_1
2	The confidential information of individuals (or organizations) was stolen	NT\$ Rev_2	P_ratio_2
3	Attacker detection the device weakness (the device can be computer or server)	NT\$ Rev_3	P_ratio_3
4	Be attacked by multiple sources, resulting in the system (or service) operate abnormal	NT\$ Rev_4	P_ratio_4
5	Cause the system (or service) operate abnormal	NT\$ Rev_5	P_ratio_5

Table 2. The hazard rating of corporate customers

Hazard level (l)	Harmful behavior	Charge	Compensation ratio
1	Be attacked by multiple sources, resulting in the system (or service) operate abnormal	NT\$ Rev_1	P_ratio_1
2	Cause the system (or service) operate abnormal	NT\$ Rev_2	P_ratio_2
3	Be unauthorized manipulation of the computer (or server)	NT\$ Rev_3	P_ratio_3
4	The confidential information of individuals (or organizations) was stolen	NT\$ Rev_4	P_ratio_4
5	Attacker detection the device weakness (the device can be computer or server)	NT\$ Rev_5	P_ratio_5

Table 3. The SLA example of the general customers

Select	Defense Services	Fee / compensation
	Denial-of-service (DoS)	NT\$ Rev_5 / -NT\$ P_1
	The Distributed Denial-of-service (DDoS)	NT\$ Rev_4 / -NT\$ P_2
	Vulnerability scanning (Scan)	NT\$ Rev_3 / -NT\$ P_3
	Backdoor (Spyware)	NT\$ Rev_2 / -NT\$ P_4

Table 4. The Protection Type Profile (PTP)

Number(t)	Defense type	Defense costs	Defense time
1	Denial-of-service (DoS)	r_1	$ProtectionTime_1$
2	The Distributed Denial-of-service (DDoS)	r_2	$ProtectionTime_2$
3	Vulnerability scanning (Scan)	r_3	$ProtectionTime_3$
4	Backdoor (Spyware)	r_4	$ProtectionTime_4$
5	Trojan, Bot Detection and Prevention	r_5	$ProtectionTime_5$

Table 5. The parameter description Table

Parameter	Explain	Value
E	The collection of events detected during a certain time	1,...,m
S	The customers collection, $S = S_1 \cup S_2$, S_1 is the Collection for enterprise customers, S_2 is the collection of general customers	1,...,n
T	As a defensive type collection	1,...,5
ε_{est}	When value equal 1, indicating that the target of the event for the e times attack is s customer, the type of event is t	0 or 1
σ_{st}	Represent that whether there are attacks during the s customer in t defense services	0 or 1
δ_{st}	Represent that the whether there are demand for s customers in t defense services	0 or 1
P_{st}	Represent the amount of **compensation** of the defense services of the s customers in t defense services	
C_{st}	Represent the amount of **charge** of the defense services of the s customers in t defense services	
r_t	Represent that defense type t need to consume how many of the defense resources (Eg: How many of rules the demand has to set ?)	
F	Represent the maximum available total defense resources for the defense system	

6   The Analysis of Defense Resources Usage

A.   Fig.s and Tables

Based on the above planning service environment, as well as refer to the statistical results of the attack with intent [6] and major network security company Network Threat
statistics [7] [8] to conFig. the types of fees and compensation, further to conFig. each
network attacks and the proportion of the types of customers, to do the statistical analysis of the behavior of defense resources usage. In addition assume that the network service provider to provide network security and defense services, which the available
resources of the defense system is 2000 (F = 2000). Table 6 and Table 7 are the parameter settings for each fee type. Table 8 represent the PTP information set.

The following analysis will be mainly focus on the defense resources of a single
security domain, analyze the resource usage by using the model which we proposed.
The following major analyze the influence between the number of services and profit
for different types of customers, which control variable is to control the proportion of
customer types, the operating variable is the number of customers in the security domain, and the fixed factors are the maximum available resources for the defense system, the number and proportion of each event type when the events occur.

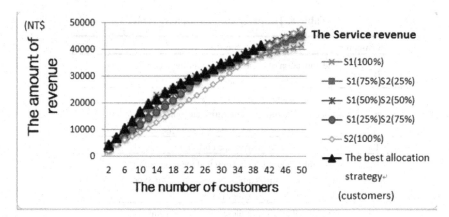

Fig. 6. The chart of Service revenue

Table 6. The hazard rating of the general customers

Hazard level (l)	Harmful behavior	Charge	Compensation ratio
1	Be unauthorized manipulation of the computer (or server)	NT$ 400	50%
2	The confidential information of individuals (or organizations) was stolen	NT$ 350	45%
3	Attacker detection the device weakness (the device can be computer or server)	NT$ 150	40%
4	Be attacked by multiple sources, resulting in the system (or service) operate abnormal	NT$ 200	15%
5	Cause the system (or service) operate abnormal	NT$ 150	15%

Fig. 6 indicates that represent the proportion of enterprise customers, and represent the proportion of general customers. This Fig. can be seen the more proportion of enterprise customers, the more pre-earnings will be. When the defense resources become the full load, the earnings growth will be less. In the late, the lower proportion of enterprise customers will be more income. For the service provider's point of view, we can make an inference to the ideal situation based on the above data. The ideal situation is no matter how many the customers are, the amount of the proceeds must be the best. After analyzing the allocation strategy of the various types of customers, we found that when the defense resources is sufficient, we can give the priority to accept the enterprise customers, when either adequate defense resources, began to accept the general customers, but no longer accept enterprise customers, as the triangle curve in Fig. 6.

The statistical analysis data of the best allocation strategy to compare the other five types of the different proportion of customers, we found that the best customer allocation strategy with the type of ［ (25%), (75%)］ proportion, their final income and the number of customers is the most similar. So use the strategy that the final proportion of customers will be close to ［ (25%), (75%)］ .

Table 7. The hazard rating of corporate customers

Hazard level (l)	Harmful behavior	Charge	Compensation ratio
1	Be attacked by multiple sources, resulting in the system (or service) operate abnormal	NT$ 650	95%
2	Cause the system (or service) operate abnormal	NT$ 500	90%
3	Be unauthorized manipulation of the computer (or server)	NT$ 400	80%
4	The confidential information of individuals (or organizations) was stolen	NT$ 380	75%
5	Attacker detection the device weakness (the device can be computer or server)	NT$ 100	50%

Table 8. The Protection Type Profile (PTP)

Number(t)	Defense type	Defense costs	Defense time
1	Denial-of-service (DoS)	5	5-days
2	The Distributed Denial-of-service (DDoS)	8	5-days
3	Vulnerability scanning (Scan)	1	5-days
4	Backdoor (Spyware)	4	5-days
5	Trojan, Bot Detection and Prevention	6	5-days

7   Conclusion

In this paper, according to the operation of the overall system, we propose a model for defense resources management basis on the behavior of the usage of resources, and further assume that the service environment and the analysis of defense resources usage. We found that the more proportion of the enterprise customer, the more initial income will be, but with increasing in the number of customers will make the resources into full, the growth of earnings will become slower. Through the observation of a variety of data of the proportion of customers, and to design the best strategy to satisfy the customer's demand from the provider perspective. As for the best strategy for defense resources, when the resources are sufficient, then priority by adding enterprise customers, when the resources became the full load, began to accept the general customers. Finally, as the load of resources become full, we can choice one type of allocation of defense resources to design a defense resource management mechanism, while in the future, we can based on the above results applied to defense system of resource management to implement.

References

1. Aib, I., Boutaba, R.: PS: A Policy Simulator. IEEE Communications Magazine 45(4), 130–136 (2007)
2. Su, H.-K., Yau, Z.-Z., Wu, C.-S., Chen, K.-J.: Session-Level and Network-Level SLA Structures and VoIP Service Policy over DiffServ-Based MPLS Networks. IEICE Transactions on Communications E89-B(2), 383–392 (2006)
3. Marilly, E., Martinot, O., Betge-Brezetz, S., Delegue, G.: Requirements for service level agreement management. In: Proc. IEEE Workshop on IP Operations and Management (2002)
4. Yu, M.-R.: Implementation of SLA-Based Security Policy Management for Cooperative Defense Network (2010)
5. Chain, J.-S.: Design of SLA-Based Cooperative Security and Management Mechanism on Soft Network. In: TANet 2008(2008)
6. Lee, W.-H.: On Investigation of Malicious Software's Activities - A Case Study on a Company's Internet Connections (2005)
7. Taiwan Computer Emergency Response Team and Coordination Center,
   http://www.cert.org.tw/resource/

A New Approach for Detecting SMTPFA
Based on Entropy Measurement

Hsing-Chung Chen[1,*], Jai-Zong Sun[2], Shian-Shyong Tseng[1], and Chien-Erh Weng[3]

[1] Department of Computer Science and Information Engineering,
Asia University, Taichung County, Taiwan 41354
[2] Institute of Computer Science and Information Engineering, Asia University,
Taichung County, Taiwan 41354
[3] Department of Electronic Communication Engineering,
National Kaohsiung Marine University Kaohsiung, Taiwan
{cdma2000,sstseng}@asia.edu.tw, asiaphd10026@gmail.com,
ceweng@mail.nkmu.edu.tw

Abstract. In this paper, we propose a new approach of detecting a kind of Simple Mail Transfer Protocol Flooding Attack (SMTPFA for short) based on entropy measurement. We will calculate the entropy values from the received packets flow. Further checking its entropy value compared with the values of abnormal entropy, we then use it to detect this server whether is suffered some attacks from hacker. The scheme can easily detect SMTPFA, and monitor the real-time status of SMTP server.

Keywords: SMTP, Entropy, Attack detecting, SMTP flooding attack.

1 Introduction

In recent years, with the rapid development of the networks, people communicate of long range gradually shift from use the traditional post letter becoming to use e-mail delivery. Today, e-mail has become one of necessary communication tools for Internet users. In 1982, the early stage of e-mail development, the SMTP (Simple Mail Transfer Protocol) is formulated in RFC 821[5]. Owing to RFC 1939 [7], RFC 2821 [6] and RFC 3461 [8] are formulated in the RFC standard, the e-mail protocol has been gradually completed.

A simple e-mail server (SMTP server, for short hereinafter) has a lot of users, so it became an important attacked target in the network. The ways of attacks includes SMTP Flooding Attack (SMTPFA), spam attacks and the malicious attachment etc. in e-mail [1, 2, 10, 12]. The SMTPFA will increase the loading of the server. In this paper, we propose a new approach for detecting SMTPFA based on entropy operation. Then, we use the entropy operation to analyse the received packets, in order to distinguish normal packets and abnormal packets from SMTP message flow, and then calculate the corresponding information parameters. Therefore, the information parameter will be

---

* Corresponding author.

J.J. Park et al. (Eds.): NPC 2012, LNCS 7513, pp. 349–359, 2012.

used to describe the status of the serving server. According to the value of this status, the server will determine whether it is suffered by SMTPFA.

The remainder of this paper is organized as follows. Section 2 describes the SMTP and entropy operation related work. In the Section 3, we propose a new approach for detecting SMTPFA based on entropy operation, and describe how to calculate the parameters of server status. Finally, we draw conclusions in Section 4.

2   Related Work

In our proposed approach, we use the entropy measurement to detect the behaviour of the SMTPFA. Therefore, in Section 2, we will describe the normal message flows of SMTP standard [5, 8], and the entropy operations [2, 3].

2.1   SMTP

First, SMTP had been defined in the RFC 821[5]. It is an independent subsystem in special communication system. In this communication system, it only needs a reliable channel to transmit the related sequence message flows. SMTP has an important simple delivering e-mail protocol which it can forward an e-mail between two different networks. The architecture of SMTP is shown in Fig. 1. In the SMTP architecture, it consists of a Sender, a sender-SMTP, a receiver-SMTP and a Receiver. When a Sender (user or file server) will connect to another receiver, it will send a request message of Establishes Connection to the sender-SMTP. Then, the sender-SMTP will establish a two-way transmission channel in order to connect the Receiver. The receiver-SMTP will be as a destination point or a relay point. Thus, the sender-SMTP will send the related SMTP commands to the receiver-SMTP. Finally, the receiver-SMTP will follow these commands to send back a SMTP response message to sender-SMTP. According to the above steps, if the command-respond pair has been completed during one normal time-period, it means that a round of SMTP session has been completed. The established SMTP message flows are divided into seven stages [5, 8] as below: Establishes Connection, HELO, MAIL FROM, RCPT TO, DATA, DATA TRANSFER, and QUIT. The SMTP message flows are shown in Fig. 2.

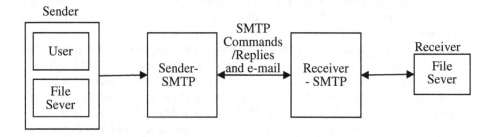

Fig. 1. The SMTP architecture

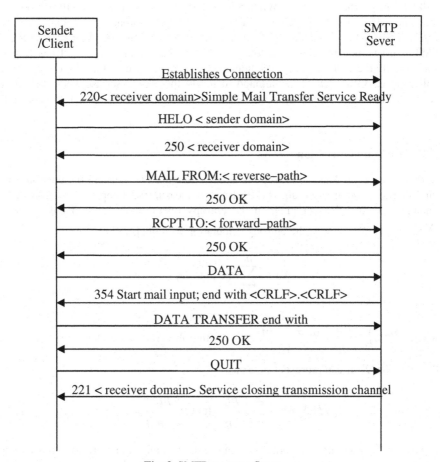

Fig. 2. SMTP message flows

At first, in Establishes Connection, Client (e-mail sender) will send a request of Establishes Connection to SMTP server, and prepare to forward an e-mail. After SMTP server getting the requesting connection, it will send a message '220' which means the SMTP server has prepared completely. When client gets the message "220" from SMTP server, it will send a command as "HELO < sender domain>" to SMTP server. After SMTP server gets the command as "HELO", a buffer will be initialized, and sent back the message "250 < receiver domain>" which means the command of Client is correct. Then, Client will write the source address into "MAIL FROM: < reverse–path>" command. The main purpose of this step is that when some errors have occurred during e-mail delivered path, it will return error messages of the e-mail to Client via reverse-path. If the e-mail address is inerrancy, the SMTP server will response the message "250", else it will response the message "550" which means the e-mail address doesn't exist. After Client gets the message "250", it will send back the "RCPT TO :< forward–path>" command. When the above steps have been completed, the client will use the "DATA" command to notify the SMTP server. Then, the data will be sent via the file server. When SMTP server gets command, it will response the message "354" to notify Client "You can start to upload the e-mail, and add "<CRLF>.<CRLF>" at the end of this e-mail. After getting "<CRLF>.<CRLF>", the SMTP server then responses the message "250" that means the e-mail has finished successfully the work. Finally, if Client doesn't want to uses e-mail functions, she/he will send back the "QUIT" command to notify the SMTP server. Then, the SMTP server further response the message "221" which means as "shut down the connected service".

2.2   Entropy Operation

In the Information Theory, Entropy is an approach used to measure the uncertainty or randomness in random variable [4, 9]. Entropy measurement approach is proposed by Shannon [3] and Weaver [11]. In the entropy operation, a random entropy value $X \in \{x_1, x_2, x_3, ..., x_n\}$, the entropy calculation formula [4, 9] as below:

$$H(X) = -\sum_{i=1}^{n} P(x_i) \log P(x_i)$$ (1)

where $P(x_i) = \dfrac{m_i}{m}$, $m = \sum_{i=1}^{n} m_i$, m_i is the observation frequency or numbers of the x_i from X. It can represent [4, 9] as:

$$H(X) = -\sum_{i=1}^{n} \left(\frac{m_i}{m}\right) \log P\left(\frac{m_i}{m}\right)$$ (2)

For example, if we throw a coin according to the formula (1) and (2), the positive and negative entropy values will be shown as follows:

$$H(positive) = -\left(0.5 \log_2 \frac{0.5}{1} + 0.5 \log_2 \frac{0.5}{1}\right) = 1 = H(negative)$$

Throwing a coin will face the probability of 99%, the positive entropy value is as

$$H(positive) = -\left(0.99 \log_2 \frac{0.99}{1}\right) \cong 0.014.$$

And the negative entropy value is as

$$H(negative) = -\left(0.01 \log_2 \frac{0.01}{1}\right) \cong 0.066.$$

From the example above, we know that the coin is thrown according to the positive and negative probability to determine the entropy. The entropy value is inversely proportional to the probability value. With this feature, the value of results we calculate has dependability.

3   A New Approach for Detecting SMTPFA

When SMTP server is under the SMTPFA, it will have a large number of request packets into SMTP server. In SMTPFA, the request packets will sent to SMTP server from clients, and the connection will be established with the SMTP server. But clients will not be sent the command packets again. At the same time, there have request packets from another client into SMTP server. Therefore, the server resources will be reduced ceaselessly, further increasing the loading of the server. In this session, we propose a new approach for detecting SMTPFA based on entropy operation. This approach can quickly to detect SMTPFA. In order to detect SMTPFA, we mark a server command packet and a client message packet become to a pairs. A normal packets pair (hereinafter referred to as the NPP) include one command packet and one message packet; an abnormal packets pair (hereinafter referred to as the APP) just include one message packet and no command packet. Then, we calculate the normal and abnormal packets entropy value in the SMTP message flow. By using this entropy to determine whether the server was affected by SMTPFA.

In general, when SMTPFA has starting, the device other than the server may not work. However, in our proposed method, we assume that the SMTP server crashing by SMTPFA. This represents the SMTPFA will attack the server directly, and does not affect the router and bandwidth. We will describe the process of SMTP message flow matching as below. Then, we will explain how to use the entropy operations to calculate the SMTP server status value. Finally, we describe a server status change of entropy situation when a server is under SMTPFA. Some notations used in the paper are given in Table 1.

Table 1. Notations

Notations	Definitions	Notations	Definitions
$Port_i$	The i-th port number	D_{loss}	The fail packets are sent from client to SMTP server.
S_{port_i}	The i-th message flow packet pair, for the port number $port_i$, which is send from SMTP server. It includes two packets: $S_{S\_port_i}$ and $S_{D\_port_i}$.	T_w	The w-th unit of time slide window, w=1, 2, 3, ..., n,
$S_{D\_port_i}$	The i-th packet is delivered from client to SMTP server, which is one of the packet pair S_{port_i}.	P	The total SMTP message flow pair numbers, where $P = P_n + P_a$.
$S_{S\_port_i}$	The i-th packet is delivered from SMTP server to client, which is one of the packet pair S_{port_i}.	P_n	The number of normal SMTP message flow pair, where $P_n = \left\{ P_{n_1}, P_{n_2}, P_{n_3}, ..., P_{n_j} \right\}$, j=1, 2, 3, ..., n

Table 2. (*Continued*)

D_{port_i}	The i-th message flow pair, for the port number $port_i$, which is delivered from client to SMTP server. It includes both packets: $D_{S\_port_i}$ and $D_{D\_port_i}$.	P_a	The number of abnormal SMTP message flow pair, where $P_a = \{P_{a_1}, P_{a_2}, P_{a_3}, ..., P_{a_j}\}$, j=1, 2, 3, ..., n。
$D_{S\_port_i}$	The i-th packet is delivered from SMTP server to client, which is one of the packet pair $D_{D\_port_i}$.	$H(X)$	An entropy value set. $X = \{x_1, x_2, x_3, ..., x_j\}$, j=1, 2, 3, ..., n。
$D_{D\_port_i}$	The i-th packet is delivered from SMTP server to client, which is one of the packet pair D_{port_i}.	S	The status value of SMTP Server

3.1   SMTP Message Flow

Definition 1. A completion SMTP message flow contains six rounds, which not include the steps of Establishes Connection and Service closing transmission channel. The round 0 is represented to the packet pair of establishment connection, and the round 7 is represented the packet pair of closing transmission channel. There is only one packet in the round 0 and round 7. After the SMTP connection being established, the message flow will be divided into a pair of two packets matching. The packet pair is (S_{port_i}, D_{port_i}), where $(S_{port_i}, D_{port_i}) = ((S_{S\_port_i}, S_{D\_port_i}), (D_{D\_port_i}, D_{S\_port_i}))$. It is recorded by the SMTP server.

According to Definition 1, In SMTP message flow; there have two packets in one pair. Every packets pair includes a source and destination port number, and it is used to identify the sender and the receiver. For example, in the round 1, SMTP server will send a message "220: Service already" to client. The packet pair is called $(S_{S\_port_i}, S_{D\_port_i})$, it means the packet that send to Client form SMTP server. When the destination of client gets the packet, it will send a HELO packet to SMTP server, it is called $(D_{D\_port_i}, D_{S\_port_i})$. This packet means that send to SMTP server form Client. Therefore, this transmission process is called a successful packet pair (S_{port_i}, D_{port_i}).

If there has a packet is transmission fail or over the SMTP server waiting time from client, it's called a fail packet pair (S_{port_i}, D_{loss}), and record into the SMTP server.

SMTP packets pair message flow as shown Fig. 3.

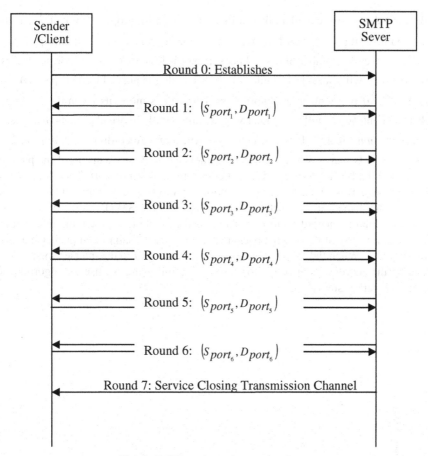

Fig. 3. SMTP packet pair message flows

3.2   A Approach for Detecting SMTPFA Using Entropy

Definition 2. In the SMTP, it has a NPP at least, to represent the SMTP server and the client has completed at least the starting of SMTP connection steps.

In the approach of detecting the SMTPFA, SMTP message flows are divided into two one-group pairing according to the description of Section 3.1. Then, we use the entropy operation to calculate the SMTP packets pair entropy values for the normal message flows and abnormal message flows. The entropy formulas are listed as follows.

$$Entropy: H(x_1) = -\left(\sum \frac{P_n}{P} \log_2 \frac{P_n}{P}\right), \tag{3}$$

$$Entropy: H(x_2) = -\left(\sum \frac{P_a}{P} \log_2 \frac{P_a}{P}\right), \tag{4}$$

where $P = P_n + P_a$.

By formula (3), we calculate the normal packets pair entropy $H(x_1)$ at T_w. If the normal number of packets pair is more, its mean the normal packets pair entropy P_n will less. Otherwise, the number of normal packets pair is less, its mean the normal packets pair entropy P_n will more. In formula (4), we calculate the normal packets pair entropy $H(x_2)$ at T_w. If the number of abnormal packets pair is more, its mean the abnormal packets pair entropy P_a will less. Otherwise the number of abnormal packets pair is less; it means the abnormal packets pair entropy P_n will more. According to Definition 2, if all of the packets pair is abnormal in SMTP message flow, it means all of the packets are lost, and the SMTP server and Client connections will not start. Therefore, in the SMTP message flow must be at least a normal packets pair to represent server and client is established a connection, and complete the SMTP steps of establish connection. Finally, according to formula (1) and formula (2), we get the intersection point of the entropy of the normal packets pair entropy and abnormal packets pair, as shown in Fig.4. When the server status values are more near to the intersection point, it indicating the server's security will be lower. The following we use the algorithm to describe the server status value.

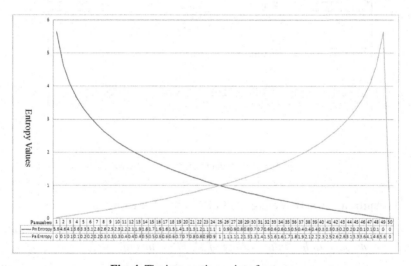

Fig. 4. The intersection point of entropy

Algorithm

Input: $(H(P_n), H(P_a))$, a SMTP message flow pair is including two Entropy value for normal packets and abnormal packets in T_w.

Output: Result values S of The SMTP server status in T_w. The value is 0, 1 or -1, where its safety, threshold limit value, dangerous, respectively.

Begin

$$H(P_n) \leftarrow -\left(\sum \frac{P_n}{P} \log_2 \frac{P_n}{P}\right)$$

$$H(P_a) \leftarrow -\left(\sum \frac{P_a}{P} \log_2 \frac{P_a}{P}\right)$$

for $P_n = P$ to $P - P_n$ do

    for $P_a = P$ to $P - P_a$ do

        Generate $(H(P_n), H(P_a))$;

    if $H(P_n) - H(P_a) < 0$ **then**

        return -1;

        else if $H(P_n) - H(P_a) \cong 0$ **then**

        return 0;

        else $H(P_n) - H(P_a) > 0$ **then**

        return 1;

        end

      end

    end

    return S;

end

□

Both NPP entropy value and APP entropy value are same almost, then $H(P_n) - H(P_a) \cong 0$, and return 0 mean the status on behalf of the server in the security value of the critical point. When the NPP entropy value adds the APP entropy value will less than 0, $H(P_n) - H(P_a) < 0$, its mean the SMTP server is under the danger status. If the server in this case, it will be attacked by SMTPFA or the SMTP server will overload. When the NPP entropy value adds the APP entropy value will greater than 0, $H(P_n) - H(P_a) > 0$, its mean the SMTP server is safe status. Finally, return the server status value S, and according to the value determine whether the SMTP server was affected by SMTPFA.

3.3   An Example for Detecting of SMTPFA

In the time slide window $T_w = \{T_1, T_2, T_3, ..., T_{10}\}$, the SMTP packets pair is 100 in a time slide window, and the packets total is 1000, where:

$$P_n = \{P_{n_1}, P_{n_2}, P_{n_3}, ..., P_{n_{10}}\} = \{100, 95, 87, 85, 76, 67, 51, 32, 22, 19\}$$

P_{n_1} entropy: $H\left(P_{n_1}\right) = -\left(\sum \dfrac{P_{n_1}}{P}\log_2 \dfrac{P_{n_1}}{P}\right) = -\dfrac{100}{100}\log\dfrac{100}{100} = 0$

P_{n_2} entropy: $H\left(P_{n_2}\right) = -\left(\sum \dfrac{P_{n_2}}{P}\log_2 \dfrac{P_{n_2}}{P}\right) = -\dfrac{95}{100}\log\dfrac{95}{100} = 0.074$

$$\vdots$$

$P_{n_{10}}$ entropy: $H\left(P_{n_{10}}\right) = -\left(\sum \dfrac{P_{n_{10}}}{P}\log_2 \dfrac{P_{n_{10}}}{P}\right) = -\dfrac{19}{100}\log\dfrac{19}{100} = 2.396$

$H(P_n) = \{0, 0.074, 0.201, 0.234, 0.396, 0.578, 0.972, 1.644, 2.185, 2.396\}$ Then,

$P_a = \{P_{a_1}, P_{a_2}, P_{a_3}, \dots, P_{a_{10}}\} = \{0, 5, 13, 15, 24, 33, 49, 68, 78, 81\}$

P_{a_1} entropy: $H\left(P_{a_1}\right) = -\left(\sum \dfrac{P_{a_1}}{P}\log_2 \dfrac{P_{a_1}}{P}\right) = -\dfrac{0}{100}\log\dfrac{0}{100} = 0$

P_{a_2} entropy: $H\left(P_{a_2}\right) = -\left(\sum \dfrac{P_{a_2}}{P}\log_2 \dfrac{P_{a_2}}{P}\right) = -\dfrac{5}{100}\log\dfrac{5}{100} = 4.322$

$$\vdots$$

$P_{a_{10}}$ entropy: $H\left(P_{a_{10}}\right) = -\left(\sum \dfrac{P_{a_{10}}}{P}\log_2 \dfrac{P_{a_{10}}}{P}\right) = -\dfrac{81}{100}\log\dfrac{81}{100} = 0.304$

$H(P_a) = \{0, 4.322, 2.944, 2.737, 2.059, 1.6, 1.029, 0.556, 0.358, 0.304\}$.

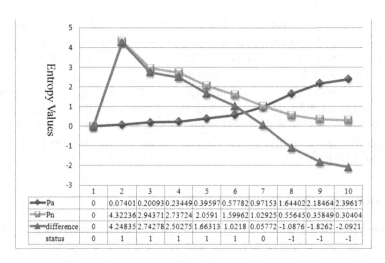

	1	2	3	4	5	6	7	8	9	10
Pa	0	0.07401	0.20093	0.23449	0.39597	0.57782	0.97153	1.64402	2.18464	2.39617
Pn	0	4.32236	2.94371	2.73724	2.0591	1.59962	1.02925	0.55645	0.35849	0.30404
difference	0	4.24835	2.74278	2.50275	1.66313	1.0218	0.05772	-1.0876	-1.8262	-2.0921
status	0	1	1	1	1	1	0	-1	-1	-1

Fig. 5. The status of SMTP server, $H(P_a)$ and $H(P_n)$

In the above calculation process, $H(P_n)$ is NPP entropy, $H(P_a)$ is APP entropy. We prove that the description of Section 3.2 is correct: the smaller the entropy value, the number of normal packets pair will be greater; the smaller the value, the fewer the number representing the abnormal packets. Then, we will add $H(P_a)$ and $H(P_n)$ in the same time slide window T_w, and calculate the status value to behalf the SMTP server status. Finally, the SMTP server status, $H(P_a)$ and $H(P_n)$ are show in Fig. 5.

4   Conclusions

In this paper, we propose a new approach for detecting SMTPFA based on entropy measurement. By using this method, we can quickly analyse the current status of the SMTP server, and determine whether the server is attacked by SMTPFA or not. This approach can not only be applied to different SMTP servers, but also monitor the real-time status of SMTP server. Finally, according to the status value of STMP server by using the entropy measurement we proposed, it can detect SMTPFA easily and quickly.

Acknowledgements. This work was supported in part by Asia University, Taiwan, under Grant 100-asia-34, also by the National Science Council, Taiwan, Republic of China, under Grant NSC99-2221-E-468-011.

References

1. O'Donnell, A.J.: The Evolutionary Microcosm of Stock Spam. IEEE Security & Privacy, 70–75 (2007)
2. Bass, T., Watt, G.: A simple framework for filtering queued SMTP e-mail. In: MILCOM 1997 Proceedings, vol. 3, pp. 1140–1144 (1997)
3. Shannon, C.E.: A mathematical theory of communication. Bell System Technical Journal 27, 379–423, 623–656 (1948)
4. Information Entropy,
   http://www.absoluteastronomy.com/topics/Information_entropy
5. Postel, J.B.: A Simple Mail Transfer Protocol. RFC821 (1982)
6. Klensin, J.: Simple Mail Transport Protocol. RFC2821 (2001)
7. Myers, J., Rose, M.: Post Office Protocol - Version 3. RFC 1939 (1996)
8. Moore, K.: Simple Mail Transfer Protocol (SMTP) Service Extension for Delivery Status Notifications (DSNs). RFC 3461 (2003)
9. Russell, S., Norvig, P.: Artificial Intelligence - A Modern Approach 3/E (2011)
10. Bass, T., Freyre, A., Gruber, D., Watt, G.: E-Mail Bombs and Countermeasure: Cyber Attack on Availability and Brand Integrity. IEEE Network 12(2), 10–17 (1998)
11. Weaver, W., Shannon, C.E.: The Mathematical Theory of Communication (1949); republished in paperback (1963)
12. Wang, X., Chellappan, S., Boyer, P., Xuan, D.: On the effectiveness of secure overlay forwarding systems under intelligent distributed DoS attacks. IEEE Transactions on Parallel and Distributed Systems, 619–632 (2006)

A Multi-constraint Resource Search Algorithm for P2P-SIP Conference Services

Hui-Kai Su[1,*], Wen-Hsu Hsiao[2], Jian-Ting Pan[3], Chen-Hung Liao[4],
Kim-Joan Chen[3], and Chien-Min Wu[5]

[1] Dept. of Electrical Engineering, National Formosa University,
Yun-Lin 632, Taiwan
hksu@nfu.edu.tw
[2] Department of Computer Science and Information Technology, WuFeng University,
Chia-Yi 621, Taiwan
[3] Dept. of Electrical Engineering, National Chung-Cheng University,
Chia-Yi 621, Taiwan
[4] Telecommunications Laboratories, Chunghwa Telecom Co. Ltd., Taoyuan, Taiwan
[5] Dept. of Computer Science and Information Engineering, Nan-Hua University,
Chia-Yi 622, Taiwan

Abstract. Peer-to-peer conference is an interactive multi-users conferencing application that improves the issues of concentrated loading, single-point failure and expensive infrastructure cost for the traditional centralized conference model, according to the conference resource shared by each other. The benefit of non-centralized system can be achieved by using P2P-SIP. However, unlike the traditional centralized architecture, the conference resource is provided by each peer user. How to search the heterogeneous resource efficiently is a key point in the dynamic and distributed environment. Thus, we proposed a multi-constraint resource search algorithm for P2P-SIP conferencing services. In the full distributed environment, users can search a usable resource to reduce the call-setup time and save the conferencing cost according to the conferencing scale and the quality requirements.

Keywords: Peer-to-Peer, Session Initiation Protocol, Resource Search Algorithm.

1 Introduction

In the centralized architecture of the traditional multimedia conferencing model, several high-performance equipment has to be purchased by the conferencing service provider. With the user increasing, the loading of the conference server becomes heavy. More conference high-end servers should be deployed to support a highly-scale conferencing service and keep the conference quality. Thus, the conferencing service provider has to invest more money in the conferencing-service infrastructure.

According to the Peer-to-Peer (P2P) concept, users share their resource to each other. Consequently, the infrastructure cost of conference servers can be reduced.

---

* Corresponding author.

J.J. Park et al. (Eds.): NPC 2012, LNCS 7513, pp. 360–372, 2012.
© IFIP International Federation for Information Processing 2012

Additionally, the P2P conference system is unlike the centralized conference system. Due to no centralized conference server to handle conferences, the conference resource have to be looked up by using a P2P resource discovery mechanism, e.g., participants' address, available P2P focus and available P2P mixer, etc. Based on the P2P resource discovery mechanism, the available conference resource can be searched out by cooperating with other peers. However, although P2P conference service can be achieve by P2P-SIP related works[1–3], the present scheme cannot support constraint-based conference resource discovery. In a heterogeneous P2P conference environment, the capacity of each peer is difference. How to search out an available and feasible resource efficiently to satisfy the conference requirements is very significant in a real environment.

This paper proposed a multi-constraint resource search algorithm for P2P-SIP conferencing services in a heterogeneous overlay network. According to the peer capacity, peers are classified and managed with an abstract and logical tree structure. The specified tree structure can provide a conference resource discovery functionality with multiple constraints. Thus, the resource requirements of a conference can be satisfied and supported by other peers, such P2P focus and P2P mixer.

2 Background

Recently, multimedia conferencing service is more and more popular. The IETF has organized some related working groups that develop standards for multimedia conferencing and discuss related issues. Many RFC documents were proposed, such as RFC 4353[4], RFC 4579[5] and RFC 5850[6]. The architecture models, components and protocols of SIP conference were discussed.

P2P SIP composes of the characteristics of P2P distributed architecture and centralized client-server model. The resource locating and message transmission services for full distributed environment is provided by using an P2P overlay network. The advantages of decentralization, low cost, high robustness and high scalability are included. The problems of single-point failure and loading concentration can be reduced. Nowadays, P2PSIP is based on the SIP-over-P2P framework. a P2P protocol, e.g., Chord, provides resource store and discovery for SIP. The registration and addressing of SIP users are achieved. Other applications can also be applied.

P2PSIP working group was organized in 2007, and several related drafts were proposed. The working group make efforts in the development of P2PSIP standards. The reference [7] proposed a resource discovery mechanism with P2PSIP. The mechanism can store the resource information into the distributed P2P network dynamically. However, the peer heterogeneity is not considered. An unsuitable resource may be searched out to support a large multimedia conference. Consequently, its quality would be unstable and the conference may be crashed.

3 A Multi-constraint Resource Search Algorithm for P2P-SIP VoIP Services

In this section, the design of multi-constraint resource search algorithm over the P2P network is proposed. The resource discovery in DHT can be divided into two methods usually. The first method is random walk[8]. The nodes would randomly probe their neighbors to ask if they are resource providers. This method brings a huge network overhead and inefficient search. The second one is putting resource information and corresponding index into the overlay, then getting resource information by retrieving the index from the overlay, such as [9].

In addition, no service discovery usage standard for RELOAD was proposed. In order to find a suitable resource for P2P-SIP in the distributed network, P2P-SIP Working Group also proposed the related draft for service discovery, i.e., Recursive Distributed Rendezvous (ReDiR)[7].

In [7], it discovers the nearest resource with Node-ID because the resource is distributed and discovered based on Node-ID. Furthermore, ReDiR requires O(log n) messages (or discovery hops) to find resource. In the situation, the searched resource could not support the conference sometimes, such as limiting in its mixing capacity or transport capacity. The resource discovery procedure may be re-performed until the suitable resource is found. For conferencing, it means the call setup time increases with the messages (or discovery hops) and peer capacity. Thus, we propose a multi-constraint resource search algorithm to reduce the call setup time.

On the other hand, the heterogeneity and availability of resource is a important subject for dynamic peer-to-peer network. As an improvement, we also develop a dynamic resource registration method to achieve distributed loading and efficient discovery.

3.1   System Environment

The P2P-SIP multimedia conference network is formed by peers, and the logical conferencing overlay network is constructed. Each peer connects to other peer in the overlay and maintains the overlay routing information by the DHT. Some peers also have to provide the storage space to storage the index information which is assigned by the DHT.

Peers can share the resource to other peer in the overlay. It can be a role such as a P2P Focus or P2P Mixer in the multimedia conference network.

- *Focus* deals with the session initialization, management, and coordination of conferences. It does not require complex computing, but need to handle all of conference sessions.
- *Mixer* provides the functionalities of video and audio mixing for conferences. Moreover, it also handles the receiving and delivering of video and audio streams for all conference participants.

In the centralized system, powerful conference servers would be deployed. On the contrary, the capacity of each P2P-SIP peer is weak and heterogeneous. In P2P-SIP, a peer which has enough capability to be a Focus or Mixer has to register information to the overlay. When a User Agent want to make a conference, the resource discovery mechanism is used to find suitable resource and establish this session. Figure 1 illustrates an example that a caller makes a conference. (1) P2P conference servers, i.e., P2P Focus and P2P Mixer, register their information to the P2P overlay network. (2) When the caller wants to create a conference, he will discovery the conference resource that provides the functionality of Focus and Mixer. (3) Based on the resource discovery

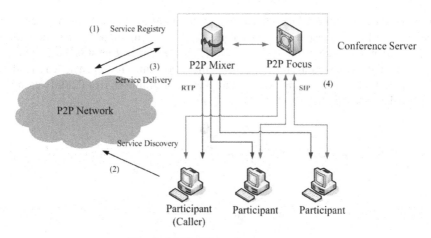

Fig. 1. A P2P-SIP conference system

mechanism, the suitable P2P Focus and P2P Mixer are selected. (4) Finally, the selected P2P Focus and P2P mixer handle the conference operations, such as conference initialization, release, media processing, etc.

3.2   Resource Indexing

The capability of resources which are provided by peers change dynamically with the resource assignment or reconfiguration. If resource provider registers the index of current capability to the overlay, the caller might find the older resource index since the overlay information has not been updated rapidly. In order to avoid this problem, the resource registration has to find and delete the last record. Therefore, it may involve high network overhead and long resource search time due to the dynamical available resource information.

Unlike the previous method, we define two class for resource capability, fixed attribute and dynamic attribute. Fixed attribute is the maximal capability of resource, and the dynamic attribute is available capability of resource. The all attributes show in Table 1.

Table 1. The attributes of service resource

	P2P Focus	P2P Mixer
Fixed attributes	Maximal connection capacity	1) Maximal mixing capacity, 2) maximal transport capacity, and 3) highest SVC-layer surpporting
Dynamic attributes	Available connection capacity	1) Available mixing capacity, and 2) available transport capacity

Table 1 shows the attributes of P2P Focus and P2P Mixer. In our P2P-SIP conference service, each service has its service index, and builds a *Constraint Tree* by the fixed attribute. The *Constraint Tree* adopts the concept of range search. Using a tree-based data structure which called data partitioning tree, can divide the resource attribute into different segment. For example, the P2P Focus supposes that the system can provide maximal connection capacity to 12 connections, at least is 3 connections, and it can build a Constraint Tree as Fig. 2. In the Constraint Tree, each node is a index, called Node-Index. By the same way, Figure 3 is a Constraint Tree of P2P Mixer, it has three fixed attributes.

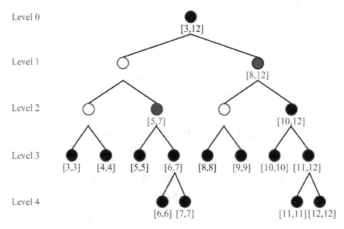

Fig. 2. A Constraint Tree for P2P focus

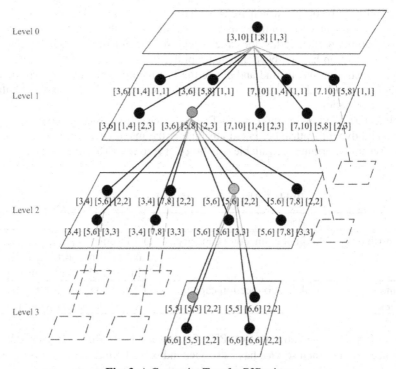

Fig. 3. A Constraint Tree for P2P mixer

3.3   Resource Registration

If the peer in the overlay shares the resource to others, it has to register the index which includes service name, resource attributes, and the location information to the overlay network. In our system, we use DHT to maintain a structured overlay. Keys, correspondingly, play the role of indices of this database. We use "Hash(Service Name; Node Index)" as a key. Node Index, the fixed attribute which is provided by peer belong to leaf node in the Constraint Tree. For example, Hash(P2P Focus; 9) indicates that a P2P Focus can provide 9-connections resource to support conferences.

Unlike the traditional segment tree, when a peer receive the information belongs to it. If the peer is not the root of Constraint Tree, then it duplicates the information to its parent node. In this way, each node keeps the information of its children just as Fig. 4.

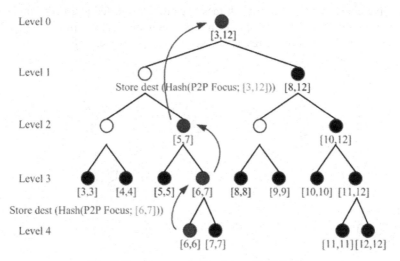

Fig. 4. The resource duplications of P2P Focus

3.4   Resource Search

In traditional P2P-SIP system, users create a conference through resource discovery because users are unaware of where the available conference resources are. Resource discovery in our approach can find the feasible conference resource to support the conference according to the Constraint Tree information.

First, each resource requester establishes a Constraint Tree according to the service type, P2P Focus or P2P Mixer. Second, resource requester finds the tree node on the constraints of resource requirements. For example, a caller want to make a conference with five participants, he has to look up a P2P Focus which can handle five connections at least. In the Constraint Tree, many tree nodes may satisfy the requirement, but the minimal tree nodes will be selected in order to minimize query messages. Third, the index of each selected tree node is converted into Resource-ID (key) by DHT. Resource requester stores the keys of the selected tree nodes to its register.

The resource requester selects *s* Resource-IDs (keys) from its register and send the Fetch messages to the *s* destinations in parallel. *s* is a parameter which is assigned by system or users. For example, it sends one Fetch message when *s*=1. If *s* is larger than the size of its register, all of the keys in the register will be selected, and then send to the *s* destinations with the Fetch messages in parallel. If the peer which receives the Fetch message has the enough available resource, it will reply a response message to the resource requester. The response message contains the *k* resources, such as the suitable *k* P2P Focuses.

Based on [10], we propose a range query algorithm for conference resource discovery with Constraint Tree. According to [10], the node [5,7] and node [8,12] can be converted into Resource-IDs(keys), and then stored to the register. Figure 2 illustrates the Constraint Tree of a P2P Focus resource. If the requester wants to make a five-people conference, it sends Fetch messages to the selected tree nodes in the P2P Focus Constraint Tree. The selected tree nodes which are [5,7] and [8,12] in Fig. 2 can guarantee the P2P Focus of the responded keys can support the conference.

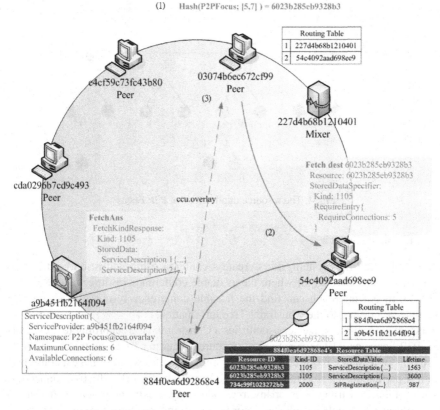

Fig. 5. The data flow of service discovery with P2P focus

Figure 5 illustrates the data flow of resource discovery. The requester wants find a P2P Focus that can support five to seven connections. (1) The key is calculated with a Hash function. (2) Based on DHT mechanism which is Chord in our system, the Fetch message can be delivered to P2P Focus whose capacity is between five and seven. (3) The peer (tree node [5,7]) replies a response message include service (resource) description to the requester, i.e., the service descriptions of k P2P Focuses.

 .The requester receives the response, and then contacts with the resource candidate immediately according to the result, or waits until all response messages are received. From the response results, if no peer can support the conference, the next s Resource-IDs (keys) from its register would be selected again. By the same way, the suitable peer would be looked up, finally. However, if the register is empty and no suitable peer can be selected, it means that no peer can support the exacting conference requirement.

4   System Operation

In this section, the flow diagram of a P2P-SIP conference setup is explained. Figure 6 illustrates the process of the call setup.

1. The caller has to set the conference profile before call setup.
2. Using our multi-constraint resource search algorithm, caller can find the available P2P Focus from the overlay network.
3. And then the caller sends a SIP-invite message which is a request for create a P2P-SIP conference to the Focus. At the meanwhile, the caller send a list which contains all the conference member by SDP [11] through the SIP-invite message according to RFC 5366 [12].
4. If Focus receives the request, it has to find members in the overlay according to the list in the SIP-invite message. And then it find the IP address of all members through the overlay which is create by DHT.
5. In addition, Focus has to search a suitable P2P Mixer using our mechanism from the overlay according to the conference profile.
6. When Focus finds a suitable Mixer, it send a SIP-invite message as the request to the Mixer.
7. If Mixer accepts the SIP-invite request, it response a 200 OK message to the Focus which contains the Media Mixing Level information by SDP.
8. After the above process, Focus send SIP-invite messages to all members. The messages include the information about Mixer.
9. All callees join the conference and establish the media streaming connection with Mixer according to the above information.

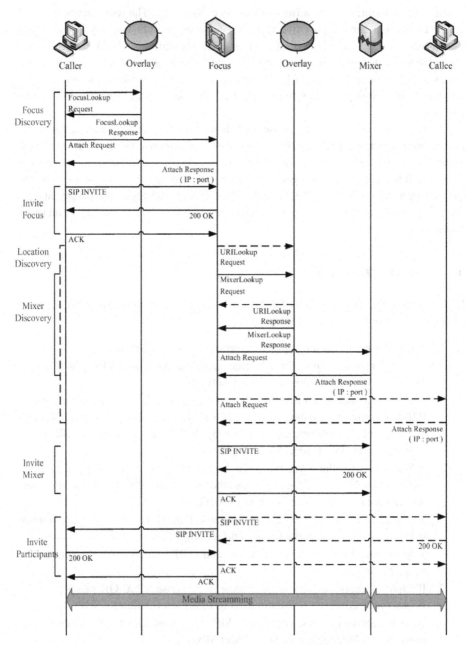

Fig. 6. The message sequence chart of a P2P-SIP conference setup

5 Simulation and Results

5.1 Simulation Environment

Our multi-constraint resource search algorithm based on RELOAD was implemented on Oversim [13, 14]. Oversim is a P2P simulation framework which is based on OMNet++ [15].

The heterogeneous P2P conference overlay network was simulated. There are 1000 nodes in our simulated overlay. We carried out the simulations on heterogeneous capacity scenarios. The resource density of P2P Focus is 20% in the overlay, and the P2P Mixer is same. But the two conditions are independent. For instance, a peer could be a P2P Focus and P2P Mixer simultaneously. And the DHT is the Chord using 160-bits SHA-1 to hash the key. Table 2 shows the distribution of resources which include the range and the attributes in the overlay. Assume each peer in the overlay creates h calls one hour, and then the conference arrival rate is $1000h$.

Table 2. The resources of conference service

Node class	Attribute	Value	Random Distribution
P2P focus	Maximal connection capacity	[3 50]	Uniform
P2P mixer	Maximal mixing capacity	[2 200]	Uniform
	Maximal transport capacity	[1 50]	Uniform
	highest SVC-layer surpporting	[1 3]	Uniform
Peer	-	-	-

Table 3. The conference profile

Attribute	Value
Conference member	3 40 participants
Frame quality	1 3 layers
Session time	60 180 minutes

Table 4. The resource prfile of P2P mixer

Resolution	Frame rate (frames/sec)	Quality	Bitrate (Mbps)	Occupied mixing resource
352x240	6.25	1	0.4	1
		2	0.75	2
		3	1.2	4

We randomly generate a Conference Profile as a call. The different Conference Profile maps to the different value of resource. Table 3 and Table 4 show Conference Profile and Resource Profile Mapping, respectively. In Table 4, Bitrate is the requirement of transport capacity and Mixing is the requirement of Mixing capacity. The levels of Quality are defined from Bitrate and Mixing. It can provide more higher quality frame when the resources in overlay achieve the requirement. We discover the resources in the Resource Profile to setup the conference using our mechanism.

We simulate 12 hours and there are three phases in our simulation. It builds the overlay network topology in the initial phase. The transition phase begin to simulate the behavior of P2P-SIP conference. Finally, the measurement phase simulate the behavior of the call and measure the simulation data simultaneously.

5.2   Simulation Results and Comparison

We implement the multi-constrain search algorithm by the P2P simulator and compare with other designs. One is ReDiR-based mechanism, which is described in section 3. We preserve the original design of [7], and then we add the capacity of service information due to [7] has not the issue about capacity. It can discover the resource using its Node-ID, and then filter the resource that cannot achieve the requirement of the call. Another one is Fixed-Partition that distributes all the resources to fixed nodes. The fixed node is similar to index server in client/server architecture. The two designs also use Table 3 and Table 4 as its conference profile.

The caller finds the suitable resources with search algorithm. If the peer has enough capacity to satisfy the caller, it response its IP address and port number to the caller. The caller will pick the most satisfied one to send SIP-invite message. Figure 7 illustrates the related performance. The definition of s is described in section 3.4. The spilt means how many index nodes the method of Fixed Partition has. Furthermore, the data structure tree is a binary tree when $branch=2$.

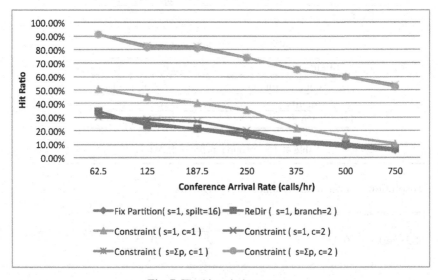

Fig. 7. The hit ratio in one step

In Fig. 7, we can see that our algorithm have high probability with one hit. Especially the method with s=parallel which means the caller can get many resource responses than s=1. As increasing the utilization of resource, the hit rate will be lower because there is no accurately way to find available resource in the distributed system. On the contrary, we use the Constraint Tree to prior capacity as a classification. Although the available resource decrease, we still can find the resource we need quickly unless there are no resources in the overlay.

In Fig.8, the average search steps for find a suitable resource is lower than other designs. It is related with the call setup time. This is because, our algorithm can avoid unnecessary search by the Constraint Tree. Even though the resources are serious shortage, we can use the range search to increase our efficiency.

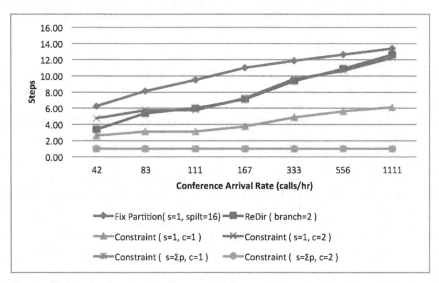

Fig. 8. The average search steps for looking a suitable resource up

6   Conclusion

In this paper, we proposed a multi-constraint resource search algorithm for P2P-SIP conference. According to the multi-constraint resource search algorithm, not only the hit ratio of P2P usable resource would be improved, but also the overall conference setup time would be reduced. The simulation shows that our proposed method has high efficiency for resource search. Comparing with other algorithms, the efficiency of P2P-conference resource search can be improved. Even if the conference arrival rate is increasing, it can also find the suitable resource efficiently. Additionally, our mechanism also has good flexibility; it can be extended to other structured peer-to-peer systems, such as Pastry, CAN, etc.

Acknowledgment. We would like to thank the National Science Council (NSC) in Taiwan. This research was supported in part by the NSC under the grant number NSC100-2221-E-150-077.

References

[1] Jennings, C., Lowekamp, B., Rescorla, E., Baset, S., Schulzrinne, H.: Resource Location and Discovery (RELOAD) Base Protocol (2010),
http://draft-ietf-p2psip-base-08.txt

[2] Oredope, A., Liotta, A., Roper, I., Morphett, J.: Peer-to-peer session initiation protocol in highly volatile environments. In: Next Generation Mobile Applications, Services and Technologies (NGMAST 2008), September 16-19, pp. 76–82 (2008)

[3] Baumgart, I.: P2pns: A secure distributed name service for p2psip. In: Sixth Annual IEEE International Conference on Pervasive Computing and Communications, PerCom 2008, pp. 480–485 (March 2008)

[4] Rosenberg, J.: A framework for conferencing with the session initiation protocol (SIP). RFC 4353 (2006)

[5] Johnston, A., Levin, O.: Session Initiation Protocol (SIP) Call Control - Conferencing for User Agents. RFC 4579 (2006)

[6] Mahy, R., Sparks, R., Rosenberg, J., Petrie, D., Johnston, A.: A Call Control and Multi-Party Usage Framework for the Session Initiation Protocol (SIP). RFC 5850 (May 2010)

[7] Maenpaa, J., Camarillo, G.: Service Discovery Usage for Resource Location and Discovery, RELOAD (2012),
http://draft-ietf-p2psip-service-discovery-05.txt

[8] Lv, Q., Cao, P., Cohen, E., Li, K., Shenker, S.: Search and replication in unstructured peer-to-peer networks. In: Proceedings of the 16th International Conference on Supercomputing, ICS 2002, pp. 84–95. ACM, New York (2002)

[9] Buford, J., Wang, A., Hei, X., Liu, Y., Ross, K.: Discovery of in-band streaming services in peer-to-peer overlays. In: Global Telecommunications Conference, GLOBECOM 2007, pp. 242–247. IEEE (2007)

[10] Zheng, C., Shen, G., Li, S., Shenker, S.: Distributed segment tree: Support range query and cover query over dht. In: Proceedings of the Fifth International Workshop on Peer-to-Peer Systems, IPTPS (February 2006)

[11] Handley, M., Jacobson, V., Perkins, C.: SDP: Session Description Protocol. RFC 4566 (2006)

[12] Camarillo, G., Johnston, A.: Conference Establishment Using Request-Contained Lists in the Session Initiation Protocol (SIP). RFC 5366 (2008)

[13] The OverSim P2P Simulator, http://www.oversim.org/

[14] Baumgart, I., Heep, B., Krause, S.: Oversim: A flexible overlay network simulation framework. In: 2007 IEEE Global Internet Symposium, pp. 79 –84 (November 11, 2007)

[15] The OMNeT++ Network Simulation Framework, http://www.omnetpp.org/

The Effects of Governmental Subsidy on the Quality of Education in Taiwan's Private Universities and Colleges

Ching-Hui Shih

Department of Accounting and Information Systems, Asia University
500, Liufeng Rd., Wufeng, Taichung, Taiwan 41354 (ROC)
chshih@asia.edu.tw

Abstract. The government arranges subsidies for private colleges annually with excellent academic performance. In order to justify if government subsidies can enhance the quality of education, this paper will investigate the relationship between governmental subsidy and education quality of Taiwanese private universities and colleges through data envelopment analysis and regression analysis on research data. Empirical results for the principles of the current government allocation of funds to provide advice, expect to enhance the quality of education, more limited government resources for the best allocation.

Keywords: governmental subsidy, educational quality, DEA.

1 Introduction

In view of the need for innovation and knowledge in the 21st century, countries around the world have been actively nurturing talents and this task has inevitably fall into the hands of universities around the world. Universities have become the place for competing for knowledge, innovation and human resource, thus causing the competitiveness of a country's university to be the index for the country's national competitiveness. Development of higher education in Taiwan has gone from 4 universities in 1949 to 163 universities in 2011 and total number of students has also increased from 5000 to 1,340,000. There are 54 public universities (33.13%) with 440,000 students (33.84%) enrolled in it and 109 private universities (66.87%) with 900,000 students enrolled (67.16%) (Ministry of Education Statistics 2011). These facts have shown the intention by the Taiwan government to provide better educational advancement path and higher education for more Taiwanese citizens. However, the Taiwan government is concerned if the quality of education provided to the students is able to be kept at a high level.

Article 13 of the Taiwan fundamental law of education states that "The government and the people may conduct education experiments as needed and strength research and assessment of education to improve education quality and promote education development." C.S. Wu feels that improving the quality of education not only fulfills the demands of the society, but also ensures the competitiveness of the schools is maintained at a high level, proving the importance of education quality [16].

J.J. Park et al. (Eds.): NPC 2012, LNCS 7513, pp. 373–380, 2012.
© IFIP International Federation for Information Processing 2012

Geuna and Martin pointed out in their studies that universities in Europe and Asia-Pacific are given subsidies based on the results of their performance appraisal [4]. The Taiwan government has adopted the "Private School Law" to improve the quality of education in private colleges and reduce the advantage in resources available that public colleges have over private colleges. The government also arranges subsidies for private colleges annually and offers scholarships to students with excellent academic performance. Annual subsidy for private colleges has increased by 46.43% over the years, from NT$ 4.7 billion in 1996 to NT$ 6.9 billion in 2009. However, there has been a lack of literatures discussing if the subsidies are beneficial for improving education quality.

There are many papers in Taiwan discussing about the education quality in Taiwan. There are papers discussing about education quality assurance [12] [1] [8] [15] [5] and theory to education quality [16] [17] [2] [3] [14]. However, there is a lack of papers verifying the effect of government subsidies has on education quality. Therefore, this paper will perform research on Taiwan private universities and discuss about the relationship between government subsidy and education quality.

2   Literature Review

2.1   Reward, Subsidy Revenue

According to "Implementation Regulations for Establishing an Accounting System Regarding School Endowment Corporations and Private Schools" and "Regulations under the agreement for Establishing an Accounting System Regarding School Endowment Corporations and Private Schools", schools that have accepted donations and subsidies from government agencies, local organizations or individuals have to be categorized by the school as "revenue from donations and subsidies". Subsidies from government agencies have to be further categorized as "subsidy revenue" and donations from foreign government agencies, local organizations and individuals have to be further categorized as "donation revenue".

The Ministry of Education in Taiwan has set the working standard for the audit of rewards and subsidies for private schools. The grant of rewards is evaluated based on the performance, administrative operations, school-running character, reward implementation performance and policy performance. Subsidies are divided into school size subsidy and overall resource subsidy. The 2011 Ministry of Education award for administrative Affairs in Private Schools development plan states that subsidies takes up 20% of the total funds and rewards takes up 80% of the total funds. This shows that the Ministry of Education are emphasizing on school performance, causing every university to perform at its best to obtain the rewards. Schools can use this as an evidence of excellent school performance and attract students to enroll.

Lai Y.U., Hu W.H., Kuo C.J. pointed out in their research that the better the school performance of private universities, the more the government subsidy will be and these lead to more disclosure of financial information. [7] Therefore, there is a positive relationship between school performance of private universities and government subsidies. Moreover, financial information disclosure of private universities and colleges also has a positive relationship with government subsidies.

2.2   Endowment

Research results by Lin C.L., Ho Y.c has shown that there is a positive correlation between information transparency and endowments and there is a negative correlation between endowment and financial manipulation. [10] Therefore, higher transparency of financial information results in lesser chance of mismatch in endowment records due to the positive correlation of the two. However, higher level of financial manipulation will cause a negative perception from donators and potential donators due to the negative correlation.

Lai Y.U., Hu W.H., Kuo C.J. pointed out in their research that private universities and colleges performance does not have a significant correlation with private donations and financial records have shown that private donations have not reached a significant level for private universities and colleges. [7]

It is a common for large scale organizations to attract people for private donations due to their access to more resources allowing them to easily become the concern of the public. Lin C.L., C.C. Hsieh feels that the scale of the organization will affect the endowments of not-for-profit organizations.   [9]

2.3   Education Quality

Sallis feels that it is difficult to judge the quality of education because quality of education is a subjective concept. [11] Juran pointed out that education quality is the requirement for achieving the final objective of education and fits the requirement of legal law. [6] It allows the students receiving the education to be effective in their production and services in the work force.

Wang R.J. thinks that in addition to teaching and research, higher education quality standards should also include administrative and management activities of the university.

The current trend in colleges is being able to provide functions that focus on teachings, researches and services. Therefore, Wu C.S. reckons that education quality should be judged by "learning quality", "teaching quality", "administrative quality", "environment quality", "research quality" and "social service quality". [16]

Yang F.F., C.Y. Huang performed regression analysis using variables such as ratio of teachers with doctorate title, number of publications by department teachers, faculty academic research funds, student-teacher ratio, amount of resources in the library per students and equipment funds per student. [13]

3   Research Methods

3.1   Data Source and Sampling

The main objective of this paper is to discuss the relationship of Taiwanese private university subsidy and education quality. The data source will come from the official website of Ministry of Education and the financial statement page of various universities. Source of the data comes from 109 private universities and data will 2006 till 2008 will be sampled. There will be a total of 309 data samples excluding incomplete data.

3.2   Variables

I. Subsidy

All subsidies should only be used by the school and the main source of the subsidies comes from government agencies. Data for this subsidy can be acquired from financial reports made public by the school's accountant.

II. Education Quality

Judgment of education quality is difficult because education quality is a subjective concept. [14] This paper uses data envelopment analysis and judge the education quality based on concepts coming from the first article of University Act, "Universities shall encourage academic research, cultivating talent, enhancing culture, serving society and accelerating the development of the country." Therefore, factors used to judge the quality of education includes teaching, research and services. These factors are similar to the indications for evaluation of teachers in every school. For "teaching", number of students will be the measureable variable and for "research", the measureable variable will be the cooperative education revenue from National Science Council and Industry-University research funds. Lastly, the measureable variable for "services" will be the promotion revenue. Judgment concept factors are divided into manpower and funding. The quality and quantity of teachers will be the main factors affecting manpower. Quantity of the teachers refers to the number of teachers with position higher than assistant professors and quality of teachers refers to the degree the teachers hold. Finally, library resources, recurrent expenditures and capital expenditure will be the factors affecting funding.

III. Endowments

All endowments coming from foreign government agencies, local organizations and individual donations have to be classified as endowments by the school receiving them. The main sources are the founder or affiliated companies and a small portion of endowments comes from alumni and the public. This small portion should be made public on the report by the school accountant.

IV. Scale of the School

Fang J.J. pointed out the scale of the school will affect the quality of education. [5] Research will be done based on this fact and the scale of the school will be directly proportional to the total assets of the school.

V. Nature of the School

The schools will be categorized into 1) universities in general and 2) technical and vocational training universities.

VI. Teaching Expenditure

All expenditures used on teaching, research, guidance and discipline will be included and this data shall be made public by the school's accountant.

3.3   Assumptions

Guena and Martin stated that evaluation results of university performance are used as indications for government subsidy for schools in Europe and Asia-pacific. [7] Based on the working standards for the audit of rewards and subsidies for private schools by Ministry of Education in Taiwan, 80% of the total subsidy is allocated based on indications such as "university evaluations", "education character", "administrative performance" and "planning and execution of funding". Therefore, if a school is capable of receiving more subsidies, this indicates that they have a better education quality. It can be deduced that subsidy income has a positive correlation with education quality.

Assumption 1. Taiwan private university's subsidy has a positive correlation with education quality.

3.4   Empirical Models

The model below will be used to verify if the previous assumption stands.

$$EQ = \beta_0 + \beta_1 GSR + \beta_2 DR + \beta_3 Size + \beta_4 TE + \beta_5 SC + \varepsilon$$

In the above model, EQ refers to education quality, GSR is grants and subsidies received from the government, DR is donations received, Size is the size of the school, TE is teaching expenses, SC is the school character and lastly ε is error term.

4   Empirical Results and Analysis

4.1   Descriptive Statistics and Correlation Coefficient Analysis Results

Table 1 show the descriptive statistics results of each variable. From the table, it can be observed that the mean value for education quality of the private universities is 0.8258. The government subsidy has a mean value of NT$150,319 thousand. The maximum amount of subsidy is NT$625,968 thousand and the minimum amount of subsidy is NT$0. The average amount of endowments is NT$53,971 thousand, maximum amount of endowments is NT$625,968 thousand and minimum amount of endowments is NT$0. The size of the school has a mean value of NT$4,042,319 thousand. The largest size is NT$22,345,737 thousand and the smallest size is NT$1,046 thousand. The mean amount of teaching expenses is NT$686,140 thousands. The maximum amount of teaching expenses is NT$2,310,121 thousand and the minimum amount of teaching expenses is NT$64,267 thousand.

From Table 1, the average government subsidy of NT$150,319 thousand for private universities takes up only 21.91% of the average teaching expenses (NT$686,140 thousand), taking up a small portion of the teaching expenses. Donations from board of directors make up for the majority of the endowments for a newly established university in 2007. The average endowment over the three years is NT$53,971 thousand and it only makes up for 7.87% of the average teaching expenses (NT$686,140 thousand), taking up a small portion of teaching expenses too.

Table 1. Descriptive Statistics for each variable

Variable	Unit	Min. Value	Max. Value	Mean	Standard Deviation
GSR	NT$ thousand	0.000	625,968	150,319.33	118,945.141
DR	NT$ thousand	0.000	3,210,620	53,970.65	267,512.390
Size	NT$ thousand	1,046	22,345,737	4,042,318.86	4,011,100.692
TE	NT$ thousand	64,267	2,310,121	686,139.98	453,544.696
SC				1.67	0.471

GSR: Grants and Subsidies Received, DR: Donations Received,EQ: Education Quality
DEA: DEA efficiency value,Size: Size of the school,SC: School character,TE: Teaching Expenses

4.2   Regression Analysis Results

Table 2 shows the empirical results based on assumption 1. The coefficient after adjustment to regression mode is found to be 0.069 and F value is 5.567 (P value is 0.0000). The standardized coefficient is -0.237 and this shows that Taiwan private universities' subsidy has a negative correlation with education quality. This result does not match with assumption 1 that "Taiwan private university's subsidy has a positive correlation with education quality." This means that higher subsidy from the government does not lead to better education quality.

On the controllable variables, the regression coefficient for donations is 0.028 and this shows an insignificant level. This means that donations do not have a huge influence on education quality. Regression coefficient of school size is -0.252, showing a significant level. This means that the bigger the size of the school, the worse the education quality is. Teaching expenses have a regression coefficient of 0.432 and this significant level means higher teaching expenses leads to better education quality. Lastly, school character has regression value of 0.107 and this value is of low significance. This means that the character of the school has no influence on the education quality.

Table 2. Empirical results for regression analysis of independent variables and education quality

Variable	Non-standardized coefficient	Standardized Coefficient	T Value	VIF
Intercept	0.741		13.985[***]	
Subsidy	-3.490	-0.237	-2.237[**]	3.702
Donations	1.821	0.028	0.431	1.376
School Size	-1.101	-0.252	-2.800[***]	2.677
Teaching Expenses	1.669	0.432	3.971[***]	3.907
School Character	0.040	0.107	1.587	1.491

Note: R^2 value after adjustment is 0.069. F value is 5.567, $p < 0.0001$ [*]P<0.05 , [**]P<0.01

5   Conclusions and Suggestions

5.1   Conclusions

A total of 103 private universities and colleges from 2006 – 2008 are sampled in this research to investigate the relationship between subsidy and education quality. Research results have shown that private universities have negative correlations between subsidy and education quality. This correlation does not match with the assumption that subsidy and education quality has positive correlations and this can be a pondering subject. One of the reasons is there are currently 109 private universities and there are a total of 163 universities including public universities. The intense competition between the universities and the decrease from 300,000 to 200,000 in the number of students enrolling in universities has caused every school to gain crisis awareness. They believe they have to enhance their education quality by recruiting high quality students to improve the performance of the school. Therefore, every school offers hefty scholarships to attract good quality students to the school. Moreover, schools have encouraged teachers and professors to strive for funding such as subsidies from National Science Council and Industry-University Cooperation Funds. Another possible reason is government subsidy does not have a significant effect on the school expenses to improve education quality. The average amount of subsidy per school is NT\$150,319 and the average expenses per school is NT\$686,140. The subsidy takes up 21.91% of the total expenses, showing an insignificant effect on the expenses.

Control variables "teaching expenses" and "education quality" have a positive correlation. "Size of school" and "education quality" has a negative correlation. These conclusions have shown that "teaching expenses" and "size of school" are two factors affecting education quality. Endowments and education quality have shown a negative correlation but the level is insignificant.

5.2   Suggestions

(1) Review the Allocation of Funding to Gain Maximum Benefit
In 2011, the Ministry of Education has split funding into subsidy and rewards. Subsidies are further split into subsidy for size of school and general resources subsidy. These subsidies take up 20% of the total funding. Rewards are split into evaluation performance, school character, administrative operation, reward subsidy operation performance and policy performance. These take up 80% of the total funding. This distribution does not have a significant effect in improving education quality. Therefore, the government has to reconsider the distribution to achieve maximum benefits.

(2) Encourage Public Donations to Gain Finance
The paper has shown that donations from the public are relatively low compared to other donations. Every school has to improve their transparency and promote the school's advantage. Schools can also either work together with companies of the same idea or create school enterprises. This will improve the revenue of the school and combine theory with practical work, allowing for a win-win situation.

(3) Strengthen Financial Autonomy to Pursue Sustainable Development
With the country facing increasingly difficult finance, the government has decreased the subsidies towards higher education. Therefore, Taiwanese universities are encouraged to raise funds to improve the finance of the universities. The best solution is to couple traditional basic researches with consideration for future finance development. Schools should strengthen their applied research field and commercialize the knowledge such as offering short-term professional courses, various job training or technology consulting services. The funding received will be a hefty amount and will be able to compensate for the lack of government subsidies.

References

1. Chan, Y.: A study on the quality assurance in the European higher education area. Educational Policy Forum 10(1), 1–50 (2007)
2. Chen, Y.S.: The research of education quality. Quality Magazine. Chinese Society for Quality 44(2), 75–78 (2008)
3. Fang, J.J.: A study on the size of the school and education quality. Educational Resources and Research 27, 51–57 (1999)
4. Geuna, A., Martin, B.R.: University research evaluation and funding: an international comparison. Minerva 41, 277–304 (2003)
5. June, I.F.: The Implications of European, American and Chinese quality management models to improving education quality. Quality Magazine. Chinese Society for Quality 45(12), 17–23 (2009)
6. Juran, J.M.: A universal approach to management for quality. Quality Process 12, 19–24 (1986)
7. Lai, Y.U., Hu, W.H., Kuo, C.J.: Effects of school performance and financial information disclosure of private universities and colleges on government financial support and private donation. Educational Policy Forum 14(2), 65–89 (2011)
8. Lim, D.: Quality assurance in higher education: A study of developing countries. Ashgate, Aldershot (2001)
9. Lin, C.L., Hsieh, C.C.: Determinants of donations in not-for-profit organizations. Third-Sector Review 7, 45–71 (2007)
10. Lin, C.L., Ho, Y.C.: Implications of information Transparency and financial manipulation on donations: Empirical evidences from Not-for-profit organizations in Taiwan. Taiwan Journal of Applied Economics 86, 139–184 (2009)
11. Sallis, E.: Total quality management in education, 3rd edn. Kogan Page, London (2002)
12. Tang, Y.: A comparative study of higher education quality assurance mechanisms-In Britain, The United States, Germany, Australia, Japan, and France. Taiwan Education Review 619, 50–61 (2003)
13. Yang, F.F., Huang, C.Y.: The application of a hedonic model to a quality-adjusted price index for private universities of Taiwan. Journal of Education Studies 7, 139–174 (2006)
14. Wang, B.J.: An analysis of the contents of the evaluation model of elementary and junior high school. Journal of Education Research 91, 52–62 (2001)
15. Wang, R.J.: International experience of higher education quality management system. Taiwan Education Review 632, 21–29 (2005)
16. Wu, C.S.: The essence of education quality management. Quality Magazine. Chinese Society for Quality 42(6), 60–63 (2006)
17. Wu, C.S.: Education promoting education quality for educational competitiveness. Quality Magazine. Chinese Society for Quality 43(8), 62–66 (2007)

Examining the Effectiveness of a Distant Learning Education Program: Use of Patient Safety and Reporting Law and Ethics as Example

Chiou-Fen Lin[1], Meei-Ling Shyu[1], Meei-Shiow Lu[2], and Chung-I Huang[3,4]

[1] School of Nursing, Taipei Medical University
[2] The National Union of Nurses' Associations ROC
[3] School of Health Care Administration, Taipei Medical University
[4] Department of Technology Application and Human Resource Development,
National Taiwan Normal University, Taiwan

Abstract. This study was to test a distant learning education program aiming to improve nurses' understanding of law and ethics regarding to patient safety and reporting in Taiwan. With stratified randomized sampling of 3 medical centers, 12 regional and 50 local hospitals, 2,323 questionnaires were distributed to nurses working at the sampled hospitals. Questionnaire return rate was 99.5% with 2,312 valid returned. Based on this survey, the researchers designed a distant learning education course targeting the knowledge deficits. The results indicated that 57.7% of the sampled nurses passed the patient safety and reporting law and ethic test before the education program was instituted by the National Union of Nurses Associations. 38,603 nurses completed the distant learning course and 94.8% passed the test. This study demonstrated that the distant learning education program is effective, and should be considered as a way to improve access to and reduce cost of continuing education.

Keywords: Distant Learning Education Program, Patient Safety, Reporting, Law, Ethics.

1 Introduction

According to the Taiwanese Nursing Professional law no. 8, nurses should apply their practice license at the governing institute where the nurses practice. After register and receiving the practice license, the nurses can start nursing practice. The practicing nurses should receive certain hours of continuing education within 6 years in order to review the practice license (National Regulation Database, 2011). Therefore, all nursing associations have been providing all kinds of seminars and conferences to promote the accessibility of continuing nursing education. However, due to the time limitation and location issues, many nurses may not be able to participate in continuing education courses. Thus there is a need to explore the feasibility and effectiveness of distant learning education programs.

J.J. Park et al. (Eds.): NPC 2012, LNCS 7513, pp. 381–385, 2012.

2   Study Purposes

The purposes of this study were:

1. To assess nurses' knowledge of patient safety and reporting law and ethics.
2. To design the content of the distant learning education course on patient safety and reporting law and ethics.
3. To examine the effectiveness of the distant learning education course on patient safety and reporting law and ethics.

3   Study Methods

Multiple methods were used in this study, which included systematic review of literature, cross-sectional survey, distant learning education and outcome evaluation. This study comprised of three stages in implementation. The first stage was to appraise current literature. According to the study purposes, we searched and reviewed domestic and international nursing literature related to patient safety and reporting law and ethics. Based on the review findings, we constructed a draft of assessment tool, Knowledge Assessment of Patient Safety and Reporting Law and Ethics, to assess nurses' understanding of the topic. Expert validity and internal consistency were assessed. A pilot study was conducted with randomized sampling. Data were collected and analyzed to identify the final items of the assessment tool. The second stage was to conduct the knowledge assessment using the finalized tool. Based on the assessment results, we designed a distant learning education course specifically targeting the knowledge deficit. The third stage was to publish the distant learning education course content in the Newsletter of The National Unions of Nurses' Association, R.O.C. A post-test assessment was included. After studying the distant learning education course regarding to patient safety and reporting law and ethics, nurses completed the post-test assessment and faxed it back to The National Unions of Nurses' Association. Continuing education credits were granted to those passed the course evaluation.

4   Study Population and Sampling Method

The study population for assessing the knowledge of patient safety and reporting law and ethics was the domestic nurses working at the local or regional hospitals or medical centers (including those qualified based on the New Hospital Accreditation) for at least 6 months. Stratified random sampling method was used to select the hospitals from three different levels: medical centers (including those judged to be outstanding hospital based on the accreditation), regional hospitals (including those judged to be excellent hospital based on the accreditation), and local hospitals (including those judged to be qualified hospital based on the accreditation), according to the 2007-2009 hospital and teaching hospital accreditation results published by the Department of Health. Sample hospitals were selected from each of the three clusters to ensure the appropriate sample size in each cluster. Sample size was calculated based on the rule of having 10-20 samples in each concept or variable. Considering the size of the nursing population, we applied the large population sampling principle (Chiou, 2007) and estimated 1% attrition rate. This study planned to select about 11% of the nurses in Taiwan. We randomly selected three medical centers from 19 qualified medical centers, 12 regional hospitals from 92 regional hospitals, and 50 local hospitals from 432 local hospitals. The final sample included the day shift nurses working at one of these 65 hospitals for at least 6 months.

5   Study Materials

The demographic information was collected from the nurse participants, which included hospital, unit, professional level, years of working experience, age, gender, and educational level. The assessment tool, Knowledge Assessment of law and Ethics Regarding to Patient Safety and Reporting, included contents and performance of nurses' execution of patient safety reporting, knowledge of relevant law and ethics such as the purposes, benefits, types, ethics, and laws of reporting adverse events. A score was assigned to each item: the right answer received score 1 and the wrong answer score 0. The total scores indicate the nurse's assessment score; the higher score the better knowledge on the patient safety and reporting laws and ethics. The final tool comprised of 16 multiple choice questions. To pass the assessment, nurses should correctly answer at least 12 questions (70%).

1. Validity Test: Content validity of the assessment tool was evaluated by 10 experts of the patient safety and reporting system, from industry, regulation, and academics. The importance and suitability of each item were assessed. The content validity indexes were 0.8 and above. We also invited 5 nurses to assess the readability and wording. Revision was done to ensure the readability of the tool.
2. Reliability Test: Reliability was evaluated using the completed knowledge assessment tool from 92 nurses of a northern regional hospital. The results indicated that the internal consistency of the items, using Cronbach's α to express, ranged from 0.65 to 0.74.
3. Discriminant Validity Test: The tool, Knowledge Assessment of Patient Safety and Reporting Law and Ethics, was further assessed for discriminate power. We grouped the nurses with the highest 27% total scores into the high performance group, and the nurses with the lowest 27% total scores in the low performance group. The different score in each item between the high performance and low performance groups formed the discriminant index. The original tool contained 20 items. We removed 4 items with discriminant index of 0.2 or below. The final tool contains a total of 16 items.

6   Data Analysis and Statistics

Knowledge Assessment of Patient Safety and Reporting Law and Ethics. Based on the stratified randomization, we obtained the consents from the sample hospitals for conducting research. During unit/ward morning meeting, a research staff explained the study purposes and invited the day shift nurses to participate in this study. After consenting, the nurse participants were given the knowledge assessment tool with name removed. A written instruction was given to the participating nurses for how to complete the study. The knowledge assessment tool was returned and examined for completeness upon return. A total of 2323 questionnaires were sent out with 2312 valid return. The valid return rate was 99.5%. Data were entered into a computer software database and then analyzed using the Statistic Package for Social Study (SPSS, version 15.0). The nurse participants' demographic information were analyzed with descriptive statistics, including frequency, percentage, mean, and standard deviation. T-test, one way Analysis of variance (ANOVA) with Scheffe's posteriori comparison, and Pearson's correlation were used as inference statistics.

Evaluation of the Distant Learning Education Program. For each of the 16 items, it would be scored as 1 if the nurse's answer was correct and 0 if the answer was wrong. The total possible score was 16 if the nurse answered all items correctly. The pass score was set as 12 (70%).

7   Study Results

Prior to conducting the distant learning education, there were only 57.7% of the participating nurses passed the knowledge assessment of patient safety and reporting law and ethics. The most frequent score was 12 (18.4%), and the next frequent score was 11 and 13 (16.3%). The mean score was 11.67 with standard deviation of 2.44. There were 364 nurses, 15.8% of the nurse participants, received score of 10 or below. Nurses' knowledge on patient safety and reporting law and ethics was lower than their knowledge on patient safety. Among the 16 multiple choice questions, the majority of the nurses (62.8%) answered wrong on the question, the reporting type for delaying medication administration due to computer out of order. The next common mistaken question was what kind of ethical conduct would be if the nurse helps the patient and his/her family to communicate with other medical professionals about the safety issues they concerned. About 57.1% of the participating nurses answered the question wrong. The results demonstrated that among the nurses' knowledge of patient safety and reporting law and ethics, there was particular needs to improve nurses' understandings of adverse event reporting type and ethical principles and rules. cm

The distant learning education course was distributed through the Newsletters of the National Union of Nurses' Association. There were 38603 nurses read the distant learning education content and 94.8% of the participating nurses passed the knowledge assessment.

8   Conclusions and Recommendations

This study applied systematic review of literature, collected and compiled the relevant references on patient safety and reporting law and ethics. A cross-sectional survey was used to broadly and swiftly assess the nurses' knowledge related to patient safety and reporting law and ethics. Data analysis indicated that only 57.7% of the nurse participants passed the assessment. There was a need to improve nurse' knowledge on this topic. After implementing the distant learning education, the nurses increased their knowledge on patient safety and reporting law and ethics. There were 38603 nurses participated in the distant learning program and 94.8% passed the knowledge assessment. The nurse participants received immediate feedback from the distant learning education course and obtained the continuing education credits as a second gain. This study demonstrated the effectiveness of a distant learning education program on increasing nurses' knowledge of patient safety and reporting law and ethics. We recommended applying distant learning education programs in the future for national education topics, in order to improve the accessibility of continuing education and reduce the cost of delivering of the education.

Acknowledgement. This study was supported by the research fund from the Department of Health (DOH099-TD-M -113-099003). We thank the research team members for their active participation and the experts for taking time to attend the meetings. We also would like to express our gratitude to those nurses from the three medical centers, 12 regional hospitals, and 50 local hospitals and who completed the study assessment tool.

References

1. Chiou, H.J.: Quantitative research method (1): study design and data processing, Yeh Yeh, Taipei (2007) (in Chinese)
2. Nurse Act, Laws and Regulations Database of The Republic of China, Taiwan (2012), http://law.moj.gov.tw/LawClass/LawAll.aspx?PCode=L0020166 (in Chinese)

The Instructional Design of a Web-Based Self-reflective Learning Portfolio for Skill Training

Hung-Chang Lin and Yao-Hua Wang

Department of Technology Application & Human Resource Development,
National Taiwan Normal University, Taiwan
{jasonlin,wang}@ntnu.edu.tw

Abstract. Technical education mainly focuses on the development of students' motor skills. At vocational educational schools in Taiwan, technical teachers usually teach skills in a big class. Therefore, those teachers always face the problems of not realizing students' learning process and difficulties; the evaluation is also deficient in credibility and validity.

The learners' self-reflection can help teachers understand their learning process. In this study, the researchers analyze the objectives, strategies and introspection emphasis in the skill-training stages and provide recommendations for students to reflect in each phase. Then the researchers apply these recommendations as the basis of introspection to build a Web-based learning portfolio (WBLP) for skill training.

The results of this study reveal that the Moodle platform conforms to the requirements of building a Web-based self-reflective learning portfolio for technical training purpose. Besides, this paper has mapped out the Moodle Modules that provide the self-reflection features for a technical-training WBLP.

Keywords: Moodle, Web-based learning portfolio, Technical training, Self-reflective learning, Instructional design.

1 Introduction

Technical education mainly focuses on the development of technical skills of students. Students are trained to gain better technical operating ability and this has become one of the main objectives of technical education. Traditionally, technical training has been taught through the demonstration and guidance of teachers and students learn skills through imitation or repetitive practices. However, teachers often face some problems in the traditional technical training courses. For instance, it is difficult for teachers to be aware of students' initial skill level; also, due to the huge number of students in a class, teachers often have difficulties realizing students' learning process and problems. Therefore, teachers are unable to provide feedbacks at the appropriate time to assist students' learning. Moreover, it is difficult for teachers to evaluate individual performance from a team work project with credibility and validity.

Self-reflection allows students to reflect on their learning process. With the reflection, teachers can further understand the students' learning process and adjust their

J.J. Park et al. (Eds.): NPC 2012, LNCS 7513, pp. 386–393, 2012.

teaching and evaluation. Therefore, the objective of this paper is to explore the possibility of utilizing Moodle (Modular Object-Oriented Dynamic Learning Environment)
to build a Web-based self-reflective learning portfolio for technical training.

2   Web-Based Self-reflective Portfolio

2.1   Self-reflection vs. Learning

Dewey [1] is the creator of the concepts to self-reflection in education. He believes
that self-reflection is reflecting on knowledge through initiation, continuous thinking
and careful thinking. However, Schon [2] believes self-reflection is the reconcile
process of individual's past experience, actions, beliefs and convictions gained
through learning. The process finally builds a knowledge and meaning that belongs
only to the individual. Montgomery [3] stated that life experiences can be fully utilized through the process of self-reflection and further build on new life experiences.
Repeated cycle of self-reflecting, usage of knowledge and forming new experiences
can reach the effect of learning.

Keeping a reflective journal is a form of record and it has to be easily inspected by
the instructors so that instructors are able to effectively judge the level of students'
reflective thinking [4, 5]. Several researches have attempted to identify students' reflective thoughts and measure the depth of their reflective thinking. Bain, Ballantyne,
Packer & Mills [6]suggest a framework for reflective thoughts. This framework divides reflective thoughts into 8 levels (see Table 1) and this can be a reference for
evaluating the contents of students' reflective thinking.

Table 1. Framework of Reflective Thoughts Suggested by Bain (Bain et al., 1999)

Category	Description of the Contents of Reflective Thinking
Nonsense	Meaningless contents
Simple	Yes/No answers
Incomplete	Incomplete or lost contents
Reporting	Contents are reported with no individual opinions or views
Responding	1. Low amount of concept involved 2. Describes observations with no causes 3. Describes personal emotions
Relating	1. Contents are related to personal experience 2. Brief explanation of what happened
Reasoning	1. Has a good reasoning to what have happened 2. In-depth discussion of the relationship between the theory and the real situation
Reconstructing	1. Students present a high level of inference 2. Combines self-experience with reasoning and makes a systematic conclusion to the theory

2.2   Self-reflection Learning Portfolio

The use of learning portfolio (or called portfolio) is a new trend in education[7]. The
portfolio collects the learners' projects over a period of time. The contents of the

learning portfolio describe students' learning process. Each portfolio is exclusive to each student. Viewers of the portfolio can understand information such as the learner's personal information, learning process and learning attitude through the narration kept in the portfolio [8-10].

The self-reflection learning portfolio is the portfolio with self-reflection as its main purpose. It provides students opportunities for systematic and continuous reflective thinking. They can help the learners improve their understanding of their work and often provide beneficial feedbacks [5]. The self-reflection learning portfolio not only reflects on the learning transfer of the learners, but it also provides materials for students for self-reflection purposes [10].

Some information in the portfolio that is difficult to record in words (such as illustration portfolio, project process) can be recorded and saved using digital media methods. Discussion among students can also be recorded in terms of audio files, images or video recordings to provide a more realistic overview of the student's effort in the learning process [11]. E-portfolio is a combination of a learning portfolio and multimedia [12]. The contents not only include interpretation of the learning portfolio, it also incorporates with the features of multimedia. There is the addition of multimedia resources and files to enrich the contents of the portfolio.

Other than the produce portion, Barrett [13]suggests the e-portfolio should also include the process portion, which should contain how students gather multimedia materials, the production process of project works, students' reflective journals, and the interaction between students and teachers. Therefore, the learning portfolio should not only present the results of learning, but it also present evidence of the learner's growth and development in academic [14, 15].

3   Development of the Web-Based Self-reflection Learning Portfolio for Skill Training

Course Management System (CMS) provides a platform for students and teachers to conveniently upload and download teaching materials files. The system also provides a platform for discussion and this provides additional benefits to traditional teaching method and creates a totally new teaching environment. Barret [9] argues that the addition of adequate reflection activities and feedback mechanism on a CMS, such as reflection, learning journals, self-evaluation, peer evaluation and feedbacks, can build up a self-reflection learning portfolio.

3.1   Reflective Thinking in Different Stages of Technical Training

Due to the different teaching objectives in different stages of technical training, teachers should design the appropriate self-reflection activities for each stage based on the different teaching objectives. Table 2 lists the suggestions for resources for reflective thinking for technical training stages based on the categorization of reflection contents in an e-learning portfolio [10].

Table 2. Teaching Points, Teaching Strategies, Points of Reflective Thinking, and Reflection Contents in Different Stages of Technical Training

Stages of Technical Training	Teaching Points	Teaching Strategies	Points of Reflective Thinking	Reflection Contents
Stage 1: Building up cognitive knowledge	• Introduce the objectives of the skill, functions, tools, process, principle and outcome • Explain the possible experiences, errors and dangers during operation	• Initiate learning motivations • Build up overall concepts about technical operation	Enhance the learner's reflective thinking about cognitive skills.	• Teaching objectives • Textbooks • References • Related websites • Related rules • Lecture notes • Related resources • Peer feedback • After-class reflective thoughts
Stage 2: Demonstration	• Demonstrate motor skills (How) • Explain When and Why to execute specific motor skills • Explain the key points of techniques through continuous operation	• Explanation and interpretation: 1. Action demonstration (overall → details) 2. Master the methods and skills • Preliminary practice	Make learners think about the procedure and reasons in order to strengthen the impression of operation.	• Operation procedure • Different versions of operation demonstrations and results • Observation records • In-class photos • In-class videos • Peer feedbacks • Qualitative reflective journals
Stage 3: Guidance and Practices	• Allow learners to practice skills 1. Fragment skill practice 2. Complete skill practice • Offer scenarios to practice skill operations	• Cooperative learning • Combine detailed actions into a large scale action through practices • Individual guidance and team guidance	Allow learners to discover problems encountered during operation in order to find the key points of the practice.	• Operation procedure • Semi-finished work • Records from design to formation stage • Records of practice procedure • Project work of all stages • Observation records • In-class photos • In-class videos • Peer feedbacks • Qualitative reflective journals

Table 2. (*Continued*)

Stage 4: Mastering the techniques	• Offer scenarios to simulate practices • Offer high level practices to learners • Practice skills to the level of automation	• Individual guidance and team guidance • Learning through pondering • Guide learners to solve problems using the developed skills	Offer learners to think how to apply basic theory to solve problems presented in scenarios	• Final products • Grades • Reflective thoughts on final products • Quantitative evaluation on self-reflection • Peer feedbacks • Peer assessment • In-group evaluation • Between-group evaluation • Qualitative reflective journals

3.2   The Application of Moodle for Building the Self-reflection Learning Portfolio Mechanism

Moodle (Modular Object-Oriented Dynamic Learning Environment) is a learning management system (LMS). Moodle provides several teaching modules which allow instructors to design teaching activities for classes.

The advantage of modular programming is the instructors are able to utilize different program modules based on the needs of the class when designing teaching activities. These program modules have clear, simple and high portability features, and the modular structure is beneficial to the development of Moodle e-portfolio [16-18]. Furthermore, the standardized nature of a learning portfolio set up by Moodle allows evaluation to be more objective.

Based on the analysis of technical training stages and the discussion of designing a self-reflection learning portfolio, Table 3 shows the functional description of a self-reflection learning portfolio which is built with Moodle's modular features.

Table 3. Moodle Modules that Provide Self-reflection Features for Different Stages of Technical Training

Technical Training		Moodle Modules that Provide Self-reflection Features	
Stages	Reflection Contents	Moodle Modules	Description of Moodle Modules
Stage 1: Building up cognitive knowledge	• Teaching objectives • Related websites • Related rules • Lecture notes • Related resources	• Class documents (Provide Reflection Contents)	• Provide learning contents and related resources
	• Peer feedbacks	• Chat rooms • Forums	• Provide social network features • Provide cooperative activities and discussion records

Table 3. (*Continued*)

	• Textbooks • References • Class notes • Reflective thoughts	• Blog	• Provide student learning process records • Keeping reflective journals
Stage 2: Demonstration	• Peer feedbacks	• Chat rooms • Forums	• Provide social network features • Provide cooperative activities and discussion records
	• Operation procedure • Demonstration and results of different versions of operations, observation records • In-class photos • In-class videos • Qualitative reflective journals	• Blog	• Provide student learning process records • Keeping reflective journals
Stage 3: Guidance and practice	• Peer feedbacks	• Chat rooms • Forums	• Provide social network features • Provide cooperative activities and discussion records
	• Periodic project work	• Assignments submission • Database • Grades	• Record cases and evidence of improvements • Provide peer evaluations and instructor's evaluation on student's reflective thoughts (database)
	• Operation procedure • Semi-finished work • Records from design to formation stage • Records of practices • Observation records • In-class photos • In-class videos • Qualitative reflective journals	• Blog	• Provide student learning process records • Keeping reflective journals
Stage 4: Mastering the techniques	• Peer feedbacks	• Chat rooms • Forums	• Provide social network features • Provide cooperative activities and discussion records
	• Final finished product • Self-reflection on the project • Grades	• Assignments submission • Database • Grades	• Provide course work assessment • Provide summative assessment • Instructor's evaluation and feedbacks • Record cases and evidence of improvements • Provide peer evaluations and instructor's evaluation on student's reflective thoughts (database)

Table 3. (*Continued*)

• Peer assessment • In-group evaluation • Between-group evaluation	• Workshop	• Provide feedbacks and evaluations among the learners • Provide evaluation and feedbacks of project works among groups • Provide evaluation and feedbacks within the group • Self-evaluation and self-feedback
• Qualitative reflective journals	• Blog	• Provide student learning process records • Keeping reflective journals
• Course comments	• Feedback form	• Provide reflections and comments for the course by students

4   Conclusions and Suggestions

The Instruction and evaluation of motor skills have encountered several difficulties. The main cause is the instructors having problems realizing the learners' learning process. In order to improve the learner's learning efficiency and assist instructors to understand the learner's learning process, the use of a self-reflection learning portfolio is a possible solution.

Moodle provides several convenient teaching modules for instructors to easily develop teaching activities. This paper investigates the technical training procedure and points out the required reflection based on the teaching objectives of each training stage for learners. Finally, student's reflective thoughts are retained through appropriate Moodle's teaching modules to build up a complete self-reflection learning portfolio.

The design of a self-reflection learning portfolio provides students with the opportunity to self-reflect in every stage of technical learning and improve their learning. Moreover, the instructors are able to understand more about students' learning process. Based on students' learning process and reflective activities, the instructors are able to provide a more complete evaluation and feedback for the students.

Acknowledgements. The authors thank the National Science Council of the Republic of China, Taiwan, for financially supporting this research under Contract No. NSC 100-2511-S-003-011.

References

[1] Dewey, J.: How we think. D. C. Heath, Boston (1933)
[2] Schön, D.: Educating the Reflective Practitioner, San Francisco. The Jossey-Bass Higher Education Series (1987)
[3] Montgomery, J.R.: Reflection, a meta-model for learning, and a proposal to improve the quality of university teaching (1993)

[4] Bell, A., Kelton, J., McDonagh, N., Mladenovic, R., Morrison, K.: A critical evaluation of the usefulness of a coding scheme to categorise levels of reflective thinking. Assessment & Evaluation in Higher Education 36, 797–815 (2011)

[5] Dyment, J.E., O'Connell, T.S.: Assessing the quality of reflection in student journals: a review of the research. Teaching in Higher Education 16, 81–97 (2011)

[6] Bain, J.D., Ballantyne, R., Packer, J., Mills, C.: Using journal writing to enhance student teachers' reflectivity during field experience placements. Teachers and Teaching: Theory and Practice 5, 51–73 (1999)

[7] Chang, C.-C.: Enhancing self-perceived effects using Web-based portfolio assessment. Computers in Human Behavior 24, 1753–1771 (2008)

[8] Paulson, F.L., Paulson, P.R., Meyer, C.A.: What makes a portfolio a portfolio? (1991)

[9] Barrett, H.C.: Electronic portfolios as digital stories of deep learning (2004)

[10] Chang, C.-C., Chou, P.-N.: Effects of reflection category and reflection quality on learning outcomes under a Web-based portfolio assessment environment: A case study of high school students in computer application course. The Turkish Online Journal of Educational Technology 10, 101–114 (2011)

[11] Chang, C.-C., Tseng, K.-H., Yueh, H.-P., Lin, W.-C.: Consideration factors and adoption of type, tabulation and framework for creating e-portfolios. Computers & Education 56, 452–465 (2011)

[12] Barrett, H.C.: Electronic Teaching Portfolios: Multimedia Skills + Portfolio Development = Powerful Professional Development (2000)

[13] Barrett, H.C.: Balancing the two faces of eportfolios (2010)

[14] Stiggins, R.J.: Student-centered classroom assessment. Maxwell Macmillan, New York (1994)

[15] Chang, C.-C.: Construction and evaluation of a web-based learning portfolio: An electronic wdqauthentic assessment tool. Innovations in Education and Teaching International 38, 144–155 (2001)

[16] Sweeney, J., O'Donoghue, T., Whitehead, C.: Traditional face-to-face and web-based tutorials: A study of university students' perspectives on the roles of tutorial participants. Teaching in Higher Education 9, 311–323 (2004)

[17] Masterman, E., Jameson, J., Walker, S.: Capturing teachers' experience of learning design through case studies. Distance Education 30, 223–238 (2009)

[18] Ellis, R.A., Goodyear, P.: Students' experience of e-learning in higher education. Taylor & Francis, Abingdon (2010)

The Difference Analysis between Demographic Variables and Personal Attributes – The Case of Internal Auditors in Taiwan

Li-Jia Chiu and Neng-Tang Norman Huang

Department of Technology Application and Human Resource Development,
National Taiwan Normal University, Taiwan
chiu.judy1188@gmail.com, nthuang@ntnu.edu.tw

Abstract. Internal control plays a pivotal role in enhancing security operations and quality control in an organization. From the perspective of management, internal auditors work for ensuring effective operations and improving performance for all the management systems within the organization. They bear great responsibility and play a key role. This study aimed to explore the internal audit staff demographic variables of personality traits differences. This research selected samples of the internal auditors from domestic companies, i.e. members of the Institute of Internal Auditors, in Taipei, Hsinchu, Taichung, and Kaohsiung. A total of 567 questionnaires are issued and the number of valid questionnaires is 272.

Keywords: Internal auditors, personal attributes, demographic variables.

1   Introduction

1.1   Background

The major business scandals occurring in the recent years, such as the Eron case in 2001, which filed for bankruptcy, and the WorldCom case in 2002, whose CEO, Bernard Ebbers, was forced to resign due to his loans to the company in personal name, have drawn worldwide attention to corporate governance, and revealed the importance of the roles and functions of internal auditors.

The Five Factors Model (FFM) of the personality traits is the most influential model in personality theory. The perspective of characteristics provides the general principle of the thinking on human beings' behavior. After rigorous scientific testing, the model has been approved by the circle of personality psychology. FFM, also known as Big Five, is one kind of characteristic perspective. It is NEO-PI-R personality inventory developed by Costa & McCrae (1992a). According to past literature, job satisfaction is relatively influenced by the employees' personality traits. Thus, this study treats internal auditors of firms as the subjects, and analyzes the personality traits of internal auditors' different statistical variables. Based on the research results, the suggestions are proposed for the reference of the business circle.

J.J. Park et al. (Eds.): NPC 2012, LNCS 7513, pp. 394–400, 2012.

Guilford (1959) suggested that personality is the combination of personal characteristics, attributes and properties. Thus, individuals have persistent and unique characteristics different from others. According to Smith & Tyler (1997), the society includes the groups defined upon population and members are decided by personal bodies or social attributes. Demographic statistics reveal quality and characteristics which include personality traits and common psychological capabilities. It is the individual difference of psychological process and behavior (Brand, Egan, & Deary, 1993).

Personality is the unique composition of personal characteristics, and it determines the interaction between human beings and environment. Personality also interacts with the situations. Allport (1937, 1961) suggested that personality is the dynamic organization in the individuals' psychological system and the unique form which determines a person's "adaption to external environment" and "thinking & behavior". Therefore, the individuals' behavior reflects the unique personality characteristics. When the characteristics continuously appear in different situations, they are called personality traits. However, in the studies on personality traits, FFM is more commonly used and accepted by the scholars. In recent years, the psychologists have generalized a more proper theoretical framework to describe the employee difference in personnel matter arrangement. Tupes & Christal (1961), Norman (1963) and other studies suggested that FFM is legitimate to be the classification criterion of personality construction. According to the literatures on personality, FFM can be the principle framework for the researchers. Mount & Barrick (1995) suggested that FFM can be applied to personality measurement, particularly the selection of employees. Goldberg (1990) demonstrated the FFM framework of Norman. FFM of Costa & McCrae (1992) is identified the most: agreeableness, conscientiousness, extraversion, neuroticism and experience openness.

1.2   Research Purposes

Based on research background and motivations above, this study intends to find the relationship between internal auditors' demographic variables and personality traits. The findings can serve as the references for the recruitment of internal auditors. The research purpose is to find if internal auditors' demographic variables have significant differences on personality traits. According to above research purpose and literature review, this study assumes that internal auditors' personality traits will be significantly different according to different demographic variables.

2   Methods

2.1   Sample

This study conducted a questionnaire survey on the internal auditors in the branches of four regions in the Institute of Internal Auditors, R.O.C., and distributed the questionnaires on site. A total of 567 questionnaires were distributed to the internal auditors who participated in the project lecture on the day of survey, and 376 copies were retrieved, with a return rate of 66%. After eliminating 104 invalid samples, there were 272 valid samples, with a valid return rate of 48%.

2.2   Instrument

This study measured personality traits by NEO Five-Factor Inventory (NEO-FFI) developed by Costa & McCrace (1992b), and adopted their Form S. After the revision, there were 35 items in this inventory. Cronbach's alpha of the dimensions is extraversion 0.7181, agreeableness 0.6268, neuroticism 0.7926 and conscientiousness 0.7343.

3   Results

3.1   Dimensions of Demographic Variables

The sample structure is based on gender, age, education level, subordination level, job title and working years. Among the valid samples, 33.1% are males and 66.5 % are females; most of them are 26~35 years old (45.6%), followed by 36~45 years old (39.0%), 46~55 years old (12.1%), above 55 years old (2.6%) and below 25 years old (0.4%). There are few subjects aged below 25 years old and above 55 years old, and thus, they are respectively allocated in "26~35" and "46~55" and are revised as "below 35" and "above 46". Regarding education level, most of the subjects are graduated from universities (65.8%), followed by college (17.3%), above master (14.7%) and senior high school (vocational school) (1.8%). Generally speaking, 80.5% subjects are at least graduated from universities. Since few samples are graduated below senior high schools (vocational schools), they are allocated in "college" and it is revised as below (including) college. As to subordination level of internal auditors, according to sample distribution, general manager (office) is the most (50.4%), followed by president (office) (27.6%) and the board of directors (12.9%). Some do not belong to above (8.1%) (such as vice general manager, financial unit, etc.). In terms of job title, basic auditors (34.2%) are the most, followed by experienced auditors (31.3%) and general auditors (19.5%). Since job titles for internal auditors in different firms are varied, "others" are 14.7%; in addition, as to total working years as internal auditors, "below 3 years" is the most (38.2%), followed by "3~5 years" (29.0%), "6~10 years" (23.9%), "11~15 years" (4.8%) and above 16 years (2.2%). Since there are few subjects above 16 years, they are allocated in "11~15 years" and revised as "above 11 years" .

3.2   Difference Analysis between Gender and Personality Traits

Analysis is conducted to find if gender has a significant difference on four dimensions of personality traits. Independent sample t test is conducted on males and females to find if male and female internal auditors have a significant difference on the dimensions of personality traits. According to the findings, gender does not have a significant difference on dimensions of personality traits, indicating that internal auditors are not influenced by gender as a variable. Most of the valid samples are females, and this suggests that the firms prefer hiring the females. The analytical results do not indicate the difference, as shown in Table 1.

Table 1. Differences between the various dimensions of gender in personality

Variable	Gender	Sample Size	M	SD	t	p
Extraversion	M	90	3.6611	.58337	.127	.722
	F	181	3.6961	.54918		
Agreeableness	M	90	3.8519	.46234	1.901	.169
	F	181	3.8131	.43485		
Neuroticism	M	90	2.5653	.56533	.317	.574
	F	181	2.5311	.59130		
Conscientiousness	M	90	3.8386	.46375	.805	.370
	F	181	3.9517	.46668		

3.3 Difference Analysis between Age, Education Level, Subordination Level, Job Title, Working Years and Personality Traits

Analysis is conducted to find if age, education level, subordination level, job title and working years have significant differences on four dimensions of personality traits. One-way ANOVA is conducted on variables with at least two categories to find if there is significant difference among the groups of variables. Scheffe post hoc comparison is conducted on the groups with significant differences to compare the difference of pair groups.

According to Table 2, internal auditors are not influenced by education level in different variables. Among the subjects, most of them are graduated from universities (65.8%), indicating that education level is a necessary condition for internal auditing; however, it is not the key factor of the variables. Internal auditors of different subordination levels do not show significant differences in the dimensions of personality traits, suggesting that internal auditors are not influenced by different subordination levels in the variables.

Job title has a significant difference on "conscientiousness" in personality traits. Scheffe post hoc comparison finds that "others" in conscientiousness is higher than entry-level auditors. However, "others" cannot be classified; thus, the analytical result cannot be indicated. In addition, according to one-way ANOVA, F value of job title on "extraversion" in personality traits is significant. However, Scheffe post hoc comparison does not show that the mean of any pair groups is significantly different. Although extraversion is different on the cognition of subordination level, it is uncertain if the supervisors or non-supervisors show a higher degree. Working years has a significant difference on "conscientiousness" in personality traits. Scheffe post hoc comparison finds that the degree of total working years for 6~10 years is higher than total working years below 3 years. In other words, when internal auditors' working years are longer, their conscientiousness is stronger. In addition, one-way ANOVA finds that F value of working years on "extraversion" in personality traits is significant; however, Scheffe post hoc comparison does not show a significant difference of mean in any two groups.

Mean and standard deviation of dimensions of personality traits are shown in Table 2. Regarding personality traits, average score of each item is 3.4369 and it is medium. Among the dimensions, the score of conscientiousness is the highest (mean =3.9164). It shows that internal auditors' characteristics of competency, responsibility, self-requirement, carefulness, persistence and goal orientation are more significant. Score of neuroticism is the lowest (mean =2.5409). It means that internal auditors' neuroticism is insignificant, indicating that internal auditors should have the characteristics to be calm under the pressure.

Table 2. The demographic variables in the personality differences between the various dimensions

Variable			N	M	SD	F	Scheffe Post hoc comparison
Extra-version	Age	(1) under the age of 35	125	3.6560	.59709	.343	
		(2) 36-45 years old	106	3.7005	.51457		
		(3) More than 46 years old	40	3.7313	.56440		
	Educa-tion level	(1) College below	52	3.7548	.40972	.621	
		(2) University	179	3.6592	.58040		
		(3) Master above	40	3.7063	.63521		
	Subor-dination level	(1) Board of directors	35	3.7357	.51429	2.367	
		(2) Chairman of the board	75	3.5633	.57992		
		(3) General Manager	137	3.7591	.56017		
		(4) Other	22	3.5795	.50819		
	Job Title	(1) Chief Auditor	53	3.7972	.54609		n. s.
		(2) Senior auditor	85	3.7676	.51291	3.123*	
		(3) Primary auditor	93	3.5538	.57678		
		(4) Other	40	3.6625	.58984		
	Work-ing years	(1) less than three years	104	3.6250	.58397	3.906**	n. s.
		(2) 3-5 years	79	3.5886	.57601		
		(3) 6-10 years	65	3.8192	.49511		
		(4) More than 11 years	19	3.9474	.46082		
Holistic				**3.6847**	**.55891**		
Agreea-bleness	Age	(1) under the age of 35	125	3.7760	.50184	1.491	
		(2) 36-45 years old	106	3.8648	.38566		
		(3) More than 46 years old	40	3.8792	.38302		
	Educa-tion level	(1) College below	52	3.8750	.36436	.396	
		(2) University	179	3.8156	.45916		
		(3) Master above	40	3.8083	.47223		
	Subor-dination level	(1) Board of directors	35	3.7333	.35974	1.182	
		(2) Chairman of the board	75	3.8000	.37066		
		(3) General Manager	137	3.8735	.51032		
		(4) Other	22	3.7879	.28257		
	Job Title	(1) Chief Auditor	53	3.8648	.44585	1.473	
		(2) Senior auditor	85	3.8882	.35485		
		(3) Primary auditor	93	3.7581	.52963		
		(4) Other	40	3.8000	.37780		
	Work-ing years	(1) less than three years	104	3.7981	.43117	1.367	
		(2) 3-5 years	79	3.7785	.49694		
		(3) 6-10 years	65	3.9179	.40731		
		(4) More than 11 years	19	3.8333	.39675		
Holistic				**3.8272**	**.44335**		

Table 2. (*continued*)

Variable			N	M	SD	F	Scheffe Post hoc comparison
Neuroticism	Age	(1) under the age of 35	125	2.6050	.66720	1.755	
		(2) 36-45 years old	106	2.4623	.47908		
		(3) More than 46 years old	40	2.5594	.53032		
	Education level	(1) College below	52	2.6130	.60292	.789	
		(2) University	179	2.5405	.59781		
		(3) Master above	40	2.4594	.47399		
	Subordination level	(1) Board of directors	35	2.4893	.51034	1.147	
		(2) Chairman of the board	75	2.6200	.60349		
		(3) General Manager	137	2.5365	.59682		
		(4) Other	22	2.3750	.52893		
	Job Title	(1) Chief Auditor	53	2.5566	.51862	.994	
		(2) Senior auditor	85	2.5206	.52605		
		(3) Primary auditor	93	2.6062	.63362		
		(4) Other	40	2.4219	.64592		
	Working years	(1) less than three years	104	2.5793	.60114	1.722	
		(2) 3-5 years	79	2.5997	.60625		
		(3) 6-10 years	65	2.4000	.53728		
		(4) More than 11 years	19	2.5132	.44467		
Holistic				**2.5409**	**.58146**		
Conscientiousness		(1) under the age of 35	125	3.8510	.51994	2.286	
	Age	(2) 36-45 years old	106	3.9788	.41529		
		(3) More than 46 years old	40	3.9625	.40252		
	Education level	(1) College below	52	4.0120	.41440	1.423	
		(2) University	47	4.0426	.41725		
		(3) Master above	40	3.9250	.38998		
	Subordination level	(1) Board of directors	35	3.9607	.44014	.856	
		(2) Chairman of the board	75	3.8633	.42523		
		(3) General Manager	137	3.9124	.51122		
		(4) Other	22	4.0284	.30602		
	Job Title	(1) Chief Auditor	53	3.9410	.45836	3.567*	(4)>(3)
		(2) Senior auditor	85	3.9559	.39420		
		(3) Primary auditor	93	3.8038	.51453		
		(4) Other	40	4.0688	.46336		
	Working years	(1) less than three years	104	3.8666	.46617	3.450*	(3)>(1)
		(2) 3-5 years	79	3.8671	.49531		
		(3) 6-10 years	65	4.0731	.41156		
		(4) More than 11 years	19	3.8289	.42738		
Holistic				**3.9164**	**.46686**		

*p<.05   **p<.01

4   Discussion

The results showed that job title has a significant difference on extraversion and conscientiousness in personality traits; total working years has a significant difference on extraversion and conscientiousness in personality traits; job title and total working years have significant differences on conscientiousness in internal auditors' personality traits. Internal auditors with total working years above 6-10 years have the strongest conscientiousness. In other words, internal auditors' conscientiousness varies according to working years. The auditors with longer working years have stronger conscientiousness.

In business operation and management, the role of internal auditing will become more important and influential. In the future, the firms will value the function and benefits of internal auditing, thus making internal auditors' personality traits a critical factor in the recruitment process, so that they could fulfill the important and effective roles.

This study suggests that when selecting internal auditors, the firms can use various "personality traits evaluation scales". They should select internal auditors with personality traits such as "extraversion", "agreeableness" and "conscientiousness". These auditors are more competent, they enjoy internal auditing and will have higher job performance.

The findings show that internal auditors having total working years less than 3 years account for the majority (38.2%), indicating that their turnover rate is high. Holland (1985) found that when personality traits match the jobs, the employees will have the highest job satisfaction and work efficiency, as well as the lowest turnover rate.

Therefore, it is suggested that senior managers should value internal auditors' job satisfaction, identify the problems, and improve them by proper measures in order to reduce the turnover of internal auditors and ensure that they can function properly in the organizations, enjoy the work, and contribute to the firms.

References

1. Allport, G.W.: Personality: A Psychological Interpretation. Holt, Rinehart, & Winston, New York (1937)
2. Allport, G.W.: Pattern and Growth in Personality. Holt, Rinehart & Winston, New York (1961)
3. Brand, C.R., Egan, V., Deary, I.J.: Personality and general intelligence. In: Bonaiuto, P., van Heck, G.L., Nowack, W., Deary, I.J. (eds.) Personality Psychology in Europe, vol. 4, Tilburg University Press, Tilburg (1993)
4. Costa Jr., P.T., McCrae, R.R.: Four Ways Five Factors are Basic. Personality and Individual Differences 13, 653–665 (1992a)
5. Costa Jr., P.T., McCrae, R.R.: Professional Manual for The NEO PI-R and NEO-FFI. Psychological Assessment Resources, Inc., Odessa (1992b)
6. Goldberg, L.R.: An Alternative Description of Personality: The Big Five Factor Structure. Journal of Personality and Social Psychology 59, 1216–1229 (1990)
7. Guilford, J.P.: Personality. McGraw-Hill, New York (1959)
8. Holland, J.L.: Making Vocational Choices: A Theory of Vocational Personalities and Work Environments. Prentice-Hall, Englewood Cliffs (1985)
9. Mount, M.K., Barrick, M.R.: The Big Five Personality Dimensions: Implications for Research and Practice in Human Resources Management. In: Ferris, G.R. (ed.) Research in Personnel and Human Resources Management, vol. 13, pp. 153–200. JAI Press, Greenwich (1995)
10. Norman, W.T.: Toward and Adequate Taxonomy of Personality Attributes: Replicated Factor Structure. Journal of Abnormal and Social Psychology 66, 574–583 (1963)
11. Smith, H.J., Tyler, T.R.: Choosing the right pond: the impact of group membership on self-esteem and group-oriented behaviors. Journal of Experimental Social Psychology 33, 146–170 (1997)
12. Tupes, E.C., Christal, R.E.: Recurrent Personality Factors Based on Trait Ratings. Journal of Personality 60, 225–251 (1961)

Success Factors and Problems Encountered in the Workplace Learning of University/College of Technology Students in Taiwan: A Five-Star Hotel as an Example

Mey-Tyng Wang and Guo-Hong Lei

Department of Technology Application and Human Resource Development
National Taiwan Normal University
libra@gate.sinica.edu.tw, Bernie23203@yahoo.com.tw

Abstract. In order to help students in universities/colleges of technology close the education-employment gaps, Taiwan's educational authorities promoted workplace-learning programs. However, what are the success factors and problems encountered? This article reaches three defined conclusions: 1) student can internalize knowledge and skills over time, and apply them to workplace except for improving performance; 2) student can develop initiative characters, improve innovation, and even activate industries to think with novel ideas; 3) and, the lacking earnest attitude as well as deficiency of communication ability affect the performance which should be. Following with these conclusions, three recommendations are offered: 1) it would be proper to strengthen student's professional intellect for future development; 2) it would be proper to strengthen student's vocational capability in practice, including individual personality; 3) and, it would be proper to offer related testing or scaling tools to help student get awareness and thus upgrade their attitude during workplace-learning.

Keywords: university/college of technology, workplace learning, success factor, hospitality industry.

1 Introduction

Due to the widespread of higher education, upgrading of vocational technical education, and the changing of economics, society, and enterprise structure, it is necessary for high level vocational education institutions–including university/college of technology, and junior college of technology–to adapt themselves timely. Not only the teaching of vocational education institutions have to be implemented under such principles that discriminate none and cater to specific nature of the individual, but also those vocational education institutions have to face changing manpower needs in business, as well as to coordinate with government policy. Therefore, The most significant difference between vocational education institutions and general universities is that vocational education institutions emphasis pragmatic approach that s gaps between learning and performance, and combine theory and practicein order that students could be capable of applying their skills and capability to workplace (Ministry of Education, 2010a).

J.J. Park et al. (Eds.): NPC 2012, LNCS 7513, pp. 401–408, 2012.

There were critics that most higher education students have difficulty to join in the workplace after graduation. Under government policy, universities/colleges of technology currently are strengthening their internship programs in order to help students to experience workplace earlier, shorten career exploring period, recognize what workplace needs, establish correct working attitude, and thus expand their career opportunities. As a result, it would be necessary and realistic trend forthe school to pay attention on WL. However, in the light of the fact that there are so many WL approaches, it is worth to understand if those approaches could effectively help students to learn in WL, and benefit both of students and industry. Therefore, this research aims to: 1) understand the factors leading to success in WL for students in universities/colleges of technology; and 2) understand what WL obstacles that those students would encounter. Via literature review as well as interviews with students and managerial level of a hotel, this research also aims to provide the schools and industries involving in WL program with suggestions and recommendations.

2   Literature Review

2.1   Current Condition and Trend of WL in Taiwan

In a broad sense, WL includes learning activities in workplace, semi-workplace, and community. In the US, the most popular six categories of internship that university/college students participate in are: cooperative education (co-op), field experience, practicum, service learning, externship, and apprenticeship (Lee, L. S., & Lai, C. C., 2011, quoted from WetFeet, u.d.). Among these six categories, cooperative education is a policy mode promoted by government and is also a strategic integration of higher education and the industry. And as Meng (2003) points out, it is a kind of cooperation between the industries and schools. Encompassing their main subjects, the design of WL is to encourage students go to workplace to meet development requirements of individual career and professional skill (Linn, Ferguson, & Egart, 2004). Despite of different modes, WL could still help students to utilize their knowledge, intellects, and interpersonal relationship to have a real-world view of workplace earlier. Furthermore, along with the refined curricula designs for students, a proper combination of academic intellects and working experience could be achieved by giving high commitment, as well as offering suitable working environment (Parsons, Caylor, & Simmons, 2005). Taiwan's Ministry of Education has integrated cooperative education-related affairs, such as off campus internship, college-internship matchmaking, industry's participation of internship mechanism, and competence rebuilding, into a unified program (Ministry of Education, 2010c). The promulgation of *Off-Campus Students Internship Implementation Program* (amendment) in 21 January, 2011 by the Ministry aims to offer experiential learning earlier to establish proper attitude towards work for students, increase pragmatic teaching resources for the school and career positions for students, and reduce orientation training cost for the industry (Ministry of Education, 2011).

2.2   Situated Learning Perspectives

Under the concept of cooperative education, WL aims to form a real situation, in which situated learning model could be used to improve the students' learning effectiveness, and provide the educators with different thinking in order to inspire more innovative teaching approaches. Situated learning is considered as a society participation process, and both community and culture would affect the members' learning models. During this socialization process, the interaction between experienced and inexperienced members would deliver recessive and dominant knowledge and then a common interpretation of a matter could be reached (Lave & Wenger, 1991). In terms of workplace, learning behaviors could be seen in every aspect of WL situation, and the learning effectiveness could be evaluated by degree of participation. By doing so, students who have different learning requirements could have more understandings about the diversity and difference of education. Therefore, situated learning put the emphasis on realized relations between learning and social culture, as well as the interaction between learners and environment, and thus the efficiency of WL could be improved.

2.3   Factors Leading to Successful WL

Critical factors leading to successful WL could be divided into absorptive capacity in workplace and mission objectives for WL. WL is not only limited in schools, but also includes internships based on cooperative education; thus, through WL, students could combine theory and practice , and then transform and apply learned knowledge, skill and capacity (Hui-Hua Chiu, 2006). Therefore, students have to firstly acquire related knowledge and skills, follow with the process of self-transform and internalize, and then apply learned knowledge and skills to WL.

2.3.1   Perspective of Absorptive Capacity

Due to the perspective of absorptive capacity (ACAP) proposed by Zahra and Gerard (2002), the importance of absorptive capacity has caught those eyes of strategic management, technology management, international business, and organizational economics. There are two forms of absorptive capacity: potential absorptive capacity (PACAP) and realized absorptive capacity(RACAP). PACAP includes knowledge acquisition and assimilation capacities; while RACAP includes knowledge transformation and exploitation. A model of ACAP is as figure 1.

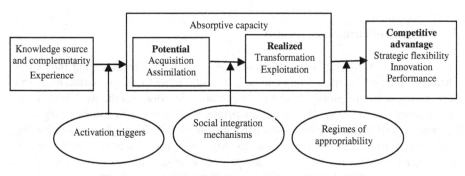

Fig. 1. A model of ACAP Source: Zahra & Gerard, 2002

2.3.2   Systemic View of WL

According to "What Makes for Good Workplace Learning" prepared by Australian National Training Authority, ANTA (2003), the ultimate goal of WL should be business competitiveness and innovative capacity. An ideal WL, some important channels such as networks and partnerships should be included. These channels will be transformed, after socialized process, into capability to reach the WL goals of improving competitiveness and innovative capacity. A systemic view of workplace learning is as figure 2.

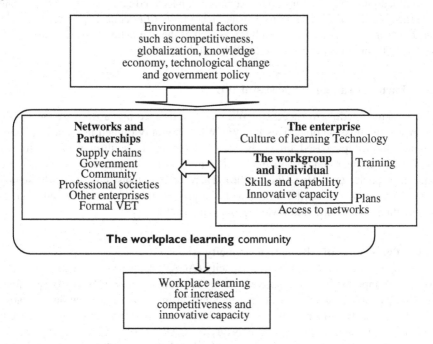

Fig. 2. A systemic view of workplace learning
Source: NCVER, 2003

3   Findings and Discussion

This research put the emphasis on tourism–one of the Six Key Emerging Industries. Therefore, the authors specifically choose a five-start hotel locates in northern Taiwan as research subject regarding its good transportation location and the worldwide business service it provides. The hotel cooperate with eight universities/colleges of technology, and there are 24 students participating in WL. Through case studies and semi-constructive interview, the authors interview with participants who join cooperative education, including one senior manager, one administrative personnel, and three internship students in third or forth grade of college/university. Questionnaire writings are prepared in accordance with literature review and research outlines. If uncertainties are found during the review of interview materials, there will be e-mails or telephone calls to enquire further information to make sure that all contents in questionnaire are keeping in consistence and meeting the requirements of this research so that this research could contribute to credibility and validity. After systematically sorting out, factors leading to success or problems resulting from obstacle in WL for students of universities/colleges of technology are detailed below.

3.1   Factors Leading to Success in Workplace for Students of Universities/Colleges of Technology

3.1.1   Students' Capabilities to Absorb, Internalize, and Apply
Analysis in this research consists with the theories raised by Zahra & Gerard (2002), and Lave & Wenger (1991).Students could acquire knowledge from school, gain practical experiences of society from hotel, merge them together and then to apply them in the workplace.

3.1.2   Five-Start Hotel Can Lead to Innovation Skills
Analysis in this research consists with the theory raised by ANTA (2003). It shows that active and practical learning could improve the innovative capacity for students and activate the innovative thinking for the industry; meanwhile, the hotel could also offer professional trainings to improve practical operation capability.

3.2   Problems Resulting from Obstacle in Workplace Learning for Students in Universities/Colleges of Technology

3.2.1   Theory Learned in School Could Be Applied to Hotel Business in Those But Could Not Improve Its Effectiveness
In the interview results, show that professional knowledge teaching remains inadequate due to students' desire for more professional knowledge. The above information represents that professional knowledge could only be applied to basic practices in the industry but could not improve its effectiveness, which means that the mission objectives of the industry could not be reached. This also demonstrates that the knowledge learned in the school could not reach ANTA's perspective of a WL that could improve competitiveness (ANTA, 2003).

3.2.2   Deficiency of Communication Ability
The environment of global competition requires the capability performing with knowledge, skills, and attitudes (Hunter, 2004; Schejbal & Irvine, 2009). Analysis against interview results that students are lacking basic knowledge and proper attitude. As a result, students need to be more capable in terms of communication, language, and positive attitude.

4   Conclusion and Suggestions

4.1   Conclusions

4.1.1   Student Could Internalize Knowledge and Skills over Time, and Apply Them to Workplace Except for Improving Effectiveness

By internalizing professional knowledge and practice, the students could flexibly apply their knowledge and experiences to workplace and accomplish general working mission and goals. However, in terms of cost saving and improving service quality, the effectiveness is limited.

4.1.2   Student Could Develop Initiative Characters, Improve Innovation, and Even Activate the Industry to Think with Novel Ideas

Students would be more capable after receiving basic professional knowledge, and know how to reason and logically analyze, systematically criticize, and make decision. By experiencing practical operation in hotel, active and energetic students who have received multi-dimensional   trainings would become more flexible. Their innovative capability would be also upgraded.

4.1.3   The Lacking Earnest Attitude as Well as Deficiency of Communication Ability Would Affect the Performance Which Should Be

The quality and effectiveness of students in workplace are largely decided by their attitudes and communicating capacity, such as values, oral expression, listening, English speaking, respect and acceptance, interaction with people from different departments, interpersonal relationship, and teamwork.

4.2   Suggestions

4.2.1   It Would Be a Proper Way to Strengthen Student's Professional Intellect for Further Development

Facing different unexpected situations, students would usually respond with being at a loss or unable to react. As a result, it would be better for hotel to offer more advanced training in legal knowledge, management skills, service professions, cost control. By doing so, related rights of both students and business owner could be protected, the students could also have more opportunities to shorten the adaptation period because they have become more capable of multiple capabilities as well as competitiveness.

4.2.2   It Would Be a Proper Way to Strengthen Student's Vocational Capability in Practice, Including Individual Personality

Universities/colleges of technology should consider efforts to improve students' positive mind and characters, empathy and sense of morality, values judging, recognizing professional functions of business organization, in order to strengthen their capabilities in practical operation. Additionally, students should be encouraged to share, exchange the knowledge the have learned, and join healthy activities such as professional speech, preschool or nursing home visiting.

4.2.3 It Would Be a Proper Way to Offer Related Testing or Scaling Tools to Help Student Gaining Awareness and Thus Upgrade Their Attitude during Workplace Learning

Hotel managers are encouraged to provide aptitude test before conducting interview. If any student with negative attitude are found during interview, hotel managers are advised to explain to him/her the hardship would have to face in order to reduce the possibility that students might not be able to accomplish mission and thus the effectiveness could be improved.

References

1. Australian National Training Authority: What makes for good workplace learning (2003), http://www.ncver.edu.au/publications/1004.html (retrieved December 3, 2010)
2. Chiu, H.H.: An Empirical Study on Relationship Among Learning Environment, Personal Attributes and Absorptive Capacity – An Example of Students from Department of Hotel and Restaurant Management of S School Under Rotary Cooperative Education Program. Unpublished master's thesis, Shu-Te University, Kaohsiung (2006)
3. Hunter, W.D.: Knowledge, skills, attitudes, and experiences necessary to become globally competent. Unpublished doctoral dissertation, Lehigh University, Bethlehem, PA (2004), http://www.globalcompetence.org/pub-pres/HunterDissertation.pdf (retrieved October 10, 2011)
4. Meng, J.-L.: New Thinking for Academic-Industry Collaboration. Technological and Vocational Education Bimonthly 76, 17–20 (2003)
5. Lave, J., Wenger, E.: Situated learning: legitimate peripheral participation. Cambridge University Press, New York (1991)
6. Lee, L.S., Lai, C.C.: The Improvement towards Technical Colleges off-campus Internship Design. Quarterly Journal of Technological and Vocational Education 1(3), 1–5 (2011)
7. Lin, J.C.: Four Major Strategies for Workplace Learning. T&D Fashion 31, 1–5 (2005)
8. Linn, P.L., Ferguson, J., Egart, K.: Career exploration via cooperative education and lifespan occupational choice. Journal of Vocational Behavior 65(3), 430–447 (2004)
9. Ministry of Education: New Program for Technical Education—Cultivating Excellent Professional Personnel, Department of Technological & Vocational Education (2010a), http://www.tve.edu.tw/Public/Publish/20102251128375334.pdf (retrieved October 15, 2010)
10. Ministry of Education: MOE Promotes Academic-Industry Collaboration Plan, Department of Technological & Vocational Education (2010b), http://www.tve.edu.tw/HotNews.asp?NewsId=276 (retrieved November 19, 2010)
11. Ministry of Education: MOE Grant Directions Regarding Technical College off-camp Internship (Amended on January 1, 2011), http://edu.law.moe.gov.tw/LawContentDetails.aspx?id=FL050926&KeyWordHL=&StyleType=1 (retrieved February 20, 2012)

12. Parsons, C.K., Caylor, E., Simmons, H.S.: Cooperative Education Work Assignments: The role of organizational and individual factors in enhancing ABET competencies and co-op workplace well-being. Journal of Engineering Education 94(3), 309–318 (2005)
13. Schejbal, D., Irvine, G.: Global Competencies, Liberal Studies, and the Needs of Employers. Continuing Higher Education Review (The Journal of the University Continuing Education Association) 73, 125–142 (2009)
14. Zahra, S.A., George, G.: Absorptive Capacity: A review, reconceptualization, and extension. Academy of Management Review 27(2), 185–203 (2002), http://frontiers.sauder.ubc.ca/Zahra_George_AMR_2002.pdf (retrieved December 3, 2010)

Cross-Cultural Training Programs and Expatriate Adjustment Effectiveness

Shiang-Lan Kuo

Department of Technology Application and Human Resource Development,
National Taiwan Normal University, Taiwan

Abstract. The purpose of the study reported here was to explore cross-cultural training programs and expatriate adjustment effectiveness that increase effective cross-cultural interaction. Effective cross-cultural training increases trainees' knowledge, encourages them to see the personal and organizational benefits of cultural diversity and cross-cultural competence, and increases their skill and capacity to work with cultural diversity. Cross-cultural training is an effective strategy in the achievement of organizational performance targets and multicultural policy objectives. Addressing the identified limitations of current practice in CCT will increase its contribution to the development and enhancement of organizational and individual cultural competence. Moreover, developing cross-cultural training programs could add value to the firm and its people.

Keywords: Cross-Cultural Competence, Cross-Cultural Training, Expatriate Adjustment, Multinational Corporations.

1 Introduction

Multinational corporations (MNCs) are having difficulty retaining expatriates for their global operations. It is estimated that 10–80% of expatriates sent on foreign assignments return home prematurely. One of the reasons for expatriates' failure has been cited as the inability of these managers and/or their spouses to adapt to the host-country's culture. As a result, cross-culture training programs provided to employees and their families by MNCs have become crucially important for successful international operations (Okpara & Kabongo, 2011).

Gertsen (1990) argues that cross-cultural training can be classified into two major categories: (1) conventional training, where the information is transmitted through a unidirectional communication, as is the case in colleges, universities and management development centers and (2) experimental training, where the trainer gets the trainees to participate by simulating real life and hands on situations. Gertsen (1990) also identified two other possible training orientations where the training emphasis is based on the notion of culture in general and aims at sensitizing participants to the notion of culture, or focuses on one specific culture and aims at making trainees more competent in that particular culture. Gertsen (1990) argued that the combination of these two dimensions reveals four types of training (Okpara & Kabongo, 2011), as shown in Figure 1.

The purpose of the study reported here was to explore cross-cultural training programs and expatriate adjustment effectiveness that increase effective cross-cultural interaction.

J.J. Park et al. (Eds.): NPC 2012, LNCS 7513, pp. 409–413, 2012.

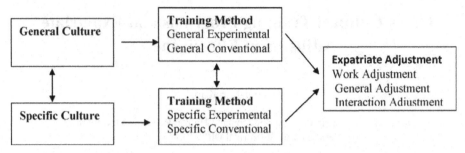

Fig. 1. Dimensions of cross-cultural training methods
Source: Adapted and modified from Gertsen (1990, p. 354)

2   Definition and Contents

2.1   Cross-Cultural Competence

The range of definitions of cross-cultural competence could be synthesized as: The ability to function or work effectively in culturally diverse situations in general and in particular encounters with people from different cultures. Because of the   hidden or invisible nature of one's own culture and the historically tribal, territorial and parochial nature of nations and societies, cross-cultural competence is not an innate characteristic of human nature. Rather, it is learned — as is culture — through experience, education and training. Individuals and organizations do not choose their native culture, but they can choose to acquire and place value on cross-cultural competence. The level or degree of cultural competence required for effective functioning is determined largely by context. It is also largely dictated and measured by the perceptions of the individuals in cross-cultural encounters; one person's idea of the cultural competence required in the situation may be different from another's (Bean, 2006).

Australian papers and reports (Miralles & Migliorino, 2005; Eisenbruch, 2004) have proposed a model comprising the following four dimensions of cultural competence (Bean, 2006):

(a)Systemic cultural competence — requires effective policies and procedures, monitoring mechanisms and sufficient resources to foster culturally competent behavior and practice at all levels.
(b)Organizational cultural competence — requires skills and resources to meet client diversity, an organizational culture which values, supports and evaluates cultural competency as integral to core business.
(c)Professional cultural competence — depends on education and professional development and requires cultural competence standards to guide the working lives of individuals.
(d)Individual cultural competence — requires the maximization of knowledge, attitudes and behaviors within an organization that supports individuals to work with diverse colleagues and customers.

2.2   Cross-Cultural Training (CCT)

CCT is defined as that which increases the competence of individuals to function in cross cultural situations domestically and abroad. In broad terms, CCT programs focus on the following broad categories (Bean, 2006):

(a)managing and working with culturally-diverse employees and colleagues;
(b)working and living internationally;
(c)designing and delivering products and services to culturally-diverse   customers.

CCT is generally delivered in three models (Bean, 2006);

(a)General awareness and communication training — focuses on developing generic cross cultural skills and sensitivity to assist with interactions in any culture the participant may encounter.
(b)Ethno- or country-specific training — focuses on a single ethnic group or country to increase participants' knowledge, understanding and ability to function effectively in that environment or with that group.
(c)Training in working with interpreters and translators — focuses on developing the technical skills involved and also includes those elements of cross-cultural communication that influence the process.

Pre-departure training is the traditional form for CCT and it is conducted apart from the actual experience of realities in the host culture. Traditionally, pre-departure CCT programs are administered about a month before departure. Such post-arrival training need not necessarily take place immediately upon the expatriate's arrival; some CCT may be more effective if it is delayed until the expatriate tries to cope with culture shock. Hence, such training could start about three to six months after arrival in the host country. Expatriate CCT aims to increase the applicability of new behaviors, which are more appropriate to the host culture. However, an individual's capacity for efficient learning ebbs and flows during the expatriate period. Therefore, CCT may preferably be sequential, progressing in steps starting at pre-departure and continuing to the post-arrival phases. Sequential CCT would provide continuous guidance for the incremental restructuring of the expatriate's frame of reference towards greater consistency with the host culture (Selmer, 2010).

Through observation, interview, and material analysis, it looks at five essential and practical considerations in cross-cultural program adjustment – spoken communication, material translation, silent communication, local trainers, and empowerment and localization (Chang, 2009). Furthermore, cultural adjustment is considered to be a prerequisite for expatriate success abroad. One way to enhance adjustment is to provide employees with knowledge and awareness of appropriate norms and behaviors of the host country through cross-cultural training (Puck, Kittler, & Wright, 2008).

3   Implementation Steps

The steps of implementing cross-cultural training programs, as follows (Bean, 2006):

Step 1: Define the organizational context and training objectives
Establish the relationship of cultural competence to the organizational, legal and people management contexts. Define the training needs and objectives. Ensure strong organizational support for the training program.

Step 2: Understand cultural competence and cross-cultural training
Before embarking on a cross-cultural training program, be clear on the nature of cultural competence, the range of cross-cultural training approaches and the criteria for an effective cross-cultural training trainer.

Step 3: Promote the value of cross-cultural training to the organization
Demonstrate the value of cross-cultural training to all stakeholders with the statistical evidence and qualitative comments.

Step 4: Design and conduct cross-cultural training effectively
Study the range of options for cross-cultural training and resources that will ensure the training objectives are met. Select the appropriate trainers and work closely with them. Organize and conduct the program for maximum effectiveness.

Step 5: Evaluate and follow-up the cross-cultural training program
Design and carry out a rigorous evaluation process. Identify and implement strategies to ensure that learning is applied to performance and enhancing the organization's cultural competence.

4   Discussion and Conclusions

Effective cross-cultural training increases trainees' knowledge, encourages them to see the personal and organizational benefits of cultural diversity and cross-cultural competence, and increases their skill and capacity to work with cultural diversity. A recent review of Bennett's Developmental Model of Intercultural Sensitivity (Hammer, Bennett, & Wiseman, 2003) suggests that a higher degree of acceptance/adaptation to cultural differences among employees would result in the following benefits (Bean, 2006):

(a) Less stress.
(b) More satisfaction with living/working in a foreign culture.
(c) Greater job accomplishment in culturally-diverse environments.
(d) Lower levels of prejudice and discrimination.
(e) Less resistance to diversity initiatives.

At the systemic and organizational levels, cultural competence must be closely linked to policy requirements and organizational values and service delivery objectives and expressed in high levels of political, leadership and managerial support for CCT. At the professional level, cultural competence must be integrated into the standards and competency and performance frameworks of professions and occupations. At the individual level, CCT is most effective when it addresses the concerns and motivations of participants and is provided within an organizational context that provides opportunities and incentives for applying acquired cross-cultural knowledge and skills to the workplace. To effectively facilitate the development of cultural competence, cross-cultural trainers need support in the areas of professional and resource development. Cross-cultural training is an effective strategy in the achievement of organizational performance targets and multicultural policy objectives. Addressing the identified limitations of current practice in CCT will increase its contribution to the development and enhancement of organizational and individual cultural competence (Bean, 2006). Moreover, developing cross-cultural training programs could add value to the firm and its people (Qin & Baruch, 2010).

Since expatriate training is essential, how to design effective training programs is an important issue for business managers. It suggests that an effective training program is contingent upon certain environmental factors. Among these factors, the fit between expatriate learning style and instructor learning mode, and the perceived cross cultural differences between host country and home country were regarded as the two main moderating (or contingency) factors to evaluate the influences of expatriate training on training effectiveness(Lee & Li, 2008).

References

1. Bean, R.: Cross-Cultural Competence and Training in Australia. Cultural Competence in the Health Care Industry 14(1), 14–22 (2006)
2. Bean, R.: The Effectiveness of Cross-Cultural Training in the Australian Context (2006), http://www.immi.gov.au/media/publications/research/cross_cultural/Contents_Executive_Summary.pdf
3. Chang, W.-W.: Cross-cultural adjustment in the multinational training programme. Human Resource Development International 12(5), 561–569 (2009)
4. Eisenbruch, M.: The Lens of Culture, Lens of Health: Toward a Framework and Toolkit for Cultural Competence. In: UNESCO Asia-Pacific Regional Training Workshop, Bangkok (2004)
5. Gertsen, M.: Intercultural competence and expatriates. International Journal of Human Resource Management 1(3), 341–362 (1990)
6. Hammer, M.R., Bennett, M.J., Wiseman, R.: Measuring Intercultural Sensitivity: The Intercultural Development Inventory. International Journal of Intercultural Relations 27(4), 421–443 (2003)
7. Lee, L.-Y., Li, C.-Y.: The moderating effects of teaching method, learning style and cross-cultural differences on the relationship between expatriate training and training effectiveness. The International Journal of Human Resource Management 19(4), 600–619 (2008)
8. Miralles, J., Migliorino, P.: Discussion Paper: Increasing Cultural Competency for Healthier Living. National Health and Medical Research Council, Canberra (2005)
9. Okpara, J.O., Kabongo, J.D.: Cross-cultural training and expatriate adjustment: A study of western expatriates in Nigeria. Journal of World Business 46(1), 22–30 (2011)
10. Puck, J.F., Kittler, M.G., Wright, C.: Does it really work? Re-assessing the impact of pre-departure cross-cultural training on expatriate adjustment. The International Journal of Human Resource Management 19(12), 2182–2197 (2008)
11. Qin, C., Baruch, Y.: The impact of cross-cultural training for expatriates in a Chinese firm. Career Development International 15(3), 296–318 (2010)
12. Selmer, J.: Expatriate cross-cultural training for China: views and experience of "China Hands". Management Research Review 33(1), 41–53 (2010)

Soft Power: A Critical Factor for the Effectiveness and Development of a School

Hui-Min Ko

Department of Technology Application and Human Resource Development
National Taiwan University, Taiwan

Abstract. This research aims to explore the contents of a school's soft power, including culture, strategy, leadership, learning, marketing and innovation. Managing soft power not only is critical for a school's development, but also should be regarded as a indispensible asset of schools. The measures for a school to establish its soft power are: establishing core values, shaping a learning school, emphasizing on knowledge management, innovating, and introducing a more adaptive marketing strategy. A school could become more perspective and sustainable through soft power, and thus be able to deal with a fast-changing educational environment and meet practical requirements.

Keywords: soft power, organizational culture, learning school, marketing strategy.

1 Introduction

Prof. Joseph S. Nye of Harvard University proposed his idea of "soft power" in 2004. Soft power, in accordance with Nye, is an ability to achieve goal through its own attraction rather than threats or seduction, and such an attraction comes from a country's culture, political values, and diplomatic policies. Since then, global research and application of soft power began; meanwhile, most countries also vigorously enhance their own soft power and regard it as an important strategic factor for domestic and international development. Currently, researches on and applications of soft power are so popular that soft power is discussed worldwide. Even most governments, enterprises and schools all have an idea to establish their own soft power in order to meet today's challenges. In the light of that schools play an important role in matters such as education and academic exchange, and that the establishment and management of soft power in the mean time are critical for a school's development, this research aims to explore the contents of soft power and establish some measures for soft power to improve a school's effectiveness and competitiveness, and thus the school's goal of sustainable management could be achieved.

2 The Contents of School Soft Power

The comprehensive power of a school includes hard power and soft power. Hard power is apparent and easy to evaluate, which includes buildings, facilities, teachers and

J.J. Park et al. (Eds.): NPC 2012, LNCS 7513, pp. 414–420, 2012.

funds. Soft power, on the other hand, is less obvious and more difficult to evaluate, which includes visions, spirits, culture, system, management, image and reputation. Internally, the soft power of a school represents a kind of cultural power, and, externally, an attraction and influence. It is the sum of a school's cultural power, strategic power, leadership power, learning power, innovation power, and marketing power (Chang, Ming-hui 2009).

2.1   Cultural Power

School culture is a school system composed by various codes, values, and meanings, which is shared and utilized by all the school members; it is also a legacy of ideology, including codes, systems, values, beliefs, rituals, and traditions, which could be divided into faculty culture, student culture, executive culture, community culture, material culture and spiritual culture (Zhang, Duo-yan, 2007). The power of these cultures is intangible but unlimited. They could not only enrich educational system, but also work in areas that system is unable to touch, and that is why they keep a school alive. The development of school culture could increase the performance of the school members, and help a school become more effective (Tsai, Chin-hsiong, 2000).

2.2   Strategic Power

Strategy is a form of integrating and coordinating resource allocation. In terms of an uncertain future, it is also a process analyzes the quality of internal and external resources, adapts the change of overall environment, and proposes the most adaptive way to achieve the goal of an organization (Tang, Chih-ming, 2009). A school's strategic power, therefore, is a set of plans that are determined in accordance with that school's goals, characteristics, and its own conditions, and aims to achieve the goal of sustainable operation. This set of plans defines a school's area of operation; it is also the blue print, procedure and measure to achieve goals of a school (Hax, 1991). An excellent strategic power of operation could outline the future development. A school head should have an overview of the environment and adopt proper operation strategy so as to survive and excellence, especially during a time when resources are limited and competition is fierce.

2.3   Leadership Power

Leadership is an art to influence people and stimulate them to complete missions and improve organizational behavior through providing motives, directions and goals, as well as utilizing personal charm, effective management and encouragement (Xie, Yu-lin, 2008). Leadership is to help a team to achieve its goals, maintain its integrity, and encourage it members (Wu, Ching-shan, 2006). The quality of leadership influences not only an organization's performances, atmosphere and future development, but also how much of its members' need could be met. A school leader's leadership style would have a profound influence on the performance and development of his or her school, and the satisfactory degree and performances of school members. Furthermore, the leadership style is the major power to develop the school's soft power.

2.4   Learning Power

The purpose of organizational learning is to endow an organization with learning power, making its members have a core value of being eager to learn, personal mastery and willing to change and innovate; it also aims to commence organizational transformation, and encourage members in an organization to examine themselves, learn from each other, ponder problems and take actions to solve them (Xie, Hui-juan, 2004). School learning activities are the extension of organization learning. A school's learning power could improve the quality of its members, develop a team learning environment, and promote the value of teamwork.   This fact has a significant influence on a school's integration, innovation and organizational culture development.   This fact also could encourage a school to learn and progress. Learning power, one of a schools' soft powers, emphasizes the fact that people could learn whenever and wherever, and that everyone is a learner.   Such a learning system includes the learning activities of the student, the faculty and leader (Zhang, Ming-hui, 2005).

2.5   Marketing Power

School marketing is a concept that regards school as a market, and applies the idea of marketing to the daily life in a school.   Through activities such as analysis, planning and execution, this concept aims to make faculty, community, parents, and general public understand a school's visions, teacher's quality and curriculum. A successful school marketing includes enhancing prestige, increasing competitiveness, solving recruiting difficulty, gaining more external resources, and effectively reaching an internal consensus (Xu, Xiao-jun, 2011). Measures for school marketing include internal marketing, external marketing and interactive marketing (Wu, Ching-shan, 2005).

2.6   Innovation Power

Innovation has the meanings of "make change" or "introduce new things" (Wu, Ching-shan, 2005).   School innovation is "a process that adapts creative ideas and translates them into services, products, or means that deal with things in a school environment in order to develop a school's characteristics, improve its effectiveness, and thus to achieve the goal of education" (Wu, Ching-shan, 2003). The major functions of innovation are to display educational dynamics and creativities, enrich educational contents and activities, ensure schools' survival and development, and improve and excellence education quality. Innovation includes the change of ideas, technologies, services, operational procedures, activities and environments (Wu, Ching-shan, 2003).

3   Ways to Develop School Soft Power

3.1   Establishing Core Values

A school's core value comes from its history, culture and characteristics, as well as the spirit of the times. The core value is the stem and soul of school culture. It is also a prerequisite and foundation of a school's soft power. It reflects the common value and vision of the faculty and student, and represents a school's goals and visions. Based on school's characteristics and needs for development, the principles to establish a core value are: reviewing its own history; analyzing current situation; widely inquiring comments and suggestions from students, faculty, and people who concern the school; extracting merits from the school's tradition; forming a core value with profound and unique connotation; and making this value become a common belief and principle for each and every school member.

3.2   Shaping a Learning School

The idea of learning school develops from learning organization. The concept of learning organization is based on Peter M. Senge's "The Fifth Discipline", which is composed by system thinking, improving mental models, personal mastery, building shared vision and team learning. To thoroughly understand the fifth discipline is the foundation for the establishment of learning organization.

In addition to integrate the fifth discipline into school's learning strategy and major task, I feel that the essence of the idea of learning school is "learning".   All the school head, faculty, student and parents of the community should be the main body of a learning school.   The ways to form a learning school are: setting learning goals, transforming school leaders into learning ones, developing the student's self-directed learning ability, encouragement and rewarding.

3.3   High Quality School Leadership

A school leader should have characteristics that could lead, improve, and excel his or her school, and should also have a respectable personality to win respect from school members and make them follow his or her leadership wholeheartedly.   In addition, one should notice that although there are various leadership theories, research results show that no one single type of leadership could be applied to everyone and everywhere. A leader should be able to adjust his or her leadership in accordance with circumstance. Therefore, a school head should choose an effective way to lead in accordance with the characteristics of faculty, student and environment so as to meet school's requirements, and to lead the school effectively and efficiently(Wu, Ching-shan, 2006).

3.4   Emphasizing Knowledge Management

In accordance with Zhang, Ji-cheng (2006), knowledge management is "a knowledge activity that promotes the accumulation, spread, sharing, creation, value-adding or efficiency of knowledge in an organization through development and effective utilization of knowledge by using of the tool of information management". The knowledge management in a school, therefore, is to establish an effective knowledge management system in order that the knowledge in school organization could be effectively created, circulated and added more values, and thus that more innovative professional knowledge of education could be produced constantly. In order to improve school knowledge management, there should be support and promotion from the leader, specially-assigned persons to be in charge of knowledge management matters, and a knowledge management strategy that encourages organization members to create and contribute special knowledge, and rewards anyone who do so. Furthermore, a knowledge base, data base and information circulation system should be established in order to transform any useful knowledge into information, systemize the knowledge, make the knowledge more accessible, and constantly update knowledge.   Meanwhile, knowledge should also be permanently stored in computer software so that users could access to and utilize knowledge more efficiently and that the experience and knowledge of a school could be shared on information platform.

3.5   A More Adaptive School Marketing Strategy

A school should establish a service- and customer-centered culture.   Under this culture, a school could more concern about customer while making decision, teaching and holding an activity.   Under this culture, a school could improve its service quality to win the customer's heart and acquire more recognition and support.   Furthermore, in prior to marketing itself, a school should have several discussions and brainstorming on matters such as upper guidance, school environment, internal and external resources, teacher's specialty, student's need, and expectation from parents, in order to reach a consensus between school members.   Thus, school characteristics could be developed, reputation could be established, and recognition and support from the public could be gained.

3.6   Innovative Operation

Innovative operation demonstrates that fact that school operation concept is changing and school culture is reforming.   The sustainable development of innovative operation is based on learning organization.   School leaders should have an innovative mind set and shape a new organizational culture, atmosphere, environment and condition in order to establish a decision-making model composed by brainstorming, mutual discussion, and tolerance.   They should be able to encourage school members to actively participate in school operation, work as a team, brainstorm, discuss mutually, and tolerant dissenting views so as to improve competitive edge of the school (Zhang, Ming-hui, 2009). The following measures could be used to promote innovative operation: creating a special team to promote innovative operation, encouraging cooperation and sharing among school members, learning from other schools, establishing a platform for innovation, providing adequate resources, and rewarding those who make significant contributions to innovative operation.

4   Conclusion

With the trend of globalization and commercialization of education, schools of all levels are facing a fierce competition and serious challenge. The establishment and development of soft power are critical for a school to survive and excel. Developing soft power is a lengthy and accumulative process that requires wisdom. The six components of school soft power proposed in this research include: cultural power, strategic power, leadership power, learning power, marketing power, and innovation power. The six soft powers that are interconnected and complemented each other could cohere, stabilize, influence, innovate, and develop a school organization. One who would like to bring soft power into full play should: establish profound and unique core values and translate these values into a common belief and code for all the members in the school; create a learning environment to promote group learning, encourage school members to work coherently and induce organization teamwork; develop high quality leadership to boost morale and improve organization efficiency; emphasize knowledge management in order to share and learn knowledge and experience; have the courage to change and innovate to fill the school with energy, So as to make sure a more forward looking, sustainable, adaptive, and responsive educational environment and requirements.

References

1. Cai, J.-X.: Leadership Transformation and School Effectiveness, pp. 76–77. National Taiwan Normal University Press, Taipei (2000)
2. Chang, M.-H.: An Research on School Operation and Management: Vision, Integration and Innovation, pp. 85–89. Pro-Ed Publishing Company, Taipei (2005)
3. Chang, M.-H.: The Soft Power of School Operation. Journal of Educational Research (188), 27–35 (2009)
4. Hax, A.C.: Redefining the Concept of Strategy and the Strategy Formation Process. Engineering Management Review 19(1), 19–24 (1991)
5. Nye Jr., J.S.: Soft Power, The Means to Success in World Politics, p. 25. Public Affairs, New York (2004)
6. Senge, P.M.: The Fifth Discipline: The Art and Practice of the Learning Organization, Chinese version, trans. by Jin-lun Guo, pp. 10–17. Military History and Translation Office, Ministry of National Defense, Taipei (2002)
7. Tang, Z.-M.: School Strategic Management. Friends of National Education 60(4), 1–2 (2009)
8. Xie, H.-J.: Planning and Practice of a Learning School. Inservice Education Bulliten 21(1), 13 (2004)
9. Xie, Y.-L.: The: New Area of Military in Economy-Based Knowledge Era: Military-Based Knowledge. National Defense Journal 23(6), 70–71 (2008)
10. Xie, Y.-L.: On the Communication Art of Strategic Leadership. National Defense Journal 23(2), 93 (2008)
11. Wu, Z.-L.: The Marketing Strategy for School Management. Educational Information and Research (53), 61–69 (March 2004)
12. Wu, C.-S.: School Administration, pp. 165–196. Psycological Publishing Co., Taipei (2006)
13. Wu, C.-S.: The Ehtablishment of a School's New Management Strategy. Secondary Education 56(3), 2–26 (2005)

14. Wu, C.-S.: Innovative Managment. Educational Information and Research (53), 134–135 (July 2003)
15. Xu, X.-J.: The Application of School Mketing Srategy on Public Relations of a School. Journal of National Taichung University: Education 25(1), 121–137 (2011)
16. Zhang, D.-Y.: Introduction to Education, pp. 66–67. National Open University, Taipei (2007)
17. Zhang, J.-C.: Management and Innovation of Knowledge, p. 67. Chuan Hua Science & Technology Book Co., Taipei (2004)

Merging Grid into Clustering-Based Routing Protocol for Wireless Sensor Networks

Ying-Hong Wang, Yu-Wei Lin, Yu-Yu Lin, and Hang-Ming Chang

Computer Science and Information Engineering
Tamkang University
Tamsui Taipei, Taiwan, R.O.C.
inhon@mail.tku.edu.tw, {harry040,jerry198926}@hotmail.com,
chmcice174723@gmail.com

Abstract. After sensors are deployed, it cannot be recharged in Wireless sensor networks. Therefore, the energy of sensors is limited. In this situation, how to design a routing algorithm is very important. An effective algorithm can reduce energy consumption and prolong network lifetime. In this proposal, we proposed a routing protocol. And it can reduce the energy consumption of nodes and use energy effectively to sense by clustering. Finally, we compare the methods we proposed with the others by simulation.

Keywords: Cluster, Power saving, Routing protocol, WSNs.

1 Introduction

In recent years, wireless application and wireless communication markets have become more popular due to the rapid development of wireless communications technology. Moreover, the advance in micro technology has led to wide adoption of multiple wireless network technologies consisting mainly of wireless sensor networks [1]. In wireless sensor networks, micro-manufacturing technology continues to increase capabilities in environmental sensing, information processing, wireless communications, computing ability, and storage capacity. In order to take full advantage of these advances, reducing energy consumption to extend network lifetime of wireless sensors is critical, and thus an important topic for research.

The characteristics of wireless sensor design calls for small footprint, low cost, power saving, and accurate sensing ability. The current areas of research can be divided into the following several categories: routing protocol, target tracking, locating, data aggregation, fault tolerance, sensor node deployment and energy management. Each sensor node has data processing, communication, and data sensing responsibilities, all consume a limited energy resource. In this premise, a wireless sensor node achieves the greatest benefit from an increase in energy consumption efficiency. Therefore, how to design an effective routing protocol is a very important topic. In the wireless sensor network applications using the environment as a static target and more under consideration, we hope that the node does not have too strong computing power and

J.J. Park et al. (Eds.): NPC 2012, LNCS 7513, pp. 421–428, 2012.

other additional equipment in order to achieve as much as possible to reduce energy consumption and cost effectiveness. To achieve this goal we propose a cluster-based routing protocol for wireless sensor network that is Merging Grid into Clustering-based Routing Protocol for Wireless Sensor Networks, MGCRP.

2   Related Work

There are numerous papers on using routing protocols to make wireless sensor networks stable, effective and power saving. [2, 3] introduces the concept of using routing protocols in wireless networks.

Recently, there are three leading ways of routing .They are chain-based, cluster-based and tree-based; our paper will focus on cluster-based. In cluster-based routing nodes are divided into clusters and the cluster head will send the data collected from normal nodes to sink.

Low Energy Adaptive Clustering Hierarchy (LEACH) [4] is proposed by Heinzelman. This routing protocol divides nodes into several clusters by their location, and the nodes can only communicate with in the same cluster.

Energy-Balanced Chain-cluster Routing Protocol (EBCRP) [5] is proposed by Xi-Rong Bao. It is a cluster-based distributed algorithm that builds a path of chains through the use of a ladder algorithm.

3   Merging Grid into Clustering-Based Routing Protocol

Our proposed routing protocol is divided into two phases: Clustering Phase and Routing Phase, and we will add Cluster-Head Rotation Mechanism to maintain routing persistence in the Routing Phase.

3.1   Network Environment and Assumption

We assume the wireless sensor network is composed of a sink and a large number of static sensor nodes randomly deployed in the target area.

a.   System Environment

We assume n sensor nodes randomly distributed in the area to be monitored are continuouly sensing and reporting events. These sensor nodes are static. We use S_i to indicate the i-th node, sensor nodes set $S = \{S_1, S_2, ..., S_n\}$, and the number of S is n. We make the following assumptions about the sensor nodes and the network module.

i)   The sink is deployed in a region away from the sensors and we assume that the energy of the sink is infinite.

ii)   Sensor nodes will be assigned a unique identifier before deployed in the sensing area.

iii)   All nodes have the same computing, storage and energy capabilities.

iv)   The sensor node's transmission power can be changed according to the distance from the receiver.

v)   All sensor nodes are static. In addition, each sensor node knows its own location and the sink knows their location though the use of the location mechanism.

b. *Energy Consumption Module*

Our paper is uses [7] the communication energy consumption module, and follows the formula:

$$E_T(k, d) = E_{Tx}k + E_{amp}(d)k \tag{1}$$

$$E_R(k) = E_{Rx}k \tag{2}$$

$$E_{fuse}(k) = E_{fuse}k \tag{3}$$

Formula (1) means the sensor nodes have an energy cost when transmitting data, (2) means the sensor nodes have an energy cost when receiving data, (3) means the sensor nodes have an energy cost when the data fuses. In these three functions, where k is data packet size, E_{Tx} is energy cost for transmitting one unit data of the sensor node, E_{Rx} represents the energy cost when node receives one unit data, E_{fuse} is energy cost of the fusing the data. When the sensor nodes transmit amplification is required, so transmitting nodes have an additional $E_{amp}(d)k$ energy cost. The value of $E_{amp}(d)k$ can be determined by formula (4).

$$E_{amp}(d)k = \varepsilon_{FS}d^2 \tag{4}$$

Where d is the distance between two nodes, ε_{FS} represents the amplified electric power energy cost.

c. *Sensor Node and Cluster Information*

Table 1. is the sensor node information table, which is used to record information about itself. Next we will introduce each field of the table. Node_ID is the identification of the node. Res_Energy is the residual energy of the node. Head_ID is the identification of the cluster head in its own cluster, if the Head_ID and Node_ID are the same, the node itself is the cluster head. Cluster_ID is the cluster number the sensor node belongs to. Next_Hop is the next sensor node to forward data to. Table 2. is the cluster table, it records information of every cluster member and including the following fields Node_ID, Res_Energy, and Cost. Node_ID is the identification of member of the node in the cluster. Res_Energy is the residual energy of the node in the cluster. Cost is transmission cost between two nodes. Table 3. Is Head List, it is used to record information one neighboring cluster heads. The fields include Node_ID, Cluster_ID and Cost. Node_ID is the identification of the neighboring cluster head. Cluster_ID is the cluster number of the neighboring of cluster head. Cost is transmission cost between two cluster heads.

Table 1. Sensor node information table

Node_ID	Res_Energy	Head_ID	Cluster_ID	Next_Hop

Table 2. Cluster_Table

Node_ID	Res_Energy	Cost

Table 3. Head_List

Node_ID	Cluster_ID	Cost

3.2   Clustering Phase

a. Clustering

Before discussing the clustering step, first, we must are define the routing protocol parameters and variables.

Rectangle Unit Block (Block): This is a rectangular block. The user defined value of N divides the network into several blocks which are the same size and are not overlapping.

Center of Block (BC): After dividing the network into several grids, we will calculate the center coordinates of the grids resulting in a vector of coordinates. We assume Block_Center i (BC_i) is the i-th center coordinates of the block.

Cluster: Cluster can be regarded as a set C which is includes several sensor nodes. We can represent a set C as C = $\{S_j\}, S_j \in S, j=1,2,...,n$. Where j is the number of sensor nodes. We assume the Cluster_ID is i which represent the cluster number of the grid. In any cluster (C_i), if any member of the sensor nodes are not in a cluster, it is an invalid cluster, otherwise, it is valid cluster.

Distribution: We define a new parameter in a valid cluster Distribution it is used to evaluate the distribution of nodes in a valid cluster. The number of nodes within a valid cluster closer to BC are the best. The formula (5) is used to calculate the distribution of the cluster. Where $d(S_m, BC_i)$ is the distance between the member of the sensor nodes in cluster and the BC of the cluster and where $N(C_i)$ is the number of sensor nodes in the cluster. After defining these parameters and variables, the following details the description of each step.

Step 1: Network Gridding

After the deployment of the sensor nodes, we will make a grid of the network. In this paper, we assume that the sensor nodes in the network can be arranged to an M*M area, and assume every length of block is N. The network will be divided into $(\frac{M}{N})^2$ same size blocks. Where the user defined the N value and M value is the length of the sensor network.

Step 2: Calculate Center of Grid

Formula (6) calculates the center of the grid. BC_i is the two-dimensional coordinate vector, where $i=1,2,...,(\frac{M}{N})^2$, this is used to indicate the number of the grid, and also is also the Cluster_ID. The numbering starts from the (0,0) position along the X axis towards the right, Sequenced 1, 2, ..., until numbered to the right- border of the sensor network, then back to left-border of the sensor network. In this moment, shift the Y-axis direction one unit block down, then repeat the sequencing step until the grid is complete. Then use the number of grids and formula (6) to get each center of grid.

Step 3: Calculate Distribution (C_i) of Valid Cluster

In this step, we will calculate the Distribution of the valid cluster. First, we give a set VC that includes all valid clusters in the network. N(VC) expresses the number of valid clusters. We will only calculate the Distribution of clusters in the VC set. After each Distribution in each cluster has been calculated, we will start the cluster merging process.

$$Distribution(C_i) = \frac{\left[\sum_{S_m \in S} d(S_m, BC_i)\right]}{N(C_i)} \qquad (5)$$

$$BC_i = \left(\left[(i-1)\% \left(\frac{M}{N}\right) + \frac{1}{2}\right] * \frac{M}{N}, \left[\left[(i-1)/\left(\frac{M}{N}\right)\right] + \frac{1}{2}\right] * \frac{M}{N}\right) \qquad (6)$$

Step 4 : Merge Valid Cluster

First, we choose the fewest number of nodes and the cluster with the largest Distribution value from the VC set. Assume a cluster from the VC set that meets the above conditions is C_A, where $C_A \in VC$, A=1,2,...,$(\frac{M}{N})^2$, then we will start the merge. Let the distance between S_a and S_b be minimal, where $S_a \in C_A$, $S_b \in C_B$, B=1,2,...,$(\frac{M}{N})^2$, $C_B \in VC$ and $C_B \neq C_A$. Then we add all the sensor nodes to C_B from C_A. In other words, let all the Cluster_IDs of the sensor nodes from C_A change to C_B, and remove from the VC C_A, resulting in one less N(VC) .

Step 5: Clustering Finish

Assume the variable K is the user set up number of clusters in the network. The value of K will affect the efficiency of network, so we must decide the variable K according to the network size and number of nodes. The operation of clustering in step 4 will be repeated until N(VC)=K. After clustering finishes, the sink will send related information to the sensor node for an update.

b.   Cluster Head Selection

The main task of the cluster head is to fuse data that sensor nodes sensed within a cluster, receive other cluster heads' sensed data, and, send to sink, after clustering finishes and, cluster head must be selected from each cluster. To do so, the sink will broadcast a Head_Elect Message packet to every sensor node in each cluster in the network. When a sensor node gets this packet, it will generate a random variable P between 0 and 1, where P is used to differentiate between the same residual energy from other sensor nodes. After sensor node got a random variable P, then immediately to calculate itself residual energy. The residual energy is then calculated.

The member nodes of the same cluster compare each of their residual energies according to the transmission power to obtain cost between them. Sensor nodes with the most residual energy will be selected as the cluster head. If more than one sensor nodes have the same residual energy in the same cluster then the sensor node with the larger P value will be selected as cluster head. After each of the cluster heads of cluster has been selected, each cluster head will send a Head_Confirm packet to the sink. The packet format is shown in Table 4. Each Head_Confirm packet contains three fields, they are Header, Node_ID and Cluster_ID. The Header records the name of packet, Node_ID expresses the Node_ID of the sensor node that is the cluster head, Cluster_ID expresses the Cluster_ID of the cluster to where the cluster head belongs. After the sink received all the Head_Confirm packets, it will consolidate the information and forward it to each cluster head allowing them to, update their Head_List table.

Table 4. Head_Confirm packet

Header	Node_ID	Cluster_ID

3.3   Route

In our paper, the transmission route can be divided into two parts: inner-cluster transmission route and outer-cluster transmission route. Inner-cluster transmission route refers to the path between cluster head and sensor nodes within the same cluster. Outer-cluster transmission route refers to the path between cluster heads.

Our proposed path selection method is mainly based on transmission cost between the sensor nodes. So we use Bellman-Ford shortest path algorithm[6] for the route selection method. We arrange the network as a graph, and assume the sensor nodes in the network are the vertexes of graph and the transmission cost between nodes are edges of the graph. Through the Bellman-Ford algorithm we can calculate the lowest cost of each sensor node to the other.

a.   Inner-Cluster Transmission Route Build
Inner-cluster transmission routes are the path between sensor nodes within the same cluster. The sink broadcasts to all the sensors nodes their minimum path cost to the cluster head in their cluster using the Bellman-Ford algorithm according to member cost in the Cluster_Table. In (7), $C(i, j)$ defines the cost between node i and node j, where $P_t(i, j)$ is the transmission power of node i to node j during transmission. After the sensor node receives the minimum cost between the node and the cluster head, it then records the next hop target in the Next_Hop field. When the node wants to transmit data, it sends data to the sensor node based on Next_Hop field. During the transmission, if the sensor node dies or cluster head changes, the Bellman-Ford algorithm is invoked to re-calculate the minimum cost path and the Next_Hop field is updated.

b.   Outer-Cluster Transmission Route Build
The outer-cluster transmission route and inner-cluster transmission route have the same algorithm, but in the outer-cluster, the send object changes to cluster head to cluster head. The cluster head receives the data that members sent in the cluster and, then it integrates the received data and forwards it to its neighboring cluster head. According to the Cost field of Head_List and through the use of the Bellman-ford algorithm, the cluster head selects the next hop. After the calculation, the cluster head will record the transmission object. If the cluster head has been replaced, then the new cluster head will request a member to re-calculate the minimum cost between cluster heads.

c.   Cluster Head Rotation Mechanism
The cluster head not only senses the environment but integrates the data from members of the same cluster, and transmits data to other cluster heads. In order to reduce the early death of sensor nodes, we add the cluster head rotation mechanism to distribute the energy consumption. We assume time divided into continuous periods of T, in the beginning T the sink will send a Cluster_Head Rotation Message to the sensor network. After a normal node receives this message, they will immediately send their residual energy information to the cluster head. Then the cluster head will select the node of with the most residual energy to be the new cluster head. At the same time, the cluster head will broadcast to members within cluster the new identify of the cluster head and update Head_ID of the normal node and send Head_Confirm packet to the sink. The sink will gather all the new cluster head information, consolidate, and send the data to all the cluster heads so they can update Head_List

table. During *T*, the sink will repeat the above action to replace the cluster head until the energy of members within cluster is less than the energy defined by the cluster head threshold.

4   Simulation and Analysis

This paper uses the Dev C++ simulation environment. The condition of the sensor network and its related values is shown on Table 5. A round is defined by data that is transmitted to sink safely; a conclusion that is made from the average of 50 kinds of conditions. We can observe that MGCRP is better than LEACH and EBCRP via Fig.1 and Fig.2, The selection of cluster head principle of EBCRP is better than LEACH because it chooses the nodes which are closer to sink to be clusters. The design does not have the transmission distance limitation of clusters in LEACH, but the routing of EBCRP is a chain which is connected by nodes resulting in redundant data transmissions. In this paper, MGCRP combines nodes which are closer to others in a cluster and when the nodes are distributed unevenly, it shortens the distance between nodes and the cluster head to attain power savings. To not overload any one member, we add cluster head rotation mechanism, to equally to distribute energy consumption to the members in the cluster prolonging the network lifetime.

Table 5. Experimental Parameters

Parameter	Value
Sensing range (m^2)	(0,0)~(100,100)
Sink location	(50,150)
Sensor node numbers (n)	100
Sensor node initial energy (E0)	0.5 J
E_{Tx}, E_{Rx}	50 nJ/bit
ε_{FS}	10 pJ/(bit•m^2)
E_{fuse}	5 nJ/(bit•single)
Data packet size	4000 bits
Grid length (N)	10 m
Cluster number (K)	5

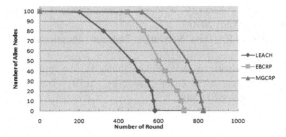

Fig. 1. Relation between the number of alive nodes and number of round with different routing protocol

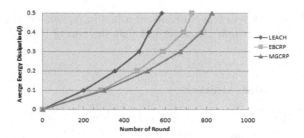

Fig. 2. Relation between consumption of average energy and number of round with different routing protocol

5   Conclusions

In this routing protocol, we grid the network and then combine these grids based on a user defined value, There are several advantages of this protocol show below. First, sensors will be allocated by high density in the same cluster no matter what the condition is. Second, we add the cluster head rotation mechanism, and it could allot workload equally to every node. Through effective clustering, the routing protocol which we proposed could save more energy and prolong the network lifetime.

References

1. Akyildiz, I.F., Weilian, S., Sankarasubramaniam, Y., Cayirci, E.: A survey on sensor networks. IEEE Communications Magazine 40(8), 102–114 (2002)
2. Al-Karaki, J.N., Kamal, A.E.: Routing techniques in wireless sensor networks: a survey. IEEE Wireless Communications 11(6), 6–28 (2004)
3. Qiangfeng, J., Manivannan, D.: Routing protocols for sensor networks. In: Proceedings of First IEEE Consumer Communications and Networking Conference, CCNC 2004, pp. 93–98 (January 2004)
4. Heinzelman, W.R., Chandrakasan, A., Balakrishnan, H.: Energy-efficient communication protocolfor wireless microsensor networks. In: Proceedings of the 33rd Annual Hawaii International Conference on System Sciences, vol. 2, p. 10 (January 2000)
5. Bao, X.-R., Zhang, S., Xue, D.-Y., Qie, Z.-T.: An Energy-Balanced Chain-Cluster Routing Protocol forWireless Sensor Networks. In: Proceedings of the 2010 2nd International Conference on Networks Security Wireless Communications and Trusted Computing (NSWCTC), pp. 79–84 (April 2010)
6. Bertsekas, D., Gallager, R.: Data Networks, 2nd edn. Prentice-Hall, Englewood Cliffs (1992)
7. Heinzelman, W.B., Chandrakasan, A.P., Balakrishnan, H.: An application-specific protocol architecture for wireless microsensor networks. IEEE Transactions on Wireless Communications 1(4), 660–670 (2002)

A Termination Detection Technique Using Gossip in Cloud Computing Environments

JongBeom Lim[1], Kwang-Sik Chung[2], and Heon-Chang Yu[1,*]

[1] Department of Computer Science Education, Korea University
[2] Department of Computer Science, Korea National Open University
{jblim,kchung0825,yuhc}@korea.ac.kr

Abstract. Termination detection is a fundamental problem in distributed systems. In previous research, some structures are used (e.g., spanning tree or computational tree) to detect termination. In this work, we present an unstructured termination detection algorithm, which uses a gossip based algorithm to cope with scalability and fault-tolerance issues. This approach allows the algorithm not to maintain structures during runtime due to node joining and leaving. These dynamic behaviors are prevalent in cloud computing environments and little attention has been paid by existing approaches. To measure the complexity of our proposed algorithm, a new metric, *self-centered message complexity* is used. Our evaluation over scalable settings shows that the unstructured approach can have a significant merit on performance over existing algorithms.

Keywords: Termination Detection, Gossip Algorithm, Cloud Computing.

1 Introduction

In the termination detection problem, a set of nodes in the system collectively execute a distributed computation. Determining whether a distributed computation has terminated is a non-trivial task because no node has complete knowledge of the global state, and there is no notion of global time or global memory. Each node only knows its own local state and local time, and communication among nodes can be done only by message passing.

Termination detection problem has been extensively studied for static distributed systems where all of the nodes are stationary in terms of node joining and leaving from the beginning to the end (e.g., [1, 2, 3, 4, 5, 6]). One of systems that termination detection algorithms can be used in is the cloud computing system in which constituent nodes can easily join and leave with dynamic behavior due to loosely-coupled environments. However, although much research for the termination detection problem in recent years mainly focuses on reducing message complexity, little attention has been paid to the aforementioned dynamic behavior. Most of the studies assumed that the system does not change anymore without considering node failures and joining which are vital aspects in cloud computing environments that should not be dismissed.

---

* Corresponding author.

J.J. Park et al. (Eds.): NPC 2012, LNCS 7513, pp. 429–436, 2012.
© IFIP International Federation for Information Processing 2012

Recently, gossip-based algorithms have received much attention due to its inherent scalable and fault-tolerant properties which offer additional benefits in distributed systems [7]. Correctness of a gossip-based protocol is presented in [8, 9]. In gossip-based algorithms, each node maintains some number of neighbors called a partial view. With this partial view, at each cycle (round), every node in the system selects f (fanout) number of nodes at random and then communicates using one of the following ways: 1) Push, 2) Pull, and 3) Push-pull mode. Gossip-based algorithms guarantee message delivery to all nodes with high probability and their variation can be found in [10, 11, 12, 13, 14]. Applications of gossip-based algorithms include message dissemination, failure detection services, data aggregation etc.

In this paper, we present an unstructured termination detection algorithm based on the gossip-based algorithm. The use of the gossip-based algorithm for the termination detection problem is a desired approach to deal with scalability and dynamic behavior in cloud computing systems. Having partial view in the gossip-based algorithm is the essential key to achieve the scalability issue. In other words, each node does not have to maintain all the nodes in the system, but the small number of nodes. Furthermore, in structured termination detection algorithms (using spanning tree or computational tree), reconstruction of the structure of algorithms is needed when node joining and leaving. Otherwise, detecting the termination of a distributed computation is virtually impossible since node connection is broken.

The rest of the paper is organized as follows. We present the system model and formally describe the termination detection problem in Section 2. Section 3 provides our gossip-based termination detection algorithm. Simulation results for the algorithm and their interpretation are given in Section 4; this section also analyzes the message complexity. Finally, Section 5 gives our conclusions.

2   Model and Problem Specifications

2.1   System Model

We assume that the cloud computing infrastructure consists of numerous nodes of resources, and individual nodes process arbitrary programs to achieve a common goal. Because of the absence of shared memory, each process or node should communicate with other nodes only by message passing through a set of channels. In addition, we assume that all channels are reliable and FIFO (first-in, first-out), meaning all messages within a channel are received in the order they are sent to. And the message delay is bounded. There is no global clock. However, it is assumed that each node synchronizes its time by gossiping with other nodes. This approach has been justified by [15]. Furthermore, the communication model is asynchronous. In other words, a sender does not have to wait for acknowledgements of receivers (non-blocking).

2.2   Specifications of the Problem

Termination detection is a fundamental problem in distributed systems; it is not an exception in cloud computing systems. The importance of determining termination derives from the observation that some nodes may execute several sub-problems, and in some cases, there are precedence dependencies among them. Because there is no shared memory, message passing is the only way to deal with the termination detection problem satisfying following properties:

- **Safety:** If the termination detection algorithm announces termination, then the underlying computation has indeed terminated.
- **Liveness:** If termination holds in the underlying computation, then eventually the termination detection algorithm announces termination and henceforth termination is not revoked.
- **Non-interference:** The termination detection algorithm must not influence the underlying computation.

The definition of termination detection is as follows: Let $P_i(t)$ denote the state (active or passive) of process P_i at time t and $C_{i,j}(t)$ denote the number of messages in transit in the channel at time t from process P_i to process P_j. A distributed computation is said to be terminated at time t if and only if:

$$(\forall i :: P_i(t) = passive) \wedge (\forall i,j :: C_{i,j}(t) = null)$$

2.3   Performance Metrics

Traditionally, the following metric has been used to measure the performance of termination detection algorithms:

- **Message Complexity:** The number of messages required to detect the termination.

In addition to the message complexity, we propose a new metric called self-centered message complexity. Self-centered message complexity counts the number of message requited to detect the termination from the requester point of view rather than from the whole nodes in the system. We conjecture that this is more flexible and simpler metric to measure the structured and unstructured termination detection algorithms because some algorithms are not always intuitive and observable at the high-level domain. Self-centered message can be defined as follows:

- **Self-centered Message Complexity:** The number of messages required to detect the termination from the requester point of view.

3   Termination Detection Technique

In this section, we first review the basic gossip-based protocol based on [16] to describe our gossip-based termination detection algorithm. The termination detection algorithm proposed in this section can be viewed as an extension of the gossip-based algorithm to support the termination detection functionality.

3.1   Termination Detection Technique Using the Gossip Algorithm

In the gossip-based algorithm, there are two different kinds of threads in each node: active and passive. At each cycle (round), an active thread selects a neighbor at random and sends a message. The active thread then waits for the message from the receiver. Upon receiving the message from the neighbor, the active thread updates local information with the received message and its own information. A passive thread waits for messages sent by active threads and replies to the senders. Afterwards, the passive thread updates its local information with the received message from the sender accordingly.

The function *getNeighbor()* returns a random neighbor identifier from its partial view, not from the entire set of nodes in our algorithm. It is noted that according to the system parameter f (fanout), *getNeighbor()* returns f number of neighbor identifiers. Additionally, before the gossiping is initiated, the partial view of nodes is constructed by the middleware called peer sampling service [16], which returns a uniform random sample from the entire set of nodes in the system.

A simple way to solve the termination detection problem is to use distributed snapshots (e.g., [3]). If a consistent snapshot of a distributed computation is taken after the distributed computation has terminated, the snapshot will capture the termination of the computation. However, the algorithm that uses distributed snapshots broadcasts to all other nodes when a process goes passive; this involves a large number of request messages. Furthermore, detecting whether all the other processes are taken a snapshot is not a trivial job even though all the other processes are passive and taken a snapshot.

Hence, we take the distributed approach with the gossip-based algorithm. To let a process decide whether all of nodes are passive and distributed computation is terminated, we use the piggybacking mechanism by which a node adds additional information of neighbors to the message during gossiping. By using the piggybacking mechanism, any node wishing to detect termination can eventually detect whether distributed computation is terminated or not.

In the previous researches using the distributed approach, however, they assumed that the number of nodes is static. Few studies have focused on the dynamic behavior such as adding and removing nodes while request operations are ongoing, which is that we want to deal with. In the dynamic scenario, it is assumed that each node can learn about newly added and removed nodes by the middleware before each cycle begins.

3.2   Unstructured Termination Detection Algorithm

The unstructured termination detection algorithm using a gossip-based approach is summarized in Figure 1. We explain only our extensions to the gossip algorithm. We assume that each process has a unique identifier and can be indexed by from 1 to n, where n is the number of processes (nodes) in the system. Henceforth, the terms a node and a process are used interchangeably.

- *Initial local state for process P_i*
  - **array of states** : $State_i[j] = passive, \forall j \in \{1 \ldots n\}$
- *During gossiping*: Process P_i executes the followings during gossiping with target P_j (where $j \neq i$):
  1. When P_i sends a basic message to P_j:
     (a) $State_i[j].state = State_j[j].state = active$;
     (b) $State_i[j].timestamp = State_j[j].timestamp = LC_{current}$;
  2. When P_j sends a basic message to P_i:
     (a) $State_i[i] = State_j[i] = active$;
     (b) $State_i[i].timestamp = State_j[i].timestamp = LC_{current}$;
  3. Updating states array:
     (a) Update each element of $State_i[k]$ and $State_j[k]$, where $\forall k \in \{1 \ldots n\}$, according to timestamp
- *When local computation is completed*:
  1. Updating local state:
     (a) $State_i[i].state = passive$;
     (b) $State_i[i].timestamp = LC_{current}$;
- *Deciding for termination*:
  1. Checking states array:
     (a) Check if $State_i[k].state == passive, \forall k \in \{1 \ldots n\}$
     (b) if (a) is true, then termination is detected.
     (c) if (a) is false, then termination is not detected.

Fig. 1. The proposed unstructured termination detection algorithm

Each process P_i maintains the following data structures:

- $State_i[1 : n]$: An array of states for P_i. This data structure consists of two elements for each array: state and timestamp. State value can be active or passive and timestamp value is logical time at which state value is updated.

We describe our extensions as follows:

1. If process P_i selects process P_j during gossiping following states are performed:
   (a) When P_i sends a basic message to P_j, State array is updated as follows:
       (i) jth elements (i.e., state and timestamp) of array of both processes are updated with *active* and $LC_{current}$.

(b) When P_j sends a basic message to P_i, State array is updated as follows:
  (i) ith elements (i.e., state and timestamp) of array of both processes are up-dated with *active* and $LC_{current}$.
(c) Each element of *State[k]* of both processes, where $\forall k \in \{1 \ldots n\}$, is updated with the one whose timestamp value is larger.
2. When local computation is completed, State values are updated as follows:
  (a) $State_i[i]$.*state* and $State_i[i]$.timestamp are updated with *passive* and $LC_{current}$, respectively.
3. In order to decide whether local computation of whole processes is completed, fol-lowing states are performed:
  (a) State array is checked:
    (i) If $State_i[k]$.*state* == *passive*, where $\forall k \in \{1 \ldots n\}$, then it concludes that termination is detected.
    (ii) Otherwise, it concludes that termination is not detected and local computa-tion of some processes is ongoing.

4   Experimental Evaluation

In this section, we present simulation results for the gossip-based termination detec-tion algorithm using the PeerSim simulator [17], which supports extreme scalability and dynamicity of nodes, and is implemented in Java. To compare our algorithms' performance, we implemented the simple broadcast algorithm that is similar to [3], which involve n-1 request messages and n-1 acknowledge messages. During entire experiments, a fanout parameter f is set to 1.

We first evaluated effects of the size of PartialView and the number of nodes. In Figure 2, we can see the results for the requisite number of cycles to detect termina-tion with varying the size of PartialView from 5 to 30 by increments of 5 for 10^4 nodes, and the number of nodes from 10^2 to $10^{4.5}$ with a PartialView size of 20. It is noted that in this experiment, we let each node update its state when a request mes-sage is received.

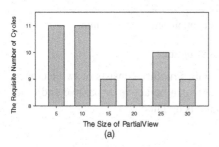
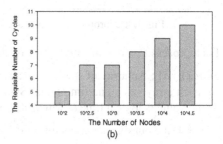

(a)   (b)

Fig. 2. The requisite numbers of cycles to detect termination. The number of nodes is set to 10^4 in (a). The size of PartialView is set to 20 in (b).

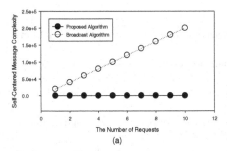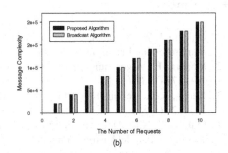

Fig. 3. The comparisons of self-centered message complexity (a) and message complexity (b) between the proposed algorithm and the broadcast algorithm

We have confirmed that effects of the size of PartialView is insignificant when the size is larger than 15 when the number of nodes is 10^4. Notice that in Figure 2(b), the requisite number of cycles grows linearly as the total number of nodes increases exponentially.

Figure 3 shows the results of message complexity. It is noted that in this experiment, the number of nodes is set to 10^4, and the size of PartialView is set to 20. When we compare self-centered message complexity of the proposed algorithm and the broadcast algorithm, our algorithm performed better than the broadcast algorithm about a 111100% improvement.

During experiments we also have confirmed that if each node changes its state to passive when local computation is finished, rather than when a request message received, the requisite number of cycles to detect termination using our unstructured algorithm is 2. In this regard, when we compare the two algorithms, message complexity is close to each other. In other words, the proposed algorithm generates $2n$ messages, while the broadcast algorithm generates $2(n-1)$ messages. This signifies that our unstructured termination detection algorithm and the broadcast algorithm have no big difference in message complexity, but in our algorithm, messages are diffused among nodes without a bottleneck.

5   Conclusion

In this work, we have presented the termination detection algorithm using a gossip-based approach to cope with scalability and fault tolerance issues. A cloud environment where the behavior of their constituting nodes is active and dynamic (i.e., joining and leaving at any time) is an example that our algorithm will be applied to. Furthermore, our gossip-based termination detection algorithm could be embedded seamlessly into other existing gossip-based algorithms. In other words, if a gossip-based algorithm is implemented for the failure-detection service, then the termination detection algorithm proposed in our work can be embedded in the existing gossip-based algorithm.

References

1. Dijkstra, E.W., Scholten, C.S.: Termination detection for diffusing computations. Information Processing Letters 11, 1–4 (1980)
2. Mattern, F.: Algorithms for distributed termination detection. Distributed Computing 2, 161–175 (1987)
3. Huang, S.-T.: Termination detection by using distributed snapshots. Inf. Process. Lett. 32, 113–120 (1989)
4. Mahapatra, N.R., Dutt, S.: An efficient delay-optimal distributed termination detection algorithm. J. Parallel Distrib. Comput. 67, 1047–1066 (2007)
5. Mittal, N., Venkatesan, S., Peri, S.: A family of optimal termination detection algorithms. Distributed Computing 20, 141–162 (2007)
6. Livesey, M., Morrison, R., Munro, D.: The Doomsday distributed termination detection protocol. Distributed Computing 19, 419–431 (2007)
7. Ganesh, A.J., Kermarrec, A.M., Massoulie, L.: Peer-to-peer membership management for gossip-based protocols. IEEE Transactions on Computers 52, 139–149 (2003)
8. Allavena, A., Demers, A., Hopcroft, J.E.: Correctness of a gossip based membership protocol. In: Proceedings of the Twenty-Fourth Annual ACM Symposium on Principles of Distributed Computing, Las Vegas, NV, USA, pp. 292–301. ACM, Las Vegas (2005)
9. Gurevich, M., Keidar, I.: Correctness of gossip-based membership under message loss. In: Proceedings of the 28th ACM Symposium on Principles of Distributed Computing, pp. 151–160. ACM, Calgary (2009)
10. Ganesh, A.J., Kermarrec, A.-M., Massoulié, L.: HiScamp: self-organizing hierarchical membership protocol. In: Proceedings of the 10th Workshop on ACM SIGOPS European Workshop, pp. 133–139. ACM, Saint-Emilion (2002)
11. Voulgaris, S., Gavidia, D., van Steen, M.: CYCLON: Inexpensive Membership Management for Unstructured P2P Overlays. Journal of Network and Systems Management 13, 197–217 (2005)
12. Matos, M., Sousa, A., Pereira, J., Oliveira, R., Deliot, E., Murray, P.: CLON: Overlay Networks and Gossip Protocols for Cloud Environments. In: Meersman, R., Dillon, T., Herrero, P. (eds.) OTM 2009, Part I. LNCS, vol. 5870, pp. 549–566. Springer, Heidelberg (2009)
13. Jelasity, M., Montresor, A., Babaoglu, O.: T-Man: Gossip-based fast overlay topology construction. Comput. Netw. 53, 2321–2339 (2009)
14. Lim, J., Lee, J., Chin, S., Yu, H.: Group-Based Gossip Multicast Protocol for Efficient and Fault Tolerant Message Dissemination in Clouds. In: Riekki, J., Ylianttila, M., Guo, M. (eds.) GPC 2011. LNCS, vol. 6646, pp. 13–22. Springer, Heidelberg (2011)
15. Iwanicki, K., van Steen, M., Voulgaris, S.: Gossip-based clock synchronization for large de-centralized systems. In: Proceedings of the Second IEEE International Conference on Self-Managed Networks, Systems, and Services, pp. 28–42. Springer, Dublin (2006)
16. Jelasity, M., Guerraoui, R., Kermarrec, A.-M., van Steen, M.: The Peer Sampling Service: Experimental Evaluation of Unstructured Gossip-Based Implementations. In: Jacobsen, H.-A. (ed.) Middleware 2004. LNCS, vol. 3231, pp. 79–98. Springer, Heidelberg (2004)
17. Montresor, A., Jelasity, M.: PeerSim: A scalable P2P simulator. In: IEEE Ninth International Conference on Peer-to-Peer Computing, P2P 2009, pp. 99–100 (2009)

OEIRM: An Open Distributed Processing Based Interoperability Reference Model for e-Science

Zhiming Zhao, Paola Grosso, and Cees de Laat

System and Network Engineering Research Group
Informatics Institute, University of Amsterdam
Science Park 904, 1098XH, Amsterdam, The Netherlands
{Z.Zhao,P.Grosso,C.T.A.M.Delaat}@uva.nl

Abstract. E-Science applications are often interdisciplinary and require resources from different infrastructures; the interoperability between heterogeneous infrastructures is an important requirement for constructing large scale experiments. Analyzing interoperability issues by including both application and infrastructure aspects promotes a global view on interoperability of different layers, and we argue it can converge to an optimal reference model to guide the development of service layers in e-Science infrastructures. This paper proposes an Open Distributed Processing based interoperability reference model for e-Science.

Keywords: e-Science, Open Distributed Processing, Interoperability, Cloud, Grid.

1   Introduction

E-Science applications are characterized by big data and interdisciplinary approaches, and require not only large computing and storage capacities, but also effective cooperative computing model to handle the application complexity [1]. Collaborating different infrastructures essentially enable the construction of large scale experiments; however, the technical diversities between infrastructures often make such collaboration difficult, and the service layer interoperability between different infrastructures has been highlighted as a key functional requirement [2].

Historically, e-Science infrastructures are often developed for specific application domain(s); the diverse application requirements result in different focuses on the infrastructure services. Even started with homogenous architecture, the evolution of technologies may still push the infrastructure upgrade towards different directions. Therefore, the interoperability between different infrastructures and the compatibility with the legacy applications from the early infrastructures will remain as a requirement in e-Science for a long term [3]. Many of the existing interoperability solutions focus on specific layers in the context e-Science: between infrastructures [4, 5], between middleware [6], and between workflows [7], and typically via iterative steps: building adapters or connectors between two infrastructures and then deriving new service layer models for standardization via certain community efforts. Such

J.J. Park et al. (Eds.): NPC 2012, LNCS 7513, pp. 437–444, 2012.

iterations can continuously promote the evolution of standards for infrastructures and the above service layers, but will not completely solve the interoperability problems when the diversity between infrastructures and the missing links between standards remain [36]. Providing interoperability solutions only at a specific layer without a global view of the entire e-Science context hampers the convergence of service layer evolution. An interoperability reference model is needed to complement the model of the application and infrastructure [8].

In this paper, we propose an interoperability reference model to analyze related issues and review the existing solutions in e-Science. We discuss how the interoperability issues should be handled in the context of the application life-cycle. The research is conducted in the context of EU F7 project ENVRI [9].

2   An Open Distributed Processing Based Reference Model

The Open Distributed Processing (ODP) model captures the design and development issues in complex distributed systems into five viewpoints, namely enterprise, information, computational, engineering and technology [10]. Although it is originally developed in the enterprise IT context, its decomposed view on system design and development contributes valuable model for analyzing the interoperability in e-Science. Following the ODP methodology, we highlight five viewpoints in analysing the interoperability in the e-Science context: scientific, information, computational, middleware and infrastructure, as shown in Fig. 1.

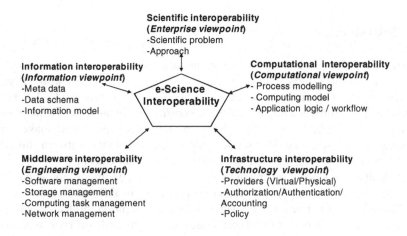

Fig. 1. An Open e-Science Interoperability Reference Model (OEIRM)

In the next section, we will review the available solutions of the interoperability using this model.

3   Interoperability in e-Science: From Infrastructure to Application

The five viewpoints proposed in Fig. 1 model the interoperability related issues not only in the service layers in infrastructure but also the characteristics of scientific domain and applications.

3.1   The Scientific Interoperability

From the scientific viewpoint, e-Science activities often require technologies or software components originally developed by different domains. The interoperability between different scientific domains and disciplines has been highlighted as the basic approach in e-Science. For instance, modeling and simulation based computing methods extend traditional laboratory based experimental sciences such as chemistry, physics and finance [11, 12], and semantic web technologies have been promoted as basis for building information models and system integration in large collections fields [13]. Moreover, many simulation models have also exhibited their power in different contexts, for instance finite element simulation model shows its strong power not only in fluid dynamics but also in studying financial problems [14]. In specific fields, the BRIDGE project aims at the distributed optimization using different simulation models and cross both ChinaGrid and EU SIMDAT [15]. These types of interoperability comprises of the basis of the interdisciplinary activities in e-Science.

3.2   The Information Interoperability

The information interoperability refers to not only data content but also meta metadata, information models and all kinds of descriptions of the services that e-Science applications need. The solutions can be roughly classified into two groups. The first one is to map diverse information models using connectors, for instance the Advanced Resource Connector ARC between EGEE and NorduGrid [16]. Semantic level interoperability enables the data exchange at the meta level, for instance the Linked Open Data principles proposed by the EU environmental sciences is for sharing scientific data [17], semantic web services based mediators [4], and semantic information preprocessing framework [18]. The second one is to synchronize diverse information representation mechanisms to one common model, for instance OGF promotes a solution named Grid Laboratory Uniform Environment (GLUE) [19]. TPT (Taiwan prescription template) is an information level interoperability solution proposed by Kuo to enable the medical exchange among different infrastructure, and is promoted as the standards for improving the patient information [20]. The information interoperability potentially realizes the semantic level information exchange between different e-Science domains.

3.3   The Computational Interoperability

From the computational viewpoint, 1) the application can be interoperable with the others by sharing and exchanging the intelligence in e-Science applications, i.e. the composition of the application logic 2) the execution engine of the application can be interoperable to execute applications from the other engines. Currently, the scientific workflow management systems from scientific computing context, and the MapReduce related Cloud computing model from large internet companies such as Google are two main forces pushes the evolution of the cooperative computing model. Although aiming at different types of data and application contexts, these two models merging from different perspectives to get benefits from each other, for instance MapReduce is included as an execution model in Kepler [20], or DAG is include in MapReduce to extend its flow control [21]. Workflow bus was proposed to realize engine level interoperability between different systems [22]. The computational interoperability focuses on the runtime issues of the e-Science applications.

3.4   The Middleware Interoperability

The middleware interoperability refers to cross invocation of services among different service layers, and mainly deals with the diversity between middleware in invoking services, in managing data involved by the service invocation. Typical approach is to provide a gateway node to map the invocation interface of both sides. Wang proposed a gateway between the submission tool in gLite and the CNGrid GOS environment, and a scheduler decides the jobs from the gateway queue to middleware of which side [23]. Another way to solve such interoperability issues is to adopt a standardized service interface for job submission, storage and network management; OGF promoted a standards named HPC basic profile (HPCBP) towards this direction [24]. Web services interoperability (WS-I) is another initiative to promote the interoperability for the web service stacks [25], although it faces several challenges to commit is final mission. An important problem that in the middleware interoperability is how to efficiently utilize the resources from different domains after the middleware interoperability has been enabled. Saga deals with the load balance issue in this context by proposing a HPCBP gateway, so that the jobs from other infrastructures will be checked against the allocation table of the local infrastructure scheduler with certain load balance constraints [26]. The Grid meta scheduler (GMS) can schedule computing tasks of workflows among several middleware gLite, Unicore and Globus environments, but mainly batch and job farming based tasks [27]. GridARS is another example but focuses on reserving the resources among different infrastructures [28].

3.5   The Infrastructure Interoperability

From the infrastructure viewpoint, distributed resources have been aggregated and virtualized as different stack of services; from Clusters, Grids and Clouds. There are several standardization initiatives for Cloud models, for instance Open Cloud Computing Interface(OCCI) [29], Open Virtualization Format [30], and Cloud data management interface (CDMI) [31]. Moreover, whole organization related issues such as management policies for sharing data and resources, including authorization, authentication and accounting issues are included, for instance security level interoperability [32,33], using model checking approach to verify the policies and rules [34].

Table 1 summarizes the existing work in one table.

Table 1. Interoperability in e-Science

	Involved issues	Approach and examples
Scientific interoperability	-Scientific problems - Scientific methods	-Problem to large system scale, and involve different domains. Interdisciplinary optimization, Bridge project [15]. -Computational sciences in many fields [11,12] Simulation models extended to different fields [14]
Information interoperability	-Scientific data -Resource description, meta data, information model	- Community based ontology framework, Linked Open Data [7] - Ontology mapping , Semantic based information preprocessing[18], ARC[16], Semantic Web Services mediators[4], - Standardized information model, GLUE [18], TPT[19],
Computational interoperability	-Joint computing model -Runtime embedding -cross invocation	- MapReduce in Scientific workflow [20], flow control in MapReduce [21] - Runtime engine: Workflow bus[22],
Middleware interoperability	-Cross data access -Cross job submission -Cross infrastructure load balance	- Gateway based protocol mapping [23] - HPCBP [24], WS-I [25] - GridARS [28], GMS [27],
Infrastructure interoperability	-Authentication/Authorization/ Accounting/Security/Policy -Infrastructure model	- Authentication/Authrization/Accounting: SAML, X.509 [32,33], XACML[34] -OCCI [29], OVF[30], CDMI[31]

4   Related Work

Interoperability has been recognized as a key issue in different contexts, and several reference models have been proposed. Riedel proposed an Infrastructure Interoperability Reference Model (IIRF) [35], which is now in the OFG community effort. The main idea of the IIRF is to fill the missing links between the existing earlier interoperability related middleware or standards, in particular the interoperability between infrastructure for High performance computing and high throughput computing. Open Grid Forum set up a working group called Grid Interoperability Now! (GIN) [36]. The IIRF focuses on the different standards in the existing Grid middleware; however, its basic concepts are compatible with model presented in this paper.

5   Summary

The research presented in this paper is conducted in the context of the EU ENVRI project; we aim at an interoperability model for promoting the resource sharing among infrastructures from different environmental science domains [9]. Using the Open Distributed Processing (ODP) model, we proposed an interoperability reference model named OEIRM, and analyzed the interoperability issues in the life cycle of e-Science applications using five different viewpoints of the model.

The diversity of the scientific domains drives the interdisciplinary research in e-Science from various angles; solving the diversity by providing interoperability support only promotes the evolution of scientific domains and all kinds of support technologies, but will not eventually remove such diversity. From this point of view, interoperability will be a continuous problem exists in the e-Science context. Different interoperability technologies as we see from the above analysis play a central role in enabling the collaborations in different contexts, but they also raises a challenge problem for the e-Science researchers: how we should deal with the interoperability issues in an evolutionary vision of the infrastructure and e-Science applications? As the next step, we will develop the reference model to guide the development of future e-Science application and service layers of infrastructures.

Acknowledgments. We would like to thank the FP7 EU funded Integrated project ENVRI project (project number 283465) and the Dutch national and education network SURFnet, through the GigaPort Research on Network (RoN) project for sponsoring this research.

References

1. Francis, J., Alexander, A., Alexander, S.: Big data. Computing in Science and Engineering 13, 10–13 (2011)
2. Geraci, A.: IEEE Standard Computer Dictionary: Compilation of IEEE Standard Computer Glossaries. IEEE Press, Piscataway (1991)
3. Charalabidis, Y., Janssen, M., Glassey, O.: Introduction to cloud infrastructures and interoperability minitrack. In: Hawaii International Conference on System Sciences, p. 2177 (2012)
4. Ngan, L., Feng, Y., Rho, S., Kanagasabai, R.: Enabling interoperability across heterogeneous semantic web services with owl-s based mediation. In: Asia-Pacific Conference on Services Computing, pp. 471–476. IEEE (2011)
5. Arcieri, F., Fioravanti, F., Nardelli, E., Talamo, M.: A layered it infrastructure for secure interoperability in personal data registry digital government services. In: International Workshop on Research Issues in Data Engineering, pp. 95–102 (2004)
6. Blair, G., Grace, P.: Emergent middleware: Tackling the interoperability problem. IEEE Internet Computing 16, 78–82 (2012)
7. Zhao, A., Belloum, A., Laat, C., Hertzberger, B.: Using jade agent framework to prototype an e-science workflow bus. In: 7th IEEE International Symposium on Cluster Computing and the Grid, pp. 655–660 (2007)
8. White, L., Wilde, N., Reichherzer, T., El-Sheikh, M., Goehring, G., Baskin, A., Hartmann, B., Manea, M.: Understanding interoperable systems: Challenges for the maintenance of soa applications. In: Hawaii International Conference on System Sciences, pp. 2199–2206 (2012)
9. EU 7th framework programme. Common operations of environmental research infrastructures, grant agreement no. 283465, http://www.envri.eu
10. Linington, P., Milosevic, Z., Tanaka, A., Vallecillo, A.: Building enterprise systems with ODP. CRC press, Taylor & Francis Group (2012)
11. Cassel, L.: Interdisciplinary computing is the answer: now, what was the question? ACM Inroads 2(1), 4–6 (2011)
12. Smarkusky, D., Toman, S.: An interdisciplinary approach in applying fundamental concepts. In: Proceedings of the 10th ACM Conference on SIG-Information Technology Education, SIGITE 2009, pp. 224–228 (2009)
13. Vattan, S., Goel, A.: Semantically annotating research articles for interdisciplinary design. In: Proceedings of the Sixth International Conference on Knowledge Capture, K-CAP 2011, pp. 165–166 (2011)

14. Qiu, G., Kandhai, B., Sloot, P.: Understanding the complex dynamics of stock markets through cellular automata. Phys. Rev. E 75, 046116 (2007)
15. Wang, Y., Roberto, D., Boniface, M., Qian, D., Cui, D., Jiang, J.: Cross-domain middlewares interoperability for distributed aircraft design optimization. In: IEEE International Conference on eScience, pp. 485–492 (2008)
16. Ellerta, M., Grnagerb, M., Konstantinovc, A., et al.: Advanced resource connector middleware for lightweight computational grids. Future Generation Computer Systems, 219–240 (2007)
17. Hausenblas, M.: Utilising linked open data in applications. In: Proceedings of the International Conference on Web Intelligence, Mining and Semantics, pp. 7:1–7:4 (2011)
18. Zhao, Z., Taal, A., Grosso, P., Laat, C.: Resource discovery in large scale network infrastructure. In: IEEE Int'l conf. on Networking Architecture and Storage (2011)
19. Field, L., Andreozzi, S., Konya, B.: Grid information system interoperability: The need for a common information model. In: IEEE International Conference on e-Science, pp. 501–507 (2008)
20. Kuo, C., Li, Y., Lee, P., Wu, Y.: An interoperability infrastructure with portable prescription for improving patient safety – the framework of a national standard in taiwan. In: World Congress on Computer Science and Information Engineering, vol. 1, pp. 293–297 (2009)
21. Budiu, M., Delling, D., Werneck, R.: Dryadopt: Branch-and-bound on distributed data-parallel execution engines. In: International Parallel and Distributed Processing Symposium, pp. 1278–1289 (2011)
22. Zhao, Z., Booms, S., Belloum, A., Laat, C., Hertzberger, B.: Vle-wfbus: a scientific workflow bus for multi e-science domains. In: Proceedings of the 2nd IEEE International Conference on e-Science and Grid Computing, pp. 11–19 (2006)
23. Wang, Y., Scardaci, D., Yan, B., Huang, Y.: Interconnect egee and cngrid e-infrastructures through interoperability between glite and gos middlewares. In: International Conference on e-Science and Grid Computing, pp. 553–560 (2007)
24. Ruiz-Alvarez, A., Smith, C., Humphrey, M.: Bes++: Hpc profile open source c implementation. In: IEEE/ACM International Workshop on Grid Computing, pp. 41–48 (2008)
25. Schoenberger, A., Schwalb, J., Wirtz, G.: Has ws-i's work resulted in ws-* interoperability? In: IEEE International Conference on Web Services, pp. 171–178 (2011)
26. Kazushige, S., Aida, K., Miura., K.: Mutual job submission architecture that considered workload balance among computing resources in the grid interoperation. In: IEEE/ACM International Workshop on Grid Computing, pp. 19–25 (2011)
27. Mirto, M., Passante, M., Aloisio, G.: A grid meta scheduler for a distributed interoperable workflow management system. In: IEEE Symposium on Computer-Based Medical Systems, pp. 138–143 (2010)
28. Takefusa, A., Nakada, H., Takano, R., Kudoh, T., Tanaka, Y.: Gridars: a grid advanced resource management system framework for intercloud. In: Proceedings of the Conference on Cloud Computing Technology and Science, pp. 705–710 (2011)
29. Open Grid Forum. Open cloud computing interface infrastructure,
    http://forge.ogf.org/sf/wiki/do/viewPage/
    proejcts.occi-wg/wiki/Infrastructure
30. Distributed management task force. Open virtualization format specification. In dsP0243 version 1.1.0 (2010)
31. Storage networking industry association. Cloud data management interface. Storage networking industry association. Tech. Report (2010)

32. Cantor, J., Philpott, P., Maler, E.: Assertions and protocols for the oasis security assertion markup language. OASIS Standard (2005)
33. Moses, T., et al.: extensible access control markup language. OASIS Standard (2005)
34. Maarabani, M., Cavalli, A., Hwang, I., Zaidi, F.: Verification of interoperability security policies by model checking. In: IEEE International Symposium on High-Assurance Systems Engineering, pp. 376–381 (2011)
35. Riedel, M., Memon, M., Memon, A., Mallmann, D., Lippert, T., Kranzlmuller, D.: e-science infrastructure integration invariants to enable htc and hpc interoperability applications. In: IEEE International Symposium on Parallel and Distributed Processing Workshops, pp. 922–931 (2011)
36. Riedel, M., Laure, E., Soddemann, T., Field, L., et al.: Interoperation of world-wide production e-science infrastructures. Concurr. Comput.: Pract. Exper. 21(8), 961–990 (2009)

Using PCI Pass-Through for GPU Virtualization with CUDA[*]

Chao-Tung Yang[**], Hsien-Yi Wang, and Yu-Tso Liu

Department of Computer Science, Tunghai University, Taichung 40704,
Taiwan ROC
ctyang@thu.edu.tw, wiath.wang@gmail.com,
vvvv6502@hotmail.com

Abstract. Nowadays, NVIDIA's CUDA is a general purpose scalable parallel programming model for writing highly parallel applications. It provides several key abstractions – a hierarchy of thread blocks, shared memory, and barrier synchronization. This model has proven quite successful at programming multithreaded many core GPUs and scales transparently to hundreds of cores: scientists throughout industry and academia are already using CUDA to achieve dramatic speedups on production and research codes. GPU-base clusters are likely to play an important role in future cloud data centers, because some compute-intensive applications may require both CPUs and GPUs. The goal of this paper is to develop a VM execution mechanism that could run these applications inside VMs and allow them to effectively leverage GPUs in such a way that different VMs can share GPUs without interfering with one another.

Keywords: CUDA, GPU virtualization, Cloud computing, IaaS, PCI pass-through.

1 Introduction

GPUs are really "manycore" processors, with hundreds of processing elements. A graphics processing unit (GPU) is a specialized microprocessor that offloads and accelerates graphics rendering from the central (micro-) processor. Modern GPUs are very efficient at manipulating computer graphics, and their highly parallel structure makes them more effective than general-purpose CPUs for a range of complex algorithms. We know that a CPU has only 8 cores at single chip currently, but a GPU has grown to 448 cores. From the number of cores, we know that GPU is appropriately to compute the programs which are suited massive parallel processing. Although the frequency of the core on the GPU is lower than CPU's, we believe that massively parallel can conquer the problem of lower frequency. By the way, GPU has been used on supercomputers. In top 500 sites for November 2010, there are three supercomputers of the first 5 are built with NVIDIA GPU [2].

---

[*] This study was supported in part by the National Science Council, Taiwan ROC, under grant numbers NSC 100-2218-E-029-004 and NSC 100-2622-E-029-008-CC3.
[**] Corresponding author.

J.J. Park et al. (Eds.): NPC 2012, LNCS 7513, pp. 445–452, 2012.

In recent years, virtualization environment on Cloud [1] become more and more popular. The balance between performance and cost is the most important point that everybody focused. For more effective to use the resource on the server, virtualization technology is the solution. Running many virtual machines on a server, the resource can be more effective to use. But the performance of virtual machines has their own limitations. Users will limit by using a lot of computing on virtual machine.

Proper use of hardware resources and computing power to each virtual machine is the Infrastructure as a Service (IaaS), which is one of the architecture of Cloud Computing. But the virtual machine has its limitations, system virtual environment does not support CUDA [4], CUDA high performance computing unable to GPU virtualization. In this paper, by using PCI pass-through technology, making the virtual machines in a virtual environment able to use the NVIDIA graphics card, and then we can use the CUDA high performance computing. Finally, we will compare the two open source virtualization environment hypervisor, whether it will be after PCI pass-through CUDA performance differences. Through the experiment, we will be able to know which environment will be the best in a virtual environment using CUDA.

Therefore, there is a new topic that let the virtual machines using the physical GPGPU (General-Purpose computing on Graphics Processing Units) in the real machine to help compute. Because GPU is really many-core processors, the computing power of virtual machines will increase by using GPU. In this paper, we introduce some of the hypervisor environment for virtualization and different virtualization types on cloud system. And we also introduce some types of hardware virtualization. This paper implements a system with virtualization environment and using PCI pass-through technology let the virtual machines on the system can use GPU accelerator to increase the computing power. Final, we discuss the performance of GPU between virtual machines and native machine.

2   Background

Virtualization [5] technology is a technology that creation of a virtual version of something, such as a hardware platform, operation system, a storage device or network resources. The goal of virtualization is to centralize administrative tasks while improving scalability and overall hardware-resource utilization. By using virtualization, several operating systems can be run on a single powerful server without glitch in parallel.

2.1   Full-Virtualization

Unlike the traditional way that put the operation system kernel to Ring 0 level, full-virtualization use hypervisor instead of that. Hypervisor manage all instructions to Ring 0 from Guest OS. Full-virtualization [6] uses the Binary Translation technology to translate all instructions to Ring 0 from Guest OS and then send the requirement to hardware. Hypervisor virtualized all hardware until, Guest OS access the hardware just like a real machine. It has highly independence. But Binary Translation technology reduces the performance of virtual machine. The architecture of full-virtualization is shown in Figure 1.

2.2   Para-Virtualization

In para-virtualization [7], does not virtualize all hardware until. There is a unique Host OS called Domain0. Domain0 is parallel with other Guest OS and use Native Operating System to manage hardware driver. Guest OS accessing the real hardware by calling the driver in Domain0 through hypervisor. The requirement sent by Guest OS to hypervisor is called Hypercall. To make the Guest OS sending the hypercall instead of sending requirement directly to hardware, the Guest OS's kernel needs to rewrite, so that some non-open-sourced operation systems cannot support.

In para-virtualization, does not virtualize all hardware until. There is a unique Host OS called Domain0. Domain0 is parallel with other Guest OS and use Native Operating System to manage hardware driver. Guest OS accessing the real hardware by calling the driver in Domain0 through hypervisor. The requirement sent by Guest OS to hypervisor is called Hypercall. To make the Guest OS sending the hypercall instead of sending requirement directly to hardware, the Guest OS's kernel needs to rewrite, so that some non-open-sourced operation systems cannot support. The architecture of para-virtualization is shown in Figure 2.

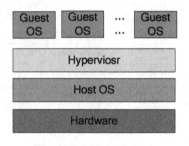

Fig. 1. Full-Virtualization

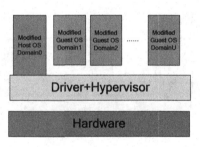

Fig. 2. Para-Virtualization

2.3   Xen

The VM Layer of Host OS type deploys on Host OS, such like Windows or Linux, and then installs other operation system on top of VM Layer. The operation systems on top the VM Layer are called Guest OS. Xen's hypervisor is installed directly in the host, and the other operation systems we want deploy are on top of it. It is easier to manage CPU, Memory, Network, Storage and other resource. The main purpose of Xen [3] uses hypervisor type and its VMM (Virtual Machine Monitor) is more efficient and safety to control the host CPU, Memory and other resource.

Xen uses a unit called Domain to manage virtual machines. Domain is divided into two types as shown in Figure 3, one of them is called Domain0, played like Host OS, has control AP of Xen, used for management. Another type called DomainU is a field that Guest OS installed on it. When using physical resource, DomainU cannot call the hardware driver directly, it must be through Domain0 to deal with.

2.4   Related Work

There are some approaches that pursue the virtualization of the CUDA Runtime API for VMs such as rCUDA [12], vCUDA, GViM [13] and gVirtuS [14]. The solutions feature a distributed middleware comprised of two parts, the front-end and the back-end. Figure 4 shows that the front-end middleware is installed in the virtual machine, and the back-end middleware with direct access to the acceleration hardware, is running by host OS with executing the VMM.

rCUDA using Sockets API to let the client and server have communication with each other. And client can use the GPU on server through that. It is a production-ready framework to run CUDA applications from VMs, based in a recent CUDA API version. We can use this middleware to make a customized communications protocol and is independent.

VMGL [16] is the OpenGL hardware 3D acceleration for virtual machines, OpenGL apps can run inside a virtual machine through VMGL. VMGL can be used on VMware guests, Xen HVM domains (depending on hardware virtualization extensions) and Xen paravirtual domains, using XVnc or the virtual frame buffer. VMGL is available for X11-based guest OS's: Linux, FreeBSD and OpenSolaris. Finally, VMGL is GPU-independent: we support ATI, nVidia and Intel GPUs.

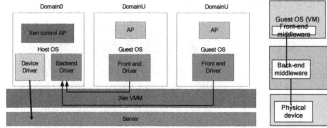

Fig. 3. Domain0 and DomainU

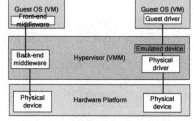

Fig. 4. Front-End and Back-End

The key idea in vCUDA is: API call interception and redirection. With API interception and redirection, applications in VMs can access graphics hardware device and achieve high performance computing applications. It allows the application executing within virtual machines to leverage hardware acceleration. They explained how to access graphics hardware in VMs transparently by API call interception and redirection. Their evaluation showed that GPU acceleration for HPC applications in VMs is feasible and competitive with those running in a native, non-virtualized environment [8].

GViM is a system designed for virtualization and managing the resources of a general purpose system accelerated by graphics processors. GViM uses Xen-specific mechanisms for the communication between front-end and back-end middleware. The GViM virtualization infrastructure for a GPGPU platform enables the sharing and consolidation of graphics processors. Their experimental measurements of a Xen-based GViM implementation on a multi-core platform with multiple attached

NVIDIA graphics accelerators demonstrate small performance penalties for virtualized vs. non-virtualized settings, coupled with substantial improvements concerning fairness in accelerator use by multiple VMs.

In J. Duato's work, he uses remote GPU for virtual machine. Although his virtualization technique noticeably increases execution time when using a 1 Gbps Ethernet network, it performs almost as efficiently as a local GPU when higher performance interconnects are used. Therefore, the small overhead incurred by our proposal because of remote use of GPUs is worth the savings that a cluster configuration with less GPUs than nodes reports [11].

Atsushi Kawai and Kenji Yasuoka proposed DS-CUDA, a middleware to virtualize a GPU cluster as a distributed shared GPU system. It simplifies development of a code that uses multiple GPUs distributed on a network. Results with good scalability were shown in their paper. Also the usefulness of the redundant calculation mechanism is confirmed.

3   System Implementation

To use GPU accelerator on virtual machines, this paper plans using PCI pass-through to implement the system for better performance. For performance, near-native performance can be achieved using device pass-through. This technology is perfect for networking applications or those that have high disk I/O or like using hardware accelerator that have not adopted virtualization because of contention and performance degradation through the hypervisor. But assigning devices to specific guests is also useful when those devices cannot be shared. For example, if a system included multiple video adapters, those adapters could be passed through to unique guest domains.

VT-d Pass-Through is a technique to give a DomU exclusive access to a PCI function using the IOMMU[17] provided by VT-d. It is primarily targeted at HVM (fully virtualized) guests because Para-Virtualized pass-through does not require VT-d .There is an important thing that your hardware must support that. In addition to the motherboard chipset and BIOS also your CPU must have support for IOMMU IO virtualization (VT-d). VT-d is disabled by default, to enable it, need "iommu" parameter to enable it. The system architecture and user point of view are shown in Figures 5 and 6, respectively.

4   Experimental Results

Previously, we have conducted the design principle and implementation methods. We present here several experiment conducts on two machines. The node's hardware specification is listed in Table 1. In Table 1, we use a machine with the Xeon E5506, 12GB memory, CentOS 6.2 with Xen. Quadro NVS 295 is using for primary graphics card. Tesla C1060 is the one we using for computing and passing through to virtual machine.

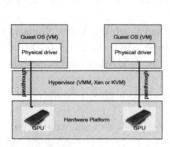

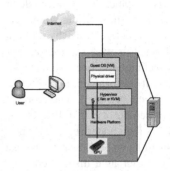

Fig. 5. System architecture   **Fig. 6.** User point of view

Table 2 is the hardware/software specification of virtual machines. We want discuss that the CPU number will or not affect the performance of virtual machine in PCI pass-through. So we will use 1, 2 or 4 CPUs in our virtual machine to see the difference between each other. These of virtual machines' virtualization type are full, because we found out that PCI pass-through is not working in para-virtualization in our research.

Table 1. Hardware/Software Specification

Hardware/Software Specification						
	CPU	Memory	Disk	OS	Hypervisor	GPU
Node	Xeon E5506	12GB	1TB	CentOS 6.2	Xen	Quadro NVS 295/ Tesla C1060

Table 2. Hardware/Software Specification of Virtual Machines

Hardware/Software Specification of Virtual Machine							
	CPU	Memory	Disk	OS	Hypervisor	GPU	Virtualization
VM1	1	1024MB	12GB	CentOS 6.2	Xen	Tesla C1060	Full
VM2	2	1024MB	12GB	CentOS 6.2	Xen	Tesla C1060	Full
VM3	4	1024MB	12GB	CentOS 6.2	Xen	Tesla C1060	Full

We use seven benchmarks for performance comparison: alignedTypes, asyncAPI, BlackScholes, clock, convolutionSeparable, fastWalshTransform and matrixMul. These seven benchmarks are part of CUDA SDK. From many benchmarks in the suite, we select 7 representative SDK benchmarks of varying computation loads and data size which use different CUDA feature. These benchmarks are executed with the default options. And we also test the bandwidth between GPU and virtual machine. We want to see that the PCI pass-through technology will affect the bandwidth or not.

The first experiment is performance comparison between native and virtual machine. We will present how much GPU performance will be reduced with PCI pass-through. The second experimental result is performance comparison among three virtual machines with one CPU, two CPUs and four CPUs, respectively. We will demonstrate the number of CPU used in virtual machines will affect the GPU performance or not. All SDK benchmarks' execution time is measured by the Linux command 'time' in the CentOS 6.2.

We first analyze the performance of the CUDA SDK benchmarks running in a VM using PCI pass-through, and compare their execution times with those of a native environment —i.e., using the regular CUDA Runtime library in a non-virtualized environment. Figure 10 shows that the execution time on processing the SDK benchmark in native and virtual machine using one CPU on Xen. We can see the real time of these benchmarks on virtual machine is less than native machine.

Figure 11 shows that the different execution time between virtual machines which one has one CPU, another has two CPUs. In this figure, we can see that the number of CPUs does not affect the user time, which means the GPU computing time is not changed when the number of CPU changed one to two. Figure 12 shows that the execution time between two CPUs and four CPUs in virtual machines which based on Xen. In this figure, we can see more clearly about the number of CPU does not affect the performance of GPU. In Figures 10, 11 and 12, we can demonstrate that the execution time is very close. Only the system time is significantly different.

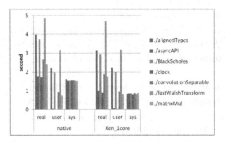

Fig. 7. Execution Time between Native and Virtual Machine

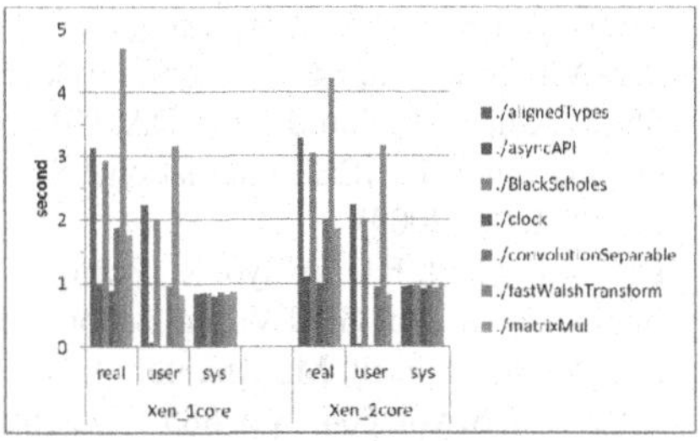

Fig. 8. Execution Time between 1 Core and 2 Core Virtual Machine

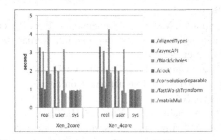

Fig. 9. Execution Time between 2-Core and 4-Core Virtual Machines

5   Conclusions

As we know, the method of CUDA is famous in parallel programming. The performance could get better after the serial codes translated to the codes which using this method. Virtualization is also a famous thing in recent year. Through the virtualization technology, we can use the resource on the serve more efficient. Using the PCI pass-through to implement that computing with GPU accelerator in virtual machines is very helpful. In our work, we can see the performance of GPU is the same between native and virtual machine. No matter how many CPU in virtual machine, the GPU provide the same performance by PCI pass-through. Even we using virtual machine, the system time are less than real machine. And the system time of the virtual machine using one CPU is less than the four. The inner communication in virtual machine is not through the real hardware but just in the memory on the real machine. Using the PCI pass-through to implement that computing with GPU accelerator in virtual machines is saving more resource, and has the same performance with real machine in computing overall.

References

1. Cloud computing, http://en.wikipedia.org/wiki/Cloud_computing
2. NVIDIA, http://www.nvidia.com.tw
3. Xen, http://www.xen.org/
4. CUDA, http://en.wikipedia.org/wiki/CUDA
5. Virtualization, http://en.wikipedia.org/wiki/Virtualization
6. Full Virtualization,
   http://en.wikipedia.org/wiki/Full_virtualization
7. Para Virtualization, http://en.wikipedia.org/wiki/Paravirtualization
8. Shi, L., Chen, H., Sun, J.: vCUDA: GPU accelerated high performance computing in virtual machines. In: IEEE International Symposium on Parallel & Distributed Processing, IPDPS 2009 (2009)
9. Duato, J., Igual, F.D., Mayo, R., Peña, A.J., Quintana-Ortí, E.S., Silla, F.: An Efficient Implementation of GPU Virtualization in High Performance Clusters. In: Lin, H.-X., Alexander, M., Forsell, M., Knüpfer, A., Prodan, R., Sousa, L., Streit, A. (eds.) Euro-Par 2009. LNCS, vol. 6043, pp. 385–394. Springer, Heidelberg (2010)
10. Duato, J., Peña, A.J., Silla, F., Mayo, R., Quintana-Ort, E.S.: rCUDA: Reducing the number of GPU based accelerators in high performance clusters. In: Proceedings of the 2010 International Conference on High Performance Computing & Simulation (HPCS 2010), pp. 224–231 (June 2010)
11. Duato, J., Peña, A.J., Silla, F., Mayo, R., Quintana-Orti, E.S.: Performance of CUDA virtualized remote GPUs in high performance clusters. In: International Conference on Parallel Processing, ICPP (September 2011)
12. D. Inf. de Sist. y Comput., Univ. Politec, Enabling CUDA acceleration within virtual machines using rCUDA. In: 2011 18th International Conference on High Performance Computing (HiPC) (December 2011)
13. Gupta, V., Gavrilovska, A., Schwan, K., Kharche, H., Tolia, N., Talwar, V., Ranganathan, P.: GViM: GPU-accelerated virtual machines. In: 3rd Workshop on System-level Virtualization for High Performance Computing, pp. 17–24. ACM, NY (2009)
14. Giunta, G., Montella, R., Agrillo, G., Coviello, G.: A GPGPU Transparent Virtualization Component for High Performance Computing Clouds. In: D'Ambra, P., Guarracino, M., Talia, D. (eds.) Euro-Par 2010, Part I. LNCS, vol. 6271, pp. 379–391. Springer, Heidelberg (2010)
15. Yang, C.T., Huang, C.L., Lin, C.F.: Hybrid CUDA, OpenMP, and MPI Parallel Programming on Multicore GPU Clusters. Computer Physics Communications 182(1), 266–269 (2010)
16. VMGL, http://sysweb.cs.toronto.edu/vmgl
17. Amit, N., Ben-Yehuda, M., Yassour, B.-A.: IOMMU: Strategies for Mitigating the IOTLB Bottleneck. In: Varbanescu, A.L., Molnos, A., van Nieuwpoort, R. (eds.) ISCA. LNCS, vol. 6161, pp. 256–274. Springer, Heidelberg (2011)

Parallel Valuation of the Lower and Upper Bound Prices for Multi-asset Bermudan Options

Nan Zhang and Ka Lok Man

Department of Computer Science and Software Engineering,
Xi'an Jiaotong-Liverpool University, China
{nan.zhang,ka.man}@xjtlu.edu.cn

Abstract. We present a parallel algorithm and its multi-threaded implementation for computing lower and upper bound prices of multi-asset Bermudan options. Our baseline sequential algorithm follows Longstaff and Schwartz's least-squares Monte Carlo method in computing the lower bound and Andersen and Broadie's simulation-based procedure with sub-optimality checking for the upper bound. The parallel implementation uses POSIX Threads for thread manipulation and Intel's MKL functions for random number generation and linear algebra operations. Tests were made on Intel x86 multi-core processors using the same option examples as the previous work, and the runtimes of the same computations were reduced from minutes to a few seconds.

Keywords: Parallel computing, option pricing, multi-asset Bermudan options, Monte Carlo simulation.

1 Introduction

An equity call or put option is a financial contract that gives its holder the right without obligation to buy or sell a unit of the underlying asset at a pre-agreed strike price K until a future expiration time T. In exchanging for this right, the buyer of such an option must pay the seller a certain amount of premium. The problem of option pricing is to compute the fair price of such an option contract. A buyer of a European-style option can only exercise the right of buying or selling at the expiration time T. In contrast, an American-style option can be exercised any time before T. Closed-form analytical formulas have been derived for the prices of many European options under a variety of models, the most widely-used being the Black-Scholes formula [3] under the geometric Brownian motion model. However, for American options, because of the early-exercise feature, closed-form expressions have not been found. For this reason, their prices are often computed using numerical procedures.

Various finite-difference schemes and lattice-based methods are such procedures often used to price American options. With these methods the early-exercise boundary of an American option can be easily determined. Whenever the payoff from exercising exceeds the option's continuation value at an exercise time it is assumed that the option should be exercised. However, when an option's value depends on a basket of assets it is not efficient to model the dynamics of the asset prices using either of these two methods. Instead, simulation-based approaches can easily incorporate multiple assets, but the determining of continuation values at early exercise times is not as easy.

J.J. Park et al. (Eds.): NPC 2012, LNCS 7513, pp. 453–462, 2012.
© IFIP International Federation for Information Processing 2012

Regression-based methods [5,13,11] have been proposed to estimate the continuation values, and, thus, to enable Monte Carlo simulations to be applied in computing the prices of multi-asset American options. Longstaff and Schwartz [11] apply linear least-squares regression at every exercise time spot using observed continuation values on all in-the-money paths to find the coefficients of an assumed linear relationship between true continuation values and prices of the underlying assets. Algorithms like this produce low-biased estimations for the true price of an American option because the exercise strategies generated using the regressions are often sub-optimal. Hence, these algorithms compute lower bounds for the prices of multi-asset American options.

Andersen and Broadie [2] proposed a duality-based algorithm that computes upper bounds for multi-asset American options. The algorithm works with any lower bound estimator and presents the upper bound as the sum of the lower bound and a penalty term. The penalty term is a non-negative quantity representing a compensation for the potential incorrect exercise decisions made by following a sub-optimal strategy. Nested Monte Carlo simulations were used in [2] to compute the term. Optimisations were proposed in [4] for improving and accelerating the computing of the lower and upper bounds.

We present in this paper a parallel algorithm for computing the lower and upper bounds of multi-asset Bermudan[1] options. The algorithm parallelises the least-squares Monte Carlo lower bound estimator [11] and the primal-dual upper bound algorithm [2]. The sub-optimality checking discussed in [4] is also incorporated into the upper bound computation. The parallel algorithm was implemented via POSIX Threads, and works on shared-memory x86 multi-core processors. Highly-optimised functions from Intel's Math Kernel Library (MKL) [9,10] were used in the implementation for linear algebra operations and random number generation. Experiments on an entry-level dual-core processor (2.4GHz Intel P8600) showed that the computational times for the same five-asset max-call Bermudan options were reduced from several minutes (as reported in [4] Table 3) to just a few seconds.[2] All the source codes for this work is freely available via email.[3]

In Section 2 we briefly present the lower and upper bound algorithms [11,2,4]. The parallel algorithm is presented in Section 3. Experimental results are reported in Section 4. Related work is discussed in Section 5. Conclusions and future work are found Section 6.

2   Sequential Computing the Lower and Upper Bounds

Assume a Bermudan option has d exercise opportunities within time period 0 to T. These exercise times are denoted by $0 < t_1 < t_2 < \cdots < t_d = T$. The Bermudan option's value depends on a basket of n assets whose state $\boldsymbol{S}_i = (S_i^1, S_i^2, \ldots, S_i^n)^4$ at time t_i, $i \in [1, d]$, follows a vector-valued Markov process on $\mathbb{R}^n$ with initial value $\boldsymbol{S}_0$.

---

[1] Bermudan options are American-style options that can be exercised at a series of discrete time spots.

[2] Admittedly, the tests in [4] were made on a 2.0GHz Intel Pentium 4, a model much older than the processor we used in our tests.

[3] Email: nan.zhang@xjtlu.edu.cn

[4] We use the subscript i for t_i. So $\boldsymbol{S}_i$ is actually $\boldsymbol{S}_{t_i}$.

Let B_t denote the time t value of one unit of cash invested in a risk-free money market account at time 0. Let h_i denote the payoff from exercising the option at the stopping time t_i, where $t_i \in \mathcal{F} = \{t_1, t_2, \dots, t_d\}$. The price Q_0 of the Bermudan option is, therefore, $Q_0 = \sup_{t_i \in \mathcal{F}} \mathbb{E}_0(h_i/B_i)$, where $\mathbb{E}_i$ denotes the expectation conditional on the information available until time t_i. The algorithm described in [11] computes not Q_0 but L_0, where $L_0 = \mathbb{E}_0(h_i/B_i) \leq Q_0$. The quantity L_0 is a low-biased price of the option obtained by following some specific exercise policy rather than the optimal one.

To compute L_0 using Monte Carlo simulations we have to estimate the continuation values at each exercise time, so that on a path j at time t_i, $i \in [1, d]$, if the immediate payoff exceeds the continuation value the option is assumed to be exercised. The computation starts from time $t_d = T$, at which it is assumed that the option is exercised for all in-the-money paths. The payoffs h_d on all simulated paths are then used as the observed continuation values for the estimation of the continuation value at time t_{d-1}. The algorithm [11] assumes a linear relationship between the true continuation value C_{d-1} at time t_{d-1} and the state variable S_{d-1} such that $C_{d-1} = e_{d-1}^1 f_1(S_{d-1}) + e_{d-1}^2 f_2(S_{d-1}) + \dots + e_{d-1}^m f_m(S_{d-1})$. The m functions $f_1, f_2, \dots, f_m$ are the pre-defined basis functions, and $e_{d-1}^1, e_{d-1}^2, \dots, e_{d-1}^m$ are the coefficients whose values are estimated by the following least-squares regression.

Assume totally N_R simulation paths are launched and at time t_{d-1} there are p in-the-money paths. We use $1, 2, \dots, p$[5] to index these in-the-money paths. We form a p-by-m (p rows and m columns) design matrix A_{d-1} whose jth row, $j \in [1, p]$, is $A_{d-1}^j = (f_1(S_{d-1}^j), f_2(S_{d-1}^j), \dots, f_m(S_{d-1}^j))$, where S_{d-1}^j is the n-dimensional vector-valued state variable at time t_{d-1} on the jth in-the-money path. Then we form the p-dimensional vector $V_{d-1} = (B_{d-1}h_{d-1}^1/B_d, B_{d-1}h_{d-1}^2/B_d, \dots, B_{d-1}h_{d-1}^p/B_d)$, where $B_{d-1}h_{d-1}^j/B_d$ is the observed discounted continuation value on the jth in-the-money path at time t_{d-1}. Now we can set up a linear system and solve the m-dimensional vector $E_{d-1} = (e_{d-1}^1, e_{d-1}^2, \dots, e_{d-1}^m)$ for the exercise time t_{d-1} by minimising the merit function $\chi^2 = \Sigma_{i=1}^p (V_{d-1}^i - A_{d-1}^i E_{d-1}^\mathrm{T})^2$, where V_{d-1}^i is the ith component of vector V_{d-1} and A_{d-1}^i is the ith row of the matrix A_{d-1}. The merit function is a measure for the aggregated difference between the observed continuation values and the estimated continuation values.

The linear system can be solved by using either QR or LQ factorisation, depending on whether it is over-determined or under-determined. Alternatively, the more robust singular value decomposition can be used at a higher computational cost. In our implementation the MKL function LAPACKE_dgels is used for solving the linear system. More details about the MKL functions for the factorisations can be found in the online reference [10]. Once E_{d-1} has been computed the p-dimensional vector $\hat{C}_{d-1}^\mathrm{T} = A_{d-1}E_{d-1}^\mathrm{T}$ can be derived, which contains the estimated continuation values for the p in-the-money paths. This process proceeds backwards from time t_{d-1} to t_1 and outputs the d-by-m coefficient matrix E, whose ith row, $i \in [1, d-1]$, stores the coefficients for the exercise time t_i. The dth row of E is filled by zeroes.

After the estimated exercise policy coefficient matrix E is obtained, another N_L simulation paths are launched. On a jth path at the first exercise time t_i, $i \in [1, d]$,

---

[5] These are not their indexes in the whole N_R simulated paths.

when $h_i^j > (f_1(\boldsymbol{S}_i^j), f_2(\boldsymbol{S}_i^j), \ldots, f_m(\boldsymbol{S}_i^j))\boldsymbol{E}_i{}^{\mathrm{T}}$, the option is assumed to be exercised, and the time 0 value of the resulted cashflow is h_i^j/B_i. The low-biased option price L_0 is the mean of such cashflows on all the N_L simulated paths.

The upper bound U_0 of the option is defined in [2] as $U_0 = L_0 + \Delta_0$, where Δ_0 is a penalty term defined as $\Delta_0 = \mathbb{E}_0(\max_{t_i \in \mathscr{F}}(h_i/B_i - \pi_i))$. The process π_i is a martingale defined in [4] by $\pi_{i+1} = \pi_i + L_{i+1}/B_{i+1} - Q_i/B_i$ at time t_{i+1}, $i \in [1, d-1]$. At time 0 and time t_1 it is defined as $\pi_0 = L_0$ and $\pi_1 = L_1/B_1$. The process L_{i+1}/B_{i+1} is the discounted lower bound price at time t_{i+1} and is computed by $L_{i+1}/B_{i+1} = \mathbb{E}_{i+1}(h_{\tau_{i+1}}/B_{\tau_{i+1}})$, where τ_{i+1} is the first exercise time instance starting from time t_{i+1} at which exercise is indicated. The algorithm in [4] with sub-optimality checking suggests computing π_i only at those exercise times when exercise is suggested.

To estimate Δ_0 we simulate N_H paths, each of which has $d + 1$ time steps, corresponding to the n-dimensional vector state variables $\boldsymbol{S}_0, \boldsymbol{S}_1, \ldots, \boldsymbol{S}_d$. On a jth simulated path, starting from time t_1 we ignore all exercise times at which continuation is suggested by the exercise policy. For a time t_i, $i \in [1, d]$, if exercise is suggested, we follow one of the two procedures listed below.

1. If time t_i is the first exercise time on the jth path at which exercise is suggested, we set π_i^j to the discounted option's payoff, which is also the discounted option value in this case, and so we have $\pi_i^j = h_i^j/B_i$. We then launch N_S simulation trials to estimate $Q_i/B_i = \mathbb{E}_i(h_{\tau_i}/B_{\tau_i})$. This is the discounted option's continuation value from time t_i if continuation is enforced. As above, stopping time τ_i is the first exercise time instance starting from time t_i at which exercise is suggested. The penalty term Δ_i^j is set to 0.

2. If, otherwise, time t_i is not the first exercise time on the jth path at which exercise is suggested, we set $\pi_i^j = \pi_l^j + h_i^j/B_i - Q_l/B_l$, where t_l is the previous exercise time on the jth path at which exercise is suggested. By the time when π_i^j is computed the values of π_l^j and Q_l/B_l are already available. We then launch N_S simulation trials to estimate $Q_i/B_i = \mathbb{E}_i(h_{\tau_i}/B_{\tau_i})$ for later use. The penalty term Δ_i^j in this case is set to $\Delta_i^j = h_i^j/B_i - \pi_i^j$.

The penalty term Δ^j for the jth path is then set to $\Delta^j = \max(\Delta_1^j, \Delta_2^j, \ldots, \Delta_d^j)$. The penalty terms for the exercise times at which continuation is suggested are set to zeroes. After the penalty terms have been computed for all the N_H paths, the upper bound increment Δ_0 is set to the mean of all the penalty terms. The upper bound U_0 is therefore $U_0 = L_0 + \Delta_0$. Fig. 1 shows an example path of the simulation using a single-asset Bermudan call option.

Note that the above-listed procedure is derived from the simplified definition of π_i and Proposition 4.1 in [4]. If $\hat{L}_0$ is the lower bound estimation obtained by N_L simulation trials with a sample standard deviation $\hat{s_L}$ and $\hat{\Delta}_0$ is the estimation for the increment using N_H trials with a sample standard deviation $\hat{s_\Delta}$, as in [2], a $100(1-\alpha)\%$-probability confidence interval for the price Q_0 of the Bermudan option can be computed as $[\hat{L}_0 - z_{1-\alpha/2}\hat{s_L}/\sqrt{N_L}, \ \hat{L}_0 + \hat{\Delta}_0 + z_{1-\alpha/2}\sqrt{\hat{s_L}^2/N_L + \hat{s_\Delta}^2/N_H}]$ with z_x denoting the xth percentile of a standard Gaussian distribution.

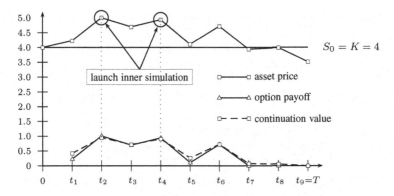

Fig. 1. A simulation path for a single-asset Bermudan call option, which can be exercised at times $t_1, t_2, \ldots, t_9 = T$. On this path, at times t_2 and t_4 the payoff exceeds the continuation value, and so the inner simulation is only launched at these two time spots.

3   The Parallel Computing of the Lower and Upper Bounds

In computing the L_0 and Δ_0, besides the procedures explained in Section 2, there are auxiliary steps, such as generating random numbers and constructing simulation paths for computing the coefficient matrix E. A complete sequence of the steps for computing the L_0 and Δ_0 is found in Fig. 2.

In a parallel computer system having c processors, we denote the processors by $p_1, p_2, \ldots, p_c$. In our program, the parallelisation was achieved through POSIX Threads which works on shared-memory multi-processor systems. However, the parallel algorithm is not confined by such platforms. The construction of the N_R simulation paths for estimating the coefficient matrix E needs ndN_R standardised normally distributed random numbers ($\mathcal{N}(0, 1)$). With c processors, this task is equally divided such that each processor generates ndN_R/c random numbers and then constructs N_R/c paths. For each processor p_i, $i \in [1, c]$, it starts generating random numbers from the $(i-1)ndN_R/c$ position in the stream, so that there is no overlap between the processors.

The computing of the coefficient vectors $E_{d-1}, E_{d-2}, \ldots, E_1$ needs $d - 1$ iterations. In each of the iterations, cross-sectional information needs to be collected, which makes this phase not as natural to be parallelised as the others. However, the MKL function LAPACKE_dgels and other functions for linear algebra we used support multithreading, and as a result of that this phase was not explicitly threaded.

After obtaining the matrix E, the lower bound L_0 is computed over N_L paths where maximumly ndN_L random numbers may be needed. Each of the c processors completes an equal fraction of this task.

The estimation of Δ_0 is also equally divided among the c processors. Like the computation of L_0, the exact number of random numbers to be needed is unknown beforehand. However, in this case, the maximum number $nd^2N_HN_S$ is so large that, often, they cannot all be generated and stored as 8-byte double-precision floats. Hence, we

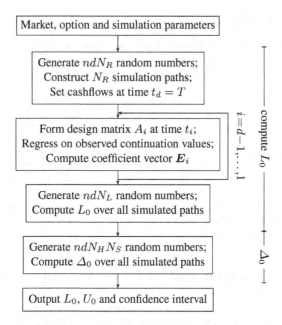

Fig. 2. Steps for computing lower bound L_0 and upper bound $U_0 = L_0 + \Delta_0$

only generated $ndN_H N_S$ random numbers with each processor generating an equally-lengthed segment without overlapping. For any processor p_i, $i \in [1, c]$, in the simulation if the numbers in its segment are used up, it will roll back to the beginning of the segment.

When the program starts, the main thread is bound onto processor p_1. When using the c processors for explicit threading, the main thread spawns $c - 1$ child threads and binds each of them onto one of the processors $p_2, p_3, \ldots, p_c$. After generating the child threads, the main thread is given an equal fraction of the task to complete. During this course we disable the multi-threading feature of the MKL functions to avoid resource contention [9]. This can be done by using the MKL function `mkl_set_num_threads` to set the number of threads used by MKL to 1. However, when estimating the coefficient vectors we enable the multi-threading feature by setting the number to c. Nevertheless, the MKL functions may dynamically adjust the number of threads they actually use during the computation. The sequence of the parallel computing is shown in Algorithm 1.

4   Experimental Results

We used the same multi-asset symmetric Bermudan max call options [2,4] to test our sequential and parallel implementations. Each of these Bermudan options depends on a basket of n uncorrelated equity assets. The risk-neutral dynamics of their prices all follow geometric Brownian motion processes. For a jth, $j \in [1, n]$, asset in the basket, its price dynamic at time t is modelled by the equation $dS_t^j = (r - \delta)S_t^j dt + \sigma S_t^j dW_t^j$, where r is the annual risk-free interest rate, δ is the dividend yield of the equity asset,

---

Algorithm 1. Parallel computing of L_0 and U_0 using c processors $p_1, p_2, \ldots, p_c$

Input: Market, option and simulation parameters.
Output: L_0, Δ_0, U_0 and a $100(1-\alpha)\%$-probablity confidence interval.

1 **begin**
2 | Bind main thread onto processor p_1.
3 | Set the number of threads used by MKL to 1.
4 | Spawn $c - 1$ child threads and bind each of them onto one of $p_2, p_3, \ldots, p_c$.
5 | **with** c threads **in parallel do**
6 | | Generate ndN_R standardised normally distributed random numbers.
7 | | Construct N_R simulation paths.
8 | Allow main thread to reside on any one of the c processors.
9 | Set the number of threads used by MKL to c.
10 | Compute coefficient matrix $E = (\mathbf{0}, \boldsymbol{E}_1, \ldots, \boldsymbol{E}_{d-1}, \mathbf{0})^{\mathrm{T}}$.
11 | Bind main thread onto processor p_1.
12 | Set the number of threads used by MKL to 1.
13 | Spawn $c - 1$ child threads and bind each of them onto one of $p_2, p_3, \ldots, p_c$.
14 | **with** c threads **in parallel do**
15 | | Generate ndN_L standardised normally distributed random numbers.
16 | | Compute cashflows on the N_L simulated paths.
17 | Set L_0 to the mean of the cashflows.
18 | Spawn $c - 1$ child threads and bind each of them onto one of $p_2, p_3, \ldots, p_c$.
19 | **with** c threads **in parallel do**
20 | | Generate $ndN_H N_S$ standardised normally distributed random numbers.
21 | | Compute increments of the N_H simulated paths.
22 | Set Δ_0 to the mean of the increments.
23 | Set $U_0 = L_0 + \Delta_0$.
24 | Compute the confidence interval.
25 **end**

σ is the annual volatility and W_t^j is a standard Brownian motion process. The time t value of one unit of cash invested at time 0 is $B_t = \exp(rt)$. The d exercise times for the options are equally spaced at times $t_i = iT/d$, $i = 1, 2, \ldots, d$. On the simulated paths, from a time t_i to time t_{i+1}, $i \in [0, d-1]$, the price of a jth asset is updated by $S_{i+1}^j = S_i^j \exp((r - \delta - \sigma^2/2)(t_{i+1} - t_i) + \sigma\epsilon\sqrt{t_{i+1} - t_i})$, where ϵ is a $\mathcal{N}(0, 1)$ random number. The options' strike prices are K, and so the payoff of such an option at time t_i, $i \in [1, d]$, is $h_i(\boldsymbol{S}_i) = (\max(\boldsymbol{S}_i^1, \boldsymbol{S}_i^2, \ldots, \boldsymbol{S}_i^n) - K)^+$. For comparison purposes we used the same values for the market and simulation parameters as in [2] and [4]. We set $K = 100$, $r = 0.05$, $\delta = 0.1$, $T = 3$, $\sigma = 0.2$, $d = 9$, $N_R = 200,000$, $N_L = 2,000,000$, $N_H = 1,500$, $N_S = 1,000$ and $\boldsymbol{S}_0 = (S, S, \ldots, S)$. For the five-asset Bermudan options we used the same 18 basis functions found in Appendix A.2 [4]. For the three-asset Bermudan options we used the first 10 functions and the first 8 for the two-asset Bermudan options.

The sequential and parallel implementations were programed in C/C++. The NPTL (native POSIX thread library) 2.12.1 was used for the threading. The tests were made on

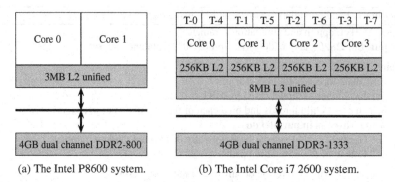

(a) The Intel P8600 system.   (b) The Intel Core i7 2600 system.

Fig. 3. Multi-core machines used in tests

Intel multi-core systems running Ubuntu Linux 10.10 (64 bit). The binary executables were compiled by the Intel compiler icpc 12.0 for Linux.

We first present in Table 1 the results from three groups of tests using the Bermudan max call options when $n = 2, 3, 5$. Some data reported in Table 2 [2] and Table 3 [4] are included in the table for comparison. These groups of tests were made on a 2.4GHz dual-core Intel P8600 processor (Fig. 3(a)). We show the results on this entry-level multi-core processor to demonstrate that our sequential and parallel implementations are practical on common personal computers.

From the data reported in Table 1 we can see that the $\hat{L}_0$s and $\hat{U}_0$s produced by the parallel program are very close to the data reported in [2] and [4], yet the runtimes were much shorter. We also ran tests using the seven five-asset Bermudan options on a 3.4GHz (turbo boost to 3.8GHz) quad-core (8 threads with hyperthreading) Intel Core i7 2600 processor (Fig. 3(b)). It took the sequential program 27.19 seconds to compute the $\hat{L}_0$s and $\hat{U}_0$s for the seven options and the parallel program 11.66 seconds using eight threads.

5   Related Work

Choudhuryet al. [6] parallelised Longstaff and Schwartz's lower bound algorithm. The lower bound estimating algorithm was divided into three phases: path simulation, calibration (in which the least-squares regressions are performed) and valuation. They used singular value decomposition in preference of its robustness, and they explicitly parallelised the calibration phase, exploiting the fact that the decomposition of the design matrices is mutually independent. The parallel algorithm was implemented using the Quantlib open-source library [1]. A speedup of 18 times for the whole lower bound algorithm was achieved on a 32 processor Blue Gene system. Doan et al. [7] presented two parallel Monte Carlo based algorithms for pricing multi-asset Bermudan options. The first of the two algorithms parallelises the approach proposed by Ibanez and Zapatero [8] which computes the optimal exercise boundary of an option through parameterisation. The second parallelises the algorithm proposed by Picazo [12] which computes continuation values through classification. Their algorithms were evaluated in a desktop grid environment.

Table 1. Computational and timing results on Intel dual-core 2.4GHz P8600

S_0	$\hat{L}_0$	T_L	$\hat{U}_0$	T_U	T_P	T_S	T'_S	95% CI	95% CI'
$n = 2, m = 8$									
90	8.048	1.80	8.051	0.48	2.28	2.59		[8.043, 8.068]	[8.053, 8.082]
100	13.886	1.71	13.891	0.52	2.23	2.88		[13.881, 13.912]	[13.892, 13.934]
110	21.341	1.82	21.345	0.59	2.41	3.14		[21.335, 21.370]	[21.316, 21.359]
Total runtime					6.91	8.61			
$n = 3, m = 10$									
90	11.254	2.06	11.257	0.70	2.75	4.00		[11.249, 11.277]	[11.265, 11.308]
100	18.653	2.45	18.660	0.76	3.21	4.50		[18.647, 18.684]	[18.661, 18.728]
110	27.546	2.66	27.556	0.83	3.49	4.82		[27.539, 27.584]	[27.512, 27.663]
Total runtime					9.44	13.31			
$n = 5, m = 18$									
70	3.899	2.74	3.901	1.02	3.76	5.63	46.2	[3.895, 3.912]	[3.880, 3.913]
80	9.024	3.30	9.029	1.07	4.37	6.52	54	[9.019, 9.046]	[8.984, 9.033]
90	16.612	4.25	16.618	1.17	5.42	7.88	85.2	[16.607, 16.641]	[16.599, 16.686]
100	26.125	5.10	26.143	1.23	6.33	9.03	121.8	[26.119, 26.170]	[26.093, 26.194]
110	36.746	5.30	36.771	1.28	6.58	9.33	151.2	[36.740, 36.802]	[36.681, 36.819]
120	47.890	5.31	47.909	1.33	6.63	9.44	168.6	[47.883, 47.943]	[47.816, 48.033]
130	59.352	5.33	59.379	1.33	6.66	9.47	198	[59.345, 59.415]	[59.199, 59.437]
Total runtime					39.75	57.29			

Notes: The estimations $\hat{L}_0$, $\hat{U}_0$ and the 95% CI were computed by our parallel program. T_L is the parallel runtime for computing the $\hat{L}_0$ and T_U is the parallel runtime for computing the $\hat{U}_0$. T_P is the total parallel runtime, $T_P = T_L + T_U$. T_S is the runtime of our sequential program in computing $\hat{L}_0$ and $\hat{U}_0$. T'_S is the runtime reported in the middle panel of Table 3 [4]. There, the original runtimes were measured in minutes. Here, they are converted to seconds. The data of 95% CI' for $n = 2, 3$ are copied from Table 2 [2], and that for $n = 5$ are copied from the middle panel of Table 3 [4]. No timing result was found in Table 2 [2], and, therefore, data for T'_S when $n = 2, 3$ are not included in the table.

6 Conclusions

We have presented a parallel algorithm and its implementation that computes the lower and upper bound prices of multi-asset Bermudan options. The algorithm parallelises the lower bound estimator proposed in [11] and the upper bound estimator proposed in [2] with the sub-optimality checking discussed in [4]. The parallel implementation uses POSIX Threads for multi-threading and Intel's high-performance MKL functions for random number generation, QR or LQ factorisation and vector and matrix operations. Tests were made using the same symmetric five-asset Bermudan max call options as in [2,4]. The results on an entry-level 2.4GHz dual-core Intel P8600 showed that it took the parallel program a few seconds to price anyone of the Bermudan options, while in [4], some of the same tasks needed several minutes on a 2.0GHz Intel Pentium 4.

The factorisation of the design matrix for different exercise times is independent of each other, although the overall procedure for the least-squares regressions is sequential.

This fact can be exploited to explicit parallelise the factorisations as the approach presented in [6]. The reason we did not exploit this opportunity in our parallel algorithm was that through testing we found that in the tested examples the cost of the explicit multi-threading exceeded that of the implicit multi-threading of the MKL functions. However, in our future work, for examples of larger scales we may explicit parallelise the factorisations at different exercise times to achieve better scalability.

Another possible direction for future work is that we may work on implementing the parallel algorithm on general-purpose GPUs using CUDA or OpenCL to achieve further better performance.

References

1. Quantlib: A Free/Open-source Library for Quantitative Finance,
   http://quantlib.org/index.shtml
2. Andersen, L., Broadie, M.: Primal-Dual Simulation Algorithm for Pricing Multidimensional American Options. Management Science 50(9), 1222–1234 (2004)
3. Black, F., Scholes, M.: The Pricing of Options and Corporate Liabilities. The Journal of Political Economy 81(3), 637–659 (1973)
4. Broadie, M., Cao, M.: Improved Lower and Upper Bound Algorithms for Pricing American Options by Simulation. Quantitative Finance 8(8), 845–861 (2008)
5. Carriere, J.F.: Valuation of the Early-Exercise Price for Options using Simulations and Non-parametric Regression. Insurance: Mathematics and Economics 19(1), 19–30 (1996)
6. Choudhury, A.R., King, A., Kumar, S., Sabharwal, Y.: Optimizations in Financial Engineering: The Least-Squares Monte Carlo Method of Longstaff and Schwartz. In: Proceedings of the 2008 IEEE International Symposium on Parallel and Distributed Processing (IPDPS), pp. 1–11. IEEE (April 2008)
7. Doan, V., Gaikwad, A., Bossy, M., Baude, F., Stokes-Rees, I.: Parallel Pricing Algorithms for Multi-Dimensional Bermudan/American Options using Monte Carlo Methods. Mathematics and Computers in Simulation 81(3), 568–577 (2010)
8. Ibáñez, A., Zapatero, F.: Monte Carlo Valuation of American Options through Computation of the Optimal Exercise Frontier. Journal of Financial and Quantitative Analysis 39(2), 253–275 (2004)
9. Intel Corporation: Intel Math Kernel Library for Linux OS: User's Guide, Document Number: 314774-018US (2011), http://software.intel.com/en-us/articles/intel-math-kernel-library-documentation/
10. Intel Corporation: Intel Math Kernel Library Reference Manual, Document Number: 630813-044US (2011), http://software.intel.com/en-us/articles/intel-math-kernel-library-documentation/
11. Longstaff, F.A., Schwartz, E.S.: Valuing American Options by Simulation: A Simple Least-Squares Approach. The Review of Financial Studies 14(1), 113–147 (2001)
12. Picazo, J.A.: American Option Pricing: A Classification-Monte Carlo (CMC) Approach. In: Monte Carlo and Quasi-Monte Carlo Methods 2000: Proceedings of a Conference Held at Hong Kong Baptist University, pp. 422–433. Springer (December 2000)
13. Tsitsiklis, J.N., Roy, B.V.: Optimal Stopping of Markov Processes: Hilbert Space Theory, Approximation Algorithms, and An Application to Pricing High-Dimensional Financial Derivatives. IEEE Transactions on Automatic Control 44(10), 1840–1851 (1999)

Insight of Direct Search Methods and Module-Integrated Algorithms for Maximum Power Point Tracking (MPPT) of Stand-Alone Photovoltaic Systems

Jieming Ma[1,2,*], Ka Lok Man[1,3], T.O. Ting[1], Hyunshin Lee[3], Taikyeong Jeong[3], Jong-Kug Sean[4], Sheng-Uei Guan[1], and Prudence W.H. Wong[2]

[1] Xi'an Jiaotong, Liverpool University, China
[2] University of Liverpool, UK
[3] Myongji University, South Korea
[4] LS Industrial Systems, South Korea
jieming@liv.ac.uk

Abstract. By detection of input signal, Maximum Power Point Tracking (MPPT) algorithms are used to maximize the potential output power. Since Perturbation and Observe (P&O) method was first applied in a Photovoltaic (PV) system, a myriad of MPPT algorithms has been proposed. With the pros and cons of various MPPT algorithms, a detailed analysis of several typical direct search and module-integrated MPPT algorithms is presented in this paper. Directions of future work for implementing new MPPT algorithms are also outlined.

Keywords: Maximum Power Point Tracking (MPPT) algorithms, Photovoltaic (PV) system, Perturbation and observe (P&O) method.

1 Introduction

To address the environmental issue, Photovoltaic (PV) solar generation has attracted increasing attention as one of the most potential and promising alternative energy sources. By taking the advantage of directly converting solar energy into current electricity, PV stands as a paradigm of reducing carbon dioxide emission, and the use of PV has been proposed by many countries.

Recent research has shown that the performance of PV modules is sensitive to the operating environment [9], and therefore the output Current-Voltage (I-V) characteristic curve of commercial PV modules exhibited nonlinear characteristics. Fig. 1 shows the variation of the I-V curves under different irradiation and temperature conditions. It can be observed that the Maximum Power Point (MPP) [3], at which the PV generator delivers the maximum output power, varies with these weather conditions.

In order to gain maximum energy conversion efficiency, researchers have proposed a series of novel algorithms for tracking the MPPs. In terms of the control strategies, Maximum Power Point Tracking (MPPT) algorithms can be classified as direct search methods and module-integrated algorithms. Direct search methods, which

---

* Corresponding author.

J.J. Park et al. (Eds.): NPC 2012, LNCS 7513, pp. 463–471, 2012.

profit from its simple implementation, have been most commonly used in practice for a long time. Based on the measurements of PV electricity, direct seeking methods locate the operating point without considering any environment factors. Module-integrated algorithms, however, usually require a large number of experimental data or mathematical functions deduced from the physical properties of PV materials. In most cases, thermometers and light meters are applied in module-integrated PV systems to evaluate the atmospheric factors. Not only the additional measurements increase the hardware cost, but their accuracy also affects the performance of MPPT algorithms. Thus, traditional module-integrated approaches were thought to be expensive and unreliable [14]. That is the most likely reason why one particular direct MPPT algorithm (e.g. Perturb-and-Observe (P&O) [8]) with imperfect tracking performance claimed by many researchers, continuously has exuberant vitality.

With recent advances in the field of Integrated Circuit (IC) manufacturing technology, the performance of hardware toolkits has been improved tremendously while the cost has dropped significantly. All these aspects have led to a renewed interest in module-integrated MPPT algorithms. Many module-integrated microcontroller-based PV systems have shown flexibility and reliable performance in MPPT compared with conventional direct approaches [4].

The advantages and disadvantages of direct search methods for MPPT are discussed in the next section. Section 3 illustrates two practical module-integrated algorithms: Particle Swarm Optimization (PSO [4]) and Golden Section Search (GSS [15]). The last section is devoted to discussions and conclusions along with directions for future work.

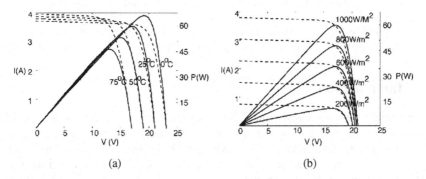

(a)   (b)

Fig. 1. The variation of the P-V and I-V curves under (a) varying temperature and (b) varying irradiance

2   Direct Search MPPT Methods

Since Hill Climbing algorithms appeared in literature on power electronics in 80's of the last century, many new direct MPPT methods have emerged in a rapid succession [8, 2, 13, 7]. The common advantage of the cohort of algorithms is their environment-independent features. Environmental measurements and sampling technologies have not been widely used over the last two decades due to their immaturity and faultiness. A small quantity of measurements not only means the lower cost that can be attained, but also indicates the higher accuracy and reliability that can be achieved.

2.1   Perturbation and Observe (P&O) Method

P&O is a well-known practical MPPT algorithm and is presented in the literature as a reference method. On the basis of the Power-Voltage (P-V) characteristics curve of a PV module, P&O method perturbs the operating point and determines the change of direction by comparing the power with the historical reference value.

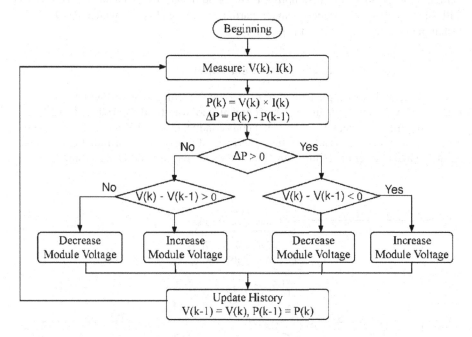

Fig. 2. Conventional Perturbation and Observe algorithm flowchart

Fig. 2 shows a flowchart for the basic algorithm for the most basic form. Starting from the measures of the operating voltage and current, the algorithm firstly obtains the sign of ΔP, which denotes the difference between the current operating power and the reference power. When the sign of ΔP is positive, the direction of assigned increment is identical to that of the perturbation of the operating voltage. On the contrary, it is opposite as long as the ΔP is negative.

A P&O algorithm is independent of PV generator characteristics and thus its simplicity and flexibility are widely recognized by many the researchers. However, the shortcomings of P&O have been proven in numerous papers since P&O was firstly applied in PV systems. Even in an ideal environment, the operating point oscillates around the MPP, which significantly affects the tracking efficiency. The easiest way of improving the oscillation is to apply smaller increments. However, this approach will slow down the tracking speed. A clever variable perturbation step size is introduced in [2]. The flexible increment can avoid intense oscillation while at the same time keeping the acceptable efficiency from the start of tracking stage. The minor disadvantage comes from the approximation module based framework, which increases the complexity of the algorithm. The accuracy of the module, like many used in module-integrated methods, directly affects the seeking efficiency.

The weather conditions, which are transformers of P-V characteristic, are hard to predict and are usually non-linear. Since P&O algorithm refers to a particular hill-like P-V curve monotonously, the weakness of tracking changing MPP is obvious. As has been illustrated in [8], P&O method fails under rapidly changing atmospheric conditions. The seeking direction may be set wrong as long as the irradiance and/or temperature change(s) within a sampling time. In addition, the P-V characteristic curve will show multi-peak property under partial shadows [11], in which P&O MPPT technique may fail in tracking the global MPP.

2.2   Incremental Conductance (IncCond) Method

IncCond method was implemented to overcome the limitations of P&O MPPT algorithms under a rapidly changing environment and was firstly introduced in [8]. By comparing the incremental and instantaneous conductance of PV modules, the control process can detect the variety of atmospheric conditions (e.g. solar radiation and temperature) and correct the failure situation of the conventional P&O algorithm.

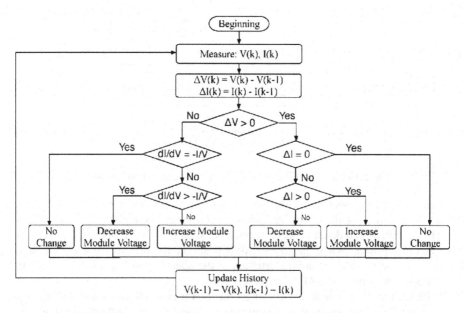

Fig. 3. Conventional Incremental Conductance algorithm flowchart

An algorithm flowchart of the IncCond method is shown in Fig. 3. The IncCond algorithm starts from detecting the changes of weather conditions. The increase of the irradiation can be recognized by dV = 0 and dI > 0, while dV = 0 and dI < 0 can determine the decrease of the irradiation. The increment voltage is given as the direction of the irradiation. If changes in voltage and current are both detected, the control of the operating voltage will be based on the relationship between the location of operating point in P-V curve and the sign of module conductance. When the operating point is located at the left side of MPP, the sign of the conductance is negative. On the contrary, the conductance turns out to be positive as long as the operating point is at the right-hand side of MPP. The value of the conductance drops to zero when it reaches the MPP. Since

$$\frac{dP}{dV} = \frac{d(V \cdot I)}{dV} = I + V \frac{dI}{dV} \tag{1}$$

these relationships can be given by

$$\frac{\Delta P}{\Delta V} = -\frac{I}{V}, \text{ at MPP}$$

$$\frac{\Delta P}{\Delta V} > -\frac{I}{V}, \text{ left of MPP}$$

$$\frac{\Delta P}{\Delta V} < -\frac{I}{V}, \text{ right of MPP} \tag{2}$$

Though IncCond method fills in the blank of environment consideration, many of the inherent drawbacks, like oscillation and disability of particle shadow conditions, limit its application.

3   Module-Integrated MPPT Algorithms

Direct method is able to drive the operating voltage near MPP gradually, yet it usually requires much sampling time to obtain a satisfactory accuracy. Moreover, the characteristic of PV modules is shown nonlinear and related to many weather factors. It is difficult to determine the search direction in terms of the current and voltage only. Module-integrated MPPT algorithms are implemented based on the mathematical functions obtained from empirical data and can calculate the MPP directly. [4] also showed the flexibility and low cost of module-integrated methods. However, the conventional module-integrated MPPT algorithms were thought to be unfeasible since the performance is dependent on the accuracy of sensors and approximation modules. The complexity of the algorithm is significantly increased due to the calculation of the electrical property of the PV module (e.g. current, voltage or power). Even in a simple MPPT algorithm, more sampling time is required as long as the number of power point evaluation is large. It is well-known that the weather condition changes quickly at some times. If the sampling time is long, the operating voltage, which was estimated for the condition of the previous sample time, may be not proper for the current environment. The tracking efficiency is therefore limited by the lag of the control. Recent advances on PV module modeling and sensing technologies have led a renewable interest in module-integrated method. Two optimization algorithms were applied in [4] and [15], which describe the application of Particle Swarm Optimization and Golden Section Search in PV system respectively. The simulation results proved the MPPT efficiency of such algorithms is superior to that of direct search approaches.

3.1   Particle Swarm Optimization (PSO)

Particle Swarm Optimization (PSO) [10] is one of the prominent algorithms in the category of nature-inspired algorithms and it has been one of the most successful numerical optimization algorithms applied in many fields. One of the advantageous features of PSO is due to its ability to converge quickly to a potential solution. In other words, PSO is faster compared to many evolutionary algorithms such as Genetic Algorithm (GA) [5].

PSO works as follows. Firstly, candidate solutions (or commonly known as particles) are initially seeded onto the search space in a random manner. These particles will then move through the problem space with the aim of finding the global optimum. The movement is guided by the essentially important ingredient formulas:

$$X_i^{t+1} = X_i^t + wV_i^{t-1} + 2r_1(X_i^t - Pbest_i^t) + 2r_2(X_i^t - Gbest_i^t) \qquad (3)$$

whereby V_i^t is the velocity for i^{th} dimension at time t, w is the inertia weight, usually is set to 0.5, X_i^t is the current position of ith dimension at time t, $Pbest_i^t$ is the best position for i^{th} dimension at time t of a particle, also known as personal best, $Pbest_i^t$ is the best solution among all participating particles for i^{th} dimension at time t, also known as global best, r_1 and r_1 are independent uniform random numbers within [0, 1].

In each iteration, all particles will be evaluated through a similar cost function. Then, update of Pbest and Gbest values are performed instantly. In other words, the asynchronous update is adopted here. The reason for asynchronous update is that the information of Pbest and Gbest can be feedback into the whole population instantly without delay and this will accelerate the convergence rate.

During the update of velocity through [10], the limit of Vmax and Vmin is imposed, usually within 10%, 50% or 100% of search space. The value chosen for Vmax and Vmin is not really crucial and does not affect the performance drastically. Also, after the update through (2), checking is done to ensure that particles only explore the predefined search space. Many techniques are used to handle this boundary values. Simply set the value to boundary limit is one of the alternatives. Another alternative will be to impose re-initialization within the search space upon violation. The later alternative is preferred as this will increase the diversity of the population and hence assist in avoiding local optima. The similar boundary handling technique is adopted in this work. As the number of iteration increases, particles accelerate towards those with better fitness until maximum iteration is reached.

3.2   Golden Section Search (GSS)

GSS is named after the function values of three testing points, whose distances form a golden ratio. As shown in Fig. 4, a line starting from X_l and ending at X_u can be divided into two line segments by the intermediate points X_l. The ratio of the whole line to the larger segment is equal to the ratio of the larger segment to the smaller segment. The relationship can be described in a mathematical way as:

$$\frac{l_1+l_2}{l_1} = \frac{l_1}{l_2} \qquad (4)$$

where l_1 is the length of the larger segment and l_2 is the length of the smaller one. If l_1/l_2 is defined as φ, the Equation (4) can be further express as:

$$\varphi^2 - \varphi - 1 = 0 \qquad (5)$$

After solving the above equation, the positive root is the golden ratio which is equal to 1.61803398874989. Like bisection search [6], GSS releases another intermediate point X_2 , whose position is also chosen in terms of the golden ratio but in an opposite direction.

By successively comparing the values of intermediate points and replacing the upper or lower bound with the internal point, the searching range can be gradually narrowed and the MPP is obtained as the midpoint of a small interval at last. As cleverly placing the intermediate points, recalculation of the integrated module is not required and thus the algorithm speed is improved. However, GSS only works for an unimodal function. When PV modules work under a partial shadow condition, a global search technique is required to assist the tracking process.

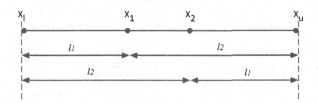

Fig. 4. Intermediate points set of GSS algorithm

4   Experimental Results

The performance of MPPT algorithms is verified by using computer simulation. The PV system introduced in [12] is selected in this paper. It consists of a PV module (MSX60 [1]), a micro-controller, a DC-DC converter and a resistive load (5Ω). The MPPT algorithms are performed by the micro-controller and the computed operating voltage is used to maximize the output power. Fig. 5 shows the testing environment data. As is defined in [8], the feasibility of the MPPT algorithms is evaluated by the MPPT efficiency, which can be expressed as

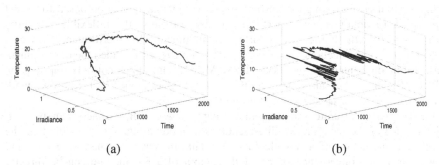

| (a) | (b) |

Fig. 5. Testing environments (a) a sunny day and (b) a cloudy day

$$\eta_{MPPT} = \frac{\int P_{actual}(t)dt}{\int P_{max}(t)dt} 100\% \tag{6}$$

where P_{actual} and P_{max} are the simulated PV power and the theoretical maximum PV power respectively.

Table 1 compares the performance of MPPT algorithms. By comparing the incremental and instantaneous conductance of the PV array, IncCond algorithm gains slightly higher accuracy than P&O method. However, the accuracy of the two direct search methods are reduced about 10% as the input data of a cloudy day was chosen. GSS shows high speed and MPPT efficiency both in a cloudy day and a sunny day.

Table 1. Performance comparison of MPPT algorithms

Algorithms	Parameters	Environment	MPPT efficiency	Elapsed fictime
P&O	Increment=0.01 V	Sunny day	99.9699%	5.697698s
		Cloudy day	90.7315%	6.855091s
IncCond	Increment=0.01 V	Sunny day	99.9722%	0.980223s
		Cloudy day	90.7850%	0.999242s
GSS	Absolute error=0.01 V	Sunny day	99.9999%	25.8170s
		Cloudy day	99.9992%	26.2450s
PSO	Absolute error=0.01 V. Population size=15, Inertia weight=0.5	Sunny day	99.9937%	105.1850s
		Cloudy day	99.9773%	109.5920s

5   Discussion and Conclusion

Several direct search methods and module-integrated MPPT algorithms are presented in this paper. Also, the effectiveness and efficiency of these algorithms are analyzed. Algorithm complexity, tracking speed, robustness and range of effectiveness are all the factors affecting PV system efficiency. With the ease of implementation, acceptable MPPT efficiency and low cost sensors, the direct search algorithms have been widely used for a long time. Many improvements have been proposed for direct approaches to obtain a better performance. Nevertheless, the inflexible searching method becomes the bottleneck of further development. High-performance low-cost IC technologies and accurate modeling manners have recently widen the development space for module-integrated methods. These MPPT algorithms not only improve the MPPT efficiency, but also enhance the processing capability for rigorous work environment (e.g. partial shadow conditions).

Based on the accurate sampling data, many new design manners can be considered. One of the most known disadvantages of module-integrated methods is the complex computation of a module function. This increases the hardware cost and slows down the convergence speed. If the output of a PV module can be directly expressed as a mathematical expression in terms of several environment variables, many negative features of module-integrated algorithms can be eliminated. Furthermore, more practical optimization techniques, such as gradient method, can be applied in a multivariable controlled system. The specially designed PV system will be much cheaper and faster than the computational intelligence algorithm, whereby tracking MPP is based on a large number   of random points.

References

1. 60-Watt Multicrystalline Photovoltaic Module ovoltaic Module Datasheet. BP (2002)
2. Al-Amoudi, A., Zhang, L.: Optimal control of a grid-connected pv system for maximum power point tracking and unity power factor. In: Seventh International Conference on Power Electronics and Variable Speed Drives (Conf. Publ. No. 456), pp. 80–85 (September 1998)
3. Castaner, L., Silvestre, S.: Modelling Photovoltaic System using PSpice. John Wiley & Sons Inc. (2002)
4. Chen, L.R., Tsai, C.H., Lin, Y.L., Lai, Y.S.: A biological swarm chasing algorithm for tracking the pv maximum power point. IEEE Transactions on Energy Conversion 25(2), 484–493 (2010)
5. Deb, K., Pratap, A., Agarwal, S., Meyarivan, T.: A fast and elitist multiobjective genetic algorithm: Nsga-ii. IEEE Transactions on Evolutionary Computation 6(2), 182–197 (2002)
6. Foster, I., Kesselman, C.: Practical Optimization: Algorithms and Engineering Applications. Springer (2007)
7. Hua, C., Lin, J., Shen, C.: Implementation of a dsp-controlled photovoltaic system with peak power tracking. IEEE Transactions on Industrial Electronics 45(1), 99–107 (1998)
8. Hussein, K.H., Muta, I., Hoshino, T., Osakada, M.: Maximum photovoltaic power tracking: an algorithm for rapidly changing atmospheric conditions. IEE Proceedings Generation, Transmission and Distribution 142(1), 59–64 (1995)
9. Ishaque, K., Salam, Z., Syafaruddin: A comprehensive matlab simulink pv system simulator with partial shading capability based on two-diode model. Solar Energy 85(9), 2217–2227 (2011)
10. Kennedy, J., Eberhart, R.: Particle swarm optimization. In: Proceedings of IEEE International Conference on Neural Networks, vol. 4, pp. 1942–1948 (November/December 1995)
11. Nguyen, D., Lehman, B.: An adaptive solar photovoltaic array using model-based reconfiguration algorithm. IEEE Transactions on Industrial Electronics 55(7), 2644–2654 (2008)
12. Oi, A.: Design and Simulation of Photovoltaic water pumping system. California Polytechnic State University (2009)
13. Salameh, Z., Taylor, D.: Step-up maximum power point tracker for photovoltaic arrays. Solar Energy 44(1), 57–61 (1990)
14. Salas, V., Olas, E., Barrado, A., Lzaro, A.: Review of the maximum power point tracking algorithms for stand-alone photovoltaic systems. Solar Energy Materials and Solar Cells 90(11), 1555–1578 (2006)
15. Shao, R., Chang, L.: A new maximum power point tracking method for photovoltaic arrays using golden section search algorithm. In: Canadian Conference on Electrical and Computer Engineering, CCECE 2008, pp. 619–622 (May 2008)

Pricing Bermudan Interest Rate Swaptions via Parallel Simulation under the Extended Multi-factor LIBOR Market Model

Nan Zhang[1], Ka Lok Man[1], and Eng Gee Lim[2]

[1] Department of Computer Science and Software Engineering,
Xi'an Jiaotong-Liverpool University, China
{nan.zhang,ka.man}@xjtlu.edu.cn
[2] Department of Electrical and Electronic Engineering,
Xi'an Jiaotong-Liverpool University, China
enggee@xjtlu.edu.cn

Abstract. We present a parallel algorithm and its implementation that computes lower and upper bounds for prices of Bermudan swaptions. The evolving of the underlying forward rates is assumed to follow the extended multi-factor LIBOR market model. We follow the Longstaff-Schwartz least-squares approach in computing a lower bound and the Andersen-Broadie duality-based procedure in computing an upper bound. Parallelisation in the implementation is achieved through POSIX threading. High-performance Intel MKL functions are used for regression and linear algebra operations. The parallel implementation was tested using Bermudan swaptions with different parameters on Intel multi-core machines. In all the tests the parallel program produced close results to those reported in the previous studies. Significant speedups were observed against an efficient sequential implementation built for comparison.

Keywords: Parallel computing, Bermudan swaption pricing, LIBOR market model, Monte Carlo simulation.

1 Introduction

An interest rate swap is an agreement between two parties to exchange cash flows equal to interest at a pre-determined fixed rate on a notional principal for cash flows equal to interest at a floating rate on the same principal for a pre-determined number of years. The exchanges of cash flows take place on pre-scheduled dates which usually span equal length of periods known as the accrual period, often three or six months. The floating rate in most interest rate swaps is the LIBOR (London Interbank Offered Rate) rate. The party who pays out fixed-rate interests and receives floating-rate interests is known as the fixed payer of the swap. A Bermudan swaption is an option which gives the holder the right to enter an interest rate swap at each date in a series of exercise dates, provided this right has not been exercised before. Bermudan swaptions are one of the most important and widely traded derivatives in fixed-income markets.

The LIBOR market model framework [4,9,11] and its extensions [2] are often used to compute the prices of Bermudan swaptions. Due to its large number of state variables,

J.J. Park et al. (Eds.): NPC 2012, LNCS 7513, pp. 472–481, 2012.

lattice-based methods are not feasible for this model class, and the pricing generally requires Monte Carlo simulations. To make Monte Carlo simulation be able to handle the built-in early exercise feature in Bermudan-style options Longstaff and Schwartz [10] proposed the least-squares Monte Carlo approach, which determines the early exercise boundary through linear regressions. Prices for Bermudan options computed using this regression-based method are biased low to the true values, because the exercise strategies generated by the regressions are inferior to the optimal ones. For upper bounds on Bermudan options Andersen and Broadie [3] proposed a Monte Carlo algorithm that uses the duality representation of the options' value function. Combining the low- and high-biased pricing algorithms gives valid confidence intervals for the true price of a Bermudan swaption.

However, the lower and upper bound pricing algorithms are computationally demanding. The upper bound algorithm requires nested simulations. To accelerate the algorithms we developed parallel solutions to the Longstaff-Schwartz method for lower bound and the Andersen-Broadie method for upper bound, and applied them to the pricing of Bermudan swaptions in the extended multi-factor LIBOR market model. The parallel algorithms are designed to work on shared-memory x86 multi-core processors that dominate today's PC markets. The parallelisation was achieved through fine-tuned POSIX threads. Mathematical functions from Intel's highly optimised Math Kernel Library (MKL) [7,8] were used for linear algebra operations. Various source code optimisations, such as common sub-expression elimination, were hard coded into the programs. The parallel implementation was tested on common Intel multi-core processors using the same examples as in [3]. The longest execution time was found in the valuation of the 8% fixed rate 11-year contract. On the quad-core 3.4GHz Intel Core i7-2600 used in the tests it took about eleven seconds to find the swaption's lower and upper bound prices using eight threads.

In Section 2 we briefly discuss the extended multi-factor LIBOR market model. The lower and upper bound estimations for Bermudan swaptions are discussed in Section 3. The parallel algorithm is presented in Section 4. Experimental results are reported in Section 5. Conclusions are summarised in Section 6.

2 Model Setup

Define an increasing maturity structure $0 = t_0 < t_1 < t_2, \ldots, < t_K$ and time t_i price $P(t_i, t_j)$ of a zero-coupon bond paying off \$1 at time t_j for $i \leq j$ and $i, j \in \{0, 1, 2, \ldots, K\}$. The LIBOR market model in general does not put any restriction on the increasing maturity structure, but our implementation assumed that any two successive time spots in the structure span an equidistant accrual period, often three or six months in practice. While the function $P(,)$ can be defined on any time spots not necessarily coinciding with the dates in the maturity structure, we define it on dates in the maturity structure to simplify the problem and, thus, to serve the purpose of our implementation. The discrete forward rate $F_{t_j}(t_i)$ for any t_i and t_j when $i \leq j$ and $i, j \in \{0, 1, 2, \ldots, K-1\}$ that applies to period between t_j and t_{j+1} observed at time t_i is defined as

$$F_{t_j}(t_i) = F_j(i) = \frac{1}{\delta_j}\left(\frac{P(t_i, t_j)}{P(t_i, t_{j+1})} - 1\right), \quad \delta_j = t_{j+1} - t_j \tag{1}$$

With this definition for forward rates, the definition for $P(t_i, t_j)$ can be written as

$$P(t_i, t_j) = P(i, j) = \prod_{k=i}^{j-1}\left(\frac{1}{1 + \delta_k F_k(i)}\right), \quad i \le j, \ i, j \in \{0, 1, 2, \dots, K\} \tag{2}$$

Note that in Equation (2) the production is performed up to time t_{j-1}, because the forward rate $F_{j-1}(i)$ applies to the period from time t_{j-1} to time t_j. In the extended LIBOR market model [2], knowing the initial forward rates $F_j(0)$ for all $j \in \{0, 1, 2, \dots, K - 1\}$ forward rates observed at future times can be approximated by

$$\hat{F}_j(i+1) = \hat{F}_j(i)\exp\left(\frac{\varphi(\hat{F}_j(i))}{\hat{F}_j(i)}\boldsymbol{\lambda}_j^{\mathrm{T}}(i)\left[\left(\hat{u}_j(i) - \frac{1}{2}\frac{\varphi(\hat{F}_j(i))}{\hat{F}_j(i)}\boldsymbol{\lambda}_j(i)\right)\Delta_i + \epsilon_i\sqrt{\Delta_i}\right]\right) \tag{3}$$

Equation (3) is obtained by applying Euler scheme to the dynamics of the forward rate in continuous time. For the equation to hold we have the obvious condition $i + 1 \le j \le K - 1$. Function $\varphi(.)$ in the equation is the skew function, $\boldsymbol{\lambda}_j(i)$ is the m-dimensional volatility vector, and $\hat{u}_j(i)$ is the m-dimensional drift vector defined as

$$\hat{u}_j(i) = \sum_{k=i+1}^{j}\boldsymbol{\lambda}_k(i)\frac{\delta_k\varphi(\hat{F}_k(i))}{1 + \delta_k\hat{F}_k(i)} \tag{4}$$

The ϵ_i in Equation (3) is a m-dimensional vector of independent standard Gaussian variables and $\Delta_i = t_{i+1} - t_i$. Using Equation (3) with Monte Carlo simulation paths of forward rates can be generated. The equation guarantees the generated rates are positive. It should be pointed out that 1) in computing the drift term $\hat{u}_j(i)$ the summation starts from time t_{i+1}, thus excluding the term $\boldsymbol{\lambda}_i(i)\delta_i\varphi(\hat{F}_i(i))/(1 + \delta_i\hat{F}_i(i))$, and 2) the same m-dimensional vector ϵ_i applies to the generation of all forward rates $F_j(i+1)$ for $j = i+1, i+2, \dots, K-1$ from $F_j(i)$.

A Bermudan swaption gives the holder the right of exercising to enter a swap agreement in which the holder pays fixed cashflows $\theta\delta_{j-1}$ at time t_j for $j = s+1, s+2, \dots, e$, in exchange for LIBOR on a \$1 notional, assuming t_s being the first exercise date and t_e being the last payment date. Payments for periods between t_j and t_{j+1} are exchanged at time t_{j+1} (paid in arrears). A Bermudan swaption is characterised by three dates: the lockout date t_s, the last exercise date t_x and the final swap maturity t_e. Our implementation assumed that all these three dates coincide with dates in the maturity structure and $t_s \le t_x = t_{e-1} = t_{K-1}$, that is, the last exercise date t_x is the second last date in the maturity structure and the swap matures at time t_K. A Bermudan swaption characterised by t_s, t_x and t_e (assuming $t_e = t_{x+1}$), can be exercised once at any time between t_s and t_x. The first payments are exchanged at time t_{s+1}, and the last at time $t_e = t_{x+1}$.

For such a Bermudan swaption exercised at t_j for $j \in \{s, s+1, \dots, x = e-1\}$ we define a strictly positive process $B(t_i, t_j)$ for $i \le j$ as

$$B(t_i, t_j) = B(i, j) = \sum_{k=j}^{x} \delta_k P(i, k+1) \tag{5}$$

The par-rate $R(t_i, t_j)$ observed at time t_i if the swaption is exercised at time t_j assuming the swap maturing at time $t_e = t_{x+1}$ is

$$R(t_i, t_j) = R(i, j) = \frac{P(i, j) - P(i, x+1)}{B(i, j)} \tag{6}$$

This rate is also known as the swap rate at time t_i that makes the payoff of the swap exercised at time t_j and maturing at time $t_e = t_{x+1}$ equal to zero, thus, being fair to both the parties. With the above definitions the payoff $S(t_j)$ of the swaption exercised at time t_j for the fixed payer is

$$S(t_j) = S(j) = B(j, j)(R(j, j) - \theta)^+ = B(j, j) \left(\frac{1 - P(j, x+1)}{B(j, j)} - \theta \right)^+ \tag{7}$$

where θ is the fixed coupon rate. The time 0 value of this payoff $S(j)$ received at exercise time t_j is $P(0, j)S(j)$.

Equipped with the above-mentioned definitions Monte Carlo simulation can be used to evaluate lower and upper bounds for prices of Bermudan swaptions in an extended m-factor LIBOR market model.

3   Lower and Upper Bounds for Bermudan Swaption

Use Q_0 to denote the fair time 0 price of a Bermudan swaption. The price equals to the discounted payoff of the swaption if it is exercised at an optimal exercise time between t_s and t_x. Using $\aleph$ to denote the set $\{t_s, t_{s+1}, \dots, t_x\}$ of exercise times, Q_0 is computed by

$$Q_0 = \sup_{\tau \in \aleph} \mathbb{E}^Q \left(P(0, \tau)S(\tau) \right) \tag{8}$$

where $\mathbb{E}^Q$ denotes the expectation under the spot measure (see [2] for more details about the spot measure), $S(\tau)$ is the payoff to the fixed payer if exercise takes place at time τ and $P(0, \tau)$ discounts the payoff to time 0. If τ^* is the optimal exercise strategy that solves Equation (8) the task of computing Q_0 is down to finding τ^*.

With Monte Carlo simulation various methods have been proposed to approximate the optimal exercise strategy τ^*. Andersen [1] used an optimisation procedure to determine the exercise boundary. Sided with the work in [6], we applied the regression-based Longstaff-Schwartz method [10] in searching for the approximations. This method computes low-biased price $L_0 = \mathbb{E}^Q(P(0, \tau)S(\tau)) \leq Q_0$ for a Bermudan swaption.

Knowing the initial forward curve, we first simulate N_R paths of forward rates, over which an exercise strategy is computed. On a particular path at an exercise time t_j for

$j \in \aleph$ we use a constant c, the swap rate $R(j, j)$ observed at time t_j if exercise takes place at that time, $R(j, j)^2$ and $R(j, j)^3$ as basis functions for the regression. After the strategy generation we launch another group of N_L paths with an $N_L \gg N_R$. The lower bound L_0 is estimated over these N_L paths based on the strategy.

The upper bound U_0 is computed by the simulation-based algorithm [3] proposed by Andersen and Broadie. The sub-optimality checking discussed in [5] was integrated into our implementation. The upper bound U_0 is set as the sum of the lower bound L_0 and a penalty term Δ_0. We launch N_H simulated paths to compute Δ_0 as $\Delta_0 = \mathbb{E}^Q(\max_{\tau \in \aleph}(P(0, \tau)S(\tau) - \pi_\tau))$. On any simulated path, at time t_i the computation for Δ_i takes place only if exercise is suggested by the exercise strategy. The computation follows one of the two procedures.

1. If time t_i is the first exercise time on the path at which exercise is suggested, π_i is set as $\pi_i = P(0, i)S(i)$, the discounted payoff from the exercise. We then launch N_S inner simulation trials to estimate the swaption's discounted continuation value $P(0, i)Q_i = \mathbb{E}^Q(P(0, j)S(j))$ where $t_j \in \{t_{i+1}, t_{i+2}, \ldots, t_x\}$ is the first exercise time instance at which exercise is suggested after time t_i. The penalty term Δ_i is initialised as 0.

2. If, otherwise, time t_i is not the first exercise time on the path at which exercise is suggested, we set $\pi_i = \pi_l + P(0, i)S(i) - P(0, l)Q_l$, where t_l is the previous exercise time on the path at which exercise is suggested. By the time when π_i is computed the values of π_l and $P(0, l)Q_l$ are already available. We then launch N_S inner simulation trials to estimate $P(0, i)Q_i = \mathbb{E}^Q(P(0, j)S(j))$, where $t_j \in \{t_{i+1}, t_{i+2}, \ldots, t_x\}$ is the first exercise time instance at which exercise is suggested after time t_i, for later use. The penalty term Δ_i is set as $\Delta_i = P(0, i)S(i) - \pi_i$.

Note that the above procedure is deduced from Proposition 4.1 in [5]. Applying Equation (15) in [5] to a Bermudan swaption, at exercise time t_i where exercise is suggested process π_i is defined as

$$\pi_i = \pi_{i-1} + P(0, i)S(i) - P(0, i-1)Q_{i-1} \tag{9}$$

If time t_i is the first exercise time on a path at which exercise is suggested, according to Proposition 4.1(1) in [5], $\pi_{i-1} = P(0, i-1)S(i-1)$. At an exercise time where continuation is suggested such as time t_{i-1}, the swaption's payoff is equal to its continuation value, and, so, we have $\pi_{i-1} = P(0, i-1)Q_{i-1}$. Substitute $P(0, i-1)Q_{i-1}$ for π_{i-1} in Equation (9) we get $\pi_i = P(0, i)S(i)$. The penalty term $\Delta_i = P(0, i)S(i) - \pi_i = 0$. If, however, time t_i is an exercise time, but not the first one, at which exercise is suggested, according to Proposition 4.1(2), $\pi_{i-1} = \pi_l - P(0, l)Q_l + P(0, i-1)S(i-1)$, where time t_l is the previous exercise time on the path at which exercise is suggested. Because at time t_{i-1} the swaption's payoff equals to its continuation value, we have $\pi_{i-1} = \pi_l - P(0, l)Q_l + P(0, i-1)Q_{i-1}$. Substitute this expression for π_{i-1} in Equation (9) we get $\pi_i = \pi_l + P(0, i)S(i) - P(0, l)Q_l$. Fig. 1 shows an example where inner simulations are launched at exercise times t_{s_1} and t_{s_4} where exercises are suggested.

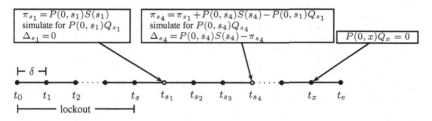

Fig. 1. Inner simulation on a constructed forward rate path. Note that time t_{s_1} is the first exercise time instance on the path at which exercise is suggested, and t_{s_4} is the second.

If $\hat{L}_0$ is the lower bound estimation over N_L simulation trials with a sample standard deviation $\hat{s_L}$ and $\hat{\Delta}_0$ is the estimation for the penalty term using N_H trials with a sample standard deviation $\hat{s_\Delta}$, as in [3], a $100(1-\alpha)\%$-probability confidence interval (CI) for the price Q_0 of the Bermudan swaption can be computed as

$$100(1 - \alpha)\% \text{ CI} = \left[\hat{L}_0 - \frac{z_{1-\alpha/2}\hat{s_L}}{\sqrt{N_L}}, \ \hat{L}_0 + \hat{\Delta}_0 + z_{1-\alpha/2}\sqrt{\frac{\hat{s_L}^2}{N_L} + \frac{\hat{s_\Delta}^2}{N_H}} \right] \quad (10)$$

with z_x denoting the xth percentile of a standard Gaussian distribution.

4 The Parallel Computing

On a parallel computer with c processors, the computation for L_0 over N_L paths and that for Δ_0 over N_H paths are evenly distributed onto all processors through POSIX threads. In the generation of random numbers, each individual processor generates a segment for its own use, skipping a certain amount from the beginning of a random number stream. Take the ith processor (processor index starting from 0) as an example. In computing L_0 it will generate $m(N_L/c)(t_e/\delta)$ standardised normally distributed random numbers, m being the model factor. This segment starts from the $(im(N_L/c)(t_e/\delta))$th position of the random stream, assuming a constant accrual period divisible by the final swap maturity. The ith processor will then construct N_L/c complete paths and compute a $\hat{L}_0$ over these paths. The $\hat{L}_0$ over all N_L paths are obtained by averaging all $\hat{L}_0$s computed by each of the c processors.

The phase of optimal exercise strategy approximation is not explicitly threaded. The computation starts from the second last exercise time t_{x-1} and proceeds backwards until reaching exercise time instance t_s. At each time step payoffs and swap rates on all in-the-money paths are collected for the least-squares regression. The regression is performed by Intel's MKL function LAPACKE_dgels. Other MKL functions are used for linear algebra operations, such as vector-vector multiplication. These MKL functions by default support threading. During execution they are allowed to use any processor available in the system.

To minimise execution time of the approximation the necessary preprocessing that can be parallelised through threading is separated from the backward computation where the collection of the cross-sectional information makes explicit parallelisation

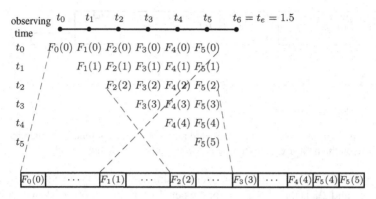

Fig. 2. A single forward rate path and its one-dimensional storage in memory

difficult. The preprocessing includes random number generation, path construction and payoff calculation. These tasks are parallelised and evenly distributed onto all processors.

A path of forward rates conceptually is a two-dimensional structure. To save storage space in memory we map it onto an one-dimensional array. Fig. 2 illustrates the mapping using an example where $t_e = 1.5$ and $\delta = 0.25$. A mapping function $I(i,j) = \sum_{k=0}^{i-1}(t_e/\delta - k) + (j - i)$ is designed to return the index position in the array where rate $F_j(i)$ should be stored. For this function to work we need the obvious constraints $i \leq j$ and $i, j \in \{t_0, t_1, \ldots, t_x = t_{e-1}\}$.

When generating a forward rate using Equation (3), in computing the drift function $\hat{u}$, repetitive evaluation of common sub-expressions should be avoided. For example, in generating $\hat{F}_3(3)$ drift function $\hat{u}_3(2)$ needs to be evaluated according to Equation (4). Let $D_j(i)$ denote the term inside the summation in Equation (4), that is, $D_j(i) = \lambda_j(i)(\delta_j\varphi(\hat{F}_j(i)))/(1 + \delta_j\hat{F}_j(i))$. Using this notation we have $\hat{u}_3(2) = D_3(3)$. Now, when $\hat{F}_4(3)$ is computed from $\hat{F}_4(2)$, drift function $\hat{u}_4(2) = D_3(3) + D_4(3)$ needs to be evaluated. However, by this time $D_3(3)$ has already been computed in the generation of $\hat{F}_3(3)$, and, so, its value should not be evaluated again. In our implementation, whenever $\hat{F}_{i+1}(i+1)$ is computed we have a buffer initialised for drift function $\hat{u}_{i+1}(i) = D_{i+1}(i+1)$. Next, when generating $\hat{F}_j(i+1)$ for $t_j \in \{t_{i+2}, t_{i+3}, \ldots, t_x = t_{e-1}\}$ only $D_j(i+1)$ is computed and its value is added to the accumulated value in the buffer to form the value for drift function $\hat{u}_j(i)$. This optimisation significantly reduced execution times of the path generations, especially for the nested simulations in computing the upper bound penalty term Δ_0. The routine in our implementation for computing the payoff $S(j)$ defined in Equation (7) not only returns the payoff but also the swap rate $R(j, j)$ to save the rate being computed separately.

In computing the penalty term Δ_0 the inner simulation generates forward rates based on rates in existing path. For example, if on one of the N_H paths at exercise time t_i exercise is suggested, the inner simulation will be launched, which will then generate N_S paths to estimate the discounted continuation value. These N_S paths all originate from the time instance t_i on the original path, and so they all have the same forward rates observed between time t_0 and time t_i along the original path.

5   Experimental Result

The parallel implementation was programed in C/C++. For comparison purpose an efficient sequential program was also implemented. The NPTL (native POSIX thread library) 2.12.1 was used for threading. Tests were made on a quad-core 3.4GHz Intel Core i7-2600 processor (Fig. 3(b)) and two quad-core 2.0GHz Intel Xeon E5405 processors (Fig. 3(a)). Both the systems ran Ubuntu Linux 10.10 64-bit version. The binary executables were compiled by Intel's C/C++ compiler icpc 12.0 for Linux with -O3 optimisation.

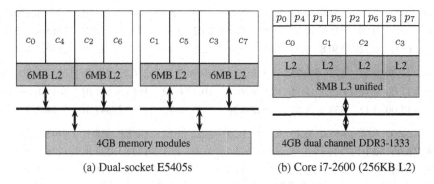

(a) Dual-socket E5405s   (b) Core i7-2600 (256KB L2)

Fig. 3. Multi-core systems used in tests

The implementations were tested using Bermudan swaptions under different lockouts t_s, final swap maturities t_e and fixed coupon rates θ. We used the same examples as in [3]. In all the tests, forward rates were generated in an extended two-factor LIBOR market model according to Equation (3). The parameters were set to the same values as in [3]: $\varphi(x) = x$, $\delta = 0.25$, $F_j(0) = 0.1$ for $j \in \{t_0, t_1, \ldots, t_{x-1}\}$, and $\lambda_j(i) = (0.15, 0.15 - \sqrt{0.009(t_j - t_i)})$ for $i \le j$. For the simulations we had $N_R = 5000$, $N_L = 50000$, $N_H = 750$ and $N_S = 300$. The testing results on the Intel Xeon E5405s are reported in Table 1. The runtimes were measured in seconds as wall clock times. Data from Table 4 in [3] are included for comparison. In all the tests we assumed $t_x = t_{e-1}$.

From the speedup (S_P) data it can be seen that the parallel program demonstrated significant accelerations against the sequential program. Comparing the data in the last two columns we can see that the figures are quite close, although not identical. While exercise strategies were generated by an optimisation procedure in [3], we generated them using the regression-based method. In computing $\hat{L}_0$ the work in [3] used antithetic sampling, but we did not use any variance reduction technique.

On the quad-core 3.4GHz Intel Core i7-2600 the same tests were made. For the 11-year contract with 0.08 fixed coupon rate the parallel program finished the whole computation in 11.63 seconds and demonstrated 5.2 times speedup against the sequential program.

Table 1. Lower and upper bounds of Bermudan swaptions and timing results on two quad-core 2.0GHz Intel Xeon E5405s

t_s	t_e	θ	$\hat{L}_0$	T_L	$\hat{\Delta}_0$	T_U	T_P	S_P	95% CI	95% CI'
0.25	1.25	0.08	183.6	0.12	0.022	0.23	0.35	2.14	[183.6, 183.6]	[183.9, 184.1]
0.25	1.25	0.10	42.3	0.05	0.031	0.12	0.17	2.71	[42.3, 42.3]	[43.1, 43.6]
0.25	1.25	0.12	5.2	0.05	0.010	0.11	0.16	2.0	[5.2, 5.2]	[5.5, 5.7]
1.00	3.00	0.08	341.5	0.13	0.094	0.54	0.67	4.13	[341.5, 341.6]	[339.2, 340.6]
1.00	3.00	0.10	126.1	0.09	0.214	0.35	0.44	4.07	[126.1, 126.3]	[125.1, 127.2]
1.00	3.00	0.12	36.8	0.14	0.217	0.27	0.41	2.76	[36.8, 37.0]	[36.4, 37.6]
1.00	6.00	0.08	751.0	0.33	0.966	3.24	3.57	6.64	[751.0, 752.0]	[749.0, 755.2]
1.00	6.00	0.10	315.9	0.36	3.152	1.66	2.02	5.41	[315.8, 319.0]	[315.6, 323.5]
1.00	6.00	0.12	130.8	0.35	1.957	0.89	1.23	4.45	[130.8, 132.8]	[126.5, 131.6]
1.00	11.00	0.08	1236.5	0.95	11.310	19.02	19.98	7.14	[1236.5, 1247.9]	[1245.1, 1269.0]
1.00	11.00	0.10	613.3	1.11	17.619	9.62	10.73	6.29	[613.3, 631.0]	[618.4, 645.0]
1.00	11.00	0.12	334.2	1.05	13.022	4.20	5.26	6.70	[334.2, 347.3]	[324.7, 345.0]
3.00	6.00	0.08	458.0	0.29	0.218	1.23	1.52	5.17	[458.0, 458.3]	[443.6, 446.6]
3.00	6.00	0.10	234.4	0.34	0.403	0.86	1.20	4.53	[234.4, 234.8]	[225.5, 229.5]
3.00	6.00	0.12	110.8	0.32	0.776	0.65	0.97	3.90	[110.8, 111.6]	[105.9, 109.0]

Notes: The estimations $\hat{L}_0$ and $\hat{\Delta}_0$ and the confidence intervals are reported in basis points. T_L is the parallel runtime in computing $\hat{L}_0$, T_U is the parallel runtime in computing $\hat{\Delta}_0$, and $T_P = T_L + T_U$ is the total parallel runtime. S_P is the speedup of the parallel implementation in computing $\hat{L}_0$ and $\hat{\Delta}_0$ against the sequential implementation running under the same settings. Data in the last column are copied from the seventh column of Table 4 in [3]. They are included for purpose of comparison.

6   Conclusions

We have presented a parallel algorithm that computes lower and upper bounds for prices of Bermudan swaptions under the extended multi-factor LIBOR market model. The algorithm uses the Longstaff-Schwartz least-squares Monte Carlo method in generating early exercise boundary for a swaption. This boundary is later used for estimating the lower and upper bounds. In computing the upper bound we follow the duality-based procedure proposed by Andersen and Broadie. Sub-optimality checking is incorporated into the upper bound estimation to reduce its computational cost.

The implementation of the parallel algorithm was tested for its correctness and performance. The implementation works on shared-memory x86 multi-processor systems. Parallelisation was achieved through explicit POSIX threading, except in the generation of exercise boundary, in which Intel MKL functions' threading ability is exploited. Source code optimisations, such as elimination of common sub-expressions, were applied to the programs to speedup the simulations. Conceptually two-dimensional forward rate paths are mapped onto one-dimensional arrays in memory to save storage space. The implementation was tested on Intel multi-core systems. All the tests were completed by the parallel program in reasonable length of time periods. Significant speedups were observed against an efficient sequential implementation.

References

1. Andersen, L.: A Simple Approach to the Pricing of Bermudan Swaptions in the Multi-Factor Libor Market Model. The Journal of Computational Finance 3(2) (1999)
2. Andersen, L., Andreasen, J.: Volatility Skews and Extensions of the Libor Market Model. Applied Mathematical Finance 7, 1–32 (2000)
3. Andersen, L., Broadie, M.: Primal-Dual Simulation Algorithm for Pricing Multidimensional American Options. Management Science 50(9), 1222–1234 (2004)
4. Brace, A., Gatarek, D., Musiela, M.: The Market Model of Interest Rate Dynamics. Mathematical Finance 7(2), 127–155 (1997)
5. Broadie, M., Cao, M.: Improved Lower and Upper Bound Algorithms for Pricing American Options by Simulation. Quantitative Finance 8(8), 845–861 (2008)
6. Hippler, S.: Pricing Bermudan Swaptions in the LIBOR Market Model. Master's thesis, University of Oxford (June 2008)
7. Intel Corporation: Intel Math Kernel Library for Linux OS: User's Guide (2011), Document Number: 314774-018US, http://software.intel.com/en-us/articles/intel-math-kernel-library-documentation/
8. Intel Corporation: Intel Math Kernel Library Reference Manual, Document Number: 630813-044US (2011), http://software.intel.com/en-us/articles/intel-math-kernel-library-documentation/
9. Jamshidian, F.: LIBOR and Swap Market Models and Measures. Finance and Stochastics 1(4), 293–330 (1997)
10. Longstaff, F.A., Schwartz, E.S.: Valuing American Options by Simulation: A Simple Least-Squares Approach. The Review of Financial Studies 14(1), 113–147 (2001)
11. Miltersen, K.R., Sandmann, K., Sondermann, D.: Closed Form Solutions for Term Structure Derivatives with Log-Normal Interest Rates. The Journal of Finance 52, 409–430 (1997)

Evolving Linear Discriminant in a Continuously Growing Dimensional Space for Incremental Attribute Learning

Ting Wang[1,2,*], Sheng-Uei Guan[2], T.O. Ting[3], Ka Lok Man[2], and Fei Liu[4]

[1] Department of Computer Science, University of Liverpool, Liverpool L69 3BX, UK
[2] Department of Computer Science and Software Engineering
[3] Department of Electrical and Electronic Engineering
Xi'an Jiaotong-Liverpool University, Suzhou 215123, P.R. China
[4] Department of Computer Science & Computer Engineering, La Trobe University,
Victoria 3086, Australia
ting.wang@liverpool.ac.uk, {steven.guan,toting}@xjtlu.edu.cn,
kalok2006@gmail.com, f.liu@latrobe.edu.au

Abstract. Feature Ordering is a unique preprocessing step in Incremental Attribute Learning (IAL), where features are gradually trained one after another. In previous studies, feature ordering derived based upon each individual feature's contribution is time-consuming. This study attempts to develop an efficient feature ordering algorithm by some evolutionary approaches. The feature ordering algorithm presented in this paper is based on a criterion of maximum mean of feature discriminability. Experimental results derived by ITID, a neural IAL algorithm, show that such a feature ordering algorithm has a higher probability to obtain the lowest classification error rate with datasets from UCI Machine Learning Repository.

Keywords: pattern classification, incremental attribute learning, data preprocessing, feature ordering, neural networks.

1 Introduction

Incremental Attribute Learning (IAL) is a machine learning strategy where features in the problem are often gradually trained one by one. Such a machine learning approach is usually employed to solve complex pattern recognition problems. During the solution process, features with greater discriminability are distinguished and separated from features with weaker discriminability by some criteria in the first place. After that, some approaches like neural networks and genetic algorithms can be employed to complete the incremental training. Therefore, there are two important steps in the processing. One is the criterion for the differentiation of features with great discriminability; while the other is the machine learning approach for pattern recognition. In the first step, features are sorted in some order from high discriminability to low discriminability. In the second step, ordered features are trained by incremental attribute

---

* Corresponding author.

J.J. Park et al. (Eds.): NPC 2012, LNCS 7513, pp. 482–491, 2012.

machine learning approaches for classification or regression. Consequently, the criterion of feature ordering is regarded as the key to enhancing performance of final results from incremental machine learning.

In previous research, feature ordering criteria have been developed based on some feature selection approaches [1-3]. Generally, these criteria can be divided into two types: wrappers and filters. The former is based on each feature's individual contribution to classes; while the latter is based on the score of each feature according to some ranking mechanisms like Linear Discriminant or Correlation.

In this study, an evolutionary feature ordering criterion is presented. According to this criterion, feature ordering preprocess of IAL aims to use an evolutionary algorithm to search the training sequence of features where the mean of features' discriminabilities calculated in this sequence is the maximum one compared with the other feature orderings. In this paper, IAL and feature ordering are reviewed in section 2. An Accumulative Linear Discriminant for the calculation of feature discriminability is presented in section 3. Section 4 illustrates the maximum discriminability mean criterion, and an evolutionary algorithm of the criterion is interpreted in section 5. Experimental results and analysis for benchmarks from UCI machine learning dataset are illustrated in section 6. Finally, section 7 concludes this study with key findings.

2   Incremental Attribute Learning with Ordered Features

2.1   Feature Ordering in IAL

Incremental Attribute Learning is a "divide-and-conquer" machine learning strategy where features are gradually trained in stages. Compared with Incremental Learning (IL) where the number of training patterns is gradually increasing, IAL focuses on the increasing of the feature number in a machine learning process. IAL aims to solve easy problems earlier and cope with difficulties later. Because of the segmentations of features, IAL can avoid the curse of dimensionality in high-dimensional problems. It is also applicable for problems with newly imported features.

Previous studies showed that IAL can improve final performance in pattern recognition. Particularly, IAL can bring along more accurate results than conventional approaches where features are imported to training by batch. For example, based on UCI datasets, classification errors of Diabetes, Thyroid and Glass derived by ILIA [4] and ITID[1], two neural IAL algorithms, reduced by 8.2%, 14.6% and 12.6%, respectively [1, 2]; moreover, based on OIGA, testing error rates derived by IGA of Yeast, Glass and Wine declined by 25.9%, 19.4% and 10.8% [5] in classification. Furthermore, i⁺Learning and i⁺LRA, two kinds of IAL decision trees, were employed to run 16 different UCI datasets. Results indicated that algorithms based on IAL can get better performance than ITI in 14 datasets of the total [6]. In addition, a study on incremental SVM extended IAL to a wider application field [7]. All of these previous IAL studies showed that IAL can indeed promote the performance of pattern recognition.

Moreover, in previous studies, the significance of feature ordering to improving final results in pattern recognition [2, 5] has been discovered. Feature ordering is seldom used in conventional methods where features are trained in one batch, in contrast, feature ordering affects the training results from IAL. Thus, feature ordering is unique to IAL.

Previous studies sorts feature ordering in two different ways: ranking-based filters and contribution-based wrappers. Such a division is similar to those approaches in feature selection. Previous studies have validated that ranking-based feature ordering approaches are better than the contribution-based ones usually at least in two different aspects: time [8] and error rate [9]. Different from feature selection, which attempts to search a feature subset or reduce feature weights for the optimal results, feature ordering aims to sort features for IAL purpose by some criteria. It is obvious that different criteria produce different feature ordering that may produce different results.

2.2   Incremental Neural Networks

ITID [1], a representative of neural IAL based on ILIA [4], is different from traditional approaches which train features by batch. It divides all input dimensions into several sub-dimensions, each of which corresponds to an input feature. Instead of learning input features altogether as an input vector in training, ITID learns inputs through their corresponding sub-networks one after another and the structure of neural networks gradually grows with an increasing input dimension as shown in Fig. 1. During the training, information obtained by a new sub-network is merged together with the information obtained by the old network. ITID has a pruning technique which is adopted to find the appropriate network architecture. With less internal interference among input features, ITID achieves higher generalization accuracy than conventional methods [1].

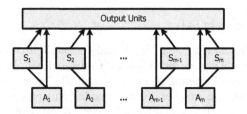

Fig. 1. The basic network structure of ITID [1]

3   Linear Discriminant for Feature Ordering

Linear discriminant is usually employed to evaluate feature discriminability in the dimensional space where feature number is stable. However, feature dimension in IAL is dynamic, thus conventional linear discriminant should be adapted.

3.1   Fisher's Linear Discriminant

FLD, a linear statistical classifier, provides simple ways to estimate the accuracy of classification problems. It firstly assumes that the datasets used in FLD are Gaussian conditional density models, where data have normal distributed classes or equal class covariance. The Fisher criterion aims to search a direction where the distance between different classes is the farthest and the distance of each pattern within every class is the closest. Thus, in this direction, the ratio of distance between-classes and within-classes is the largest compared with other directions. Such a direction often leads to the simplest classification. Mathematically, FLD in two-category classification is

$$J(w) = \frac{(\tilde{\mu}_2 - \tilde{\mu}_1)^2}{s_1^2 + s_2^2} \tag{1}$$

where $\tilde{\mu}_1$ and $\tilde{\mu}_2$ are two means of projected classes, and s_1 and s_2 are within-class variances. The objective of FLD is to search the matrix w for maximum $J(w)$. The larger the $J(w)$, the easier in the classification.

However, due to the fact that $J(w)$ is impacted by two classes, it will be difficult to calculate $J(w)$ for patterns belonging to three or more classes at a same time. Therefore, (1) should be revised for this demand.

3.2 Standard Deviation Linear Discriminant in IAL

In IAL, each feature's discriminability can be estimated in this feature's one-dimensional space. Features can be ordered by the ranking value of feature discriminability. For two-class classification problems c_2, based on formula (1), discriminability of feature f_i can be given by

$$D(f_i) = \frac{(\mu_2 - \mu_1)^2}{s_1^2 + s_2^2} \tag{2}$$

where μ_1 and μ_2 are two means of classes, and s_1 and s_2 are within-class variances.

However, (2) is too simple to cope with multi-category classifications, because the between-class scatter is difficult to describe merely by distance between patterns. Here, the difference between the centers of these multiple classes should be replaced by standard deviations of centers and standard deviations of patterns, so that the influence brought by classes whose mean is not the smallest or the largest among all means of classes can be measured.

Definition 1. Single Discriminability (SD) is a ratio of a feature by the standard deviation of all class centers and the sum of standard deviations of all patterns in each class.

SD for both two-category and n-category classification problems can be unified as

$$D(f_i) = \frac{std\left[\left(\mu_{f_{i,j}}\right)_{j=1}^{j=n}\right]}{\sum_{j=1}^{j=n} std\,(f_i)_j} \tag{3}$$

where n is the total number of classes, and two $stds$ are standard deviations, one for all patterns belonging to c_j in feature i, and the other for the vector consisting of the means of all classes. Let $\mathbf{x}$ be the vector for standard deviation calculation, the standard deviation of $\mathbf{x}$ is

$$std(\mathbf{x}) = \sqrt{\frac{\sum_{k=1}^{k=r}(x_k - \mu)^2}{r - 1}} \tag{4}$$

where the vector$\mathbf{x} = \{x_k\}_{k=1}^{k=r}$,$x_k$ is the value of kth pattern, and r is the total number of patterns. Obviously, in equation (4), the part of $(x_k - \mu)$ is a distance between k^{th} pattern and its mean. Thus, let *dist* replace this part, (4) can be re-written as:

$$std(\mathbf{x}) = \sqrt{\frac{\sum_{k=1}^{k=r} dist_{x_k,\mu}^2}{r - 1}} \tag{5}$$

where$dist_{x_k,\mu}$denotes the distance of kth pattern in x and its mean μ.

3.3   Linear Discriminant for a Growing Feature Space

With the increasing number of new features in IAL, the dimension number of feature space is also growing. A growing feature space has been regarded as one of the most manifest characteristics of IAL. In such a growing feature space, the standard deviation, which is the core of evolving linear discriminant, should be upgraded from that in one dimension. More specifically, the standard deviation in one dimensional space is based on the distance between each pattern and their mean of the same class. This distance should be extended to a higher dimensional space, when the feature space is growing. If $\|D\|$ is the Euclidean norm of d-dimensional feature space, (5) can be given in a high-dimensional style by

$$std(\mathbf{x}) = \sqrt{\frac{\sum_{k=1}^{k=r} \|D_{x_k,\tilde{\mu}}\|^2}{r - 1}} \tag{6}$$

where$\tilde{\mu}$ is the barycenter of x, and

$$\|D_{x_k,\tilde{\mu}}\| = \sqrt{\sum_{i=1}^{d} (x_{k,i} - \mu_i)^2} \tag{7}$$

where d is the total number of features imported so far. Therefore, to calculate standard deviation of r patterns in two dimensions, (6) can be written as

$$std(\mathbf{x}) = \sqrt{\frac{\sum_{k=1}^{k=r} \left[(x_{k,1} - \mu_1)^2 + (x_{k,2} - \mu_2)^2\right]}{r - 1}}, \tag{8}$$

$$\mathbf{x} = \{x_{k,d}\}_{k=1,d=1}^{k=r,d=2} \in \mathbb{R}_{feature}^{r \times 2}$$

and for a tri-dimensional space, the equation is

$$std(\mathbf{x}) = \sqrt{\frac{\sum_{k=1}^{k=r} \left[(x_{k,1}-\mu_1)^2 + (x_{k,2}-\mu_2)^2 + (x_{k,3}-\mu_3)^2\right]}{r-1}} \tag{9}$$

where$\mathbf{x} = \{x_{k,d}\}_{k=1,d=1}^{k=r,d=3} \in \mathbb{R}_{feature}^{r \times 3}$

Accordingly, multidimensional standard deviation of r patterns in an m-dimensional space is

$$std(\mathbf{x}) = \sqrt{\frac{\sum_{k=1}^{k=r}\sum_{i=1}^{i=m}(x_{k,i} - \mu_i)^2}{r-1}}, \mathbf{x} = \{x_{k,d}\}_{k=1,d=1}^{k=r,d=m} \in \mathbb{R}_{feature}^{r\times m} \tag{10}$$

Based on (10), when some new features are incrementally introduced into the system, formula (3), the standard deviation based linear discriminant of IAL in one feature dimension, should be upgraded to fit in this gradually increasing dimensional space, because (3) has little consideration on gradually importing of new features.

Definition 2. Accumulative Discriminability (AD) is the ratio in d-feature space between the multidimensional standard deviation of all class centers and the sum of all multidimensional standard deviations of all patterns in each class.

If $\{f_1, f_2, ..., f_m\}$ is the pool of input features, $\mathbf{f} = \{f_{k,d}\}_{k=1,d=1}^{k=r,d=m} \in \mathbb{R}_{feature}^{r\times m}$, when the $d^{th}(1\leq d\leq m)$ feature is imported, AD is

$$AD(f_1, f_2, ..., f_d) = \frac{std\left[(\tilde{\mu}_j)_{j=1}^{j=n}\right]}{\sum_{j=1}^{j=n} std\left[(f_i)_{i=1}^{i=d}\right]_j}, (1 \leq d \leq m) \tag{11}$$

where $\tilde{\mu}_j$ is the barycenter of vector $(f_1, f_2, ..., f_d)$ with patterns belonging to j.

Therefore, results of (11) are dynamic when new features are gradually imported into training. To obtain better classification results, it is necessary to ensure the result of (11) being the maximum in every step of feature importing.

4   Maximum Mean Discriminative Criterion

To obtain the most accurate classification result in IAL, it is necessary to ensure data-sets have the greatest discriminability in every step when a new feature is imported into the predictive system and the feature dimension is increased from d to $d+1$. Therefore, the ratio in (11) will be the largest all the time, which guarantees different classes always can be separated in the easiest way. Therefore, the criterion for optimal classification results, also the greatest discriminability, is to produce an optimal feature ordering which contains the greatest discrimination ability in each round of feature importing. Obviously, after all features are imported, the optimal feature ordering will have the largest sum or mean of features' discriminability calculated in each step of the process. Hence such a criterion for obtaining the optimal feature ordering can be given with maximum discriminability mean by

$$\max \frac{1}{d}\sum_{d=1}^{d} AD(\mathbf{f}_{1:d}), (1 \leq d \leq m) \tag{12}$$

where $\mathbf{f}_{1:d}$ is the feature subset of $\{f_1, f_2, ..., f_m\}$ during the feature importing process.

Usually, feature with greater SD calculated by (3) may not always get the greater AD, because (11) has an additional value produced by the Euclidean distance in high dimensional space. Such a value is disproportionate with the value in (3). Thus features which have greater SD may also have weaker AD in IAL feature importing. Therefore, for IAL classification, (12) will likely produce more accurate results than (3).

5   Evolution of the Optimal Feature Ordering

An evolutionary algorithm can be employed to obtain the maximum mean of features' discriminability for optimal feature ordering. An algorithm modified by Genetic Algorithms (GA) is employed.

Firstly, the algorithm randomly produce a set of seeds in different feature orderings. Secondly, more than two places in the ordering of each seed are exchanged to generate a new ordering. Such an exchange is similar to crossover and mutation in GA. According to criterion (12), if the seed gets the greatest mean of discriminability in its history, it will be recorded, and after several epochs of evolution, the recorded feature ordering of each seed will be compared with one another, and a seed with the greatest mean will be selected as global optimization.

In global optimization, sometimes because of the large feature number and limitations of the evolutionary generation number, the selected seed is only a potential global optimal solution, which is close to the real optimal solution. Therefore, this seed should be evolved again to search for the real one (global optimum). Here, only the potential seed is evolving. After a number of evolutions, if there is no better one, the recorded global feature ordering seed will be regarded as the truly optimal one. Therefore, usually there is a limitation to the maximum mean of discriminability.

To guarantee final feature ordering has the maximum mean, it is necessary to repeat global optimization searching process for several times. If most of repetitions produce the same results, and the results have the greatest mean of discriminability, these same results can be concluded as a global optimum.

Obviously, the ordering transformed data based on the global optimal feature ordering can be directly employed in training, validation and testing. The speed of producing such a transformed dataset depends on the feature dimensional numbers, the number of evolving generations and the number of random seeds.

6   Experiments

A summary of four benchmarks, Diabetes, Cancer, Glass, and Thyroid, from UCI Machine Learning Repository in our experiments is show in Table 1.

Table 1. Brief information of datasets

	DIABETES	CANCER	GLASS	THYROID
PATTERN	768	699	214	7200
INPUT NUMBER	8	9	9	21
OUTPUT	2	2	6	3

In the experiments, 50% patterns were randomly selected as training data, 25% for validation and 25% for testing. Moreover, for AD optimal feature ordering, 100 seeds were generated in a 10-generation evolution. Potential global optimum feature ordering was obtained and repeated for 10 times to confirm the optimization status. Diabetes, Cancer, and Glass have 200 generations in each confirmation round, while Thyroid has 5000 epochs, because of its large feature number. Results based on ITID and feature orderings derived by AD were compared with those results obtained in previous studies, where feature orderings were derived based on original orderings [2], wrappers [4], correlation-based mRMRs [9, 10], and conventional approaches [4]. Here, ITID was randomly initialized by 20 different structures, and the final results were the statistical average of these 20 different initial neural networks. Table 2-5 show the comparison results of classification error rate and the means of AD. Results derived in this study have been highlighted in bold.

Table 2. Diabetes results comparison

APPROACHES	FEATURE ORDERING	CLASSIFICATION ERROR RATE
ITID-AD (AD)	**2-6-7-8-5-4-1-3**	**21.61458%**
ITID-SD (SD)	2-6-8-7-1-4-5-3	21.84896%
MRMR-DIFF.(MRMRD)	2-6-1-7-3-8-4-5	22.86459%
MRMR-QUO. (MRMRQ)	2-6-1-7-3-8-5-4	22.96876%
WRAPPERS (WRA.)	2-6-1-7-3-8-5-4	22.96876%
ORIGINAL (ORI.)	1-2-3-4-5-6-7-8	22.86458%
CONVENTIONAL (CON.)	IN ONE BATCH	23.93229%

Table 3. Cancer results comparison

APPROACHES	FEATURE ORDERING	CLASSIFICATION ERROR RATE
ITID-AD	**3-2-6-7-5-1-8-4-9**	**1.551726%**
ITID-SD	3-2-6-7-1-8-4-5-9	1.695405%
MRMR-DIFFERENCE	2-6-1-7-3-8-5-4-9	2.29885%
MRMR-QUOTIENT	2-6-1-7-8-3-5-4-9	2.29885%
WRAPPERS	2-3-5-8-6-7-4-1-9	2.4999985%
ORIGINAL ORDERING	1-2-3-4-5-6-7-8-9	2.902299%
CONVENTIONAL	IN ONE BATCH	1.867818%

Table 4. Glass results comparison

APPROACHES	FEATURE ORDERING	CLASSIFICATION ERROR RATE
ITID-AD	**3-8-2-4-6-7-1-5-9**	**34.33964%**
ITID-SD	3-8-4-2-6-5-9-1-7	34.81133%
MRMR-DIFFERENCE	3-2-4-5-7-9-8-6-1	39.05663%
MRMR-QUOTIENT	3-5-2-8-9-4-7-6-1	35.28304%
WRAPPERS	4-2-8-3-6-9-1-7-5	36.4151%
ORIGINAL ORDERING	1-2-3-4-5-6-7-8-9	45.1887%
CONVENTIONAL	IN ONE BATCH	41.226405%

Table 5. Thyroid results comparison

App.	Feature Ordering	Error Rate
AD	**21-18-19-15-20-17-13-7-12-5-4-8-3-9-16-6-14-1-11-10-2**	**1.525001%**
SD	21-19-17-18-3-7-6-16-13-20-10-8-2-4-5-1-11-12-14-15-9	1.927777%
mRMRd	3-7-17-10-6-8-13-16-4-5-12-21-18-19-2-20-15-9-14-11-1	1.619443%
mRMRq	3-10-16-7-6-17-2-8-13-5-1-4-11-12-14-9-21-15-18-19-20	1.625001%
wra.	17-21-19-18-1-2-3-4-5-6-7-8-9-10-11-12-13-14-15-16-20	2.505556%
Ori.	1-2-3-4-5-6-7-8-9-10-11-12-13-14-15-16-17-18-19-20-21	2.0500015%
Con.	In One Batch	1.8638875%

According to Tables 2-5, comparing with all the other approaches based on different criteria, it is obvious that ITID-AD, which was derived by the evolving linear discriminant with the criterion of maximum AD means in a growing feature space, exhibits the lowest error rate.

7   Conclusion

An evolving linear discriminant for feature-based incremental learning is presented in this paper. This linear discriminant has the same basic concept with FLD, but it can be employed for pattern classification with IAL in a growing feature space. With the criterion of maximum means of AD during the process of feature importing, such a linear discriminant is applicable to search the optimal feature ordering by an evolutionary searching algorithm. Experimental results showed that the approach using the evolving linear discriminant with the criterion of maximum discriminability mean is more feasible to reduce the classification error rate than some other methods. It indicates that the evolving linear discriminant demonstrated in this paper exhibits effective performance with the discriminability's maximum mean criterion and evolutionary searching algorithm. For classification problems with an increasing dimensional feature space to be solved with IAL, the approaches presented in this paper can be regarded as a solution likely to get better performance.

Acknowledgement. This research is supported by National Natural Science Foundation of China under Grant 61070085.

References

1. Guan, S.U., Liu, J.: Incremental Ordered Neural Network Training. Journal of Intelligent Systems 12(3), 137–172 (2002)
2. Guan, S.U., Liu, J.: Incremental Neural Network Training with an Increasing Input Dimension. Journal of Intelligent Systems 13(1), 43–69 (2004)
3. Wang, T., Guan, S.U., Liu, F.: Ordered Incremental Attribute Learning based on mRMR and Neural Networks. International Journal of Design, Analysis and Tools for Integrated Circuits and Systems 2(2), 86–90 (2011)

4. Guan, S.U., Li, S.C.: Incremental Learning with Respect to New Incoming Input Attributes. Neural Processing Letters 14(3), 241–260 (2001)
5. Guan, S.U., Zhu, F.M.: An Incremental Approach to Genetic Algorithms Based Classification. IEEE Trans. on Systems, Man and Cybernetics Part B 35(2), 227–239 (2005)
6. Chao, S., Wong, F.: An incremental decision tree learning methodology regarding attributes in medical data mining. In: Proceedings of the Eighth Int'l Conference on Machine Learning and Cybernetics, Baoding, pp. 1694–1699 (2009)
7. Liu, X., Zhang, G., Zhan, Y., Zhu, E.: An Incremental Feature Learning Algorithm Based on Least Square Support Vector Machine. In: Preparata, F.P., Wu, X., Yin, J. (eds.) FAW 2008. LNCS, vol. 5059, pp. 330–338. Springer, Heidelberg (2008)
8. Bermejo, P., Ossa, L., Gámez, J.A., Puerta, J.M.: Fast wrapper feature subset selection in high-dimensional datasets by means of filter re-ranking. Knowledge-Based Systems 25(1), 35–44 (2012)
9. Wang, T., Guan, S.-U., Liu, F.: Feature Discriminability for Pattern Classification Based on Neural Incremental Attribute Learning. In: Wang, Y., Li, T. (eds.) ISKE2011. AISC, vol. 122, pp. 275–280. Springer, Heidelberg (2011)
10. Peng, H., Long, F., Ding, C.: Feature selection based on mutual information: criteria of max-dependency, max-relevance, and min-redundancy. IEEE Transactions on Pattern Analysis and Machine Intelligence 27(8), 1226–1238 (2005)

Compact Multiplicative Inverter for Hardware Elliptic Curve Cryptosystem

M.M. Wong[1,*], M.L.D. Wong[1,2], and Ka Lok Man[2]

[1] School of Engineering, Computing and Science,
Swinburne University of Technology Sarawak Campus, Malaysia
mwong@swinburne.edu.my
[2] Xi'an Jiaotong-Liverpool University, Suzhou, China
{Dennis.Wong,ka.man}@xjtlu.edu.cn

Abstract. This paper presents a compact design of a multiplicative inverter for elliptic curve cryptosystems. Using a methodology based on the composite field arithmetic, we propose a combinatorial solution to mitigate the usage of look up tables as commonly adopted by the conventional software based approach. In particular, we perform further isomorphism in the subfield, such that the required arithmetic are constructed using logical AND and XOR gates only. In this work, we demonstrate our proposed methodology with the field $GF((2^8)^{41}) \cong GF((((2^2)^2)^2)^{41})$ in optimal normal type II basis. The chosen field is both secure and results in efficient computation. An analysis of the resultant hardware complexity of our inverter is reported towards the end.

Keywords: Elliptic curve (EC) cryptosystems, composite field arithmetic (CFA), Itoh and Tsujii inversion algorithm (ITIA), multiplicative inversion.

1 Introduction

Finite fields play an essential role in the modern cryptographic applications. As such, the complexity of its underlying field's arithmetic will determine the amount of resources required in the final cryptosystem. Therefore, the first, and the most essential step in constructing a compact and efficient elliptic curve (EC) hardware cryptosystem is to choose the suitable field for ECC computation. Therefore, composite field, which offers greater computational efficiency compared to other finite fields, is a favourable choice. The prior studies in composite field EC cryptosystems had emphasized on software implementations where look-up tables (LUTs) were utilized in the subfield arithmetic [1-4]. Consequently, the unbreakable delays of LUTs will determine the maximum attainable clock rate of the final hardware circuitry. This drawback can be avoided by employing combinatorial approaches, i.e. using only the combinatorial logic for the hardware construction.

---

* The work of M. M. Wong was supported by Swinburne University of Technology Sarawak Campus under a Ph.D. studentship.

J.J. Park et al. (Eds.): NPC 2012, LNCS 7513, pp. 492–499, 2012.

In particular, the scalar multiplication, kP, is the most crucial and yet the most complicated operation in any elliptic curve cryptography (ECC) [5, 6] applications. It involves a repetition of point additions and point doublings, which requires inversions over the finite field when defined in affine coordinate system [7]. Therefore, in this work, we propose a compact and efficient inversion circuit through the exploitation of composite field arithmetic (CFA) for EC hardware cryptosystem. Two main criteria are taken into consideration during the construction, which are the **security** aspect and the **complexity** of the underlying arithmetic. In short, we need to select an optimal field that is insusceptible to the known attacks and also results in combinatorial inversion circuitry without the need of LUTs.

2   Composite Field Inversion for Elliptic Curve Cryptography

Construction of the composite field inverter in EC cryptosystem requires three major steps. The first and also the most important step is choosing an appropriate field that would circumvent the cryptographic attacks on the elliptic curve discrete logarithm problem (ECDLP) [8-9]. ECDLP is defined as follows. Given an elliptic curve E, defined over a finite field $GF(q)$, a point $P \in E(GF(q))$ of order r, and a second point $Q \in \langle P \rangle$, determine the integer $l \in [0, r-1]$ such that $Q = lP$. The ECDLP is of particular interest because its apparent intractability would form the basis for the security of EC cryptographic schemes [10].

In 2000, Gaudry, Hess and Smart (GHS) [11] showed that the Weil descent attack methodology (see [12]), can be used to reduce any instance of the ECDLP to an instance of discrete logarithm problem (DLP) in the Jacobian of a hyperelliptic curve over $GF(2^N)$. Only for the case where $N \in [160, 600]$ is prime, $GF(2^N)$ is secure from the GHS attack [13]. In other words, the use of elliptic curves over $GF(2^N)$ with N is a composite number is not recommended.

In the later date, the applicability of the GHS attack on the ECDLP for elliptic curves over $GF(2^N)$ for composite $N \in [160, 600]$ was further analyzed by Maurer et al. in [10]. The elliptic curves of composite field $GF((2^n)^m)$ that are susceptible to the GHS attack were identified and listed precisely in their paper. Therefore, this allows us to select the composite field that is not weak under GHS attack.

For security purposes, the extension field, m, has to be a considerably large prime number, while the subfields, n, is chosen to be relatively smaller in order to simplify the computation. Hence, we have chosen $GF((2^8)^{41})$ for our design.

In the second step, after the field selection, we consider algorithmic optimization to achieve area reduction in the inverter design. While the previous studies focused on two-level isomorphism composite field, we propose to perform further isomorphisms in the subfield $GF(2^8)$, such that it is further reduced to $GF(((2^2)^2)^2)$. With this, we can derive a combinatorial inverter circuitry without the use of LUTs. Furthermore, normal basis representation is often a preferred choice over the polynomial basis representation in hardware implementation. Among the normal bases, the optimal normal basis (ONB) manages to further reduce the complexity of the complicated normal basis multipliers. As we have decided the extension field, m, to be a prime number, ONB type II representation is sought here.

Last, we employ the Itoh and Tsujii inversion (ITI) algorithm [14, 15] to perform the efficient and compact multiplicative inversion over the selected composite field. The ITI algorithm presented below as Theorem 1 is a Fermat's Little Theorem (FLT)-based inversion algorithm which can efficiently reduce the inversion in the extension field $GF((2^n)^m)$ to the inversion in its subfield, $GF(2^n)$.

Theorem 1 (Itoh & Tsujii Inversion [14]). *Let* $A \in GF((2^n)^m)$, $A \neq 0$ *and* $r = \frac{(n^m-1)}{(n-1)}$. *The inverse of an element A can be computed as* $A^{-1} = (A^r)^{-1}. A^{r-1}$, *with* $A \in GF(2^n)$.

Overall, in this work, we derive a combinatorial inverter over $GF((((2^2)^2)^2)^{41})$ for EC cryptosystems in ONBII representation using the ITI algorithm. Detailed description of our proposed inverter will be presented in the next section. To the best of our knowledge, this is the first reported work on using ITI for the aforementioned configuration.

3   Design and Implementation

Our composite field inverter using ITI algorithm can be accomplished through the following four steps. Here after, we denote our field as $GF(q^m)$ with $q = (((2^2)^2)^2)$ and $m = 41$.

Step 1: Exponentiation of $A^{r-1} \in GF(q^m)$. The exponent $r - 1$ can be expressed as a sum of powers $q^{40} + q^{39} + q^{38} + \cdots + q^2 + q$. Through a series of repeated power raising and multiplication, the exponentiation is accomplished as follows;

$$A^{q^2} = (A^q)^q$$

$$A^q. A^{q^2} = A^{q^2+q}$$

$$\left(A^{q^2+q}\right)^{q^2}. \left(A^{q^2+q}\right) = A^{q^4+q^3+q^2+q} = A^{\sum_{i=1}^{4} q^i}$$

$$\left(A^{\sum_{i=1}^{4} q^i}\right)^{q^4}. \left(A^{\sum_{i=1}^{4} q^i}\right) = A^{q^8+q^7+\cdots+q} = A^{\sum_{i=1}^{8} q^i}$$

$$\left(A^{\sum_{i=1}^{8} q^i}\right)^{q^8}. \left(A^{\sum_{i=1}^{8} q^i}\right) = A^{q^{16}+q^{15}+\cdots+q} = A^{\sum_{i=1}^{16} q^i}$$

$$\left(A^{\sum_{i=1}^{16} q^i}\right)^{q^{16}}. \left(A^{\sum_{i=1}^{16} q^i}\right) = A^{q^{32}+q^{31}+\cdots+q} = A^{\sum_{i=1}^{32} q^i}$$

$$A^{r-1} = \left(A^{q^{32}+q^{31}+\cdots+q}\right)^{q^8}. A^{q^8+q^7+\cdots+q} \tag{1}$$

The complexity to compute A^{r-1} using addition chain (see (1)) is found to be 6 multiplications in $GF(q^{41})$ and 40 exponentiations to the qth power. While the exponentiation requires only q cyclic shifts, the $GF(q^{41})$ multiplier needs to be implemented using a normal basis multiplier.

Step 2: Multiplication of A and A^{r-1} that yield $A^r \in GF(q)$. In the second step, multiplication of two operands $A, A^{r-1} \in GF(q^{41})$ will result in $A^r \in GF(2^q)$. ubsequently, we need a specific multiplier that compute the first coefficient in the general multiplication in $F(q^{41})$. This step can be accomplished with 81 multiplications and 81 additions over $GF(2^q)$. Note that in the finite field of characteristic 2, both subtraction and addition are implemented using a XOR operation.

Step 3: Inversion in $GF(2^n)$ yields $(A^r)^{-1}$. Instead of using LUTs, we utilize a combinatorial circuitry to perform the inversion over the composite field $GF(((2^2)^2)^2)$. The inversion involves three level of isomorphisms which requires three field polynomials stated (in a general form) below:

$$r(y) = y^2 + y + v, \text{extension of } GF(2^8)/GF(2^4) \tag{2}$$

$$s(z) = z^2 + Tz + 1, \text{extension of } GF(2^4)/GF(2^2) \tag{3}$$

$$t(w) = w^2 + w + 1, \text{extension of } GF(2^2)/GF(2) \tag{4}$$

The inverter architecture is described with reference to their respective field polynomials in general. First, for the isomorphism between $GF(2^8)/GF(2^4)$, we have the element of field $GF(2^8)$, δ, expressed as $\gamma_1 Y^{16} + \gamma_0 Y$, where $\gamma_0, \gamma_1, v \in GF(2^4)$ and using both roots of $r(y)$ as $r(y) = (y + Y)(y + Y^{16})$. Second, for the isomorphism between $GF(2^4)/GF(2^2)$, we have the element of field $GF(2^4)$, Δ, expressed as $\Gamma_1 Z^4 + \Gamma_0 Z$, where $\Gamma_1, \Gamma_0, T \in GF(2^2)$ and $s(z) = (z + Z)(z + Z^4)$. Last, for the isomorphism between $GF(2^2)/GF(2)$, we let element of field $GF(2^2)$, d, expressed as $g_1 W^2 + g_0 W$, where $g_0, g_1 \in GF(2)$ and $t(w) = (w + W)(w + W^2)$.

Hence, the multiplicative inverse of $\gamma_1 Y^{16} + \gamma_0 Y$ can be computed as stated in (5),

$$(\gamma_1 Y^{16} + \gamma_0 Y)^{-1} = [\gamma_1 \Theta]Y^{16} + [\gamma_0 \Theta]Y \tag{5}$$

where $\Theta = [\gamma_0 \gamma_1 + (\gamma_0^2 + \gamma_1^2)v]^{-1}$. The arithmetic in (5) can be decomposed into several subfield operations, namely the multiplications and the inversions. To summarize, the arithmetic required over the inversion is tabulated in Table 1 and as depicted in Figure 1. The total complexity of our inverter is 36 ANDs and 96 XORs.

Step 4: Multiplication of $(A^r)^{-1}.A^{r-1}$. In this final step, we need to multiply $A^{r-1} \in GF(q^m)$ (from Step 1) and $(A^r)^{-1} \in GF(q)$ (from Step 3) to duce A^{-1}. This step requires $m = 41$ multiplications in $GF(q)$. Let $g, h \in GF(((2^2)^2)^2)$ be $\{\gamma_1 Z^8 + \gamma_0 Z\}$ and $\{\delta_1 Z^8 + \delta_0 Z\}$ respectively. Multiplication of g and h is then derived in (6),

$$(\gamma_1 Z^8 + \gamma_0 Z)(\delta_1 Z^8 + \delta_0 Z)$$
$$= (\gamma_1 \delta_1)(Z^8)^2 + (\gamma_1 \delta_0 + \gamma_0 \delta_1)Z^8 Z + (\gamma_0 \delta_{01})Z^2$$
$$= [(\gamma_1 + \gamma_0)(\delta_1 + \delta_0)v + \gamma_1 \delta_1]Z^8 + [(\gamma_1 + \gamma_0)(\delta_1 + \delta_0)v + \gamma_0 \delta_0]Z \qquad (6)$$

with a complexity of 27 ANDs and 81 XORs.

Table 1. Multiplicative Inverse for $GF(((2^2)^2)^2)$

Operation	Equation
Inversion in $GF(2^8)$	$\delta_1 = [\gamma_1 \gamma_0 + (\gamma_1^2 + \gamma_0^2)v]^{-1}\gamma_0$
	$\delta_0 = [\gamma_1 \gamma_0 + (\gamma_1^2 + \gamma_0^2)v]^{-1}\gamma_1$
	$v\gamma^2 = [(\Gamma_0 + \Gamma_1)^2]Z^4 + N^2 \Gamma_0^2$
Inversion in $GF(2^4)$	$\Delta_1 = [\Gamma_1 \Gamma_0 T^2 + (\Gamma_1^2 + \Gamma_0^2)]^{-1}\Gamma_0$
	$\Delta_0 = [\Gamma_1 \Gamma_0 T^2 + (\Gamma_1^2 + \Gamma_0^2)]^{-1}\Gamma_1$
	$\Gamma^2 = g_0 W^2 + g_1 W$
	$\Gamma T = (g_0 + g_1)W^2 + g_1 W$
Inversion in $GF(2^2)$	$d_1 = g_0$
	$d_0 = g_1$
Multiplication in $GF(2^4)$	$(\Gamma_1 \Delta_1)(Z^4)^2 + (\Gamma_1 \Delta_0 + \Gamma_0 \Delta_1)Z^4 Z$
	$\qquad\qquad + (\Gamma_0 \Delta_0)Z^2$
Multiplication in $GF(2^2)$	$[(g_1 + g_0)(d_1 + d_0) + g_1 d_1]W^2$
	$+[(g_1 + g_0)(d_1 + d_0) + g_0 d_0]W$

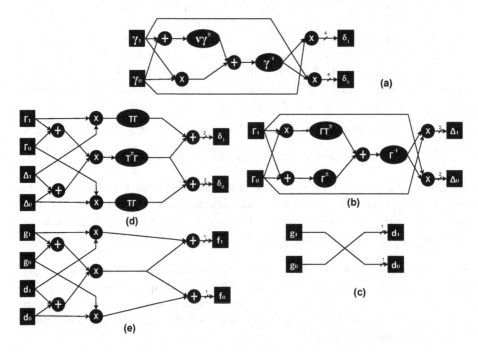

Fig. 1. Inversion over $GF(2^8)$ using CFA. (a) Inversion in $GF(2^8)$, (b) Inversion in $GF(2^4)$, (c) Inversion in $GF(2^2)$, (d) Multiplication in $GF(2^4)$, (e) Multiplication in $GF(2^2)$.

4   Discussion and Results

To demonstrate the efficacies of our inverter in EC hardware cryptosystem, its computational cost is benchmarked with the previous works. To our best knowledge, the most recent and comparable work from the literature was presented by Guajardo and Paar in 1997 [4]. They employed ITI algorithm for inversion over two levels composite field of $GF((2^n)^m)$ in polynomial basis representation, and the subfield $GF(2^n)$ arithmetic was computed using the LUT approach.

The LUT approach employed in the previous works of the composite field EC cryptosystems [1-4] was performed using *log* and *antilog* conversion. In this approach, three and two tables of 2,048 bits were used to calculate the multiplication and the inversion of the field elements respectively. Meanwhile, without using any LUT, our $GF(((2^2)^2)^2)$ inverter and multiplier are constructed using 36 ANDs and 96 XORs, and 27 ANDs and 81 XORs respectively.

Due to the large amount of subfield multiplier are required, the complexity of the subfield multiplier determines the hardware cost (area and power) and the performance of the inverter architecture. Here, we point out the advantages of using combinatorial $GF(((2^2)^2)^2)$ multiplier as opposed to the LUT approach in hardware implementation. Having both architectures implemented in Cyclone III EP3C120F780I7 FPGA, the summary of the hardware requirements are tabulated in Table 2. Based on the result in Table 2 our combinatorial circuitry is capable of promoting a significant saving in term of hardware resources and with higher overall performance compared to the conventional LUT approach, which is based on *log* and *antilog* conversion method.

Table 2. Hardware analysis of FPGA implementation for $GF(((2^2)^2)^2)$ multiplier using (i) combinatorial circuity as proposed in our work and (ii) log and antilog conversions

	(i) Combinatorial Circuity	(ii) Log and Antilog Conversions
Total LE	51	432
Total Combinatorial Functions	51	432
Dedicated Logic Register	0	0
Total Register	8	0
Total Memory Bits	0	2,048
Fmax (MHz)	142.76	95.15
Total Thermal Power Dissipation (mW)	79.83	80.61
Core Dynamic Thermal Power Dissipation (mW)	2.90	3.65
Core Static Power Dissipation (mW)	68.26	68.27
I/O Thermal Power Dissipation (mW)	8.67	8.70

Furthermore, we also include the existing EEA-based inverter architectures over binary field, $GF(2^m)$ [16-18] for benchmarking. The complexity of these architectures working in $GF(2^{328})$, together with the work by Guajardo and Paar in $GF((2^8)^{41})$ and our work are summarized in Table 3. The analytical results in Table 3 proved that composite field results in compact architecture design compared to the binary field. Therefore, composite field that is insusceptible towards cryptographic attacks is highly desirable in hardware EC cryptosystem implementation.

Table 3. Analytical comparison of various inverter architectures

	Guajardo and Paar [14]	Guo and Wang [16]	Wu at al. [17]	Yan and Sarwate [18]	Our Work
Finite Field	$GF((2^8)^{41})$	$GF(2^{328})$	$GF(2^{328})$	$GF(2^{328})$	$GF((((2^2)^2)^2)^{41})$
OR gates	0	0	1,312	0	0
NOT gates	0	0	656	0	0
AND gates	0	645,504	654,504	430,336	275,652
XOR gates	315,688	430,336	215,168	430,336	986,340
XOR3 gates	0	215,168	215,168	0	0
Adder	7,812	656	0	0	0
Mux	0	860,672	654,504	645,504	0
LUT (2048 bits)	8,279	0	0	0	0

5   Conclusion

This work presented of a secure and compact combinatorial inverter for EC cryptosystems over $GF((((2^2)^2)^2)^{41})$ in ONBII representation. Unlike the previous works, we performed further isomorphisms in the subfield, $GF(2^8) \cong GF(((2^2)^2)^2)$, such that the need for LUTs can be eliminated completely. Using the ONBII representation, we chose the extension field m, to be a prime number while allowing the 40 exponentiations be implemented easily using   simple cyclic shifts. In addition to that, we have shown the advantages of using combinatorial circuitry for EC hardware cryptosystem   as opposed   to the LUT approach. Furthermore, we has proven our composite field inverter is more compact than those binary field inverters which were reported in the literature.

References

1. Harper, G., Menezes, A., Vanstone, S.A.: Public-Key Cryptosystems with Very Small Key Lengths. In: Rueppel, R.A. (ed.) EUROCRYPT 1992. LNCS, vol. 658, pp. 163–173. Springer, Heidelberg (1993)
2. Beauregard, D.: Efficient algorithms for implementing elliptic curve public-key schemes. Master's thesis, ECE Dept., Worcester Polytechnic Institute (1996)
3. Win, E.D., Bosselaers, A., Vandenberghe, S., Gersem, P.D., Vandewalle, J.: A fast software implementation for arithmetic operations in GF(2^n). In: Proceedings of the International Conference on the Theory and Applications of Cryptology and Information Security: Advances in Cryptology, pp. 65–76. Springer, London (1996)
4. Guajardo, J., Paar, C.: Efficient Algorithms for Elliptic Curve Cryptosystems. In: Kaliski Jr., B.S. (ed.) CRYPTO 1997. LNCS, vol. 1294, pp. 342–356. Springer, Heidelberg (1997)

5. Koblitz, N.: Constructing Elliptic Curve Cryptosystems in Characteristic 2. In: Menezes, A., Vanstone, S.A. (eds.) CRYPTO 1990. LNCS, vol. 537, pp. 156–167. Springer, Heidelberg (1991)

6. Miller, V.S.: Use of Elliptic Curves in Cryptography. In: Williams, H.C. (ed.) CRYPTO 1985. LNCS, vol. 218, pp. 417–426. Springer, Heidelberg (1986)

7. Hankerson, D., Menezes, A.J., Vanstone, S.: Guide to Elliptic Curve Cryptography. Springer-Verlag, New York, Inc. (2004)

8. Menezes, A., Teske, E., Weng, A.: Weak Fields for ECC. In: Okamoto, T. (ed.) CT-RSA 2004. LNCS, vol. 2964, pp. 366–386. Springer, Heidelberg (2004)

9. Menezes, A., Teske, E.: Cryptographic implications of Hess' generalized GHS attack. Applicable Algebra in Engineering, Communication and Computing 16, 439–460 (2006), 10.1007/s00200-005-0186-8

10. Maurer, M., Menezes, A., Teske, E.: Analysis of the GHS Weil Descent Attack on the ECDLP over Characteristic Two Finite Fields of Composite Degree. In: Pandu Rangan, C., Ding, C. (eds.) INDOCRYPT 2001. LNCS, vol. 2247, pp. 195–213. Springer, Heidelberg (2001)

11. Gaudry, P., Hess, F., Smart, N.: Constructive and destructive facets of Weil descent on elliptic curves. Journal of Cryptology 15, 19–46 (2002), 10.1007/s00145-001-0011-x

12. Frey, G.: Applications of arithmetical geometry to cryptographic constructions. In: Proceedings of the Fifth International Conference on Finite Fields and Applications, pp. 128–161. Springer

13. Menezes, A., Qu, M.: Analysis of the Weil Descent Attack of Gaudry, Hess and Smart. In: Naccache, D. (ed.) CT-RSA 2001. LNCS, vol. 2020, pp. 308–318. Springer, Heidelberg (2001)

14. Itoh, T., Tsujii, S.: A fast algorithm for computing multiplicative inverses in $GF(2^m)$ using normal bases. Inf. Comput. 78, 171–177 (1988)

15. Guajardo, J., Paar, C.: Itoh-Tsujii inversion in standard basis and its application in cryptography and codes. Designs, Codes and Cryptography 25, 207–216 (2002), 10.1023/A:1013860532636

16. Guo, J.H., Wang, C.L.: Hardware-efficient systolic architecture for inversion and division in $GF(2^m)$. IEE Proceedings Computers and Digital Techniques 145(4), 272–278 (1998)

17. Wu, C.H., Wu, C.M., Shieh, M.D., Hwang, Y.T.: Systolic VLSI realization of a novel iterative division algorithm over $GF(2^m)$: a high-speed, low-complexity design. In: The 2001 IEEE International Symposium on Circuits and Systems, ISCAS 2001, vol. 4, pp. 33–36 (May 2001)

18. Yan, Z., Sarwate, D.: New systolic architectures for inversion and division in $GF(2^m)$. IEEE Transactions on Computers 52(11), 1514–1519 (2003)

Space Exploration of Multi-agent Robotics via Genetic Algorithm

T.O. Ting[1,*], Kaiyu Wan[2], Ka Lok Man[2], and Sanghyuk Lee[1]

[1] Dept. Electrical and Electronic Eng.,
[2] Dept. Computer Science and Software Eng.,
Xi'an Jiaotong-Liverpool University, Suzhou, China
{toting,kaiyu.wan,ka.man,sanghyuk.lee}@xjtlu.edu.cn

Abstract. Robots play an important role in space exploration whereby the presence of human is almost impossible in some environments. Instead of using a robot, we incorporate a group of robots working together to achieve the definitive goal. Evolutionary algorithm, namely Genetic Algorithm is applied in the multi-agent robotics for space exploration. Hereby, the core focus of this paper is to study the effect of crossover rate upon the convergence of the exploration. As from our results, choosing the right parameter value is crucial for optimal coverage of the potential area.

Keywords: Genetic Algorithm, Multi-agent Robotics, Space Exploration.

1 Introduction

An agent can be defined as a computational system that tries to fulfill a set of goals in a complex, dynamic environment [1]. It has sensors which provide information on the surrounding environment, and its actions are controlled by the agent's actuators. An agent can take upon many forms, depending upon its application and environment. Important properties that an agent possesses are autonomy, reactivity and proactiveness. Additional properties include being able to describe information states, deliberative states and motivational states. An agent is called autonomous if operates completely autonomously – that is, if it decides itself how to relate its sensory data to motor commands in such a way that its goals are attended to successfully [2]. An agent is said to be adaptive if it is able to improve its goal-achieving competence over time. Autonomous agents constitute a part of study in artificial intelligence.

Recently, growing interest has been shown in systems composing several interacting autonomous agents, instead of a single agent. They can be applicable in domains that cannot be handled by centralized systems. Nowadays, a solid platform of computer and network technology is available for realizing complex multi-agent systems. By having multiple robots cooperating, there are many advantages compared to using a single robot. The robots have a larger range of task domains, which can be seen through the wide range of applications discussed later. If the robots exchange information with each other whenever they sense each other, they can localize themselves

J.J. Park et al. (Eds.): NPC 2012, LNCS 7513, pp. 500–507, 2012.
© IFIP International Federation for Information Processing 2012

faster and more accurately. As there are many robots performing a single task to achieve a common goal, redundancy is introduced. Thus, it has higher fault tolerance than using a single-robot system. Being more robust, it can accomplish tasks more efficiently. As an example, in the year 2003, a mission called Beagle 2, attempting to explore planet Mars and collect soil samples from the planet. A spacecraft was sent with a single robot in it. This is a centralized system where the robot is controlled via wireless communication. The mission failed because the robot's antenna was damaged during landing, thus, no signal is received from the robot. Thus, if a decentralized multiple-robot system was used instead, this problem would not have occurred, since the robots can still perform work without one member. The only downfall is a slower speed as communications between agents take up an amount of precious time.

With multiple-robot systems, more robots would be needed and produced. This will greatly reduce the economic cost of a single robot, making it more marketable. Also, with multiple robots at a few different places, a wider area can be covered. This introduces distributed sensing and action, where the system can sense at one place and performs an action at another place. An example of a natural multi-agent society is an ant colony. Within this colony, you can see many different tasks being carried out by many ants, working together to achieve a single goal. You see as many as a few hundred ants carrying big chunks of food back to their nest, or attacking a predator much larger than themselves, for example a praying mantis. This is an inspiration for multi-agent robotic systems researches, knowing that this field yields many opportunities and benefits, as many applications unfold.

2 Evolutionary Robotics

One critical goal in multi-agent robotic systems development is to design a distributed control infrastructure for the robots to perform their tasks over a problem-solving period without human supervision. They must be capable of dealing with dynamic changes occurring over time, such as unpredictable changes in environment, or even variations in their own performance capabilities. To improve a robot's likelihood of survival in a changing environment, learning, evolution and adaptation are important. They help by inducing appropriate competition or cooperation with other agents/robots. Learning is a strategy for an agent to adapt to its environment. Adaptation refers to an agent's learning by making adjustments with respect to its environment. Evolution is considered as a strategy for a population of agents to adapt to the environment [1].

When there is an environmental change or an unpredictable event occurs, an agent, through its experience, attempts its best response action. By evaluating how well that action responded, it learns something. If the evaluation result is bad, which means that the response action doesn't really work well, the agent will most likely avoid using that action again for that particular event / change or something similar to it. On the other hand, if the evaluation results is good, when that event / change occurs the next time around, the agent will more likely respond with the previous action. And so, the learning process continues, and the agent attempts to adapt to the environment. From the learning process, new behaviors or processes can be generated. For living creatures, evolution is a process of selective reproduction and substitution. This process takes a long time, and spans over generations. This means that animals need to mate in order to evolve. But, robots can't mate. Instead, in multi-agent robotics, the agents evolve its controllers – also known as its brain or processor – via evolutionary algorithms, which is discussed in the following section.

3   Genetic Algorithm

Genetic Algorithm (GA) is adaptive method that may be used to solve search and optimization problems [3, 4]. It applies the nature's law of survival of the fittest that only allows the organisms that best adapt to the environment to live. It may also be regarded as 'a hill-climbing search method that finds near-optimal solutions by subjecting a population of points in a search space to a set of biologically inspired operators.

3.1   Representing Hypotheses in GA

A chromosome can be represented by anything in a universal set – colored strings, decimal numbers, or even as simple as bit strings of zeros and ones. Hypotheses can have many descriptions. For example, we take the attribute "weather". Some possible values are sunny, rainy, cloudy, etc. We also can use bit strings to represent these values, but it is quite complex to do so. For example, we can take 010 to represent cloudy, 011 to represent any two possible values of cloudy or rainy, 111 to represent any weather condition, etc. If the second attribute is the football field condition, and the values range from dry to wet, we can represent the field condition in 4 levels. In binary string, we can take 00 to represent very dry, to 11 to represent very wet. To make computation easy for genetic operations such as mutation and crossover, hypotheses are usually described by bit strings.

3.2   GA for Multi-agent Robotics

By applying evolutionary computation for solving optimization problems, robotics is one of the fields in which researchers have found many applications, ranging from control strategy synthesis to geometric motion planning. For motion planning, a chromosome represents a path that consists of straight-line segments. A path may or may not be feasible. The initial population of chromosomes is a group of paths. Chromosomes are evaluated and selected according to their fitness. Genetic operators are used for possible improvement. In this case, the fitness function is used to evaluate the feasibility, length, smoothness, clearness of a path [1]. Three commonly used genetic operators are selection, crossover and mutation. In selection, candidates with higher fitness have higher chances to survive in the next generation. Crossover recombines two parent paths into two new paths whereas mutation tunes the node coordinates in a feasible path for sharp adjustment.

3.3   Fitness Function

In behavior evolution, the fitness function used to select the best next location consists of two terms: one is the general fitness, and another is called special fitness. The general fitness term encourages the group robots to explore the potential field in new, less confident regions, and at the same time avoid repeating the work of other robots. It is defined as:

$$s_g = \prod_{i=1}^{m} \left\{ (1 - \max\{w_i'^k\}) \prod_{j=1}^{m_e} \sqrt[4]{d_{ij} - R_1} \right\} \tag{1}$$

where $\max\{w_i'^k\}$ denotes the maximum confidence weight corresponding to the location of robot i. m denotes the number of robots that are grouped together during one evolutionary movement step, according to a special fitness term. When the special fitness term is concerned with spatial diffusion, m becomes m_d. m_e denotes the number of robots that do not belong to m, and have just selected and executed their next motion strategies. d_{ij} refers to the distance between robots i and j, which is greater than a predefined distance threshold, R_1. In addition to the general fitness, we also define two special fitness terms corresponding to the criteria of multi-robot spatial diffusion and area coverage, respectively. They are:

1. Spatial diffusion:

$$s_1 = \prod_{i=1}^{m_d - 1} \prod_{j=i+1}^{m_d} \sqrt{d_{ij} - R_2} \tag{2}$$

2. Area coverage:

$$s_2 = \frac{\sqrt{\Delta V}}{\prod_{i=1}^{m_c} \zeta_i} \tag{3}$$

where m_d denotes the number of spatially diffusing robots whose inter-distances d_{ij} are greater than the threshold R_2. ΔV denotes the total number of locations visited by a group of m_c area-covering robots, based on their selected motion directions. ζ_i denotes a significant proximity distance between robot i and other robots in the environment. Having defined the general and special fitness terms, the complete fitness function used in the evolution of group robots can be given as follows:

$$F = \begin{cases} s_g \cdot s_1, & \text{for spatially diffusing robots} \\ s_g \cdot s_2, & \text{for area covering robots} \end{cases} \tag{4}$$

Thus, given a certain stimulus, a robot first applies some genetic operations to a population of chromosomes representing possible next locations.

4   Simulation and Results

This simulation aims to study the effect of the different values of crossover probability on the efficiency of the system. The relevant toolbox is downloaded from [6]. The environment of exploration space is as depicted in Fig. 1 with relevant true potential field map shown in Fig. 2. The size is 300 x 300 pixels. It contains three medium-sized obstacles – two oval-shaped and one rectangular. Six robots are used in this experiment. Their initial positions are at the bottom left corner. These can be seen as small dots in Fig. 1. As suggested by most GA researchers [7, 8, 9, 10], the probabilities of crossover which are used in this experiment range from 0.5 to 0.9. The other simulation parameters are given in Table 1.

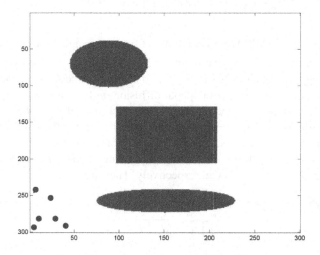

Fig. 1. The environment used for Simulation

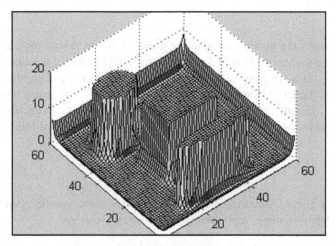

Fig. 2. True potential field map for simulation

Table 1. Parameters used in the simulation

Parameter	Symbol	Unit	Value
Number of robots	M		6
Sensory section	N		16
Environment size		grid	300x300
Map resolution		grid	5
Map locations			60x60
Maximum movement step	d_m	location	7
Robot initial locations		location	(5, 5) (10, 40) (20, 10) (20, 30) (45, 25) (55, 5)
Behavior vector increment	ψ		0.2
Chromosome length	$(2L) \cdot M$	bit	96
Population size	P		120
Generations per step	G		48
Crossover probability	p_c		0.5-0.9
Mutation probability	p_m		0.1/0.05/0.005
Number of run steps			20

The mutation rate is already adaptively regulated according Equation (5) below.

$$p_M = \begin{cases} 0.1, & \text{if } 1 \leq generation < 40 \\ 0.05, & \text{if } 40 \leq generation < 80 \\ 0.005, & \text{if } 80 \leq generation < 120 \end{cases} \tag{5}$$

The percentage of the unaccessed environment is monitored throughout the experiment. This is shown in the graph of Fig. 3. The lower the percentage of unaccessed area, the

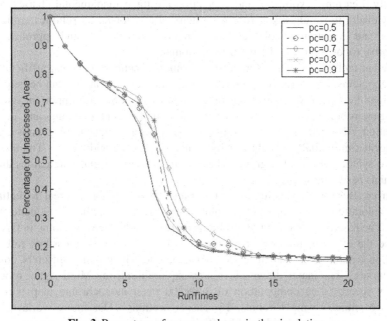

Fig. 3. Percentage of unaccessed area in the simulation

better it is. It is clear from the graph that the system works best when $p_c = 0.8$. Also, $p_c = 0.5$ yields almost the same result. The system is worst at $p_c = 0.7$. After RunTimes = 14, the percentage of unaccessed area for all crossover probabilities converges to about 17%. This value refers to the area covered by the obstacle. Thus the exploration of the map converges at approximately 14 run steps. The value of crossover rate do not affect much on this map, as it may be too small to see apparent results, and there are not enough obstacles. Simulations can be done using bigger maps in the future, but will take a much longer time. For one simulation of a single crossover probability value, it took 16 minutes on this 300×300 pixels monochrome map.

5   Conclusions

Behavior-based robotics, collective robotics, and evolutionary robotics have been inspired by biology, ethnology, sociology and other related fields. The three approaches are interrelated. They all aim at generating complex, adaptive and goal-driven group behaviors from simple local interactions among individuals in multi-agent robotic systems. However, they also produce different forms of autonomy, adaptability, task complexity, and intelligence in multi-agent systems. For example, although behavior based approaches are robust for many task environments, they are not necessarily adaptive. An evolutionary system can, on the other hand, improve the adaptability to the changes in a dynamic environment.

Multi-agent robotic system design is challenging because the performance of such a system depends significantly on issues that arise from the interactions between robots. Distributed approaches are appealing due to their properties of scalability and reliability. Learning, evolution, and adaptation are three fundamental characteristics of individuals in a multi-agent robotic system. Behavior-based robotics, collective robotics, and evolutionary robotics have offered useful models and approaches for cooperative robot control in the multi-robot domain.

Different techniques of reinforcement learning, genetic algorithms, artificial life, immune systems, probabilistic approaches, and multi-agent planning can be helpful in the design of cooperative controllers for multiple robots. Several important issues in multi-agent robotics, such as self-organization, multi-agent planning and control, coevolution, emergent behavior, reactive behavior, heterogenous/homogenous design, multi-agent simulation, and behavior dynamics need to be addressed. The ultimate aim is to synthesize complex group behaviors from simple social interactions among individuals based on simple strategies.

As a conclusion, the evolutionary multi-agent robotics has a great potential in space exploration. The core of our evolutionary algorithm applied is Genetic Algorithm. The reactive movement of a robot is represented by a chromosome in GA. We analyzed the effect of the crucial parameter in GA, namely the crossover rate. The simulation results show that different crossover rate will produce different convergence curves. The major drawback in area exploration using Multi-Agent robots is the slow speed. One computation of 300×300 pixel monochrome map will take around 16 minutes using 6 robots, 16 sensory sections. Our future works will be focusing on speed reduction alongside efficient exploration of the search area.

References

1. Liu, J.M., Wu, J.-B.: Multi-Agent Robotic Systems. CRC Press LLC, Florida (2001)
2. Mataric, M.J.: Autonomous Robots (1997); Referred by J.M. Liu and J.B. Wu (2001)
3. Song, Y.H., Wang, G.S., Wang, P.T., Johns, A.T.: Environmental/Economic Dispatch Using Fuzzy Logic Controlled Genetic Algorithms. IEEE Proceedings on Generation, Transmission and Distribution 144(4), 377–382 (1997)
4. Khatib, O.: Real-time Obstacle Avoidance for Manipulators and Mobile Robots. International Journal of Robotics Research 5(1), 90–98 (1996)
5. Liu, J.M., Wu, J.-B., Maluf, D.A.: Evolutionary Self-Organization of an Artificial Potential Field Map with a Group of Autonomous Robots. IEEE (1999)
6. Multi-Agent Robotics Matlab Toolbox,
   http://www.crcpress.com/product/catno/2288
7. Yun, Y.S., Gen, M.: Performance Analysis of Adaptive Genetic Algorithms with Fuzzy Logic and Heuristics. Fuzzy Optimization and Decision Making 2, 161–175 (2003)
8. Mak, L.K., Wong, Y.S., Wang, X.X.: An Adaptive Genetic Algorithm for Manufacturing Cell Formation. International Journal of Manufacturing Technology 16, 491–497 (2000)
9. Srinivas, M., Patnaik, L.M.: Adaptive Probabilities of Crossover and Mutation in Genetic Algorithms. IEEE Transaction on Systems, Man and Cybernetics 24(4), 656–667 (1994)
10. Wu, Q.H., Cao, Y.J., Wen, J.Y.: Optimal Reactive Power Dispatch Using an Adaptive Genetic Algorithm. Electrical Power & Energy Systems 20(8), 563–569 (1998)

Weightless Swarm Algorithm (WSA) for Dynamic Optimization Problems

T.O. Ting[1,*], Ka Lok Man[2], Sheng-Uei Guan[2], Mohamed Nayel[1], and Kaiyu Wan[2]

[1] Dept. Electrical and Electronic Eng.
[2] Dept. Computer Science and Software Eng.
Xi'an Jiaotong-Liverpool University, Suzhou, China
{toting,ka.man,steven.guan,mohamed.nayel,
kaiyu.wan}@xjtlu.edu.cn

Abstract. In this work the well-known Particle Swarm Optimization (PSO) algorithm is applied to some Dynamic Optimization Problems (DOPs). The PSO algorithm is improved by simplification instead of introducing additional strategies into the algorithm as done by many other researchers in the aim of improving an algorithm. Several parameters (w, V_{max}, V_{min} and c_2) are being excluded from the conventional PSO. This algorithm is called Weightless Swarm Algorithm (WSA) as the prominent parameter, inertia weight w does not exist in this proposed algorithm. Interestingly, WSA still works effectively via swapping strategy found from countless trials and errors. We then incorporate the proven clustering technique from literature into the framework of the algorithm to solve the six dynamic problems in literature. From the series of tabulated results, we proved that WSA is competitive as compared to PSO. As only one parameter exists in WSA, it is feasible to carry out parameter sensitivity to find the optimal acceleration coefficient, c_1 for each problem set.

Keywords: dynamic optimization, swapping, weightless swarm.

1 Introduction

Particle swarm optimization (PSO) [1] is one of the prominent algorithms in the category of nature-inspired algorithms and it has been one of the most successful numerical optimization algorithms applied in many fields [2]. One of the advantageous features of Particle Swarm Optimization is its ability to converge quickly to a potential solution. In other words, PSO is faster compared to many evolutionary algorithms such as Genetic Algorithm (GA) [3], Evolutionary Programming (EP) [4], Evolutionary Strategies (ES) [5], Differential Evolution (DE) [6] etc.

This is how PSO works. Firstly, candidate solutions (or commonly known as particles) are seeded onto the search space in a random manner. These particles will then move through the problem space in the aim of finding the global optimum. The movement is guided by the essentially important ingredient formulas:

$$V_i^t = w \times V_i^{t-1} + 2r_1\left(Pbest_i^t - X_i^t\right) + 2r_2\left(Gbest_i^t - X_i^t\right) \tag{1}$$

---

* Corresponding author.

J.J. Park et al. (Eds.): NPC 2012, LNCS 7513, pp. 508–515, 2012.

$$X_i^{t+1} = X_i^t + V_i^t \tag{2}$$

where by:

V_i^t	is the velocity for ith dimension at time t
w	is the inertia weight , usually set to 0.5
X_i^t	is the current position of ith dimension at time t
$Pbest_i^t$	is the best position for ith dimension at time t of a particle, also known as personal best
$Gbest_i^t$	is the best solution among all participating particles for ith dimension at time t, also known as global best
r_1, r_2	These are independent uniform random numbers within [0, 1]

In each iteration, all the particles will be evaluated through a similar cost function. Then, the update of *Pbest* and *Gbest* values are performed instantly. In other words, the asynchronous update is adopted here. The reason for asynchronous update is that the information of *Pbest* and *Gbest* can be feedback into the whole population instantly without delay and this will accelerate the convergence rate. In literature, many works prefer asynchronous update [7, 8].

During the update of velocity, V through (1), the limit of Vmax and Vmin is imposed, usually within 10%, 50% or 100% of search space. The value chosen for Vmax and Vmin is not really crucial and does not affect the performance of PSO drastically. Also, after the update through (2), checking is done to ensure that particles only explore the predefined search space. There are many techniques to handle these boundary limits, which are beyond the scope of this paper. By simply set the value to boundary limit is one of the alternatives. Another alternative will be to impose re-initialization within the search space upon violation. The later alternative is preferred as this will increase the diversity of the entire population and hence assists in avoiding local optima. The similar boundary handling technique is adopted in this work. As the number of iteration increases, particles accelerate towards those with better fitness until maximum iteration is reached.

By careful inspection of (1) and (2), the following interpretations are valid in regards to PSO:

i.   *The velocity somehow acts as short-term memory retention and plays a crucial role in the update process.*

ii.   *The update of a dimensional value is guided by Pbest and Gbest. Simply, this means that a particle moves between Pbest and Gbest.*

iii. *The independent random numbers r_1 and r_2 control the ratio of movement towards Pbest and Gbest.*

In this work, instead of using conventional Particle Swarm Optimization (PSO), a much simpler yet robust variant is presented to solve Dynamic Optimization Problems

(DOPs). This novel algorithm is given the name, Weightless Swarm Algorithm (WSA) as the inertia weight introduced by Shi and Eberhart in the year 1998 [9] is not present in this algorithm. The work on WSA is novel and thorough work will be carried out in future to stabilize its performance. The exclusion of inertia weight reduces several other parameters such as *Velocity*, V_{max} and V_{min}. Due to this, WSA is faster compared to its original form. As the complexity of the algorithm is reduced, the tuning of the algorithm is much easier in this work.

The rest of the paper is organized as follows. Section 2 describes the essence of WSA; this includes the explanation of the strategies incorporated to enable PSO to work without inertia weight. Parameter settings and experimental results are given in Section 3 and 4 respectively. Lastly is the conclusion in Section 5.

2   The Essence of Weightless Swarm Algorithm

Weightless Swarm Algorithm (henceforth abbreviated as WSA) has the same form as the canonical PSO. Without the inertia weight, the updated equation is simplified from two-line equation to a single line:

$$X_{i,d}^{t+1} = X_{i,d}^{t} + r_1 c_1 \left(Gbest_{i,d} - X_{i,d}^{t} \right) + r_2 c_2 \left(Pbest_{i,d} - X_{i,d}^{t} \right) \tag{3}$$

whereby Xi,d is the position of dth dimension of ith particle. *Pbest* is the best position found in the search history of a particle whereas *Gbest* is the best solution found in the entire search history. r_1 and r_2 are two independent uniform random number generators within [0, 1]. The acceleration coefficient, c_1 and c_2 are both set to 1.7. Following the theoretical analysis by Clerc and Kennedy [10], a constriction factor $K = 0.729$ is introduced on the basis of $|c_1+c_2| \leq 4.1$. If we assume $c_1=c_2=2.05$ and $K=0.729$, the new coefficients will have the value of $0.729 \times 2.05=1.49445$. Furthermore, new results presented in [11] based on the theory of dynamic systems for analysis of a particle trajectory have been carried out with different parameter set ($w=0.6$ and $c_1=c_2=1.7$) which showed slightly superior performance. The WSA introduced here agreed to these parameter settings even without the present of inertia weight. By setting $c_1=c_2=1.7$, results are slightly improved as compared to 1.5. Interestingly, the default setting for c_1 and c_2 of PSO in EAlib [12] is also 1.7. From the results on static numerical problems, we found that equation (1) can be further simplified as:

$$X_{i,d}^{t+1} = X_{i,d}^{t} + r_1 c_1 \left(Gbest_{i,d} - X_{i,d}^{t} \right) \tag{4}$$

Using Equation (4) works effectively as when swapping is done during the update of *Pbest* and *Gbest* values; many *X* values are actually the previous *Pbest* values. Hence, it is not really necessary to learn from oneself.

Therefore, in WSA, several parameters prominent in PSO are omitted. The well-known inertia weight, w is now not present. Hence, it means that the velocity, V is also unnecessary. Without V, a user also discards the concern of the bound for this parameter, namely V_{max} and V_{min}. Also, by adopting (4) in WSA, one of the acceleration coefficients is automatically discarded. Thus, the proposed algorithm has a much simpler form compared to canonical PSO. By this form of algorithm, the complexity present is greatly reduced and we only need to tune c_1 for optimal performance; this has been done successfully in this work.

The reduction in the complexity of the algorithm thereby results in a lower computational cost of the relevant computer program. By running both programs (PSO and WSA) concurrently, it is observed that at the point whereby WSA is completing 20 runs, the PSO is only at its 4th run. It means that the proposed method solves dynamic optimization problems five times faster compared to PSO. This is due to simpler code and more resource effective as memory allocation for both w and V are commented in the existing C++ EAlib program, available from [12].

2.1   The Trick in WSA

The secret of WSA is extremely simple and this is indeed the core in this proposed methodology. In the canonical PSO, setting w to zero value resulted in stagnant search; the algorithm does not seem to work. During the update of *Pbest* and *Gbest*, it has been a traditional practice that these values are replaced by better particles. However, in our proposed WSA, instead of doing replacement, swapping of values is adopted. By swapping, we increase the diversity of the population and accelerate the convergence rate. This is due to the reason that when swapping is imposed, the probability of particle X equal to *Pbest* or *Gbest* is significantly reduced. For instance, in the case of replacement scenario in PSO, for a given iteration, if *Pbest* is updated for 5 times, there are 5 ineffective positional updates as the term $\left(Pbest_{i,d} - X_{i,d}^{t} \right) = 0$. These ineffective updates are avoided in WSA, resulting in better accuracy and faster convergence given the same number of function evaluations.

2.2   Implementation of WSA

The implementation of WSA is pretty simple and can be implemented into any existing PSO algorithm with the following steps:

i.   *Set inertia weight = 0,*
ii.   *Discard the Pbest term by setting c_1 in equation (1) to zero.*
iii. *Swapping is done during Pbest update. The swapping for Gbest may not be necessary as in many algorithm implementations; one of the Pbest values is actually the Gbest.*

The above three steps are simple yet they improve the performance of the algorithm drastically without the need of inertia weight. This simple strategy can be implemented easily into any existing PSO algorithm.

3   Parameter Settings

In this work, as PSO is the best algorithm in undetectable dynamic environments from the results presented in [13, 14], it is adopted for comparison in this work. The settings for both algorithms are as follows:

3.1   PSO

The inertia weight, w is linearly decreased from 0.6 to 0.3 and acceleration coefficients, $c_1 = c_2 = 1.7$.

3.2   WSA

Inertia weight is not present; therefore it is in fact zero. The acceleration coefficient, c_1 is found through parameter sensitivity analysis and $c_2 = 0$.

4   Experimental Results

Six dynamic problems from [15] are adopted as test bed in this work. Problems such as Sphere, Rastrigin, Griewank and Ackley are well-known problems in the area of numerical optimization. The descriptions of the different change strategies T1, T2, T3… are available from [15]. Simulation results are presented in Tables 1-4 with Tables 5 recording the mean and standard deviation for results in Table 4. From Table 2, it is observed that the performance of WSA is close to PSO in Table 1. As from Table 1, the PSO recorded total overall performance of 39.98494 whereas WSA recorded a figure of 38.74686. It means that the solution of WSA is competitive compared to its predecessor. As the nature of WSA may not be the same as PSO, the parameter sensitivity analysis is carried out to obtain the optimal settings for both diversity and overlapping ratio. From the analysis, the diversity: α=0.6 and overlapping ratio: β=0.9 are suggested for optimal performance. Results of parameter sensitivity analysis are not included to avoid extended paper. Results using these settings are recorded in Table 3, now with overall performance of 40.10769 (even closer to PSO's). It is interesting to note that with the optimal parameter setting, the performance of each problem set is slightly improved.

As WSA can perform effectively even without learning from *Pbest*, equation (2) is used for the results depicted in Table 4, now with independent values of acceleration coefficient. These values are depicted in the second column of the table, The total overall performance is now improved up to 41.14739. From our analysis, it is found that c1 ranges from 1.9 to 3.5. With different changing ratio for the case of F1, it is interesting to note that the value of c1 increases in a similar pattern; the greater changing ratio favors greater value of c1. From this behavior, the feasibility of adaptive c1 is observed. This will be one of the promising directions for future work. The composition of Rastrigin problem set seems to be most challenging in this study as this is a multimodal problem with many local optima residing close to one and other. For such a case, long jump or step is favored by setting c1=3.5 and this helps in reducing chances of falling into a local optimum in the light of dynamic environment. Again, it is interesting to note that the performance of each problem set is slightly improved compared to the one in Table 4. Mean values and standard deviation (STD) are tabulated in Table 5.

Table 1. Performance of PSO on F1-F6, Overlapping ratio = 0.1, Diversity = 0.3 and Popsize = 40 / 10

Problem	Changing ratio	T1	T2	T3	T4	T5	T6
F1	0.3	0.987776	0.982685	0.993593	0.970057	0.993230	0.959536
	0.7	0.916581	0.957208	0.985420	0.975387	0.991905	0.976794
	1.0	0.949945	0.926093	0.953148	0.971681	0.994805	0.957577
F2	1.0	0.892211	0.878057	0.854241	0.872302	0.845164	0.866242
F3	1.0	0.757464	0.500827	0.556597	0.591180	0.629322	0.565224
F4	1.0	0.729952	0.698798	0.688129	0.693392	0.684277	0.688200
F5	1.0	0.840236	0.825325	0.826304	0.802516	0.831110	0.811447
F6	1.0	0.830845	0.755024	0.737995	0.747123	0.809007	0.733006
Total overall performance = 39.98494							

Table 2. Performance of WSA on F1-F6 ($c_1=c_2=1.7$) Overlapping ratio = 0.1, Diversity = 0.3 and Popsize = 40 / 10

Problem	Changing ratio	T1	T2	T3	T4	T5	T6
F1	0.3	0.985672	0.976931	0.980326	0.922440	0.992259	0.912831
	0.7	0.899224	0.954392	0.980958	0.933082	0.992136	0.933062
	1.0	0.934711	0.904565	0.948396	0.946560	0.994972	0.941083
F2	1.0	0.877429	0.850753	0.831603	0.837051	0.843487	0.801454
F3	1.0	0.551327	0.480017	0.565144	0.666168	0.600981	0.568956
F4	1.0	0.591770	0.676461	0.631459	0.673681	0.658180	0.676794
F5	1.0	0.833339	0.782035	0.798453	0.767672	0.823851	0.738357
F6	1.0	0.814561	0.738476	0.719556	0.708658	0.814662	0.690929
The overall performance = 38.74686							

Table 3. Performance of WSA on F1-F6 ($c_1=c_2=1.7$) Overlapping ratio = 0.9, Diversity = 0.6 and Popsize = 40 / 10

Problem	Changing ratio	T1	T2	T3	T4	T5	T6
F1	0.3	0.988957	0.983702	0.995235	0.963875	0.996286	0.959345
	0.7	0.928869	0.965581	0.987264	0.975389	0.994323	0.970561
	1.0	0.953625	0.936263	0.957113	0.962115	0.996393	0.959473
F2	1.0	0.886155	0.859200	0.838945	0.840452	0.831960	0.824130
F3	1.0	0.776315	0.551812	0.604169	0.617472	0.706699	0.592349
F4	1.0	0.730942	0.690995	0.718009	0.685624	0.708417	0.662063
F5	1.0	0.845622	0.807329	0.816988	0.784206	0.848746	0.774031
F6	1.0	0.820322	0.763701	0.751292	0.749416	0.822872	0.723090
The overall performance = 40.10769							

Table 4. Performance of WSA on F1-F6 (c_1 varies) Overlapping ratio = 0.9, Diversity = 0.6 and Popsize = 40 / 10

Problem	c_1	Changing ratio	T1	T2	T3	T4	T5	T6
F1	1.9	0.3	0.989761	0.983868	0.995160	0.978730	0.997635	0.967037
	2.2	0.7	0.925635	0.967005	0.988625	0.977918	0.996809	0.975176
	2.5	1.0	0.961981	0.943873	0.960278	0.974210	0.996547	0.961759
F2	2.5	1.0	0.925925	0.896458	0.882685	0.899841	0.867598	0.864477
F3	3.5	1.0	0.814633	0.541270	0.605347	0.638468	0.723133	0.604509
F4	2.5	1.0	0.748691	0.729934	0.721208	0.718273	0.718745	0.698000
F5	2.3	1.0	0.892377	0.862897	0.856936	0.843768	0.880029	0.826867
F6	2.5	1.0	0.838275	0.808686	0.780733	0.796042	0.852256	0.767322
The overall performance = 41.14739								

Table 5. Mean Values and STD for Results in Table 4

Problem	Changing ratio	T1	T2	T3	T4	T5	T6
F1	0.3	0.58±0.52	1.35±0.88	0.29±0.32	0.00±1.38	0.00±0.01	1.43±2.06
	0.7	4.85±5.27	2.74±2.02	0.36±0.37	1.12±1.40	0.00±0.02	0.88±1.39
	1.0	1.74±2.25	2.47±2.50	2.25±0.54	0.23±0.50	0.00±0.00	0.30±0.71
F2	1.0	0.83±0.92	1.25±1.81	2.22±2.97	0.67±1.49	1.20±0.81	1.44±2.34
F3	1.0	4.02±5.06	89.8±172	45.9±91.8	54.0±96.0	11.3±35.7	64.2±108
F4	1.0	6.40±11.2	6.59±9.84	8.14±8.54	5.34±8.81	14.0±21.3	7.40±12.4
F5	1.0	0.71±1.46	1.09±2.36	1.30±2.57	1.08±1.87	0.47±0.71	1.40±2.55
F6	1.0	3.50±4.11	4.26±4.04	6.89±7.45	2.58±3.68	1.42±1.22	3.71±4.17

5   Conclusions

In this work, it is proven that PSO works effectively even without the present of the prominent inertia weight on Dynamic Optimization Problems. Thus, the proposed algorithm is called Weightless Swarm Algorithm (WSA). The strategy can be incorporated into any existing PSO algorithm by discarding the inertia weight and changing the update strategy to swapping instead of replacement. From the series of results, it is shown that the nature of WSA is different from PSO and therefore parameter sensitivity analysis is done to obtain the optimal parameters (overlapping ratio and diversity). The performance of WSA is only slightly less compared to PSO without inertia weight. The simplicity of WSA allows the tuning of acceleration constant, c1 independently in order to obtain better results. Thus, it is evident that WSA has superior properties alongside extremely simple strategy and cheaper computational costs. Future work will be done to find the underlying properties yet to be discovered.

References

1. Kennedy, J., Eberhart, R.: Particle Swarm Optimization. In: Proceedings of 1995 IEEE International Conference on Neural Networks, vol. 4, pp. 1942–1948 (1995)
2. Robinson, J., Rahmat-Samii, Y.: Particle Swarm Optimization in Electromagnetics. IEEE Transactions on Antennas and Propagation 52, 397–407 (2004)
3. Deb, K., Pratap, A., Agarwal, S., et al.: A Fast and Elitist Multiobjective Genetic Algorithm: NSGA-II. IEEE Transactions on Evolutionary Computation 6, 182–197 (2002)
4. Yao, X., Liu, Y., Lin, G.: Evolutionary Programming made Faster. IEEE Transactions on Evolutionary Computation 3, 82–102 (1999)
5. Francois, O.: An Evolutionary Strategy for Global Minimization and its Markov Chain Analysis. IEEE Transactions on Evolutionary Computation 2, 77–90 (1998)
6. Brest, J., Greiner, S., Boskovic, B., et al.: Self-Adapting Control Parameters in Differential Evolution: A Comparative Study on Numerical Benchmark Problems. IEEE Transactions on Evolutionary Computation 10, 646–657 (2006)
7. Gazi, V.: Asynchronous Particle Swarm Optimization. In: IEEE 15th Signal Processing and Communications Applications, SIU 2007, pp. 1–4 (2007)
8. Rada-Vilela, J.: Random Asynchronous PSO. In: 2011 5th International Conference on Automation, Robotics and Applications (ICARA), pp. 220–225 (2011)
9. Shi, Y., Eberhart, R.: A Modified Particle Swarm Optimizer. In: Proceedings of 1998 IEEE International Conference on Evolutionary Computation, pp. 69–73 (1998)
10. Clerc, M., Kennedy, J.: The Particle Swarm - Explosion, Stability and Convergence in a Multidimensional Complex Space. IEEE Transactions on Evolutionary Computation 6, 58–73 (2002)
11. Trelea, I.C.: The Particle Swarm Optimization Algorithm: Convergence Analysis and Parameter Selection. Information Processing Letters 85, 317–325 (2003)
12. EAlib (open platform to test and compare the performances of EAs),
    http://people.brunel.ac.uk/~csstssy/ECiDUE/
    ECDOP-Competition12-TestPlatform.tar.gz
13. Yang, S., Li, C.: A Clustering Particle Swarm Optimizer for Locating and Tracking Multiple Optima in Dynamic Environments. IEEE Transactions on Evolutionary Computation 14, 959–974 (2010)
14. Li, C., Yang, S.: A Clustering Particle Swarm Optimizer for Dynamic Optimization. In: IEEE Congress on Evolutionary Computation (CEC 2009), pp. 439–446 (2009)
15. Technical Benchmark Generator for the IEEE WCCI-2012 Competition on Evolutionary Computation for Dynamic Optimization Problems (2012),
    http://people.brunel.ac.uk/~csstssy/ECiDUE/
    TR-ECDOP-Competition12.pdf

Design of a Reliable XOR-XNOR Circuit
for Arithmetic Logic Units

Mouna Karmani[1,*], Chiraz Khedhiri[1], Belgacem Hamdi[1],
Amir-Mohammad Rahmani[2], Ka Lok Man[3], and Kaiyu Wan[3]

[1] Electronics & Microelectronics Laboratory, Monastir, Tunis University, Tunisia
[2] University of Turku, Finland
[3] Xi'an Jiaotong-Liverpool University, China
{mouna.karmani,chirazkhedhiri}@yahoo.fr,
Belgacem.Hamdi@issatgb.rnu.tn, amir.rahmani@utu.fi,
{ka.man,Kaiyu.Wan}@xjtlu.edu.cn

Abstract. Computer systems used in safety-critical applications like space, avionic and biomedical applications require high reliable integrated circuits (ICs) to ensure the accuracy of data they process. As Arithmetic Logic Units (ALUs) are essential element of computers, designing reliable ALUs is becoming an appropriate strategy to design fault-tolerant computers. In fact, with the continuous increase of integration densities and complexities ICs are susceptible to many modes of failure. Thereby, Reliable operation of ALUs is critical for high performance safety-critical computers. Given that XOR-XNOR circuits are basic building blocks in ALUs, designing efficient reliable XOR-XNOR gates is an important challenge in the area of high performance computers. The reliability enhancement technique presented in this work is based on using a Concurrent Error Detection (CED) based reliable XOR-XNOR circuit implementation to detect permanent and transient faults in ALUs during normal operation in order to improve the reliability of highly critical computer systems. The proposed design is performed using the 32 nm process technology.

Keywords: XOR-XNOR circuits, Concurrent Error Detection, fault-secure property, self-testing property, fault model.

1 Introduction

With the continuous increase of integration densities and complexities, IC design has become a real challenge to ensure the necessary level of quality and reliability especially for high performance applications [1-2]. Thus, computer systems used for instrumentation, measurement, and advanced processing in safety-critical applications like avionic, automotive and biomedical applications require high reliable ICs to ensure the accuracy of analytical data they process [3]. In fact, a microprocessor is an internal hardware component that performs the mathematical calculations required for

---

* Corresponding author.

J.J. Park et al. (Eds.): NPC 2012, LNCS 7513, pp. 516–523, 2012.
© IFIP International Federation for Information Processing 2012

computers to run programs and execute commands while ALUs in microprocessors are combinatorial circuits allowing computers to add, subtract, multiply, divide and perform other logical operations at high speeds. Thanks to advanced ALUs, modern microprocessors are able to perform very complicated operations which make ALUs among the essential elements of computers. Consequently, designing efficient reliable ALUs is an important challenge in computer-based safety-critical systems [4]. Thus approaches and techniques to increase the reliability of these digital blocks are gaining more importance.

Interest in on-line error detection continues to grow as VLSI circuits increase in complexity [5]. The property of verifying the results delivered by a circuit during its normal operation is called Concurrent Error Detection (CED) [6]. Concurrent checking is increasingly becoming a suitable characteristic thanks to its ability to detect transient faults that may occur in a circuit during normal operation. CED also provides an opportunity for self-diagnosis and self-correction within a circuit design, especially in specific applications domains requiring very high levels of reliability [4].

Since XOR-XNOR circuits are basic building blocks in Arithmetic Logic Units, the performance and reliability of these digital circuits is affected by the individual performance of each XOR-XNOR included in them [7-8]. Thus, XOR-XNOR circuits should be designed such that they indicate any malfunction during normal operation. In this paper, we propose a CED based reliable new design XOR-XNOR circuit implementation using the 32 nm process technology. The circuit is analysed in terms of fault-secure and self-testing properties with respect to the set of fault models including logical stuck-at faults, transistor stuck-on and transistor stuck-open faults.

The organization of this manuscript is as follows: the CED based reliable circuits technique is first presented in Section 2, followed by the proposed XOR-XNOR circuit implementation in Section 3. Finally, the circuit's fault analysis with all parasitic is illustrated in Section 4.

2   The CED Based Reliable Circuits

Concurrent error detection verifies the results delivered by a circuit during its normal operation. Concurrent error can be achieved by means of duplication and comparison. However, this technique requires more than 100% hardware overhead [9]. In fact, the CED technique presented in this paper is achieved by means of output duplication technique. The output of a circuit has a certain property that can be monitored by a checker. If an error causes a violation of the property, the checker gives an error indication signal [10]. The concurrent error detection property can be used for verifying the fault secure or/and the self-testing properties for circuits requiring high level of reliability and availability.

The Fault-Secure property: A circuit is fault-secure for a set of faults, if for any valid input code word and any single fault, the circuit either produces an invalid code word on the output or doesn't produce the error on the output [4]. In fact, ensuring the fault-secure property is essential for achieving safety and reliability in critical systems. Another useful property is the self-testing one.

The Self-Testing property: For each modelled fault there is an input vector occurring during normal operation that produces an output vector which do not belong to the output code. This property avoids the existence of redundant faults. If the circuit is both fault-secure and self-testing it is said Totally Self Checking (TSC property) [9]. The concept of TSC circuits was first proposed in [11] and then generalized and detailed in [12]. Thus, the combination of the fault secure and the self-testing properties offers the highest level of protection. The fault secure property is the most important one, since it guarantees error detection under any single fault, but it is also the most difficult to achieve [9].

3   The Proposed XOR-XNOR Circuit Implementation

In this paper, a novel XOR-XNOR circuit designed in modified pass transistor logic is presented. This gate has dual inputs (A, A~, B and B~) and generates dual outputs (XOR, XNOR). The circuit implementation is performed with six MOS transistors. In the current XOR-XNOR circuit implementation, errors caused by faults will be detected only by checking the complementarity principle between the XOR and XNOR functions. The proposed XOR-XNOR circuit and the correspondent layout are respectively given by Fig. 1 and Fig. 2.

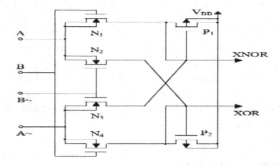

Fig. 1. The proposed XOR-XNOR circuit implementation

The XOR-XNOR circuit is implemented in full-custom 32 nm technology [13]. SPICE simulations of the circuit extracted from the layout, including parasitic, are used to demonstrate that the circuit has an acceptable electrical behaviour.

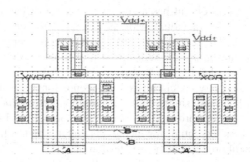

Fig. 2. Layout of the XOR-XNOR circuit in full-custom 32 nm process technology

SPICE simulation of the circuit without any fault is illustrated by Fig. 3.

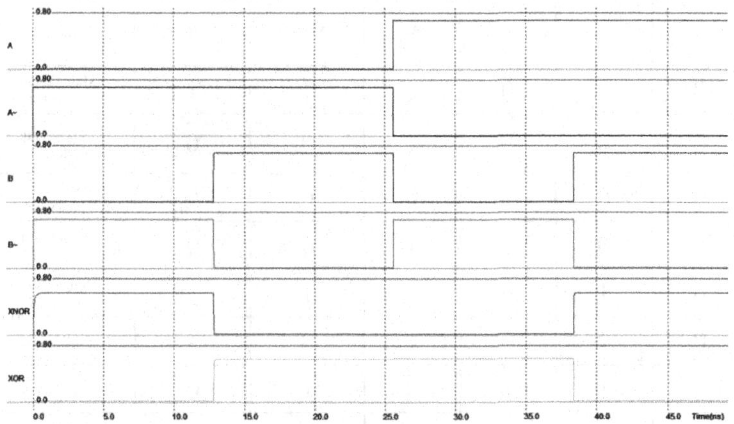

Fig. 3. SPICE simulation of the XOR-XNOR circuit in 32nm technology without faults

In Fig.3, we can remark that XOR and XNOR the outputs obtained by simulating the fault-free XOR-XNOR circuit are complementary.

4   The XOR-XNOR Circuit Fault Analysis

In the following sub-sections, we analyse the behaviour of the proposed XOR-XNOR circuit in terms of fault-secure and self-testing properties with respect to the set of fault models including logical stuck-at faults, transistor stuck-on and transistor stuck-open faults.

4.1   The Stuck-at Fault Model

The most common model used for logical faults is the single stuck-at fault. It assumes that a fault in a logic gate results in one of its inputs or the output is fixed at either a logic 0 (stuck-at-0) or at logic 1 (stuck-at-1) [14]. In the following, we analyze the behaviour of the XOR-XNOR gate shown in Fig. 1 in terms of fault secure and self-testing properties with respect to the logical stuck-at faults. For inputs, we consider the logical stuck-at fault model. Table 1 gives the response of the gate for all inputs combinations.

From Table 1, we can conclude that for primary logical stuck-at faults, all single and multiple faults on primary inputs will result in a non-valid code by producing no complementary outputs. In fact, each fault will be detected when there are non complementary (XOR, XNOR) outputs, because normally XOR and XNOR should be complementary data. Consequently, the proposed circuit is fault-secure and self-testing for single and multiple stuck-at faults.

Table 1. The Gate Response for all inputs combinations

A	A~	B	B~	XOR	XNOR	Conclusion
0	0	0	0	1	1	Multiple fault (detected)
0	0	0	1	0	0	Single fault (detected)
0	0	1	0	0	0	Single fault (detected)
0	0	1	1	0	0	Multiple fault (detected)
0	1	0	0	1	1	Single fault (detected)
0	1	0	1	0	1	Valid input
0	1	1	0	1	0	Valid input
0	1	1	1	0	0	Single fault (detected)
1	0	0	0	1	1	Single fault (detected)
1	0	0	1	1	0	Valid input
1	0	1	0	0	1	Valid input
1	0	1	1	0	0	Single fault (detected)
1	1	0	0	1	1	Multiple fault (detected)
1	1	0	1	1	1	Single fault (detected)
1	1	1	0	1	1	Single fault (detected)
1	1	1	1	1	1	Multiple fault (detected)

In addition, by analyzing the table above we can remark that when a fault type stack-at occurs, in the major case, it will affect the XOR output. In fact, when such faults occur we will obtain a faulty XOR and a fault-free XNOR output for all cases if the input A is equal to the low level. Otherwise, if the input A is equal to the high level we will obtain a faulty XOR output only when the logic product A~B is equal to the high level. Thereby, this remark can give us lots of ideas to consider when designing an error correction approach to ensure the fault tolerance property in the current XOR-XNOR circuit implementation. Next, we consider the stuck-on and stuck-open transistor fault model. We will examine all possible single transistor stuck-on and transistor stuck-open faults within the circuit of Fig. 1 in next two sub-sections.

4.2   The Transistor Stuck-on Fault Model

A transistor stuck-on fault may be modelled as a bridging fault from the source to the drain of a transistor [14]. In order to analyse the circuit behaviour in the presence of stuck-on faults with realistic circuit defects, we simulate the considered XOR-XNOR circuit in the presence of faults. Faults are manually injected in the circuit layout of Fig. 2.

Table 2. The Gate Response for Transistor Stuck-on faults

Transistor Stuck-on	Input vectors detecting the fault A B	XOR	XNOR
N1	0 0	0	0
	1 0	1	1
N2	0 1	0	0
	1 1	1	1
N3	0 1	1	1
	1 1	0	0
N4	0 0	1	1
	1 0	0	0
P1	0 1	1	1
	1 0	1	1
P2	0 0	1	1
	1 1	1	1

From Table 2, we can conclude that for any valid input code word, any injected single stuck-on fault within the gate produces an invalid code word (non complementary (XOR, XNOR) outputs), therefore the Fault-Secure property is verified for this set of faults. On the other hand, the self-testing property signify that for each single stuck-on fault within the gate there is at least one input vector occurring during the circuit normal operation that detects it. In fact, by analysing the simulation results summarized in Table 2, we can say that the self-testing property is also verified for this set of faults. Thus, the combination of the fault-secure and the self-testing properties makes the circuit Totally Self Checking for the stuck-on fault model.

4.3   The Transistor Stuck-Open Fault Model

A stuck-open transistor involves the permanent opening of the connection between the source and the drain of a transistor [14]. In order to analyse the circuit behaviour in the presence of stuck-open faults, faults are manually injected in the circuit layout of Fig. 2. Let's examine the behaviour of the XOR-XNOR circuit under any single transistor open fault to make the proof that it is fault secure for this class of faults. Given that the XOR-XNOR circuit contains six transistors, there are six possible transistor open faults. SPICE simulation results of the circuit obtained by rendering the NMOS transistor N1 stuck-open are illustrated by Fig. 4.

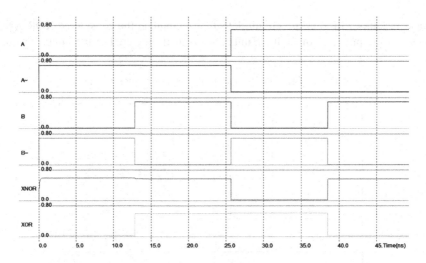

Fig. 4. SPICE simulation of the XOR-XNOR circuit with N1 stuck-open

In Fig. 4, we show that for the combination (0,0), (1,0) and (1,1) of the inputs (A,B) the circuit does not produce any error and both XOR and XNOR outputs are fault-free while for the combination (0,1) the circuit produce a fault-free XOR and a faulty XNOR. In fact, the Fault secure property require that for any valid input code word, any single transistor open fault within the gate produces an invalid code word on the output or does not produce an error on the output. Knowing that the considered fault will be detected because normally XOR and XNOR should be complementary data, we are sure that the fault secure property will not be lost. In the same way, we have simulated all possible single stuck-open faults within the XOR-XNOR circuit and simulation results show that the Fault-Secure property is verified for this set of faults.

Regarding the self-testing property, simulation results show that this property is verified for the NMOS transistors stuck-open. However, a stuck-open injected in any PMOS transistor (P1 or P2) don't produce any error in the circuit outputs and both XOR and XNOR outputs are fault-free. Thus, the fault will be undetectable because it has no effect on the circuit outputs. Theoretically, the self testing property is not ensured since a P1 or a P2 stuck-open transistor is undetectable but this is not catastrophic because firstly the fault-secure property is the most important one and secondly, we are sure that these two faults if they occur separately or even at the same time they have no effect on the outputs of the proposed circuit.

5   Conclusion

As modern processors and semiconductor circuits move into 32 nm technologies and below, designers face the major problem of process variations which affects the circuit performance and introduces faults that can cause critical failures. Therefore, integrated circuits are more and more required to guarantee reliability for safety-critical applications in the presence of permanent and transit faults. Thus, to cope with the growing difficulty of off-line testing, the concurrent error detection property is indispensable when designing complex nanometer VLSI circuits ALUs. This paper presents a new design 6-transistors XOR-XNOR circuit that can be used to ensure the on-line detection of faults occurring in computer systems during the manufacturing process. The proposed circuit, designed using the 32 nm CMOS technology, is analysed in terms of fault-secure and self-testing properties with respect to the set of fault models including logical stuck-at faults, transistor stuck-on and transistor stuck-open faults.

References

1. Bushnell, M., Agrawal, V.: Essentials of Electronic Testing for Digital, Memory, and Mixed-Signal VLSI Circuits (2002)
2. White, M., Chen, Y.: Scaled CMOS Technology Reliability Users Guide. NASA Electronic Parts and Packaging (NEPP) Program (2008)
3. Edward, W.: Performance and Reliability of Integrated Circuits within Computing Systems. EE Times Design Article (2011)
4. Hamdi, B., Chiraz, K., Rached, T.: Pass Transistor Based Self-Checking Full Adder. International Journal of Computer Theory and Engineering 3(5), 608–616 (2011)
5. Nicolaidis, M.: On-line testing for VLSI: state of the art and trends. Integration, the VLSI Journal 26(1-2), 197–209 (1998)
6. Mouna, K., Chiraz, K., Belgacem, H., Kalok, M., Lei, C., Lim, E.: A Concurrent Error Detection Based Fault-Tolerant 32 nm XOR-XNOR Circuit Implementation. In: Proceedings of the IAENG International MultiConference of Engineers and Computer Scientists - IMECS 2012, Hong Kong (2012)
7. Nicolaidis, M., Duarte, R.O., Manich, S., Figueras, J.: Fault-Secure Parity Prediction Arithmetic Operators. IEEE Design & Test of computers 14, 60–71 (1997)
8. Chowdhury, S.R., Banerjee, A., Roy, A., Saha, H.: A High Speed Transistor Full Adder Design using Novel 3 Transistor XOR Gates. International Journal of Electronics, Circuits and Systems II, 217–223 (2008)
9. Nicolaidis, M.: Carry Checking / Parity Prediction Adders and ALUs. IEEE Transactions on Very Large Scale Integration Systems 11(1), 121–128 (2003)
10. Zeng, C., McCluskey, E.J.: Finite State Machine Synthesis with Concurrent Error Detection. In: Proc. International Test Conference, pp. 672–679 (1999)
11. Anderson, D., Metze, G.: Design of totally self-checking check circuits for m-out-of-n codes. IEEE Trans. on Computers 22(3), 263–269 (1973)
12. Pradhan, K., Stiffler, J.: Error correcting codes and self-checking circuits in fault-tolerant computers. IEEE Computer Magazine 13, 27–37 (1980)
13. Etienne, S.: Microwind and Dsch version 3.1. INSA Toulouse (2006) ISBN 2-87649-050-1
14. Lala, P.K.: An introduction to logic circuit testing, pp. 1–9. Morgan & Claypool (2009)

New Electronic Acupuncture System Using Intelligence

You-Sik Hong[1], Hongkyun Kim[2], Cheonshik Kim[3], and Geuk Lee[4]

[1] School of Information and Communication Engineering, Sang JI University, Wonju,
Kangwon, 220-702, Korea
[2] Dept. of Electronic Engineering at the Hanbat National University in Taejon, Korea
[3] Dept. of Computer Science, Sejong University, Seoul, Korea
[4] Dept. of Information & Communication, Han-nam University, Daejon, Korea
yshong@sangji.ac.kr, mipsan@paran.com

Abstract. In recent years, scientific studies of traditional oriental medicine are accelrating. Furthermore, researches of medical examinations and treatments through collaboration of oriental medicine and western medicine is in progress. This paper will seek for spots on the body suitable for acupuncture using special features that skin impedance values are different. The computer simulation results have shown that Electro-Acupuncture administered by using the medical diagnosis system developed in this study is more effective than the conventional method.

Keywords: Pulse wave, Fuzzy Rules, Acupuncture.

1 Introduction

In oriental medicine, the term 'pulse' has several meanings. The pulse is considered an important factor in herbal remedies, since observation of a person's pulse rate may reflect their health and illness[1-3]. The observation of heart palpitations is critical as the cessation of a person's heart palpitations classify them as dead. Therefore, the condition of the instant heart change is observed in both western medication and eastern medication, and we can diagnose it by feeling the pulse. Since ancient times, oriental doctors have considered pulse rate as an important data in diagnosis. Accordingly, a doctor who was competent in checking the pulse of their patient was considered a creditable doctor. However, the current blood pressure pulse analyzer may be considered flawed, since it is uncertain whether the blood pressure pulse analyzing sensor is located precisely on the radial artery. Furthermore, the analogue type blood pressure pulse analyzer has the issue of objectifying the blood pressure pulse. Although some people may have the same forearm length, the thickness of their blood vessel may differ, and therefore there is no set of data that is considered reliable enough to judge the accuracy of blood pressure pulse rates. [4-7] In this paper, in order to calculate the best optimal time of Electronic-Acupuncture, it will consider the patient's physical conditions, age conditions and disease conditions[8-12]. As the computer simulation resulted, Electronic-Acupuncture using the intelligence had proven to be more efficient than the existing method. The composition of this paper is

J.J. Park et al. (Eds.): NPC 2012, LNCS 7513, pp. 524–531, 2012.

as follows: section 2 discusses the multipad with a built-in Electronic-Acupuncture ; section 3 discusses the fuzzy rules based on pulse wave analysis. Section 4 reports the results of Electronic-Accupuncture simulation and section 5 concludes this paper.

2   E-Acupuncture Pad with Built-In Multi-active

What is a multi-pad with a built-active JEUNJACHIM (Electronic-Acupuncture) depending on a patient's current body status? Based on this information, the patient meets the voltage and current self-oscillation. The frequency with the ability to automatically advanced procedure is called JEUNJACHIM. In order to perform these functions simultaneously with the sensing of JEUNJACHIM, one is required to possess the ability to perform surgery, derive accurate analysis from fuzzy logic and process statistical data. Electrical resistance of the body including long-term resistance, internal resistance and the surface can be divided into exposed skin. Resistance of the body when the DC voltage is based on the pure resistive component can be considered only based on the basis, when the impedance of the AC voltage should be considered. That body electrical conductors if you think skin, blood, muscles and other body each part of the voltage and current for the resistive component and capacity components are separated by impedance and its size, the electrical conduction path, the contact voltage, the contact area, and energizing time, is applied differently depending on the frequency may occur.

Fig. 1. Multipad with a built in electronic acupuncture

Figure1 illustrates the basic theory of Electronic-Acupuncture. In addition, these changes in a person's age, gender, humidity, temperature, weight and fat accumulation is based on the changes. The requirements when considering the electrical resistance of human skin in general is based on the amount of approximately 2500Ω. However, the same voltage and current is applied even if the amount of contact area and pain change in resistance over time are different. In the electrical resistance of human body tissues, regardless of the DC and AC power is almost constantly appear if time longer JUAL heat due to temperature rise of tissue resistance is slightly reduced. When the electricity in the human body typically conduct a minimum of power to feel the flow of the AC voltage is 1mA ~ 2mA for men. In contrast, direct the flow of power is smaller than the stimulus at least five double-road sensing current flow caused by the voltage applied, even though I do not feel the flow of electricity. Thus, in the treatment of **JEUNJACHIM,** electricity is AC rather than DC voltage with the voltage of the aneurysm and the frequency and voltage, over current change as a real hand acupuncture procedures, a small battery that has the same effect as a treatment is likely to be seen.In the experiment, according to AC current that can safely come off as self a man 16mA (60Hz) women 10.5mA (60Hz) is about the human body can withstand DC current is approximately 74mA men for women is approximately 50mA .But it also including a person's body size and weight may appear slightly different depending on the requirements. In this paper, the voltage between 15V ~ 50V AC voltage to the change of 5Hz ~ 1.2Khz and current 500uA ~ 1500uA given in the current experiments were carried out. Figure 2 illustrates the electronic acupuncture circuit

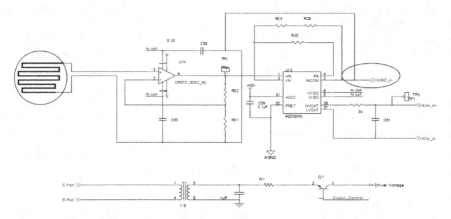

Fig. 2. Electronic acupuncture circuit

3   Fuzzy Rules Considering the Patient's Condition

The general algorithm comes to a conclusion of B on the assumption of 'A → B and equals A'. In this case the latter A should be completely consistent with the former A (of conditional clause). This kind of inference is called Modus Ponens and the Fuzzy algorithm is trying to expand as follows which will be called GMP (Generalized Modus Ponens);

Assumption 1: If x equals A,y will be B.
Assumption 2: x equals A'.
Conclusion : y equals B'.

When you use the Fuzzy Rules, the knowledge to judge a patient's health by using the pulse wave will be expressed in Fuzzy R and you will be able to carry out modeling like the following to observe Output (or Symptom) B to clarify Input (or Cause) A.

If you are not careful for actual pulse feeling, often you may be confused that floating pulse, sliding pulse, and big pulse are powerful while submerging pulse and small pulse aren't. However, some floating pulse, big pulse, and sliding pulse are weak and some submerging pulse and small pulse are strong.

If 4 patients, a, b, c, and d are in their terminal stage, the left figure will be ranging from 0.8 to 1.0 and if in the middle stage, from 0.4 to 0.7 and if in the initial stage, from 0.1 to 0.3. The figure in the middle indicates the patient's physical condition. For example, if a patient is 150 cm high and weighs less than 45 kg, the figure will range from 0.1 to 0.3, if he is 151 - 170 high and weights 46 - 70kg, from 0.4 to 0.7, and if he is 171 - 200 cm high and weighs 71 - 130kg, from 0.8 to 1.0. This illustrates the Fuzzy conversion factor to adjust the correlation coefficient in consideration of the weight, age, gender, and physical condition when you analyze patient health condition.

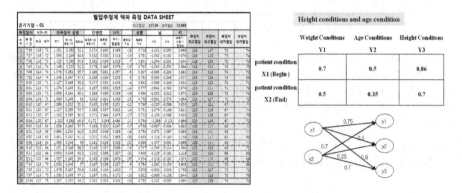

Fig. 3. Patient Health Condition using Fuzzy Rules

The evidences of this kind of hypothesis are atopic disease, acne, and age spot. This skin related troubles happen because the diseased spots have high resistance of electricity. High resistance to electricity means inappropriate oxygen provision therefore the skin disorder occurs in various ways such as atopic disease or age spot. Existing blood pressure pulse analyzing system doesn't consider patient's sex, age, and condition therefore there is an inadequacy of choosing the right amount of pressure to press the needle into patient's skin. It also has a problem of inaccuracy in finding the right acupuncture points. Therefore if a needle is used on an aged patient or a young patient with weak skin it might leave bruises or wounds. In this paper, it tried to solve these problems using intelligent fuzzy rules.

e=R-Y
Ce=e2-e1

Where, Y: optimum pulse feeling judgment

R: Criteria Input
e: Error
Ce: Error Displacement
e2: Current Error

A global priority reflects the importance of an element with respect to the focus of the problem. The derivation of local priorities is carried out through the use of a comparison scale and a pair wise comparison matrix. A comparison matrix for deriving the priority vector

$w^T = (\ w_1,\ w_2,\ w_3,\ w_4,\ \cdots\ )$ is associated with 3 elements in a specific level with respect to a single element in a level immediately about it. Such a matrix is denoted by A.

$$
A = \begin{bmatrix}
w_1/w_1 & w_1/w_2 & w_1/w_3 & w_1/w_4 \\
w_2/w_1 & w_2/w_2 & w_2/w_3 & w_2/w_4 \\
w_3/w_1 & w_3/w_2 & w_3/w_3 & w_3/w_4 \\
w_4/w_1 & w_4/w_2 & w_4/w_3 & w_4/w_4
\end{bmatrix}
$$

In this matrix every element a_{ij} is the result of a pair wise comparison denoting the dominance of element i relative to element j. A comparison is also being made of the jth element with the ith element. The fuzzification membership functions in a fuzzy rule base are triangular typed ones defined by equation (1) with $a, b, u \in U$. The fuzzy rule base composes of MISO (Multi Input Single Output) typed rule base. Each fuzzy membership function in a fuzzy rule base has a membership value area $[0,1]$, and should be normalized in this area.

$$
y = \begin{cases}
\dfrac{2}{b-a}(x-a), & a \le u \le b, \quad u \in U \\
0, & otherwise
\end{cases}
\tag{1}
$$

This interval includes all possible values for the variable in universe of discourse(U). All fuzzy sets in a fuzzy rule base have the same support interval $[a,b]$. The equation can be represented all types of fuzzy membership functions both fuzzy and non-fuzzy membership functions. The oriental medicine is adopting 4 diagnosis methods such as seeing, hearing, inquiring, and touching but among those is there tongue feeling system in which a doctor will see a patient's tongue for diagnosis. This method has been used to observe the tongue condition or fur deposited on it to diagnose any disease and its kind from the ancient times. Observation of the tongue is mainly used to understand functioning of the heart and spleen. If the tongue fur is white, the corresponding disease is in its initial stage or light, indicating False Symptom, Cold Symptom, and Humid Symptom. If it is yellow, it indicates heat is accumulated in internal organs, most commonly acute fevers.

   Fig. 4 illustrates the automatic detection of RGB images which is most similar to the patient's health judgment condition among those tongue feeling images to make the oriental medicine scientific. Moreover, this thesis has developed an algorithm for more accurate judgment of the quantity of tongue furs and the sublingual veins by using the ultraviolet ray and infrared methods.

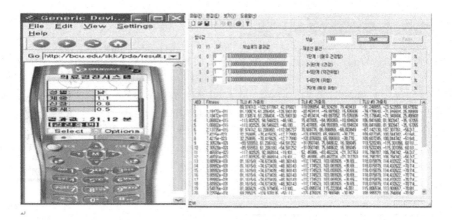

Fig. 4. Pulse wave decision system using fuzzy rules

Fig. 4 illustrates the Pulse wave decision system using fuzzy rules which depending on the patient's physical condition. In this paper, it is tried to classify the difference in physical characteristics such as thickness of skin and blood vessel, skin impedance, glandular nature of skin in order to come up with an accurate pulse analysis.

4   Simulation

In this paper, in order to solve this kind of problem, it uses compositional inference while using the fuzzy rule. Fuzzy compositional rule of inference is applied to come up with a calibrating constant in order to derive an accurate result (considering the patient's physical condition) in analyzing the blood pressure pulse. In existing method, an oriental doctor infers one pulse wave out of 28 pulse wave and diagnoses the patient. Fuzzy compositional rule of inference is a rule made in order to come up with an inference by using fuzzy production rule which includes fuzzy variables. The form of fuzzy compositional rule of inference is as in the following.

Belief of fuzzy composite function: If fuzzy compositional rule of inference is applied in fuzzy production rule then belief of fuzzy evaluation function can't be used. So in order to calculate the belief of fuzzy function, the belief of fuzzy composite function is used.

$\beta c = \beta comp(\beta(\beta f, \beta r))$
$= \min (\max (\beta (\beta fp, \beta rpq)))$

In here, p=1, 2, ⋯, m, q = 1, 2, ⋯, n. m, n are the number of each fuzzy thesis in premise and conclusion. Belief of fuzzy union function in type 1 and 2 of fuzzy production rule which are the minimized version of type 5 and 6 can come up with the same node or conclusion using different inference. In this kind of node, same conclusion has two or more different belief of function. In this type of situation, in order to recalculate the belief of fuzzy function, fuzzy union function is used.

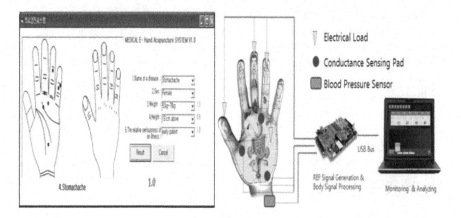

Fig. 5. Intelligence DSP Board Firmware

Fig. 5 shows the sequence of DSP Board Firmware. The sequence can be classified into 4 major categories. They are Main Part for main process, Sensor Signal Input & Processor, Data Indexing Processer to create accurate information data on the basis of the sensed data and Fuzzy Logic Driver to create the result data. After power supply, all the register functions of DSP and related memories and variables are initialized. Then, the electric route creation part outputs the electric pattern by the patient condition and A/D and D/A is executed to process the pattern after delivered from the sensor. In this paper, the blood pressure is converted into a form for facilitating judgement via 1st and 2nd derivative and the electrode to measure the conductivity filters each delivered signal to create the input data required by the Fuzzy logic.

5   Conclusion

This paper calculates the optimal time for Electronic-Acupuncture using fuzzy rules. In order to calculate the exact acupuncture time, it considers physical condition, illness conditions and age conditions. However, this classification scheme depending on the patient's illness conditions vary greatly. To improve these problems, it adjusts the acupuncture time depending on the patient physical conditions. Since the oriental medicine can check human's health and disease condition by observing the pulse beating condition, the herbal treatment considers the pulse very importantly. The oriental doctor has regarded the pulse as an important data in diagnosis from the past. However, the existing pulse stethoscope was not good enough to confirm if the pulse wave detection sensor was positioned exactly on the aorta radial. Furthermore, it was difficult to feel for accurate pulse of a person with a thick forearm and different body type to the person with a thin forearm. The health judgment by using existing pulse feeling has generated ambiguous problems with accurate judgment due to an oriental doctor's subjective data analysis. In this paper, we applied the Fuzzy algorithm to analyze such a problem and draw an inference from objective data in view of pretreatment and applied the electrical characteristics of pain parts which respond to acupuncture antidune in view of post-treatment to propose the scientific pulse feeling system algorithm and simulation experiment.

Acknowledgments. This work was supported by the Security Engineering Research Center, granted by the Korea Ministry of Knowledge Economy.

References

1. Lee, Y.J., Lee, J., Lee, H.J., Yoo, H.H., Choi, E.J., Kim, J.Y.: Study on the characteristics of blood vessel pulse area using ultrasonic. Korea Institute of Oriental Medicine Researches 13(3), 111–119 (2007)
2. Lee, J., Lee, Y.J., Lee, H.J., Choi, E.J., Kim, J.Y.: Designing a stabilized process of pulse analyzing method using sigma 6. Korea Institute of Oriental Medicine researches 12(2), 85–92 (2006)
3. Lee, Y.G.: Diagnostic atlas 2 analyzing pulse, pp. 11–14. Chungdam Books (2003)
4. Gunal, S., Edizkan, R.: Subspace based feature selection for pattern recognition. Information Sciences (2008)
5. http://www.etnews.co.kr/etnews/word
6. Garg, M.L., Ahson, S.I., Gupta, D.V.: A Fuzzy Petri-nets for Knowledge Represent- ation and Reasoning. Information Processing Letters 39, 165–171 (1992)
7. Genrich, H.J., Lautenbach, K.: System Modelling with High-level Petri Nets. Theoretical Computer Science 13, 109–136 (1981)
8. Leung, K.S., Lam, W.: Fuzzy Concepts in Expert Systems. IEEE Computer, 43–56 (September 1988)
9. Looney, G.C., Alfize, A.A.: Logical Controls via Boolean Rule Matrix Transformation. IEEE Trans. on SMC, 1077–1082 (November/December 1987)
10. Looney, G.C.: Fuzzy Petri Nets for Rule- based Decision Making. IEEE Trans. on SMC 18(1) (January/February 1988)
11. O'Rourke, M.F., Kelly, R.P., Avolio, A.P.: The Arterial Pulse, 1st edn. Lea & Febiger, Philadelphia (1992)
12. Gong, Y., Chen, H., Pu, J., Lian, Y.M., Chen, S.: Quantitative investigation on normal pathological tongue shape and correlation analysis between hypertension and syndrome. In: China Journal of Traditional Chinese Medicine and Pharmacy (2005)
13. Gunal, S., Edizkan, R.: Subspace based feature selection for pattern recognition. Information Sciences (2008)
14. Hong, Y.-S., Lee, S.-S., Nam, D.-H., Lee, W.-B., Kim, H., Song, Y.J., Kim, K.-B., Lee, G., Kang, J.-J., Kumar, R., Jin, H., Moon, C., Lee, Y., Chung, C.: Smart Pulse Wave Detection System Using Intelligence. In: Lee, G., Howard, D., Ślęzak, D. (eds.) ICHIT 2011. LNCS, vol. 6935, pp. 213–220. Springer, Heidelberg (2011)

A Runtime Environment for Distributed Mashups in Multi-device Scenarios

Oliver Mroß and Klaus Meißner

Faculty of Computer Science
Technische Universität Dresden, Germany
{oliver.mross,klaus.meissner}@tu-dresden.de

Abstract. Multi-device scenarios pave the way for new applications that allow the user to interact collaboratively with other users or enhance the interaction through the combination of different devices. To realize such applications, a new development paradigm is needed. Traditional methods do not support the dynamic extension or alteration of the application's feature set. Our approach is based on the idea of modeling the composition and distribution of several application components, so that the component implementations and their assignment to specific execution environments (component distribution) can be determined dynamically. All application components are linked together as an overlay network in the context of the multi-device environment. Therefore, we propose an architecture of a runtime environment and an overview of the component distribution process during the load-time of a multi-device mashup.

Keywords: Multi-Device Environment, Distributed Mashups, Runtime Environment, Model-based Mashup Development.

1   Introduction

The quickly growing popularity of mobile devices and their rich feature set are leading to the need for applications, in which several interactive devices can be used in combination. Such applications allow the user to collaborate with other users across the borders of their personal devices. These scenarios range from simple data sharing to complex applications, in which multiple users can connect with each other and create a shared view on distributed content that can be modified from different devices, e. g., a collaborative decision making application. In each of these scenarios the devices are providing a distributed user interface of the application.

The device mobility can cause the dynamic adaption of the distribution state during the application's runtime. If another person and her Smartphone, for example, are entering the interaction environment, the application could integrate a new UI element that allows the person to take part in the collaboration. To distribute the user interface in the context of a multi-device environment the application developer has to provide a specific UI for each device. The problem here is the development effort to create multi-device applications. Another problem is the dynamic availability of mobile devices. The application developer has no knowledge of the configuration of the

J.J. Park et al. (Eds.): NPC 2012, LNCS 7513, pp. 532–541, 2012.

multi-device environment. This means that a static distribution of the user interface is not possible during the application's design-time.

In our approach, we address both problems through the use of the development methods from the mashup domain. Hence, we denote such applications as model-based distributed mashups. From the perspective of the application developer, these methods allow to reduce the development effort, because they introduce a strict separation between the application and the UI development. The application developer describes only the composition of the application, the communication between the application components and their distribution as part of an application model. We assume there are several classes of UI components and each class contains device specific UI component implementations. They are provided in a public component repository service that allows registering reusable black-box application components. To address the problem of the dynamic device availability, the composition and distribution descriptions declare properties of required application components and runtime environments, i. e., they do not include concrete assumptions about the availability of application components or devices. To make clear what we understand by the notion of a distributed model-based mashup application, we will give a simple development example now.

Example 1. An application developer defines an application model that includes the description of three application components. The first one is a UI component, which is responsible for the presentation and manipulation of a UML diagram in the context of a Smart TV. The second one is a service component that transforms all raw data of the acceleration and position sensor of a Smartphone into a two-dimensional representation, which is used as input parameter for the previously mentioned UI component. The third component has the same functionality as the second, but it has to be executed on a Tablet computer. Besides the component requirements, the distribution and the communication requirements between the application components are described in the application model as well. In this scenario it contains two communication channels. The first one connects the UI component with the service component that should be executed on the Smartphone. The second communication channel connects the previously mentioned UI component with the service component that should be executed on the Tablet computer.

To generate and execute the distributed mashup, a new kind of runtime environment is needed, which we will explain in this paper. Hence, the remaining paper is structured as follows. Related work will be discussed in the following Sect. 2. In Sect. 3 we will give an overview of the architecture of a runtime environment that enables the execution of a distributed mashup. After that, we will sketch the individual phases of the dynamic loading process of a model-based distributed mashup in Sect. 4. In the final Sect. 5 we draw conclusions and will give an outlook on the next research steps.

2   Related Work

In [1] the vision of a new model of pervasive applications is based on three precepts. The second precept says that different devices can be seen as portals to one virtual application. We share this view, but we understand the notion of a virtual application as a network of components that are distributed and executed on different devices in a distributed runtime environment. In the CRUISe project [2] a model-based development method and a browser-based thin-server-runtime [3] of mashup applications were developed. The application's composition on the presentation layer is defined as part of the composition model. It contains component templates that are matched and ranked against a set of already existing mashup components, i. e., the mashup application is generated dynamically during the application's load-time. However, the CRUISe approach does not support the execution of components in distributed runtime environments nor it provides needed operations to distribute UI components dynamically on a set of heterogeneous devices. Our current project DoCUMA is based on the CRUISe research results and will extend the mashup development methods to create applications for collaborative multi-device scenarios. To model the distribution of UI components during the design time of an application a meta-model was developed in [4]. Its entities represent digital and physical elements of the smart environment on a high-level abstraction layer. Specific aspects like the distribution requirement description that is needed to compute the dynamic distribution of application components are not part of the meta-model. The approaches in [5,6] describe the use of UI properties to characterize the distribution of abstract UI elements on model layer – the CARE-properties [7]. They allow to bind an abstract UI to a concrete device of the smart environment during the design time. Our approach addresses the dynamic distribution of black-box UI components, thus a static binding between UI components and their runtime environment is not feasible. Hence, a runtime environment descriptor for each interactive device is needed to compute the mashup component distribution dynamically. In [8] the device description model of the UPnP standard [9] is transferred into an ontological representation. It allows the dynamic determination of the valid mapping between the set of required mashup components and the set of their appropriate runtime environments.

Finally, in [10] a distributed runtime environment is described that enables the migration of UI components between heterogeneous devices. It is based on a reverse engineering process that comprises the generation of an abstract user interface model from a UI implementation, which is the starting point of a model-to-code transformation. The result of the transformation is a device specific UI. In our approach we use black-box UI components, which do not allow a reverse engineering in the way of the approach in [10]. To allow the migration of UI components between heterogeneous devices, we will focus on the concept of adapting the component implementation by replacing the migrating application component [11] with an optimal component that is a device specific variant of the same component class during the application's runtime.

3   Overview of the Architecture

In this Sect., the architecture of the runtime environment of a distributed mashup application is presented. In the remainder of this paper it is denoted as the **Client-Server-Runtime (CSR)**. Figure Fig. 1 visualizes the main parts of the CSR – the client- and the server-side runtime environment. Both can execute different

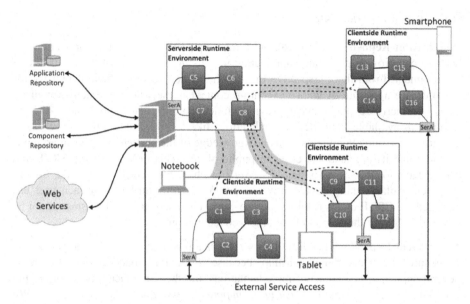

Fig. 1. Overview of the CSR

application components in parallel, which are linked together as an overlay network that is built on top of the connected devices.

In this paper, the client-side part of the CSR is denoted as **CRTE** (*Client Side Runtime Environment*) and the server-side is denoted as **SRTE** (*Server Side Runtime Environment*). The CRTE is responsible for the instantiation, initialization, execution and visualization of the mashup UI components. Further, it encapsulates all communication features that are needed to execute a distributed mashup successfully. These include local and remote communication features, e. g., the creation of local and distributed communication channels. To migrate and replicate UI components between different devices, each CRTE provide serialization and deserialization capabilities that allow the exchange of component state information between different devices.

The SRTE is responsible to register multiple applications. Hence, it provides a service that allows the application developer to register several application models, which describe the application composition and communication patterns of several mashup components. Another feature is the dynamic discovery and registration of multiple devices and their runtime environment descriptions. Furthermore, the SRTE mediates messages between all distributed application components and between the runtime environments. Another important feature of the SRTE is the execution of the application's loading process, in which the application components and the appropriate CRTEs are determined dynamically. This is discussed in Sect. 4.

In the left part of Fig. 1 several services are depicted, which are needed to load and execute a distributed mashup application. In the following Sect., we will dwell on this aspect.

3.1   Services of the CSR

Application Repository (AppRe). With the help of this service the application developer can provide predefined application models in the context of the multi-device environment. From this perspective the *AppRe* service acts as a central registry for multi-device applications whose execution context is the whole interactive environment. Furthermore, the service provides functionalities that enable the SRTE to publish all available multi-device applications like a broadcaster. This is necessary, because we assume that the user has no knowledge of the existence of the smart environment and its applications, e. g., in public places. This means that the SRTE and CRTE have to provide automatic discovery mechanisms, which enables the user to discover available multi-device applications. We assume further, that each user has installed the CRTE on his (mobile) device, since the discovery mechanisms cannot be realized only with the help of client-side web technologies.

Component Repository (CoRe). This service is a fundamental part of the generation procedure of the distributed mashup, because it provides functionalities to access several application component implementations and their interface descriptors in the SMCDL format *(Semantic Mash-up Component Description Language)* [2]. We assume that for each platform (Smartphones, Tablet computers, Desktops), there are specific application components, which provide the foundation of generating a distributed mashup across the borders of heterogeneous devices. Another fundamental function of this service is the registration of several application components. This includes the registration of device-specific components, which encapsulate services of the interactive device, e. g., the access to embedded sensors or in- and output devices.

After we have given an overview of our approach of a distributed runtime environment, we will describe the dynamic loading process of a model-based distributed mashup and its individual phases in the next Sect. 4.

4   Loading Process of a Distributed Mashup

In our approach the load-time of a model based distributed mashup can be divided into the following phases. Each phase uses runtime environment features that are distributed on the client- and server-side. A more detailed description on what middleware components are used in which phase, is not part of this paper.

4.1   Process Phases

Discovery. During this phase the SRTE collects several pieces of information. The first ones are characterizing the device and the software platform that forms the foundation to execute future application components (*CRTE discovery*). The second part of information are the user credentials (*user discovery*), which are needed to determine the valid set of available applications. In other words every user has a predefined application set that depends on the user preferences and the associated user role. The applications per user are the third information piece (*application discovery*).

Once the user has logged in, he can choose to join an active or load an associated application. The first case is out of the scope of this paper.

Application Selection. After the completion of the discovery phase, the next step of the loading process is the presentation of the determined application set to the user. Therefore, the SRTE analyses every application description in the set of the available applications and sends a reduced information set to present all available application models as visual entries in the context of the client device. That means that the user can initiate the loading process of a distributed mashup from his personal device. We denote it as the *initial device*. After the user selects a model reference, a message is sent from the user's CRTE to the SRTE, where it causes the initiation of the server-side model interpretation procedure.

Interpretation. The main goal of this phase is to determine what mashup components are needed by the application, what components are available and what CRTEs could be used to realize the specified distributed mashup (represented by application model). Therefore, following steps are executed. First, the SRTE resolves the associated application model from the received model reference that was selected by the user. The model is used as input parameter during the invocation of the server-side mashup loading process. Second, all CRTE descriptors are retrieved and used as input parameter during the loading procedure invocation. That means that every CRTE could be used as a potential execution environment of the mashup components. Besides these two input parameters, the third information set – the interface descriptors of all application components – is already provided by third party component developers as entities of the previously mentioned *CoRe* service. After the SRTE has retrieved all required information, the interpretation procedure will be triggered. The knowledge of the needed application components is extracted from the application model. It encompasses functional properties of the required application components, e. g., supported properties, operations and event messages. Furthermore, the knowledge of the component distribution is extracted from the application model too, because in our approach the application developer defines the distribution per mashup component explicitly, i. e., there is an association between the description of the needed mashup component and the description of the required distribution context. The distribution context spans several aspects, e. g., device characteristics like the display resolution or context characteristics like the maximum distance between the initial device (that represents the user's position) and the needed execution context of the bound mashup components. The characteristics of the available CRTEs are determined from the registered runtime descriptors. They include runtime environment aspects, e. g., the supported in- and output modalities and the software platform aspects, such as provided APIs or available rendering capabilities (audio and video player features, etc.). With the help of this information the SRTE can derive what application component is executable within the context of which CRTE.

Matching and Ranking. The main goal of this phase is the computation of the final distribution set that describes the distribution of those mashup components, which correspond on one side with the functional requirements and on the other side with the distribution requirements that are both part of the application model. In our approach the algorithm to compute the distribution set consists of the following steps. First, the interpreted information of the application model is used to determine the set of usable CRTEs. Therefore, the SRTE needs to consider the registered runtime environment descriptions, which characterize the functional and non-functional properties of the corresponding CRTE. In other words, the CRTE descriptors are matched against the descriptions of the required distribution context in the application model. In our approach, each distribution context description represents one required CRTE per mashup component. After the corresponding CRTE was determined, the associations between the distribution contexts and the functional component requirements are used to create a matrix that comprises the mapping between a CRTE and a mashup component requirement. In the second step of our algorithm, each entry of the previously mentioned matrix is used to compute the best matching application component implementation. The result of our distribution algorithm is a refined matrix (*distribution set*) that describes the mapping between the entries of the set of usable CRTEs and the entries of the set of available mashup component implementations.

Apportionment. In our approach a distributed mashup application is characterized as a network of communicating mashup components, which are executed in the distributed context of several runtime environments (CRTEs). This involves the execution of multiple application components in the context of a single CRTE. To integrate these components successfully, the communication description of the application model is needed during the integration process. That is, the model has to be apportioned into several model fragments, to reduce the communication overhead between the SRTE and CRTE. These fragments have to be bound to these mashup components, which are part of the previously mentioned distribution set. Hence, the set has to be extended with modal data, for example, communication channel descriptions per mashup component. The result of this phase is an extended distribution set that contains several entries and each entry incorporate the following information units: a unique identifier of the mashup component, a component descriptor (functional and non-functional component properties) in the SMCDL format, the executable code of the mashup component, model fragment information and the identifier of the corresponding CRTE.

The first parameter is created in the context of the SRTE, because it is responsible to route all communication messages between the distributed mashup components. The second parameter incorporates all information that is necessary to integrate the component in a remote execution context, e. g., external software libraries. The third parameter covers all information that is necessary for instantiating and executing the application components. The fourth parameter contains the model data, e. g., the description of the communication behavior between the mashup components. The last parameter represents the CRTE, in which context the application components should be executed.

Integration. After the extended distribution set was created, the last phase of the loading process will begin – the distributed integration of all included mashup components. It covers the instantiation, initialization and the optional layout- and rendering-process of several mashup components in the remote context of different

CRTEs. For this purpose the SRTE has created a bidirectional communication channel to every CRTE during the aforementioned discovery phase. In our approach we will use Web Sockets, which allow the SRTE to push application specific messages to the client-side. As input parameter the extended distribution set is used in this phase. First the set is sorted under the criteria of the CRTE, because this allows to group the distribution set and each group covers all mashup components that are executed in the same context. Second, for each group an integration command message is created, which causes the associated CRTE to start a client-side integration procedure, in that each delivered mashup component is instantiated and initialized. This message contains all information of each group member (component ID, component description, executable code and model fragment data) that is needed for the remote integration procedure.

5 Conclusion and Further Work

In this paper, we presented our approach to realize a distributed mashup application for multi-device scenarios. We used model-based development methods that are known from the mashup domain, e. g., modeling the composition and communication of application components. To distribute mashup components on heterogeneous devices further conditions must be fulfilled during the load-time. To address the problem of the dynamic availability of mobile devices every personal device has to provide a discovery feature that allows the server-side device registration and the client-side application selection. Modern web browser do not provide such discovery features, that means we need to extent the browser capabilities to use it as a universal runtime environment for mashup components. Furthermore, in our approach an application is provided and executed by the multi-device environment and not by the device itself. Hence, the personal device of the user has to communicate with a central server that provides all available applications.

Another problem that we address is the heterogeneity of multiple interactive devices. To overcome this issue, in our approach for every device a specific mashup component implementation has to be registered in a public component repository service. Each mashup component is associated with a descriptor that contains functional and non-functional property information, such as supported operations and capabilities. Especially, the non-functional component description part contains requirement descriptions from the perspective of the component developer, e. g., needed device-specific sensors or in- and output resources. That means that the client-side runtime environment has to provide self-descriptive properties that condition the deployability of a mashup component. Hence, each potential runtime environment provides a generic interface that allows aggregating the runtime environment descriptors on the server-side during the discovery phase.

As further research, we will investigate the possibilities to express the distribution requirements per needed mashup component as part of the application model with the help of semantic technologies, e. g., SPARQL-queries[1]. We assume that this will help us to simplify the matching process, because these queries can be used directly in the matching phase of the application loading process. No additional interpretation and transformation operations have to be implemented. Furthermore, we will extend existing standards for device description, e. g., the UPnP standard, with additional non-functional properties, because we need to describe what device-specific (in- and output) and what software-specific conditions must be fulfilled to execute a mashup component. For example, a component developer wants to annotate that his mashup component is only executable on a smartphone with a camera and a Webkit-based browser. Therefore, we plan to describe these runtime environment properties in an ontological representation format, because we assume that semantic technologies will help us to reduce the implementation effort and improve the quality of the dynamic matching between required distribution contexts and the available runtime environments.

Acknowledgement. The work of Oliver Mroß is founded by the European Social Fund (ESF), Free State Saxony (Germany) and T-Systems Multimedia Solutions GmbH (Germany, Dresden) and is filed under ESF-080951831.

References

1. Banavar, G., Beck, J., Gluzberg, E., Munson, J., Sussman, J., Zukowski, D.: Challenges: An Application Model for Pervasive Computing. In: Proceedings of the 6th Annual International Conference on Mobile Computing and Networking - MobiCom 2000, pp. 266–274. ACM Press, New York (2000)
2. Pietschmann, S., Radeck, C., Meißner, K.: Semantics-based discovery, selection and mediation for presentation-oriented mashups. In: Proceedings of the 5th International Workshop on Web APIs and Service Mashups - Mashups 2011, p. 1. ACM Press, New York (2011)
3. Pietschmann, S., Waltsgott, J., Meißner, K.: A Thin-Server Runtime Platform for Composite Web Applications. In: Proceedings of the 2010 Fifth International Conference on Internet and Web Applications and Services, ICIW 2010, pp. 390–395. IEEE, Washington, DC (2010)
4. Demeure, A., Sottet, J.S., Calvary, G., Coutaz, J., Ganneau, V., Vanderdonckt, J.: The 4C Reference Model for Distributed User Interfaces. In: Proceedings of the Fourth International Conference on Autonomic and Autonomous Systems (ICAS 2008), pp. 61–69. IEEE, Washington, DC (2008)
5. Manca, M., Paternò, F.: Flexible support for distributing user interfaces across multiple devices. In: Proceedings of the 9th ACM SIGCHI Italian Chapter International Conference on Computer-Human Interaction Facing Complexity - CHItaly, p. 191. ACM Press, New York (2011)
6. Blumendorf, M., Roscher, D., Albayrak, S.: Dynamic user interface distribution for flexible multimodal interaction. In: International Conference on Multimodal Interfaces and the Workshop on Machine Learning for Multimodal Interaction on - ICMI-MLMI 2010, p. 1. ACM Press, New York (2010)

---

[1] http://www.w3.org/TR/rdf-sparql-query/

7. Coutaz, J., Nigay, L., Salber, D., Blandford, A., May, J., Young, R.M.: Four easy pieces for assesing the usability of multimodal interaction: the CARE properties. In: Nordby, K., Helmersen, P.H., Gilmore, D.J., Arnesen, S.A. (eds.) INTERACT. IFIP Conference Proceedings, pp. 115–120. Chapman & Hall (1995)
8. Togias, K., Goumopoulos, C., Kameas, A.: Ontology-Based Representation of UPnP Devices and Services for Dynamic Context-Aware Ubiquitous Computing Applications. In: 2010 Third International Conference on Communication Theory, Reliability, and Quality of Service, pp. 220–225. IEEE (2010)
9. UPnP Forum: UPnP Device Architecture (2008), http://upnp.org/specs/arch/UPnP-arch-DeviceArchitecture-v1.1.pdf
10. Nickelsen, A., Paternó, F., Grasselli, A., Schmidt, K.-U., Martin, M., Schindler, B., Mureddu, F.: Open: open pervasive environments for migratory interactive services. In: Proceedings of the 12th International Conference on Information Integration and Web-based Applications & Services - iiWAS 2010, p. 639. ACM Press, New York (2010)
11. Ketfi, A., Belkhatir, N., Cunin, P.-Y.: Automatic Adaptation of Component-based Software: Issues and Experiences. In: Proceedings of the International Conference on Parallel and Distributed Processing Techniques and Applications - PDPTA 2002, vol. 3, pp. 1365–1371. CSREA Press (2002)

A Location-Based Algorithm for Supporting Multicast Routing in Mobile Ad-Hoc Networks

Le The Dung[1] and Beongku An[2]

[1] Dept. of Electronics & Computer Engineering in Graduate School, Hongik University, Korea
thedung_hcmut@yahoo.com
[2] Dept. of Computer & Information Communications Engineering, Hongik University, Korea
beongku@hongik.ac.kr

Abstract. In this paper, we propose a location-based algorithm for supporting multicast routing in mobile ad-hoc networks. Instead of having routing paths in advanced to forward data packets from source node to multicast receivers, this algorithm let each node which receives data packets independently, adaptively determines the routing paths to forward data packets based on the information of its neighbor nodes. Before forwarding data packets, mobile node checks and uses one of its neighbor nodes as the next hop. Therefore, the availability of routing segments is ensured, providing high performance even in high mobility environment. The performance of this algorithm for multicast routing is validated via simulation using OPNET.

Keywords: Mobile ad-hoc networks, Multicast routing, Mobile node's location.

1 Introduction

Ad-hoc networks are decentralized, self-organizing networks, able to form a communication network without relying on any fixed infrastructure. Each mobile node in an ad-hoc network is equipped with radio transceiver which allows it to communicate with other nodes over wireless channel. Moreover, mobile node may use GPS device to obtain its location, velocity, moving direction to orient the routing decision. Since the transmission range of mobile nodes in ad-hoc networks is limited, communication among them is often multi-hop. Therefore, nodes may operate, if needed, as relays for data packets to be routed to the intended destination.

Ad-hoc networks have advantages over conventional networks. For example, they are more economical because they do not need to build fixed infrastructure, they increase mobility and flexibility because they can be brought up and torn down in a short time.

The multicast routing protocol in mobile ad-hoc networks (MANET) is currently getting the attraction from researchers because of the development of considerable number of multicast applications. The advantage of multicast routing is its capacity to efficiently save network resources by allowing source node to send data in a single transmission to a group of receivers. The classification of multicast routing protocols is presented in detailed in [1]. As in [1] multicast routing protocols can be grouped

J.J. Park et al. (Eds.): NPC 2012, LNCS 7513, pp. 542–549, 2012.

according to their topologies which use two different taxonomies, i.e. reactive/proactive/hybrid and flat/hierarchical multicast routing protocols.

Recently, due to the availability of small, inexpensive, low power GPS receivers and techniques for finding relative coordinates based on signal strength, the location-based routing method can be used in mobile ad-hoc networks. Geocast [2] is an approach to delivery multicast data packets to a set of node within a specified geographic region. Several schemes for geocasting are proposed in [3]. In those schemes, all multicast receivers reside in a multicast region. Geomulticast routing was proposed in [4] for the case that multicast receivers reside in several regions. In Geomulticast routing, mobile nodes periodically send mobility information to their neighbor nodes. Then a mobile node is grouped into cluster if its mobility is less than a threshold. Cluster head is selected as the node which has the lowest id. By using the same process, several clusters may be merged to parent clusters. A multicast mesh is formed among cluster heads. Multicast data are delivered through this clustered head based limit mesh structure. In RSGM [5], the network area is divided into many square zones. Each mobile node uses its current location pos (x, y) to calculate its zID (a, b). The center of zone is also calculated. A zone leader is the node which is nearest to the zone center. Zone leaders flood LEADER packets in their zones periodically to announce their leadership, members in each zone send REFRESH packets to their zone leader to notify their membership. When a multicast member moves into a new zone, if that zone leader is unknown, it queries the neighbor node in the zone for the leader information. If it fails to get this information it will announce itself as a leader by flooding LEADER packet into the zone. The zone leaders are responsible for sending REPORT packets periodically to update zone membership information to the source node. Source node starts the multicast session by flooding ANNOUNCE packet into the network. Multicast packets are sent along the virtual distribution tree rooted at the source node to the multicast members.

The rest of this paper is organized as follows. The location-based algorithm consisting of mobile node's location updating, multicast data packet forwarding, and adaptive update interval of mobile's node location is described in Section 2. The performance results of this location-based algorithm are discussed in Section 3. Finally, the paper is concluded in Section 4.

2   The Proposed Location-Based Algorithm

2.1   Basic Concepts

Our proposed location-based algorithm for multicast routing uses the information of multicast receivers' locations and neighbor nodes at each mobile node to choose the next hop for data packet forwarding. By using that information, the data packet forwarding algorithm can choose available best intermediate nodes to forward multicast data packets. Also, receivers and intermediate nodes can adaptively choose the information updating rate based on their mobility and network status.

2.2   Mobile Node's Location Updating

In this section, we describe detailed steps of how to get the necessary information to guide the routing and how multicast data packets are sent from source node to multicast receivers.

Step 1: Each mobile node advertises its id and location by sending Introduce packet at adaptive rate. The format of Introduce packet is as follow.

Node ID	Node Location	TTL

Fig. 1. The format of Introduce packet

Step 2: To join the multicast group, each multicast receiver sends Join packet to source node. The Join packets sent by multicast receivers consist of the IDs and current location of receivers. The format of Join packet is below.

Src Location	Rcv Location	Seq_Num

Fig. 2. The format of Join packet

Step 3: After source node receives these Join packet, it send multicast data packets to every multicast receivers using the following data packet forwarding algorithm.

2.3   Location-Based Packet Forwarding Algorithm

Location-based packet forwarding algorithm is used for both Join packets and data packets. According to this algorithm, each mobile node independently chooses the next hop to forward packets (i.e. Join packets and data packets) based on the following priorities:

1. A node chooses the neighbor node which is the farthest node from it (i.e. having largest BH in Fig. 3).

where
$$BH = \frac{AB^2 + BC^2 - AC^2}{2 \times AC} \tag{1}$$

2. If there are more than two nodes satisfying the above criteria, the node which is the nearest to the source node – receiver line (i.e. having smallest AH in Fig. 3) is selected.

where
$$AH = AB \sin\left(\frac{AB^2 + BC^2 - AC^2}{2 \times AB \times AC}\right) \tag{2}$$

3. Finally, if these two criteria are still met, the node which has the lowest ID is selected.

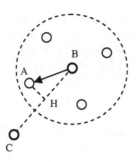

Fig. 3. Algorithm for choosing next hop to forward data packets

To reach multicast receivers, data sent by source node consist of next hop ids determined by previous location-based packet forwarding algorithm. The information of receivers at source node is from Join packets sent by receivers to source node regularly. When source node receives Join packets, it will add the receiver information to Receiver Record Table (RRT) entry and set the timer. If any multicast receiver does not want to participate in multicast session, it simply stops sending Join packet to source node. After not receiving Join packet from a receiver, the timer of entry in RRT for that receiver expires and it is removed from RRT.

Node receiving data packet checks if its id matches one of the next-hop ids in data header. If yes, it will use the packet forwarding node to select next hope ids to forward the data packet. It eliminates unnecessary receiver information. It only keeps the receiver information (i.e. receiver location) to which data packets are forwarded. Fig. 4 illustrates how multicast data packets are forwarded from source node to multicast receivers.

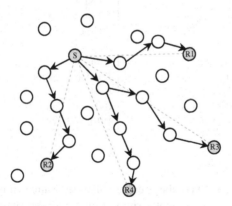

Fig. 4. Multicast data sending from source node (S) to multicast receivers (R1, R2, R3, R4)

2.4   Adaptive Update Interval of Mobile Node's Location

To eliminate unnecessary Introduce packets sent by mobile nodes to update its location information to their neighbor nodes, we propose the idea of adaptive update interval of mobile node's location. All mobile nodes will listen to the data packets regardless of being intended receivers or not. If the chance of receiving data packet of a mobile node is small, its information (i.e. id, location) is not important to packet routing. Then it reduces the rate of sending Introduce packets to its neighbor nodes. If a mobile node receives data packets often, it knows that it may play an important role in packet routing. Therefore it sends Introduce packets more frequent. The data receiving rate is calculated as

$$Data\operatorname{Re}ceivingRate = \frac{num\_of\_data \times data\_rate}{elapsed\_time} \qquad (3)$$

3   Performance Evaluation

3.1   Simulation Environment

The following table shows the settings of simulation parameters. We simulate one multicast group which has one multicast source and varying number of multicast receiver. Multicast receivers are chosen randomly. Source sends packet at constant rate of 20 packets per second. Each data packet has 512 bytes.

Members join the multicast group at the beginning of simulation and remain as members during the simulation. Source begins to send data right after it receives the Join packet and continues sending the data throughout the simulation.

Table 1. Simulation parameters

Environment Factors	Defined Configuration
Simulator	OPNET
Simulation Area	1000m × 1000m
Simulation Time	300sec
Number of Nodes	50
Radio Range	250m
Mobility	Random Waypoint
Node Speed	0~60km/h
Node Pause Time	0~10sec (randomly)
MAC Protocol	IEEE 802.11

3.2   Simulation Results

We run the simulation and take the average values to evaluate how our proposed multicast routing protocol can efficiently support the multicast routing services by using following metrics:

- *PDR*: the ratio of the number of data packets received at multicast receivers to the number of data packets transmitted at source node.
- *Normalized control overhead*: the ratio of total number of control overheads to the number of data packets received at multicast receivers.

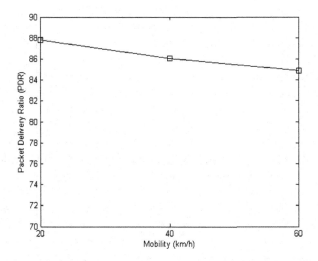

Fig. 5. PDR (Packet Delivery Ratio) as a function of node mobility

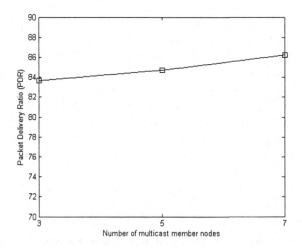

Fig. 6. PDR (Packet Delivery Ratio) as a function of number of multicast member nodes

Fig. 5 and Fig. 6 present PDR as functions of node mobility and number of multi-cast member nodes (i.e. scalability of the network), respectively. As we can see in Fig. 5 and Fig. 6, our proposed algorithm still maintains high PDR under high node mobility and scales well as the number of multicast member node increases because each node adaptively selects next hop to forward data based on the updated informa-tion of its neighbor nodes. The update interval of node's location is optimized by using adaptive strategy, giving latest neighbor node's information with the lowest number of control overheads.

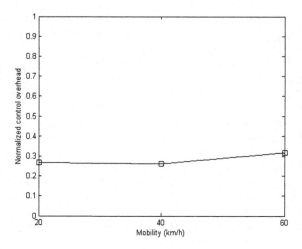

Fig. 7. Normalized control overhead as a function of number of node mobility

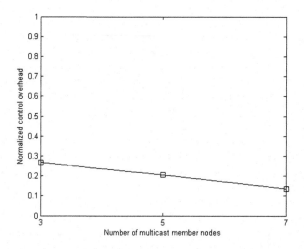

Fig. 8. Normalized control overheads as a function of number of multicast member nodes

Fig. 7 and Fig. 8 present the normalized control overhead as functions of node mobility and multicast member nodes, respectively. In our proposed algorithm, approximately for every 4 multicast data packets successfully delivered at receivers, a control overhead is needed at node mobility of 20km/h and 40km/h. While approximately for every 3 multicast data packets successfully delivered at receivers, a control overhead is needed at node mobility of 60km/h. As the number of multicast member nodes increases, our proposed location-based algorithm shows efficient multicast data transmission (i.e. for every 4, 5, and 7 multicast data packets successfully delivered at receivers, a control overhead is needed) because a node may use its neighbor information to select several next nodes for multicast data packet forwarding.

4   Conclusions

In this paper, we propose a location-based algorithm for supporting muticast routing in mobile ad-hoc networks. This algorithm sends multicast data packets based on the location information of multicast receivers. Each node uses packet forwarding algorithm to adaptively select next nodes for multicast data forwarding. The update interval of mobile node's location used in packet forwarding algorithm is optimized by adaptive strategy at each node.

The performance evaluation using OPNET of our proposed algorithm shows that it can support efficient multicast routing with high PDR under high node mobility and scales well as the number of multicast member nodes increases.

Acknowledgment. This research was supported by Basic Science Research Program through the National Research Foundation of Korea (NRF) funded by the Ministry of Education, Science and Technology (2011-0025907).

References

1. Junhai, L., Danxia, Y., Liu, X., Mingyu, F.: A Survey of Multicast Routing Protocols for Mobile Ad-Hoc Networks. IEEE Communications Survey & Tutorials 11(1), 78–91 (2009)
2. Navas, J.C., Imielinski, T.: Geocast – geographic addressing and routing. In: Proc. of ACM/IEEE Int. Conf. on Mobile Computing and Networking, pp. 66–76 (1997)
3. Ko, Y.-B., Vaidya, N.H.: Geocasting in Mobile Ad Hoc Networks: Location-Based Multicast Algorithm. In: Proc. of Second IEEE Workshop on Mobile Computing Systems and Applications, pp. 101–110 (1999)
4. An, B., Papavassiliou, S.: Geomulticast: architectures and protocols for mobile ad hoc wireless networks. Journal of Parallel and Distributed Computing 63, 182–195 (2003)
5. Xiang, X., Wang, X., Yuanyuan: Stateless Multicasting in Mobile Ad Hoc Networks. IEEE Transactions on Computer 59(8), 1076–1090 (2010)

Nibble-CRC for Underwater Acoustic Communication

Imtiaz Ahmed Khan, Nam-Yeol Yun, and Soo-Hyun Park

Ubiquitous System Lab., Graduate School of BIT, Kookmin University, Seoul, Korea
{fish786,anuice,shpark21}@kookmin.ac.kr

Abstract. Underwater acoustic sensor networks (UWASNs) are complex in design due to the characteristics of underwater medium. The underwater communication environment and the medium vary on time, geographical location and depth. Sensor nodes are also born with some limitations such as fixed amount of energy, small size memory and node mobility. Signals travel inside a noisy acoustic channel which required checking errors after receiving. Secure communication is one of the main characteristics of any networks. UWASNs also maintain a security protocols in each layer. Moreover, data link layer performs the main task of error check. To protect unauthorized access to our network and for a common line of defense against the errors, it requires attentions during the protocol design. Depends on the several error detection mechanisms, cyclic redundancy check (CRC) performs better than other mechanisms in respects of the different underwater factors. In this paper, we discuss about the CRC: how it is different from other mechanisms in terms of carrying functions that helps to check double error (running sum) but correct checksum. The trade-offs between error detection system designs (using a nibble size CRC) and underwater communication system designs.

Keywords: UWASNs, Error Detection, Network Efficiency, Energy Efficiency, CRCs.

1 Introduction

Underwater acoustic sensor networks are attracted lots of interest because of the capabilities to solutions of underwater related applications and researches [1-5]. To monitor underwater environment and research works such as, oceanic geographic data collection, oceanic environmental monitoring, resource investigation, disaster prevention and tactical surveillance application, underwater acoustic communication is the fundamental technology for these applications [6].

Moreover, monitoring underwater quality and examining the water quality in rivers and canals for industrial water pollutions after technical disaster in different regions that could be put an effect on our fishes and underwater vegetables. Recent Japanese tsunami which destroy one nuclear power generation plant and radiated a large area of radio activity in environment as well as rivers and connecting oceans. Short term sensor network can be deployed to measure the pollution level and polluted area for

J.J. Park et al. (Eds.): NPC 2012, LNCS 7513, pp. 550–558, 2012.

our civilians and sensor network is the only solution for this as it is economical and easy to deploy.

The error checking is one of the vital issues as the channel is a noisy and unsecure. Different error checking mechanisms are used depends on the system design. According to our previous study [7], one byte CRC performs better among checksum, parity bit, longitudinal redundancy check (LRC), vertical redundancy check (VRC) different FEC and ARQ mechanisms.

We realized that as our data size was much smaller than RF based terrestrial networks. We need to reduce the duration of communication between base stations to sensor nodes (end-to-end delay). The nibble size CRC is our first try to integrate real time communication in our robot fish and sensor networks. Though nibble size CRC is not enough in terms of accuracy, it performs better than checksum or parity bits as it works on polynomial arithmetic GF (Galois field with two elements) finite algebra theory. In this paper, we describe our nibble size CRCs and its theoretical error detection capabilities and finally we analyze the performance of CRC-8, CRC-16, CRC-32, and CRC-64.

2   Related Works

The characteristics of UWASNs are different from the RF based terrestrial networks. The propagation speed of acoustic signals in the water is about 1.5×10^3 m/s and also affected by many factors such as path loss, multi path, noise and Doppler spread. For these reasons, the error rate is very high in acoustic channel. The channel also works as half duplex communication which requires long time for communication between senders to receivers usually takes tens milliseconds. The node mobility due to water current is 3-6 kilometers per hour which change the topology of the networks [8], [10]. The main problem is the limited energy. Still there is no way to recharge the power cells. The architect of UWASNs is also 2D vs. 3D [1-2].

Electromagnetic wave (EM) in radio frequencies and, conventional radio frequency does not work well in underwater due to nature of the medium and can propagate at short distances through conductive sea water only at extra low frequencies (30-300Hz) which required large antenna and high transmission power [8-9]. Optical signals are suitable for surface clean water and short distance (10-100 meters) and high bandwidth (10-150Mps) communication [10]. Moreover, transmission of optical signals requires high precision in pointing the narrow laser beams, which is not very easy due to the mobility of the sensors depends on water current. For signaling, among different physical waves (like sound, radio & optical), due to the extraordinary characteristics of sound, acoustic wave is the only signal that can travel rapidly with lower attenuation in underwater environment than other signals.

The communication among underwater sensors and autonomous/unmanned underwater vehicle (AUV/UUV) is a great challenge. Moreover, different error checks mechanisms are used in different layers for reliable data communication and the secured data transmission. But data link layer performs the main task of error check. Signals coming from different directions with different speeds bit by bit towards the receiver are transferred to the data link layer. Error detection mechanisms are playing an important role as they are used every time when some data exchanges in-side networks.

2.1 Theory of CRC

CRCs performance is the best as it works based on polynomial arithmetic GF (2) (Galois field with two element) Finite Algebra theory. Among various error detection methods the CRC, mechanism performed well in MAC layer as an error detection mechanism. Most of the error detection mechanisms using running-sum which could make a lot of possibility for receiving wrong code words as the error is undetected due to alter double bit position.   But CRC is used for detect double bit errors.

CRC works on binary field and the binary polynomials that facilitate the definition of cyclic redundancy codes. Simply, it can be said that a field is an algebraic system which the operation of addition, subtraction, multiplication and division can be performed. Fields can be finite or infinite and these finite binary fields only denoted by two numbers 0 and 1. Mathematical equation is something like if we have k bits messages, if we want to send it, we add some redundancy bits that is called n bits,   and n bits code words always > k. How many redundancy bits we add in the message $(n-k)$ bits = r (redundancy bits). Based on some formulas or methods, the code word created some times exclusive or operation, sometimes polynomial equations, or some block calculated method.

The selection of a code for a specific application depends on a number of factors including the amount of protections required, the overhead involved, the cost of implementation, the error control strategy employed and the nature of the errors. It is shown that $n-k$ check bits of a code forming the overhead directly affect the error control capability of a code. In general the more check bits in a code, the greater its power of error detection is. A fix number of check bits, the relative overhead of a code can be kept low by using a large number of message blocks k [11].

CRC also known as polynomial codes which used such a code word by using associated polynomials are multiplies of a certain polynomials g(x) called generator polynomials. The main error detection power depends on the generator polynomials which are made of combination of prime numbers.

Let M(x) be the message polynomial, G(x) generator polynomial, G(x) is fixed for a given CRC scheme. And G(x) is known by both sender and the receiver. Now we can create a block polynomial F(x) based on M(x) and G(x) such that F(x) is divisible by G(x).

Sending

1. Message M(x) multiply by x^n
2. Divide $x^n M(x)$ by G(x)
3. Ignore the quotient and keep the reminder C(x)
4. Make a block form and send   f(x)= $x^n M(x)$ =C(x)

Receiving

- Receiving F'(x)
- Divide F'(x) by G(x)
- Accept if remainder is 0, otherwise an error occurred rejected.

Working principle

$x^nM(x) + C(x)$ is divided by $G(X)$, so $x^nM(x) = G(x)Q(x) + C(x)$
$x^nM(x) + C(x) / G(x) = G(x)Q(x) / G(x) + C(x)+C(x) / G(x)$ { binary   modular addition is equivalent to binary modular subtraction $(C(x)+C(x)=0)$}

2.2   Different Error Detection by CRC [12]

Let's thing we send message $F(x)$ but it received $F'(x) = f(x) + E(x)$. $E(x)$: Error due to some noise.

Single Bit Error
$E(x) = x^i$ If $G(x)$ has two or more terms, $G(x)$ will not divide $E(x)$.

Two Isolated Single Bit Errors (double errors)
$E(x) = X^i + X^j$, Where $I > J$, $E(x) = x^j(x^{i-j}+1)$ It was found that $G(x)$ is not divisible by x , a sufficient condition to detect all double error is $G(x)$ does not   divide (x^t+1) for any t up to i-j (i.e., block length)

Odd Number of Bit Errors
If $(x+1)$ is a factor of $G(x)$ all odd number of bit errors are detected. Let's assume that an odd number of Errors has $x+1$ as a factor. then $E(x) = (x+1)T(x)$, then Evaluate $E(x)$ for $x=1$, then $E(x)= E(1)= 1$ since there are odd number of terms $(x+1) = 1+1 =0$, $(X+1) T(x)= (1+1) T(1) = 0$, $E(x)= (x+1)T(x)$

Short Burst Errors ((Length T<=n, number of redundant bits),
Where $E(x) = x^j (x^{t-1}+.....+1)$ length t, Start at bit position J, if $G(x)$ has an x^0 term $t<= n$, $G(x)$ will not divide $E(x)$. So, all errors up to length n are detected.

Long Burst Errors (Length T=n+1)
Undetected able only if burst error is the same as $G(x)$, $G(x) = x^n+.....1$, n-1 bits is in a position between x^n and x^0, $E(x) = 1+....1$, must match probability of not detecting the error is $2^{-(n-1)}$.

Longer Burst Error (length t >n+1)
Probability of not detecting the error is 2^{-n}, number of redundant bits.

2.3   Selecting the Polynomial Generator

Selecting a polynomial for our communication system of limited packet size up to 23 byte is something different as there is a trade of something different between the theoretical analysis and the real field adjustment. Moreover, in real field we have to measure several factors that can impact the system. We are going to use this in our MAC board in a limited memory space and computation power. With the 4 bits long limited space we have the five prime factors $(10)_2 = (X)$, $(11)_2 = (x+1)$, $(111)_2 = x^2+x+1$, $(1011)_2 = x^3+x+1$, and $(1101)_2 = x^3+x^2+1$ that could be used as generator polynomial for our system.   A good polynomial generator needs to have the following characteristics:

  1. It should have at least two terms.
  2. The coefficient of the term x^0 should be 1.
  3. It should not divide x^t+1, for t between 2 and n − 1.
  4. It should have the factor $x + 1$.

First 3 are too short and not good enough but the last one decimal value $(13)_{10}$ binary $(1101)_2$ and the polynomial x^3+x^2+1 is best among them. As it can detect 3 bits of burst errors and able to detect two different single bit error in a code word. A code word with two isolated errors up to 8 bits apart can be detected by this generator. x^3+x^2+1 is better among others in respect of 4 bit   polynomial.

3   Considering Factor of Error Detection System for UWASNs

Our main issue is real time data communication in UWASNs. Due to low propagation speed of acoustic signal that causes very large end to end delay. If we can reduce the end-to-end delay then we can improve data throughput from our network. Equations used to our simulations parts.

$$\text{Data throughput}(\tau) = \frac{\text{Number of original data packets}}{\text{time to successfully send packets}}$$

One end-to-end cycle operation time (€) = number of original data packets / time to successfully send packets. So we want to use nibble size CRC for our UWASN system. It will reduce our pay load size compared to CRC-8, CRC-12, CRC-16, and CRC-32.

Energy Consumption
In UWASNs the energy is another important factor. The less size payload, less the energy consumes. Though it is very small, it will save small fraction of our energy in every cycle operation. Nibble-CRC consumes less energy than others.

$$\text{Energy Consumption} = \text{total transmitting time} \times \text{Unit Power}$$

Transmission Efficiency
In communication system this is the main factor that we pay attention in this paper. For receiving data is only very small as it collect some environmental information of water temperature of the river, P_H factor and Oxygen (O_2) level of some particular area.

$$\text{Transmission Efficiency} = \frac{\text{Information bytes}}{\text{Total bytes}}$$

High Channel Error Probability

In UWSNs error rate is also very high due to various types of noises, multipath problem and reliable data transport is a great problem. Some recent studies show that the end-to-end approach is in feasible for sensor networks. The high error channel probability makes the probability of successfully transferring data from end to end is uncertain as too many retransmission required for successful data delivery [13-15]. Our nibble CRC will need strong error detection mechanism that can detect errors in a certain level.

Limited hard ware infrastructural support likes lower data transmission speed and half duplex operation which is also a cause of slower communication [16-18]. The total time delay from base to sensor required time, usually takes tens of milliseconds [19].

4   Performance Analysis

Our packet size is 22 byte, modem speed is 200bps and the modem consume 2watt during data transmission and during lasting 0.75watt. Simulation area is 100m by 100m. Sound speed is 1500m/s, also channel error rate 20% for small data packets and 30 to 40% for large data packets.

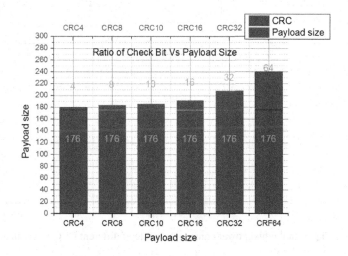

Fig. 1. Payload size with check bits

Our Figure 2 shows that power consumption rate of CRC-4 is lowest among others. Which help the lifespan of the deployed sensors and AUVs.

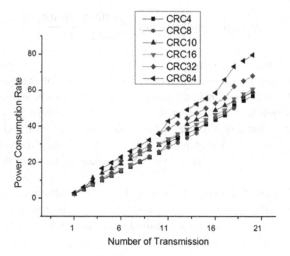

Fig. 2. Power consumption rate of different CRCs

Figure 3 shows power consumption between two sensors in fixed networks. CRC-4 consumes the lowest power in networks.

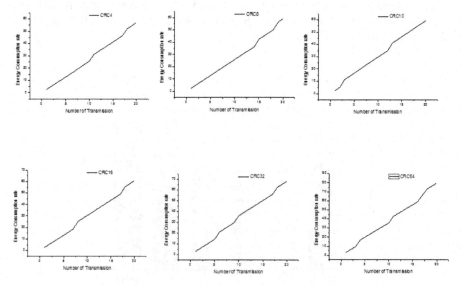

Fig. 3. Individual power consumption rate of different CRC mechanism

We illustrate 20 transmission with calculated transmission errors in respect of channel error rate based on small size CRC and large size. CRC32 and CRC64 3~4 times errors. And 2 times for CRC4, CRC8, CRC10 and CRC16. The performances of different type of CRC mechanisms are simulated and it was found that nibble CRC pay load size is the lowest among others. Our proposed nibble CRC, CRC-4 network efficiency rate is also better than others CRC-8 or CRC-16 or CRC-32 bit polynomial. But the error detection rate of our nibble CRC is not so good like CRC-8, CRC-16 or CRC-32 where 99.9984% error detection is possible [20]. But if we compare with RF based networks, (2010 bit: 128 bit) large size payload also ISO and IEEE declared as a standard error detection mechanism CRC-16 and CRC-32 for RF based networks. In underwater, our small size packets nibble size CRC may perform better as high channel error probability and peculiar underwater characteristics. Small amount of energy also can increase the life time of the sensor networks as we cannot recharge our battery.

5   Conclusion

In this paper, we try to find out a small size CRC that can be used for small size packet especially for underwater environment. CRC is well suited in the domain of error detection. Previously, we used CRC-8 for our lab experiment in our test bed and real deployment area. We observed our communication system in Han River, Seoul and other one location in Seoul and another city in Busan, Korea, in different distance and different location. We did not face any big difference though we change out location. This is first time we try to find smaller nibble size CRC and in the future we want to observe the performance of error detection rate and the performance of our nibble size CRC how it works in real fields.

References

1. Akyildiz, I.F., Pompili, D., Melodia, T.: Challenges for Efficient Communication in Underwater Acoustic Sensor Networks. ACM SIGBED Review 1(1) (July 2004)
2. Cui, J.-H., Kong, J., Gerla, M., Zhou, S.: Challenges: Building Scalable Mobile Underwater Wireless Sensor Networks for Aquatic Applications. Special Issue of IEEE Network on Wireless Sensor Networking (May 2006)
3. Heidemann, J., Ye, W., Wills, J., Syed, A., Li, Y.: Research Challenges and Applications for Underwater Sensor Networking. In: IEEE Wireless Communications and Networking Conference, Las Vegas, Nevada, USA (April 2006)
4. Proakis, J., Sozer, E., Rice, J.A., Stojanovic, M.: Shallow Water Acoustic Networks. IEEE Communications Magazines, 114–119 (November 2001)
5. Xie, G.G., Gibson, J.: A Networking Protocol for Underwater Acoustic Networks. In: Technical Report TR-CS-00-02, Department of Computer Science, Naval Postgraduate School (December 2000)
6. Park, S., Jo, B., Han, D.-S.: An Effective Mac Protocol for Data Collection in Underwater wireless sensor networks. In: Proceeding MILCOM 2009 Proceedings of the 28th IEEE Conference on Military communications (2009)
7. Khan, I.A., Yun, N.-Y., Muminov, S., Park, S.-H.: A Reliable Error Detection Mechanism in Underwater Acoustic Sensor Networks. In: Kim, J.-H., Lee, K., Tanaka, S., Park, S.-H. (eds.) AsiaSim2011. PICT, vol. 4, pp. 190–199. Springer, Heidelberg (2012)

8. Koopman, P., Chakravarty, T.: Cyclic Redundancy Code (CRC) Polynomial Selection for Embedded Networks. In: The International Conference on Dependable Systems and Networks, DSN 2004 (2004)
9. Liu, L., Zhou, S., Cui, J.-H.: Prospects and Problems of Wireless Com-munication for Underwater Sensor networks. Wiley WCMC Special Issue on Underwater Sensor Networks, INVITED (2008)
10. Anguita, D., Brizzolara, D., Parodi, G.: Prospects and Problems of Optical Diffuse Wireless Communication for Underwater Wireless Sensor Networks. Wireless Sensor Networks: Application-Centric Design
11. Xie, P., Cui, J.-H.: An FEC-based Reliable Data Transport Protocol for Underwater Sensor Networks. In: Proceeding of 16th International Conference on Computer Communications and Networks, ICCCN 2007 (2007)
12. Forouzan, B.: Data Communications and Networking, 4th edn (2007)
13. Freitag, L., Grund, M., Singh, S., Partan, J., Koski, P., Ball, K.: The WHOI Micro-Modem: An Acoustic Communications and Navigation System for Multiple Platforms. In: IEEE Oceans Conference, Washington DC (2005)
14. Wan, C.-Y., Campbell, A.T., Krishnamurthy, L.: PSFQ: A Reliable Transport Protocol for Wireless Sensor Networks. In: WSNA 2002, Atlanta,Georgia, USA (September 2002)
15. Kim, S., Fonseca, R., Culler, D.: Reliable Transfer on Wireless Sensor Networks. In: Frist IEEE International Conference on Sensor and Ad Hoc Communication and Networks, SECON 2004 (October 2004)
16. Shin, S.-W., Yun, N.-Y., Cho, H.-J., Kim, J.-E., Lee, J.-Y., Khan, I.A., Park, S.-H.: The UMO (Underwater Moving Object) Firmware Design and Implementation Based on Underwater Acoustic Communication. In: EUC 2011 (2011)
17. Yun, N.-Y., Kim, Y.-P., Muminov, S., Lee, J.-Y., Shin, S.Y., Park, S.-H.: Sync MAC Protocol to Control Underwater Vehicle Based on Underwater Acoustic Communication. In: EUC 2011 (2011)
18. Kim, Y.-P., Namgung, J.-I., Yun, N.-Y., Cho, H.-J., Khan, I.A., Park, S.-H.: Design and Implementation of the Test-bed for Underwater Acoustic Sensor Network Based on ARM9 Processor. In: EUC 2010 (2010)
19. Stann, F., Heidemann, J.: RMST: Reliable Data Transport in Sensor Networks. In: First IEEE International Workshop on Sensor Net Protocols and Applications(SNPA), Anchorage, Alaska, USA (May 2003)
20. Khan, I.A., Yun, N.-Y., Muminov, S., Park, S.-H., Kim, C.-H.: A Standard Error Detection Mechanism for Underwater Acoustic Sensor Networks. In: The 12th International Conference on Intelligent Autonomous System (IAS-12) Jeju Island, Korea

An Optimized Sub-texture Mapping Technique
for an Arbitrary Texture Considering Topology Relations

Sangyong Lee[1], Cheonshik Kim[2], and Seongah Chin[3,*]

[1] Department of Computer Science and Engineering, Korea University, Seoul, Korea
[2] Department of Computer Engineering, Sejong University, Seoul, Korea
[3] Division of Multimedia Engineering, Sungkyul University, Anyang-City, Korea
{xyleez,solideochin}@gmail.com, mipsan@paran.com

Abstract. In recent years, texture mapping techniques have become more advanced as providing real-time rendering tasks. However, few methods have been conducted in optimizing a sub-texture mapping for an arbitrary texture. In this paper, we present a method to optimize sub-texture mapping by reflecting topology relations in which an arbitrary sub-texture source has to be represented as minimizing distortions of the sub-texture source. We have defined a manipulating mechanism that helps a user control a texture source using a track ball interface in order to minimize loss of the texture source. And a sub-texture frame has to be aligned to dominant geometric structures of 3d model by employing some transformations. We have shown experimental results to verify the proposed method as well.

1 Introduction

In general, texture mapping is one of the fundamental techniques which are broadly used to enhance the final appearance of a 3d model by attaching a texture source into the 3d model. In recent years, 3d video games have extensively utilized some advanced texture mappings in real-time rendering such as normal mapping, parallax mapping and displacement mapping etc [1][2][3]. Even in game industry it is becoming more and more important to create cinematic appearance of digital scenes. In certain applications, we need to attach sub-textures like face paintings, scars, wounds, and decorations. Texture parameterization between a set of object mesh and a sub-texture source is critical to minimize texture stretch or texture deviation [4][5][6]. However very few researches concerning sub-texture mapping techniques for an arbitrary sub-texture have been reported, which implies they do not seem to reflect topology relations between the geometric structures of a 3d model and a sub-texture source. This fact causes some loss of the texture source that has to be appeared when the sub-texture source is clapped or scaled. If the sub-texture is larger than the region of meshes where a user wants to attach it then the source has no choice but to lose the boundary area. In the case we reduce the source image so that some parts mostly

---

* Corresponding author.

J.J. Park et al. (Eds.): NPC 2012, LNCS 7513, pp. 559–564, 2012.
© IFIP International Federation for Information Processing 2012

around the boundary of meshes would be filled with background source. In fact, we have to make alignment of the sub-texture source corresponding to the geometric structures by employing interactive interface manipulated by a general user in order to keep the sub-texture source as closely as we really want.

Hence, in this approach, we propose an optimized sub-texture mapping for an arbitrary texture by reflecting topology relations between a 3d models and a sub-texture source. The motivation of the approach is to avoid loss of the sub-texture source. At first, a trackball interface is defined to manipulate a 3d model, which helps a user control a texture source in order to minimize loss of the texture source. Rotation and scaling transformations are required to align the texture source to dominant geometric structures of 3d model. We have shown experimental results to verify the proposed method as well.

2   The Proposed Approach

The fundamental idea of the approach comes from how to attach a sub-texture image as is without losing any parts. A texture coordinate of a source image has to be accurately matched into a vertex on a 3d mesh model, where a user wishes to attach. However it is not easy to succeed in what we want since geometric structures of a 3d mesh model are not necessarily corresponding to a texture source frame. Hence, we have to seek a proper method to align a sub-texture source to suitable match of the vertices of a 3d model.

2.1   Trackball Interface

We have to keep in mind that a proper match between geometric structures of a 3d mesh and a sub-texture source needs to be solved when texture mapping is carried out. At first, we fix the sub-texture source on the screen then we have employed a trackball interface that makes us keep adjusting transformation of the 3d model until we acquire what we want to have with the sub-texture source. This trackball interface is suitable since it can provide flexible controls to let a user manipulate the 3d model.

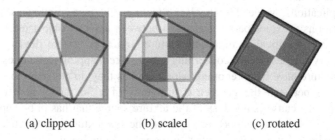

(a) clipped   (b) scaled   (c) rotated

Fig. 1. Variant occurrences of texture mapping

As shown in Fig. 1, there are several cases that we may expect when doing sub-texture mapping. A user picks a specific mesh on a 3d model where he wants to represent a sub-texture. A sub-texture can be clipped as shown in (a). Reduction of a sub-texture source is shown in (b). A wanted mapping appears in (c) after rotations of the sub-texture source. A user can utilize a trackball interface in an interactive way that may provide flexible control to match what they want to represent with a sub-texture by rotating the 3d model. In particular, it is critical to provide an accurate matching when a sub-texture source seems to be complex enough with sophisticated patterns since we do not want to expect lots of losing the sub-texture source. To realize a trackball interface, Eq. (1) is used.

$$R_{zyx} = R_z(\theta_z) R_y(\theta_y) R_x(\theta_x)$$

$$= \begin{bmatrix} \cos\theta_y \cos\theta_z & \sin\theta_x \sin\theta_y \cos\theta_z - \cos\theta_y \sin\theta_y & \cos\theta_x \sin\theta_y \cos\theta_z + \sin\theta_y \sin\theta_y \\ \cos\theta_y \sin\theta_z & \sin\theta_x \sin\theta_y \sin\theta_z + \cos\theta_x \cos\theta_z & \cos\theta_x \sin\theta_y \sin\theta_z - \sin\theta_x \cos\theta_z \\ -\sin\theta_y & \sin\theta_x \cos\theta_y & \cos\theta_x \cos\theta_y \end{bmatrix}, \quad (1)$$

where the rotation angles with x, y, and z axis are θ_x, θ_y and θ_z. And $R_x(\theta_x)$, $R_y(\theta_y)$ and $R_z(\theta_z)$ indicate the transformations of rotations.

2.2   Texture Alignment

Let a center mesh that a user clicks and wants to attach a sub-texture source be f_p source. This center mesh is composed of three line segments. Let the longest line segment be f_q among three line segments. Then we can acquire the rotation angle θ using inner product of two vectors as shown in Fig. 2(a). Once we have carried out the rotation then the sub-texture source is aligned to the mesh model. The final appearance looks as shown in Fig. 2 (b).

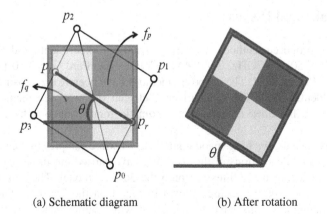

(a) Schematic diagram   (b) After rotation

Fig. 2. Conceptual diagram of rotation

2.3   Scaling Interface

If the mesh that a user selects is skewed and stretched along one direction and a sub-texture source is like a square or round shaped, we require a scaling transformation in order to represent the sub-texture sources that we want to attach. If we do not deal with the surroundings, then some parts of the sub-texture source cannot be appeared since the mesh looks skewed. To solve this, we understand that 3d coordinates on the mesh model are projected onto the screen coordinates. In the processing this procedure, the normalization has to be done using the maximum and minimum coordinates which will be used as texture coordinates. In Fig. 3, we display the conceptual diagrams to help us comprehend the approach of scaling. The mesh is shown in Fig. 3(a). Horizontal scaled texture mapping and vertical scaled one appear in Fig. 3(b) and (c) respectively given the texture source in (d). The screen coordinates can be translated into texture coordinates using Eq (2).

$$(x', y') = (\frac{x}{\max(x) - \min(x)}, \frac{y}{\max(y) - \min(y)}), \qquad (2)$$

where (x, y) is the screen coordinates and $(x'y')$ is the texture coordinate.

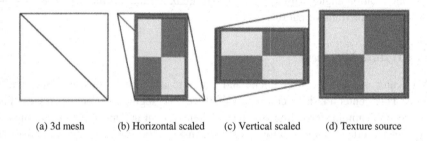

| (a) 3d mesh | (b) Horizontal scaled | (c) Vertical scaled | (d) Texture source |

Fig. 3. Conceptual diagram of scaling

3   Results and Discussion

To verify the proposed methods, we have carried out experiments under Intel Core (TM) i5 CPU 750@2.67GHz, 2.99RAM, NVIDIA GeoFore GTS 250 (VGA) with Windows XP Professional. The proposed methods have been realized using Microsoft MFC and OpenGL API. The comparisons between the proposed methods and the general method that does not consider automatic transformations have been conducted.

In the experiments, we have made a number of texture samples that can be used in face paintings and decorations of the face. We have carried out the proposed texture mapping by attaching the sub-texture onto the 3d face model. The sub-textures are composed of face painting pictures shown in Fig. 4 on the first row. Face painting sub-texture mapping results have been created with scaling factors 1, 0.9, and 0.8 shown in the first, second and third respectively from the left in Fig. 4. The proposed

method and mesh models are shown in the fourth and last column in Fig. 4. As we
have shown here, the proposed method creates the sub-textures as good as the original
ones comparing to the other results mostly showing loss of the sub-textures.

Fig. 4. The first row shows the sub-texture sources. Face painting sub-texture mapping results
are shown with scaling factors 1, 0.9, and 0.8 in the first three columns. The proposed method
and mesh models are shown in the fourth and last from the left column.

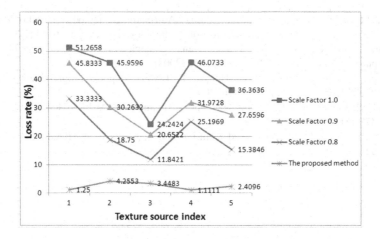

Fig. 5. Loss rate comparisons

In Fig. 5, we have shown loss rate (%) comparisons computed by the number of loss mesh in Fig. 4 indicating that the proposed method in the fourth column in Fig. 4, shows better loss rate than others created by scaling factors observed in the first, second and third column in Fig. 4.

Authors want to mention that mesh tagging tasks are skipped in this article, which will be reported in the other article, since mesh tagging tasks required for sub-texture mapping are beyond the scope of the proposed method.

4   Concluding Remarks

In this paper, we present a technique that makes it possible to automatically create an optimized sub-texture mapping. This basic idea is from matching topology relations between geometric structures of a 3d model and a sub-texture source. The approach starts with providing a trackball interface that utilize a convenient user control when texture mapping. Once a user gains a sub-texture source then a 3d model can be manipulated using the trackball functions until the user is satisfied with the texture appearance. This functionality makes the sub-textures be as good as the appearance the user wants to attach with keeping the sub-texture source as much as we represent.

Acknowledgement. This work was partially supported by Korea Science and Engineering Foundation (NRF) grant funded by the Korean government (No. 2012-0002889).

References

1. Sloan, P.: Normal Mapping for Precomputed Radiance Transfer. In: Proceedings of the 2006 Symposium on Interactive 3D Graphics and Games, pp. 23–26. ACM, New York (2006)
2. Gao, R., Yin, B., Kong, D., Zhang, Y., Si, H.: An Improved Method of Parallax Mapping. In: IEEE Conf. on Computer and Information Technology, Sydney, pp. 30–34 (2008)
3. Szirmay-Kalos, L., Umenhoffer, T.: Displacement Mapping on the GPU — State of the Art. Computer Graphics Forum 27(6), 1567–1592 (2008)
4. Sander, P., Snyder, J., Gortler, S., Hoppe, H.: Texture Mapping Progressive Meshes. In: ACM SIGGRAPH 2001, pp. 409–416 (2001)
5. Praun, E., Finkelstein, A., Hoppe, H.: Lapped Textures. In: ACM SIGGRAPH 2000, pp. 465–470 (2000)
6. Neyret, F., Cani, M.: Pattern-based texturing revisited. In: ACM SIGGRAPH 1999, pp. 235–242 (1999)

Research on a Smart Input Device Using Multimodal Bio-signal Interface

HyunJu Lee[1], Taehyun Kim[1], Dongkyoo Shin[1], HeeWon Park[2],
Soohan Kim[2], and DongIl Shin[1,*]

[1] Dept.of Computer Engineering and Science, Sejong University,
In 98 Gunja-Dong, Gwangjin-Gu, Korea
[2] Samsung Electronics Co., LTD VD R&D,
416 Metan-3 dong, Yeongtong-gu, Suwon-city, Korea
{nedkelly,crowlid82}@gce.sejong.ac.kr,
{shindk,dshin}@sejong.ac.kr, {Heewonpark,ksoohan}@samsung.com

Abstract. This paper presents a smart input device based on multimodal analysis methods using human bio-signals. The core of the smart input device is software modules, which consist of an intelligent driving function and an analysis processing function for bio-signals. The smart input device utilizes a multimodal interface that analyzes and recognizes human bio-signal patterns. The multimodal analysis system can recognize a user's emotional and stress status by analyzing an electrocardiogram (ECG), and it can determine the user's level of concentration from electroencephalogram (EEG) patterns. To analyze the concentration, stress, and emotional status of the user, the EEG rendering system and ECG analysis system use five signal values, i.e., MID_BETA, THETA, ALPHA, DELTA, GAMMA, and the P, Q, R, S and T waves. A reformation of SVM and a clustering algorithm were applied to the user's EEG and ECG signal patterns for body context recognition. In our experiment, the on/ off status of the user's stress status controls the difficulties of the game, such as the selecting the type of race course or the number of obstacles. In addition, the speed of the car can be controlled depending on the concentration or non-concentration status of the user. The stress status of the user was predicted with an accuracy of 83.2% by the K-means algorithm, and the concentration status was predicted with an accuracy of 71.85% by the SVM algorithm. We showed that a bio-signal interface is quite useful and feasible for new games.

1   Introduction

Today, even though computer science and technology in the 21st century are developing very rapidly, humans still know themselves only to a very limited extent. Most of all, advances in human computer interaction and virtual reality techniques are very important. Computing environments are moving to the human body or to human

---

* Corresponding author.

J.J. Park et al. (Eds.): NPC 2012, LNCS 7513, pp. 565–574, 2012.
© IFIP International Federation for Information Processing 2012

residence space from computer space in hardware development. Until intelligence inundates "to create intelligence how" the problem which is than "to deliver how" to be important, this becomes conclusion with problem of interface. Currently, it is entering the stage in which the progress of technique surpasses users' requirements, so the interface will become an efficient means for reducing the gap between the product and the user. Renovation of the interface will become an efficient means of making a priority of the effect over performance upgrade. The multimodal biology interface uses analyzed ECG and EEG signal results. Making the multimodal biology interface technique more natural and effective is the focus of the field of virtual reality, which has been developed with techniques associated with the visual/ auditory sense centers. Biofeedback games use various sensor links in the body, and the user's electroencephalogram/ electrocardiogram/ electromyograms signals are reflected in real time. Preschoolers and disabled people, for example, find existing edutainment contents difficult to use (e.g., by keyboard, mouse). The multimodal biology interface is based on this new concept, so production paradigms of the new contents are needed.

This paper presents a smart input device that consists of a multimodal signal processing interface. For this study, equipment was used to measure the user's EEG and ECG signals, which are used to determine the condition of the driver. A smart device is used to ensure safe driving and to prevent risks to the driver. Users can know location using normalized values between 0 to 100. At the same time, an ECG is used to determine the emotional state and stress of the user while the user is concentrating on driving. Acquiring such biological information is applicable to the existing embodied system based on Bayesian theory. This device is suitable for driving whether or not there is a follow-up operation based on the user's location. During the process, a safe angle of rotation and safe vehicle speeds are cleverly controlled. So, the input device environment that is provided is able to cope with any emergency situations that the user may encounter. A similar situation occurred in the present experiment compared with the previous simulation environment. So, the intelligent module distinguishes the event once or repeats it by checking section status and using stored data. The intelligent module determines whether the event is temporary or ongoing. Finally, the intelligent module warns of a rapid change in risk in a specific section based on degree of similarity value.

In chapter 3 explains the composition of multimodal biology interface. Section 4 presents the results of an experimental evaluation of clustering accuracy using the reformed k-means based on EM algorithm to compare human emotion recognition performance.

2   Previous Work

The complexity context of the human body's signals to interactively recognize emotions relies on the detection of a physiological change attributable to an affective stimulus, followed by adequate classification of the change. Previously, most of the methods used to classify emotions using physiological signals have been based on off-line analysis of statistical features extracted from large quantities of data [1]. Systems to dynamically detect, classify, and utilize emotions, based on instantaneous responses from the input device, are still lacking. Using a combination of auto associative neural networks (AANNs) and sequential analysis, a novel mechanism was developed to detect changes in physiological signals associated with emotional states [2]. Brain Computer Interface (BCI) technology represents a rapidly growing field of research, with applications ranging from prosthetics and control systems to medical diagnostics. In this research, the experiment considers only BCI technologies that use sensors that measure and interpret brain activity (commonly referred to as neural bio-recorders [5]) as a source of input. The oldest established method of neural bio-recording, which was developed in 1927 by Berger [4], is the application of electrodes that survey the changes in field potential over time arising from synaptic currents. "In 2003, taxonomy by Mason and Birch identified MEG, PET, and fMRI as unsuitable for BCI applications, due to the equipment required to perform and analyze the scan in real time, but more recent attempts to use fMRI as a BCI input device have demonstrated significant future potential in this area [3]." Brain-computer interfaces have become a topic of research interest, both as a means for obtaining user input and for studying responses to stimuli.

In our research, we controlled the speed of the car by concentration value of brain signals and the color of the car by emotional context at driving simulation content. Also, when the stress value was excessively high, the car files for overcome obstacles.

3   Design of Smart Input Device Using Physiological Signals

3.1   Acquisition Devices of Physiological Signals

We developed two different devices to measure EEG and ECG signals. The device on the right upside of Fig. 1 acquires brainwave signals from the frontal lobe of the brain. The four sensors must be attached to the forehead positions of the human brain. The EEG device has four channels with electrode disposition. To acquire the users' ECG signals, we also developed the ECG sensor device. The device on the left upside of Fig. 1 was used to measures the user's ECG signals. Both devices send the detected signals to a computer by Bluetooth.

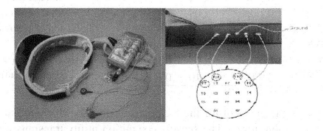

Fig. 1. The External of EEG(right) and ECG(left) sensor device

3.2   Overall Architecture

Software modules were divided into two parts. The first part is the network software module with an I/O device, and the second part is the context manager software module for biometric data. The first part has two base modules, i.e., a client module and a server module. The client module consist of an EEG/ ECG network, and it has three modules, i.e., the initialize module, the connect module, and the data manager module. The data manager module takes charge of the radio communication data reception department, a data processing department, and the data transmission department. The server module consists of modules that interpolate game contents. The contents network server module also has three parts, i.e., an initializer module to initialize the server, a client manager module that manages the EEG/ ECG data from the client module, and a module for receiving data from the client with a Command Processor that processes the received data. According to concentration values in the range of 0 – 100, it transmits SPEED_UP or SPEED_DOWN commands and the value of the contents. Thus, it is possible to control the speed of the car in the game through concentration. The brain wave extraction is so advanced that it can extract an electromyogram signal from the blinking of the eyes.

Eye blinking occurs at regular intervals, and it delivers a left-turn command to contents. When the eye is winked twice, a right-turn command is delivered to contents. In addition, it recognizes emotion and the changes in emotion that results from the color of the car, i.e., a happy state was associated with a red car, and a sad or fearful state was associated with a blue car. Table 1 provides a definition of the interlock protocol for the physiological signal I/O device between software modules and contents. This emotion feedback technique is useful in additional contents, e.g., games and simulations. For instance, if the users are hiding from an enemy, the enemy can locate them when their emotions (stress, fear) are heightened. Thus, it is important for the mind to be calm.

Table 1. Interlock protocol list of the device

Command	To Server	From Client ACK	From Client Value	Comment
SPEED_UP	0 x 02	0 x 02	0 ~ 100	Concentration Value
SPEED_DOWN	0 x 03	0 x 03	0 ~ 100	
LEFT	0 x 04	0 x 04		Blink one time
RIGHT	0 x 05	0 x 05		Blink two times
FLY ON	0 x 06	0 x 06	0 ~ 100	Stress and Non Stress State
FLY DOWN	0 x 07	0 x 07	0 ~ 100	
HAPPY	0 x 09	0 x 09	0 ~ 100	Analyze Emotion as 2 Part
SAD	0 x 10	0 x 10	0 ~ 100	(Happy, Sad)

Table 2 shows the protocol for the ECG sensor device, which communicates with the sensor recognition utility. The sensor recognition utility transmits one byte value (0 x 08 and 0 x 09) to the electrocardiogram sensor to acquire the user's temperature and pulse.

Table 2. Command list of the ECG device

Command	To Sensor	From Sensor				Command
		ACK	#1	#2	#3	
Sensor on	0 x 03	0 x 30				Power On
Sensor off	0 x 04	0 x 40				Power Off
Normal Mode	0 x 05	0 x 50				Set up Normal Mode
Stream Mode	0 x 06	0 x 6F	#D1	#D2	...	Set up Stream Mode
Battery Status	0 x 07	0 x 71	#B			Battery(MIN)0 x 00~0 x ff(MAX)

Fig. 2 shows the structure of the context manager for various signals (e.g., biology). The context manager processes context in two steps to analyse the pattern of the various contexts acquired from the sensor devices. First, the context extractor normalizes the seven contexts between 0.1 and 0.9; all normalized contexts are used as input values to the predictor. Second, the context manager stores all contexts in the database for creation of association rules.

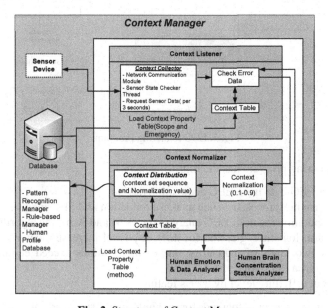

Fig. 2. Structure of Context Manager

The design of the biometric (EEG, ECG) analyzing algorithm has three parts, as listed below:

1) Normalization Module: In about biometric signal from person deviation by normal function
2) Post-Processing Module: Analysis function of wavelet by signals/ nonlinear dynamics/ high dimensional statistical/ Laplacian mapping
3) Analytical Study Module: Analytical function of user's intention about biometric signals

4   Experimental Environment

4.1   Implementation of Physiological Analysis Program

We are developing a program to analyze a user's concentration status from brainwave signals. Fig. 3 shows the program that classifies EEG signals. It measures the dimension of the power of concentration with EEG signals, and it finds the direction in which the power of concentration is displayed by winking the eye. This program can identify concentration easily to use progress bar. Also, we can detect the blink action from an image on the screen.

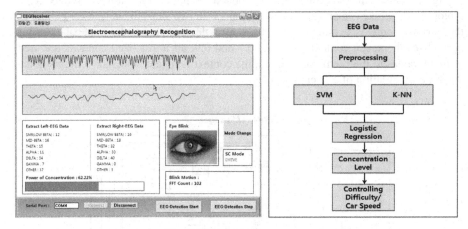

Fig. 3. EEG rendering program

The EEG rendering program has the following steps:

1) Input EEG data from EEG acquisition device
2) Perform pre-processing such as noise reduction and FFT analysis
3) Computation result of EEG analysis by SVM and K-means algorithm
4) Perform logistic regression for difficulty level increase/ decrease expression then two kinds of indicators, one or more values exceed certain limits of concentration status
5) Output difficulty level by user's feeling

We used a non-parametic method for quantitative assessment of the EEG. Fast Fourier transformation can be used to convert the time-domain function to a frequency-domain function.

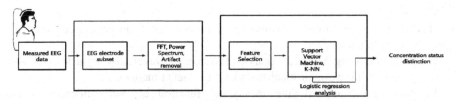

Fig. 4. System architecture for mining the EEG feature

Fig. 5 shows how the ECG signals are acquired and analyzed. This program assesses and displays the user's current state of emotion or stress.

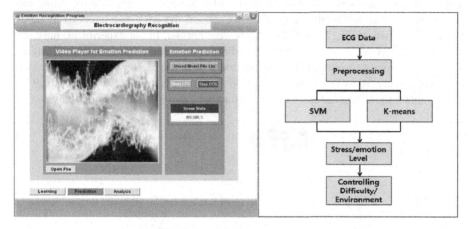

Fig. 5. Human Emotion Analyzer

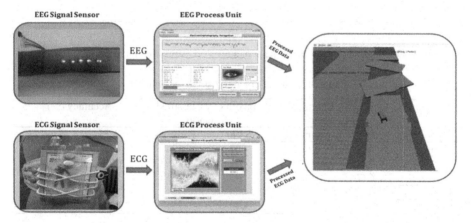

Fig. 6. Overview of contents apply multimodal biology interface

Fig. 6 shows the overview screen of the contents applied in the multimodal biology interface. The direction of the input device was decided by an eye blink (EMG signal) of the user, and the input device moves according to the state of intensity of the EEG. Further, when the user feels plentiful concentration or is stressed, the input device slows down or overcomes obstacles with its flying skill, embodied with the artificial intelligence model.

4.2   Performance Results

The EM-based, K-means algorithm, which is applied in this experiment and see reformation, uses unsupervised learning with supervised learning algorithms. To verify the performance of the Human Emotion Analyzer, we used a protein data set as the input value of the human emotion analyzer. The Human Emotion Analyzer acquires electrocardiogram data (P, Q, R, S, and T waves) from the electrocardiogram sensor device and applies the peak of all waves and the RRV (r-r interval) as input values. As shown in Fig. 7, all distributions were normal. In our experiment, only the R-R interval and the R peak showed small differences in emotion and stress changes. The neural emotion showed the highest accuracy, with the range of the three emotions at approximately 56 to 75%. Stress recognition showed a high performance result of 83%. Table 3 shows the accuracy of the performance results based on our analysis.

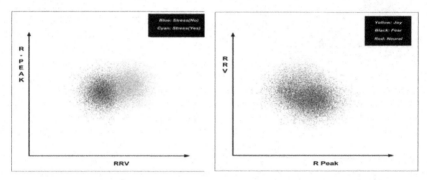

Fig. 7. Distribution of RRV and R peak of stress/ non stress and three emotions states

Table 3. Result of emotion / stress recognition

Emotion	Correctly Classified Instances		Incorrectly Classified Instances		Accuracy (%)	
Algorithm	SVM	K-means	SVM	K-means	SVM	K-means
Fear	503	662	683	524	42.4	55.8
Neural	737	891	449	295	62.1	75.1
Joy	637	801	549	385	53.7	67.5
Stress(yes)	1058	1247	440	251	70.6	83.2
Stress(no)	1058	1247	440	251	70.6	83.2

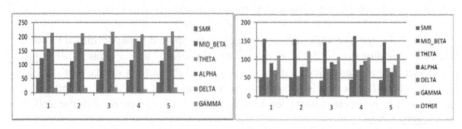

Fig. 8. Brain wave data of non-concentration state (left) and concentration state (right)

Fig. 8 show experimental data of the non-concentration and concentration states from brain waves, respectively. The EEG rendering system extracts the brain wave feature set using the FFT algorithm. Before we decrease error factor by trend removal technique.

The concentration formula is as follows:

$$\text{Concentration Indicators} = \text{Power Ratio of (SMR + M − Beta) / Theta} \qquad (1)$$

Theta rhythm decreases in the concentration state, and the SMR and Mid-beta rhythms indicate increases in unfocused and focused attention, respectively. Therefore, focus indicators can be quantified by the ratio of (SMR + M − beta rhythm) to Theta rhythm. Also, we convert absolute power to relative power of the FFT value for sophisticated results. The EEG rendering program calculates the concentration distinction value using SVM and the K-NN algorithm. The SVM in these experiments used the set of parameters that resulted in the highest correct rate of classification among all SVMs tested. SVMs were tested with RBF kernels with σ = 0.5. The SVMs were trained and tested using Platt's sequential minimal optimization (SMO) algorithms [6, 7, 8].

Table 4. Result of concentration recognition

Classifier	Concentration State	Non-Concentration State	Average Accuracy (%)
SVM	71.5	72.2	71.85
k-NN	67.5	71.3	69.40

5   Conclusion and Future Work

In this paper, we have reported efforts to produce architecture for building intelligent content effects that have more efficiency than the requirement of a user's status recognition and an expedient environment. This paper describes an intelligence and complexity context analysis system using ECG and EEG patterns. The Human Emotion Analyzer evaluates differences in emotion or stress levels. We also demonstrated a sensor device that acquires continuous brainwave signals from the frontal lobe.

In this experiment, we developed a technique that analyzes the multimodal physiological signal for contents. In this paper, we proposed a method for supplying optimized information within a car and provided analysis of human body biometric signals in a driving environment to allow a user to become easily live in comport to driving in the contents. Also, physical value examined theory to achieve basic physics feedback anything. Technology than can analyzes brain waves and recognize the status of the human body is very important and can provide a foundation for research in the future. The analysis method and the intelligent system presented in this paper can be used in a wide range of diverse fields of study in future research work.

Acknowledgments. This research is supported by Ministry of Culture, Sports and Tourism(MCST) and Korea Creative Content Agency(KOCCA) in the Culture Technology(CT) Research & Development Program 2009.

References

1. Picard, R., Vyzaz, E., Healey, J.: Toward Machine Emotional Intelligence/ Analysis of Affective Physiological State. IEEE Transl. Pattern Analysis and Machine Intelligence 23(10), 1175–1191 (2001)
2. Kramer, M.A.: Auto associative Neural Networks. Computers and Chemical Engineering 16(4), 313–328 (1992)
3. Vaughan, T., et al.: Brain-computer interface technology: a review of the second international meeting. IEEE Transactions on Neural Systems and Rehabilitation Engineering 2, 94–109 (2003)
4. Haynes, J.D., Rees, G.: Decoding mental states from brain activity in humans. Nature Neuroscience 7(7) (2006)
5. Poli, R., Cinel, C., Citi, L., Sepulveda, F.: Evolutionary Brain Computer Interfaces. In: Giacobini, M. (ed.) EvoWorkshops 2007. LNCS, vol. 4448, pp. 301–310. Springer, Heidelberg (2007)
6. Platt, J.C.: Fast training of support vector machines using sequential minimal optimization. In: Scholkopf, B., Burges, C., Smola, A. (eds.), Advances in Kernel Methods—Support Vector Learning, pp. 185–208. MIT Press, Cambridge (1998)
7. Platt, J.C.: Using analytic QP and sparseness to speed training of support vector machines. In: Kearns, M.S., Solla, S.A., Cohn, D.A. (eds.) Advances in Neural Information Processing Systems, vol. 11, MIT Press, Cambridge (1999)
8. Platt, J.C., Nello Cristianini, N., Shawe-Taylor, J.: Large margin DAG's for multiclass classification. In: Solla, S.A., Leen, T.K., Müller, K.-R. (eds.) Advances in Neural Information Processing Systems, vol. 12, pp. 547–553. MIT Press, Cambridge (2000)

Cryptanalysis of an RFID Tag Search Protocol Preserving Privacy of Mobile Reader

Eun-Jun Yoon[*]

Department of Cyber Security, Kyungil University,
33 Buho-Ri, Hayang-Ub, Kyungsan-Si, Kyungsangpuk-Do 712-701, Republic of Korea
ejyoon@kiu.ac.kr

Abstract. RFID tag search system can be used to find a particular tag among numerous tags. In 2011, Chun et al. proposed an RFID tag search protocol preserving privacy of mobile reader holders. Chun et al. claimed that their proposed protocol can withstand five attacks to be considered in serverless search protocols, such as tracking, cloning, eavesdropping, physical, and Denial of Service (DoS) attacks. However, this paper points out that the Chun et al.'s protocol still can be vulnerable to the DoS attack.

Keywords: RFID, Privacy, DoS attack, Serverless search, Passive tag.

1   Introduction

Recently, Radio frequency identification (RFID) technology has been applied to many real-life applications [1]. Basically, RFID technology is used to identify RFID tags automatically. RFID tag search system can be used to find a particular tag among numerous tags [2,3]. RFID tag search system has many applications such as inventory management, supply chain, and search for books in the library. In 2009, Tan et al. [4] proposed secure serverless search protocols to treat the security and privacy concerns in RFID tag search system. Tan et al.'s protocols enable users with mobile readers to search specific tags even though the mobile readers cannot connect to a backend server. Tan et al.'s protocols also provide the robustness against the losses of mobile readers. Since mobile readers can be easily lost or stolen, the losses of mobile readers lead to leakage of sensitive information such as identifiers or secret keys of tags. Various RFID tag search protocols [5–9] have been proposed to meet security and privacy requirements based on Tan et al.'s protocols.

In 2011, Chun et al.[9] proposed a new RFID tag search protocol which can preserve privacy of mobile reader holders unlike related protocols. In the security analysis, Chun et al. claimed that their proposed protocol can withstand five attacks to be considered in serverless search protocols, such as tracking, cloning, eavesdropping,

---

[*] Corresponding author.

J.J. Park et al. (Eds.): NPC 2012, LNCS 7513, pp. 575–580, 2012.
© IFIP International Federation for Information Processing 2012

physical, and Denial of Service (DoS) attacks. However, this paper points out that the Chun et al.'s protocol still can be vulnerable to the DoS attack.

The paper is organized as follows. Section 2 reviews the Chun et al.'s RFID tag search protocol and then shows its weakness in Section 3. Finally, Section 4 concludes the paper.

2   Review of Chun et al.'s RFID Tag Search Protocol

The Chun et al.'s RFID tag search protocol is composed of two phases, which are an initial setup and a tag search. In the initial setup phase, from a backend server, each reader receives an access list of which each entry is encrypted with the identifiers of the reader and a tag. Then, in the tag search phase, the reader searches a specific tag using this list. Some of the notations used in the Chun et al.'s protocol are defined as follows:

- R_j, T_i : Mobile RFID reader and tag, respectively.
- RD_j, ID_i : Identity of R_j and T_i, respectively.
- $SE = (E, D)$: Efficient symmetric encryption algorithm, e.g. AES-128.
- t_i : Secret encryption key of the RFID tag T_i
- λ : Bit length of a plaintext and a ciphertext.
- $x \leftarrow E_t(m)$: A deterministic polynomial-time algorithm that takes as input a symmetric key $t \in \kappa_D$ and a message $m \in \{0,1\}^\lambda$, outputs a ciphertext $x \in \{0,1\}^\lambda$.
- $m \leftarrow D_t(x)$: A deterministic polynomial-time algorithm that takes as input a private key t and a ciphertext x, outputs a plaintext m.
- $\oplus$: Bit-wise exclusive-OR (XOR) operation.

2.1   Initial Setup Phase

The phase consists of two parts. The first part is performed to generate information for an RFID tag T_i and the second for a mobile reader R_j.

S.1 For each RFID tag T_i, the backend server generates a tag identifier ID_i and a secret encryption key t_i and then stores the pair (ID_i, t_i) with the additional tag information into its own central database. Each tag T_i stores the pair (ID_i, t_i).

S.2 For a mobile reader R_j, the backend server generates an access list L_j as follows: If the mobile reader R_j is assumed to access to the tags $T_i (1 \leq i \leq n)$, the backend server computes each ciphertext $E_{t_i}(RD_j \oplus ID_i)$ for $i = 1,...,n$ by encrypting $RD_j \oplus ID_i$ with the secret key t_i under the given encryption algorithm $E()$. Then, the backend server adds the pairs $(ID_i, E_{t_i}(RD_j \oplus ID_i))$ $(1 \le i \le n)$ in the access list L_j. The backend server also transmits the access list L_j to the mobile reader R_j over a secure channel.

Table 1. Access list L_j for a mobile reader R_j

ID	PW
ID_1	$E_{t_i}(RD_j \oplus ID_1)$
ID_2	$E_{t_i}(RD_j \oplus ID_2)$
...	...
ID_n	$E_{t_i}(RD_j \oplus ID_n)$

2.2   Tag Search Phase

The Chun et al.'s tag search protocol is illustrated in Fig. 1 and is performed as follows:

T.1 $R_j \rightarrow T_i$: $\alpha \| n_r$

When R_j wants to search T_i, R_j first chooses a λ-bit random number n_r and computes $\alpha = E_{ID_i}(RD_j \oplus n_r)$, then broadcasts $\alpha \| n_r$ to T_i.

T.2 $T_i \rightarrow R_j$: $\beta \| n_t$

Each tag T_i who receives a message $\alpha \| n_r$ obtains RD_j by computing $D_{ID_i}(\alpha) \oplus n_r = D_{ID_i}(E_{ID_i}(RD_j \oplus n_r)) \oplus n_r$ using its own identifier ID_i and n_r. Then, each tag T_i computes $K_i = E_{t_i}(RD_j \oplus ID_i) \oplus n_r$ with its own secret key t_i. Finally, each tag T_i chooses a λ-bit random number n_t and computes $\beta = E_{K_i}(ID_i \oplus n_t)$, then sends $\beta \| n_t$ to R_j.

T.3 R_j computes $K_i = E_{t_i}(RD_j \oplus ID_i) \oplus n_r$ using the random number n_r chosen before and the stored value $E_{t_i}(RD_j \oplus ID_i)$ in the access list L_j. Then, R_j obtains ID_i' by computing $D_{K_i}(\beta) \oplus n_t = D_{K_i}(E_{K_i}(ID_i \oplus n_t)) \oplus n_t$ using K_i and n_t. Finally, R_j checks whether $ID_i' ? = ID_i$ or not. If $ID_i' == ID_i$ then R_j knows that T_i exists nearby R_j.

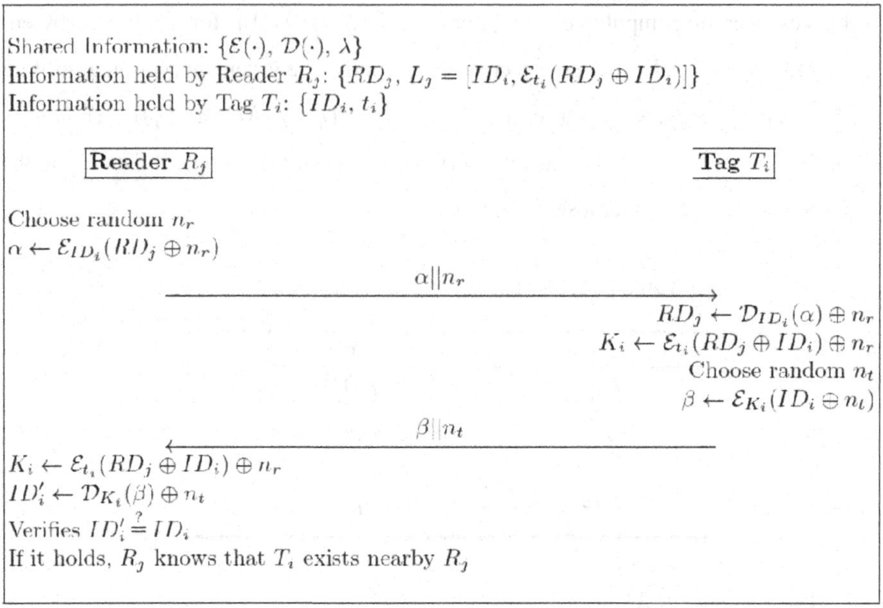

Shared Information: $\{\mathcal{E}(\cdot), \mathcal{D}(\cdot), \lambda\}$
Information held by Reader R_j: $\{RD_j, L_j = [ID_i, \mathcal{E}_{t_i}(RD_j \oplus ID_i)]\}$
Information held by Tag T_i: $\{ID_i, t_i\}$

| Reader R_j | | Tag T_i |

Choose random n_r
$\alpha \leftarrow \mathcal{E}_{ID_i}(RD_j \oplus n_r)$

$$\xrightarrow{\quad \alpha \| n_r \quad}$$

$\qquad\qquad\qquad\qquad\qquad\qquad RD_j \leftarrow \mathcal{D}_{ID_i}(\alpha) \oplus n_r$
$\qquad\qquad\qquad\qquad\qquad\qquad K_i \leftarrow \mathcal{E}_{t_i}(RD_j \oplus ID_i) \oplus n_r$
$\qquad\qquad\qquad\qquad\qquad\qquad$ Choose random n_t
$\qquad\qquad\qquad\qquad\qquad\qquad \beta \leftarrow \mathcal{E}_{K_i}(ID_i \ominus n_t)$

$$\xleftarrow{\quad \beta \| n_t \quad}$$

$K_i \leftarrow \mathcal{E}_{t_i}(RD_j \oplus ID_i) \oplus n_r$
$ID_i' \leftarrow \mathcal{D}_{K_i}(\beta) \oplus n_t$
Verifies $ID_i' \stackrel{?}{=} ID_i$
If it holds, R_j knows that T_i exists nearby R_j

Fig. 1. Chun et al.'s RFID tag search protocol

3   Denial of Service Attack against Chun et al.'s Protocol

The Chun et al.'s RFID tag search protocol is vulnerable to Denial of Service (DoS) attack. DoS attack is one category of attacks on RFID systems. An adversary tries to find ways to fail target tag from receiving services. Almost all resources in an RFID system can become target of the DoS attack, including tag, reader, or backend server. Attacks on the air interface include shielding tags, flooding the reader field with a multitude of tags or selectively jamming the reader field. The goal is usually to sabotage specific resources of an RFID system, such a digital supply chain, effectively making the system unavailable to its intended users.

In the tag search phase, all tags T_i nearby a mobile reader R_j must respond to the request of R_j. Especially, in Step T.2 of the Chun et al.'s RFID tag search phase, all tags T_i always must compute 3 times symmetric encryption operations to respond the request of R_j. These computations can be vulnerable to the following an adversary Adv's DoS attack which is illustrated in Fig. 2.

A.1 $Adv \rightarrow T_i: \ \alpha \| n_r$

Suppose that an adversary Adv intercepts $\alpha \| n_r$ from Step T.1. Adv broadcasts $\alpha \| n_r$ to T_i.

A.2 $T_i \rightarrow Adv$: $\beta \parallel n_t$

All tags T_i nearby Adv will respond to the request of Adv as follows:

Each tag T_i who receives a message $\alpha \parallel n_r$ will obtain RD_j by computing $D_{ID_i}(\alpha) \oplus n_r = D_{ID_i}(E_{ID_i}(RD_j \oplus n_r)) \oplus n_r$ using its own identifier ID_i and n_r. Then, each tag T_i will compute $K_i = E_{t_i}(RD_j \oplus ID_i) \oplus n_r$ with its own secret key t_i. Finally, each tag T_i will choose a λ -bit random number n_t and compute $\beta = E_{K_i}(ID_i \oplus n_t)$, then send $\beta \parallel n_t$ to Adv.

A.3 Adv drops $\beta \parallel n_t$ and then broadcasts $\alpha \parallel n_r$ to T_i continuously until success DoS attack.

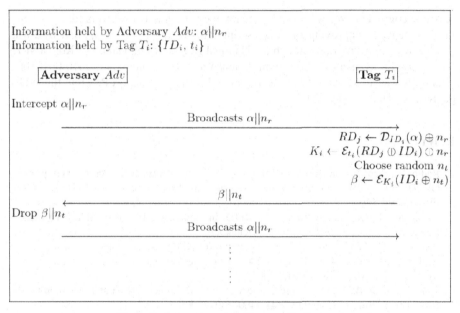

Fig. 2. DoS Attack against Chun et al.'s Protocol

From the computation results of above Step A.2, we can see that all tags T_i automatically must compute 3 times symmetric encryption operations to respond the request of Adv. These 3 times symmetric encryption operations of the RFID passive tag T_i can be quite expensive operations because T_i uses a low-power microcontroller for sensing and communication with the RFID reader R_j.

Therefore, if Adv broadcasts the intercepted $\alpha \parallel n_r$ continuously, all tags T_i cannot respond to the request of the legitimate leaders. Moreover, Adv can simply perform the above described DoS attack by choosing a random $\alpha^* \| n_r^*$ without intercepting the R_j's sending message $\alpha \| n_r$.

As a result, the Chun et al.'s RFID tag search protocol is vulnerable to the above described DoS attacks.

4   Conclusions

This paper analyzed the security of Chun et al.'s RFID tag search protocol preserving privacy of mobile reader holders. We presented a denial of service (DoS) attack against this protocol. Further works will be focused on improving the protocol which can not only withstand the DoS attack but also provide more computational efficiency.

Acknowledgments. We would like to thank the anonymous reviewers for their helpful comments in improving our manuscript. This research was supported by Basic Science Research Program through the National Research Foundation of Korea(NRF) funded by the Ministry of Education, Science and Technology(No. 2010-0010106). This study was also supported by the Intramural Research Support Program funded by the Kyungil University in 2012.

References

1. Radio Frequency Identification(RFID).: A focus on information security and privacy. OECDWorking Party on Information Security and Privacy, DSTI/ICCP/REG (2007)9/FINAL, 70 (2008)
2. Vaudenay, S.: On Privacy Models for RFID. In: Kurosawa, K. (ed.) ASIACRYPT 2007. LNCS, vol. 4833, pp. 68–87. Springer, Heidelberg (2007)
3. Feldhofer, M., Wolkerstorfer, J.: Strong crypto for RFID tags-a comparison of low-power hardware implementations. In: Proc. 2007 IEEE International Symposium on Circuits and Systems (ISCAS), pp. 1839–1842 (2007)
4. Tan, C., Sheng, B., Li, Q.: Secure and serverless RFID authentication and search protocols. IEEE Trans. Wireless Commun. 7(4), 1400–1407 (2008)
5. Ahamed, S.I., Rahman, F., Hoque, E., Kawsar, F., Nakajima, T.: 3PR: secure server-less search protocols for RFID. In: Proc. 2nd International Conference on Information Security and Assurance (ISA), pp. 187–192 (2008)
6. Ahamed, S.I., Rahman, F., Hoque, E., Kawsar, F., Nakajima, T.: Secure and efficient tag searching in RFID systems using serverless search protocol. Int. J. Security and Its Applications 2(4), 57–66 (2008)
7. Won, T.Y., Chun, J.Y., Lee, D.H.: Strong authentication protocol for secure RFID tag search without help of central database. In: Proc. 2008 IEEE/IFIP International Conference on Embedded and Ubiquitous Computing (EUC), pp. 153–158 (2008)
8. Hoque, M.E., Rahman, F., Ahamed, S.I., Park, J.H.: Enhancing privacy and security of RFID system with serverless authentication and search protocols in pervasive environments. Wireless Personal Communications 55(1), 65–79 (2009)
9. Chun, L.J., Hwang, J.Y., Lee, D.H.: RFID tag search protocol preserving privacy of mobile reader holders. IEICE Electronics Express 8(2), 50–56 (2011)

Cryptanalysis of Goriparthi et al.'s Bilinear Pairing Based Remote User Authentication Scheme

Hae-Jung Kim[1] and Eun-Jun Yoon[2,*]

[1] College of Liberal Education, Keimyung University,
1000 Sindang-dong, Dalseo-Gu, Daegu 704-701, Republic of Korea
[2] Department of Cyber Security, Kyungil University,
33 Buho-Ri, Hayang-Ub, Kyungsan-Si, Kyungsangpuk-Do 712-701, Republic of Korea
hjkim325@hanmail.net, ejyoon@kiu.ac.kr

Abstract. Recently, many user authentication schemes with bilinear pairings have been proposed for client-server environment. In 2009, Goriparthi et al. proposed an improved bilinear pairing based remote user authentication scheme. Goriparthi et al. claimed that the improved scheme can withstand replay, forgery and insider attacks. However, this paper shows that the improved scheme is not only insecure against off-line password guessing, remote server impersonation, Denial of Service, and insider attacks, but also has mutual authentication problem.

Keywords: Cryptography, Authentication, Security, Attack, Smart card, Bilinear pairing.

1   Introduction

A remote user authentication scheme allows users to access various services offered by the remote server. In 1981, Lamport [1] first introduced well-known password authentication scheme with one-way hash function, but the scheme suffers from high hash computation overhead and password resetting problems. Thereafter, many authentication schemes have been proposed based on hash function and on public key cryptography [2–7]. The identity-based public-key system with bilinear pairings defined on elliptic curves offers a flexible approach to achieve simplifying the certificate management [8]. Bilinear pairings are an effective method to reduce the complexity of the discrete log problem in a finite field and provides a good setting for the bilinear Diffie-Hellman problem (BDHP). In the past, many user authentication schemes with bilinear pairings have been proposed for client-server environment [9–11].

In 2004, Das et al. [9] first proposed a remote user authentication scheme using bilinear pairings. However, Chou et al. [10] pointed out that Das et al.'s scheme is insecure to replay attack and the proposed a modified scheme to over- come replay

---

* Corresponding author.

J.J. Park et al. (Eds.): NPC 2012, LNCS 7513, pp. 581–588, 2012.
© IFIP International Federation for Information Processing 2012

attack. In 2009, Goriparthi et al. [11] showed that Chou et al.'s modified scheme still suffers from the replay attack and then proposed another improved GDS scheme to overcome replay, forgery and insider attacks.

Nevertheless, this paper shows that the GDS scheme is not only insecure against off-line password guessing, remote server impersonation, Denial of Service (DoS), and insider attacks, but also has secure mutual authentication problem. As a result, the GDS scheme cannot be applicable to real client-server communication environments.

This paper is organized as follows: Section 2 describes the basic definition and properties of the bilinear pairings. Section 3 reviews the GDS scheme; then Section 4 discusses its weaknesses. The conclusions are presented in Section 5.

2   Preliminaries

This section describes the basic definition and properties of the bilinear pairings[8–11].

2.1   Bilinear Pairings

Let G_1 be an additive cyclic group of prime order q and G_2 be the multiplicative cyclic group of the same order. Practically we can think of G_1 as a group of points on an elliptical curve over Z_q^*, and G_2 as a subgroup of the multiplicative group of a finite field $Z_{q^k}^*$ for some $k \in Z_q^*$. Let P be a generator of G_1. A bilinear pairing is a map $e : G_1 \times G_1 \to G_2$ having the following three properties:

1.   Biliearity: $e(aP, bQ) = e(P, Q)^{ab}$, for all $P, Q \in G_1$ and $a, b \in Z_q^*$.
2.   Non-degeneracy: For all P, where P is not a generator, there exists $Q \in G_1$. such that $e(P, Q) \neq 1$.
3.   Computability: There is an efficient algorithm to compute $e(P, Q)$ in polynomial time for all $P, Q \in G_1$.

2.2   Computational Problems

Many pairing-based cryptographic schemes are based on the hardness of the following problems. No algorithm is known to be able to solve any of them so far.

Definition 1. *Given a group* G_1 *of prime order* q, *a generator* P *of* G_1, *the computational Diffie-Hellman problem (CDHP) is to compute* abP *given* (P, aP, bP) *for* $a, b \in Z_q^*$.

Definition 2. *Given two groups* G_1 *and* G_2 *of the same prime order* q *, a bilinear map* $e: G_1 \times G_1 \to G_2$ *and a generator* P *of* G_1 *, the bilinear Diffie-Hellman problem (BDHP) in* (G_1, G_2, e) *is to compute* $h = e(P, P)^{abc}$ *given* (P, aP, bP, cP) *for* $a, b, c \in Z_q^*$.

Definition 3. *Given a group* G_1 *of prime order* q *, a generator* P *of* G_1 *, the elliptic curve factorization problem (ECFP) is to find* xP *and* yP *given* $xP + yP$ *for* $x, y \in Z_q^*$.

Definition 4. *Elliptic curve discrete logarithm problem (ECDLP): Given a group* G_1 *of prime order* q *, two elements* P *and* Q *, find an integer* $a \in Z_q^*$ *, such that* $Q = aP$ *whenever such an integer exists.*

3 Review of GDS Scheme

GDS scheme [11] consists of three phases namely Registration; Login and Verification; and Password Change Phases and the phases work as follows. Throughout the paper, notations are employed in Table 1.

Table 1. Notations used in GDS scheme

U, RS	The user and the remote server, respectively.
ID	The identity of U.
e	A bilinear map, $e: G_1 \times G_1 \to G_2$.
P	A generator of group G_1.
PW	Password of U.
N	A user friendly random number of U.
s	The private key of RS in Z_q^*.
P_S	The public key of RS such that $P_S = sP$.
sk	A common session key shared between U and RS.
$H(\cdot)$	A map-to-point function, $H : \{0,1\}^* \to G_1$.
$h(\cdot)$	One way hash function, $h : \{0,1\}^* \times G_1 \to \{0,1\}^k$, where k is output length.

3.1 Registration Phase

This phase is depicted in Figure 1. When the user U wants to register to the remote server RS.

R1. $U \rightarrow RS:$ (ID, PW)

   U submits his/her identity ID and password PW to the RS.

R2. $RS \rightarrow U:$ $(ID, R_{ID}, H(\cdot), h(\cdot))$

   (a) RS computes U's private key $R_{ID} = sH(ID) + H(PW)$ by using the private key s.

   (b) RS personalizes the smart card with $(ID, R_{ID}, H(\cdot), h(\cdot))$ and hands it to U securely.

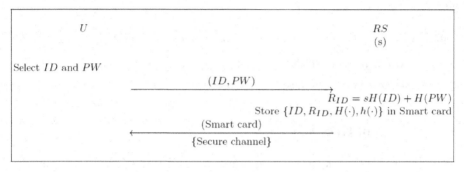

Fig. 1. Registration phase of GDS scheme

3.2   Login and Verification Phase

In this phase, the user U wants to communicate with the powerful server RS. This phase is depicted in Figure 2. The detailed communication steps are described as follows:

L1. $U \rightarrow RS:$ (ID, DID, V, T)

   (a) U inserts smart card in a terminal and submits ID and PW.

   (b) After validating the ID, the smart card randomly chooses an integer $r \in Z_q^*$.

   (c) The smart card computes $V(V_x, V_y) = rP_S$.

   (d) The smart card computes $DID = (r + h(T, V_x, V_y))[R_{ID} - H(PW)]$, where T is the user system's timestamp.

   (e) The smart card sends (ID, DID, V, T) to RS over a public channel.

L2. $RS \rightarrow U:$ (Accept or Reject)

   RS receives (ID, DID, V, T) at time T^* and verifies the validity of the time interval between T^* and T, by checking if $(T^* - T) \leq \Delta T$. If it holds, checks whether

$$e(DID, P) \overset{?}{=} e(H(ID), V + h(T, V_x, V_y)P_S) \tag{1}$$

If it holds, RS accepts the login request, rejects otherwise.

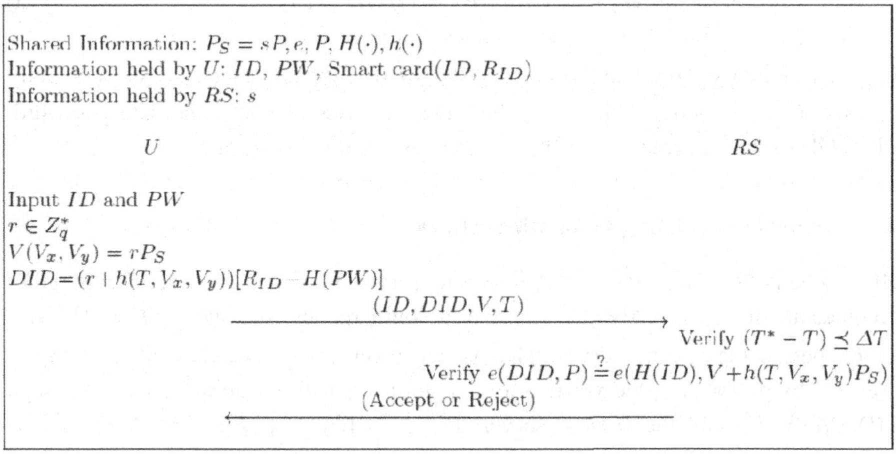

Shared Information: $P_S = sP, e, P, H(\cdot), h(\cdot)$
Information held by U: ID, PW, Smart card(ID, R_{ID})
Information held by RS: s

$\qquad\qquad U \qquad\qquad\qquad\qquad\qquad\qquad\qquad\qquad\qquad\qquad\qquad RS$

Input ID and PW
$r \in Z_q^*$
$V(V_x, V_y) = rP_S$
$DID = (r \mid h(T, V_x, V_y))[R_{ID} - H(PW)]$
$\qquad\qquad\qquad\qquad\qquad\qquad (ID, DID, V, T)$
$\xrightarrow{\hspace{7cm}}$
$\qquad\qquad\qquad\qquad\qquad\qquad\qquad\qquad\qquad$ Verify $(T^* - T) \preceq \Delta T$
$\qquad\qquad\qquad\qquad$ Verify $e(DID, P) \overset{?}{=} e(H(ID), V + h(T, V_x, V_y)P_S)$
$\qquad\qquad\qquad\qquad$ (Accept or Reject)
$\xleftarrow{\hspace{7cm}}$

Fig. 2. Login and verification phase of GDS scheme

3.3 Password Change Phase

P1. U inserts the smart card into a terminal and submits ID and password PW.

P2. The smart card verifies the entered ID with the stored one in the smart card. If ID is matched, it prompts U for a new password PW^*.

P3. U submits a new password PW^*.

P4. The smart card computes

$$\begin{aligned} R_{ID}^* &= R_{ID} - H(PW) + H(PW^*) \\ &= sH(ID) + H(PW^*) \end{aligned} \tag{2}$$

and replaces the previously stored R_{ID} by R_{ID}^*.

4 Cryptanalysis of GDS Scheme

This section shows that the GDS scheme is not only insecure against off-line password guessing, remote server impersonation, Denial of Service, and insider attacks, but also has mutual authentication problem.

4.1 Off-Line Password Guessing Attack

GDS scheme is vulnerable to the off-line password guessing attack as follows. Suppose that an adversary has obtained $(ID, R_{ID}, H(\cdot), h(\cdot))$ stored in the stolen smart card, the adversary can guess a candidate password PW_a^*, and then check whether

$$e(R_{ID} - H(PW_a^*), P) = e(H(ID), P_S)$$ (3)

If the check holds valid, which implies $PW = PW_a^*$, the adversary has success- fully guessed U's password. Otherwise, the adversary tries another candidate password. Thus, GDS scheme cannot resist the off-line password guessing attack.

4.2   Remote Server Impersonation Attack

GDS scheme is vulnerable to the remote server impersonation attack. In GDS scheme, anyone can verify the validity of login request message (ID, DID, V, T) of U beside the remote server. That is, an adversary can easily authenticate the user U by performing the verification equation (1) with the login request message (ID, DID, V, T) and the remote server RS's public key $P_S = sP$. We can see that the verification equation (1) does not require the remote server RS's private key s. It means that an adversary can perform the following remote server impersonation attack. Suppose that an adversary has intercepted (ID, DID, V, T) in the login and verification phase and obtained the RS's public key $P_S = sP$, then he/she can easily check the validity of the timestamp T and whether $e(DID, P) ?= e(H(ID), V + h(T, V_x, V_y)P_S)$. If both checks hold valid, the adversary accepts the login request, rejects otherwise. Thus, GDS scheme cannot resist the remote server impersonation attack.

4.3   DoS Attack on Password Change Phase

Suppose that an adversary temporarily gets U's smart card in the password change phase of the GDS scheme, then he/she can arbitrarily input two passwords PW_{old} and PW_{new} as the old and the new ones, respectively. In this case, the smart card will compute

$$\begin{aligned} R_{ID}^* &= R_{ID} - H(PW_{old}) + H(PWnew) \\ &= sH(ID) + H(PW) - H(PW_{old}) + H(PWnew) \end{aligned}$$

and replace R_{ID} with R_{ID}^*. As a result, this will make U's original password PW never be used in subsequent login and verification phase and thus cause denial of service.

4.4   Mutual Authentication Problem

GDS scheme does not provide secure mutual authentication. Mutual authentication means that both client and server are authenticated to each other within the same protocol. In Step L2 of the GDS scheme, RS can authenticate U by checking the equation (1) because only a valid U can compute DID of the equation (3). However, U cannot authenticate RS because RS does not send any authentication message to U for mutual authentication. It means that an attacker can easily impersonate a legal remote server to cheat the user U without performing the authentication procedure. Therefore, the GDS scheme cannot achieve mutual authentication.

4.5   Insider Attack

GDS scheme is vulnerable to the insider attack. The insider attack means that the insider attacker of RS can directly obtain the user U's password PW in the registration phase [23, 24]. In the GDS scheme, users' passwords PW will be directly revealed to RS because they are transmitted to RS as plaintext, so RS can get all the users' passwords PW in the registration phase. The insider attacker of RS can use these passwords to access other servers to provide useful services or information instead of U. In practice, users offer the same password to access several remote servers for their convenience. Thus the insider attacker of the remote server may try to use PW to impersonate U to login to the other remote servers that U has registered with outside this server. If the targeted outside remote server adopts the normal password authentication scheme, it is possible that the insider attacker of the remote server could successfully impersonate U to login to it by using PW. Although it is also possible that all the insiders of the remote server can be trusted and that U does not use the same password to access several servers, the implementers and the users of the scheme should be aware of such a potential weakness [12,13]. Therefore, GDS scheme is vulnerable to the insider attack.

5   Conclusions

This paper showed that the GDS scheme is not only insecure against off-line password guessing, server impersonation, DoS, and insider attacks, but also has secure mutual authentication problem. Thus, the GDS scheme cannot be applicable to real client-server communication environments. Further works will be focused on improving the GDS scheme which can be able to provide greater security and provides computation efficiency.

Acknowledgments. We would like to thank the anonymous reviewers for their helpful comments in improving our manuscript. This study was supported by the Kyungil University Grant.

References

1. Lamport, L.: Password authentication with insecure communication. Communications of the ACM 24(11), 770–772 (1981)
2. Chang, C.C., Liao, W.Y.: A remote password authentication scheme based upon ElGamal's signature scheme. Computers & Security 13(2), 137–144 (1994)
3. Jablon, D.P.: Strong password-only authenticated key exchange. ACM Computer Communications Review 26(5), 5–20 (1996)
4. Wang, Y.Y., Liu, J.Y., Xiao, F.X., Dan, J.: A more efficient and secure dynamic ID-based remote user authentication scheme. Computer Communications 32(4), 583–585 (2009)
5. Kim, S.K., Chung, M.G.: More secure remote user authentication scheme. Computer Communications 32(6), 1018–1021 (2009)
6. Xu, J., Zhu, W.T., Feng, D.G.: An improved smart card based password authentication scheme with provable security. Computer Standards & Interfaces 31(4), 723–728 (2009)
7. Li, C.T., Hwang, M.S.: An efficient biometrics-based remote user authentication scheme using smart cards. Journal of Network and Computer Applications 33(1), 1–5 (2010)
8. Joux, A.: A One Round Protocol for Tripartite Diffie-Hellman. In: Bosma, W. (ed.) ANTS 2000. LNCS, vol. 1838, pp. 385–394. Springer, Heidelberg (2000)
9. Das, M.L., Saxena, A., Gulati, V.P., Phatak, D.B.: A novel remote user authentication scheme using bilinear pairings. Computers & Security 25(3), 184–189 (2006)
10. Chou, J.S., Chen, Y., Lin, J.Y.: Improvement of Das et al.'s remote user authentication scheme. Cryptology ePrint Archive, Report 2005/450 (2005)
11. Goriparthi, T., Das, M., Saxena, A.: An improved bilinear pairing based remote user authentication scheme. Computer Standards & Interfaces 31(1), 181–185 (2009)
12. Ku, W.C., Chuang, H.M., Tsaur, M.J.: Vulnerabilities of Wu-Chieu's improved password authentication scheme using smart cards. EICE Transactions on Fundamentals of Electronics, Communications and Computer Sciences E88-A(11), 3241–3243 (2005)
13. Yoon, E.J., Yoo, K.Y.: Two security problems of efficient remote mutual authentication and key agreement. In: Proceedings of Future Generation Communication and Networking (FGCN 2007), vol. 2, pp. 66–70 (2007)

Energy-Efficiency Protocol for Securing the Wireless Sensor Networks[*]

Luu Hoang Long[1] and Eunmi Choi[2,**]

[1] Nexcel Solutions, Hochiminh, Vietnam
longluu229@gmail.com
[2] Department of Information System, Kookmin University,
Jeongneung-Dong, Seongbuk-Gu, Seoul, 136-702, Korea
emchoi@kookmin.ac.kr

Abstract. Wireless Sensor Networks (WSNs) are used in many application areas because of its characteristics of easy installation and deployment of sensor nodes in any place and any form. In most of cases, WSNs are typically deployed in un-trusted environment so that security of data communication becomes the essential demand. Secure data transfer in sensor networks requires complicated consideration, compared to conventional desktop computers with the limited processing power, storage, bandwidth, and energy. In this paper, we provide a secure protocol for WSNs which is not only trying to achieve all major issues in security, but also satisfies the low-power consumption as well. We provide and develop secure protocols for data communication and algorithmic mechanisms which ensure energy-saving processing to maximize the performance of communication.

Keywords: Wireless Sensor Networks (WSN).

1 Introduction

A wireless sensor network consists of spatially distributed autonomous sensors to cooperatively monitor physical or environmental conditions, such as temperature, sound, vibration, pressure, motion or pollutants. The development of wireless sensor networks was motivated by military applications such as battlefield surveillance. They are now used in many industrial and civilian application areas, including industrial process monitoring and control, machine health monitoring, environment and habitat monitoring, healthcare applications, home automation, and traffic control.

In wireless sensor networks, sensors usually communicate with each other using a multi hop approach. The biggest problem of sensor networks is power

---

[*] This research was supported by Basic Science Research Program through the National Research Foundation of Korea(NRF) funded by the Ministry of Education, Science and Technology(2012-0002774).
[**] Corresponding author.

J.J. Park et al. (Eds.): NPC 2012, LNCS 7513, pp. 589–598, 2012.

consumption, which is greatly affected by the communication between nodes. To solve this issue:

- *Aggregation points* are introduced to the network. This reduces the total number of messages exchanged between nodes and saves some energy. Usually, aggregation points are regular nodes that receive data from neighboring nodes, perform some kind of processing, and then forward the filtered data to the next hop.
- Similar to aggregation points is *clustering*. Sensor nodes are organized into clusters, each cluster having a "cluster head" as the leader. The communication within a cluster must travel through the cluster head, which then is forwarded to a neighboring cluster head until it reaches its destination, the base station.
- Another method for saving energy is *setting the nodes to go idle* (into sleep mode) if they are not needed and wake up when required.

In this paper, we develop an energy-saving and practically efficient sensor-level secure protocol. We divide sensor nodes into a number of clusters and propose the usage of super sensor node as a control center in that cluster. In addition, we establish three types of keys for each sensor node according to each type of communication patterns: an individual key shared with the base station, a cluster key shared with multiple neighboring nodes, and a group key that is shared by all the nodes in the network.

We provide security for sensor networks by including a message authentication code (MAC) with each packet. A MAC can be viewed as a cryptographically secure checksum of a message. We use symmetric encryption algorithms for encrypting the message because the asymmetric encryption is impractical in such the constrained environments as sensor networks. The block cipher algorithm is chosen for encrypting the transmission message.

In our implementation, we try to achieve all security requirements in wireless sensor networks: data confidentiality, data authenticity, data integrity, data freshness, and semantic security. We achieve data confidentiality, data authenticity, data integrity primitives by using encryption mechanism and add MAC with each packet. We achieve data freshness and semantic security primitives through adding an IV into the MAC. For the whole protocol implementation, we use block cipher encryption as a default encryption algorithms due to its high-performance in resource constrained environments such as wireless sensor networks.

The rest of this paper is structured as follow. Section 2 introduces related works of research on security for WSNs. The system overall architecture will be presented in section 3. In section 4, we analyze our secure protocol. We conclude our paper and show future works in section 5.

2   Related Works

There are many protocols for securing data communication in wireless sensor networks. Among those protocols, SPINS [1], TinySec [2] and LEAP [3] emerge with more dominant features.

The SPINS is a suite of security building blocks proposed by Perig et all. It is optimized for resource constrained environments and wireless communication. SPINS has two secure building blocks: SNEP and μTESLA. SNEP provides data confidentiality, two-party data authentication, and data freshness. μTESLA provides authenticated broadcast for severely resource-constrained environments. All cryptographic primitives (i.e. encryption, message authentication code (MAC), hash, random number generator) are constructed out of a single block cipher for code reuse. This, along with the symmetric cryptographic primitives used reduces the overhead on the resource constrained sensor network. However, wireless sensor networks using SPINS can be the victim of DoS attack (Denial of Services) because SPINS rely on a shared counter between the sender and receiver for the block cipher in counter mode. Hence, each sensor node has to store the counter for each its senders.

The TinySec is the first fully-implemented link layer security architecture for wireless sensor networks. A link-layer's security architecture can detect unauthorized packets when they are first injected into the network. TinySec provides the basic security properties of message authentication and integrity (using MAC), message confidentiality (through encryption), semantic security (through an Initialization Vector) and replay protection. TinySec supports two different security options: authenticated encryption (TinySec-AE) and authentication only (TinySec-Auth). With authenticated encryption, TinySec encrypts the data payload and authenticates the packet with a MAC. The MAC is computed over the encrypted data and the packet header. In authentication only mode, TinySec authenticates the entire packet with a MAC, but the data payload is not encrypted.

LEAP (Localized Encryption and Authentication Protocol) is a key management protocol for sensor networks that is designed to support in-network processing, while restricting the security impact of a node compromise to the immediate network neighborhood of the compromised node. The design of the protocol is motivated by the observation that different types of messages exchanged between sensor nodes have different security requirements, and that a single keying mechanism is not suitable for meeting these different security requirements. Hence, LEAP establishes four types of keys for each sensor node – an individual key shared with the base station, a pair-wise key shared with another sensor node, a cluster key shared with multiple neighboring nodes, and a group key that is shared by all the nodes in the network. LEAP also includes an efficient protocol for inter-node traffic authentication based on the use of one-way key chains. The drawback of LEAP is it requires every node has space for storing up to hundreds of bytes of keying materials.

3   Architecture

In this section, we describe our secure protocol design and techniques/mechanisms that are used to build the secure protocol. The overall system architecture will be shown with our keying mechanisms.

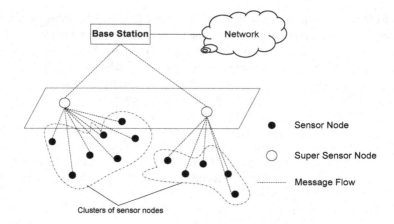

Fig. 1. Overall System Architecture

3.1   Overall System Architecture

Based on the prior research works of sensor secure protocols, we develop an energy-saving and practically efficient sensor-level secure protocol which achieves all the major issues of security in wireless sensor networks such as data confidentiality, data authenticity, data integrity, data freshness, and semantic security. As shown in Figure 1, there are three main actors in our protocols: the base station, the super sensor nodes, and the sensor nodes.

- **Base Station:** communicates with Super Sensor Nodes and Sensor Nodes.
- **Super Sensor Node:** A super sensor node communicates with other super sensor nodes. With this communication, a cluster communicates with other clusters. Also, a super sensor node communicates with sensor nodes in its cluster and the base station.
- **Sensor Node:** A sensor node communicates with other sensor nodes in a cluster through its super sensor node. Particularly, the super sensor node acts as an intermediate node for transmitting the packet sent from a sensor node to another in its cluster. A sensor node communicates with its super sensor node and the base station. A sensor node may send an alert to the base station if it observes any abnormal or unexpected behavior by a neighboring node.

3.2   Keying Mechanisms

In this section, we describe for each kind of nodes in our secure protocol. We assume that only the base station can generate the keys for the whole secure protocol. It means any key setup process for any kind of node in the network has to pass through the base station. In succession, we will consider the keys setup for the super sensor node and the sensor node.

In case of adding a new super sensor node S into a sensor network, the global key and individual key are pre-loaded into to S before its deployment. S is a new super sensor node, so that S does not need to care about the list of keys/counters shared with each sensor node in the cluster at this moment.

The things that S should do now are establishing the cluster key and list of keys shared with other super sensor nodes. These keys can be established through 3 steps:

- Step 1: Neighbors discovery. In this step, S broadcasts a message to discover all super sensor nodes near by it. The broadcasting message contains the ID of S. After receiving the message from S, S's neighbors response with their ID. S lists out its neighbors' ID in a list called LNID.
- Step 2: Generate Keys. S sends LNID to the base station and asks the base station for generating keys. The packet that is sent in this step is encrypted using the individual key shared between S and the base station.
- Step 3: Deliver Keys. After generating keys, the base station sends appropriate keys to S and S's neighbors. The transmission packets in this step are encrypted using the individual key shared between the base station and each node.

In case of adding a new sensor node N into a sensor network, the global key and individual key are pre-loaded into to S before its deployment. The cluster key can be transmitted after N successfully established a secret key with its super sensor node. The secret key establishing process gets through 3 steps which are described as follow:

- Step 1: Super Sensor Nodes Discovery. In this step, N broadcasts a message to discover all super sensor nodes near by it. The broadcasting message contains the ID of N. After receiving the message from N, only the super sensor nodes (which are near by N) response with their ID.
- Step 2: Choose Cluster to Join. From the super sensor nodes' IDs from the previous step, N chooses one cluster to join (in this case, a cluster is represented by n super sensor node's ID).
- Step 3: Secret Key Generation. N sends the chosen cluster's ID to the base station and asks for the secret key generation. The packet that is sent in this step is encrypted using the individual key shared between S and the base station.
- Step 4: Keys Delivery. After generating keys, the base station sends appropriate keys to N and N's super sensor node. The transmission packets in this step are encrypted using the individual key shared between the base station and each node.

3.3   Packet Format

Based on above consideration, we create the packet format for our secure protocol as follows.

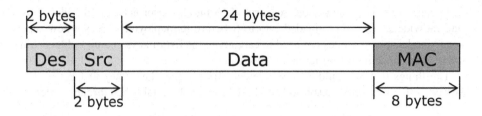

Fig. 2. Packet Format in Secure Protocol

As you can see in Fig. 2, the transmission packet in our secure protocol includes four parts: Des‖Src‖Data‖MAC. Where:

- Des is the ID of destination node and it will not be encrypted. The size of Des is 2 bytes.
- Src is the ID of node that sends the packet and it will not be encrypted. The size of Src is 2 bytes.
- Data is the information that be sent. In our secure protocol, this information will be encrypted by key K_{enr} before sending. The output's size of skipjack algorithm is 8 bytes so that we chose the size of data is 24 bytes which is the multiple of 8 bytes.
- MAC is security checksum for the whole packet. A key K_{mac} is used to create MAC. We chose the size of MAC is 8 bytes to decrease the size of whole packet as much as possible.

For example, A and B are principals, such as communicating nodes. The complete message that A sends to B is:

$$A \rightarrow B: (B\_ID \parallel A\_ID \parallel \{Data\}K_{enr} \parallel \{M\}K_{mac})$$

Now we will describe what are included in M (in previous state) before it is encrypted by the K_{mac}. Assume that in the hexa-mode:

- Two bytes of A's ID are A_1 and A_2,
- Two bytes of B's ID are B_1 and B_2.
- Two bytes of the counter C shared between A and B are C_1 and C_2,
- The first eight bytes of $\{Data\}K_{enr}$ are $D_1, D_2, \ldots, D_7, D_8$.

As MAC acts as the checksum value for the transferring packet, MAC should contain all parts of the packet's information. Particularly, MAC contains A_1 & A_2, B_1 & B_2, and C_1 & C_2. There are two more bytes for representing the data; and the last two bytes of data D_7&D_8 are chosen. Then, the content of M before it is encrypted by key K_{mac} should be:

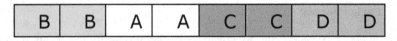

Fig. 3. The structure of MAC

Finally, we describe the mechanism that is used to create K_{enr} and K_{mac}. As discussed above, each node shares with the base station a key called individual key. Moreover, each sensor node shares with its super sensor node a secret key. These kinds of keys are used for securing the node-to-node transmission packet. In this section, we call them "symmetric key" so that it is easier to describe our mechanism.

We surveyed of cipher block chaining algorithms for software implementation on embedded microcontrollers and found that RC5 and Skipjack are most appropriate. RC5 is slightly faster Skipjack. However, for good performance, RC5 requires the key schedule to be pre-computed, which uses 104 extra bytes of RAM per key [5]. Because of these drawbacks, the default block cipher in our protocol is Skipjack.

Assume that node A shares with node B a symmetric key K_S. The size of K_S is 10 bytes. The mechanism of creating K_{enr} and K_{mac} from Ks is shown in the figure below:

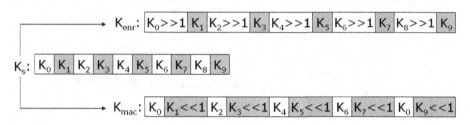

Fig. 4. The mechanism of generating K_{enr} and K_{mac}

As you can see in Fig. 4, all even bytes in 9 bytes of symmetric key will be right-shift one step to create the K_{enr} and all odd bytes in 9 bytes of symmetric key will be left-shift one step in order to create the K_{mac}. The reason that we used shifting mechanism is this approach is very fast so that we can save the sensor's energy.

4   Experimental Results

We made the simulation for assessing the performance of our protocol comparing to Typical Protocol and LEAP. In this simulation, we sequentially added sensors to create sensor networks. The number of sensors varies from 100 to 600 sensors and compute:

- The time for creating a sensor network and establishing keys.
- The number of packets for sending and receiving of each sensor

We implemented the simulation using C++ programming language. The resources we chose to perform comparison tests are: Windows XP; Intel® Core™ 2 Duo T7300 2.00 GHz, 200 GHz; RAM 2.00 GB. The experimental results are visually shown below.

In Figure 5, you can see that when the number of sensors increases, the time for creating the sensor network and establishing keys of our secure protocol is much better than in case of typical protocol. When the sensor's density increases, the number of neighbors of each sensor will be increased. In case of the typical protocol, the more neighbors each sensor has the more key generating step and delivering key step must be done at that sensor. That is the reason why the times are significantly increased in case of the typical protocol. In our protocol, the sensors just need to establish the key with its directly super sensor and the key generation process is done at the base station so that our secure protocol's times are slightly increased.

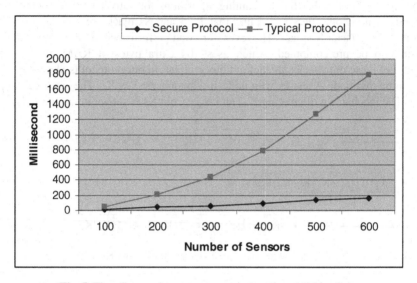

Fig. 5. Time for creating a sensor network and establishing keys

We run the simulation and collect the number of packets each sensor sent and received to make comparison between our secure protocol and LEAP. The results are shown in Figure 6.

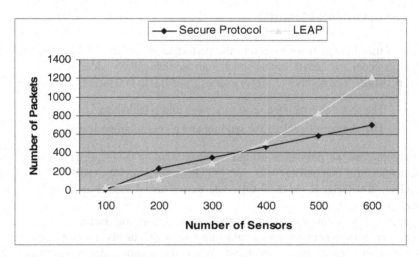

Fig. 6. The number of packets received to create sensor networks

The above figure shows that with the low sensor density, the number of packets each sensor received in LEAP is lower than in case of our secure protocol. However, with the high sensor density (this case is commonly in wireless sensor networks), our secure protocol is much better. In our secure protocol, we divided the sensing area into number of clusters. Each cluster is controlled by one super sensor. When adding a new sensor, this sensor just needs to communicate with its super sensor. This approach helps to reduce the number of packets received to create sensor networks.

5   Conclusion

In summary, this paper describes an energy-saving and practically efficient sensor-level secure protocol in wireless sensor networks. We establish three types of keys for each sensor node according to each type of communication patterns: an individual key shared with the base station, a cluster key shared with multiple neighboring nodes, and a group key that is shared by all the nodes in the network. Each key for each type of communication patterns provides more security for our protocol.

We also come up with a simulation to analysis the performance of our secure protocol. Through the simulation, we experience our protocol by comparing the time for creating a sensor network and establishing keys to a typical protocol; and comparing the number of packets sent and received to LEAP. The experimental results show that our secure protocol performance is potential especially when the sensor density of the sensor network is high.

References

1. Perrig, A., Szewczyk, R., Wen, V., Culler, D., Tygar, J.D.: SPINS: Security Protocols for Sensor Networks. In: The Seventh Annual International Conference on Mobile Computing and Networking (MobiCom 2001), (2001)
2. Karlof, C., Sastry, N., Wagner, D.: TinySec: A Link Layer Security Architecture for Wireless Sensor Networks. In: ACM SenSys 2004, November 3-5 (2004)
3. Zhu, S., Setia, S., Jajodia, S.: LEAP: Efficient Security Mechanisms for Large-Scale Distributed Sensor Networks. In: The Proceedings of the 10th ACM Conference on Computer and Communications Security (2003)
4. Saraogi, M.: Security in Wireless Sensor Networks. In: ACM SenSys 2004 (2004)
5. Casado, L., Tsigas, P.: ContikiSec: A Secure Network Layer for Wireless Sensor Networks under the Contiki Operating System. Identity and Privacy in the Internet Age, September 30 (2009)
6. Law, Y.W., Doumen, J., Hartel, P.: Survey and Benchmark of Block Ciphers forWireless Sensor Networks. ACM Transactions on Sensor Networks (TOSN) 2(1), 65–93 (2006)
7. Wang, S., Liu, K.Z., Hu, F.P.: Simulation of Wireless Sensor Networks Localization with OMNeT. In: 2005 2nd International Conference on Mobile Technology, Applications and Systems, November 15-17, pp. 1–6 (2005)
8. Rivest, R.L., Robshaw, M.J.B., Sidney, R., Yin, Y.L.: The RC6 Block Cipher. AES submission (June 1998)

9. Perrig, A., Canetti, R., Song, D., Tygar, J.D.: Efficient and secure source authentication for multicast. In: Network and Distributed System Security Symposium, NDSS 2001 (February 2001)
10. Bellare, M., Kilian, J., Rogaway, P.: The security of the cipher blocks chaining message authentication code. Journal of Computer and System Sciences 61(3), 362–399 (2000)
11. Carman, D.W., Kruus, P.S., Matt, B.J.: Constraints and approaches for distributed sensor network security, NAI Labs Technical Report No. 00010 (2002)
12. Rivest, R.L.: The RC5 encryption algorithm. In: Workshop on Fast Software Encryption, pp. 86–96 (1995)
13. Stajano, F., Anderson, R.: The Resurrecting Duckling: Security Issues for Ad-Hoc Wireless Networks. In: Malcolm, J.A., Christianson, B., Crispo, B., Roe, M. (eds.) Security Protocols 1999. LNCS, vol. 1796, pp. 172–182. Springer, Heidelberg (2000)
14. Douceur, J.R.: The Sybil Attack. In: Druschel, P., Kaashoek, M.F., Rowstron, A. (eds.) IPTPS 2002. LNCS, vol. 2429, pp. 251–260. Springer, Heidelberg (2002)
15. Karlof, C., Wagner, D.: Secure Routing in Sensor Networks: Attacks and Counter measures. To appear in Proc. of First IEEE Workshop on Sensor Network Protocols and Applications (May 2003)

A Novel Time Reversal-Least Sidelobe Scheme to Minimize ISI and MUI

Do-Hoon Kim, Jungwook Wee, and Kyu-Sung Hwang[*]

Korea Electronics Technology Institute, Seoul, Korea
Department of Computer Engineering, Kyungil University, Gyeongbuk, Korea
{speedno,jwwee}@keti.re.kr, kshwang@kiu.ac.kr

Abstract. In this paper, the scheme that combines a prefilter for sidelobe minimization with the time-reversal prefilter in the ultra wide band wireless communication system is proposed. The proposed scheme can be used in the variable symbol interval situation. When the system has the symbol interval which is larger than one-tap, the proposed scheme exploits the symbol interval to minimize the ISI. In the multi user environment, the proposed scheme is combined with space-time multiplexing scheme to alleviate multi user interference (MUI). Through numerical simulations, we examine the bit error rate (BER) performance of the proposed scheme in single user and two-user environment, and show that the proposed scheme can offer some BER performance gains comparing to the conventional TR scheme.

Keywords: UWB communication, Time-reversal, Sidelobe suppression, Additional prefilter.

1 Introduction

Recently, in indoor wireless communication environment, ultra wideband (UWB) multimedia wireless communication systems that can transmit high capacity and high speed multimedia data has caught major attentions, because it is able to support high speed transmission of the huge data. However, the UWB operates in a frequency selective fading environment, such that intersymbol interference (ISI) arises and degrades overall performances. In order to overcome the ISI is the time-reversal (TR) scheme in [1] which applies time-reversed complex conjugated channel impulse response (CIR) as a prefilter at transmitter. The TR scheme focuses the signal energy which is scattered by the frequency selective fading to maximize SNR and reduce ISI. In addition, the TR scheme focuses spatial signal energy to the intended receiver; it exploits the channel state information (CSI) to the intended specific position as a prefilter. Therefore, the TR scheme also reduces the multi user interference (MUI). Due to the spatial signal energy focusing property, this scheme has been applied to rich scattering environment, such as a radar system and underwater communication systems [2, 3].

---

[*] Corresponding author.

J.J. Park et al. (Eds.): NPC 2012, LNCS 7513, pp. 599–607, 2012.
© IFIP International Federation for Information Processing 2012

However, the TR scheme cannot perfectly eliminate ISI due to the residual interference that is remained in the form of sidelobe in the TR equivalent channel impulse response (CIR). In addition, the receiver at the unintended position receives MUI in the form of the cross correlation function between the transmitter to the intended receiver channel and the transmitter to the unintended receiver channel. To mitigate the residual ISI, several schemes have been proposed. In joint TR-ZF scheme [4], zero-forcing (ZF) prefilter was designed in conjunction with the TR prefilter to eliminate the residual ISI and maximize SNR. The schemes in [5, 6] exploit the symmetric property of the equivalent CIR's power to reduce the multi-user interference (MUI). In these schemes, each transmitter sends the signal, which is shifted to each other to avoid the peak-power interference from another transmitter.

In this paper, we propose a novel structure of an additional prefilter at the transmitter to suppress the residual ISI and reduce the complexity of the receiver. We consider a variable rate system that the symbol interval can be adjustable. The proposed scheme exploits the symbol interval to suppress ISI in conjunction with semidefinite relaxation (SDR) [7] technique to solve optimization problem of minimizing ISI with some constraints. The following notations are used for description throughput this paper. The operators $*$, $(\cdot)^H$, $(\cdot)^*$, and $\|\cdot\|$ indicate convolution, Hermitian transpose, complex conjugation, and norm operators respectively.

2 System Models

2.1 Indoor Wireless Channel Model

In this paper, we consider an exponential decay model in [8] for an indoor wireless channel model in order to simplify the representation and the performance analysis which is useful to express a typical frequency selective fading channel. The power delay profile (PDP) of an exponential decay model indicates the mean power at the lth tap and can be expressed as

$$\sigma_1^2 = \exp\left(\frac{(l-1)\Delta r}{\overline{\sigma}_\tau}\right) \tag{1}$$

where $\Delta\tau$ is an interval between adjacent taps, and $\overline{\sigma}_\tau$ represents the mean RMS delay spread. The coefficient at the lth tap of the channel impulse response is an identically and independently distributed circularly complex Gaussian random variable with zero mean and σ_l^2 variance.

2.2 Single User TR-LS System

Firstly, we consider a single user system that employs a TR prefilter at the transmitter side. The main advantage of this scheme is that it maximizes the transmit signal to noise ratio (SNR) since the CSI of the receiver is available at the transmitter while also greatly reducing the receiver's complexity by only employing a single-tap equalizer. However, the drawback of the TR scheme is that it has a residual ISI. The TR scheme makes an equivalent channel impulse response which is the original CIR's autocorrelation function that has maximum peak point and symmetrical sidelobes. The TR scheme maximizes the SNR but does not remove ISI completely. Thus, the performance of the system will be degraded by the residual ISI. To suppress the residual ISI, this paper proposes a scheme that employs an additional prefilter at the transmitter. The transmitter has two filters: one is a conventional TR prefilter while the other is a least sidelobe (LS) filter that minimizes the residual ISI from the TR filter. From the assumption of TR-LS system, the received signal can be written as

$$y(t) = f^{TR}(t) * g^{LS}(t) * s(t) + n(t) \tag{2}$$

where $s(t)$ is a message signal at time t, $g^{LS}(t)$ is the LS filter with length $2L-1$ and $f^{TR}(t)$ is the TR equivalent channel that can be expressed as

$$f^{TR}(t) = h(t) * g^{TR}(t) \tag{3}$$

The TR prefilter g^{TR} can be represented as

$$g^{TR}(t) = \frac{h^*(-t)}{\| h(t) \|} \tag{4}$$

where $h^*(-t)$ is time-reversed and conjugated form of the $h(t)$. In (4), the nominator means a conjugation of the time-reversed channel impulse response. Variable $n(t)$ is an additive zero-mean complex Gaussian noise. We can rewrite (3) in its discrete representation

$$f^{TR}[k] = h[k] * g^{TR}[k] \tag{5}$$

where k is a discrete sampling instant. The entire transmit prefilter is a combination of the TR filter and the LS filter which can be represented as

$$g^{TR-LS}[k] = g^{LS}[k] * g^{TR}[k] \tag{6}$$

where $g^{LS}[k]$ is a prefilter proposed in this paper. The prefilter $g^{LS}[k]$ performs peak power reduction and sidelobe expansion to minimize residual ISI. We consider the LS filter with length of $2L-1$, similar to the conventional TR equivalent channel impulse response's length. The equivalent entire system channel impulse response $f^{TR-LS}[k]$ can be represented as

$$f^{TR-LS}[k] = h[k] * g^{TR-LS}[k]. \tag{7}$$

2.3   Two User TR-LS System

For the two user TR-LS system, we consider a two transmitter-receiver pairs in the indoor wireless communication environment which can cause interference to each other. We assume the CSI of the intended receiver are available at each transmitter. However, the CSI of unintended receiver is unavailable. Since the transmitters have only the CSI of the intended user, each transmitter generate the prefilters using only the intended receiver's channels, respectively. To avoid the MUI, we introduce a scheme which combines the shifted transmission technique in [5] and the adjustment of the mainlobe's width.

Based on the proposed two user TR-LS system, the received signal at receiver1 can be written as

$$y_1[k] = f_{11}^{TR}[k] * g_1^{LS}[k] * s_1[k] + f_{21}^{TR}[k] * g_2^{LS}[k] * s_2[k] + n_1[k] \qquad (8)$$

where

$$f_{11}^{TR}[k] = h_{11}[k] * g_1^{TR}[k] \qquad (9)$$

and

$$f_{21}^{TR}[k] = h_{21}[k] * g_2^{TR}[k] \qquad (10)$$

The equivalent channel impulse response (10) can be called an interference chanel. Variable $g_1^{LS}[k]$ and $g_2^{LS}[k]$ are the least sidelobe prefilter at the transmitter 1 and 2, respectively, while s_1 and s_2 are the transmitted symbol at the transmitter 1 and 2, respectively. Similarly, the received signal at receiver 2 can be described as

$$y_2[k] = f_{22}^{TR}[k] * g_2^{LS}[k] * s_1[k] + f_{21}^{TR}[k] * g_1^{LS}[k] * s_1[k] + n_2[k] \qquad (11)$$

where

$$f_{22}^{TR}[k] = h_{22}[k] * g_2^{TR}[k] \qquad (12)$$

and

$$f_{12}^{TR}[k] = h_{12}[k] * g_1^{TR}[k] \qquad (13)$$

In (8) and (11), the first term is the intended signal, the second term is MUI, and the third term is an additive zero-mean complex gaussian noise.

3   TR-LS Scheme for ISI Suppression

This section describes out proposed scheme that exploits an additional prefilter at the transmitter to minimize the residual ISI in the TR wireless communication system. To achieve this, following subsections explain how to design the additional prefilter that minimize the sidelobe of TR equivalent impulse response.

3.1   Design of the Least Sidelobe Prefilter

Optimization Problem. Firstly, we examine how to design the least sidelobe prefilter $g^{LS}(t)$ that is designed by an optimization theory. The prefilter $g^{LS}(t)$ can be described as the matrix form, $\mathbf{g}^{LS}$. The objective of the prefilter is the minimization of residual ISI. Therefore, the optimization problem can be represented as

$$\underset{\mathbf{g}^{LS}}{\text{minimize}} \quad \left\|\tilde{\mathbf{F}}^{TR}\mathbf{g}^{LS}\right\|^2$$

$$\text{subject to} \quad \begin{aligned} \left\|\mathbf{f}^{\text{Rev}}\mathbf{g}^{LS}\right\|^2 \geq c;\, 0 \leq c \leq 1 \\ \left\|\mathbf{G}^{TR}\mathbf{g}^{LS}\right\|^2 = 1 \end{aligned} \qquad (14)$$

where $\tilde{\mathbf{F}}^{TR}$ is a matrix that represents ISI components to be minimize, and c is a peak power constraint that has a relative value to the peak power of original TR scheme. $\mathbf{f}^{TR}$ is a TR equivalent channel impulse response and $\mathbf{f}^{\text{Rev}}$ is a reversed vector of $\mathbf{f}^{TR}$. The matrix $\tilde{\mathbf{F}}^{TR}$ is a modification of the original matrix $\mathbf{F}^{TR}$. The matrix $\mathbf{F}^{TR}$ represents a TR equivalent channel.

$$\mathbf{F}^{TR} = \begin{bmatrix} f^{TR}[1] & 0 & \cdots & 0 \\ f^{TR}[2] & f^{TR}[1] & & \vdots \\ \vdots & \vdots & \ddots & 0 \\ f^{TR}[2L-1] & f^{TR}[2L-2] & & f^{TR}[1] \\ 0 & f^{TR}[2L-1] & & f^{TR}[2] \\ \vdots & 0 & \ddots & \vdots \\ 0 & \vdots & & f^{TR}[2L-1] \end{bmatrix}, \qquad (15)$$

and $\mathbf{g}^{LS}$ is a solution of this optimization problem. This solution is a vector form of the least sidelobe prefilter.

Focusing the Residual ISI within Symbol Interval. In (14), the solution minimizes ISI term. The ISI term is represented by $\tilde{\mathbf{F}}^{TR}$. This term has to be minimized by $\mathbf{g}^{LS}$. $\tilde{\mathbf{F}}^{TR}$ is a modified matrix of the equivalent TR channel matrix $\mathbf{F}^{TR}$.

In (14), central rows are nulled with zeros. Rows of $\tilde{\mathbf{F}}^{TR}$ are multiplied with $\mathbf{g}^{LS}$. Then, we can get a vector that represents ISI. The optimization solution $\mathbf{g}^{LS}$ minimizes ISI power. Thus, the multiplication of $\tilde{\mathbf{F}}^{TR}$ and $\mathbf{g}^{LS}$ has to be minimized by the solution. This is expressed by (14). When we compose $\tilde{\mathbf{F}}^{TR}$, we have to consider the focusing of ISI within the symbol interval. Thus, the solution minimizes only the symbol interval tap and outside of the symbol interval. To represent the outside of the symbol interval, we need nulling the central rows of $\tilde{\mathbf{F}}^{TR}$. Then central taps of $\tilde{\mathbf{F}}^{TR}\mathbf{g}^{LS}$ are omitted in the minimization target of the solution. Thus, in an equivalent channel impulse response, the taps inside of the symbol interval are not minimized. But they are not our concerns, because the taps do not interfere sampling time instants. The ignoring taps inside of symbol interval leads increase of the degree of freedom. Thus, the solution can exploit the increase of the degree of freedom to the suppressing ISI power. If the sytem gets more taps inside of symbol interval, more ISI power can be suppressed.

3.2   Conversion to Solvable Form

This subsection deals with the process to convert the optimization problem to solvable form. The optimization problem which discussed in previous section can be converted to a quadratic form. (14) can be converted as

$$
\begin{aligned}
\underset{\mathbf{g}^{LS}}{\text{minimize}} \quad & (\mathbf{g}^{LS})^{H} \mathbf{A} \mathbf{g}^{LS} \\
\textit{subject to} \quad & (\mathbf{g}^{LS})^{H} \mathbf{B} \mathbf{g}^{LS} \leq c;\ 0 \leq c \leq 1 \\
& (\mathbf{g}^{LS})^{H} \mathbf{C} \mathbf{g}^{LS} = 1
\end{aligned}
\tag{16}
$$

where $\mathbf{A} = (\tilde{\mathbf{F}}^{TR})^{H} \tilde{\mathbf{F}}^{TR}, \mathbf{B} = (\mathbf{f}^{Rev})^{H} \mathbf{f}^{Rev},$ and $\mathbf{C} = (\mathbf{G}^{TR})^{H} \mathbf{G}^{TR}.$

Now, the optimization problem is a quadratically constrained quadratic programming (QCQP). However, despite the conversion, the optimization problem is non-convex, because the second constraint in (16) is a quadratic form equality constraint that is a non-convex. We can use the semi-definite programming relaxation (SDR) [7] to convexity of the optimization problem. First, the QCQP has to convert to semi-definite programming (SDP). Thus, (16) can be reformulated as

$$
\begin{aligned}
\underset{\mathbf{G}^{LS}}{\text{minimize}} \quad & trace(\mathbf{A}\mathbf{G}^{LS}) \\
\textit{subject to} \quad & trace(\mathbf{B}\mathbf{G}^{LS}) \leq c;\ 0 \leq c \leq 1 \\
& trace(\mathbf{C}\mathbf{G}^{LS}) = 1 \\
& rank(\mathbf{G}^{LS}) = 1 \\
& \mathbf{G}^{LS} \succeq 0
\end{aligned}
\tag{17}
$$

(17) is a non-convex SDP, because the constraint $rank(\mathbf{G}^{LS}) = 1$ is not a convex. By the relaxation of this constraint, we can change the non-convex SDP to the convex SDP. The changed optimization problem can be described as

$$
\begin{aligned}
\underset{\mathbf{G}^{LS}}{\text{minimize}} \quad & trace(\mathbf{A}\mathbf{G}^{LS}) \\
\textit{subject to} \quad & trace(\mathbf{B}\mathbf{G}^{LS}) \leq c;\ 0 \leq c \leq 1 \\
& trace(\mathbf{C}\mathbf{G}^{LS}) = 1 \\
& \mathbf{G}^{LS} \succeq 0
\end{aligned}
\tag{18}
$$

This optimization problem can be solved by the convex SDP that can derive the solution as matrix form, $\mathbf{G}^{LS}$. However we want a solution of the vector form, $\mathbf{G}^{LS}$. The vector form solution can be extracted from $\mathbf{G}^{LS}$ by a rank-1 approximation. To extract $\mathbf{g}^{LS}$, let

$$
\mathbf{G}^{LS} = \sum_{i=1}^{r} \lambda_{i} \mathbf{q}_{i} \mathbf{q}_{i}^{H},
\tag{19}
$$

where r is a rank of $\mathbf{G}^{LS}$, and the eigenvalues of $\mathbf{G}^{LS}$ are $\lambda_1 \geq \lambda_2 \geq \ldots \geq \lambda_r > 0$, and $\mathbf{q}_1, \ldots, \mathbf{q}_r$ are the eigenvectors of $\mathbf{G}^{LS}$. We choose maximum eigenvalue and its eigenvector, $\mathbf{g}^{LS} = \sqrt{\lambda_1} \mathbf{q}_1$. This is a solution of the optimization problem.

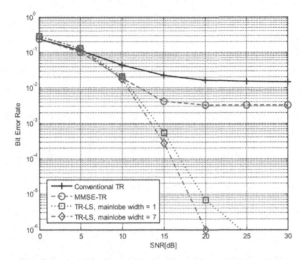

Fig. 1. BER performance comparison between the variable mainlobe width W_m = 1, 7, and conventional schemes

3.3 Single User System

In single user system which doesn't have MUI, reduction of the sidelobe can be achieved by handling the mainlobe width. To minimize ISI, we exploit the symbol interval. In previous section, we examined the wider mainlobe leads to lower side-lobe. However, if the expanded mainlobe interferes the adjacent sampling instance, ISI is occurred severely. Thus, the mainlobe width will set to a little bit shorter than adjacent sampling instance to avoid ISI from the mainlobe, therefore the mainlobe doesn't interfere to the adjacent sampling instance. The mainlobe width can be set W_m = $2T_s - 1$ where W_m is a mainlobe width and T_s is a symbol interval.

3.4 Two User System

In Two user system, we have to pay attention to MUI which cannot handle by the TR-LS prefilter due to the prefilter does not have the CSI to unintended receiver. Thus, in this paper, the proposed scheme is combined with the space time multiplexing scheme that explained in the previous chapter. To overcome MUI, the optimization problem of the TR-LS prefilter has to set the high c constraint, because the transmitter cannot mitigate MUI. Thus, the intended channel has to secure a measure of the peak power to overcome MUI. Also, the shifted transmission scheme can alleviate MUI [5].

4   Simulation Results

In this section, we provide the BER performance of the proposed TR-LS with QPSK and compare that with the conventional schemes. The simulation parameters used

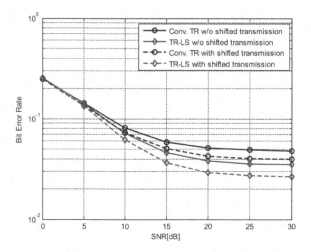

Fig. 2. BER performance comparison between the conventional TR scheme and the proposed TR-LS scheme with $W_m = 2$

in this paper is given by the channel impulse response $L = 38$, $\Delta\tau = 0.811ns$, and 100 symbols of block length. In two user environment, the space-time multiplexing scheme [5] is applied and the minimum symbol interval of 2 is used.

Figure 1 shows the comparison of BER performance in a single user environment between the proposed scheme, the conventional TR, and MMSE-TR in [9] with the fixed symbol interval, and variable mainlobe width W_m. As the mainlobe is broadening, the BER performance is improved. As shown in Figure 1, the proposed scheme has better BER performance than conventional schemes. Figure 2 gives the BER performance of the two user system. In this simulation, we set c'= 0.9. The result shows that TR-LS scheme has better BER performance than conventional TR scheme and shifted TR scheme both. Since TR-LS scheme is combined with shifted transmission scheme, BER performance is slightly improved. As shown in Figure 2, he proposed scheme reduces bit error by 26 percent as compared with conventional TR scheme.

5   Conclusion

In this paper, we proposed the TR-LS scheme to minimize ISI and MUI in UWB communication system. In the frequency selective fading channel environment, the proposed scheme exploits the symbol interval to minimize the residual ISI in the TR communication system. Since the system broadens the symbol interval, the TR-LS scheme can reduce more ISI. In addition, the proposed scheme expands the mainlobe width to reduce ISI. The expanded mainlobe width makes lower sidelobe power. Thus, the proposed scheme shows an improved signal to-ISI ratio and BER performance. From some selected simulation results, the proposed scheme shows outperform the conventional schemes.

Acknowledgements. This work was supported by the IT R&D program of MKE/KEIT.

References

1. Fink, M.: Time-reversed Acoustic. Scientific American, 67–73 (1999)
2. Jin, Y., Moura, J.M.F., Jiang, Y., Stancil, D.D., Cepni, A.G.: Time Re-versal Detection in Clutter: Additional Experimental Results. IEEE Trans. Aerospace and Electronic Systems 47, 140–154 (2011)
3. Edelmann, G.F., Song, H.C., Kim, S., Hodgkiss, W.S., Kuperman, W.A., Akal, T.: Underwater Acoustic Communications using Time Reversal. IEEE Journal of Oceanic Engineering 30, 852–864 (2005)
4. Kyritsi, P., Stoica, P., Papanicolaou, G., Eggers, P., Oprea, A.: Time Re-versal and Zero-Forcing Equalization for Fixed Wireless Access Channels. In: Asilomar Conference on Signals, Systems and Computers (2005)
5. Nguyen, H.T., Kovacs, I.Z., Eggers, P.C.F.: Time Reversal Technique for Multi-user Wireless Communication with Single Tap Receiver. Mobile and Wireless Communications Summit 16, 1–5 (2007)
6. Sigit, A.P., Choi, S.K., Lee, C.Y.: Shifted Time Reversal Technique for Two-user Wireless Communication Using Variable Rate Back-off. IEEK Journal 5, 33–39 (2011)
7. Luo, Z.-Q., Ma, W.-K., So, A.M.-C., Ye, Y., Zhang, S.: Semidefinite Re-laxation of Quadratic Optimization Problems. EEE Signal Processing Magazine 27, 20–34 (2010)
8. Vaughan, R., Andersen, J.B.: Channels Propagation and Antennas for Mobile Communications. IEE Electromagnetic Waves Series, vol. 50 (2003)
9. Strohmer, T., Emami, M., Hansen, J., Papanicolaou, G., Paulraj, A.J.: Application of Time-Reversal with MMSE Equalizer to UWB Communications. In: Global Telecommunications Conference, GLOBECOM 2004, vol. 5, pp. 3123–3127. IEEE (2004)

SNR-Based Partial Relay Selection Scheme
over Multiple Relay Network

Kyu-Sung Hwang

Department of Computer Engineering, Kyungil University,
Gyeongbuk, Korea
kshwang@kiu.ac.kr

Abstract. In this paper we propose a sub-optimal relay selection scheme over a multiple relay network where the relay node is selected if its link quality is above a certain threshold which is set to satisfy the required performance and the selected link is maintained unless its link quality does not fall below the threshold. From our derived statistics of the received output signal-to-noise ratio (SNR), we derive the end-to-end system performance in terms of the outage probability. In addition, we apply our proposed algorithm to the selection decode-and-forward protocol, and analyze its outage performances. We show from our numerical example that our proposed algorithm can provide adequate performance by setting the moderate threshold while its complexity is much lower than the one of an optimal relay selection scheme.

Keywords: Cooperative diversity, relay selection, performance analysis, opportunistic relaying and selection decode-and-forward.

1   Introduction

Recently, the cooperative diversity systems with multiple relays, based on the distributed space-time coding (DSTC) have been presented in [1, 2] to provide the spatial diversity gain in the wireless networks. However, in order to apply the conventional DSTC schemes [1–3], all the operating relay nodes need to know the channel state information (CSI) of all the standing links among the relay nodes involved in the cooperation, which may be inappropriate for the low-power required systems such as sensor network and mm-wave WPAN systems. From a practical point of view, Bletsas, et. al. in [4] proposed the opportunistic relaying to reduce the complexity in which the best relay node among relay candidates is only used and proved that it can provide the same diversity-multiplexing gain tradeoff as obtained by more complex DSTC cooperative system [1]. However, the opportunistic relaying also needs to find the best relay nodes at every transmission time, which results in high complexity since the CSI of all participating links is required. For the low complexity relay selection, authors in [5] worked on multiple relay selection schemes for the signal-to-noise ratio (SNR)-optimal/suboptimal criteria and proved their diversity orders.

J.J. Park et al. (Eds.): NPC 2012, LNCS 7513, pp. 608–615, 2012.
© IFIP International Federation for Information Processing 2012

Amarasuriya, et. al. in [6] proposed the multiple relay selection scheme with the amplify-and-forward transmission where L c relays are sequentially selected out of L relays based on the output threshold at the destination node and analyze performance bounds over the independent, identically distributed (i.i.d.) Rayleigh fading channels.

In this paper, we propose the SNR-based partial relay selection algorithm, named "switch-and-examine relay selection" (SERS) under the DF transmission using the idea of the switching diversity in [7]. In our proposed SERS scheme, an arbitrary relay node is selected and keeps selected unless it does not fall below a certain target threshold, γ_T. As we will show later on, we derive the statistics of the output signal-to-noise ratio (SNR) per hop over the independent, but non-identically distributed (i.ni.d) Rayleigh fading channels such as the cumulative distribution function (CDF), probability density function (PDF) in a closed-form expression. In addition, we discuss the outage performance of our proposed SERS under the selection decode-and-forward (SDF) transmission [8]. For probing of efficiency of SERS, we will show that our proposed SERS can achieve the same performance in terms of the end-to-end outage probability as the opportunistic relaying [4] based on the decode-and-forward (DF) transmission while it has much lowered complexity with low power consumption because it does not always need to feedback the CSI or work the channel estimations at each participating relay node.

2 System Description

2.1 System Model

In this paper we consider a DF cooperative diversity system where one source node, one destination node, and L relay nodes are utilized in a network. Consider half-duplex dual-hop communication systems from only one active relay by the proposed scheme. We denote the channel gains as source-destination, $a_{s,d}$, source-relay i, a_s, i, and relay i-destination, $a_{i,d}$, respectively. Let $\gamma_{n,m}$ be an instantaneous output SNR for each link between the node n and m which is given as $\gamma_{n,m} = |a_{n,m}|^2 / N_0$. N_0 is a noise variance at each node. When each channel undergoes the circularly symmetric complex Gaussian fading environment, an $\gamma_{n,m}$ is exponentially distributed with parameter $1/\overline{\gamma}_{n,m}$ (i.e. $\overline{\gamma}_{n,m} = E[\lambda_{n,m}]$) where $E(\cdot)$ is the expectation operator. Generally, we consider the independent and non-identically distributed (i.ni.d.) channels for each hop, and if the assumption of the independent and identically distributed (i.i.d.) channels is given, the average SNRs for source-destination, source-relay and relay-destination links are represented as $\overline{\gamma}_{s,d} = E[\gamma_{s,d}]$, $\overline{\gamma}_{s,d} = E[\gamma_{s,d}]$ and $\overline{\gamma}_{r,d} = E[\gamma_{i,d}]$, respectively. Conveniently, we denote the instantaneous output SNRs for the source-relay and the relay-destination links as Γ_1 and Γ_2, respectively.

2.2 Mode of Operation of Proposed Algorithm

During the guard periods, the source node broadcasts its pilot sequence to all relay nodes via the RTS packet, and the destination node also sends its pilot sequence to all relay nodes via the CTS packet [4]. After transmitting RTS and CTS packets, the first relay candidate[1] starts to estimate its channels. If channels of the dual-hop for the first relay are above the predetermined target threshold, the first relay candidate informs it to the source node and the remainders of relay candidates by using an acknowledgement (ACK) signal. In this situation, the remainders of possible relay nodes need not to work such as channel estimations, decoding processes and retransmissions. More specifically, we first estimate the output SNR, $\gamma_{s,1}$, between the source node and the first relay candidate. If $\gamma_{s,1}$ is acceptable (i.e. $\gamma_{s,1} \geq \gamma_T$), the relay node estimates the output SNR for the relay-destination link, $\gamma_{1,d}$. When $\gamma_{1,d}$ is higher than the target threshold (i.e. $\gamma_{1,d} \geq \gamma_T$), finally, the first relay candidate is chosen as an acceptable relay node (i.e. $\Gamma_1 = \gamma_{s,1}$ and $\Gamma_2 = \gamma_{1,d}$). If the first relay candidate is not available, it sends a negative acknowledgement (NACK) signal to the source node and the remainders of relay candidates, and then the second candidate starts the channel estimations and compares them with the target threshold. Of course, when the source-relay link of the first relay candidate is unacceptable (i.e. $\gamma_{s,1} < \gamma_T$), no relay operation is performed, that is, the output SNR between the relay and destination need not be estimated. After comparison, the second relay sends its decision to others like the first one. This procedure continues up to $(L-1)$th relay candidate to find an adequate relay node. In case that $(L-1)$th relay candidate still fails to satisfy the target threshold, Lth relay candidate is used for a cooperation without comparing to the target threshold.

3   CDF and PDF

3.1   CDF and PDF

From the mode of operation, we can write the CDF of the output SNR for the source-relay link, Γ_1, in (1).

$$P_{\Gamma_1}(x) = \begin{cases} \Pr[\gamma_T \leq \gamma_{s,l} < x \,\&\, \gamma_T < \gamma_{1,d}] \\ \quad + \sum_{j=2}^{L-1} \Pr[\max\{\min\{\gamma_{s,1},\gamma_{1,d}\},...,\min\{\gamma_{s,j-1},\gamma_{j-1,d}\}\} < \gamma_T \\ \quad \,\&\, \gamma_T \leq \gamma_{s,j} < x \,\&\, \gamma_T < \gamma_{j,d}] \\ \quad + \Pr[\max\{\min\{\gamma_{s,1},\gamma_{t,d}\},...,\min\{\gamma_{s,L-1},\gamma_{L-1,d}\}\} < \gamma_T \\ \quad \,\&\, \gamma_{s,L} < x], \qquad\qquad\qquad\qquad\qquad\qquad\qquad x \geq \gamma_T, \\ \Pr[\max\{\min\{\gamma_{s,1},\gamma_{1,d}\},...,\min\{\gamma_{s,L-1},\gamma_{L-1,d}\}\} < \gamma_T \\ \quad \,\&\, \gamma_{s,L} < x], \qquad\qquad\qquad\qquad\qquad\qquad\qquad x < \gamma_T. \end{cases} \qquad (1)$$

Using the i.ni.d. assumption over relay paths, the CDF of Γ_1, $P_{\Gamma_1}(x)$, can be evaluated in terms of the individual CDF of $\gamma_{n,m}$, $P_{\gamma_{n,m}}(\cdot)$ as

---

[1] In our proposed scheme, we presume that there is the predetermined order to probe relays.

$$P_{\Gamma1}(x) = \begin{cases} (P_{\gamma_{s,1}}(x) - P_{\gamma_{s,1}}(\gamma_T))(1 - P_{\gamma_{1,d}}(\gamma_T)) \\[2mm] + \sum_{i=2}^{L-1}\prod_{j=1}^{i-1}(1-(1-P_{\gamma_{s,j}}(\gamma_T))(1-P_{\gamma_{j,d}}(\gamma_T))) \\[2mm] \times(P_{\gamma_{s,i}}(x) - P_{\gamma_{s,i}}(\gamma_T))(1 - P_{\gamma_{i,d}}(\gamma_T)) \\[2mm] + \prod_{k=1}^{L-1}(1-(1-P_{\gamma_{s,k}}(\gamma_T))(1-P_{\gamma_{k,d}}(\gamma_T)))P_{\gamma_{s,L}}(x), & x \geq \gamma_T, \\[2mm] + \prod_{k=1}^{L-1}(1-(1-P_{\gamma_{s,k}}(\gamma_T))(1-P_{\gamma_{k,d}}(\gamma_T)))P_{\gamma_{s,L}}(x), & x < \gamma_T, \end{cases} \qquad (2)$$

Note that the statistics of the output SNR for the relay-destination link, Γ_2, can be obtained in a similar way by replacing the $P_{\gamma_{s,l}}(\cdot)$ and $P_{\gamma_{l,d}}(\cdot)$ with $P_{\gamma_{l,d}}(\cdot)$ and $P_{\gamma_{s,l}}(\cdot)$ in (2), respectively[2]. In addition, we obtain the PDF of Γ_1, $p_{\Gamma_1}(x)$ differentiating $p_{\Gamma_1}(x)$ in (2) with respect to x as

$$p_{\Gamma_1}(x) = \begin{cases} (1 - P_{\gamma_{1,d}}(\gamma_T))p_{\gamma_{s,1}}(x) + \sum_{i=2}^{L-1}\prod_{j=1}^{i-1}(1-(1-R_{\gamma_{s,j}}(\gamma_T)) \\[2mm] \times(1-P_{\gamma_{j,d}}(\gamma_T)))(1-P_{\gamma_{i,d}}(\gamma_T))p_{\gamma_{s,i}}(x) \\[2mm] + \prod_{k=1}^{L-1}(1-(1-P_{\gamma_{s,k}}(\gamma T))(1-P_{\gamma_{k,d}}(\gamma_T)))p_{\gamma_{s,L}}(x), & x \geq \gamma_T, \\[2mm] + \prod_{k=1}^{L-1}(1-(1-P_{\gamma_{s,k}}(\gamma_T))(1-P_{\gamma_{k,d}}(\gamma_T)))p_{\gamma_{s,L}}(x), & x < \gamma_T, \end{cases} \qquad (3)$$

where $p_{\gamma_{n,m}}(\cdot)$ denotes the individual PDF of the output SNR between a node n and node m. For the i.ni.d. Rayleigh fading channels, the CDF and PDF of Γ_1 for SERS in (2) and (3) can be represented by exponential distributions, respectively, as

$$P_{\Gamma_1}(x) = \begin{cases} (e^{-\gamma_T/\bar{\gamma}_{s,1}} - e^{-x/\bar{\gamma}_{s,1}})e^{-\gamma_T/\bar{\gamma}_{1,d}} \\[2mm] + \sum_{i=2}^{L-1}\prod_{j=1}^{i-1}(1-e^{-\gamma_T/\bar{\gamma}_{b_j}})(e^{-\gamma_T/\bar{\gamma}_{s,i}} - e^{-x/\bar{\gamma}_{s,i}})e^{-\gamma_T/\bar{\gamma}_{i,d}} \\[2mm] + \prod_{k=1}^{L-1}(1-e^{-\gamma_T/\bar{\gamma}_{b_k}})(1-e^{-x/\bar{\gamma}_{s,r}}), & x \geq \gamma_T, \\[2mm] \prod_{k=1}^{L-1}(1-e^{-\gamma_T/\bar{\gamma}_{b_k}})(1-e^{-x/\bar{\gamma}_{s,r}}), & x < \gamma_T, \end{cases} \qquad (4)$$

---

[2] The PDF and MGF of Γ_2 are also obtained in a similar way by $P_{\gamma_{n,m}}(\cdot)$ and $p_{\gamma_{n,m}}(\cdot)$ with $P_{\gamma_{m,n}}(\cdot)$ and $p_{\gamma_{m,n}}(\cdot)$, respectively.

and

$$
P_{\Gamma_1}(x) = \begin{cases} \dfrac{1}{\overline{\gamma}_{s,1}} e^{-\left(\frac{\gamma_\Gamma}{\overline{\gamma}_{1,d}} + \frac{x}{\overline{\gamma}_{s,1}}\right)} \displaystyle\sum_{i=2}^{L-1} \prod_{j=1}^{i-1} (1 - e^{-\overline{\gamma}_T / \overline{\gamma}_{bj}}) \dfrac{1}{\overline{\gamma}_{s,i}} e^{-\left(\frac{\gamma_T}{\overline{\gamma}_{1,d}} + \frac{x}{\overline{\gamma}_{s,i}}\right)} \\[4mm] + \displaystyle\prod_{k=1}^{L-1} (1 - e^{-\gamma_T / \overline{\gamma}_{bk}}) \dfrac{1}{\overline{\gamma}_{s,L}} e^{-x/\overline{\gamma}_{s,L}}, & x \ge \gamma_T, \\[4mm] \displaystyle\prod_{k=1}^{L-1} (1 - e^{-\gamma_T / \overline{\gamma}_{bk}}) \dfrac{1}{\overline{\gamma}_{s,L}} e^{-x/\overline{\gamma}_{s,L}}, & x < \gamma_T, \end{cases}
\tag{5}
$$

where $\overline{\gamma}_{b_j} = \overline{\gamma}_{s,j} \overline{\gamma}_{j,d} / (\overline{\gamma}_{s,j} + \overline{\gamma}_{j,d})$.

4   Outage Performance of the Proposed SERS

4.1   End-to-End Outage Performance of SERS

In the end-to-end dual-hop communication where there is no direct transmission, we can define the end-to-end outage event as the case of when either one of dual links connected in series falls below the outage threshold. Thus, the outage probability can be obtained as [9]

$$
P_{out}^{ETE}(\gamma_{th}) = 1 - (1 - P_{\Gamma_1}(\gamma_{th}))(1 - P_{\Gamma_2}(\gamma_{th})),
\tag{6}
$$

where $P_{\Gamma_i}(\cdot)$ is defined in (2), and γ_{th} is a, outage threshold which can be represented as $\gamma_{th} = 2^{2R} - 1$ for R bps/Hz transmission.

4.2   Outage Performance of SERS Based on SDF Relaying

The SDF protocol for cooperative systems [8] was introduced as an efficient re-laying protocol. In SDF, the relay node operates when only the channel between the source and the relay can support the transmitted data rate, R, without error. In other words, the relay may fully decode the entire source codeword without error by a Cyclic Redundancy Check (CRC) and successfully decoded signals are retransmitted to the destination node. When the relay cannot decode, only the direct transmission is performed without a relay node. Based on SDF protocol, we can consider two outage scenarios 1) the relay is not being able to decode, then the source is repeating its transmission, 2) the relay is ability to decode and repeat the source information. Thus, we can write the mutual information of the proposed SERS based on SDF as where

$$
I_{\gamma_{tot}} = \begin{cases} \dfrac{1}{2}\log(1 + 2\gamma_{s,d}), & \gamma_{s,d} < \gamma_{th}, \\[3mm] \dfrac{1}{2}\log(1 + 2\gamma_{s,d} + \Gamma_2), & \gamma_{s,d} \ge \gamma_{th}. \end{cases}
\tag{7}
$$

Using the CDF of Γ_1 in (4) and γ_{tot} in (12), the outage probability of the proposed SERS over the i.ni.d. Rayleigh fading channels can be given as

$$P_{out}^{SDF}(\gamma_{th}) = P_{\Gamma_1}(\gamma_{th})P_{\gamma_{s,d}}(\gamma_{th}/2) + (1 - P_{\Gamma_1}(\gamma_{th}))P_{\gamma_{tot}}(\gamma_{th}). \qquad (8)$$

The closed-form expression of $P_{\gamma tot}(\gamma_{th})$ in (8) is given in Appendix A.

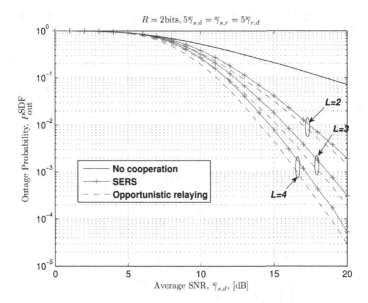

Fig. 1. Comparison of outage probability of the proposed SERS and the opportunistic relaying based on SDF protocol

5   Numerical Example

In Fig. 1, we apply our proposed SERS to SDF protocol. In this example, we set the outage threshold as 2 bps/Hz and use the optimal target threshold for our proposed SERS. Because our SERS does not maximize the total combined SNR at the destination, γ_{tot}, a little loss of outage performance is observed when comparing with the opportunistic relaying. However, the performance loss is only around 1 dB in most of SNR region of our interest whereas our proposed SERS requires a very low system complexity.

6   Conclusion

In this paper, we proposed a sub-optimal relay selection scheme, named SERS, in a dual-hop DF transmission to reduce the complexity and the power consumption at the relay nodes. Based on the derived statistics of the output SNR, we presented the outage performance of the proposed scheme. From our selected numerical examples, our proposed scheme can provide the commensurate performance gain with the optimal relay selection algorithm while it satisfies the required performance with lower complexity.

Appendix A. Statistics of Combined SNR at the Destination

Assuming the maximal ratio combining (MRC) at the destination node, the total combined SNR at the destination node can be written as

$$\gamma_{tot} = \gamma_{s,d} + \Gamma_2. \tag{9}$$

Since two random variables, $\gamma_{s,d}$ and Γ_2, are mutually independent, the PDF of γ_{tot} can be calculated as

$$p_{\gamma_{tot}} = \int_0^\infty p_{\gamma_{s,d}}(z-y) p_{\Gamma_2}(y) dy \tag{10}$$

By substituting (5) into (10) and doing some manipulations, the PDF of γ tot over the i.ni.d. Rayleigh fading channels can be given by

$$p_{\gamma_{tot}}(x) = \begin{cases} \dfrac{1}{\overline{\gamma}_{1,d} - \overline{\gamma}_{s,d}} e^{-\gamma_T/\overline{\gamma}_{b_1}} (e^{-(x-\gamma_T)/\overline{\gamma}_{1,d}} - e^{-(x-\gamma_T)/\overline{\gamma}_{s,d}}) \\[2ex] + \displaystyle\sum_{i=2}^{L-1} \prod_{j=1}^{i-1} \dfrac{1}{\overline{\gamma}_{1,d} - \overline{\gamma}_{s,d}} e^{-\gamma_T/\overline{\gamma}_{b_j}} (1 - e^{-\gamma_T/\overline{\gamma}_{b_j}}) \\[2ex] \times (e^{-(x-\gamma_T)/\overline{\gamma}_{1,d}} - e^{-(x-\gamma_T)/\overline{\gamma}_{s,d}}) \\[2ex] + \displaystyle\prod_{k=1}^{L-1} (1 - e^{-\gamma_T/\overline{\gamma}_{b_k}}) \dfrac{e^{-x/\overline{\gamma}_{s,d}} - e^{-x/\overline{\gamma}_{L,d}}}{\overline{\gamma}_{L,d} - \overline{\gamma}_{s,d}}, & x \geq \gamma_T, \\[2ex] \displaystyle\prod_{k=1}^{L-1} (1 - e^{-\gamma_T/\overline{\gamma}_{b_k}}) \dfrac{e^{-x/\overline{\gamma}_{s,d}} - e^{-x/\overline{\gamma}_{L,d}}}{\overline{\gamma}_{L,d} - \overline{\gamma}_{s,d}}, & x < \gamma_T, \end{cases} \tag{11}$$

The CDF of γ_{tot} over the i.ni.d. Rayleigh fading channels can be obtained by integrating (11) with respect to x as follows

$$P_{\gamma_{tot}}(x) = \begin{cases} \dfrac{e^{-\gamma_T/\overline{\gamma}_{b_1}}}{\overline{\gamma}_{1,d} - \overline{\gamma}_{s,d}} \left(\overline{\gamma}_{1,d}(1 - e^{-(x-\gamma_T)/\overline{\gamma}_{1,d}}) - \overline{\gamma}_{s,d}(1 - e^{-(x-\overline{\gamma}_T)/\overline{\gamma}_{s,d}}) \right) \\[2ex] + \displaystyle\sum_{i=2}^{L-1} \prod_{j=1}^{i-1} \dfrac{1}{\overline{\gamma}_{1,d} - \overline{\gamma}_{s,d}} e^{-\gamma_T/\overline{\gamma}_{b_j}} (1 - e^{-\gamma_T/\overline{\gamma}_{b_j}}) \\[2ex] \times \left(\overline{\gamma}_{i,d}(1 - e^{-(x-\gamma_T)/\overline{\gamma}_{i,d}}) - \overline{\gamma}_{s,d}(1 - e^{-(x-\gamma_T)/\overline{\gamma}_{s,d}}) \right) \\[2ex] + \displaystyle\prod_{k=1}^{L-1} (1 - e^{-\gamma_T/\overline{\gamma}_{b_k}}) \left(\dfrac{\overline{\gamma}_{L,d}(1 - e^{-x/\overline{\gamma}_{L,d}}) - \overline{\gamma}_{s,d}(1 - e^{-x/\overline{\gamma}_{s,d}})}{\overline{\gamma}_{L,d} - \overline{\gamma}_{s,d}} \right), & x \geq \gamma_T, \\[2ex] \displaystyle\prod_{k=1}^{L-1} (1 - e^{-\gamma_T/\overline{\gamma}_{b_k}}) \left(\dfrac{\overline{\gamma}_{L,d}(1 - e^{-x/\overline{\gamma}_{L,d}}) - \overline{\gamma}_{s,d}(1 - e^{-x/\overline{\gamma}_{s,d}})}{\overline{\gamma}_{L,d} - \overline{\gamma}_{s,d}} \right), & x < \gamma_T, \end{cases} \tag{12}$$

Acknowledgment. This work was supported by Kyungil University Grant.

References

1. Laneman, J.N., Wornell, G.W.: Distributed Space-time-coded Protocols for Exploiting Cooperative Diversity in Wireless Networks. IEEE Trans. Inform. Theory 49, 2415–2425 (2003)
2. Jing, Y., Hassibi, B.: Distributed Space-time coding in Wireless Relay Networks. IEEE Trans. Wireless Commun. 5, 3524–3536 (2006)
3. Anghel, P.A., Kaveh, M.: On the Performance of Distributed Space-time Coding Systems with One and Two Nonregenerative Relays. IEEE Trans. Wireless Commun. 5, 682–692 (2006)
4. Bletsas, A., Khisti, A., Reed, D.P., Lippman, A.: A Simple Cooperative Diversity Method based on Network Path Selection. IEEE J. Select. Areas. Commun. 24, 659–672 (2006)
5. Jing, Y., Jafarkhani, H.: Single and Multiple Relay Selection Schemes and Their Achievable Diversity Orders. IEEE Trans. Wireless Commun. 8, 1414–1423 (2009)
6. Amaraduriya, G., Ardakani, M., Tellambura, C.: Output-threshold Multiple-relay-selection Scheme for Cooperative Wireless Networks. IEEE Trans. on Veh. Tech. 59, 3091–3097 (2010)
7. Yang, H.-C., Alouini, M.-S.: Performance Analysis of Multibranch Switched Diversity Systems. IEEE Trans. Commun. 51, 782–794 (2003)
8. Laneman, J.N., Tse, D.N.C., Wornell, G.W.: Cooperative Diversity in Wireless Networks: Efficient Protocols and Outage Behavior. IEEE Trans. on Inform. Theory 50, 3062–3080 (2004)
9. Hasna, M.O., Alouini, M.-S.: End-to-end Performance of Transmission Systems with Relay over Rayleigh-fading Channels. IEEE Trans. Wireless Commun. 2, 1126–1131 (2003)

Robust Face Recognition in Low Resolution and Blurred Image Using Joint Information in Space and Frequency

Guoqing Li, Guangling Sun, and Xinpeng Zhang

School of Communication and Information Engineering, Shanghai University, Shanghai,China
sunguangling@shu.edu.cn

Abstract. Recognizing faces in low resolution and blurred images is common yet challenging task. Local Frequency Descriptor (LFD) has been proved to be effective for this problem and is extracted from a spatial neighborhood of each pixel of a frequency plane regardless of correlations between frequencies. To explore the frequency correlations and preserve low resolution and blur insensitive simultaneously, we propose Enhanced LFD (ELFD) in which information in space and frequency is jointly utilized so as to be more descriptive and discriminative than LFD. The selection of window size of short-term of Fourier transform adaptive to the testing image is also analyzed. In addition, linear weighting fusion of recognition results given by magnitude and phase is proposed. The experiments conducted on Yale and FERET databases demonstrate that promising results have been achieved by the proposed ELFD, adaptive window size selection and fusion scheme.

Keywords: face recognition, low resolution and blur, Enhanced Local Frequency Descriptor, frequency correlation, fusion.

1   Introduction

Due to a wide range of potential applications as well as academic challenges, face recognition has attracted much attention during the last decade. Despite great progress has been made in design of scheme robust to expressions and aging of subjects, partial occlusions, illuminations and inaccurate registrations, most of them aimed at recognizing faces in high quality image. Once coping with degraded images caused by such as blur, low resolution, noise etc, the performance will decline dramatically. Hence, in this paper, we will focus on robust blurred and low resolution face recognition.

There roughly exist three categories of ways in literature to handle face recognition from blurred and low resolution image. The first category is to deblur or super-resolve an image, then feed the restored image to the recognition engine [1, 2]. While the separated scheme is straightforward, the goal of image restoration is not consistent with recognition. And even worse, especially for blurred image, if the blur model is unknown or complex, notable artifacts introduced by deblurring will in fact decline the recognition performance. The second category is to do a direct recognition from blurred or low resolution image without deblurring or super resolution. Zhang et al [3] presented a joint blind restoration and recognition framework based on sparse representation. Once blur

J.J. Park et al. (Eds.): NPC 2012, LNCS 7513, pp. 616–624, 2012.

kernel is estimated, it is applied to blur the training set to produce a blur dictionary and the sparse coding of the blurred face using the blur dictionary is determined to give recognition result. Moreover, the kernel is estimated iteratively in a loop. We also have explored the blind blurred image recognition in which two frameworks are investigated [4]. One is first to infer the kernel as a separate step, then the kernel is used to generate a data dictionary and an adaptive SIFT feature dictionary is also obtained accordingly. The other is to integrate the kernel estimation and the adaptive SIFT dictionary inference into a common model. The two steps are alternatively executed until stop criterion is reached. The drawback of works in [3] and [4] is the low efficiency since the time consumption of blurring operation is too heavy. Li et al [5] learned two coupled mapping matrix that mapped a pair of high and low resolution image to a unique feature space. The target of the couple mapping matrix is to make the distance between two points in feature space as close as possible provide that they are corresponding to a pair of high and low resolution version of a same image. The approach is high efficiency and also without super resolution, but the mapped feature is global. The last category is to extract blur invariant or insensitive features. Heikkilä et al analyzed Local Phase Quantization (LPQ) descriptor robust to centrally symmetric blur [6]. LPQ relied on short-term of Fourier transform (STFT). They noticed that the local quantized phase information is nearly invariant in low frequency band. Clearly, only phase information is not appropriate since magnitude is also very useful for recognition shown by work [7]. Lei et al proposed Local Frequency Descriptor (LFD) that both magnitude and phase are extracted [8]. Similar to Local Binary Pattern (LBP) encoding relative relations between two pixels [9], LFD is defined in terms of relations of two local Fourier transforms of neighboring pixels of blurred image and proved to be insensitive to arbitrary type of blur kernel.

Our idea stems from the work in [8]. It has been shown that LFD is effective for recognizing low resolution face to a certain extent. We notice that the correlations between frequencies are beneficial for improving recognition performance particularly for low resolution and blurred degradations. Further, an adaptive selection of window size of STFT should be adopted. The paper is structured as follows: Section 2 reviews the LFD. Section 3 gives a detail discussion of the Enhanced LFD and the adaptive selection of window size of STFT. Sections 4 demonstrate good experimental results on Yale and FERET databases. Conclusion and future work are provided in section 5.

2   Review on Local Frequency Descriptor

LFD is based on STFT, which is calculated over a local area N_x centered at x of an image $f(x)$ as follows:

$$F_x(u) = \sum_{y_i \in N_x} f(y_i)\omega^*(y_i - x)e^{-j2\pi u^T y_i} \tag{1}$$

where $u = \{u_1, u_2, ...u_L\}$ denote a set of 2D frequencies, $\omega(x)$ denote a window function and $\omega^*(x)$ is the conjugate of it. An example of size 5×5 and 4 selected frequencies is shown in figure 1. The STFT of an image using size 5×5 and the 4 selected frequencies is demonstrated in figure 2.

Fig. 1. u1=(1/5,0); u_2=(0,1/5); u_3=(1/5,1/5); u_4=(1/5,-1/5);

(a)   (b) u_1 (c) u_2 (d) u_3 (e) u_4 (f) u_1 (g) u_2 (h) u_3 (i) u_4

Fig. 2. (a) Original face image. (b)-(i) magnitudes and phases of STFT at frequencies u_1,u_2,u_3 and u_4 from left to right.

Then local magnitude descriptor (lmd) and local phase descriptor (lpd) are extracted from magnitude and phase of STFT respectively. Similar to LBP, lmd and lpd are both dependent on binary strings describing relative relations between value of a position and its 8 neighbors. Once a binary string is obtained, it will be encoded a decimal integer.

3   Adaptive Window Size Selection and Enhanced LFD

3.1   Adaptive Window Size Selection

A low resolution or blurred image $g(\mathbf{x})$ is modeled as a convolution between a high quality image $f(\mathbf{x})$ and a blur kernel $k(\mathbf{x})$:

$$g(\mathbf{x}) = f(\mathbf{x}) \otimes k(\mathbf{x}) \tag{2}$$

Assume we focus on two positions $\mathbf{x}_i$ and $\mathbf{x}_j$ and two local regions centered at the two positions. In terms of definition of STFT, the Fourier transforms of the two local regions are as follows:

$$
\begin{aligned}
\mathrm{F}_{\mathbf{x}_i}(\mathbf{u}) &= F[\omega(\mathbf{x} - \mathbf{x}_i) f(\mathbf{x})] \\
\mathrm{F}_{\mathbf{x}_j}(\mathbf{u}) &= F[\omega(\mathbf{x} - \mathbf{x}_j) f(\mathbf{x})]
\end{aligned}
\tag{3}
$$

Suppose the size of $\omega(\mathbf{x})$ is W. Clearly, for the two local images $\omega(\mathbf{x} - \mathbf{x}_i) f(\mathbf{x})$ and $\omega(\mathbf{x} - \mathbf{x}_j) f(\mathbf{x})$, their sizes are both W. Now let the two local images blurred by blur kernel $k(\mathbf{x})$, the corresponding Fourier transforms are as follows:

$$
\begin{aligned}
\tilde{\mathrm{G}}_{\mathbf{x}_i}(\mathbf{u}) &= F\left[k(\mathbf{x}) \otimes [\omega(\mathbf{x} - \mathbf{x}_i) f(\mathbf{x})]\right] = \mathrm{K}(\mathbf{u}) \bullet \mathrm{F}_{\mathbf{x}_i}(\mathbf{u}) \\
\tilde{\mathrm{G}}_{\mathbf{x}_j}(\mathbf{u}) &= F\left[k(\mathbf{x}) \otimes [\omega(\mathbf{x} - \mathbf{x}_j) f(\mathbf{x})]\right] = \mathrm{K}(\mathbf{u}) \bullet \mathrm{F}_{\mathbf{x}_j}(\mathbf{u})
\end{aligned}
\tag{4}
$$

Suppose the size of $k(\mathbf{x})$ is K, the size of blurred local image will be the larger value between K and W. For a same frequency u_k, a blur invariant is true due to $\tilde{\mathrm{G}}_{\mathbf{x}_i}(u_k)/\tilde{\mathrm{G}}_{\mathbf{x}_j}(u_k)=\mathrm{F}_{\mathbf{x}_i}(u_k)/\mathrm{F}_{\mathbf{x}_j}(u_k)$. Nevertheless, the blur operation is first done then a local area is extracted so that for low resolution and blurred image, the STFT is as follows:

$$\mathbf{G}_{\mathbf{x}_i}(\mathbf{u}) = F\left[\omega(\mathbf{x}-\mathbf{x}_i)g(\mathbf{x})\right] = F\left[\omega(\mathbf{x}-\mathbf{x}_i)[k(\mathbf{x}) \otimes f(\mathbf{x})]\right]$$
$$\mathbf{G}_{\mathbf{x}_j}(\mathbf{u}) = F\left[\omega(\mathbf{x}-\mathbf{x}_j)g(\mathbf{x})\right] = F\left[\omega(\mathbf{x}-\mathbf{x}_j)[k(\mathbf{x}) \otimes f(\mathbf{x})]\right]$$

(5)

Similar to (3), the size of local image $\omega(\mathbf{x}-\mathbf{x}_i)[k(\mathbf{x}) \otimes f(\mathbf{x})]$ and $\omega(\mathbf{x}-\mathbf{x}_j)[k(\mathbf{x}) \otimes f(\mathbf{x})]$ are both W. Obviously, the blur insensitive will be compromised. However, we can make $\mathbf{G}_{\mathbf{x}_i}(\mathbf{u})$ and $\mathbf{G}_{\mathbf{x}_j}(\mathbf{u})$ approximate $\tilde{\mathbf{G}}_{\mathbf{x}_i}(\mathbf{u})$ and $\tilde{\mathbf{G}}_{\mathbf{x}_j}(\mathbf{u})$ respectively as close as possible by changing W. Being adaptive to the size of blur kernel of current testing image, W must be larger or at least equal to K; otherwise the blur insensitive is completely impossible. Given a general blur kernel of size 19×19, two STFT windows of sizes of 11×11 and 21×21 are utilized on high quality and corresponding blurred image, the magnitude discrepancy between high quality and blurred image corresponding to window sizes of 11×11 and 21×21 respectively have been illustrated in figure 3.We can see that the discrepancy of size of 21×21 is reduced to certain extend compared with that of size of 11×11. This result is just consistent with our analysis.

Certainly, the window size should not be too large yet for the ultimate goal of the descriptor is to characterize texture and structure of a local area. If the size is too large, the descriptor will be meaningless. Hence blur insensitive and local property is in fact a trade-off. In experiment, we choose a slightly larger window size than K.

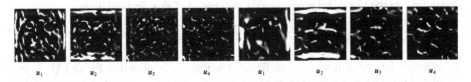

Fig. 3. Magnitude discrepancies between high quality and blurred image. The left four figures correspond window size of 11×11, the right four figures correspond window size of 21×21.

3.2 Enhanced Local Frequency Descriptor Using Joint Information in Space and Frequency

While LFD descriptor has been demonstrated to be effective for recognizing low resolution and blurred face, correlations among frequencies has not been explored since LFD only encoded the spatial neighboring relation in each single frequency plane (FP) independently. In fact, the joint representation in space and frequency is more descriptive and discriminative for recognition. To accomplish the joint representation, we propose to concatenate the binary relation of respective correlated frequencies at the same spatial locations named Enhanced LFD (ELFD). For the sake of recognition performance and efficiency, we choose arbitrary two frequencies from all frequencies as correlated frequencies. As mentioned in section 2, 4 frequencies u_1, u_2, u_3 and u_4 are selected. Accordingly, a total of 12 2-frequency combinations are produced:

$(u_1,u_2),(u_1,u_3),(u_1,u_4),(u_2,u_1),(u_2,u_3),(u_2,u_4),$
$(u_3,u_1),(u_3,u_2),(u_3,u_4),(u_4,u_1),(u_4,u_2),(u_4,u_3)$. Of a couple of correlated frequen-

cies, the former is principal FP, the latter is its correlated FP. For arbitrary a couple of correlated frequencies and a spatial location, the extended binary relations contain the 8-neighborings at the principal FP and 4-neighborings at the correlated FP. Detailed description will be given in following.

Based on the magnitude of STFT $M(u,x)$ at u and x, the enhance lmd (elmd) is defined as follows:

$$T(M(u,k),\ M(u,m)) = \begin{cases} 1 & \text{if } M(u,k) \geq M(u,m) \\ 0 & \text{otherwise} \end{cases} \tag{6}$$

where k denotes the focused position and m denotes the position of one of neighbors of pixel positioned at k. Depending on the binary relations, elmd is encoded as a decimal integer:

$$h_{\text{elmd}(u_p,u_c,k)} = \sum_{w=1}^{4} T(M(u_c,k),\ M(u_c,m))2^{w-1} + \sum_{w=5}^{12} T(M(u_p,k),\ M(u_p,m))2^{w-1} \tag{7}$$

where u_p denotes principal FP and u_c denotes its correlated FP.

Similarly, based on the phase of STFT $P(u,x)$ at u and x, the enhance lpd (elpd) is defined as follows:

$$T(P(u,k),\ P(u,m)) = \begin{cases} 1 & \text{if } P(u,k) \text{ and } P(u,m) \text{ are in the same quadrant} \\ 0 & \text{otherwise} \end{cases} \tag{8}$$

Depending on the binary relations, elpd is also encoded as a decimal integer:

$$h_{\text{elpd}(u_p,u_c,k)} = \sum_{w=1}^{4} T(P(u_c,k),\ P(u_c,m))2^{w-1} + \sum_{w=5}^{12} T(P(u_p,k),\ P(u_p,m))2^{w-1} \tag{9}$$

An example has been illustrated in figure 4 where U_1 is principal FP and U_2 is its correlated FP. The encoded integers of all positions compose a labeled image and the 12 labeled magnitude and phase images are shown in figure 5.

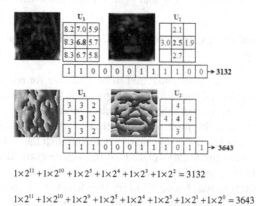

$$1\times2^{11}+1\times2^{10}+1\times2^{5}+1\times2^{4}+1\times2^{3}+1\times2^{2}=3132$$

$$1\times2^{11}+1\times2^{10}+1\times2^{9}+1\times2^{5}+1\times2^{4}+1\times2^{3}+1\times2^{1}+1\times2^{0}=3643$$

Fig. 4. The ELFD at a location and two correlated FPs

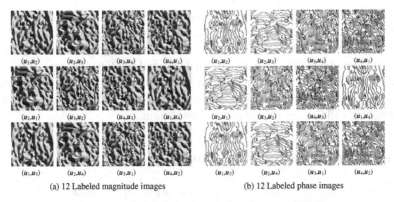

(a) 12 Labeled magnitude images   (b) 12 Labeled phase images

Fig. 5. Labeled magnitude and phase images of ELFD

Next, each of the 24 labeled images is divided empirically into 4×4=16 non-overlapping sub-regions. Thereafter a total of 16×12=192 regional label histograms are generated and concatenated into a long feature vector for both magnitude and phase. To declare the low resolution and blur insensitive properties of ELFD, for a sub-region indicated by red rectangle, two histograms of 4096 bins corresponding to original and low resolution with scale of 2 have been demonstrated in figure 6. It can be seen that the two histograms of original and low resolution image indeed stay consistently on the whole though there exists sight variations between them.

Naturally, the main drawback of ELFD is the substantially increased number of bins being 2^l, where l is the length of encoded binary string. The dimensionality of feature vector will be much higher with bins number increasing. It will introduce curse of dimensionality and make the feature unstable. We tackle it with a learning scheme: depending on training set, a global label histogram is obtained first. In a sequel,

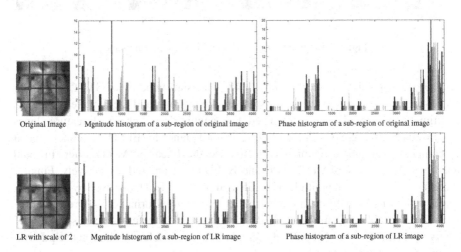

Original Image   Mgnitude histogram of a sub-region of original image   Phase histogram of a sub-region of original image

LR with scale of 2   Mgnitude histogram of a sub-region of LR image   Phase histogram of a sub-region of LR image

Fig. 6. Histograms of a sub-region

percentages of all bins are ordered and two bins of least percentage are combined into one bin and the two percentages are summed as the percentage of the combined bin. Ordering and combinations of bins are executed alternatively and iteratively until a satisfied number of bins are achieved. The final kept and combined bins are called valid bins. The original bins of a tested sub-region histogram will be adjusted and combined into a much lower number of bins in terms of the learned valid bins. The specific valid number of bins will be explained in experiment section.

4   Experimental Results and Analysis

Our proposed method ELFD and adaptive scheme are evaluated on two databases: Yale and FERET. FERET database used here is a random subset of original FERET containing 40 persons. Two low resolution degradations with down sample scale of 2 and 4, two central symmetric blur kernels including Gaussian kernel (standard deviation 3 and size 7×7) and linear motion kernel (7 pixel-length with 45 degrees), 8 complex non-parametric kernels [10] are tested. The 12 degradations of original high resolution image in figure 2(a) are depicted in figure 7.

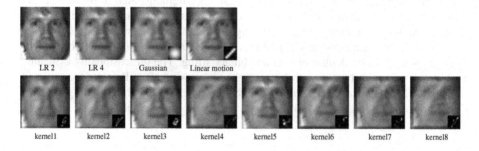

Fig. 7. 12 degradations of original high resolution image

The optimal valid number of bins is 48, Gaussian window of STFT and linear SVM classifier are adopted. Half of samples are training and the rest are testing. In addition, 5 cross validation is conducted. For magnitude and phase, all feature planes (for instance, 4 feature planes for LFD, 12 feature planes for ELFD) are concatenated to compose a complete feature vector to feed the linear SVM classifier. Fix and adaptive window size of STFT, LFD and ELFD are compared respectively. Finally, recognition results of magnitude of ELFD and phase of LFD are fused by an optimal linear weighting strategy to improve the recognition performance. All results have been listed in table 1. In this table, lmd/lpd with suffix "f" refers to fixed size and "a" refers to adaptive size. Accordingly, elmda and elpda refer to elmd and elpd with adaptive size respectively.

Table 1. Accuracy Rates of Yale and FERET (%)

Type	Yale							FERET						
	lmdf	lpdf	lmda	lpda	elmda	elpda	fusion	lmdf	lpdf	lmda	lpda	elmda	elpda	fusion
LR2	98.67	94.67	98.67	95.33	99.33	94.67	99.56	95.33	91.83	95.33	92.83	96.67	93.33	96.83
LR4	96.67	81.33	96.89	90.44	99.11	92.00	99.56	91.50	56.33	94.00	88.83	95.83	88.17	95.50
Gaussian	94.22	61.33	94.22	82.67	97.78	81.11	98.00	90.17	40.33	90.17	78.67	92.83	71.00	93.50
motion	94.00	76.44	94.00	90.89	97.78	89.56	97.78	92.33	81.33	92.33	85.50	94.67	85.00	95.83
kernel1	83.33	34.67	96.00	80.22	98.44	80.44	98.00	83.00	37.67	91.83	81.67	94.17	83.17	94.17
kernel2	80.89	48.22	94.00	68.22	97.78	71.33	97.33	78.67	45.17	90.67	75.00	92.50	73.83	91.83
kernel3	93.56	61.11	96.44	90.22	98.67	90.22	99.11	93.00	55.17	94.00	86.17	95.67	86.67	95.50
kernel4	67.56	38.89	74.22	67.78	77.33	60.44	81.78	52.83	29.17	70.33	65.17	77.50	59.50	82.83
kernel5	93.78	76.22	95.56	89.78	98.44	87.78	98.67	94.17	71.50	94.00	86.33	94.83	85.00	95.67
kernel6	82.89	62.44	91.11	78.67	94.89	78.22	95.33	81.33	57.33	87.50	78.00	90.33	78.50	91.00
kernel7	83.78	67.33	88.22	72.00	92.00	73.78	93.11	74.50	51.83	84.33	71.17	86.67	68.00	87.67
kernel8	76.67	67.33	85.56	70.89	88.44	70.67	92.67	68.00	55.67	81.17	65.33	82.67	62.67	86.67
average	87.17	64.17	92.07	81.43	95.00	80.85	**95.91**	82.90	56.11	88.81	79.56	91.19	77.90	**92.25**

- **Fixed Size versus Adaptive Size**

We test a fix size of 11×11. For adaptive size, we empirically set the size for low resolution of 2 scale and 4 scale to 11×11 and 21×21 respectively and slightly larger than kernel size for other degradations. In fact, we do not know blur kernel size in advance in reality, but the problem is simplified by assuming it is known in this paper. The great improvements obtained by the adaptive window size indicate that the feasibility and necessity of it.

- **LFD versus ELFD**

Results of both databases have shown the performance of elmd is superior to lmd but the performance of elpd is inferior to lpd in contrast. This may ascribe to curse of dimensionality since the dimensions of elmd and elpd are much higher than that of lmd and lpd. This means that if appropriate discriminant analysis is implemented, the performance of elpd will surpass lpd and the advantage of elmd will be further increased.

- **Fusion Strategy**

Through an optimal weighting value, the recognition performance could be improved by linear fusion of distance given by elmda and lpda. By an empirical search, the optimal weighting of results provided by elmda is 0.8 and the other is 0.2.

5   Conclusions and Future Work

A novel local face representation robust to low resolution and blurred degradation and other usual variations called Enhanced LFD is proposed. It improves the performance of LFD by utilizing the correlations among different frequencies so as to present a joint local descriptor of two correlated frequencies at identical spatial locations. In addition, adaptive size selection for window of STFT is proposed and a discussion in depth about it is presented. Last, a linear weighting fusion strategy is implemented. Encouraging results have been obtained on commonly used Yale and FERET database.

Future work will complement discriminate analysis for ELFD instead of direct concatenations and develop methods of automatic inference for blur kernel size of testing image.

References

1. Nishiyama, M., Hadid, A., et al.: Facial Deblur Inference Using Subspace Analysis for Recognition of Blurred Faces. IEEE Transactions on Pattern Analysis and Machine Intelligence 33(4), 838–845 (2011)
2. Liu, C., Shum, H.Y., Freeman, W.T.: Face hallucination: Theory and Practice. International Journal of Computer Vision 75(1), 115–134 (2007)
3. Zhang, H., Yang, J., et al.: Close the Loop: Joint Blind Image Restoration and Recognition with Sparse Representation Prior. In: IEEE International Conference on Computer Vision, pp. 770–777 (2011)
4. Sun, G., Li, G.: Blurred Image Classification Using Adaptive Dictionary. In: The 3rd IEEE International Conference on Intelligent Computing and Intelligent Systems, oral, vol. 3, pp. 419–423 (2011)
5. Li, B., Chang, H., Shan, S., Chen, X.: Low-Resolution Face Recognition via Coupled Locality Preserving Mappings. IEEE Signal Processing Letters 17(1), 20–23 (2010)
6. Heikkilä, J., Ojansivu, V.: Methods for Local Phase Quantization in Blur-Insensitive Image Analysis. Local and Non-Local Approximation in Image Processing, 104–111 (2009)
7. Xie, S., Shan, S., Chen, X., Chen, J.: Fusing Local Patterns of Gabor Magnitude and Phase for Face Recognition. IEEE Transactions on Image Processing 19, 1349–1361 (2010)
8. Lei, Z., Ahonen, T., et al.: Local Frequency Descriptor for Low-Resolution Face Recognition. In: IEEE International Conference on Automatic Face & Gesture Recognition and Workshops, pp. 161–166 (2011)
9. Ahonen, T., Hadid, A., Pietikainen, M.: Face Description with Local Binary Patterns:Application to Face Recognition. IEEE Transactions on Pattern Analysis and Machine Intelligence 28, 2037–2041 (2006)
10. Levin, A., Weiss, Y., Durand, F., Freeman, W.: Understanding and Evaluating Blind Deconvolution Algorithms. In: IEEE Conference on Computer Vision and Pattern Recognition, pp. 1964–1971 (2009)

Algorithms Based on Finite Automata for Testing of Z-codes[*]

Dang Quyet Thang[1], Nguyen Dinh Han[2], and Phan Trung Huy[3]

[1] Nam Dinh University of Technology and Education, Vietnam
thangdgqt@gmail.com
[2] Hung Yen University of Technology and Education, Vietnam
hannguyen@utehy.edu.vn
[3] Hanoi University of Science and Technology, Vietnam
huypt-fami@mail.hut.edu.vn, huyfr2002@yahoo.com

Abstract. In this paper, we propose an algorithm to decide whether a regular language recognized by finite automata is a Z-code or not. This algorithm has time complexity $O(n^4)$ for the general case of non-deterministic automata, $O(n^2)$ for the restricted case of deterministic automata, where n is the number of states of finite automata.

Keywords: deterministic automata, bipolar, quadratic algorithm, Z-code.

1 Introduction

The *bi-infinite* words play an important part in research infinite behaviors of system, logical models, formal dynamic systems, games and new code construction ... In coding processes, especially in transmission environment such as local networks, internet.. there are various new kinds of encoded messages that we do not know its starting and ending points, therefore its content can not be decoded. Using Z-codes for *bi-infinite* words (message), we can determine the encoding and decoding processes for any bi-infinite message by using some kind of Z-codes... Research Z-codes in formal languages, specially in theory of codes has been one of main subjects in many works [2-4,6-8,11,12], etc., which showed the interesting role of Z-codes. A very basic problem is to test wherether or not a language of finite words is a Z-code, specially, when the input is a regular language recognized by finite automata. The techniques to solve this problem provide effective methods to develop research on the related areas of codes, finite graphs and automata. The testing algorithm for Z-codes for the case of finite languages is given in [9]. However, for the general case of regular languages, such an algorithm is not known and this is the subject of this paper.

---

[*] This work is supported by Vietnamese National Foundation for Science & Technology Development (NAFOSTED).

J.J. Park et al. (Eds.): NPC 2012, LNCS 7513, pp. 625–635, 2012.
© IFIP International Federation for Information Processing 2012

Here we introduce a new testing algorithm for Z-codes with time complexity $O(n^2)$ when the input is deterministic finite automaton, and it is $O(n^4)$ when the input is non-deterministic finite automaton.

In Section 2, we recall some basic notions. In Section 3 we present some algorithms to set up a kind of extended automata. These automata permit us to establish the main result - a new testing algorithm for Z-codes in Section 4.

2   Preliminaries

We recall some notions and notations (see [1,2,6,7]). Let Σ be an alphabet. As usual, Σ^* is the free monoid generated by Σ whose elements are called *finite words*. We denote by ε the empty word. We call a nonempty word w *primitive* if it is not a proper power of any word. Set $\Sigma^+ = \Sigma^* - \{\varepsilon\}$. A subset of Σ^* is called a *language*.

In the following, our consideration is mainly based on the notion of infinite words. Let $^N\Sigma$, Σ^N, Σ^Z be the sets of left infinite, right infinite and bi-infinite words on Σ respectively. For a language L of Σ^*, we denote $^\omega L$, L^ω and $^\omega L^\omega$ the left infinite, the right infinite and the bi-infinite product of nonempty words of L respectively.

Factorizations on L of left or right infinite word are understood customarily (see [2,7]), but factorizations of a bi-infinite word need a special treatment as follows. Let $w \in \Sigma^Z$ be in the form: $w = \cdots a_{-2}a_{-1}a_0a_1a_2 \cdots$ with $a_i \in \Sigma$. An *L-factorization* of the bi-infinite word w is a strictly increasing function $\mu : Z \to Z$ satisfying $x_i = a_{\mu(i)+1} \cdots a_{\mu(i+1)} \in L$ for all $i \in Z$. Two L-factorizations μ and λ are said to be *equal*, denoted by $\mu = \lambda$ if there is $t \in Z$ such that $\lambda(i+t) = \mu(i)$ for all $i \in Z$. Otherwise, μ and λ are *distinct*, denoted by $\mu \neq \lambda$. It is easy to verify that $\mu \neq \lambda$ if and only if $\mu(Z) \neq \lambda(Z)$, or equivalently, there exists a word $u \in \Sigma^+$, two bi-infinite sequences of words of L: $\cdots, x_{-2}, x_{-1}, x_0, x_1, x_2, \cdots$ and $\cdots, y_{-2}, y_{-1}, y_0, y_1, y_2, \cdots$ such that:

$$\cdots x_{-2}x_{-1}u = \cdots y_{-1}y_0, \ |u| \leq |x_0|, \ x_0x_1x_2 \cdots = uy_1y_2 \cdots, \ |u| \leq |y_0|, \text{ with } u \neq x_0 \text{ or } u \neq y_0.$$

If every right infinite word of Σ^N has at most one factorization on L then L is said to be an *N-code* (see [7]). Analogously, if every left infinite word of $^N\Sigma$ possesses this property, we call L an $\overline{N}$-code. Obviously, L is an N-code if and only if $\overline{N} = \{\overline{x} : x \in L\}$ is an $\overline{N}$-code, where if $x = a_1a_2 \cdots a_n$ then $\overline{x} = a_n \cdots a_2a_1$.

Definition 1. A language L of Σ^+ is a *Z-code* if all L-factorizations of every bi-infinite word on L are equal.

Example 1. Every singleton $\{u\}$ is always both an N-code and an $\overline{N}$-code but it is a Z-code if and only if u is primitive. The language $L=\{ab, ba\}$ is both an N-code and an $\overline{N}$-code, but it is not a Z-code since the $...ababab...$ has two L-factorizations $...(ab)(ab)(ab)...$ and $...(ba)(ba)(ba)...$, which are verified directly to be distinct.

A *finite automaton* over Σ is a 5-tuple $A=(Q,\Sigma,E,I,F)$, where Q is a finite set of states, $E\subseteq Q\times\Sigma\times Q$ is a non-empty set of arcs, $I\subseteq Q$ is called *a set of initial states*, $F\subseteq Q$ is called *a set of terminal states*. Each arc $e\in E$ is a tuple $e=(p,a,q)$: *e starts* from p, *ends* at q and its label is a. We also say that *e leaves p for q*. A finite automaton A is called *deterministic* if $Card(I)\geq 1$ and for any $q\in Q$, $a\in\Sigma$, there is at most one arc that leaves q with the label a. A sequence of arcs $\pi=e_1e_2...e_k\in E^*$, where $e_1=(p_0,a_1,p_1),...,e_k=(p_{k-1},a_k,p_k)$ is called a *path* from p_0 to p_k. The word $w=a_1a_2...a_k$ is the label of π. A path π is called a *successful path* if its start state $p_0\in I$ and its end state $p_k\in F$. In this case, we say that the word as its label is *recognized* by A. The set of all words recognized by A is called the language recognized by A, denoted by $L(A)$.

A *directed graph* is a couple $G=(V,E)$, where V is a set of vertices and E is a set of arcs, each arc is an ordered pair of vertices: $e=(u,v)$, $u,v\in V$. If all V,E are finite we call G finite. A path from a vertex u to v consists of a sequence of vertices $x_0,...,x_n$, where $u=x_0$, $v=x_n$, $(x_i,x_{i+1})\in E$, $i=0,...,n-1$.

3 Extension of Finite Automata

We consider a kind of extended automata to establish a testing algorithm for Z-codes.

3.1 Bipolar Automat

A (non-deterministic) finite automaton A is called a *bipolar* automaton if A has only one initial state and one terminal state, and there is no arc starting from the terminal state, there is no arc ending at the initial state.

Given a finite automaton $A=(Q,\Sigma,E,I,F)$ recognizing the language $L\subseteq\Sigma^+$. From A, we construct a bipolar automaton $A'=(Q',\Sigma,E',I',F')$ recognizing the same L as follows.

(i)   Choose two new states $s,f\notin Q$, $s\neq f$, set $Q'=Q\cup\{s,f\}$. set $I'=\{s\}$, $F'=\{f\}$.

(ii)   Set $E'=E_1\cup\{(s,a,q)|(p,a,q)\in E_1,p\in I\}$, where $E_1=E\cup\{(p,a,f)|(p,a,q)\in E,q\in F\}$.

For simplicity, we denote $A'=(Q',\Sigma,E',s,f)$, and call s the in-polar, f the out-polar. The algorithm to construct A' from A is denoted by A_D has time complexity $O(|Q|+|E|)$.

Given a bipolar automaton A recognizing the language $L\subseteq\Sigma^+$, we can construct an *extended* automaton A' that recognizes L^ω (Büchi' type) by adding an ε-arc which starts at the out-polar, ends at the in-polar of A. We also denote A' by $Ex(A_D)$.

Given an extended automaton $A=(Q,\Sigma,E,s,f)$ recognizing a language L^ω, we construct a *reversed* automaton $A'=(Q',\Sigma,E',s',f')$, with $Q=Q'$, $s'=f$, $f'=s$, E' is the set of reversed arcs of E. Then A' recognizes the language $\overline{L}^\omega$. The algorithm to construct A' can be expressed by a function Reverse(A) with time complexity $O(|Q|+|E|)$.

Remark 1. Let $A=(Q,\Sigma,E,I,F)$ be a non-deterministic finite automaton and let $c=|\Sigma|$, $n=|Q|$, $m=|E|$. Then, (i) if $A'=A_D$ then $L(A)=L(A')$. (ii) in special cases, if A is deterministic then for any $q \in Q$, there are at most c arcs leaving q. Hence, A has at most $m=n.c$ arcs. When c can be seen as a constant, the time complexity of setting up A_D is $O(n)$. The number of states of A_D, and $\text{Ex}(A_D)$ is at most $n+2$. The number of arcs of A_D is at most $2m+2c=2nc+2c$ and the number of arcs of $\text{Ex}(A_D)$ is at most $2nc+2c+1$.

3.2   Products of Automata

In this paper we need to construct a new automaton $A=(Q,\Sigma,E,s,f)$ as a product of two automata (see [5]) as follows. Given two extended or bipolar automata $A_1=(Q_1,\Sigma,E_1,s_1,f_1)$ and $A_2=(Q_2,\Sigma,E_2,s_2,f_2)$, where $Q \subseteq Q_1 \times Q_2$, E is defined as follows:

(i) $\forall (q_1,a,p_1) \in E_1,\ \forall (q_2,a,p_2) \in E_2,\ a \in \Sigma \Rightarrow ((q_1,q_2),a,(p_1,p_2)) \in E$

(ii) $\forall (q_1,\varepsilon,p_1) \in E_1,\ \forall (q_2,\varepsilon,p_2) \in E_2 \Rightarrow ((q_1,q_2),\varepsilon,(p_1,p_2)) \in E$

(iii) $\forall (q_1,\varepsilon,p_1) \in E_1,\ \forall (q_2,a,p_2) \in E_2,\ a \in \Sigma \Rightarrow ((q_1,q_2),\varepsilon,(p_1,q_2)) \in E$

(iv) $\forall (q_1,a,p_1) \in E_1,\ \forall (q_2,\varepsilon,p_2) \in E_2,\ a \in \Sigma \Rightarrow ((q_1,q_2),\varepsilon,(q_1,p_2)) \in E$

(v) E has only arcs defined by above four cases.

Set $s=(s_1,s_2)$, $f=(f_1,f_2)$. The algorithm is presented by a function named $\text{Prod}(A_1,A_2)$.

Remark 2. (*i*) Similar to Mohri's analysis in [5], we see that the algorithm has time complexity $O((|Q_1|+|E_1|)(|Q_2|+|E_2|))$. By Remark 1, if A_1, A_2 are deterministic then the algorithm has time complexity $O(|Q_1||Q_2|)$. (*ii*) Let $A_1=(Q_1,\Sigma,E_1,s_1,f_1)$ be an extended automaton that recognizes L^ω. In the automaton $\text{Prod}(A_1,A_1)$, the label of a path connecting two consecutive states (f_1,q_i) and (f_1,q_j) (or (p_i,f_1) and (p_j,f_1), or (s_1,q_i) and (f_1,q_j), or (p_i,s_1) and (p_j,f_1)) is the word of L.

3.3   Union-Product of Automata

Given two extended automata $A_1=(Q_1,\Sigma,E_1,s_1,f_1)$ and $A_2=(Q_2,\Sigma,E_2,s_2,f_2)$, then the *union-products* of A_1 and A_2 is defined as $\text{ProdUni}(A_1,A_2)=(Q,\Sigma,E,I,\{(f_1,f_2)\})$, where $I=\{(f_1,q)|\forall q \in Q_2, q \neq f_2 \wedge q \neq s_2\}$, $Q \subseteq Q_1 \times Q_2$, and E is defined according to the rules from (*i*) to (*v*) in section 3.2. We add the initial state (s,s) into Q, and then add the arcs $\{((s,s),\varepsilon,(f_1,q))|\forall q \in Q_2, q \neq f_2 \wedge q \neq s_2\}$ into E. Then we have the union-product automaton with one initial state $\text{ProdUni}(A_1,A_2)=(Q,\Sigma,E,(s,s),(f_1,f_2))$.

Remark 3. (*i*) Similar to the algorithm designing the product of automata, building $\text{ProdUni}(A_1,A_2)$ has time complexity $O((|Q_1|+|E_1|)(|Q_2|+|E_2|))$. By Remark 1, if A_1, A_2 are deterministic then this algorithm has a time complexity $O(|Q_1||Q_2|)$.

(*ii*) Let $A_1=(Q_1,\Sigma,E_1,s_1,f_1)$ be an extended automaton that recognizes L^ω. In the automaton $\text{ProdUni}(A_1,A_1)$, the label of the path connecting two consecutive states (f_1,q_i) and (f_1,q_j) (or (p_i,f_1) and (p_j,f_1)) is a word of L.

4   Algorithms for Testing of Z-codes

At first we need to solve an extra problem on graph which is interesting by itseft.

4.1   A problem on Finite Graphs

Given a directed finite graph $G=(V,E)$ and two vertices: s is the *initial vertex* and f is the *terminal vertex* ($s{\neq}f$). Let $U{\subseteq}V$ be a set of vertices which are called *up-keys*, $D{\subseteq}V$ be a set of vertices which are called *down-keys* such that $U{\cap}D={\O}$ (the vertices s and f are not in $U{\cup}D$). The rest vertices are called *non-key* vertices.

Given a finite path $\pi=v_1,v_2,...,v_k$, $v_i{\in}V$, $1{\leq}i{\leq}k$ ($s=v_1$) in G. Then, (*i*) if there exist i,j, $1{<}i{<}j{<}k$ such that $v_i{\in}U$, $v_j{\in}D$ and $v_k=v_i$ then π is called *a path of type* 1.

(*ii*) if there exists i, $1{<}i{<}k$ such that $v_i{\in}U$ and $v_k=f$ then π is called *a path of type* 2.

Problem 1. Let $G=(V,E)$ be a graph defined as above. Set up an algorithm to verify if there exists any path of type 1 in G and if there exists any path of type 2 in G.

To solve this problem, we need to construct a graph $G'=(V,E')$ from G by using a "graph-copy" technique as follows:

(*i*) for each $v{\in}V$, create three vertices $(v,1),(v,2),(v,3)$ as copies of v and put to V'.

(*ii*) for each arc $(u,v){\in}E$, create three arcs $((u,1),(v,1)),((u,2),(v,2))$ and $((u,3),(v,3))$ as copies of (u,v) and put to E'. Moreover, if $u{\in}U$, create a new arc $((u,1),(v,2))$ and update to E'. If $u{\in}D$, create a new arc $((u,2),(v,3))$ and update to E'.

The algorithm to construct G' from G can be expressed by a function XCopy(G) with time complexity $O(|V|+|E|)$.

Remark 4. (*i*)   By G' constructed as above, we have: $|V'|=3n$, $|E'|{\leq}5m$ with $|V|=n$, $|E|=m$. (*ii*) The set of vertices of the type (v,k) in G' generates the subgraph G_k for each $k=1,2,3$. Each subgraph G_k is isomorphic to G. Hence G' is a version extended from the union of G_1,G_2,G_3. There are some arcs from G_1 to G_2, but not any in the reversed direction. It is similar from G_2 to G_3.

The following theorem describes the meaning of G'

Theorem 1. *Let $G=(V,E)$ be a finite graph defined as above and $G'=XCopy(G)$.*
(i) There exists a path of type 1 in G if and only if there exists a path π in G' that starts at the vertex $(s,1)$ and ends at $(v,3)$, where $v{\in}U$ and $(v,1){\in}\pi$.
(ii) There exists a path of type 2 in G if and only if there exists a path π in G' that starts at the vertex $(s,1)$ and ends at $(f,2)$.

Proof. (i) ($\Rightarrow$) There exists a path of type 1 in G: $u_1,...,u_i,...,u_j,...,u_k$ ($s=u_1$). We have $1{<}i{<}j{<}k$ such that $u_i{\in}U$, $u_j{\in}D$ and $u_i=u_k$. According to the function constructing G', there   exists   a   path π, $(u_1,1),...,(u_i,1),(u_{i+1},2),...,(u_j,2),(u_{j+1},3),...,(u_k,3)$ where $(s,1)=(u_1,1),(u_k,3)=(v,3)$. It is obviously that $v{\in}U$ and $(v,1){\in}\pi$.

($\Leftarrow$) There exists a path π in G' from $(s,1)$ to $(v,3)$, where $v\in U$ and $(v,1)\in\pi$. According to the function constructing G', π can be written as:

$(u_1,1),...,(u_i,1),(u_{i+1},2),...,(u_j,2),(u_{j+1},3),...,(u_k,3)$,   where $(s,1)=(u_1,1),(u_k,3)=(v,3)$, $1<i<j<k$, $u_i\in U$, $u_j\in D$ and $u_k=u_i$. Then, in G, there is a path of type 1: $u_1,...,u_i,u_{i+1},...,u_j,u_{j+1},...,u_k$ where $s=u_1,u_k=v$, $1<i<j<k$, $u_i\in U$, $u_j\in D$ and $u_k=u_i$.

(*ii*) It can be easily implied from the function constructing G'.   □

To test whether there exists any path of type 1 in G, we use an array *mark* as follows: a vertex (u,i) is colored WHITE, (or $mark[(u,i)]$=WHITE) to show that (u,i) has not been visited. For a vertex is considered, if its type is $(u,1)$ with $u\in U$, then it is colored BLUE, otherwise it is colored GREY. Whenever the considered vertex $(u,1)$ is colored BLUE, a corresponding vertex $(u,3)$ will be colored BLUE. This guarantees the fact that if we have a path in G' starting from $(s,1)$ and ending at $(u,3)$ which is colored BLUE then we also have a path of type 1 in G. For testing a path of type 2, we need only a path from $(s,1)$ to $(f,2)$ without using this coloring technique. A vertex is colored BLACK if it is not included in any further visiting process.

In general, the algorithm can be described as follows: (*i*) Initially, all vertices of G' are colored WHITE. (*ii*) We call a recursive function *visit* to visit all vertices of G' by using the coloring technique mentioned above. This function is modified from the DFS (Depth First Search) algorithm in [10] as follows.

```
Function int Visit(graph G', vertex (u,i),int x)
//x=1 function Visit detects path of type 1, type 2.
//x=0 function Visit only detects path of type1.
1.  if i=1 and upkey[u]=1 then
        mark[(u,1)]=mark[(u,3)]=BLUE else mark[(u,i)]=GREY
2.  for each arc ((u,i),(v,j))∈E' do
        if mark[(v,j)]=BLUE and j=3 then return 1;
        if (v,j)=(f,2) and x=1 then return 2;
        if mark[(v,j)]=WHITE then
          if Visit(G',(v,j),x)!=0 then
                    return Visit(G',(v,j),x);
3.  mark[(u,i)]=BLACK
    if i=1 and mark[(u,3)]=BLUE then mark[(u,3)]=WHITE
4.  return 0.
Function int ContainsCycle(graph G', vertex (u,i), int x)
1.  for each vertex (u,1)∈V' do
        mark[(u,1)]=mark[(u,2)]=mark[(u,3)]=WHITE
2.  return Visit(G',(u,i),x);
```

Remark 5. The algorithm ContainsCycle detecting any paths of type 1, 2 has its time complexity $O(|V|+|E|)$.

4.2   A New Algorithm for Testing of Z-codes

In this part, we present the main results of this paper. Let $L \subseteq \Sigma^*$ be a regular language recognized by a given finite automaton $A=(Q,\Sigma,E,I,F)$ which is generally non-deterministic. We consider step by step the following cases.

(*i*)   if $\varepsilon \in L$ then L is not a Z-code. To check whether $\varepsilon \in L$ reduces to determine whether $I \cap F$ is emptyset. We present I, F by two arrays as follows: $InI(q)=1 \Leftrightarrow q \in I$ and $InF(q)=1 \Leftrightarrow q \in F$. Therefore, testing whether $I \cap F$ is emptyset can be done by an algorithm Epsilon(A), with time complexity $O(n)$, $n=|Q|$.

(*ii*)   if $\varepsilon \notin L$ then $L \subseteq \Sigma^+$. Suppose that L is not a Z-code. Then there exists a word $w \in \Sigma^z$ which has two different L-factorizations. It can be one of four types as shown in Figure 1. Hence, verifying whether L is a Z-code reduces to testing whether there exists such a word w. We construct $A_1=\mathrm{Ex}(A_D)=(Q_1,\Sigma,E_1,s_1,f_1)$, $A_2=\mathrm{Reverse}(A_1)$ $=(Q_2,\Sigma,E_2,s_2,f_2)$ and from these automata we have:

Prod(A_1,A_1) induces a directed graph G_1 with the initial vertex (s_1,s_1), the terminal vertex (f_1,f_1), the set of up-keys $U_1=\{(f_1,q) \in Q_1 \times Q_1 | q \neq f_1 \wedge q \neq s_1\}$, the set of down-keys $D_1=\{(p,f_1) \in Q_1 \times Q_1 | p \neq f_1 \wedge p \neq s_1\}$, and each arc of Prod($A_1,A_1$) is an arc of G_1.

Prod(A_2,A_2) induces a directed graph G_2 with the initial vertex (s_2,s_2), the terminal vertex (f_2,f_2), the set of up-keys $U_2=\{(f_2,q) \in Q_2 \times Q_2 | q \neq f_2 \wedge q \neq s_2\}$, the set of down-keys $D_2=\{(p,f_2) \in Q_2 \times Q_2 | p \neq f_2 \wedge p \neq s_2\}$ and each arc of Prod(A_2,A_2) is an arc of G_2.

ProdUni(A_1,A_1) induces a directed graph G_3 with the initial vertex (s,s), the terminal vertex (f_1,f_1), the set of up-keys $U_3=\{(f_1,q) \in Q_1 \times Q_1 | q \neq f_1 \wedge q \neq s_1\}$, the set of down-keys $D_3=\{(p,f_1) \in Q_1 \times Q_1 | p \neq f_1 \wedge p \neq s_1\}$ and each arc of ProdUni(A_1,A_1) is an arc of G_3.

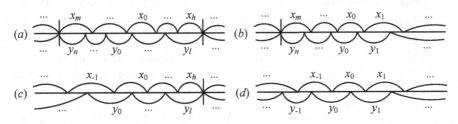

Fig. 1. Four types of two different L-factorizations of w

For the case $\varepsilon \notin L$, we establish the following result.

Theorem 2. *Let $L \subseteq \Sigma^+$ be a language recognized by a finite automaton A, let G_1, G_2, G_3 be defined as above. L is a Z-code if and only if four following conditions hold*
(i) there is no any paths of type 2 in the graph G_1;
(ii) there is no any paths of type 1 in the graph G_1;
(iii) there is no any paths of type 1 in the graph G_2;
(iv) there is no any paths of type 1 in the graph G_3.

Proof. ($\Rightarrow$) We assume by a contradiction that *L is a Z-code* and one of the conditions (*i*), (*ii*), (*iii*) or (*iv*) does not hold.

(*i*) Suppose that there exists a path of type 2 in G_1, we consider the label of this path: $(p_1,q_1)\xrightarrow{x}(p_i,q_i)\xrightarrow{y}(p_k,q_k)$, where $(s_1,s_1)=(p_1,q_1),(p_i,q_i)=(f_1,q_i)\in U_1$, $1<i<k$ and $(p_k,q_k)=(f_1,f_1)$.   Hence   we   have   a   path π: $(p_1,q_1)\xrightarrow{x}(f_1,q_i)\xrightarrow{y}(f_1,f_1)$. By Remark 2, we have $v=xy\in L^+$. With any $u\in {}^\omega L$, $z\in L^\omega$, then the word $w=uvz\in {}^\omega L^\omega$ admits two different L-factorizations. Therefore, L is not a Z-code. This contradicts the assumption.

(*ii*) Suppose that there exists a path of type 1 in G_1, we consider the label of this path: $(p_1,q_1)\xrightarrow{x}(p_i,q_i)\xrightarrow{y}(p_j,q_j)\xrightarrow{z}(p_k,q_k)$,   where $(s_1,s_1)=(p_1,q_1)$, $(p_i,q_i)=(f_1,q_i)\in U_1$, $(p_j,q_j)=(p_j,f_1)\in D_1$, $1<i<j<k$ and $(p_k,q_k)=(p_i,q_i)$. Hence, we have a right infinite path π:

$$(p_1,q_1)\xrightarrow{x}(f_1,q_i)\xrightarrow{y}(p_j,f_1)\xrightarrow{z}(f_1,q_i)\xrightarrow{y}(p_j,f_1)\xrightarrow{z}(f_1,q_i)\xrightarrow{y}\cdots$$

By Remark 2, we have $v=xyzyzyz\cdots\in L^\omega$. With any $u\in {}^\omega L$, then the word $w=uv\in {}^\omega L^\omega$ admits two different L-factorizations. Therefore L is not a Z-code. This contradicts the assumption.

(*iii*) Suppose that there exists a path of type 1 in G_2, we consider the label of this path: $(p_1,q_1)\xrightarrow{\bar{x}}(p_i,q_i)\xrightarrow{\bar{y}}(p_j,q_j)\xrightarrow{\bar{z}}(p_k,q_k)$,   where $(s_2,s_2)=(p_1,q_1)$, $(p_i,q_i)=(f_2,q_i)\in U_2$, $(p_j,q_j)=(p_j,f_2)\in D_2$, $1<i<j<k$ and $(p_k,q_k)=(p_i,q_i)$. Hence we have a right infinite path π:

$$(p_1,q_1)\xrightarrow{\bar{x}}(f_2,q_i)\xrightarrow{\bar{y}}(p_j,f_2)\xrightarrow{\bar{z}}(f_2,q_i)\xrightarrow{\bar{y}}(p_j,f_2)\xrightarrow{\bar{z}}(f_2,q_i)\xrightarrow{\bar{y}}\cdots$$

By Remark 2, we have $t=\bar{x}\ \bar{y}\ \bar{z}\ \bar{y}\ \bar{z}...\in \bar{L}^\omega$. Then, label t of π admits two different factorizations on $\bar{L}$. Correspondingly, we have $v=...\ zyzyx\in {}^\omega L$ with two differrent factorizations on L. With any $u\in L^\omega$, then the word $w=vu\in {}^\omega L^\omega$ admits two different L-factorizations. Therefore, L is not a Z-code. This contradicts the assumption.

(*iv*) Suppose that there exists a path of type 1 in G_3, we consider the label of this path: $(p_1,q_1)\xrightarrow{x}(p_i,q_i)\xrightarrow{y}(p_j,q_j)\xrightarrow{z}(p_k,q_k)$,   where $(s,s)=(p_1,q_1)$, $(p_i,q_i)=(f_1,q_i)\in U_3$, $(p_j,q_j)=(p_j,f_1)\in D_3$, $1<i<j<k$ and $(p_k,q_k)=(p_i,q_i)$. Hence, we have a bi-infinite path π:

$$\cdots(f_1,q_i)\xrightarrow{y}(p_j,f_1)\xrightarrow{z}(f_1,q_i)\xrightarrow{y}(p_j,f_1)\xrightarrow{z}(f_1,q_i)\xrightarrow{y}\cdots$$

By Remark 3, we have $w=\cdots yzyzyz\cdots\in {}^\omega L^\omega$. It implies that w admits two different L-factorizations. Therefore L is not a Z-code. This contradicts the assumption.

($\Leftarrow$) We assume by a contradiction that the four conditions (*i*)-(*iv*) hold but L is not a Z-code. Then there exists a word $u\in \Sigma^+$, two bi-infinite sequences of words of L: $\cdots,x_{-2},x_{-1},x_0,x_1,x_2,\cdots$ and $\cdots,y_{-2},y_{-1},y_0,y_1,y_2,\cdots$ such that: $\cdots x_{-2}x_{-1}u=\cdots y_{-1}y_0$, $|u|\leq|x_0|$, $x_0x_1x_2\cdots=uy_1y_2\cdots$, $|u|\leq|y_0|$, with $u\neq x_0$ or $u\neq y_0$.

We consider four cases (see Figure 1) may be happened as follows:

Case 1: There exist $m \leq 0 \leq h$, $n \leq 0 \leq l$ with $m \neq 0$ or $l \neq 0$ (Figure 1.a) such that $v = x_m x_{m+1} \cdots x_h = y_n y_{n+1} \cdots y_l$. Since $v = x_m x_{m+1} \cdots x_h$, A_1 has a path π labeled v:
$s_1 \xrightarrow{x_m} f_1 \xrightarrow{\varepsilon} s_1 \xrightarrow{x_{m+1}} f_1 \xrightarrow{\varepsilon} s_1 \cdots s_1 \xrightarrow{x_h} f_1$. Similarly, $v = y_n y_{n+1} \cdots y_l$, A_1 has a path θ labeled v: $s_1 \xrightarrow{y_n} f_1 \xrightarrow{\varepsilon} s_1 \xrightarrow{y_{n+1}} f_1 \xrightarrow{\varepsilon} s_1 \cdots s_1 \xrightarrow{y_l} f_1$.

Hence, in the graph G_1, there is a path ρ defined by π and θ as follows:
$(p_1, q_1), \ldots, (f_1, q_i), \ldots, (p_k, q_k)$ where $(s_1, s_1) = (p_1, q_1)$, $(f_1, q_i) \in U_1$, $(f_1, f_1) = (p_k, q_k)$, $1 < i < k$, or equivalently, G_1 has a path of type 2. This contradicts the condition (i).

Case 2: There exist $n, m \leq 0$ such that $v = x_m x_{m+1} \cdots = y_n y_{n+1} \cdots$ and there are no $h > m, l > n$ such that $x_h x_{h+1} \cdots = y_l y_{l+1} \cdots$ (Figure 1.b). Since $v = x_m x_{m+1} \cdots$, A_1 has a right infinite path π labeled v: $s_1 \xrightarrow{x_m} f_1 \xrightarrow{\varepsilon} s_1 \xrightarrow{x_{m+1}} f_1 \xrightarrow{\varepsilon} s_1 \cdots$ Similarly, $v = y_n y_{n+1} \cdots$, A_1 has a right infinite path θ labeled v: $s_1 \xrightarrow{y_n} f_1 \xrightarrow{\varepsilon} s_1 \xrightarrow{y_{n+1}} f_1 \cdots$

Hence, in the graph G_1, there is a right infinite path ρ defined by π and θ as follows: $(p_1, q_1), \ldots, (f_1, q_i), \ldots, (p_j, f_1), \ldots$ where $(s_1, s_1) = (p_1, q_1)$. Since ρ is a right infinite path in the finite graph G_1, there must exist vertices $(p_k, q_k) \in Q_1 \times Q_1$, $(f_1, q_i) \in U_1$, $(p_j, f_1) \in D_1$ such that $(f_1, q_i) = (p_k, q_k)$ with $1 < i < j < k$, or equivalently, G_1 has a path of type 1. This contradicts the condition (ii).

Case 3: There exist $h, l \geq 0$ such that $v = \cdots x_{h-1} x_h = \cdots y_{l-1} y_l$ and there are no $m < h, n < l$ such that $\cdots x_{m-1} x_m = \cdots y_{n-1} y_n$ (Figure 1.c). Then, we have $u = \overline{x_h} \overline{x_{h-1}} \cdots = \overline{y_l} \overline{y_{l-1}} \cdots$ with $\overline{x_h}, \overline{x_{h-1}}, \cdots, \overline{y_l}, \overline{y_{l-1}}, \cdots \in \overline{L}$ and there are no $m < h, n < l$ such that $\overline{x_m} \overline{x_{m-1}} \cdots = \overline{y_n} \overline{y_{n-1}} \cdots$. Since $u = \overline{x_h} \overline{x_{h-1}} \cdots$, A_2 has a right infinite path π labeled u: $s_2 \xrightarrow{\overline{x_h}} f_2 \xrightarrow{\varepsilon} s_2 \xrightarrow{\overline{x_{h-1}}} f_2 \xrightarrow{\varepsilon} s_2 \cdots$ Similarly, $u = \overline{y_l} \overline{y_{l-1}} \cdots$, A_2 has a right infinite path θ labeled u: $s_2 \xrightarrow{\overline{y_l}} f_2 \xrightarrow{\varepsilon} s_2 \xrightarrow{\overline{y_{l-1}}} f_2 \xrightarrow{\varepsilon} s_2 \cdots$

Hence, in the graph G_2, there is a right infinite path ρ defined by π and θ as follows: $(p_1, q_1), \ldots, (f_2, q_i), \ldots, (p_j, f_2), \ldots$ where $(s_2, s_2) = (p_1, q_1)$. Since ρ is a right infinite path in the finite graph G_2, there must exist vertices $(p_k, q_k) \in Q_2 \times Q_2$, $(f_2, q_i) \in U_2$, $(p_j, f_2) \in D_2$ such that $(f_2, q_i) = (p_k, q_k)$ with $1 < i < j < k$, or equivalently, G_2 has a path of type 1. This contradicts the condition (iii).

Case 4: There exist no h, l such that $x_h x_{h+1} \cdots = y_l y_{l+1} \cdots$ or $\cdots x_{h-1} x_h = \cdots y_{l-1} y_l$ (Figure 1.d). We have $v = x_m x_{m+1} \cdots = y y_n y_{n+1} \cdots$ with $x_m, x_{m+1}, \ldots, y_n, y_{n+1}, \ldots \in L$, $y \in \Sigma^+$ and $y \notin L$. Since $v = x_m x_{m+1} \cdots$, A_1 has a right infinite path π labeled v: $s_1 \xrightarrow{x_m} f_1 \xrightarrow{\varepsilon} s_1 \xrightarrow{x_{m+1}} f_1 \xrightarrow{\varepsilon} s_1 \cdots$ Similarly, $v = y y_n y_{n+1} \cdots$, A_1 has a right infinite path θ labeled v: $q_i \xrightarrow{y} f_1 \xrightarrow{\varepsilon} s_1 \xrightarrow{y_n} f_1 \xrightarrow{\varepsilon} s_1 \xrightarrow{y_{n+1}} f_1 \xrightarrow{\varepsilon} s_1 \cdots$ where $q_i \neq s_1, f_1$. Hence, in the graph G_3, there is a right infinite path ρ defined by π

and θ as follows: $(p_1,q_1),...,(f_1,q_i),...,(p_j,f_1),...$ where $(s,s)=(p_1,q_1)$. Since ρ is a right infinite path in the finite graph G_3, there must exist vertices $(p_k,q_k)\in Q_1\times Q_1$, $(f_1,q_i)\in U_3$, $(p_j,f_1)\in D_3$ such that $(f_1,q_i)=(p_k,q_k)$ with $1<i<j<k$, or equivalently, G_3 has a path of type 1. This contradicts the condition (iv). These complete the proof of theorem .

□

Now we formulate an effective algorithm for testing of Z-codes.

Function ZCode(A)

```
Input:  A=(Q, ,E,I,F), n=|Q|, m=|E| and L=L(A)⊆Σ*.
Output: TRUE if L is a Z-code, FALSE otherwise.
1.  if Epsilon(A) then return FALSE;
2.  A₁=Ex(A_D);
3.  G₁=Prod(A₁,A₁);
4.  G=XCopy(G₁);
5.  if ContainsCycle(G,((s₁,s₁),1),1)!=0 then return FALSE
6.  A₂=Reverse(A₁);
7.  G₂=Prod(A₂,A₂);
8.  G=XCopy(G₂);
9.  if ContainsCycle(G,((s₂,s₂),1),0)==1 then return FALSE
10. G₃=ProdUni(A₁,A₁);
11. G=XCopy(G₃);
12. if ContainsCycle(G,((s,s),1),0)==1 then return FALSE
13. return TRUE
```

Time Complexity of the Algorithm. The time complexity for Step 1 is $O(n)$, Steps 2, 6 is $O(n+m)$, Steps 3, 7, 10 is $O((n+m)^2)$, Steps 4, 5, 8, 9, 11, 12 is $O(n^2+m^2)$. Therefore, the time complexity of the whole algorithm is $O(n^4)$ in the case A is non-deterministic, and $O(n^2)$ in the case A is deterministic.

5   Conclusion

Studying on advanced automata models are paid much attention in both theoretic and application aspects. In this paper, we propose an algorithm to decide whether a regular language recognized by a finite automaton is a Z-code or not with time complexity $O(n^4)$ - for the general case of non-deterministic automata, and $O(n^2)$ for the restricted case of deterministic automata. This is a significant problem in terms of theory and practice.

References

1. Berstel, J., Perrin, D.: Theory of Codes. Academic Press Inc., New York (1985)
2. Devolder, J., Latteux, M., Litovsky, I., Staiger, L.: Codes and infinite words. Acta Cybernetica 11(4), 241–256 (1994)

3. Staiger, L.: On infinitary finite length codes. Informatique Théorique et Applications 20(4), 483–494 (1986)
4. Van, D.L.: Contribution to Combinatorics on Words. PhD thesis, Humboldt University, Berlin (1985)
5. Mohri, M., Pereira, F., Riley, M.: Speech recognition with weighted finite-state transducers. Springer, Heidelberg (2007)
6. Devolder, J., Timmerman, E.: Finitary codes for biinfinite words. Informatique Théorique et Applications 26(4), 363–386 (1992)
7. Van, D.L., Lam, N.H., Huy, P.T.: On codes concerning bi-infinite words. Acta Cybernetica 11(1-2), 97–109 (1993)
8. Lam, N.H., Van, D.L.: On a class of infinitary codes. Theoretical Infomatics and Applications 24, 441–458 (1990)
9. Madonia, M., Salemi, S., Sportelli, T.: A generalization of Sardinas-Patterson algorithm to Z-codes. Theoretical Computer Science 108, 251–270 (1993)
10. Cormen, T.H., Leiserson, C.E., Rivest, R.L., Stein, C.: Introduction to Algorithms, 3rd edn. MIT Press and McGraw-Hill (2009)
11. Van, D.L., Thomas, D.G., Subramanian, K.G., Siromoney, R.: Bi-Infinitary Codes. RAIRO Inform. Theor. Appl. 24(1), 67–87 (1990)
12. Restivo, A.: Codes and Automata. In: Pin, J.E. (ed.) LITP 1988. LNCS, vol. 386, Springer, Heidelberg (1989)

Design of the Cognitive Information Display for Water Level Control of the Steam Generator in Korean Nuclear Power Reactor

Sooill Lee

Central Research Institute, Korea Hydro and Nuclear Power co., (KHNP-CRI)
Daejeon, 305-343, Korea
kangta1@khnp.co.kr

Abstract. This paper introduces a design of the cognitive information display using EID (Ecological Interface Design) for the water level control of steam generator in Korean advance nuclear power reactor. The concept of conventional display method in NPPs (Nuclear Power Plants) mainly relies on the SSSI (Single Sensor Single Indicator) design criteria; therefore, the conventional information display method employed a method based on the type of P&ID (Piping & Instrumentation Diagram). Due to the lack or excess of the information, the operators in NPPs could not understand the overall relationship between the objective and operator's control; it leads to be a human's cognitive decision burden and human error. In this paper, we propose the design method that applies the EID to the water level control of steam generator in advanced nuclear power reactor. This design method consists of the cognitive task analysis, the selection of the example task, the design of the example task, the feasibility evaluation. Proposed design method shows the effectiveness when developing the cognitive information display in NPPs. Also, this paper shows the further study points not only for applying the EID to real NPPs, but also for applying the EID to ubiquitous maintenance applications in real NPPs to overcome the lack of the information due to small screen.

Keywords: Cognitive Information Display, Ecological Interface Design, Advanced Power Reactor, Ubiquitous maintenance, Nuclear Power Plants.

1   Introduction

An advanced digital MCR (Main Control Room) and I&C system are being applied to Korean advanced power reactor as digital techniques have improved. Also, in order to enhance the safety and human reliability in NPPs (Nuclear Power Plants), advance MMI (Man Machine Interface) based on the human's awareness has been widely studied. The MMI display for the APR1400(Advanced Power Reactor 1400MWe) MCR only relies on physical design basis such as the SSSI (Single Sensor Single Indicator) design criteria as shown in Fig. 1; therefore, the conventional information display method employed a method based on the type of P&ID (Piping & Instrumentation Diagram) on which sensor values directly indicated. In the case that the

J.J. Park et al. (Eds.): NPC 2012, LNCS 7513, pp. 636–644, 2012.

operators reach at the lack of information in the conventional personnel workstation; it leads to be a human error due to operator's poor understanding of the overall relationship between the objective and operator's control. Also, in the case of excess of the information in the LDP (Large Display Panel), it is difficult for the operator to find the proper information; it leads to the operator's burden[1]. Because the operator cannot get the insight from the conventional display and directly indicated values, integration of the information and decision could be an operator's cognitive burden. EID (Ecological Interface Design) is used to represent the internal process of human brain; therefore, it could be a method to reduce the operator's cognitive burden and human error. In this paper, we propose the design method that applies the EID to the steam generator and pressurizer water level control in advanced power reactor. This design method consists of the cognitive task analysis, the selection of the example task, the design of the example task and the feasibility evaluation.

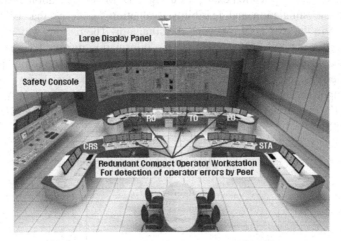

Fig. 1. Information display in APR1400 MCR

Also, this paper shows the further study points not only for applying the EID to real NPPs, but also for applying EID to ubiquitous maintenance applications in real NPPs to overcome the lack of the information due to small screen.

2   Related Work

The EID concept and its formalized approach, which is SRK taxonomy (: Skill-based, Rule-based, Knowledge-based) and AH (Abstraction Hierarchy), originated in a systematic form for the interface design of large and complex system [2]. When the abstracted information which represents on the AH gives visually to the operator, it could be an operational effectiveness at diagnosing and controlling the plant system [3]. In [4, Burns], the experiment for the information display by EID on the nuclear plant simulator shows the better situation awareness performance than the one of conventional information display [4].

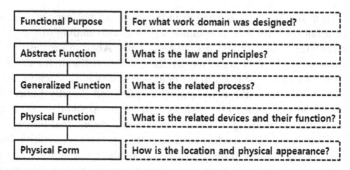

Fig. 2. Five level of abstraction hierarchy

We surveyed the application examples using EID. Most application examples have focused on the simulation and feasibility evaluation; it means that EID is rarely implemented in the real system beyond the simulator. The reasons why it is difficult to implement in the real field are that (1) the information display form is not established, (2) new EID information display design have the burden to retrain up the operator[1]. After designing the information display by EID, the feasibility evaluation is the most important to raise the performance of the information display. As shown in Figure 3, FIP (Functional Information Profile) was used to evaluate the EID design of pasteurizer [5].

Part-Whole Decomposition

	System	Sub-system	Components
Functional Purpose			
Abstract Function			
Generalized Function			
Physical Function			
Physical Form			

(Functional Decomposition — vertical axis label)

Fig. 3. Composition of the FIP

Burns (2002) validate the work domain model by training scenario [5] and Marmaras (2004) used the work-through method based on the scenario [6].

3   Proposed Design Method

The overall procedure of the proposed design method is shown in Table. 1, which consists of 5 steps (: Task selection, Cognitive task analysis, Scenario analysis, Design and evaluation of examples and Establishment of information display standard).

Table 1. Overall procedure of the proposed design method

Step	Activity	Details
1	Task selection	-
2	Cognitive task analysis	• Work domain analysis • Task analysis
3	Scenario analysis	• Procedure analysis • Expert consultant, Accident analysis
4	Design and evaluation of examples	• Display object analysis • Design of examples • Feasibility evaluation of examples
5	Establishment of information display standard	• Design of group verbal communication method • Style guide

3.1 Cognitive Task Analysis

The purpose of cognitive task analysis is to review the cognitive structure and process. In this paper, we conduct the cognitive task analysis (: work domain analysis, task analysis). The work domain analysis is conducted to decompose the task regarding steam generator control as shown in Fig. 4-6.

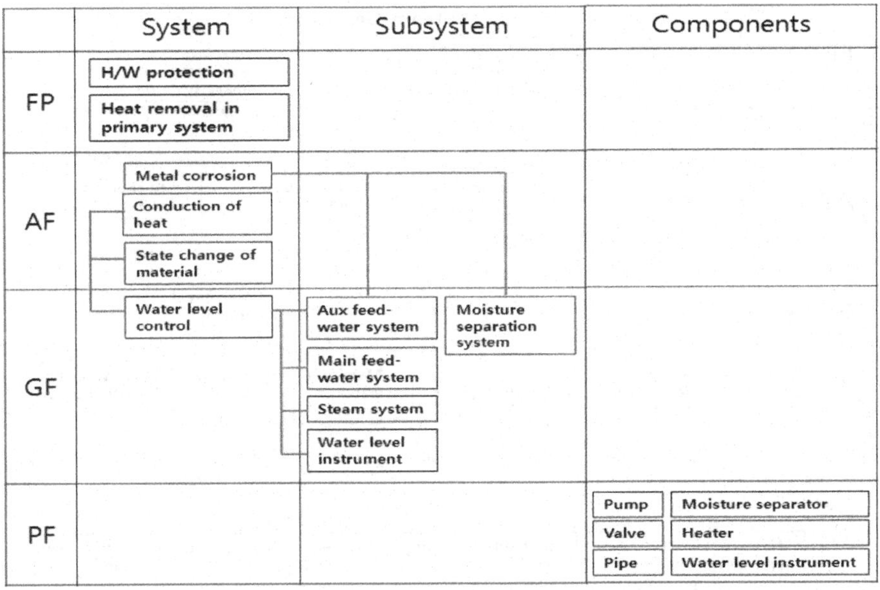

Fig. 4. FIP decomposition for water level control process of the steam generator

	System	Subsystem	Components	
FP	H/W protection Heat removal in primary system			
AF	Metal corrosion Conduction of heat State change of material			
GF	Pressure, Flow(water, steam), Water level	Pressure, Flow(water) Flow(steam) Water level	Centrifugal force, Ratio(moisture)	
PF			Centrifugal force, Ratio(moisture) Flow(water, steam)	Temperature(water) Water level Pressure

Fig. 5. Requirement driven from steam generator FIP

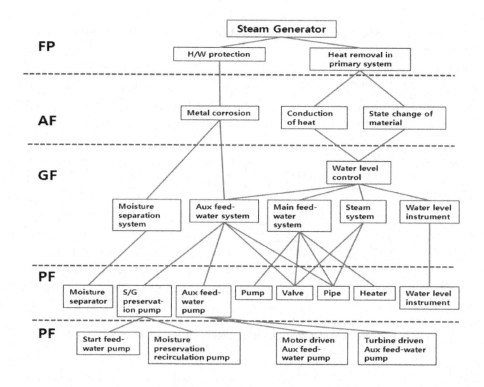

Fig. 6. Abstraction hierarchy for water level control of the steam generator

Also, we conduct the three-type task analysis on the basis of Younggwang NPP unit #5 & 6 EOP(Emergency Operating Procedure). The result of task analysis for Reactor Trip, LOCA(Loss of Coolant Accident) and SGTR(Steam Generator Tube Rupture) shows the similarity to the result of cognitive task analysis.

3.2   Scenario Analysis

The purpose of scenario analysis is to establish the information requirement. We conduct the procedure analysis on the basis of Uljin NPP unit #5 & 6 EOP, AOP(Abnormal Operating Procedure) and SOP (System Operating Procedure). Also, the expert consultant is implemented for the operation of the steam generator control as follows,

- the possibility of reactor trip from the water control of steam generator
- the task change according to automatic control of the steam generator
- the system variables for the operator during manual control
- the role of auxiliary feed water system on the task of water control of the steam generator

The accident analysis is conducted using the accident data which was taken from Korean NPPs from 2002 to 2011. Three accidents, which are related to the human error of water control, were reviewed.

3.3   Design of Example

In the conventional information display in Fig. 7, the flow vales of main feed water and main steam are indicated on the P&ID display. The operator's control means for the water control of steam generator are down-comer valve, economizer valve and the velocity of main feed water pump. In order to control by those, operator should clicks the object to load the soft control display.

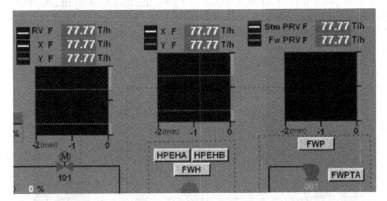

Fig. 7. Information display example of main feed water based on the P&ID

Fig. 8 shows not only the own values of feed water/steam, but also the difference/direction between the feed water flow and steam flow. The difference or direction is the abstract information not acquired from sensor; the operator can predict the water level of steam generator. The left bar means the feed water flow and the right bar means the steam flow. The direction of the arrow means that the water level of steam generator will be lower, and difference means the amount of change. The reference point means the idle point, which is an equilibrium level at which the two flows are the same, requested by the control system. The reference point can give the effect to reduce the operator's cognitive burden. Also, the left bar represents the economizer flow and down-comer flow respectively; the operator can confirm the distribution of the feed water flow according to the reactor power.

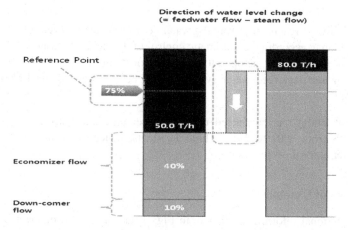

Fig. 8. Graph example of feed water and steam based on EID

Fig. 9 shows the soft controller in the VDU(Visual Display Unit) based on conventional P&ID. Due to the parallel disposition of conventional soft-controller display and the lack of plant information, it could not give the intuitive sight and overall relationship between objective and operator's control. The conventional soft controller shows the SP(Set point), PV(Process value), OP(Output demand) respectively.

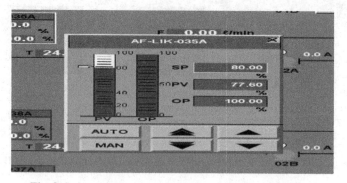

Fig. 9. Soft controller example based on conventional P&ID

Fig. 10 shows the soft controller example based on EID, and includes not only SP, PV(: feed water flow), OP(: valve open rate) respectively but also the relationship between above three values. While there are only up/down buttons in conventional soft controller, the sliding icon is employed to control the input more intuitively.

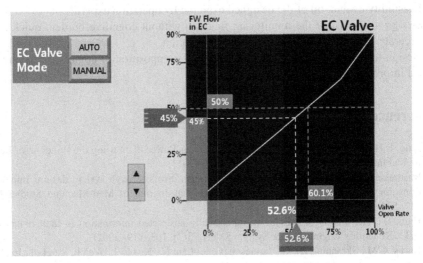

Fig. 10. Soft controller example based on EID

3.4   Consideration for Applying EID to Ubiquitous Maintenance Applications

In the industrial field as well as NPPs, there are many studies to apply ubiquitous techniques to the area of maintenance, e.g., logging, status checking, control, etc. The mobility from ubiquitous environment is the best advantage specially in the wide area such as NPPs. When maintained the complex systems in NPPs, the understanding of the overall relationship is the most important factor to maintain systems by ubiquitous devices; moreover, the device identification should be added to the display of the ubiquitous device. Considering the small screen of ubiquitous devices, we should consider further study points as shown below.

- Identification method for the proper target system for maintaining
- Design method of ubiquitous display considering portability and small screen
- Integration of P&ID display and EID to overcome the mode error(: integration method might be useful in the maintenance area of complex system)

4   Conclusion

In this paper, we introduce a design method of the cognitive information display for the water level control of steam generator, which is made up of the task selection, the cognitive task analysis, the design and evaluation of examples, the establishment of information display standard for applying the EID to real NPPs in Korea. The evaluation of the examples and the evaluation of information display standard will be carried out after the design of examples is completed. Though design experience for the cognitive information display in NPPs, we have found improvement points for a further study as summarized below.

- Feasibility evaluation of the designed example by operation expert,
- Design to consist of the monitoring function without cognitive burden, quick and accurate control function during manual operation,
- Design to reduce the mode error (e.g., proper composition of cognitive and physical information display).

References

1. Jang, B.H.: Design of Display Template in Nuclear Power Plant using the Principle of Ecological Interface Design. Master Paper, KAIST (2011)
2. Rasmussen, J., Vicente, K.J.: Coping with human errors through system design: Implications for ecological interface design. International Journal of Man-Machine Studies 31, 517–534 (1989)
3. Ham, D.: The effects of presenting functionally abstracted information in fault diagnosis tasks. Reliability Engineering & System Safety 73(2), 103–119 (2001)
4. Burns, C.M., Skraaning Jr., G., Jamieson, G.A., Lau, N., Kwok, J., Welch, R., et al.: Evaluation of ecological interface design for Nuclear process control: Situation Awareness Effects. Human Factors 50(4), 663–679 (2008)
5. Reising, D.V., Sanderson, P.: Ecological interface design for Pasteurizer II: a process description of semantic mapping. Human factors 44(2), 222–247 (2002)
6. Marmaras, N., Drivalou, S.: Design and Evaluation of Ecological Interfaces. Technical Report of THALES project, Pr. No. 65/1192 (2004)

Author Index